Hacker's Guide™ to to Visual Basic

Vincent Chen
John Montgomery

Series Editor Woody Leonhard

Addison-Wesley Developers Press

Reading, Massachusetts • Menlo Park, California • New York
Don Mills, Ontario • Harlow, England • Amsterdam
Bonn • Sydney • Singapore • Tokyo • Madrid • San Juan
Paris • Seoul • Milan • Mexico City • Taipei

Many of the designations used by manufacturers and sellers to distinguish their products are claimed as trademarks. Where those designations appear in this book, and Addison-Wesley was aware of a trademark claim, the designations have been printed in initial capital letters or all capital letters.

The authors and publishers have taken care in preparation of this book but make no express or implied warranty of any kind and assume no responsibility for errors or omissions. No liability is assumed for incidental or consequential damages in connection with or arising out of the use of the information or programs contained herein.

Library of Congress Cataloging-in-Publication Data

Montgomery, John (John I.), 1967–
    Hacker's guide to Visual Basic / John Montgomery, Vincent Chen.
      p. cm.
    Includes index.
    ISBN 0-201-87042-8 (alk. paper)
    1. BASIC (Computer program language)   2. Microsoft Visual BASIC.
  I. Chen, Vincent. II. Title.
  QA76.73.B3M663   1996
  005.265—dc20

                        96–19354
                         CIP

Sponsoring Editor: Kathleen Tibbetts
Project Manager: Sarah Weaver
Production Coordinator: Deborah McKenna
Cover design: Chris St. Cyr
Set in 11-point Times Roman by A&B Typesetters, Inc.

1 2 3 4 5 6 7 8 9 -MA- 0099989796
First Printing, July 1996

Addison-Wesley books are available for bulk purchases by corporations, institutions, and other organizations. For more information, please contact the Corporate, Government, and Special Sales Department at (800) 238–9682.

Find A-W Developers Press on the World-Wide Web at:
http://www.aw.com/devpress/

CONTENTS

FOREWORD

Starting out with Visual Basic can be a real challenge: there are a dozen or so concepts you have to "get" all at once, and if you aren't conversant with event-driven concepts, trying to bootstrap your knowledge of computers with the official documentation is an exercise in futility.

As you peel away VB's layers (and layers and layers and layers)—a process that can take years—you discover that VB exhibits all sorts of quirks. Yes, it's powerful. Yes, it's flexible. But some things don't quite work right. Techniques that work in one situation don't cut it in another. When you get right down to it, some things don't work at all. And the shortest path between two VB points may well consist of a convoluted combination of an obscure control's properties, a dozen lines of code, and a couple of calls to the Windows API: stuff that's easy to do, if you know how to do it, but awfully hard to come up with in the first place.

That's why I'm so pleased that Vince Chen and John Montgomery took on **Hacker's Guide to Visual Basic**. Aside from the fact that Vince and John are two of the smartest people I know, they're also enormously street-savvy programmers and superb writers of the off-the-wall school. As you go through these pages you'll find, over and over again, that Vince and John have uncovered astounding new ways to tackle real-world problems. You'll also find that they don't hesitate to tell you when VB is all screwed up, and what you can do to work around the problems.

This Hacker's Guide, like all Hacker's Guides, promises to tell you the unvarnished truth—even when the truth contradicts the Microsoft Party Line. The Hacker's Guide goes far beyond the official documentation, beyond the "how it should work" school of thought into the "how to get the bloody thing to work right" neighborhood. Vince and John, two of the toughest kids on VB's mean streets, will show you tips and tricks that could take a lifetime to accumulate—and at the same time reveal the big picture, so you're ready to walk the streets alone. It really is a jungle out there.

Enjoy!

Woody Leonhard
Series Hack

ACKNOWLEDGMENTS

I seem to have been only like a boy playing on the seashore, and diverting myself in now
and then finding a smoother pebble or a prettier shell than ordinary,
whilst the great ocean of truth lay all undiscovered before me.

—Sir Isaac Newton

There are too many people to thank in one page, but we'd like to tip the Hacker's Hat to Woody
Leonhard, who roped . . . uh, gave us the chance to really tear into VB[1], and to Kathleen Tibbetts,
who is, as always, patient beyond belief. We've also got to thank all the folks at Microsoft who
created VB. After all, without them, you'd be reading 700 pages of blank. Last, but not least, we
would also like to thank our families for their patience: Luna for doing double duty staying up
late taking care of a new baby while Vince was nursing HackVB, and Amy for her understanding
above and beyond the call.

---

[1] What we really mean here is, of course, Microsoft Visual Basic for Windows Version 4.0, which is a trademark of Microsoft Corp.

SECTION 1: A QUICK OVERVIEW OF VB

Speed, it seems to me, provides the one genuinely modern pleasure.

—Aldous Huxley, *Wanted, a New Pleasure*, 1949

This section is about concepts, overviews, and making sure that we're all playing with the same deck. Basically, we're going to condense Visual Basic (VB) to its essence—talking about what it is and how it works—and then delve into some of our favorite VB tips and tricks as well as some of its gotchas. We'll even translate all of *War and Peace* in this section. All in five pages. With the meaning of life thrown in for good measure.

(Hey, if you're going to promise the world, you might as well throw in the moon and stars.)

If I Were King of the Forest

VB is like a fractal image; it gets more and more complex the closer you look at it. On the surface, it's a very simple programming environment. But the more you try to explain it and understand it, the deeper you're drawn into a web of complexity so obscure that only Microsoft could have invented it.

Despite that, VB's pretty simple.

The Essence of VB

The easiest way to understand VB is to understand how you develop an application in it. You don't just sit down and start writing code. You design the user interface to your application first, and then you write whatever code you need. This flow may sound a little backwards if you're used to writing C, but it makes for very fast development in VB.

For the "design first, program later" stuff to work, VB is set up a little differently from traditional programming tools. It falls into the class known as *rapid application development,* or RAD, tools, which includes Sybase's PowerBuilder, Oracle's PowerObjects, and Borland's Delphi.

The interface consists mostly of *forms* that contain *controls.* Controls are easy to describe: They include buttons, menus, and drop-down lists. Describing a form is a little more complicated. Basically it's a group of controls and usually some kind of data. A VB application may have only one form (which would be pretty typical for, say, a simple data entry application), or it may have several forms, some of which may be dialog boxes, data entry forms, data search forms, option forms, and so on.

When you start VB, it presents you with a blank form and a bunch of controls for you to put onto it. You design the interface by putting some controls on the form. Then you modify some of the *properties* of the elements of the form and controls. Properties control how the form and controls look. Properties include the font you'll use in your text boxes and labels, the color of the background, and more complex things like which database a form is going to draw its information from.

Then you start writing code. As its name implies, VB uses a variant of good, old BASIC. You use this programming language (also called Visual Basic, just like the name of the product, as if things weren't confusing enough) to do everything from change properties of controls while the application is running to doing mathematical calculations to invoking whole other applications. Finally, you run the program.

And that's about it: Design the interface, set the properties, write the code, and run the program. In fact, it's so easy you don't even have to read the documentation. Yup, just leap in, throw the manuals away, and delete the help files. Then ask yourself why, if VB's so easy, there are so many books about it on the market.

Projects

Most computer programs consist of several files. VB programs are no different. There are form files, binary data files, code files, class files, and custom control files. VB tracks the relationships between these files via a project file, which has the extension .VBP. Figure 1.1 shows an example Project window.

Figure 1.1. VB's Project window tracks what is in your application.

Form Files

Form files have the extension .FRM. Forms correspond to displayable windows on your application. Your application may have an almost unlimited number of forms that you can choose to show or hide at your leisure. Each form file contains the information about the form's properties, controls, procedures, and even variables.

Binary Data Files

When you place binary data, like a bitmap, onto a form, VB stores that part of the form in a file with the extension .FRX.

Code Files

Code files have the extension .BAS. You use code modules to hold code that is independent of a form. A code module is a good place to put code that's common to many forms, for example, an encryption routine.

Class Files

New to Visual Basic Version 4 (VB4) are user-defined classes. These classes contain code and play a role in object linking and embedding (OLE). They have .CLS extensions.

Custom Control Files

Custom control files in VB4 have the extension .OCX. (VB3 custom control files had the extension .VBX. VB4 and VB3 custom control files are incompatible.) Custom controls contain code to perform common functions such as drawing Command buttons and making them work. (Somebody else went to the trouble of writing a lot of code so you can just drag-and-drop functionality onto your form.) You don't have to write the code; just include the custom control and use it as you would any Toolbox control. In fact, all the items in your Toolbox are custom controls. Custom controls are like free code. Can you imagine having to write the code to display something as simple and common as a Command button?

Getting Formal

Before you can finish a VB app, you have to fill out some forms. Even if there's not going to be any user interaction with the application, you have to fill out at least one form. Sad, but true.

Well, maybe it's not even sad. VB's form designer is pretty easy to use. Basically, you draw controls on the form. These controls are located in VB's Toolbox, which, by default, appears on the left side of your screen. Figure 1.2 shows a picture of the Toolbox. (Why Microsoft chose to

**Figure 1.2. The Toolbox.
You know what to do.**

call it the Toolbox when the elements inside are called controls defies explanation. Why not call it the Control Box? Or call what's inside tools? Micro-logic. Go figure.)

Until you get the hang of things, the icons in the Toolbox are probably going to make little or no sense. You can get to the popup help that tells you what each icon does by letting the cursor rest on the icon.

In the Toolbox are controls that add features to the form. These features include labels, Command buttons, text boxes, check boxes, drop-down lists, and all sorts of other useful toys. (Why not call it the ToyBox?) To add one to the form, double-click the appropriate control; doing this places in the center of your form a default-sized one of whatever you clicked. Or you can single-click and use your mouse to draw a control wherever you want it on your form.

If you're having problems visualizing what the heck you'd possibly do with these controls, imagine that you're creating an application that's going to suck the information out of a database. You'd probably want a *text box* in which users could type what they're looking for, a *data grid* to display whatever your application finds, and a *Command button* that would make the program actually go out and get data. Well, these are all controls that are available in the Toolbox.

Controls follow fairly logical rules when it comes to moving them and resizing them on a form. Click most controls on a form, and they'll display eight "handles" that you can grab. There are handles on each side of the control. Drag a handle to grow or shrink the selected side along with your mouse movement. There are also handles on the corners that work in pretty much the same way, except they grow and shrink both sides connected to them simultaneously. You can also grab the center of a control and move it around. (You may also resize and move most controls by using properties.)

VBXs and OCXs

The controls in the Toolbox are actually little programs. Microsoft wrote many of the ones that come out of the box with VB, but there are thousands more available from third parties. You can buy controls to do most anything. Say you want to write a terminal emulator. You don't need to know anything about communications protocols ("I thought kermit was a frog. And is X Modem like X Windows?"). Just buy a control that does all this for you, add it to VB, and drag it onto your form. Done. (Well, you'll have to write a little code to attach things, but that's easier than learning modem trivia.)

Such are the joys of component-based programming. Visual Basic isn't object-oriented in the strictest sense (although class modules make it a little more so), but it does enjoy one of the benefits of object orientation: You can reuse code easily. With VB3, these add-in components were called Visual Basic Custom controls (VBXs). VB4 uses OLE controls, called OCXs for short. As we said earlier in the section, VBXs and OCXs are incompatible, that is, VB4 can't use VBXs. This is a real drag because there are an awful lot of VBXs available, while OCXs are still relatively new. But developers seem to be translating their VBXs quickly, so this incompatibility shouldn't be a problem for much longer.

Observing the Properties

Properties are how VB defines how your application is going to look and how its elements are going to react when you click them, type in them, and generally muck about with them. Every object on a form has properties. There are properties, for example, to define what font your Command button will use, where it will reside on the form, and how big it'll be. In fact, it can take you longer to set all your objects' properties than it does to write the code. While some VB developers have pointed out that, yes, VB doesn't require you to write a lot of code, setting those darn properties is as much of a pain as writing code ever was. Fortunately, most properties come with intelligent default values.

The Properties window (see Figure 1.3) may look a little forbidding at first. That's mainly because it stores a lot of its information in a kind of shorthand. For example, instead of saying "red," it displays a long hexadecimal number. See, for example, BackColor in the figure. Don't worry, though. Most of the really nasty-looking properties don't require you to know this kind of arcana. Instead, they display an ellipsis (. . .) or a drop-down menu. You click on whichever to reach a self-

Properties - Form1	
Form1 Form	
Appearance	1 - 3D
AutoRedraw	False
BackColor	&H8000000F&
BorderStyle	2 - Sizable
Caption	Form1
ClipControls	True
ControlBox	True
DrawMode	13 - Copy Pen
DrawStyle	0 - Solid
DrawWidth	1
Enabled	True
FillColor	&H00000000&
FillStyle	1 - Transparent
Font	MS Sans Serif
FontTransparent	True
ForeColor	&H80000012&
Height	4635
HelpContextID	0
Icon	(Icon)
KeyPreview	False
Left	3510
LinkMode	0 - None
LinkTopic	Form1
MaxButton	True
MDIChild	False
MinButton	True
MouseIcon	(None)

Figure 1.3. Why do you treat me like I'm your property?

explanatory list. For example, you don't have to enter the hexadecimal number for a color. Instead, click the ellipsis. You'll get a color palette from which you can select the color you want.

As long as we're on the subject, for many colors the default entry is not obvious from the drop-down color palette. This is because it's not there. For instance, the hexadecimal number of the default BackColor for a Command button is &H8000000F&, which results in a medium gray. If you click the ellipses and explicitly choose the gray, you end up with the property value &H00C0C0C0&. It took a *long* time for us to figure out that VB has some color constants that represent not a specific color, but rather the colors you set for the various elements in your Windows environment. For instance, that &H8000000F& is really the constant, vbButtonFace, which means, "Use the color that all buttons in your Windows environment use." There are quite a few of these color constants.

Code-dependency

When push comes to shove, VB does require you to program. Sometimes you can get away with just a few lines of easy code. Sometimes you'll be typing until the cows come home.

VB is one of those programming languages that is very easy to pick up, particularly if you had a bit of BASIC programming in high school or have ever written macros for the likes of Word for Windows. VB statements typically look like this:

```
Text1.Text = UCase(Text1.Text)
```

In all, pretty simple stuff. VB code tends to be the kind of code that you can read out loud to yourself. While it may be a little short on plot, it has some very active characters. The one line of code above says, "Take the text in text box number 1 and make it uppercase." Or, more specifically, set the text in text box number 1 equal to what happens when you run the "UCase" function on the text in text box number 1. The shorthand can be a little confusing until you realize that, when you draw objects on a form in VB, VB gives those objects very generic names, like Command1 (a button) and Text1 (a text box). (You can easily change the name of the objects.)

Each object is made up of elements. A Command button, for example, has a caption written in the button. VB uses the period to specify which part of an object you're talking about. So Text1.Text tells VB you're talking about the text in the textbox called Text1. After the equals operator is a built-in VB function called UCase(). UCase takes whatever is in its parentheses and uppercases it, in this case, Text1.Text. The = is an assignment operator. It works a bit like the equals sign; that is, whatever is on the left becomes what's on the right.

VB is what's called an "event-driven" programming language. This means its functions react to events, such as mouse clicks. When you put a Command button on your form, you attach a procedure to the event of a mouse click. So, just as VB uses the period to separate an object from its elements, it uses an underscore to separate an object from its event. You wind up with compounds like Command1_Click. However, you'll never have to manually create these names.

Say you want an Exit button on your form. Just draw it and then double-click it to see its Code window. You'll see something like this:

```
Sub Command1_Click()
End Sub
```

Notice that VB has written two lines of code for you automatically. Your only job is to write the incredibly complex code that will exit this program, close all the windows, and destroy all the open variables. Here's what that might look like in a typically complex VB application:

```
Sub Command1_Click()
      End
End Sub
```

Not pretty, is it? The truth is, although End will close your application, you'll usually have code around the End statement that will make sure the user really wants to exit the program, as well as error-handling code and code to clean up what the application's been doing (for example, saving stuff to disk). But in hard times, you can get away with just End.

VB code can even modify properties and alter the form's appearance. So, if you really hate drawing buttons and modifying properties, you can just write code to do everything. But then you'd be better off writing in C++, which will compile down to a much tighter application that runs faster and takes up fewer resources on your PC. Put another way, VB is a very fast prototyping tool that gets applications running quickly—even if you hate to draw.

The Editor

When you write VB code, you use VB's editor, or Code window. An example is shown in Figure 1.4.

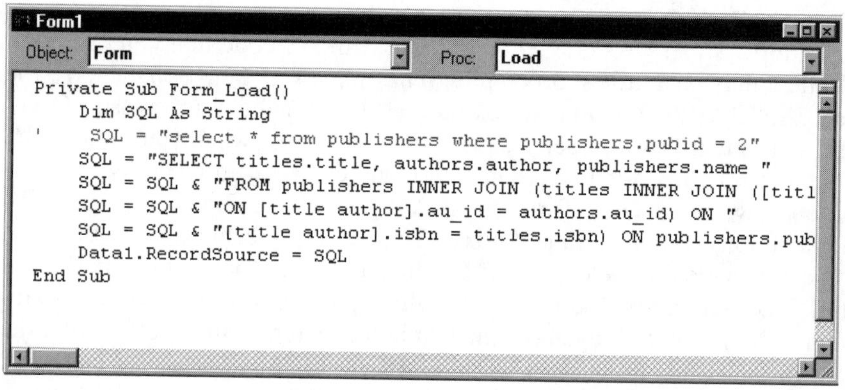

Figure 1.4. VB's Code window: Just enough features to do the job.

Let's take a tour of the Code window. Of course it has the standard Windows 95 features (Control menu box, Minimize button, Maximize button, and Exit button). At the top is the Title Bar, which contains the name of the object you're writing code for, in this case Form 1. The next line down has two drop-down list boxes: Object and Proc. Object, like the Title Bar, contains the name of the object you're working on. If you pull down the drop-down, you'll see and be able to select all the other objects in your project.

Proc is short for "procedure." It refers to all the different events that can take place for the object you've selected. For example, for a button, the default procedure is "click"—exactly what you'd expect from a button. Any events that you've already defined appear in boldface. All others represent events that are valid for the Control, but are not defined yet.

Basically, using VB's Code window is a lot like stacking pieces of paper on top of each other. You have separate sheets for each object and each procedure, neatly organized (thanks to the editor) in one pile.

The Code window is auto-parsing. As you type, it does some basic syntax checking. When you complete a line (by hitting Return or any arrow key), VB parses the line to make sure it makes sense. It doesn't actually try to figure out what the line of code will do, but it does do some elementary grammar checking (you can turn this feature off if it bothers you).

If the editor finds an error, it'll give you a virtually incomprehensible error message. Have no fear, though: you can press F1 and get an equally inscrutable explanation. At least VB's consistent.

The editor is also fastidious. As you type, it will recognize certain keywords and autoformat them. Basically, it will ensure that keywords are properly capitalized, that there is only one space between words, and that keywords and comments are color-coded so that you can find them easily.

This fastidiousness extends to capitalization of your variables. If you declare a variable at the top of a subroutine and spell it Variable and then spell it variable later, VB will correct the latter to Variable. This is mostly a good thing, although it can be a little odd having an editor correct your spelling.

VB even indents your code. It assumes that whatever you're typing should be indented by as much as the previous line was. So as you're typing your code (entering comments and indenting to make it readable), you hit Return. When you do, you won't go to the beginning of the next line; you will end up at the same column at which the last line left off. This type of indenting (which has been around in such intelligent editors as emacs for years) is nearly perfect for the typical, really short code that you write for VB.

VB indents your lines four spaces unless you tell it otherwise. Four spaces is fairly standard, although many programmers prefer three or five. To change this value, select Tools/Options/Environment, click the Editor tab, and enter the new value under Tab Stop Width. From this screen, you also can change the font and font size, the code colors, and foreground and background colors. Further, you can turn auto indent on and off and opt to view all the code in your application at once. (The alternative is to use the Object pull-down menu to move from one bit to another.) However, see the following tip.

 Don't view all code at once. Instead highlight a Function/Sub name and hit Shift+F2 to jump there. And as long as we're giving some tips, use the Split Pane capability of the editor. In the editor, locate the top of the vertical scroll bar. Move the cursor there. It will change into a pane-sizing cursor. Grab it and pull it down. Now you have two windows capable of holding two different bits of code, as shown in Figure 1.5.

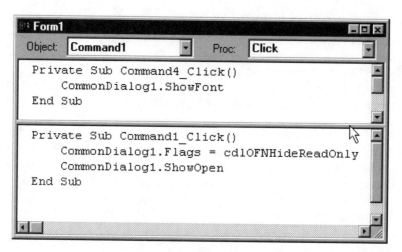

Figure 1.5. Splitting the code window.

The editor also has a pretty good search and replace engine. From the editor, select Edit/Find or press Ctrl+F. You'll see something like what is shown in Figure 1.6. Like with any word processor, you type in what you're looking for, and the editor will try to find it. Unlike with most word processors, however, you have the option of searching in the current procedure, the current module, the current project, or just the selected text. You can therefore limit your search to just the relevant areas. Most interesting on this screen is the Use Pattern Matching option. This option enables you to use wildcards to extend your search. Say you wanted to find all occurrences of the word Variable. You could search for Variable, then Variables, then Variable1, and so on. Or you could use the ? wildcard (which substitutes for any single letter) and just search for Variable?. Or you could use the *, which substitutes for multiple characters, and find Variable12.

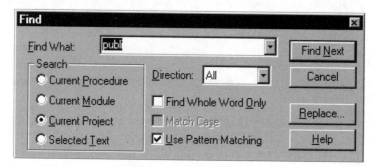

Figure 1.6. Find what? You mean it was lost?

Functions, Subs, and Procedures, Oh My

VB comes with many procedures built in, for example, Click, MouseDown, and MouseUp. You can get at these nearly any time from the editor by pulling down the Proc list box.

Often, however, these procedures aren't enough. Most of the time, you'll need to create your own. So VB has lots of facilities for creating procedures, called *general procedures* to distinguish them from the built-in procedures. There are two types of general procedure:

1. A subprogram (or Sub).

2. A user-defined function. (These are actually programmer-defined functions, but somehow the name user-defined function got attached to them back in the days of dBase for DOS, all of which is to say, call 'em functions.)

Both are called from other functions, and both contain similar code. You can tell them apart because Subs always begin with "Sub" and end with "End Sub," while functions begin "Function" and end with "End Function."

Subs and functions are the same except in one way: Subs don't return values to the calling function; functions do. So when you want the result of a procedure (say, some crunched numbers), use a function. Because functions receive and return data, you need to declare what kind of data they'll be working on. You do that when you declare the function. For example:

```
Function Crunch! (Number!)
    Dim Temp!
    Temp! = (Number! * 235)/22
    Crunch! = Temp!
End Function
```

It's not very romantic, but it does the job. There are a few things here to notice. First, the function name and variable names end in !. This is a *type declaration character.* Type-declaration characters tell VB what kind of variable it's dealing with. The ! means the variables are numbers. More specifically, the variables are what's called a *single precision floating-point number.* See the upcoming section "Variables and Data Types" for more information.

Second, notice there's something within the () of the function declaration line. This is the argument that some other function (or subprogram) is passing this function.

Finally, on the second to last line, the function name is set equal to the value of whatever mathematical wonder we've wrought. This is how you pass the result of the function back to whatever called it.

You can get into a function or Sub with the Call statement. You get out of a function or Sub with the Exit statement.

Named Arguments

Most functions and commands in VB accept named arguments, so you don't have to give the arguments in order provided you explicitly specify the argument names. For instance, the following DateAdd calls are equivalent:

```
d = DateAdd("d", 6, #Jan 5, 1996#)
d = DateAdd(Number:=6, Interval:="d", Date:=#Jan 5, 1996#)
```

In Section 2, we discuss functions and statements that can accept named arguments. These appear in the Usage part of Section 2 along with the arguments that include the colon-equals characters, such as:

Usage   *VariantValue* = DateAdd(*Interval*:=, *Number*:=, *Date*:=)

Functions and statements that do not accept named arguments include only the argument list; for example:

Usage   *BooleanValue* = CBool(*Expression*)

Optional arguments are enclosed in square brackets, as in:

Usage   *StringValue* = Error([*ErrorNumber*:=])

Variables and Data Types

Now comes the tricky part: introducing variables. You know how it is. You never know how a variable is going to act. They're just so whimsical. So unpredictable. So . . . well, variable. But seriously (semi), if you've gotten this far, you probably know what a variable is. (In case you don't, they're temporary storage for your program's information.) VB handles variables fairly well. You just declare them and use them. They're local to the procedure you're in, unless you specify otherwise. They initialize well (to 0 for numbers and to null for strings). All in all, variables in VB are very well behaved.

Numbers and Strings

Of course, things do get tricky. Programming languages don't react well when you have just one kind of variable and then stick whatever into it. This practice tends to be very inefficient. For example, storing pi to the 200th digit is very different from storing your bank balance. And both are completely different from storing the Twenty-third Psalm. If you use the same amount of memory to store all of these, you either have to truncate pi or give way too much space to your bank balance. And only God knows what's happening with that shepherd.

So, VB, like most programming languages, breaks its variables down into two types: numbers and strings. Each of these is further broken down into a few subtypes. Look at Table 1.1 to see what we mean.

Before you go about declaring variables, you have to know a few things:

- You can't give a variable the same name as that of a VB command. VB commands are reserved. If you try, VB gives you an error message.

- A variable name must begin with a letter. After that, you can use letters, hyphens, numbers, and underscores.

- A variable name can be from 1 to 40 characters long.

Table 1.1. How VB handles its variables.

DATA SUBTYPE	STORAGE SIZE	RANGE	TYPE CHARACTER
Byte	1 byte	0 to 255	None
Boolean	2 bytes	True or False	None
Integer	2 bytes	–32,768 to 32,767	%
Long	4 bytes	–2,147,483,648 to 2,147,483,647	&
Single	4 bytes	–3.402823E38 to –1.401298E–45 for negative values; 1.401298E–45 to 3.402823E38 for positive values	!
Double	8 bytes	–1.79769313486231E308 to –4.94065645841247E–324 for negative values; 4.94065645841247E–324 to 1.79769313486231E308 for positive values	#
Currency	8 bytes	–922,337,203,685,477.5808 to 922,337,203,685,477.5807	@
Date	8 bytes	January 1, 100 to December 31, 9999	None
Object	4 bytes	Any Object reference	None
String (variable-length)	10 bytes + string length	0 to approximately 2 billion (approximately 65,400 for Microsoft Windows version 3.1 and earlier)	$
String (fixed-length)	Length of string	1 to approximately 65,400	$
Variant (with numbers)	16 bytes	Any numeric value up to the range of a double	None
Variant (with characters)	22 bytes + string length	Same range as for variable-length string	None

You declare variables with the Dim, Public, Private, Global, or Static statement. The generic syntax is

```
Dim Variable [As Type]
Public Variable [As Type]
Private Variable [As Type]
Global Variable [As Type]
Static Variable [As Type]
```

And at this point, you're probably wondering how the four differ from each other. Dim, which you'll probably use the most, declares variables only in the procedure you're in. That means you can declare the same variable name in each form and code module you use without any conflicts (although doing this would probably be bad programming practice). Public must appear in the

Declarations section of a code module. Declaring a variable as Public makes it available to all procedures in all code modules in your application. You use Private to make variables available to all procedures in the module. Finally, you use Static to declare a variable that retains its value through multiple calls of the procedure. Static variables are defined only for the procedure you're in. Generally you use Static with arrays.

Variants

You don't have to declare variables. If you don't, VB defaults to its all-purpose data type, Variant. Similarly, if you omit the type of the variable, VB assumes it's a Variant variable. This practice is both good and bad. It's good because it ensures that if you forget to declare a variable fully, you'll still be able to use it. It's bad because if you forget to declare a variable (or get into the bad habit of not declaring variables and types), VB uses the least-efficient storage method. If you let VB declare all your variables, your program will take up a larger memory footprint than if you declare them yourself.

Variants store two pieces of information: the data you're storing and a data type, or, more specifically, a code number that lets VB know what kind of data it is. Data types and their codes are given in Table 1.2.

Table 1.2. Decoding Variant data types.

CODE	DATA TYPE
0	Empty
1	Null
2	Integer
3	Long
4	Single
5	Double
6	Currency
7	Date/Time
8	String

The VarType() function shows you what a Variant's data type is. You use that function like this:

```
Print VarType(Variable)
```

which would return one of the values in Table 1.2. Not that you're likely to need to know, but it's good to see what VB is up to behind your back. You can even force Variants to be a particular data type by using conversion functions like CInt. For the most part, however, don't bother. It's just good to know that you can. Like being able to drive a stick shift.

Someone (some unnamed programmer with too much time on his or her hands) once ran a series of tests by declaring the same variable in the same program with different variable types and then performing a complex calculation using the variable. The result? Integer was about ten times faster to calculate than Variant, and considerably faster than Double, too. (True to its name, Double returned a greater degree of precision.) The long and short of it: Don't declare your variables to be anything more than you need.

Variable Assignment

After you've declared your variables, you'll probably want to put stuff into them. Usually, you do this with the = operator; for example:

```
Kilobyte = 1024
```

You can even use math and other operators in your variable assignments; such as

```
Byte = 8 * Bit
Kilobyte = 1024 * Byte
```

and so on. That works fine for numbers. Words are a little different. For them, you need quotation marks:

```
President = "Abraham Lincoln"
```

And you can use operators and other variables in your declarations:

```
President = UCase("Abraham Lincoln")
```

This code would uppercase all of Honest Abe's name.

Now comes the time to use Variant. When you know what's going to go into a variable, it makes sense to declare it. When you don't know, use Variant. The prime time for using Variant is when you're pulling information out of VB's forms; for example:

```
Dim TextFromForm As Variant

TextFromForm = Text1.Text
```

Controls don't have a data type. Actually, they're a mixture of data types. So Variant is the only type you can use. Still, you should declare your variables. Doing so is good programming procedure. The next time you're reading your code, you'll thank yourself.

Variant has one other useful characteristic: It's empty. When you declare an Integer, it's set to 0. When you declare a String, it's set to "". But when you declare Variant, it's set to Empty. It's a very Zen state of being. If you plug "" or 0 into Variant, it's no longer empty.

Working with Strings: + and &

In VB3, you could join quoted phrases with + or &, like this:

"Now is the time" + "for all good men"

VB4 gets confused when you do that. The + now is reserved for mathematical operations. So you have to use the &.

Type Casting

So far, we've been giving variables a data type with the As operator, as in

```
Dim AnyNumber As Integer
```

Well, there's another way to give variables a data type: Use a variable suffix. This way has the advantage of taking fewer keystrokes, but the disadvantage of making your code a little less readable. There are six symbols that serve as data type suffixes, as shown in Table 1.3. However, there aren't enough symbols to cover all the data types, so you'd best stick with the proper, word-based declarations for readability's sake.

Table 1.3. Declaring variables with little signs.

SUFFIX	VARIABLE TYPE
$	String
%	Integer
&	Long
!	Single
#	Double
@	Currency

You can declare your variables just as you did before: with Dim, Global, Public, Private, and Static; for example,

```
Dim Number%
```

declares the variable Number to be an integer. All the other suffixes work the same way.

Note that there is no equivalent to the keyword Variant. This is because Variant is the default. So, saying

```
Dim Something As Variant
```

is the same as saying

```
Dim Something
```

Easy.

These suffixes are also useful when you're declaring what kind of value a function is going to return. If you were to write

```
Function Halitosis (NewVariable)
```

VB would assume that NewVariable is data type Variant and that the function Halitosis is going to return a Variant value. If, on the other hand, you were to write

```
Function Halitosis$ (NewVariable$)
```

you'd know that Halitosis is going to return a string and that NewVariable is a string, also.

Put another way, the following two statements are equivalent:

```
Dim a As Long
Dim a&
```

Note, however, that the type-declaration character is *not* part of the variable name. This is in contrast with some other versions of BASIC (such as WordBasic). So, if you use

```
Dim a&
```

and later use 'a' in code:

```
a = &H80
```

the same variable is still being referred to. So you can't have two variables with the same name, but different types, as in

```
Dim a&, a$
```

This would generate an error.

I Can't Hear: I'm Deftype

There's one more way to declare your variables: Use Def*type* statements. You use Def*type* statements when you want VB to know that any variable that begins with a certain character will be of one and only one data type. There are seven types of Def*type* statements, as shown in Table 1.4.

Table 1.4. Def*type* statements.

DEF*TYPE* STATEMENT	WHAT IT DECLARES
DefInt	Integers
DefLng	Long integers
DefSng	Singles
DefDbl	Doubles
DefCur	Currency
DefStr	Strings
DefVar	Variants

You use them as in this example:

```
DefInt I
```

This simple statement means that any variable beginning with the letter I is an integer. So Inscrutable and Indigo, for example, would be integers. This construct is a very fast way to define a bunch of variables at once. You can, of course, force any variable to be a different type by declaring it explicitly. The Dim statement, for example, takes precedence over a Def*type* statement.

You also can use ranges of letters, separating discrete letters with commas and ranges with hyphens; for example:

```
DefStr a, L-N
```

defines any variable beginning with the letters a, L, M, or N as a string.

Variables by Force

As we mentioned earlier in this section, VB doesn't require you to declare any variables at all. This is wonderful if you're writing a really quick program. But anyone who has had to debug a few hundred (or thousand) lines of code to find a variable that was spelled Variable when you declared it and then misspelled once, somewhere deep within the bowels of your program, will welcome the Option Explicit command.

So, where you're declaring your variables, just type Option Explicit. Then every time you use an undeclared variable, VB will advise you that doing so is not good programming practice.

Constantipation

VB also has constants. Constants work a bit like variables: You just declare them and then use them throughout your program. They differ from variables in that, true to their name, they never change. You can use them to give easy-to-understand names to numbers that you might be using a lot but that could look like gibberish to many people. A simple example is pi. You could use 3.1416. Or you could type

```
Const PI = 3.1416
```

and just use PI throughout your program when you want the value of pi. (Traditionally, constant names are all uppercase, but VB isn't case-sensitive about them, so don't sweat it.)

Constants can be declared just like variables by using the same suffixes. But because constants are more stable, VB is generally able to figure out what data type a constant should be without your telling it. So,

```
Const NAME = "Your Name Here"
```

is a string and

```
Const BIG_NUMBER = 87384787682743
```

is a long. But there are times when you don't want VB to make its assumptions, times when you really want to make sure things are done your way. So, you could say

```
Const BIG_NUMBER$ = 87384787682743
```

This time, BIG_NUMBER is a string, not a long.

You can put just about anything into a constant. The two examples we talked about are *literals*. A literal is something you put into a constant that you want interpreted literally. You can also stick in other constants. Further, you can do simple math, such as

```
Const SMALL_NUMBER = 0.002
Const LARGE_NUMBER = SMALL_NUMBER + 87837486563
```

With a wave of your magic wand, you add a big number to a SMALL_NUMBER to get a LARGE_NUMBER.

Why the heck would you ever use a constant? Mostly because they're easier to read than the number they stand in for. They also make it easy for you to change a value throughout your program. Say you defined PI as 3.14 and then later want to make it more precise, to be 3.14159. If your program used PI, defined in our earlier example as 3.14, all over the place, you'd have to find every occurrence of 3.14 and change it to 3.1415. If you defined PI as a constant, you'd just change the declaration.

Constants, like variables, have a scope—a sphere of influence. Typically, if you define a constant in a form, for example, that scope is just the procedure that you define it in. However, you can make Global Const declarations, just as you can make Global variable declarations, and your Constant will have a scope of the entire program.

There's a horde of constants already declared in the OLE objects. Just call the Object Browser (F2) and look under the Library/Project of your choice under the Constants collection.

On a final note, VB has a file called CONSTANT.TXT, which lives in the same directory as VB, that contains (you guessed it) constants. The idea is that when you need to get constants for certain things, you can just select File/Load Text/CONSTANT.TXT to pull in declarations for whatever variables you want.

Arrays

An *array* is a variable that can hold multiple (usually related) values of the same data type. You might use an array to store all the stats for your favorite major league baseball player. You could then perform operations on the elements of that array to find out how he did.

You declare arrays just like you declare variables, except you need to tell VB how big your array is going to be. You do that by adding the number of elements in parentheses after the variable name, like this:

```
Dim Array(10) As Integer
```

This statement declares an eleven-member array of integers.

You get to each element in the array by its *index*. The index is a number, 0 to *n,* where *n* is the number of elements in the array. For example, referring to Array(2) in your program would call out the third element in your array.

Arrays can even store strings, so you could create an array such as

```
Dim Array(7) As String
```

and then set the values in this array

```
Array(0) = "Monday"
Array(1) = "Tuesday"
```

and so on. You'd then reference Monday as Array(0).

As with variables, you declare arrays using your favorite keywords (Int, Single, even Variant) or those somewhat confusing symbols (#, $, @, and so on). Unlike with variables, you *must* declare arrays. Declaration serves two purposes. First, it tells VB how much memory to set aside. Second, it keeps VB from getting confused if you try to create a function with the same name as the array.

If you declare an array as Variant, you can be a little sneaky and store different data types in different indexes.

Homework Assignment

When you define a variable or a constant, you use the equals sign, which sets whatever is on the left side of the sign equal to what's on the right side. This means you are making a variable or constant (on the left) equal to a static value (on the right), like this:

```
Text1.Text = "Remember to phrase your response in the form of a question"
```

or

```
PI = 3.14
```

But it's far more useful to use an expression of some kind on the right side. In this way, you can set variables based on what's going on in your program. At the simplest level, you can do some elementary math:

```
TwoPi = 2*PI
```

But you can also perform interesting assignment feats, such as

```
Command1.Caption = Text1.Text
```

which makes the button Command1 read with whatever you typed into the text box Text1. It also makes it possible to break all rules of math with expressions like this:

```
n = n + 1
```

This expression makes no sense until you realize that you're not saying that a number is equal to one greater than itself. Rather, you're setting n equal to $n + 1$. In fact, this is how you set most counters for those times when, for example, you need to step through the elements of an array.

How Long Do I Have, Doc?

Variables don't live forever. Nor do constants. There are three rules you have to remember when you declare variables or constants:

- A procedure-level variable or constant dies with the procedure unless you declare it as Static.

- A form-level variable or constant dies when you set the form to Nothing (e.g., Set Form1 = Nothing), which also terminates the form.

- A module-level variable or constant lives as long as the program lives.

Smooth Operator

There are five types of operators:

1. Arithmetic

2. String

3. Relational

4. Logical

5. Special

Arithmetic Operators

The simplest to understand are the arithmetic, which are listed in Table 1.5.

Table 1.5. Arithmetic operators.

OPERATOR	WHAT IT DOES
+	Adds.
−	Subtracts or changes the sign.
*	Multiplies.
/	Divides.
^	Raises the number on its left to the number on its right.
\	Divides two integers.
Mod	Takes the modulus (prints the division remainder) of two numbers.

With the exception of the last two, all the operators work on all numeric data types (you can even mix and match). The last two only work on integers and long integers.

All the operators work just as you'd expect (if you remember elementary school math). Of course, in elementary school, you probably weren't taught about integer division or about taking the modulus of two numbers. Integer division works only on integers (and longs) and prints an integer as a result. Any remainder is simply discarded. This means all your answers with a fractional part will be rounded down. Also, if you feed the \ nonintegers, they will be rounded to their nearest integer and then operated on.

The modulus is a relative of \—it takes *only* the remainder. An example is 10 Mod 3—3 goes into 10 three times, with a remainder of 1.

Relational Operators

The relational operators are good for checking to see if one thing is bigger than another, smaller than another, or equal to another. They are listed in Table 1.6.

Table 1.6. Relational operators.

Operator	What It Does
=	Checks to determine if two things are equal.
<>	Checks to determine if two things aren't equal.
>	Checks to determine whether what's on the left is greater than what's on the right.
<	Checks to determine whether what's on the left is less than what's on the right.
>=	Indicates greater than or equal to.
<=	Indicates less than or equal to.

There's little to say about relational operators. You probably remember them from your early math classes. They even work on text. This may seem a little odd. But you can check to see if one string is equal to another and even check alphabetical order. For example, you may know that

```
"A rose" = "A rose"
```

but

```
"by any other name" <> "would smell as sweet"
```

Best of all, you no longer have to memorize the alphabet. VB will check it for you, as in

```
"Allosaur" < "Zebra"
```

It definitely sounds odd, but that's the way it works.

 The only caveat in using relational operators concerns floating-point values. Numerical precision may not get you exact matches between numbers. For instance, the Boolean expression, $sin(4*atn(1)) = 0$, returns False, when it should return True.

Speaking of strings, VB has an operator for joining strings: the &. In VB3, you could also use the +, but VB4 strongly encourages you to use the &—it'll give you an error if you don't. This operator is easy to use; for example:

```
"Do you know " & "how hard it is to " & "keep coming up with" & " examples?"
```

yield, "Do you know how hard it is to keep coming up with examples?" The operator even works with variables. So you could write

```
Complaint1 = "Do you know "
Complaint2 = "how hard it is "
Complaint3 = "to keep coming up with"
Complaint4 = " examples?"
```

Then when you wrote

```
WholeComplaint = Complaint1 & Complaint2 & Complaint3 & Complaint4
Print WholeComplaint
```

you'd get

```
Do you know how hard it is to keep coming up with examples?
```

Nothing to it. The & works only on strings. If you use it on numeric values, VB treats them as strings. If the strings have numeric values and you want to add them, use the + operator.

Logical Operators

The logical operators are in some ways the most confusing of the operators. For this reason, Table 1.7 shows the logical operators along with examples.

Table 1.7. Logical operators.

OPERATOR	WHAT IT DOES	EXAMPLE
Not	Negates something.	If Not (X% = Y%)
And	Joins two things.	If (X% = Y%) And (Z% = A%)
Or	Chooses one *or* two things.	If (X% = Y%) Or (Z% = A%)
Xor	Chooses one *of* two things.	If (X% = Y%) Xor (Z% = A%)
Eqv	Checks for equivalence.	If (X% = Y%) Eqv (Z% = A%)]
Imp	Checks for implication.	If (X% = Y%) Imp (Z% = A%)

These little suckers] deserve a few words of explanation. Their history goes back to the nineteenth century when an English mathematician, George Boole, decided that things should always be either true or false.[1] This is called Boolean logic. The operators that evaluate true and false expressions are called Boolean operators. (Sometimes you'll hear them called "bitwise" operators. That's because they operate on the bits of the answer they return. We'll get into that in a minute.)

The easiest of these to understand is the logical Not. Basically, it inverts the answer you'd expect if it weren't there; for example:

```
A = 1
B = 1

If Not(A = B) Then End
```

We know that A = B. If Not weren't there, the program would end (A = B would be True). But add Not, and suddenly the whole expression evaluates to False, and the program continues. There's a side effect of this wonderful operator. Consider the following example:

```
A = 5
If A Then MsgBox "True!"
If Not A Then MsgBox "True!"
```

Any numeric expression not equal to zero is True, but Not A (in our case) won't be True *unless* A = −1.

---

[1] Warning: This is a gross oversimplification. For an actual definition of Boolean logic, check with the mathematician nearest you.

Put in more general terms, if you want to figure out how a logical operator is going to behave, evaluate the expression(s) in your program as though the logical operators weren't there. All your expressions will return either True or False (0 or 1). Then apply the logical operators.

The next easiest logical operator to understand is And. This operator ensures that two expressions must both be True; for example:

```
A = 1
B = 1
C = 45
D = 45

If (A = B) And (C = D) Then End
```

This code fragment ends the program, since both statements are True. All the logical And is doing is comparing the results of the Boolean analysis of the two expressions. If they both evaluate True, And is happy. If one is True and one is False, And unhappy. And, of course, if both are False, And is unhappy.

The next logical operator is Or. Like And, Or is happy if both expressions are True. Unlike And, it's also happy if *either* of them is True. It is unhappy only when both are False. This is starting to make sense, isn't it?

Xor (pronounced Ex-Or) is a relative of Or. It stands for Exclusive Or. It is happy only when one expression is True, not when both are False and not when both are True.

Eqv is happy when the two expressions both evaluate either to True or to False, but not when one is True and the other is False. So, the code segment

```
A = 1
B = 2
C = 45
D = 46

If (A = B) And (C = D) Then End
```

causes the program to end because both expressions would evaluate to False.

Remember when we asked if this was starting to make sense? Prepare for it not to. The operator Imp makes no sense to anyone. It's based on mathematical rules that make sense only to your pet cat, and you know how he is (staring at the inside of the toilet bowl all day like it's talking or something). This is the only logical operator that really cares how you've ordered your expressions. It looks at the first operator, and if it's True, then the second operator must also be True for it to be happy. If the first operator is False, then the second can be either True or False and Imp will be happy. Odd, but true.

Program Flow

If you wrote very simple programs, they'd all execute from the first instruction straight through to the last with no interruption. Few programs are that simple. Usually, they have to make "decisions" based on user input, data files, or other variables. That is, they need to change their flow based on the conditions around them.

There are many ways to change the flow of a program. The two main ones are to use an unconditional branch or a conditional branch. You also can have the program terminate, can use conditional testing, or can have the program loop.

The Unconditional Branch

The unconditional branch is kind of odd. Some programming teachers warn beginning programmers that its use is a sign of bad programming. Whether or not this is true, the use of an unconditional branch can make a program hard to read if it's jumping around all its Subs and procedures every few lines. We cover it first because it's very simple: You just use the GoTo statement to GoTo either a line number or a label.

GoTo 1: Line Numbers and Labels

Oh, yeah, line numbers. Back in the old days of BASIC, you numbered every line and the interpreter executed them in the order you numbered them. It was a pain when you numbered your lines 10, 20, 30, and so on and then needed to add more than nine lines in a later version and so had to renumber all your lines.

VB doesn't require line numbers. But you can still use them. Just put the number at the beginning of the line, like this:

```
100 Dim VendorName As String
200 VendorName = Text1.Text
```

Now you can GoTo 200 easily if you want. Your line numbers can be up to 40 digits long. Long numbers can be hard to read. So for readability's sake (and debugging with Erl, VB's Error Line location function), keep your numbers below 65,529.

Better than line numbers are *labels*. A label is just a word with a colon after it (like in DOS batch files, if you remember those). Like a variable, a label must begin with a letter and can't be longer than 40 characters. You use them like this:

```
Dim VendorName As String
Dim VendorMunge1 As String
Dim VendorMunge2 As String
VendorName = Text1.Text

Munge1:

VendorMunge1 = UCase(VendorName)

Munge2:

VendorMunge2 = LCase(VendorName)
```

Now you have a program with two labels in it: Munge1: and Munge2:. You can GoTo Munge1: or GoTo Munge2: whenever you please. Just remember to put the colon after all label names (but not after line numbers). Also, you can't have duplicate line numbers or labels within a form or code module.

Using GoTo with Conditions

More often than you use GoTo, you'll be using If or Select Case to alter program flow. The conditions soften GoTo's arbitrariness, but still can make code hard to follow because you have to find GoTo's target (the line number of label). If is very easy to use. It follows this format: If *something is true* Then *do something;* for example:

```
If Divisor = 0 Then MsgBox "You can't divide by zero."
```

This common usage of If is called the "one-line If." You can just as easily place a Then *do something* part of the If condition on a separate line, as in the following:

```
If Division = 0 Then
      MsgBox "You can't divide by zero."
```

Doing it this way makes a lot of sense when you get into If-Then-Else conditions, like this:

```
Const MagicNumber = 143
Dim Guess As Integer

GuessPoint:
Guess = Val(InputBox$("Guess the magic number"))

If Guess = MagicNumber Then
      MsgBox "Good guess"
      End
Else
      MsgBox "Wrong. Try again."
      GoTo GuessPoint:
End If
```

Not exactly brain surgery, is it? Just remember that when you span multiple lines with an If statement, you need to include your End If. In addition to the = symbol, you can, of course, use all the standard relational operators (<>, >, <, >=, and <=).

You also can nest If tests as deeply as you want, but going too deep can make your code very hard to read. One simple example might be to have the previous code sample tell the user if he or she is within ten of the magic number, like this:

```
If Guess = MagicNumber Then
      MsgBox "Good guess"
      End
Else
      If (Guess >= MagicNumber - 10) And (Guess <= MagicNumber + 10) Then
            MsgBox "You're within 10"
            GoTo GuessPoint:
      Else
      MsgBox "Wrong. Try again."
            GoTo GuessPoint:
End If
```

If you were to develop this to one more level, your code would become virtually inscrutable. That's why VB has the ElseIf construct. ElseIf helps when your Then actions or your Else actions are more than a line or if your If instruction is longer than a line. We'd rewrite the previous code segment like this:

```
If Guess = MagicNumber Then
      MsgBox "Good guess"
      End
ElseIf (Guess >= MagicNumber - 10) And (Guess <= MagicNumber + 10) Then
      MsgBox "You're within 10"
      GoTo GuessPoint:
Else
MsgBox "Wrong. Try again."
      GoTo GuessPoint:
End If
```

Can you see how this is much easier to read? It's generally better to use ElseIf than to nest your Ifs. The general construction is

```
If X Then
      do something
ElseIf Y Then
      do something
ElseIf Z Then
      do something
Else
      do something
End If
```

You may have as many ElseIfs as you want, or you may have none. The Else is similarly optional. The only thing you must have on an If that spans more than one line is the End If statement.

Actually, this construction for our number guessing program probably isn't the best (although with so few lines, it's not a big deal). It would be better to use VB's Select Case structure. This structure is really good for If-like work when ranges of values are involved. (If is great at testing for true/false situations.) The generic construction of Select Case follows:

```
Select Case expression
      Case First set of what you're testing
            Actions
      Case Second set of what you're testing
            Actions
      Case Else
            Actions
End Select Case
```

So, we'd rewrite our previous code fragment like this:

```
Select Case Guess
      Case MagicNumber
            MsgBox "Good guess"
            End
      Case (MagicNumber - 10) To (MagicNumber + 10)
            MsgBox "You're within 10"
            GoTo GuessPoint:
      Case Else
```

```
            MsgBox "Wrong. Try Again"
            GoTo GuessPoint:
End Select
```

The second Case line introduces a new construct: To. You use To when you want to specify a range of numbers. You can also use relational operators and specify multiple ranges, but the syntax changes a little. We could rewrite that second line like this:

```
Case Is >= MagicNumber - 10, Is <= MagicNumber + 10
```

Notice the addition of Is and the comma. You use Is with relational operators (Case Is >= Magic-Number –10) and with multiple ranges. Otherwise (when specifying equality or an explicit range), you don't need it.

Case constructions are even easier to read than ElseIfs. We recommend you use them wherever you can—actually, before you resort to using ElseIf. You had to know about ElseIf before we could introduce the concept of Case, otherwise it wouldn't have made sense; otherwise we would have introduced Case first.

Feeling Loopy: Conditional Program Flow

Another way to control the flow of your programs is to use loops. VB has three kinds of loops, described briefly in Table 1.8.

Table 1.8. Going around in loops.

Type of Loop	What It Does
For/Next	Executes its instructions a set number of times.
Do/Loop	Executes its instructions until a condition is met.
While/Wend	An old version of Do/Loop. Please don't use.

The For/Next Loop

In typical constructions, your loops will do their "thinking" at the beginning. For/Next is the simplest type of loop, so we tackle it first. Basically, For/Next needs a starting value, an ending value, and an increment to count by. It then counts from start to end, performing whatever is in its instruction block until the ending value is met before going on; for example:

```
Dim I As Integer
Dim Sum As Integer
Sum = 0
For I = 0 To 100 Step 10
    Sum = Sum + I
Next I
```

This code fragment adds 10, 20, 30, 40, 50 . . . 100. (The result is 550, by the way.) You can set Step to anything you want, even negative numbers. If you don't set it, it defaults to 1. Also, For's starting and ending values don't have to be constants. They can be variables and pick up their values from elsewhere in your program. Setting the values as variables is a good way to ensure some action gets taken a set number of times.

The Do/Loop

The Do/Loop structure is considerably more versatile than that of For/Next. It executes its body until a condition that you define returns True. You can check this condition at the beginning or the end of the loop.

Do/Loops are not as simple as they may seem, primarily because they come in four varieties. Which variety a loop is depends on whether you use While or Until and whether you put the While or Until at the beginning of the loop or the end. Table 1.9 details the four varieties.

Table 1.9. Confusion with Do/Loops.

LOOP SYNTAX	WHAT IT WILL DO
Do While Boolean body Loop	Executes the body while Boolean is True. This loop doesn't have to execute at all.
Do Until Boolean body Loop	Executes the body until Boolean is True (in other words, while it's False). This loop doesn't have to execute at all.
Do body Loop While Boolean	Executes the body while Boolean is True. This loop must execute at least once (in order to reach the Loop statement).
Do body Loop Until Boolean	Executes the body until Boolean is True (in other words, while it's False). This loop must execute at least once (in order to reach the Loop statement).

Let's take a closer look at each of the different kinds of Do/Loops. First, the Do While/Loop and the Do Until/Loop. Examine the following code sample, which includes a Do While/Loop:

```
Dim I As Integer
I = 1
Do While I <= 10
     Print I
     I = I + 1
Loop
```

The result of this code fragment is the numbers from 1 to 10. If we make the Do While a Do Until/Loop, we get a different result:

```
Dim I As Integer
I = 1
Do Until I <= 10
     Print I
     I = I + 1
Loop
```

This time, the result is that nothing gets printed. That's because I is already less than 10 (it starts at 1, remember?). The Do Until sees that, and says, "OK, my job's done" and passes control to the next instruction. To make this loop work like the Do While, you'd have to change the relational operator:

```
Dim I As Integer
I = 1
Do Until I > 10
      Print I
      I = I + 1
Loop
```

Now it will print all the numbers from 1 to 10.

Next we look at the loops that do their thinking at the end, the Do/Loop While and the Do/Loop Until. Consider the following code fragment, which contains a Do/Loop While:

```
Dim I As Integer
I = 1
Do
      Print I
      I = I + 1
Loop While I <= 10
```

This code segment prints all the numbers from 1 to 10.

Do/Loop Until works like Do/Loop While. To print the numbers from 1 to 10, you would code like this:

```
Dim I As Integer
I = 1
Do
      Print I
      I = I + 1
Loop Until I > 10
```

So what's the difference between Do/While and Do/Loop While? It's easiest to see by example. Let's take the two While examples, set I = 11, and see what happens:

```
Dim I As Integer
I = 11
Do While I <= 10
      Print I
      I = I + 1
Loop
```

The result here: Nothing gets printed. Because I starts out greater than 10, the loop never gets executed. But this code will produce a result:

```
Dim I As Integer
I = 11
Do
      Print I
      I = I + 1
Loop While I <= 10
```

It prints 11 because the check isn't until after the Print statement. Now it makes sense.

Before we leave this section, let's talk briefly about exiting loops. Many times, you'll want to exit the loop. You can get out with a GoTo statement, but there's often a better way: Exit. If you want to jump out of your loop and proceed with the line of code directly after the last line of your loop, just use Exit Do (for a Do/Loop) and Exit For (for a For/Next).

You need to experiment with loops to get the hang of them. They can be a little hard to grasp because they typically involve logic embedded within logic. With simple code the easiest way to see how a loop works is to print the values of your variables at various points just to see what they are. With more complex code, take advantage of VB's debugging facilities.

Note about While/Wend loops: Many long-time BASIC programmers will remember While/Wend loops. You can still use 'em, but we recommend you use the Do While/Loop because you have the option of using Exit Do to exit the loop. Exiting from a While/Wend is harder.

File Under File

Dealing with files under VB4 is alternately very easy and unreasonably complicated. There are two basic ways that you deal with files in VB:

1. With controls on your form, for example, when you create a File/Open dialog box

2. With internal commands, such as when your application manipulates a file while it's open

Forms and Files

VB has three primary controls for selecting files:

1. Drive list box

2. Directory list box

3. File list box

That's right, three separate controls. (VB also has the Common Dialog control. We get to that in a second. But it's good to understand these three controls first.)

You use these controls just as you do any of the others: Click them and draw a box or double-click them. The most basic thing you have to know is how to create a File/Open dialog, so we'll start by creating a very simple one. First, on a blank form (preferably Form1), draw a File list box, a Directory list box, and a Drive list box. Although where you draw them really doesn't matter, it's probably best to get into good habits. So draw them as most Windows applications have them, as shown in Figure 1.7.

So far, no problem. If you ran your application now, you'd be able to select files, to change directories, and even to change drives. But none of your changes would be reflected in any of the other controls. To get that effect, you need to add one line of code to each form module. So double-click the Drive list box and under Private Sub Drive1_Change(), add the line

```
Dir1.Path = Drive1.Drive
```

Close the window and double-click the directory control. Under Private Sub Dir1_Change, add

```
File1.Path = Dir1.Path
```

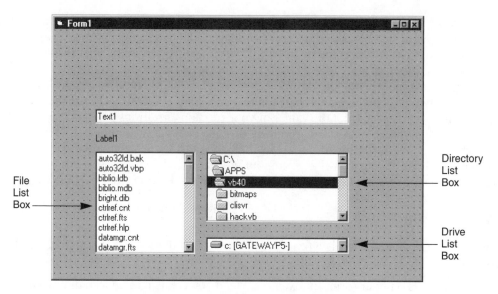

Figure 1.7. Beginning the building.

Now run your application. Change drives and directories. The program will work, unless you select a floppy drive with no disk. This will result in an error that the program doesn't know how
to handle. The actual code for getting these controls to pass information to each other *and* handle errors is a little more complex, but this is the gist of it.

For fun, you can add a text box to this small application. The goal is to write code so that
what you type into the text box becomes the current drive, path, and file. The key is to create a
text box (Text1) and then under Text1.Keypress, add the line File1.Filename = Text1.Text. The
trick is to make it so that Dir1 highlights the filename (with just this code, Dir1 will display only
the filename you type). Fortunately, this is pretty well documented.

Uncommon Dialogs

Now that we've shown you a terrible way to create your dialog boxes, how about we show you
the right way? That is, by using the Common Dialog control. This control is, by default, loaded
in your Toolbox. It looks like Figure 1.8. Using the Common Dialog control, you get dialog
boxes that look like those in all other Windows applications (for better or worse). You use this
control as you would any other: You alter its properties by sending it messages. For example, you
might place the following code under the File/Open menu item:

```
CommonDialog1.ShowOpen
```

The next thing you know, when a user selects File/Open, he or she gets the standard Windows
Open dialog box. Table 1.10 lists the top methods for the Common Dialog control. And yes, it's
as easy as it looks.

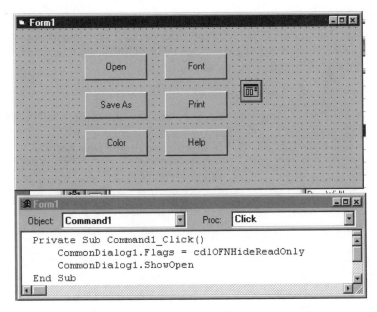

Figure 1.8. The Common Dialog control.

Table 1.10. Common Dialog control actions.

METHOD	WHAT IT DOES
.ShowOpen	Open
.ShowSave	Save As
.ShowColor	Color
.ShowFont	Font
.ShowPrinter	Print
.ShowHelp	Windows Help

A few words about the Common Dialog control. First, unlike the other controls we've dealt with so far, it won't appear on your screen at runtime. Like the Timer control, it's invisible. It just sits on your form and accepts arguments and displays dialog boxes. Also, if you have no fonts installed, the .ShowFont method will generate an error. You'll have to write error-handling code to deal with this; otherwise the application will terminate. Similarly, the .ShowHelp method requires you to give it a Windows Help filename. The Common Dialog's syntax is also changed from that in VB3, where you would write:

```
CMDialog1.Action = 1
```

to show the File/Open dialog box.

Common Dialogs also have flags (they're very patriotic). Flags alter the functioning of the dialog boxes slightly. You specify them right before you call the Common Dialog box. For example, if you placed the following line right before the CommonDialog1.ShowOpen line, the Open dialog box would have no Read Only check box:

```
CommonDialog1.Flags = cdlOFNHideReadOnly
```

Table 1.11 lists more of the flags you can use with the .ShowOpen and .ShowSave methods.

Table 1.11. File/Open and Save dialog box flags.

CONSTANT	VALUE	DESCRIPTION
cdlOFNReadOnly	0x1	Checks the Read-Only check box for Open and Save As dialog boxes.
cdlOFNOverwritePrompt	0x2	Causes the Save As dialog box to generate a message box if the selected file already exists.
cdlOFNHideReadOnly	0x4	Hides the Read-Only check box.
cdlOFNNoChangeDir	0x8	Sets the current directory to what it was when the dialog box was invoked.
cdlOFNHelpButton	0x10	Causes the dialog box to display the Help button.
cdlOFNNoValidate	0x100	Allows invalid characters in the returned filename.
cdlOFNAllowMultiselect	0x200	Allows the File Name list box to have multiple selections.
cdlOFNExtensionDifferent	0x400	The extension of the returned filename is different from the extension set by the DefaultExt property.
cdlOFNPathMustExist	0x800	Allows the user to enter only valid path names.
cdlOFNFileMustExist	0x1000	Allows the user to enter only names of existing files.
cdlOFNCreatePrompt	0x2000	Sets the dialog box to ask if the user wants to create a file that doesn't currently exist.
cdlOFNShareAware	0x4000	Sharing violation errors will be ignored.
cdlOFNNoReadOnlyReturn	0x8000	The returned file doesn't have the Read-Only attribute set and won't be in a write-protected directory.
cdlOFNExplorer	0x0008000	Use the Explorer-like Open A File dialog box template. (Windows 95 only)
cdlOFNNoDereferenceLinks	0x00100000	Do not dereference shortcuts (shell links). By default, choosing a shortcut causes it to be dereferenced by the shell. (Windows 95 only)
cdlOFNLongNames	0x00200000	Use long filenames. (Windows 95 only)

Table 1.12 shows the flags you can use with the .ShowPrinter method.

Table 1.12. Printer dialog box flags.

CONSTANT	VALUE	DESCRIPTION
cdlPDAllPages	0x0	Returns or sets the state of the All Pages option button.
cdlPDCollate	0x10	Returns or sets the state of the Collate check box.
cdlPDDisablePrintToFile	0x80000	Disables the Print To File check box.
cdlPDHidePrintToFile	0x100000	The Print To File check box isn't displayed.
cdlPDNoPageNums	0x8	Returns or sets the state of the Pages option button.
cdlPDNoSelection	0x4	Disables the Selection option button.
cdlPDNoWarning	0x80	Prevents a warning message when there is no default printer.
cdlPDPageNums	0x2	Returns or sets the state of the Pages option button.
cdlPDPrintSetup	0x40	Displays the Print Setup dialog box rather than the Print dialog box.
cdlPDPrintToFile	0x20	Returns or sets the state of the Print To File check box.
cdlPDReturnDC	0x100	Returns a device context for the printer selection value returned in the hDC property of the dialog box.
cdlPDReturnDefault	0x400	Returns the default printer name.
cdlPDReturnIC	0x200	Returns an information context for the printer selection value returned in the hDC property of the dialog box.
cdlPDSelection	0x1	Returns or sets the state of the Selection option button.
cdlPDHelpButton	0x800	Provides that the dialog box displays the Help button.
cdlPDUseDevModeCopies	0x40000	Sets support for multiple copies action; depends on whether the printer supports multiple copies.

The other methods also have flags. However, you'll probably be using Open, Save As, and Print the most, so that's what we're showing here.

So, your sample code for a File/Open menu could look like this:

```
CommonDialog1.Flags = cdlOFNHideReadOnly
CommonDialog1.ShowOpen
```

Isn't this easier than trying to create your own dialog boxes?

Types of Files

With these three controls (File, Directory, and Drive list boxes), you can create dialog boxes. But you need to be able to open files, close them, and do all sorts of other file manipulations. Piece of cake. Except you need to know that VB recognizes three kinds of files: binary, sequential access, and random access.

Binary Files. Of the three types, you're probably most familiar with binary files because they are the type of files that word processors generally use. VB thinks of binary files as streams of bytes. You can enter into the stream of bytes wherever you want and exit the stream wherever you want.

Sequential Access Files. Sequential access files are the most structured type of file. You open the file and either start reading or writing data at the beginning or the end. You can't just hop around. All records (lines) are of a length that is fixed (by you) and unchanging. This access method is good for appending records to a database.

Random Access Files. Random access files aren't really random at all. "Random" means merely that the files are somewhat less structured than sequential files because you can enter them at any specified record. Basically, you use random access file functions when you're dealing with highly-structured data (such as from a relational database) and you want to enter and exit the file at specific points (not the beginning or end).

File Manipulation

Now that you know about VB's three file types, you can start working with them. The first command to know is Open. Before you can do anything else to a file, you have to open it. Open works like this:

```
Open "FILENAME.EXT" For Append As #1
```

This line opens FILENAME.EXT and treats it as a sequential file, placing you at the end of the file. The As #1 part of the line is the number that VB associates with the open file. Each open file must have a number. If you find the numbering system cumbersome, you can let VB worry about it for you by using the following code:

```
Dim FileNumber As Integer
FileNumber = FreeFile
Open "FILENAME.TXT" For Binary As #FileNumber
```

Much easier to remember.

When you're ready to close the file, you have two options:

```
Close #FileNumber
```

or simply

```
Reset
```

which closes all open files.

Once you have a file open, what do you do with it? Well, you can write commands that read data and write data. There are all sorts of these commands. Each has a slightly different syntax depending on the kind of file you're dealing with. Table 1.13 shows some of the commands and the file types they work on.

Table 1.13. Some file statements and functions.

COMMAND	FILE TYPE	WHAT IT DOES
Get	Binary or Random	Reads data.
Input$	Any	Reads a specified number of bytes.
Input	Sequential	Reads data.
Line Input	Sequential	Reads one line of data.
Put	Binary or Random	Writes data.
Print #	Sequential	Writes undelimited data to a file.
Write	Sequential	Writes delimited data.
EOF	Any	Checks for End of File.
LOF	Any	Gets the length of the current file.
FileAttr	Any	Retrieves file attributes.
Open	Any	Opens a file.
Close	Any	Closes a file.
Reset	Any	Closes all files.

Play with these commands to see what they do. The easiest thing to do is to create a blank form (Form1) and put a text box on it (Text1). Then experiment with code, like this:

```
Private Sub Form_Load()
    Dim MyString As String

    Open "TESTFILE.TXT" For Output As #1
    Write #1, "Hello world"
    Close #1

    Open "TESTFILE.TXT" For Input As #1
    Input #1, MyString
    Text1.Text = MyString
    Close #1
End Sub
```

This code creates a file called TESTFILE.TXT and writes one line into it: Hello World. Then it closes the file, reopens it, and prints that one line in your text box. The file type we're using is sequential. If you wanted to play with random access, you could try this:

```
Private Sub Form_Load()
    Dim OutString As String
    Dim InString As String
    Dim Line As Integer

    InString = "Hello world, again"

    Open "TESTFILE.TXT" For Random As #1
    Put #1, 2, InString
```

```
      Close #1

      Open "TESTFILE.TXT" For Random As #1
      Line = 2
      Get #1, Line, OutString
      Text1.Text = OutString
      Close #1
End Sub
```

And those are the basics of file I/O. The very basics.

Menus

Most applications have menus. In fact, Microsoft recommends that all applications have File, Edit, and Help menus. You add these menus to your VB application using the Menu Editor (Tools/Menu Editor). The application is fairly self-explanatory, but we'll quickly run through how it works.

When you launch the Menu Editor, you'll see something like what's in Figure 1.9: four text boxes and a variety of buttons, check boxes, and pull-down menus. Table 1.14 explains what each does.

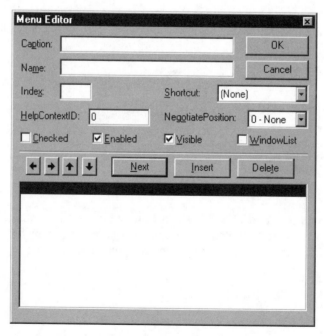

Figure 1.9. Editing menus for fun and profit.

Table 1.14. What the Menu Editor does.

ITEM	WHAT IT DOES
Caption	What you type here is what's going to appear on the user's screen.
Name	The name of the menu item as it will be used in your program. (Microsoft recommends you start all menu items "mnu.")
Index	The position of the menu item within a control array. (Index has nothing to do with the position of the item on the screen.)
HelpContextID	A number used to track context-sensitive help.
Shortcut	A drop-down menu full of shortcut options.
NegotiatePosition	Determines whether top-level Menu controls are displayed on the menu when a linked or embedded object on a form is active and displaying its menus.
Checked	Indicates whether a check mark will be displayed next to an item's name.
Enabled	Indicates whether a menu item will be grayed out.
Visible	Indicates whether a menu item will be visible. (Microsoft recommends you use Enabled instead.)
WindowList	Determines whether you want the menu to contain a list of open windows (MDI applications only).
Up Arrow	Moves an item up one line.
Down Arrow	Moves an item down one line.
Left Arrow	Moves an item to the left (promotes it).
Right Arrow	Moves an item to the right (demotes it).

The Menu Editor is easy to use. For example, if you want to create the standard menus for a typical application (for example, File/New; File/Open), you just enter items into the Menu Editor. To create the top-level File menu, enter

```
Caption:     &File
Name:  mnuFile
```

That's all you need. You then could create the New command under the File menu by entering

```
Caption:     &New
Name:  mnuFileNew
```

Then click the right arrow to demote this item to be a submenu under File. Notice the naming convention: mnuFileNew. The first three characters in the name indicate that this item is a menu; File indicates the menu is a submenu of the File menu; and New is its caption. Use this naming convention, and your life will be a lot easier. Once you have completed your basic File and Edit menus, the Menu Editor might look like Figure 1.10.

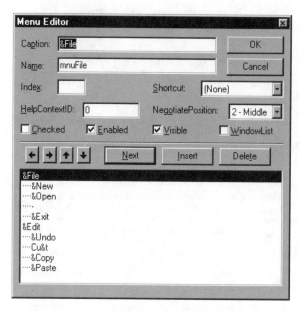

Figure 1.10. Filling in your Menu Editor.

Note that some menu items are followed by an ellipsis (...). That means that when the user selects such an item, a dialog box pops up that shows more options. It's another Windows convention you should know about.

Once you've created your application's menus, you assign code to the menu items. Go back to the form and select your menu item (for example, File/Exit). You will see the standard Code window. Enter the code you want to be executed when the user selects this menu option (in this case, it's enough to type End). Then close the Code window.

Menus also have properties, although they don't appear when you select the menu items in your form. To set properties for a menu item, go to the Properties window and pull down the list box at the top. Select the menu item for which you want to set properties. These are the same properties that you see when you're using the Menu Editor; this is just another way of looking at them.

A final note on menu properties. A menu must lead to something else. It's bad form to have a top-level menu item (for example, File) that immediately executes an action. Users are used to drop-down menus. If you make a top-level menu that doesn't have these, you'll confuse them. You can still do it, but know that your application will be unlike most Windows applications.

Adding Right-Mouse Menus

Using the right-mouse button to bring up a menu is popular these days. VB lets you create programs that do this. You start just as you do when you're going to make a normal, pull-down menu, but you hang a trigger off the MouseUp event.

Say you want the File menu to pop up when you right-click on your form. First, create the menu with the Menu Editor. Then, double-click the form (say Form1) to bring up the Code window and add the following code to the MouseUp event for the form:

```
If Button = 2 Then
      PopupMenu mnuFile, 4
End If
```

Button = 2 indicates the right-mouse button. PopupMenu is a VB method. The generic syntax looks like this:

Form.PopupMenu *Menu, Center, X, Y*

Form refers to the name of the form on which you want the menu to pop up. Menu is the name of the menu you want to pop up. Center is where you want the menu centered, relative to X and Y. (Usually you'll leave these values blank. As a result, the menu will pop up where you right-clicked.) Center can be 0, which means the left side of the menu appears under the cursor. Or it can be 4, which centers the menu on the cursor. Or it can be 8, which places the right side under the cursor.

In our code sample, we omitted Form because we were popping the menu on Form1 only. We also omitted X and Y because we wanted the menu to come up under the cursor. When you run the application and right-click the form (but not on any controls in the form), the File menu will pop up.

VB Hacks Windows

VB can talk to Windows, just like applications written in languages like C can. It may not able to reach quite as deeply into Windows's private places as those languages can, but it can look at certain system parameters and play with the Clipboard. In this section, we talk about how you can do that kind of stuff.

In the previous section, we started creating an Edit menu. However, we didn't start writing the code to actually have those menu options do anything. That's because we would have had to introduce the methods that control the Clipboard object. Those methods are shown in Table 1.15.

Table 1.15. Methods that control the Clipboard object.

METHOD	WHAT IT DOES
Clipboard.SetData	Sends pictures to the Clipboard.
Clipboard.SetText	Sends text to the Clipboard.
Clipboard.GetData()	Gets pictures from the Clipboard.
Clipboard.GetText()	Gets text from the Clipboard.
Clipboard.GetFormat()	Figures out whether it's text of a picture in the Clipboard.
Clipboard.Clear	Blows away the contents of the Clipboard.

The only one of these that's completely easy to use is Clipboard.Clear. When you call this procedure, you empty the Clipboard. Everything else requires you to have a basic understanding of Clipboard data types. There are six such data types, shown in Table 1.16.

Table 1.16. Unraveling Clipboard data types.

DATA TYPE	CONSTANT	HOW VB THINKS OF IT
Text	`CF_TEXT`	1
Bitmap	`CF_BITMAP`	2
Windows metafile	`CF_METAFILE`	3
Device-independent bitmap (.DIB)	`CF_DIB`	8
Color palette	`CF_PALETTE`	9
DDE link	`CF_LINK`	&HBF00

Give the Clipboard a test drive. Create a form. Put on it two text boxes (Text1 and Text2) and one button (Command1). Then enter the following code for Command1:

```
Private Sub Command1_Click()
    Clipboard.Clear
    Clipboard.SetText Text1.Text
    Text1.Text = ""
    Text2.Text = Clipboard.GetText(1)
End Sub
```

This procedure cuts any text from Text1 and pastes it in Text2. This is a very simple way of using the Clipboard, but it works.

Shelling and Activating Applications

VB has the power to launch other applications by using the Shell function. Generically, Shell looks like this:

`Shell(application, windowinfo)`

where *application* is the full path to the application you want to run and *windowinfo* is an integer that describes in what kind of window your shelled application is going to come up. Table 1.17 describes these integers.

Table 1.17. Values for Shell's windowinfo parameter.

VALUE	THE RESULT
1, 5, 9	A normal window with the focus
2	A minimized window with the focus (default)
3	A maximized window with the focus
4, 8	A normal window without the focus
6, 7	A minimized window without the focus

Some definitions of what's in this table. A "normal" window is one that comes up at its "normal" size. If an application normally launches less than full screen, that's what it will come up as. *Focus* means the cursor is active in that window.

[handwritten: DICG WMF   C:\PROGRAMFILE\M.oet]

AppActivate

Related to Shell is AppActivate, which transfers focus to an application that's already running. The generic syntax for AppActivate is

```
AppActivate application_title
```

Unlike with the Shell function, you don't give AppActivate the whole path to the program. AppActivate can't launch programs, so it wouldn't know what to do with the full path name. You give AppActivate the name of the program that's running—for example, AppActivate Notepad or AppActivate Word.

SendKeys

AppActivate may seem a little useless. It is—that is, until you pair it with SendKeys. SendKeys is Windows' playing Frisbee with itself: One application throws keystrokes up in the air and then transfers the focus to a second application, and you hope you focus on the second application in time to catch the keystrokes. In general, you don't want to use SendKeys. Better, use DDE (Dynamic Data Exchange) or OLE, both of which can accomplish the same basic tasks with more aplomb.

That said, SendKeys is a good tool for making a self-running demo, which every good programmer needs once he or she has a working application. So, the generic syntax is

```
SendKeys "String"[, wait]
```

So you SendKeys a string to the active application (place the string within quotes). The optional wait parameter is a Boolean value: either True, which means the keystrokes must be processed before control is returned to the procedure that called SendKeys, or False (the default), which means your procedure goes crashing happily along, while you pray that the receiving application actually caught the keystrokes.

Dynamic Data Exchange

Windows Dynamic Data Exchange (DDE) is a better way than SendKeys to have applications talk to each other. However, DDE is still prone to breaking. This is because the protocol for DDE exchanges is rather arcane and easy to foul up. A typical DDE exchange has five parts, as shown in Figure 1.11.

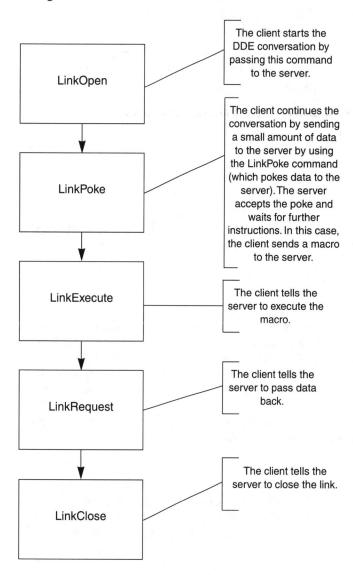

Figure 1.11. A typical DDE exchange.

As you can see, the exchange is simple. Basically, the client asks the server to do something (like a mathematical calculation) and then accepts the answer. The client (sometimes called the destination) does all the DDE work. The server (sometimes called the source) does all the other work.

DDE commands are methods, events, or properties of other objects. The main ones are shown in Table 1.18.

Table 1.18. DDE Methods

DDE COMMAND	WHAT IT IS	WHAT IT DOES
LinkOpen	Event	For a form, this event occurs when another program opens a DDE link. For labels, text boxes, and picture boxes, it occurs when the control opens a DDE conversation.
LinkExecute	Event	Sends a command string from the client to the server.
LinkNotify	Event	Tells the server to tell the client when data has changed.
LinkError	Event	Indicates an error has occurred during a DDE conversation.
LinkClose	Event	Indicates the DDE conversation has terminated. (Either application can terminate a DDE conversation at any time.)
LinkItem	Property	Returns or sets the data sent to the client.
LinkMode	Property	Specifies the type of link you're going to use and activates the connection.
LinkTimeout	Property	Specifies the amount of time a control waits for a response to a DDE message.
LinkTopic	Property	With client controls, specifies the source application and the topic. With server forms, specifies the topic to which the source form responds.
LinkSend	Method	Sends a picture from the server to the client (picture boxes only, please).
LinkPoke	Method	Sends data from the client to the server.
LinkRequest	Method	Asks the server to update the client control's properties.

Let's see this stuff in action. It's not pretty. First, you'll need a copy of Excel. Now, create a form and place a single text box on it (Text1). Then place the following code under Form1.Click:

```
If Text1.LinkMode = vbNone Then ' Test link mode.
        Text1.LinkTopic = "Excel|Sheet1"    ' Set link topic.
        Text1.LinkItem = "R1C1" ' Set link item.
        Text1.LinkMode = vbLinkManual    ' Set link mode.
        Text1.LinkRequest    ' Update text box.
    Else
        If Text1.LinkItem = "R1C1" Then
            Text1.LinkItem = "R2C1"
            Text1.LinkRequest    ' Update text box.
        Else
```

```
            Text1.LinkItem = "R1C1"
            Text1.LinkRequest    ' Update text box.
        End If
    End If
```

Now, launch your copy of Excel and type something into Cell A1. Run the application and click anywhere on the form. Whatever you typed into A1 should appear in Text1.Text.

Object Linking and Embedding

Now that we've spent far too much space on DDE, let's look at the best way of getting applications to cooperate: Object Linking and Embedding 2.0. (Some people prefer the long version, but most just say "OLE" for short, pronounced as in Oil of Olay and often accompanied by a suitable Iberian arm gesture). Superficially, OLE is like DDE—applications pass data back and forth. The difference is that DDE data is dumb—it's just the data. OLE brings across not only the data but also the formatting, menus, and toolbars of the application you call (called the host) into the application doing the calling (called the container).

OLE 2.0 has three basic features:

- *Linking.* Linking occurs when your application makes a reference to another application's data but leaves it in the native format of the other application. (For example, you use a VB program to modify some Excel data.)

- *Embedding.* Embedding occurs when you read the data into your application and store it in your app's format.

- *Automation.* Automation is something else entirely. With OLE automation, your VB application can tell another application (that supports OLE automation) what to do, how to do it, and when to do it.

Linking versus Embedding: A Simple Example

The easiest way to understand OLE is to use it. So let's start right out and do some work. Follow these steps:

1. Create a new project and make a new form.

2. Create a menu with one entry (for this example, caption it File and name it mnuFile; you don't need any code).

3. Click the OLE icon in the Toolbox and add an OLE box to your screen.

4. Select Create from File and specify a path to a data file, preferably one like a Microsoft Win-Word file (or WordPerfect—let's not be too Microsoft-bigoted) or an Excel or Lotus 1-2-3 file, one with lots of formatting. Note, this application must support OLE 2.0. Most big-name apps do; for example, Microsoft Office, Lotus SmartSuite, and WordPerfect Office.

5. Create another OLE box on your screen and specify a path to the *same* data file. This time, however, specify that this is a Link by checking the check box just under the Browse line in this dialog box.

When you're done, you should have something that looks like Figure 1.12.

Figure 1.12. Showing the difference between linking and embedding.

Now, run your application. Double-click first the document you embedded and then the document you linked. You'll see what the user will experience when you use each method of getting another application's data and formatting into your app. And you didn't even have to write any code.

Important notes:

1. When you double-click the embedded application, your simple File menu is replaced by the menus of the application that created the embedded document (in our example, we used Excel and only got Edit through Help, no File).

2. When you modify the embedded document, it doesn't affect the file on disk (it won't unless you send specific instructions to write the modified data).

3. Finally, you may notice aberrant behavior. Welcome to the bugs of OLE.

With the linked document, you'll notice that the whole application in which the embedded document was created launches when you double-click it.

Finally, notice how incredibly simple it was to make an OLE container application. Granted, this container is a bit rigid—you have to specify the data files you'll be working with at design time, for example. But basically you've built an application with all the functions of the application that you used as your OLE host.

OLE at Runtime

The previous example is a little unusual simply because it's static—at design time you chose the objects to link and embed. Likely, you'll want the people using your application to be making the decisions about what gets embedded or linked. It's pretty easy to do that.

The key to this magic is to modify four of the OLE control's properties at runtime: Class, SourceDoc, SourceItem, and Action. So, do this:

1. Draw an OLE control onto a new form. Call your form Form1 and your brand-new OLE control the default name of OLE1.

2. When the dialog box pops up asking you what kind of document you want to insert, click Cancel or press Escape.

3. Draw a button on your form called, cleverly, Command1. Double-click the button.

Now under VB3, you would have added the following code:

```
Private Sub Command1_Click()
    OLE1.Class = "Excel.Sheet.5"
    OLE1.SourceDoc = "C:\APPS\VB40\HACKVB\SAMPLE.XLS"
    OLE1.SourceItem = "R1C1:R7C5"
    OLE1.Action = 1
End Sub
```

(We're assuming you have an Excel workbook stored in C:\APPS\VB40\HACKVB\SAMPLE.XLS and its relevant data are stored in row 1, column 1 through row 7, column 5. If you want to use a different Excel workbook, feel free. You may also create one of your own and place data into some cells.)

VB4 still supports this construction (whew! mop brow), but it has a more elegant way to achieve the result:

```
Private Sub Command1_Click()
    OLE1.CreateEmbed "C:\APPS\VB40\HACKVB\SAMPLE.XLS"
End Sub
```

Or, if you want a linked object instead of an embedded one:

```
Private Sub Command1_Click()
    OLE1.CreateLink "C:\APPS\VB40\HACKVB\SAMPLE.XLS", "R1C1:R7C5"
End Sub
```

These two constructions are methods, not properties of the OLE control on your form. Notice that they are more compact (code-wise) than the VB3 way. They also execute a smidgen faster (at least on the system we tested them on). (With VB3, you specified the difference between a linked and an embedded object on the **Action =** line (0 embeds an object, 1 links it). With the two VB4 methods, you'll most likely use an If...Then...Else construction to choose between CreateEmbed and CreateLink.)

In any event (pun mildly intended), run your new application and click the button. The result should look like Figure 1.13.

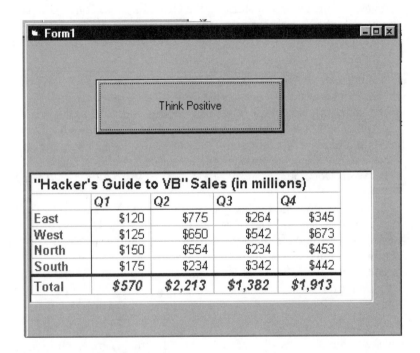

Figure 1.13. Wishful thinking? Or just an OLE application gone mad?

If you want to get fancy, your button can call up the OLE Insert Object dialog box, which will ask you which file you want to embed, and then insert that particular file into the OLE control. This is trivial, but it takes a lot of code, so we're going to save space by declining to do it here.

The preceding example introduces what you really need to know. Here's what's going on. The generic syntax of the CreateEmbed method is

```
object.CreateEmbed sourcedoc, class
```

The generic syntax of the CreateLink method is

```
object.CreateLink sourcedoc, sourceitem
```

Let's explain what's going on with these different syntaxes. It gets a bit confusing because the two methods have sourcedoc and sourceitem parameters, as well as SourceDoc and Source-Item properties of the OLE control. Bear with us as we confuse you hopelessly.

Source/Document

The source document (SourceDoc) contains the name of the file you want to embed. If you specify the filename in the code, you must enclose it in quotes. In VB3, you change the SourceDoc property. In VB4, when you use either the CreateEmbed or CreateLink methods, the value you specify for SourceDoc will override and change the value in the SourceDoc property.

When you create an object with CreateLink, the OLE container control displays an image of the file that is specified in the SourceDoc property. If you save the object, you are saving only the *link* references, not actual source data. If you want to save source data, use CreateEmbed.

You've Got Class

If you use CreateEmbed or write your code the VB3 way and you don't specify SourceDoc, your OLE control will want to know the class (or type) of the document it's going to try to read in. You have probably noticed that when you embed a link at design time, VB4 asks you what *kind* of object you're going to embed to fill in the Class property. Every Windows application that can be an OLE server (i.e., it lets you embed one of its documents into your VB application) defines a set of allowable class names. Excel 5, for example, defines Excel.Sheet.5 and Excel.Chart.5. Microsoft Word 6 has Word.Document.6 and Word.Picture.6. Visio 4 has Visio.Drawing.4. Notice the pattern?

You may be wondering how the heck we know all this stuff. Aside from the fact that we're brilliant (ahem), we know where to look. In design mode, click the OLE control and then look in the Properties window. You'll see a property called Class. Select it. Then click the ellipsis to reach a list of all the different classes available on your system. This works because every time you install an application that can be an OLE server, the application's install routine modifies the Windows Registry and inserts its class names.

SourceItems

SourceItem tells VB what part of SourceDoc to read in. It works best with programs like spreadsheets and databases, which have easily referenced (and defined) areas, but you can make word processors have SourceItems also (through bookmarks, for example).

As with the SourceDoc filename, you must surround SourceItem names with quotes. When you specify sourceitem as a part of the CreateLink method, it will override and modify the SourceItem property. If you don't specify it, CreateLink will read in as much of SourceDoc as it can. Some applications are more intelligent than others regarding how much they let you read in. Excel, for example, will feed CreateLink only the part of the worksheet that has values in it, so if you have a relatively blank spreadsheet, feel free to leave out the SourceItem parameter (or SourceItem property).

A Control of Action

The Action property is largely a VB3 holdover, although it works under VB4. This property tells the OLE control what to do with the information that it's drawing in. Table 1.19 lists the possible values of Action as well as the methods that VB4 would prefer you use instead of Action.

Table 1.19. Possible values of the Action property and what they do.

VALUE	CONSTANT	CURRENT METHOD	WHAT IT DOES
0	OLE_CREATE_ EMBED	CreateEmbed	Creates an embedded object.
1	OLE_CREATE_ LINK	CreateLink	Creates a linked object from the contents of a file.
4	OLE_COPY	Copy	Copies the object to the system Clipboard.
5	OLE_PASTE	Paste	Copies data from the system Clipboard to an OLE container control.
6	OLE_UPDATE	Update	Retrieves the current data from the application that supplied the object and displays that data as a picture in the OLE container control.
7	OLE_ACTIVATE	DoVerb	Opens an object for an operation, such as editing.
9	OLE_CLOSE	Close	Closes an object and terminates the connection to the application that provided the object.
10	OLE_DELETE	Delete	Deletes the specified object and frees the memory associated with it.
11	OLE_SAVE_TO _FILE	SaveToFile	Saves an object to a data file.
12	OLE_READ_ FROM_FILE	ReadFromFile	Loads an object that was saved to a data file.
14	OLE_INSERT_ OBJ_DLG	InsertObjDlg	Displays the Insert Object dialog box.
15	OLE_PASTE_ SPECIAL_DLG	PasteSpecialDlg	Displays the Paste Special dialog box.
17	OLE_FETCH_ VERBS	FetchVerbs	Updates the list of verbs an object supports.
18	OLE_SAVE_TO_ OLE1FILE	SaveToOle1File	Saves an object to the OLE file format.

Again, you may still use the Action property and feed it a value, but you'll likely find that the methods require less code and are easier to understand.

Other OLE Container Properties

Rather than our spending too many words on OLE container properties, have a look at Table 1.20.

Table 1.20. Properties of the OLE Container control.

PROPERTY	WHAT IT DOES
Action	Available only at runtime. Tells an OLE control what to do. Table 1.19 lists the possible values of Action and what they do.
Appearance	Available only at runtime. Returns or sets the paint style of controls on an MDIForm or Form object. Possible values are 0 (flat) and 1 (3D).
AppIsRunning	Available only at runtime. Indicates whether the application that created the object in the OLE Container control is running. Possible values are True (it's running) and False.
AutoActivate	Returns or sets a value that enables the user to activate an object by double-clicking the OLE Container control or by moving the focus to the OLE Container control.
AutoVerbMenu	Returns or sets a value that determines if a popup menu containing the object's verbs is displayed when the user right-clicks the OLE Container control.
BackColor	Returns or sets the background color of an object.
BackStyle	Returns or sets a value indicating whether a Label control or the background of a Shape control is transparent or opaque.
BorderStyle	Returns or sets the border style for an object. For the Form object and the TextBox control, read-only at runtime.
Class	Returns or sets the class name of an embedded object.
Container	Returns or sets the container of a control on a Form. Not available at design time.
Data	Returns or sets a handle to a memory object or graphical device interface (GDI) object containing data in a specified format. Not available at design time.
DataChanged	Returns or sets a value indicating that the data in the bound control has been changed by some process other than that of retrieving data from the current record. Not available at design time.
DataField	Returns or sets a value that binds a control to a field in the current record.
DataSource	Sets a value that specifies the Data control through which the current control is bound to a database. Not available at runtime.
DataText	Returns a string from or sets a string for the specified object.
DisplayType	Returns or sets a value indicating whether an object displays its contents or an icon.
DragIcon	Returns or sets the icon to be displayed as the pointer in a drag-and-drop operation.
DragMode	Returns or sets a value that determines whether manual or automatic drag mode is used for a drag-and-drop operation.
Enabled	Returns or sets a value that determines whether a form or control can respond to user-generated events.
FileNumber	Either returns or sets the file number to be used when saving or loading an object or returns the last file number used. Not available at design time.

Table 1.20 (*continued*)

PROPERTY	WHAT IT DOES
Format	Returns or sets the format when sending data to and getting data from an application that created an object. Not available at design time.
Height	Returns or sets the dimensions of an object or the width of the Columns object of a DBGrid control. For the Printer and Screen objects, not available at design time.
HelpContextID	Returns or sets an associated context number for an object. Used to provide context-sensitive Help for your application.
HostName	Returns or sets the user-readable host name of your Visual Basic application.
Index	Returns or sets the number that uniquely identifies a control in a control array. Available only if the control is part of a control array.
Left	Returns or sets the distance between the internal left edge of an object and the left edge of its container.
lpOleObject	Returns the address of the object.
MiscFlags	Returns or sets a value that determines access to one or more additional features of the OLE Container control.
MouseIcon	Sets a custom mouse icon.
MousePointer	Returns or sets a value indicating the type of mouse pointer displayed when the mouse is over a particular part of an object at runtime.
Name	Returns the name used in code to identify a form, control, or data access object.
Object	Returns the object and/or a setting of an object's method or property in an OLE Container control.
ObjectAcceptFormats	Returns the list of formats an object can accept.
ObjectAcceptFormatsCount	Returns the number of formats that can be accepted by an object.
ObjectGetFormats	Returns the list of formats an object can provide.
ObjectGetFormatsCount	Returns the number of formats an object can provide.
ObjectVerbFlags	Returns the menu state for each verb in the ObjectVerbs array.
ObjectVerbs	Returns the list of verbs an object supports.
ObjectVerbsCount	Returns the number of verbs supported by an object.
OLEDropAllowed	Returns or sets a value that determines whether an OLE Container control can be a drop target for OLE drag-and-drop operations.
OLEType	Returns the status of the object in an OLE Container control.
OLETypeAllowed	Returns or sets the type of object the OLE Container control can contain.
Parent	Returns the form, object, or collection that contains a control or another object or collection.
PasteOK	Returns a value that determines whether the contents of the system Clipboard can be pasted into the OLE Container control.

Table 1.20 (*continued*)

PROPERTY	WHAT IT DOES
Picture	Returns or sets a graphic to be displayed in a control. For the OLE Container control, not available at design time and read-only at runtime.
SizeMode	Returns or sets a value specifying how the OLE Container control is sized or how its image is displayed when it contains an object.
SourceDoc	Returns or sets the filename to use when you create an object. *Note:* You set the SourceDoc property for compatibility with the Action property in earlier versions. For current functionality, use the CreateEmbed and CreateLink methods.
SourceItem	Returns or sets the data within the file to be linked when you create a linked object.
TabIndex	Returns or sets the tab order of an object within its parent form.
TabStop	Returns or sets a value indicating whether a user can use the Tab key to give the focus to an object.
Tag	Returns or sets an expression that stores any extra data needed for your program. Unlike with other properties, the value of the Tag property isn't used by Visual Basic. You can use this property to identify objects.
Top	Returns or sets the distance between the internal top edge of an object and the top edge of its container.
UpdateOptions	Returns or sets a value specifying how an object is updated when linked data is modified.
Verb	Returns or sets a value specifying an operation to perform when an object is activated using the Action property. *Note:* The Verb property is included for compatibility with the Action property in earlier versions. For current functionality, use the DoVerb method.
Visible	Returns or sets a value indicating whether an object is visible or hidden.
WhatsThisHelpID	Returns or sets an associated context number for an object. Use to provide context-sensitive Help for your application using the What's This popup in Windows 95 Help. *Important Note:* This property requires the Microsoft Windows 95 or Microsoft Windows NT 3.51 operating system.
Width	Returns or sets the dimensions of an object or the width of the Columns object of a DBGrid control. For the Printer and Screen objects, not available at design time.

OLE Container Methods

As long as we're saving space, let's look at the OLE container's methods (Table 1.21).

Table 1.21. The OLE container methods.

METHOD	WHAT IT DOES
Close	Closes an embedded object and the connection to the host application. Has no effect on linked objects.
Copy	Copies an OLE embedded or linked object to the Clipboard.
CreateEmbed	Creates an embedded object.
CreateLink	Creates a linked object.
Delete	Deletes an object and frees the memory it was using.
DoVerb	Opens an object for whatever action you specify.
Drag	Begins, ends, or cancels a drag operation on most controls.
FetchVerbs	Gets the list of actions an OLE object supports.
InsertObjDlg	Shows the Insert Object dialog box.
Move	Moves a form or control.
Paste	Copies whatever is in the Clipboard into an OLE control.
PasteSpecialDlg	Summons the Paste Special dialog box.
ReadFromFile	Loads an object created with SaveToFile or SaveToOle1File.
Refresh	Repaints a form or control.
SaveToFile	Saves an object into a file.
SaveToOle1File	Saves an object into an OLE 1.0-compatible file.
SetFocus	Moves the focus to the specified form or control.
ShowWhatsThis	Displays the "What's this?" help for an object.
Update	Updates the data in an embedded object.
ZOrder	Moves a form or control to either the beginning or end of the Z order.

OLE Automation

One thing VB is good at is bossing other applications around. That's what OLE automation is for, after all. For example, say you want to create a WinWord document that contains the words, "This is a clever test document," and save the document. You could create a button and add the following lines of code:

```
Private Sub Command1_Click()
    Shell "c:\apps\msoffice\winword\WinWord.Exe"
    AppActivate "Microsoft Word"
    Dim WordApp As Object
    Set WordApp = CreateObject("Word.Basic")
    WordApp.Insert "This is a clever test document"
```

```
    WordApp.FileSaveAs "C:\TEMP\TESTDOC.DOC"
    Set WordApp = Nothing
End Sub
```

Now, that's an awful lot of code just to type a sentence, but it'll give you an idea of what you can do with OLE automation. Very quickly, here's what's going on.

```
    Shell "c:\apps\msoffice\winword\WinWord.Exe"
```

Starts up a new copy of WinWord for your OLE automation pleasure.

```
    AppActivate "Microsoft Word"
```

Sets focus to WinWord. (Of course, if WinWord were already running, it's even odds which copy AppActivate would activate. But that's a whole 'nother problem.)

```
    Dim WordApp As Object
```

Aha! Finally, some OLE automation code. Here we create a variable called WordApp and declare it as type Object. This is the first step in any OLE automation procedure: You need to tell VB that you're going to be mucking about with an object.

```
    Set WordApp = CreateObject("Word.Basic")
```

Step 2 in your OLE automation sojourn: Make the object variable you just declared capable of doing something. In this case, you're creating an object using WinWord's internal (and now external, thanks to the wonders of OLE automation) programming language, called WordBasic. (WordBasic somehow inherited a period halfway through its name, but that's another issue.) You can find out what to tell the CreateObject function to create by checking the WinWord WinHelp files.

```
    WordApp.Insert "This is a clever test document"
```

At this point, there's a direct line set up between your WordApp object and WordBasic, so you can start feeding WordBasic commands over the pipe. In this case, Insert, followed by this brilliant discourse:

```
    WordApp.FileSaveAs "C:\TEMP\TESTDOC.DOC"
```

You then save your words for posterity . . .

```
    Set WordApp = Nothing
```

. . . and unload the whole shebang. Usually, we'd pass a WordApp.Quit or WordApp.FileExit command first, but we seem to get errors when we do that. Anyway, setting your object equal to nothing is typically how you'd end an OLE automation transaction. It closes the connection between VB and the server app.

OLE Sample Application

It was a dark and stormy night. A Status Bar rang out. It was the work of a mad programmer, trying desperately to come up with a sample application that demonstrated how to write an OLE client and server. And this is it.

The following is a description of a very simple OLE server. It just displays a Progress Bar. A Progress Bar is useful if you're programming in an environment (such as Excel) that doesn't have fancy Progress Bars, but you'd like to show a bar anyway.

The application consists of two parts: the client and the server. The client consists of these files:

- PrgTest.vbp (the project name)

- frmTest.frm

First we create the client. Create a form, called frmTest.frm, and put one button on it: Command1. Then add this code:

```
Private Sub Command1_Click()
    Set prg = CreateObject("Progress.ProgressBar")
    prg.Caption = "MyTest"
    prg.Msg = "Progress:"
    For i = 0 To 100000
        x = Sin(2.3994)
        If i Mod 100 = 0 Then
            prg.Percent = i / 100000 * 100
        End If
    Next i
    Set prg = Nothing
End Sub
```

Right now, the For loop is just doing some simple math that will increment the Progress Bar. The server consists of these files:

- Progress.vbp (the project name)

- frmProgress.frm

- ProgressBar.cls

- modProgress.bas

- Progress.exe

As you can see, the server is a little more complex. To create a server, do this:

1. Create frmProgress.frm.

2. Add a label called lblMsg and set its Caption property to Progress:.

3. Add a Progress Bar called ProgressBar1.

4. For ease of reading, add three labels under the Progress Bar: Label1, Label2, and Label3. Set their captions to 0%, 50%, and 100%, respectively.

5. Add the following code:

```
Private Sub Form_Load()
    Left = (Screen.Width - Width) / 2
    Top = (Screen.Height - Height) / 2
End Sub
```

6. Create ProgressBar.cls (select Insert/Class Module) and add the following code:

```
Dim Frm As frmProgress

Public Property Let Caption(str As String)
    Frm.Caption = str
End Property

Public Property Let Msg(str As String)
    Frm.lblMsg = str
End Property

Public Property Let Percent(p As Integer)
    Frm.ProgressBar1.Value = p
    Frm.lblValue = p & "%"
End Property

Private Sub Class_Initialize()
    Set Frm = New frmProgress
    nInstances = nInstances + 1
    Frm.Show
End Sub

Private Sub Class_Terminate()
    Unload Frm
    Set Frm = Nothing
    nInstances = nInstances - 1
    If nInstances = 0 Then
        End
    End If
End Sub
```

7. Create modProgress.bas and add this code:

```
Public nInstances As Integer
Sub MAIN()
    nInstances = 0
End Sub
```

To get this app to work, open Progress.vbp (the server), select File/Make EXE File, and create Progress.exe. Run it. This action will register Progress in your Windows Registry. Now open PrgTest.vbp and run it. Click the Command button. The Progress Bar shows up and runs.

The Progress.exe contains a class called ProgressBar, which you access as Create–Object("Progress.ProgressBar"). Its Instancing property is set to 2 (multiple instances allowed).

modProgress.bas has the MAIN Sub as well as the global variable, nInstances, that keeps track of how many Progress Bars are being displayed. This is so that if a bar is already running, you don't have to run another copy of Progress.exe to get another one. Progress.exe exits when all Progress Bars have been dismissed.

The ProgressBar class has only properties, no methods. You set its

- caption,

- msg, and

- percent value.

That's it.

Add-Ins: A Special OLE Server

VB4 introduced Add-Ins—programs that extend VB's power. Add-Ins are neat because they are really just a special kind of OLE automation server, and one you can create in VB.

That's the good news. The bad news is that sometimes it's very hard to get VB to do what you want, *how* you want it done. For example, VB hides the features of some of its internal components, notably the editor. So if you want to create an Add-In that supplements the editor (a typical example is a tool that automatically comments selected code), you may have trouble doing it using standard methods. (We found one example of an application that did comment and un-comment code. But it seemed to rely on SendKeys rather than OLE to work the actual insertion and removal of the ' character.)

VB4 comes with two main examples of Add-Ins: Align and Spy. Unfortunately, VB4 doesn't come with very good documentation about Add-Ins. Fortunately, we found these examples to be clear, although they aren't as well documented as they could be. So, here's a skeleton Add-In that shows you the basic pieces you'll probably need to create an Add-In. Let's call it AddIn. It has four parts:

1. AddIn.vbp (the project file)

2. AddInSetup.cls

3. AddInAction.cls

4. Main.bas

Notice that there are no forms or anything else. This is a really stripped application. Create your AddIn project file and insert a class called AddInSetup. This is the class that's going to create the menu item under the VB Add-Ins menu. Also it's going to call AddInAction to actually perform whatever action you want done. Once you have created the class module, set its Instancing property to 2–Creatable MultiUse, its Name property to Connector, and its Public property to True. Then add this code:

```
'This class is what creates the menu item in VB's Add-Ins
'menu

Option Explicit

'The following variable defines the variable for our menu item
Dim AddInMenuLine As VBIDE.MenuLine
'The following variable instantiates an event handler that points to our
'event handler (AddInAction)
Dim AddInEventHandler As New AddInAction
'The following variable is a cookie that we'll pass from the Comment
'object into the AddInAction (event handler) object.
Dim AfterClickID As Long
'The following variable points to an instance of VB
Dim VBInstance As VBIDE.Application

Sub ConnectAddIn(VBDriverInstance As VBIDE.Application)
    'Save the instance of Visual Basic so we can refer to it later.
    Set VBInstance = VBDriverInstance

    'Use only one menu item, rather than a cascading menu.
    'If you select uncommented text, then the "Comment" menu
    'this Add-In will comment the code. If you selected
    'commented text, it will uncomment the code.

    'Add the menu line to VB:
    Set AddInMenuLine = VBInstance.AddInMenu.MenuItems.Add("Skeleton Add-
In")
    'Now tell the event handler which menu line to attach to:
    Set AddInEventHandler.AddInMenuLine = AddInMenuLine
    'Finally, connect our event handler with the menu line:
    AfterClickID = AddInMenuLine.ConnectEvents(AddInEventHandler)
'You can include the next line when you want to send the AfterClick
'event when VB loads:
    'AddInEventHandler.AfterClick

End Sub

Sub DisconnectAddIn(Mode As Integer)
'This code removes the menu item when you remove the Add-In using
'the Add-In manager.
    AddInMenuLine.DisconnectEvents AfterClickID
    VBInstance.AddInMenu.MenuItems.Remove AddInMenuLine
End Sub
```

Now, insert the AddInAction class module. In this module, magic occurs. Set its Instancing property to 0–Not Creatable, its Name property to AddInAction, and its Public property to False. Add the following code:

```
'This is the Class that actually creates the object
'that does the work when you select "Comment"
'from the Add-Ins menu
```

```
Option Explicit

Public VBInstance As VBIDE.Application
Public AddInMenuLine As VBIDE.MenuLine
Public Sub AfterClick()

'Insert your action code here

End Sub
```

Now create the Main.bas module. This module handles inserting your Add-In into the VB.INI file. Set its Name property to MainModule. Use this code:

```
#If Win16 Then
    Declare Function WritePrivateProfileString Lib "KERNEL" (ByVal AppName$,
ByVal KeyName$, ByVal keydefault$, ByVal FileName$) As Integer
    Declare Function GetPrivateProfileString Lib "KERNEL" (ByVal AppName$,
ByVal KeyName$, ByVal keydefault$, ByVal ReturnString$, ByVal NumBytes As
Integer, ByVal FileName$) As Integer
#Else
    Declare Function WritePrivateProfileString Lib "Kernel32" Alias
"WritePrivateProfileStringA" (ByVal AppName$, ByVal KeyName$, ByVal
keydefault$, ByVal FileName$) As Long
    Declare Function GetPrivateProfileString Lib "Kernel32" Alias
"GetPrivateProfileStringA" (ByVal AppName$, ByVal KeyName$, ByVal
keydefault$, ByVal ReturnString$, ByVal NumBytes As Long, ByVal FileName$)
As Long
#End If

Sub Main()

Dim ReturnString As String
'-- Check to see if we are in the VB.INI File. If not, add ourselves to
the INI file
    #If Win16 Then
        Section$ = "Add-Ins16"
    #Else
        Section$ = "Add-Ins32"
    #End If

    'Check to see if the AddIn.Connector entry is already in the VB.INI
file. Add if not.
    ReturnString = String$(255, Chr$(0))
    GetPrivateProfileString Section$, "AddIn.Connector", "NotFound",
ReturnString, Len(ReturnString) + 1, "VB.INI"
    If Left(ReturnString, InStr(ReturnString, Chr(0)) - 1) = "NotFound" Then
        WritePrivateProfileString Section$, "AddIn.Connector", "0", "VB.INI"
    End If
End Sub
```

You have the hard work done. Next make a couple of modifications to the project's properties. Select Tools/Options/Project. Set the Project Name to AddIn, the StartMode to OLE Server, and the Application Description to Skeleton Add-In.

To see what the Add-In does (which is basically nothing), run AddIn in one instance of VB. In a second instance, select Add-Ins/Add-In Manager and click the Skeleton Add-In check box. Click OK. Then select Add-Ins. At the bottom of this menu should be Skeleton Add-In shown as an option.

Databases in the Abstract

VB4 is supposed to be really good at getting data out of people's databases. After all, it has some extra bound data controls, doesn't it? Doesn't that make everything just peachy? Sure—especially if you happen to know SQL, 'cause that's what you're going to need if you want to do anything as mundane as, say, join two tables.

But we're getting ahead of ourselves.

A database is a place to put your stuff. Databases come in two basic types: unstructured and structured. Unstructured databases are like Folio Views, which basically sucks in a bunch of text and then indexes every word, so making searches is easy. Structured databases have tables that have rows (often called records) and columns (sometimes called attributes).

A structured database typically has several tables. Think of the tables as spreadsheets, with rows representing individual records (like employee names) and columns representing information about the rows (like salaries). These tables generally relate to each other (hence the term *relational database*). For example, one table might contain employee names, department names, and salaries and another might contain department names, locations, and budgets. These two tables share a common attribute: the department name. So you could ask this database to *join* the two tables and tell you, for example, at what location each employee works. The database would do this by looking up the employee name in the first table, finding out in what department he or she works, and then looking in the second table to find out where that department is located.

Actually, it's more complicated than that. Of course. It's made complicated by, for example, the presence of *normalization* and *indexes*. A full explanation of normalization is beyond the scope of this book, but it has to do with which information you choose to put into which tables when you're designing the database. (Okay, this is a cop-out, but normalization is pretty hairy stuff. Look it up in C. J. Date's *An Introduction to Database Systems,* Vol. I, Fifth Edition, Addison-Wesley, 1991.)

Indexes speed up searching the database. At the very highest level, an index is just an attribute that you make available for searching. Say you wanted to be able to locate employee names quickly. You could index that table on the employee names.

A special kind of index called a primary index has an extra stipulation: All elements in the attribute you choose to index must be unique. So, you probably couldn't choose employee name as a primary index (sometimes called a primary key or primary key index) because you could wind up with two employees named Leonardo Da Vinci.

And this is why most databases have really peculiar column names like Emp_ID or Cust_No. The creators of these databases wanted to have a unique attribute for every employee (or customer) and so added a column with a name that they could guarantee would be unique. Usually, they make this column a number and assign one number to every unique item in the table. Then they create a primary index on this numbered column.

You're probably wondering why you should care about primary keys. Simple. To join two tables, you must have a primary key in at least one of the tables. This makes sense when you think about it because typically you want to map unique data in one table onto nonunique data in another table.

For example, look at our original example of finding employee locations. It has two tables; call them Employee and Department. The Employee table contains a column called Department, but the values in it are nonunique (i.e., several employees can be in the same department). The Department table also contains a column called Department, but here all the values are unique; that column will be our primary key. To join the two tables, we just pull out employee names and departments from the Employee table and compare the values in that table's Department column to the values in the Department column of the Department table. Then we print the employee names from the Employee table and the location names from the Department table. Clear as mud, right?

There are many kinds of joins. *Outer joins* include information from one table even when there is no matching information in the other table(s). *Inner joins* combine information only when there is matching information in all tables. (Don't worry too much about these right now; they'll give you hangnails.)

One important consideration before we continue concerns a *transaction.* Databases often think in terms of discrete operations called transactions. For example, changing the information in a row of a database is a transaction. Adding a new row also is a transaction. A transaction hasn't really occurred, however, until it's been *committed,* that is, actually written to disk. Once a transaction is committed, the database engine has a method for undoing it (called transaction *rollback*).

How VB Gets into Databases: Jets and ISAMs

Getting into databases with VB can be as simple or complicated as you want. On the simple side, you can use VB's Data custom control. On the complex side, you can use the Open Database Connectivity (ODBC) API. In all, there are four ways VB can get to data:

1. Use VB's Data custom control. (This involves using the Jet engine—explained in the next section—but you don't need to know about Jet to do most of your work.)

2. Use a third-party custom control.

3. Use the Jet engine with VB's data access objects (DAO, explained in the next section).

4. Use APIs (e.g., ODBC or DB-Library VBSQL custom control).

   Next we discuss these ways in our order of preference (more or less).

Data Out of Control

The easiest way to get started with database access in VB is to plant a Data custom control on your form, link a control to it, and call it a night. You can do many things without writing any code; when you move around the database, modify records, or whatever, the Data custom control does the work. The control takes care of opening the database, verifying transactions, and handling all that complicated stuff by way of the Jet database engine. The Jet engine, in turn, knows about all sorts of different database formats, and abstracts them so that you don't have to know whether to write Xbase code or SQL or whatever.

I'm Leaving on a Jet Plane

The Jet engine comes with VB4. Its main job is to sit between VB's data controls and a database, abstracting the database. Like Microsoft Access, the Jet engine uses the .MDB file format, but it also can access ISAM databases such as FoxPro, dBASE, Paradox, and Btrieve, as well as non-database formats like Excel and delimited text. When you write code that uses the Jet engine, you don't have to worry about the underlying database's structure.

The Pooh of DAO

Now that you've got the Jet engine and the Data custom control down pat, we'll get confusing. To write code to modify a database, you use data access objects (DAOs). DAOs represent various parts of databases and database sessions. For example, there's a DAO called Database that itself contains objects to create tables and to start and end database sessions. These objects in turn have methods and properties of their own. The syntax you may wind up using can be downright discouraging. For example, if your form has a Data custom control called Data1 and you want to change the value in a particular field (Emp_ID) of the current record, you'll end up with code like this:

```
Data1.Recordset.Fields("Emp_ID").Value = 21
```

That's just too many periods to be good for your health.

At the top of the DAO hierarchy is DBEngine. DBEngine represents the Jet engine. It has properties that handle, among other things, security, and methods that enable you to, for example, create Workspaces. A Workspace is VB-speak for the object that contains open databases, handles security, and manages transactions. When you start using Jet, it creates a Workspace object (DBEngine.Workspace) that includes a user name and password.

Going API

If you are interested in doing ODBC work, you'll probably be interested in the VBSQL custom control. However, both ODBC and VBSQL require files and documentation that don't come with VB (not even the Enterprise Edition). So, not to put too fine a point on it, we're going to skip 'em, except to say that using APIs can give you better performance but will probably cost you in terms of development time.

The Workspace Object and Workspaces Collection

Rule number 1: If you're going to make it complicated, make it *really* complicated. So Microsoft has not just a Workspace object, but also the Workspaces collection. Workspace comprises everything—all databases, transactions, and queries—from when you log in to a database to when you log out: all the databases you opened, all the transactions you performed, and so on.

The Workspaces *collection* is the set of Workspace *objects* that one DBEngine object is dealing with.

Parts of a Workspace

A Workspace is made up of three types of collections: Group, User, and Database. Group collections are made up of Group objects; User collections are made up of User objects; Database collections are made up of Database objects. See rule number 1 in the previous subsection.

The Database object represents an open database. The User object represents a user who has access rights to the database. The Group object represents a group of User objects that share some attribute (usually security).

Parts of a Database: TableDefs, QueryDefs, Recordsets, Relations, and Containers

The collection/object relationship continues, so we're going to stop hammering the point that collections are made up of objects. We're just going to explain what these objects are. After all, why not just call 'em Tables? Why TableDefs?

'Cause they aren't quite the same. First of all, there *is* a Table object (although it's now been superseded by something called the table-type Recordset, but don't worry about that yet). Second, the Table object represents a table—data and all. A TableDef represents the table's structure, including fields, indexes, and so on, but excluding the actual data (the "rows").

QueryDefs are basically compiled queries. You write a QueryDef that operates on the Jet engine, which in turn accesses the data.

Recordsets represent data, either from a table or from a query you ran. If you've used the Table, Dynaset, and Snapshot objects in previous versions of VB, you may want to consider using these Recordset objects: the Table-type (representing a table), Dynaset-type (representing the result of a query), and Snapshot-type (representing a static copy of some data).

Databases in the Practical

Enough theory. Let's party. As we said earlier, the easiest way to go blasting around databases with VB is with the Data custom control. But before you get into using it, you need to know about the structure of the database you're about to attack. VB comes with a tool that can help with this (and even create simple databases): the Data Manager Add-In.

The Data Mangler

Under the Add-Ins menu, you'll find the Data Manager. Run it and an empty window pops up. The Data Manager (Figure 1.14) can create new databases, compact databases, and convert databases from one format into another. However, we're going to deal only with opening existing databases in order to study their design.

Figure 1.14. The Data Manager: VB's database creation and viewing engine.

For most of the examples that follow, we deal with the BIBLIO.MDB database that comes with VB (it's in the same directory as the VB executable). It's a simple example database, but it gets the job done. For now, open it and browse around its tables to see what's going on. You'll find five tables that are arranged as in Table 1.22.

As you can see, getting even simple information will likely require you to join at least two tables. If you select the items in the left column and click Design, you'll find that All Titles is actually a QueryDef, not a table, and that it's made up of a lengthy SQL statement.

Heart of All Evil: The Data Control

When you want to do anything to a database, you create a form and drop on a Data control. By itself, the Data control isn't very interesting; it just opens a channel between the form and a particular table or QueryDef in a database. It doesn't display information or do neat joins or anything. You have to do that yourself.

The Data control has four buttons and a label. The control to the farthest left (a vertical bar and a left-pointing triangle) places the current row at the beginning of the database. The next control to the right (a left-pointing triangle) goes to the previous row. The next control to the right (a right-pointing triangle) goes to the next row, and (surprise) the next control to the right (a right-pointing triangle with a vertical bar) goes to the last row in the database. (Note that the rows in a

Table 1.22. How BIBLIO is arranged.

TABLE/QUERYDEF	COLUMNS
All Titles	Title ISBN Author Year Published Company Name
Authors	Au_ID Author Year Born
Publishers	Pub_ID Name Company Name Address City State Zip
Title Author	ISBN Au_ID
Titles	Title Year Published ISBN PubID Description Notes Subject

database table aren't necessarily in any particular order that would make sense to a person. Typically they're in the order in which they were input.)

The Data control has properties, methods, and events that it responds to. Table 1.23 lists those properties that deal with data access.

Table 1.23. Some Data control properties.

PROPERTY	WHAT IT MEANS
BOFAction, EOFAction	Returns Boolean values that indicate whether the current record position is either before the first record in a table (BOFAction) or after that last record in a table (EOFAction).
Connect	Tells you what database engine created the database you have open.
DatabaseName	The database that your Data control is accessing.
RecordsetType	Tells the Data control whether you're opening a Table, a Dynaset, or a Snapshot of a table.
RecordSource	The name of the TableDef or QueryDef you're opening within the database.

So, most likely what you're going to do is open one Data control for each table you plan to access. You'll just set DatabaseName and RecordSource. Once you've set this information, you can bond other controls to the Data control. These controls will display the information in the table (or query) you actually selected.

Controls That Are into Bondage

VB includes several controls that hook up very nicely with the Data control. These are shown in Table 1.24. They usually don't require you to write any code in order to start displaying information in the database. You just set a property or two and you're off.

Table 1.24. Bonding with the Data Control.

CONTROL	DESCRIPTION
DBCombo	Just like the standard combo box, only it doesn't need any code.
DBList	Just like the regular list box, but you don't have to write any code for it.
DBGrid	Something new: a spreadsheet-like grid that lists the rows and columns presented by the Data control.
TextBox	Binds to the Data control and displays one field.
CheckBox	Binds this control to a Boolean (or bit) data field; makes a good True/False box.
ComboBox	Like the DBCombo, but you have to write some code using the AddItem method. Better to use DBCombo.
ListBox	Like DBList, but you have to write code using AddItem. Better to use DBList.
PictureBox	Displays graphical data (bitmaps, icons, and so on) from fields in the Data control. It supports properties like autoresizing.
Image	Similar to PictureBox control but uses fewer resources and is not quite as robust.

All these controls get bound to the Data control on two properties: DataSource and DataField. DataSource is the name of the Data control to read information from (e.g., Data1). DataField is the name of the attribute (like a column in a table) that you want the control to display.

Generally, the easiest way to deal with bound controls is to set the DataSource and then use the drop-down list to select the DataField. Try doing it in reverse order and you'll see what we mean: You have to type in the name of the attribute you want to select.

At this point, it's good for you to play around with the bound data controls to get an idea of how they work. They're actually pretty simple. You'll find that you can edit fields easily. When you maneuver to another row, the Data control automatically takes care of committing your changes (i.e., writing them to disk). Bound data controls support the updating of existing records, but they don't have the intrinsic capability to add or delete records. You'll have to write some code to do that. Bound data controls also don't support QueryDefs (i.e., joins). You'll have to do that in code, too. The code is fairly easy to write. But still, you'd think that VB would handle it automagically.

Code and Data Controls

The Data control and the bound controls are good at viewing information already in a database, but as we just said, you'll have to write some code to add and delete records.

Deleting Records

Let's write some code to enable you to delete records. Create a form, place on it a data control (Data1), and set DatabaseName to BIBLIO.MDB and RecordSource to Authors. Add a DBGrid (DBGrid1) and set DataSource to Data1. Then add a button (Command1) and add the following code:

```
Private Sub Command1_Click()
    Dim Msg As String
    Dim Rcd As String

    Rcd = Data1.Recordset.Fields("author")

    Msg = "You sure you wanna delete" & Chr$(10)
    Msg = Msg & Rcd
    If MsgBox(Msg, 17, "Delete?") <> 1 Then Exit Sub

    Data1.Recordset.Delete
    Data1.Recordset.MoveNext
    If Data1.Recordset.EOF Then Data1.Recordset.MovePrevious
End Sub
```

This code may not make sense to you right off. Its interesting elements are the methods to delete the current record and move to the next row and the steps we took to figure out the author's name to put it into the message box.

To tell Data1's Recordset object (the object that contains all the records in whatever object that Data1 opened) to delete the current object, just use the Delete method. To move the current record to the next record (you don't want to leave the cursor sitting on an empty row, do you?), use the MoveNext method. Then do a quick check to see whether you moved just beyond the end of the table. If you did, move back one row.

Really interesting is how we figured out the author's name. We looked into Data1's Record-set, this time at the Fields collection. (Remember, a collection is a bunch of objects.) More specifically, we looked at the intersection between the current record and the "Author" field. Technically, you don't have to include the Fields specification; Fields is what's called the *default collection* of Recordset. Some people even find it clearer to write `Data1.Recordset ("author")`. Call us old-fashioned, but doing this just seems to be inviting trouble, especially if you have several people sharing your source code.

Adding Records: Code

You use the AddNew and Update methods to add records to your table. Let's add another button (Command2) to the form in our previous example and drop in the following code:

```
Private Sub Command2_Click()
    Dim Author As String
    Dim Birthdate As Integer

    Author = InputBox("Enter author name: last, first")
    Birthdate = InputBox("Enter birth year")

    Data1.Recordset.AddNew
    Data1.Recordset.Fields("author") = Author
    Data1.Recordset.Fields("[year born]") = Birthdate
    Data1.Recordset.Update
End Sub
```

The resulting code is not very graceful, but it works. Here, we ask for the author's name and birth year. Then we create a new record and just drop those values into the fields into which we want them to go. Finally, we update the whole thing so that the new record will show up.

Adding Records: Properties

There's another way to add records. All you have to do is set a couple of properties. It's pretty easy. Just set the Data control's EOFAction property to 2–Add New and set the DBGrid's AllowAddNew property to True. Then run your program, go to the last record, press the down arrow, and start typing. When you move off the record, the Data control will automatically create a new record and verify it. If you don't type in anything, no new record is added. Using the code and properties together is a typical way to make data entry easy for the user.

Structured Bleary Language

SQL is how you get a VB application to join two tables where no join has existed before. Sure, if your database stores some queries, you can use them as the RecordSource for your Data control just as you would for a table. But the whole point of using VB is that you don't have to muck with the database; you can do it all with your client. Of course, this requires you to know SQL because the engine that's actually doing the join for you is Jet, and Jet speaks SQL.

Try this. Create a form (Form1). Put on it a Data control (Data1) and a DBGrid control (DBGrid1). Set the Data1.DatabaseName property to BIBLIO.MDB (in the VB directory). Don't set a RecordSource. Yet. Set DBGrid1.DataSource to Data1. Now, double-click Form1 and add the following code:

```
Private Sub Form_Load()
    Dim SQL As String
    SQL = "SELECT publishers.name, titles.title, authors.author "
    SQL = SQL & "FROM publishers "
    SQL = SQL & "INNER JOIN (titles INNER JOIN ([title author] "
    SQL = SQL & "INNER JOIN authors "
    SQL = SQL & "ON [title author].au_id = authors.au_id) ON "
```

```
    SQL = SQL & "[title author].isbn = titles.isbn) "
    SQL = SQL & "ON publishers.pubid = titles.pubid"
    Data1.RecordSource = SQL
End Sub
```

Frightened yet? This is the bare-bones SQL statement to display every title in the BIB-LIO.MDB database, show all the authors of these titles, and print the names of the titles' publishing companies.

The neat thing is that this join never existed before. The nasty thing is that you have to know a lot about SQL syntax and a bit about the underlying structure of the tables you're dealing with. Basically, we took four tables, linked them on three attributes, and displayed the result. It's more or less like what we have in Figure 1.15. In the figure, the boldface words are the names of the columns we presented at the end and the boxed names are the columns on which we joined the tables.

AUTHORS	TITLE	TITLES	PUBLISHERS
	AUTHOR		
		Title	
		Year Published	
	ISBN	ISBN	
Au_ID	Au_ID	Pub_ID	Pub_ID
Author		Description	**Name**
Year Born		Notes	Company Name
		Subject	Address
			City
			State
			Zip

Figure 1.15. Joining four tables to get three useful pieces of information.

The hard part of this example isn't figuring out where to join what (that's *easy*). It's getting the SQL syntax just right. First point: Several of the tables and fields in the BIBLIO database have spaces in them. SQL was designed back when filenames couldn't have spaces. So place the offending name in square brackets. Second point: Don't forget your parentheses. If you leave 'em out, you'll get an error like "Syntax error in FROM clause." (This information is available in the various manuals, but VB doesn't come with a SQL primer.)

Now we're left just with the language. We use four SQL keywords in our example: SELECT, FROM, INNER JOIN, and ON. (They don't have to be capitalized, but traditionally, SQL is. It makes the keywords easier to spot.)

- SELECT is SQL's magic-worker; it tells SQL which rows to print when whatever nasty operation the rest of your program is running completes. SELECT is actually a very easy word to get along with. You can **SELECT * FROM titles** if you want; it'll print every row and every column in the titles table. The * is a SQL wildcard.

- FROM tells SQL which table to pull the information from (in the absence of a join like the one we performed).

- INNER JOIN is one of two basic kinds of joins. As we mentioned earlier in this section, inner joins combine two fields wherever the two fields have matching values. When one field has a value and the other doesn't, the inner join ignores it. Outer joins also combine two fields, but print unmatched members. They come in two varieties: left and right. A left join prints all the values from the left (i.e., first) table, matching to values from the right table where it can. A right join prints all the values from the right table, matching to values from the left table where it can.

- ON is part of any join. It tells the join on what fields to join the two tables.

Locating Stuff in Databases

In addition to using the Data control's arrows and the various Move methods to move around a database, you can move it using the Find methods:

- FindFirst finds the first record in the database that satisfies your search
- FindLast finds the last record in the database that satisfies your search
- FindNext finds the next record in the database that satisfies your search
- FindPrevious finds the previous record in the database that satisfies your search

Typical syntax for the Find methods is

```
Data1.Recordset.FindNext "author = 'Montgomery, John' "
```

Notice that FindNext uses the = assignment operator. In general, use the Find methods with an exact comparison. For other types of comparisons, use the Seek method.

Seek finds things a little more efficiently than Find. The generic syntax of Seek is

```
table.Seek comparison, key1, key2...
```

As you can see, Seek differs from the Find family. The first, and biggest, difference is that it works only with table Recordsets, not Dynasets or Snapshots. Second, it works using an index. It doesn't have to be a primary, unique index, but you will have to select one field to be the index field. Say we wanted to find author #200 in our database. We could do this:

```
Dim MyDB As Database, MyTable As Recordset

Set MyDB = Workspaces(0).OpenDatabase("BIBLIO.MDB")
Set MyTable = MyDB.OpenRecordset("Authors", dbOpenTable)

MyTable.Index = "Au_ID"
MyTable.Seek "=", 200
```

If the table were already open with a Data control, we could just use

```
Dim MyTable As Recordset

Set MyTable = Data1.Recordset
MyTable.Index = "Au_ID"

MyTable.Seek "=", 200
```

Error Handling

Nobody's perfect. Even with a debugger, somebody somewhere is going to think up something that you didn't think up, and your app isn't going to know what to do and it's going to barf (otherwise known as "generate an error"). That's when you have to have error-handling routines. The primary way of handling errors is with the On Error statement. If you don't include On Error statements, any errors your program encounters are fatal (i.e., your app dies then and there). So, at the very least, you need a couple of error-handling calls.

On Error Resume . . .

Here's the very basic error handling approach: Your app ignores errors, for better or worse, and just proceeds to the next line of code. This approach is best for when you're accessing objects, where you can't guarantee what the object is going to do, so you have no way to trap problems.
    There are three basic forms of the On Error Resume . . . syntax:

1. On Error Resume Next goes to the statement immediately following the statement that caused the error.

2. On Error Resume *line* or *label* goes to a specific line number or label.

3. On Error Resume goes back to the statement that caused the error. Use On Error Resume to repeat an operation after you correct an error.

On Error GoTo *Line*

To jump to a specific line in the current procedure, use On Error GoTo *line*.

On Error GoTo 0

To disable the error handler in the current procedure to, use On Error GoTo 0.

Error-handling Chain

Of course, things are never this simple, right? For example, say you're in procedure B, which was called by procedure A. Both A and B have error-handling syntax. B has an error, and you drop into B's error handling; while there, B has another error. What happens? Control returns to A, which now has to deal with the error.

More generally, here's how it works. Your app encounters an error and starts doing its error-handling thing. If the error-handling code includes an On Error Resume statement, the app resumes at the level of the error handler. This is a fancy way of saying that if B drops back to A to handle its error, processing resumes in A. You will probably arrange error handling so that some errors are handled in B and some get passed back to A.

If there's an error in the error-handling routine (as in the example in the first paragraph of this subsection), the error gets passed to the calling procedure. If there's no calling procedure, you're SOL: The app displays an error message and ends. The lesson here: Keep your error-handling code simple.

Without error-handling code, your app displays a message box and ends.

Err

You can get really sophisticated in the way you deal with errors. For example, errors can return codes to tell you what happened. You can use the Err object to figure out what happened, clear the error, or even (if you're truly weird) cause an error.

Properties of Err

Err has six properties:

1. *Description:* Contains a description of the error.

2. *HelpContext:* The context ID for a topic in a Windows help file. You can use it to bring up a Help topic when an error occurs.

3. *HelpFile:* Contains a path to a Winhelp file.

4. *LastDLLError:* Works only with 32-bit Windows OSes. It returns a system error code produced by a DLL.

5. *Number:* An integer that indicates the last error that happened. In other words, you check the value of Err.Number to figure out which error occurred. You can build code into your application to fix some errors.

6. *Source:* Contains the name of the object that generated the error. You'll use it most when you're doing OLE stuff. It returns values like Word.Application.

Methods of Err

Err has two methods:

1. *Clear:* Sets the value of Err.Number back to 0.

2. *Raise:* Causes an error. Use the Raise method to pass an error back to a calling procedure or to test your own error-handling code.

Dealing with Errors as They Happen

In big applications, you'll probably want to set up a special error-handling routine that you branch to on an error. Sometimes, however, you just want to deal with errors when they come up. This is called *inline error handling.* It requires a bit of typing on your part:

- Include the On Error Resume Next statement in your code.

- After *each line of code,* check Err.Number. If Err.Number is 0, there's no error. Otherwise, Err.Number contains the value of the last error that occurred.

- Handle the error (this exercise is left to the reader).

- After you handle it, use Err.Clear to reset the error number.

The Debugger and Error Handling Code

The Debugger doesn't interact very well with error-handling code. In fact, it's downright hard to use the two of them together—VB tends to execute the error-handling code rather than breaking, so you never know that an error occurred. Oops.

Fortunately, VB has a few tricks you can use so that it will ignore your error-handling code. Start by choosing Tools/Options/Advanced. Then consider the following options:

- Break on All Errors. Click Break on All Errors, and VB now will ignore your carefully coded On Error statements and enter Break mode whenever your app has an error.

- Break in Class Module. Click Break in Class Module when you're debugging an OLE server. The OLE server will now enter Break mode rather than passing the error back to the client.

- Break on Unhandled Errors. Select Break on Unhandled Errors to have VB enter Break mode whenever it encounters an error that you don't have error-handling code for.

The Ubiquitous Sample App

Every programming book has a sample application. Some of them are just examples of what you can do with what you've learned so far. Ours is actually useful. You might think this is the result of lots of planning on our parts. Actually, when the book was already about two weeks late to our editor, John sent an e-mail to Vince (the brains of the operation) asking if he had any good sample apps lying around. Well, it turned out he did, thank heavens.

Styles, as Vince calls it, uses an OLE connection to a running copy of WinWord to find out all the styles in the current document. It then displays them in a window that will stay on top. When you want to change the style of some part of your document, you select the text and double-click the style in Styles. No more pulling down the Style menu or using finger-twisting keyboard shortcuts. Styles sends an OLE command to WinWord to change the style of the selection and then uses AppActivate to make WinWord the active window again. Very clever, and a great boon to authors of Hacker's Guides. (These books are heavily styled, and it's the authors who do most of the style tagging.)

To create Styles, follow these steps:

1. Make a form called frmStyle and drag onto it a ListBox control that you name LstStyles.

2. Drag on a Command button and set its Name to BtnGetStyles and its Caption to Get Styles.

3. Create a menu called mnuConnect. Its top menu caption is &Connect and its submenus are called mnuConnectSub (caption &Get Connection, Index 0) and mnuConnectSub (caption of &Disconnect, Index 1).

When you're done, you should have a form that looks like Figure 1.16.

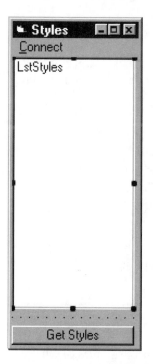

Figure 1.16. Programming with Styles.

4. Insert a Module called StyleModule.bas and put the following code into its (General) (declarations) section:

```
Declare Function SetWindowPos Lib "User32" (ByVal hwnd&, ByVal hb&, _
    ByVal x&, ByVal y&, ByVal cx&, ByVal cy&, ByVal f&) As Long

Public Const SWP_NOMOVE& = 2
Public Const SWP_NOSIZE& = 1
Public Const FLAGS& = SWP_NOMOVE Or SWP_NOSIZE
Public Const HWND_TOPMOST& = -1
Public Const HWND_NOTOPMOST& = -2

'Eventually, we'll need a way to trace Microsoft Word, so:

Public oWord As Object
```

5. In frmStyle.frm, enter the following code under the (General) (declarations) section (VB will automatically put the code in the right Objects and Procedures when it sees the Sub statements):

```
Option Explicit

Private Const CONNECT_GET As Integer = 0
Private Const CONNECT_DISCONNECT As Integer = 1

Sub GetStyles()
    'This is the code that's the Get Styles button executes.

    'We need an integer for the number of styles in the
    'active document, and a counter
    Dim nStyles As Integer, i As Integer

    'If Styles isn't connected to a running copy of
    'Word, tell the user to connect.

    If TypeName(oWord) = "Nothing" Then
        MsgBox "Not Connected! Use the Connect menu."
        Exit Sub
    End If
    frmStyle.MousePointer = vbHourglass
    LstStyles.Clear
    On Error GoTo Bye

    'OLE magic: tell word to count the number of styles
    'so we can step through them and populate LstStyles.
    'Then get the styles. These are actually WordBasic
    'commands that we're sending to the Word object.

    nStyles = oWord.CountStyles()
    For i = 1 To nStyles
        LstStyles.AddItem oWord.[StyleName$](i)
    Next i
Bye:
    On Error GoTo 0
    frmStyle.MousePointer = vbDefault
End Sub

Sub SetStyle(sName$)
    'The magic code to set the style when you double-click
    'on a style name in LstStyles
```

```
    If TypeName(oWord) = "Nothing" Then
        MsgBox "Not Connected! Use the Connect menu."
        Exit Sub
    End If
    'More OLE/WordBasic magic...
    On Error GoTo Bye
    oWord.Style sName$
    'And bring Word back to the forefront.
    AppActivate "Microsoft Word"
Bye:
    On Error GoTo 0
End Sub

Private Sub BtnGetStyles_Click()
    GetStyles
End Sub

Private Sub Form_Initialize()
    'Call the Connect menu's Click event to connect
    mnuConnectSub_Click (CONNECT_GET)
End Sub

Private Sub Form_Resize()
    'Now for the tricky part: what happens when you
    'resize the form?
    Dim success&
    If Me.WindowState = 0 Then
        'Resize list and button to "pretty" up the window
        LstStyles.Width = Me.Width - 96
        LstStyles.Height = Me.Height - 842
        BtnGetStyles.Width = Me.Width - 96
        BtnGetStyles.Top = Me.Height - 834

        'Make it the top-most window
        success& = SetWindowPos(Me.hwnd, HWND_TOPMOST, 0, _
            0, 0, 0, FLAGS)
    End If
End Sub

Private Sub Form_Terminate()
    'Call the Connect menu's click event to disconnect
    mnuConnectSub_Click (CONNECT_DISCONNECT)
End Sub

Private Sub LstStyles_DblClick()
    SetStyle LstStyles.Text
End Sub

Private Sub mnuConnectSub_Click(Index As Integer)
    'Herein lies the code for connecting to the running
    'copy of Word.

    If Index = CONNECT_GET Then
        If TypeName(oWord) = "Nothing" Then
            On Error GoTo NoConnect
            Set oWord = CreateObject("Word.Basic")
```

```
        End If
    Else
        Set oWord = Nothing
    End If
    Exit Sub
NoConnect:
    On Error GoTo 0
    Set oWord = Nothing
End Sub
```

For under one hundred lines of code, Styles is a pretty impressive app. There are, admittedly, things it doesn't do too well—deal with multiple instances of WinWord, for example. But for your typical, run-of-the-mill, down-and-dirty, style changing program, it's a keeper.

Spit and Polish

Once you've finished coding your application, you're going to want to do two things: tune it and make it distributable. This section looks at both of these.

Performance Optimization

Let's get one thing straight right now: VB is not known for creating super-speedy applications. It's not a completely compiled language like C or C++ (despite what Microsoft representatives sometimes claim). Rather, it's interpreted. VB "compiles" the code you write into pseudocode that a runtime engine (VBRUNXXX.DLL) actually executes. And as we all know from countless magazine articles, interpreted languages aren't as fast as compiled languages (this is something of a harsh generalization, but it's usually true).

Now, where were we? Ah, yes. So VB isn't fast. So what? Why make it slower than it needs to be? Start by optimizing the types of variables you use. In short, never use a variable bigger than you need. Using a Variant can be hideously slower than using an Integer if all you need is a counting variable. This is probably the easiest tip of all.

Also, don't reference properties when you can do it in a variable. If you're changing a property in a loop, for example, stick the property into a variable and then use the variable.

Use the Image control rather than the Picture control. Image is more limited in what it can do and so has less to worry about when it draws its contents. A few long-time VB users recommend using the Picture control to simulate a complicated group of controls. Each control takes time to draw, so, they figure, it's faster to draw the picture.

Another big tip is to set AutoRedraw to False. Then send a Redraw or Refresh event when something changes.

These are the main tricks for improving actual performance. But there are many tricks you can employ to make your app *seem* faster. The biggie here is to hide forms rather than unloading them. However, you'll increase the memory footprint of your application.

Here's another: You know how, during installations, you get little Status Bars that tell you how far along the installation is? Include them. They fool the user into thinking things are really zipping along—even if the user already knows it's a trick.

Memory Optimization

Generally, when you optimize for performance, you tend to take a hit on memory. However, you can do a few simple things to make sure your application doesn't hog more memory than it positively needs.

- Again: Use the right-sized variables.

- Set strings to "" when you're done with them.

- Erase (blow away) or ReDim Preserve (compress) dynamic arrays when you're not using them.

- Use LoadPicture to clear a Picture object when you don't need it any more.

Distribution

Once your app is done and ready to go, you need to create a setup routine that will install it properly on someone else's computer. If the application is simple, you can probably get away with PKZIPping the files you need into a self-extracting archive and sending that around. Unfortunately the world of Windows 95, OLE, and the Registry make ZIP a less-than-wonderful distribution method.

Why? There are four things you probably need to do for a successful distribution, only one of which PKZIP can handle:

- Copy the files to the unsuspecting victim's computer.

- Put the files into the right directories.

- Register the application in the Registry.

- Create icons, groups, and all that stuff.

In the old days (before VB4), you had to do this by writing your own setup program. So, just when you thought you were done with your application, you had to write a few hundred more lines of code—the lines that would actually be the first part of your application that users would see. Since you were tired and really didn't want to write the setup program, you may not have done a good job. So your application didn't get installed right.

SetupWizard

Well, VB4 can help. It has the SetupWizard. Like most of Microsoft's Wizards, SetupWizard is conspicuously easy to use. It asks you for information such as which project file it's going to distribute, which OLE servers it uses, and so on (there are lots of OLE questions). Then it places the distributable app either onto floppies or onto your hard disk somewhere. The SetupWizard is a standalone application that lives in a directory called SETUPKIT.

The catch is that for even a simple project (one form, no OLE, few controls), you can wind up creating 20 files at a cost of probably over 2MB. You win some, you lose some. That said, the SetupWizard is the easiest way to make your distribution stuff. It will automatically check dependencies, compress the files, copy them to disk, and create a setup program. Run it and you'll see what it does. There are really no tricks (except one, which we'll get into in a second).

Here's what's going onto your distribution media.

SETUP.EXE

This is the standard copy of SETUP.EXE that ships with VB4. It's the same one that is distributed with thousands of other VB applications. It is responsible for copying the basic files from the distribution floppies onto the user's hard disk and then executing the real setup program.

SETUP.LST

SETUP.LST is a list of the files your app needs. It includes information about which directories SETUP needs and how much disk space your app needs.

The SetupWizard creates this file. This file contains the list of the files required by your application and some general information such as default directories and disk space required. The sample SETUP.LST looks like this:

```
[BootStrap]
File1=1,,setup132.ex_,setup132.exe,$(WinPath),$(EXESelfRegister),,5/24/1995,
195584,4.0.0.2123
File2=1,,stkit432.dl_,stkit432.dll,$(WinSysPath),,$(Shared),5/24/1995,57344,
4.0.21.24
File3=1,,VB40032.DL_,VB40032.DLL,$(WinSysPath),,$(Shared),5/24/1995,739488,4
.0.21.24
File4=1,,vaen232.dl_,vaen232.dll,$(WinSysPath),,$(Shared),5/19/1995,10240,2.
0.0.5118
File5=1,,ven2132.ol_,ven2132.olb,$(WinSysPath),,$(Shared),5/19/1995,36352,2.
0.0.5118
File6=1,,mfcans32.dl_,mfcans32.dll,$(WinSysPath),,$(Shared),5/4/1995,149504,
3.1.0.2
File7=1,,msvcrt20.dl_,msvcrt20.dll,$(WinSysPath),,$(Shared),5/4/1995,250368,
2.10.0.0
File8=1,,msvcrt30.dl_,msvcrt30.dll,$(WinSysPath),,$(Shared),5/16/1995,330752
,3.0.0.5128
File9=1,,olepro32.dl_,olepro32.dll,$(WinSysPath),$(DLLSelfRegister),$(Shared
),5/16/1995,74240,4.0.0.5133
[Files]
File1=1,,GRID32.OC_,GRID32.OCX,$(WinSysPath),$(DLLSelfRegister),$(Shared),5/
24/1995,85504,4.0.21.23
File2=1,,LOAN.EX_,LOAN.EXE,$(AppPath),$(EXESelfRegister),,5/24/1995,39936,1.
0.0.0
[Setup]
Title=LoanSheet
DefaultDir=$(ProgramFiles)\LOAN
Setup=setup132.exe
AppExe=LOAN.EXE
AppPath=
```

No big deal, right?

SETUP1.EXE (16 Bit) or SETUP132.EXE (32 Bit)

These files are the *real* setup programs; SETUP.EXE is just a tool to get one of these started. They copy files, register them in the Registry, and create icons.

Miscellaneous

The SetupWizard also creates a few odds and ends, including a log file (ST4UNST.LOG) that contains information on the directories created, files copied (or skipped), Registry entries created, and groups and icons created.

It does this so that on a 32-bit system, you can uninstall your application easily (16-bit Windows doesn't support this feature). Setup will copy an uninstaller (ST4UNST.EXE) into the \WINDOWS directory. This app uses the info in ST4UNST.LOG to remove an application. Neat, huh?

Making Your Own Setup

If you want your setup program to show some kind of special dialog box or form, you can create your own with the VB Setup Toolkit—a collection of DLLs, utilities, and some sample code. Look in the SETUPKIT\SETUP1 subdirectory for the VB project file SETUP1.VBP. It contains the instructions that the SetupWizard uses to create its setup files so that when you modify the wizard, you change the behavior of your final setup program. Make it into an executable with the name SETUP1.EXE (for 16-bit apps) and SETUP132.EXE (for 32-bit ones).

Uninstalling 32-Bit Apps

Thanks to the SetupWizard, it's easy to uninstall (or de-install) applications under Windows 95 and Windows NT. Under Win 95, you just enter the Control Panel, double-click Add/Remove Programs, and follow the prompts for removing an app. Under Win NT, use the application removal utility in the Program Manager icon group.

16 versus 32 Bits

So you want your app to run under Win 3.1, too, huh? How much is it worth to you? Seriously, as you probably know, 16-bit apps run fine under the 32-bit environments, while 32-bit apps run only in 32-bit environments. Keep in mind when you're developing your app that not all features are available for 16-bit platforms, most notably these:

- Unicode strings. The 32-bit VB stores strings in Unicode format; the 16-bit version uses ANSI format. Usually, there's no problem, but. . . .

- Invoking Windows APIs. If you absolutely must invoke Windows APIs, you're going to have to invoke 16-bit APIs from the 16-bit VB and 32-bit APIs from the 32-bit version.

- Data access. 16-bit VB uses Jet 2.5; 32-bit uses 3.0. What's the diff? The Dynaset table type isn't supported with Jet 3.0.

- Long filenames. You can use long filenames only with 32-bit environments.

- Executables. For some reason, you can't cross-target your apps, that is, 32-bit VB will target only 32-bit platforms and 16-bit VB will target only 16-bit platforms.

New Stuff in VB4

VB Is Now VBA

It used to be (with VB3) that VB's programming language differed from Microsoft's Visual Basic, Applications Edition (VBA). VBA is the macro language in Excel 5. It was kind of a drag to have to learn two just-slightly-dissimilar programming languages. VB4's language engine is now VBA 2.0, which is supposed to be fully backward compatible with VBA 1.0. We haven't tested it, but if Microsoft says it is, it is. Right? Right. (Yeah. Right.) Anyway, having VBA as the common engine should make OLE automation easier.

VB Doth Object Too Much

With VB4, you can create your own objects (with their own properties, methods, events, and so on), called classes, and put them together into an object model. All you have to do is

```
Dim NewClass As New Collection
```

Then use the Add method to add some related items to your collection so that you can manipulate them as one big thing. An example of an existing collection is Workspaces, which includes all the open Workspace objects.

Creating OLE Auto Servers

Previously, your VB apps could only be OLE automation clients. With VB4 you can make servers, too (at least, you can with the Pro and Enterprise editions). These servers will expose objects and methods to applications that can act as OLE auto clients.

Custom Properties

You can now create your own properties. Sort of, anyway. What you can really do is create a property procedure (instead of **Sub...End Sub,** you use **Property()...End Property**) in a form or code module. When your application sets this "property," the code underneath gets executed.

Dealing with 32 versus 16 Bits

Now that VB comes in 32- and 16-bit versions, you need a way to target your applications correctly. For example, the 32-bit version of VB supports long filenames; the 16-bit version doesn't. VB4 has a way to deal with this (although we think it could be better): Use the #If...Then directive to build your application selectively.

Leaving on a Jet Plane

VB4 includes the Jet 3.0 database engine, which adds the capability to create new databases, alter a database's structure, and manipulate database security and referential integrity. Watch out, everybody: VB's dangerous.

Source Control

VB4, Enterprise edition, includes SourceSafe, a Source Code Control system. If it doesn't already appear on your Add-Ins menu, choose Add-In Manager from the Add-Ins menu. Then in the Available References dialog, select the Source Code Control Add-In and click OK.

New Version of Crystal Reports

For those of you who use Crystal Reports to generate your database reports, VB4 includes a new version of the Crystal Report writer.

New Variable Types

VB4 offers three new variable types: Boolean, Byte, and Date.

Edition Differences

VB4 comes in three editions: Standard, Professional, and Enterprise. Our *Hacker's Guide* focuses on the Standard ('cause it has the most features that everybody will be using). You probably have VB Pro.

Standard Edition

The Standard edition includes these features:

* Visual Basic development environment

* SetupWizard

* Setup Kit

* Other cool stuff

Professional Edition

The Professional Edition includes the Standard Edition, plus these features:

* Additional custom controls and Help

* Metafiles and bitmaps

- Microsoft Windows Help Compiler

- Crystal Reports

- A modified Data control that can open ODBC databases

- Data Access Objects (DAO)

- Image Editor

- Resource Compiler

- Code Profiler

- Help Workshop

Enterprise Edition

The Enterprise Edition includes the Professional Edition, plus these features:

- Visual Source Safe (source code control)

- Remote OLE Automation

- Remote database access tools

- Component Manager

- Data Explorer

Frequently Asked Questions

Q: I can't fit my new application on a single floppy disk anymore. Why the &#*&$ is it so (&^%^$%ing big?

A: Microsoft is forcing you to love OLE, whether you want to or not. The OLE controls that replaced VBXs are big. Microsoft's thinking (according to its home page on the World Wide Web) is that eventually all these OLE controls will be part of the operating system. Until then, VB40032.DLL alone is about 705K.

Q: I'm loading an old VB3 app into VB4, and VB4 says it's going to upgrade my controls. What should I do?

A: If you say no, your app will still run. If you say yes, your app should still run, but nobody guarantees it. Back up your app, then say yes. VB4 will replace your controls with newer (OLE) controls that basically do the same thing but that probably include some new features. It will also change the .Mak file.

Q: Do I have to change anything to have my VB3 app compile with the 16-bit version of VB4?

A: No. It'll run just like it did before.

Q: Do I have to change anything to have my VB3 app compiler with the 32-bit version of VB4?

A: Probably, for two reasons. First, if your app makes any API calls, you'll find that the 32-bit version and 16-bit version use slightly different Declare statements because the data types of the two versions are different sizes. Second, the 32-bit version uses OLE controls only; it doesn't support VBXs. You'll have to upgrade your VBXs to OCXs (OLE controls), which may mean finding out if the third-party VBX you've been using has an OCX counterpart. Don't worry about the language, though; the 16- and 32-bit versions of BASIC are compatible.

Q: Does VB4 have statements for multitasking?

A: No.

Q: If I create a DLL with VB, can I call it from other languages?

A: Yes, but you call these DLLs (called OLE DLLs) through their OLE interface, not like a true Windows DLL.

Q: Can a 32-bit VB4 app run on Win32s (the semi-32-bit environment for Windows 3.1)?

A: No.

Q: Can I create DLLs with VB4?

A: Kind of. You can make what's called an OLE DLL, which is a little like a DLL, but you get into it by using an OLE interface. Say you've created one and you now want to use it. Use the Object Browser to look at its methods and properties (just like an OLE control). You can call these "DLLs" from any application that can act as an OLE automation client.

Best Tips

Shift+<F2>

In the code module, just point to the function or subroutine, hit Shift + <F2>, and see what happens.

The Debug Window

Use the Debug Window to test code quickly. Just click the Run button and then the Pause button. Next write your code in the Debug Window. Use ? syntax to ask about function results and variable values.

Tools, Custom Controls Menu

Use to remove tools and controls you don't need and add the ones you do.

Startup Forms

By default, your application starts on Form1. But say you want something different. You can set it by choosing Tools/Options, selecting the Project tab, and setting the Startup Form. If the first thing you want your app to do is execute code in a .BAS module, create a procedure named MAIN in a .BAS file and set the startup form to Sub Main.

Error Central

Microsoft has a very good suggestion about error handling: Use a centralized error handler when you can. Try this example (obtained from somewhere in the Microsoft documentation):

```
Private Sub CodeWithErrorHandler()
      On Error GoTo ErrHandler
      '...Procedure code ...
      '...
      Exit Sub
ErrHandler:
      'Pass error to general purpose error-handling routine
      Action = HandleError(Err.Number)
      'Take action based on result of function
      If Action = MyResume Then
            Resume
      ElseIf Action = MyResumeNext Then
            Resume Next
      End If
End Sub
```

Debugging: Where Am I?

You're debugging. You're in Break mode. What procedure called the procedure that called the procedure that . . . and so on to get you where you are now? Select Tools/Calls to show the invocation chain.

Faster Startup

Normally, VB compiles your project fully before it starts. This works great when you're looking for compile-time errors. But it also means your app may be slow to start. To make it faster, select Tools/Options/Advanced and set Compile on Demand.

Compiling from DOS

DOS isn't quite dead, and VB knows this. You can easily compile your app from DOS with a command like

```
vb32 /make project application
```

Conventional Wisdom

Name your controls, forms, constants, and variables with consistent, conventional names, like **txtUserName** for a text box and **iCount** for an integer counter.

Show Me Everything

By default, the Code editor window shows you only one procedure at a time. You can display all procedures at the same time by inserting a separator line between each one. Do this by selecting Tools/Options/Editor/Full Module View.

Browsing

Use the Object Browser to navigate your application's procedures and forms. Also use it to paste function, method, and property calls into your application. (F2 is the shortcut.)

I Do Declare

Select Tools/Options/Environment/Require Variable Declaration. 'Nuff said.

Latest Bugs

 BeginTrans allows only five levels of nesting. When one user changes a database record, it may not be committed immediately (due to local caching).

If your database has more than 32 relationships or indexes, Jet cannot convert it.

A database on a NetWare 3.11 server will be opened by a Win95 client as exclusive access, even if the application specifies that it should be shared access.

SECTION 2: VISUAL BASIC FOR APPLICATIONS: FUNCTIONS AND STATEMENTS

This section describes the classes and commands in the VBA library. You'll find all of these by clicking the Object Browser icon and selecting VBA—Visual Basic for Applications.

The Collection Module

A *collection* is a named group of related components—like an array, only more potent. That's because the elements of a collection don't all have to be the same data type. For example, a collection could contain the names of OLE objects, your own arrays, and data. A collection may also be more useful than an array, since it's dynamically sized. Simply add and remove items to and from your collection. There's no need to do re-Dim.

Usage   Dim CollectionName As New Collection

Example
```
Private Sub Command1_Click()
    Dim MyStrings As New Collection
    Dim Num, NewString$, MyObject
    Do
        Num = Num + 1
        Msg = "Enter new Name:"
        NewString$ = InputBox(Msg, "Name")
        If NewString$ <> "" Then
            MyStrings.Add Item:=NewString$, KEY:=CStr(Num)
        End If
    Loop Until NewString$ = ""
    For Each MyObject In MyStrings
        List1.AddItem MyObject
    Next MyObject
    For Num = 1 To MyStrings.Count
        MyStrings.Remove 1
    Next Num
End Sub
```

Of course, you could have just added the strings to the list box directly, but this just demonstrates how you might use the Collection object.

WARNING: You can add (almost) any item to the Collection, so you must be careful to remember what you've put in it and what you've retrieved from it. To be safe, you can define user-classes that embed the Collection object functionality.

Add Method

Add adds an item to a Collection. Any objects or types can be added. There's no checking.

Usage   *object*.Add *Item*:=[, *Key*:=] [, *Before*:=] [, *After*:=]

PARAMETER	VALUE	MEANING
Item	Any expression	Required. An expression of any type that specifies the member to add to the collection.
Key	Any string expression	A unique string expression that can be used to access the item.
Before	A string (for a key) or a number	Used to manually place the item before the identified item.
After	A string (for a key) or a number	Used to manually place the item after the identified item.

All arguments are optional except *Item*. *Key* is a unique string expression that can be used to access the item, kind of like a bookmark. *After* and *Before* are used to manually place the new item either before or after the identified item; these can be strings (for keys) or numbers. As numbers, *Before/After* must be from 1 to Count (see the next item).

If you're trying to define a key and one already exists, you get an error message: "Run-time error '457', This key is already associated with an element of this collection." Good! A descriptive error message.

You can use explicit arguments such as

```
MyCollection.Add item:="me", key:="key", before:="pos1"
```

If you make a mistake or have both *Before* and *After* defined or if the *Before/After* ids don't exist, you just get a cryptic "Run-time error '5', Invalid procedure call" error message.

If *After/Before* is a number and that item does not exist, you get the error message "Run-time error '9', Subscript out of range."

 You can't add user-defined type to a Collection:

```
Type MyType
    ID As Integer
    name As String * 20
End Type

Dim MyObjects As Collection
Dim t As MyType

t.ID = 10
t.name = "who"
MyObject.Add t
```

The above code, when compiled, generates the error message "ByRef argument type mismatch" at the .Add line. You have to create a user-defined class: Insert/ClassModule and define Public variables that correspond to data members. Then you can define instances of ClassModules via Dim...New and add them to the Collection.

Count Property

Count counts the number of items in a Collection as a Long value.

Usage   *LongValue = object*.Count

You can either use this with For...Next or skip it altogether by using the For Each...Next to loop through each item. See the example for the Add method.

Item Method

Item returns a specific member of a Collection, either by its position or by a key.

Usage   *VariantValue = object*.Item(*Index*:=)
                 VariantValue = object(*Index*:=)

PARAMETER	VALUE	MEANING
Index	Number or string	Specifies the position of a member of the Collection.

This is the default method of a Collection, so *Item* is optional. The *Index* argument can be a number between 1 and Count or a string that matches a key of an item in the Collection. If the key does not exist, you get "Run-time error '5', Invalid procedure call."

All right. Why does the index start at 1? Isn't this inconsistent with the rest of the Controls numbering scheme in VB that starts at 0? Yes, it is. Welcome to VB.

In fact, if you look at the Count property in the Help file, you find this example:

```
For I = 0 To Form1.Count - 1
    Form1.Controls(I).Left = Form1.Controls(I).Left + 720
Next I
```

Remove Method

Remove removes (surprise!) a member from a Collection.

Usage   *object*.Remove(*Index*:=)

PARAMETER	VALUE	MEANING
Index	Number or string	Specifies the position of a member of the Collection.

The *Index* argument can be a number between 1 and Count or a string that matches a key of an item in the Collection. If the key does not exist, you get "Run-time error '5', Invalid procedure call."

Again, note that the numeric index starts at 1 (see rant under Item Method)!

The Constants Module

When you're adding VBA capabilities to your application, you'll probably find that memorizing the parameters and return values for all the VBA functions is a drag. Fortunately, VB defines a bunch of constants for both. The following (very, very long) table lists them.

CONSTANT	VALUE	MEANING
vbAbort	3	Return value for MsgBox
vbAbortRetryIgnore	2	Buttons argument for MsgBox
vbAlias	64 (mac only)	
vbApplicationModal	0	Buttons argument for MsgBox
vbArchive	32	Attributes argument for Dir, GetAttr, SetAttr
vbArray	8192	Return value for VarType
vbBack	Chr$(8)	Backspace character
vbBoolean	11	Return value for VarType
vbByte	17	Return value for VarType
vbCancel	2	Return value for MsgBox
vbCr	Chr$(13)	Carriage-return
vbCritical	16	Buttons argument for MsgBox
vbCrLf	Chr$(13) + Chr$(10)	Carriage-return/linefeed
vbCurrency	6	Return value for VarType
vbDataObject	13	Return value for VarType
vbDate	7	Return value for VarType
vbDefaultButton1	0	Buttons argument for MsgBox
vbDefaultButton2	256	Buttons argument for MsgBox
vbDefaultButton3	512	Buttons argument for MsgBox
vbDirectory	16	Attributes argument for Dir or GetAttr
vbDouble	5	Return value for VarType
vbEmpty	0	Return value for VarType
vbError	10	Return value for VarType
vbExclamation	48	Buttons argument for MsgBox
vbFirstFourDays	2	FirstWeekOfYear constant
vbFirstFullWeek	3	FirstWeekOfYear constant

CONSTANT	VALUE	MEANING
vbFirstJan1	1	FirstWeekOfYear constant
vbFormFeed	Chr$(12)	Form feed
vbFriday	6	FirstDayOfWeek constant
vbFromUnicode	128	Conversion argument for StrConv
vbHidden	2	Attribute argument for Dir, GetAttr, SetAttr
vbHide	0	Argument for Shell command
vbHiragana	32	Conversion argument for StrConv
vbIgnore	5	Return value for MsgBox
vbIMEAlphaDbl	7	Argument for IMEStatus (Far East versions only)
vbIMEAlphaSng	8	Argument for IMEStatus (Far East versions only)
vbIMEDisable	3	Argument for IMEStatus (Far East versions only)
vbIMEHiragana	4	Argument for IMEStatus (Far East versions only)
vbIMEKatakanaDbl	5	Argument for IMEStatus (Far East versions only)
vbIMEKatakanaSng	6	Argument for IMEStatus (Far East versions only)
vbIMENoOp	0	Argument for IMEStatus (Far East versions only)
vbIMEOff	2	Argument for IMEStatus (Far East versions only)
vbIMEOn	1	Argument for IMEStatus (Far East versions only)
vbInformation	64	Buttons argument for MsgBox
vbInteger	2	Return value for VarType
vbKatakana	16	Conversion argument for StrConv
vbLf	Chr$(10)	Linefeed
vbLong	3	Return value for VarType
vbLowerCase	2	Conversion argument for StrConv
vbMaximizedFocus	3	Argument for Shell command
vbMinimizedFocus	2	Argument for Shell command
vbMinimizedNoFocus	6	Argument for Shell command
vbMonday	2	FirstDayOfWeek constant
vbNarrow	8	Conversion argument for StrConv
vbNo	7	Return value for MsgBox
vbNormal	0	Attributes argument for Dir, GetAttr, SetAttr
vbNormalFocus	1	Argument for Shell command
vbNormalNoFocus	4	Argument for Shell command

CONSTANT	VALUE	MEANING
vbNull	1	Return value for VarType
vbNullChar	Chr$(0)	Null character
vbNullString	NULL	Use for a string argument whose value is 0
vbObject	9	Return value for VarType
vbObjectError	−2147221504 = &H80040000	Indicate error returned from VisualBasic object
vbOK	1	Return value for MsgBox
vbOKCancel	1	Buttons argument for MsgBox
vbOKOnly	0	Buttons argument for MsgBox
vbProperCase	3	Conversion argument for StrConv
vbQuestion	32	Buttons argument for MsgBox
vbReadOnly	1	Attributes argument for GetAttr or SetAttr
vbRetry	4	Return value for MsgBox
vbRetryCancel	5	Buttons argument for MsgBox
vbSaturday	7	FirstDayOfWeek constant
vbSingle	4	Return value for VarType
vbString	8	Return value for VarType
vbSunday	1	FirstDayOfWeek constant
vbSystem	4	Attributes argument for Dir, GetAttr, or SetAttr
vbSystemModal	4096	Buttons argument for MsgBox
vbTab	Chr$(9)	Tab character
vbThursday	5	FirstDayOfWeek constant
vbTuesday	3	FirstDayOfWeek constant
vbUnicode	64	Conversion argument for StrConv
vbUpperCase	1	Conversion argument for StrConv
vbUseSystem	0	FirstDayOfWeek or FirstWeekOfYear constant
vbVariant	12	Return value for VarType
vbVerticalTab	Chr$(11)	VerticalTab character
vbVolume	8	Attributes argument for Dir or GetAttr
vbWednesday	4	FirstDayOfWeek constant

CONSTANT	VALUE	MEANING
vbWide	4	Conversion argument for StrConv
vbYes	6	Return value for MsgBox
vbYesNo	4	Buttons argument for MsgBox
vbYesNoCancel	3	Buttons argument for MsgBox

The Conversion Module

There's an old joke in New England about a city slicker approaching a Vermonter (or Mainer, depending on where you're telling the joke) and asking for directions. After a lengthy series of directions (performed in your best Vermont accent), the local concludes, "Weeelll, ya can't git thar from heah." And so we introduce VB's conversion functions.

You should use the conversion functions whenever possible instead of the old Val() function because they take into account internationalization of decimal point characters, thousands separator characters, and currency symbols.

Statistical Rounding

VB uses statistical rounding for converting floating-point values to integer values. In traditional rounding, any number that is exactly half-way between two integers is rounded up to the larger integer if the number is positive and rounded down to the next smaller integer if the number is negative. For instance, 1.5 would be converted to 2, but 1.49 would be converted to 1. Similarly, –1.5 would be converted to –2 (a smaller number than –1) , but –1.49 would be converted to –1.

In statistical rounding, whether the .5 fraction is rounded up or down depends on the integer part of the number. If the integer part is odd, the number is rounded away from zero; if it is even, the number is rounded towards zero. The following table illustrates this more clearly.

NUMBER	ROUNDING RESULT
–4.5	–4
–3.5	–4
–2.5	–2
–1.5	–2
–0.5	0
0.5	0
1.5	2
2.5	2
3.5	4
4.5	4

CBool Function

CBool() converts *Expression* to a Boolean value.

Usage   *BooleanValue* = CBool(*Expression*)

Expression must evaluate to a numeric expression, but it can be a string, a number, or a comparison. If it evaluates to 0, CBool() returns False; otherwise, it returns True. If *Expression* is a string, it can *only* be True, False (with any capitalization), or a pure number expressed as a string. No expression can be put in a string.

OK	BAD
CBool(A = B)	CBool("A = B")
CBool(A)	CBool("A")
CBool(Not A)	CBool("Not A")
CBool("True")	
CBool("False")	
CBool("1")	
CBool("4.395")	
CBool(4.395)	
CBool("&H0")	
CBool("&O10")	
CBool("($5)")	
CBool("($3)")	
CBool("–$5.6")	

Or, you can look at things as in the following table, which hold true for most of the Conversion functions (except CDate):

EXPRESSION TYPE	RANGE
Numeric	Any number expressed as decimal, octal, or hexadecimal. Can be a numeric expression. 0 is converted to False. Any other number is converted to True.
Boolean	Any Boolean comparison (including use of Not).
String	Only True, False, or something that can be evaluated directly into a number.
Null	Error
Empty	Returns False.

CByte Function

CByte() converts *Expression* to an unsigned Byte value between 0 and 255, inclusive. As with CBool(), *Expression* can be a numeric expression, a comparison, or a string.

Usage   *ByteValue* = CByte(*Expression*)

 All right, this is weird (and we're pretty sure it's a bug). If *Expression* is a Boolean value—True or False—the return value is the *Boolean* value, not a Byte value. If, instead, *Expression* is a comparison that would normally return a Boolean value, CByte() returns 0 (for False) and 255 (for True).

EXPRESSION TYPE	RANGE
Numeric	Any number or a numeric expression that evaluates to a number from 0 and 255. If the number has a fractional part, CByte() rounds it to the nearest integer (see the note on statistical rounding under the previous section, "Statistical Rounding").
Comparison	Any comparison. False returns 0 and True returns 255. If expression is the value, True or False, CByte() will return the Boolean value of True or False, respectively, not 255 or 0. Don't ask us why. We didn't write the function.
String	Only something that can be evaluated directly into a number. No numeric expressions are allowed in the string.
Null	Error
Empty	Returns 0.

CCur Function

CCur() converts *Expression* to a currency value.

Usage   *CurrencyValue* = CCur(*Expression*)

Expression can be a number, a comparison, or a string. If it's a string, the string can include a currency symbol and a thousands separator. Negative values may also use parentheses, as in

```
CCur("($193,495.43)")
```

EXPRESSION TYPE	RANGE
Numeric	Any number or a numeric expression that evaluates to a number from −922,337,203,685,477.5808 to 922,337,203,685,477.5807. All numbers are rounded to four decimal places. (See the following bug.)
Boolean	Any Boolean comparison. False returns 0 and True returns −1.
String	Only something that can be evaluated directly into a number. No numeric expressions are allowed in the string.
Null	Error
Empty	Returns 0.

There's a rounding error. CCur() is supposed to use traditional rounding, not statistical rounding, but it often doesn't behave correctly when used with literal numbers. There are some conversion errors. For instance,

```
CCur(2.00005)
```

should return 2.0001, but it returns 2, while

```
CCur(2.000050000000001)
```

returns 2.0001.

CDate Function

Cdate() converts *Expression* to a Date value.

Usage   *DateValue* = CDate(*Expression*)
                VariantValue = CVDate(*Expression*:=)

Expression can be anything that can be interpreted as a date, including date literal, real numbers, strings that look like dates, and Date values. If the date is a real number, values to the left of the decimal represent the date and values to the right of the decimal represent the time of day.

The number 0 corresponds to December 30, 1899, but we couldn't get it to return that value. For instance,

```
CDate(0)
CDate(#12/31/1899#)
```

both return #12:00:00 AM#. Negative numbers smaller than or equal to −1 correspond to dates on or before December 19, 1899.

You may want to use IsDate() first to see if *Expression* is a valid date expression. This works *only* if *Expression* is a string and not a number. CDate() replaces old CVDate() from previous versions of VB, *but* with one difference: CVDate() accepts named arguments, while CDate() doesn't.

Trivia Note: We're pretty sure that the bug that made 1900 appear as a leap year is now fixed, unlike in Excel 4.x and before. On another note, it doesn't really make sense for this function to support a date like January 1, 100, since the Gregorian calendar did not come into effect until 1582 (much later in other parts of the world). The Gregorian calendar is the one we're using now, with leap years every fourth year, *except* every century *unless* the century number is divisible by 400. In 1582, Pope Gregory XIII got rid of 10 days to make the vernal equinox occur on March 21, as it had in 325 A.D., the first year of the Council of Nicaea. In 1752, Great Britain accepted the Gregorian calendar and changed the day after September 2 to September 14. (And people wonder why some of us can never remember a relative's birthday.)

EXPRESSION TYPE	RANGE
Date	Any date literal or variable from #January 1, 100 12:00:00 AM# to #December 31, 9999 11:59:59 PM#.
Numeric	Any number or a numeric expression that evaluates to a number from –657434.999988426 to 2958465.99998843. The integer part represents the date, with 0 translating to "12/30/1899," and the fractional part represents the time of day, with resolution to seconds (there are 86,400 seconds in a day).
Boolean	Any Boolean comparison. False returns "12:00:00 AM" (why not "12/30/1899" thanks to the aforementioned bug) and True returns "12/29/1899."
String	Any string that can be evaluated to a date or time from "January 1, 100 12:00:00 AM" to "December 31, 9999 11:59:59 PM."
Null	Error
Empty	Returns "12:00:00 AM."

CDbl Function

CDbl converts *Expression* to a double-precision number.

Usage   *DoubleValue* = CDbl(*Expression*)

Expression can be a number, a comparison, or a string. If it's a string, the string can include a currency symbol and a thousands separator. Negative values may also use parentheses, as in

```
CDbl("($193,495.43)")
```

EXPRESSION TYPE	RANGE
Numeric	Any number or a numeric expression that evaluates to a number from −1.797,693,134,862,31E308 to −4.940,656,458,412,47E-324 for negative values; 4.940,656,458,412,47E-324 to 1.797,693,134,862,31E308 for positive values; and 0.
Boolean	Any Boolean comparison. False returns 0 and True returns −1.
String	Only something that can be evaluated directly into a number. No numeric expressions are allowed in the string.
Null	Error
Empty	Returns 0.

CInt Function

CInt() converts *Expression* into an integer value.

Usage   *IntegerValue* = CInt(*Expression*)

    Expression can be a number, a comparison, or a string. If it's a string, the string can include a currency symbol and a thousands separator. Negative values may also use parentheses, as in

```
CInt("($5,495.43)")
```

EXPRESSION TYPE	RANGE
Numeric	Any number or a numeric expression that evaluates to a number from −32,768 to 32,767. Numbers with fractional parts are rounded to the nearest integer, except for the bug (see the note on statistical rounding in the previous section, "Statistical Rounding").
Boolean	Any Boolean comparison. False returns 0 and True returns −1.
String	Only something that can be evaluated directly into a number. No numeric expressions are allowed in the string.
Null	Error
Empty	Returns 0.

CLng Function

CLng() converts *Expression* into a Long value.

Usage   *LongValue* = CLng(*Expression*)

    Expression can be a number, a comparison, or a string. If it's a string, the string can include a currency symbol and a thousands separator. Negative values may also use parentheses, as in

```
CLng("($5,495.43)")
```

EXPRESSION TYPE	RANGE
Numeric	Any number or a numeric expression that evaluates to a number from −2,147,483,648 to 2,147,483,647. Numbers with fractional parts are rounded to the nearest integer, except For the bug (see the note on statistical rounding in the previous section, "Statistical Rounding").
Boolean	Any Boolean comparison. False returns 0 and True returns −1.
String	Only something that can be evaluated directly into a number. No numeric expressions are allowed in the string.
Null	Error
Empty	Returns 0.

CSng Function

CSng() converts *Expression* to a single-precision number.

Usage   *SingleValue* = CSng(*Expression*)

Expression can be a number, a comparison, or a string. If it's a string, the string can include a currency symbol and a thousands separator. Negative values may also use parentheses, as in

```
CSng("($193,495.43)")
```

EXPRESSION TYPE	RANGE
Numeric	Any number or a numeric expression that evaluates to a number from −3.402823E38 to −1.401298E-45 for negative values; 1.401298E-45 to 3.402823E38 for positive values; and 0.
Boolean	Any Boolean comparison. False returns 0 and True returns −1.
String	Only something that can be evaluated directly into a number. No numeric expressions are allowed in the string.
Null	Error
Empty	Returns 0.

CStr Function

CStr() converts *Expression* to a string.

Usage   *StringValue* = CStr(*Expression*)

Expression can be a number, a comparison, or a string. This function is probably preferable to Str(), since its returned string does not contain a leading space for positive numbers.

EXPRESSION TYPE	RANGE
Numeric	Any number or a numeric expression that evaluates to a number with the limits of a double-precision number.
Boolean	Any Boolean comparison. Returns False or True.
String	Any string of length up to the limits of the system.
Date	Any valid date. Returns the date in short-date format defined for the system.
Null	Error
Error	Returns string "Error" and the error number.
Empty	Returns " ", the empty string.

CVar Function

CVar() converts *Expression* to a Variant value.

Usage   *VariantValue* = CVar(*Expression*)

Expression can be any valid expression.

EXPRESSION TYPE	RANGE
Numeric	Any number or a numeric expression that evaluates to a number with the limits of a double-precision number.
Boolean	Any Boolean comparison. Returns False or True.
String	Any string of length up to the limits of the system.
Date	Any valid date.
Null	Returns Null.
Error	Returns string "Error" and the error number.
Empty	Returns " ", the empty string.

CVErr Function

CVErr() converts *Expression* to an Error value.

Usage   *ErrorValue* = CVErr(*Expression*)

Use it to generate user-defined errors. You can't use the return value directly in numeric expressions, but you can use one of the other conversion functions to first convert an error to a number.

EXPRESSION TYPE	RANGE
Numeric	Any number or a numeric expression that evaluates to a number from 0 to 65,535.
Boolean	Any Boolean comparison that evaluates to False; returns "Error 0."
String	Only something that can be evaluated directly into a number within the accepted limits. No numeric expressions are allowed in the string.
Null	Error
Empty	Returns "Error 0."

Example

```
Sub TestErr
    ret = MyFunc("Do Err")
    If IsError(ret) Then
      MsgBox "MyFunc generated error: " & CStr(ret)
    End If
End Sub

Function MyFunc(arg)
    If InStr(LCase(arg), "err") = 0 Then
        MyFunc = arg
    Else
        MyFunc = CVErr(5000)
    End If
End Function
```

The above example is rather contrived, but it does show how your functions can return any number of errors to inform the caller of specific problems.

Error Function

Error() returns the error message for a given error number as a Variant value.

Usage   *StringValue* = Error([*ErrorNumber*:=])

ErrorNumber may be either a number or a string that evaluates directly to a number. If the error number is recognized, Error() returns a description of the error. Otherwise, it returns the string "Application-defined or object-defined error." The return value is a Variant.

If no arguments are given, Error() returns the message corresponding to the most recent error. In this case, it's the same as calling Error(Err).

 This function accepts negative numbers, which are not defined ErrorNumber values.

ErrorNumber Type	Range
Numeric	Any number or a numeric expression that evaluates to a number from –2,147,483,648 to 65,535, but all negative numbers are meaningless (this is a bug).
String	Only something that can be evaluated directly into a number within the accepted limits. No numeric expressions are allowed in the string.

Hex Function

Hex() returns a string representing the hexadecimal value of a number.

Usage   *StringValue* = Hex(*Number*:=)

Number can be a number or string.

Argument Type	Range
Numeric	Any number or a numeric expression that evaluates to a number from –2,147,483,648 to 2,147,483,647 or &H0 to &HFFFFFFFF. Numbers with fractional parts are rounded to the nearest integer, except for the bug (see the note on statistical rounding in the previous section, "Statistical Rounding"). For positive numbers, Hex() returns the minimal number of digits that it would take to represent the number (no leading zeros). For negative numbers, from –1 to –32,767, Hex() returns a 4-digit number. For numbers less than –32,767, Hex() returns an 8-digit number. For example: Hex(–1) gives "FFFF." Hex(–32767) gives "8001." Hex(–32768) gives "FFFF8000." Hex(65535) gives "FFFF." Note that –1 and 65,535 both give the same results.
Boolean	Any Boolean comparison. False returns 0 and True returns FFFF.
String	Only something that can be evaluated directly into a number. No numeric expressions are allowed in the string.
Null	Returns Null.
Empty	Returns 0.

Oct Function

Oct() returns a string representing the octal value of a number.

Usage   *StringValue* = Oct(*Number*:=)

Number can be a number or string.

Argument Type	Range
Numeric	Any number or a numeric expression that evaluates to a number from –2,147,483,648 to 2,147,483,647 or &O0 to &O37777777777. Numbers with fractional parts are rounded to the nearest integer, except for the bug (see the note on statistical rounding in the previous section, "Statistical Rounding"). For positive numbers, Oct() returns the minimal number of digits that it would take to represent the number (no leading zeros). For negative numbers, from –1 to –32,767, Oct() returns a 6-digit number. For numbers less than –32,767, Oct() returns an 11-digit number. For example: Oct(–1) gives "177777." Oct(–32767) gives "100001." Oct(–32768) gives "37777700000." Oct(65535) gives "177777." Note that –1 and 65,535 both give the same results.
Boolean	Any Boolean comparison. False returns 0 and True returns 177,777.
String	Only something that can be evaluated directly into a number. No numeric expressions are allowed in the string.
Null	Returns Null.
Empty	Returns 0.

Str Function

Str() returns a string representation of a number.

Usage   *StringValue* = Str(*Number*:=)

Non-negative numbers end up with a leading space. This behavior may be a pain but will never be changed. It goes back to the early days of BASIC, and changing it would break too much existing code.

Argument Type	Range
Numeric	Any number or a numeric expression that evaluates to a number with the limits of a double-precision number.
Boolean	Any Boolean comparison. Returns False or True.
String	Any string of length up to the limits of the system.
Date	Any valid date. Returns the date in short-date format defined for the system.

ARGUMENT TYPE	RANGE
Null	Returns Null.
Error	Error
Empty	Returns 0.

Val Function

Val() returns the double-precision number contained represented by a string.

Usage $DoubleValue = Val(String:=)$

If the leading characters cannot be interpreted as a number, Val() returns 0. *All* Boolean values return 0. This is probably a bug. Val() will *not* interpret thousands-separator characters in the string or currency-symbol characters. You'll want to use one of the Cxx() functions.

The DateTime Module

The display of date and time functions is affected by the short-date format and time format set for your computer.

FORMAT NAME	DESCRIPTION
General Date	A date and/or time.
Long Date	A date according to your system's long-date format.
Medium Date	A date using the medium-date format.
Short Date	A date using your system's short-date format.
Long Time	A time in 24-hour format including hours, minutes, and seconds.
Medium Time	A time in 12-hour format including hours, minutes, and A.M./P.M.
Short Time	A time in 24-hour format including hours and minutes.

For the Date functions that take "w" as an Interval argument, pay attention to what it means. Sometimes, it means weeks, at other times, it means week*days,* and other times, it means simply days.

Date Function

Date() returns a Variant value representing the current system date. It is displayed in the short-date format set for your system.

Usage   *VariantValue* = Date

Date Statement

The Date statement sets the system date.

Usage   Date = *Date*

For MS-DOS and Windows 95 operating systems, *Date* can range from January 1, 1980, through December 31, 2099. For the Microsoft Windows NT operating system, *Date* must be in the range from January 1, 1980, through December 31, 2079. The *Date* expression can be either a literal date (enclosed in a pair of # characters) or a string that can be interpreted as a date. If *Date* contains a time, it is ignored; if it contains *only* a time and no date, it is an error.

DateAdd Function

DateAdd() adds the specified interval to a date/time value and returns the result as a Variant value.

Usage   *VariantValue* = DateAdd(*Interval*:=, *Number*:=, *Date*:=)

If *Date* is a string and the year is not specified, the current year is used. The *Interval* argument is specified as one of the strings in the following table.

INTERVAL STRING	DESCRIPTION
"yyyy"	Year
"q"	Quarter
"m"	Month
"y"	Day of year
"d"	Day
"w"	Weekday
"ww"	Week
"h"	Hour
"n"	Minute
"s"	Second

Number specifies the number of *Intervals* to add, and *Date* is a date literal or a Variant that contains a valid date.

 DateAdd() uses only the integer part of *Number,* and it is *not* rounded as indicated by the Help file.

Note that *Date* is a general term here. It can contain a Time value also. If the result is out of the range January 1, 100, 12:00:00 A.M. to December 31, 9999, 11:59:59 P.M., an error occurs.

Note that the DateAdd function is "smart" when adding months: The number of days will be adjusted so that you always get a valid date.

Example   `d = DateAdd("m", 1, #31 January 1995#)`

returns "2/28/95."

Example   `DateAdd("n", 32, Time)`

returns a time that is 32 minutes from now.

All right, quick: What's the difference between using "y," "d," and "w"? We're not sure! We think "w" should return exactly what is indicated by the Help file: add weekdays. That is, if the date is a Thursday, add 2 "w" weekdays should return the date for the following Monday. It certainly would be much more useful than having three settings that do the same thing.

 All right, we'll stop complaining and provide a solution. The following function will add number of weekdays to a date and return a Variant value.

Example

```
Function DateAddW(nWorkDays As Long, BegDate As Date) As Variant
    Dim nWeeks As Long, nDays As Integer

    If nWorkDays = 0 Then
        DateAddW = BegDate
    ElseIf nWorkDays > 0 Then
        Select Case WeekDay(BegDate)
          Case vbFriday: BegDate = BegDate + 2
          Case vbSaturday: BegDate = BegDate + 1
          Case Else
        End Select
        nDays = nWorkDays Mod 5
        If nDays + WeekDay(BegDate) > vbFriday Then
          nDays = nDays + 2
        End If
        nWeeks = Int(nWorkDays / 5#)
        DateAddW = DateAdd("ww", nWeeks, BegDate)
        DateAddW = DateAdd("d", nDays, DateAddW)
    Else
        Select Case WeekDay(BegDate)
          Case vbMonday: BegDate = BegDate - 2
          Case vbSunday: BegDate = BegDate - 1
          Case Else
        End Select
        nDays = (-nWorkDays) Mod 5
        If WeekDay(BegDate) - nDays < vbMonday Then
          nDays = nDays + 2
        End If
        nWeeks = Int((nWorkDays + 4) / 5#)
        DateAddW = DateAdd("ww", nWeeks, BegDate)
        DateAddW = DateAdd("d", -nDays, DateAddW)
```

```
            End If
         End Function
```

DateDiff Function

DateDiff() returns the number of intervals between two dates.

Usage   *VariantValue* = DateDiff(*Interval*:=, *Date1*:=, *Date2*:=[, *FirstDayOfWeek*:=[, *FirstWeekOfYear*:=]])

If *Date1* refers to a later time than *Date2,* DateDiff() returns a negative number. If *Date1* and *Date2* are strings and the year is not specified, the current year is used. Boy, this is one function with complicated arguments! The *Interval* string argument is much like that of DateAdd(), as the following table shows.

INTERVAL STRING	DESCRIPTION
"yyyy"	Year
"q"	Quarter
"m"	Month
"y"	Day of year
"d"	Day
"w"	Week (see text)
"ww"	Calendar week (see text)
"h"	Hour
"n"	Minute
"s"	Second

Now we're going to clear up (or at least make slightly less murky) the difference between using "w" and "ww" as *Interval*. The Help file talks about counting Mondays or Sundays, but not if *Date1* is a Sunday and your brother's wife's second cousin's birthday is two days on either side of . . . sheesh! Here's the real scoop:

1. With "w," DateDiff() calculates the number of full weeks (7 days) between the two dates.

2. With "ww," DateDiff() calculates the number of *calendar* weeks between the two dates. The first day of a calendar week is Sunday, but that definition may be altered by the *FirstDayOfWeek* argument.

Here's an example. Take the two dates "January 5, 1996, Friday" and "January 8, 1996, Monday." Only three days separate them—less than a full week. But Friday and Monday are part of two different *calendar* weeks, with Sunday being the start of a new week. So,

```
diff1 = DateDiff("w", #January 5, 1996#, #January 8, 1996#)
diff2 = DateDiff("ww", #January 5, 1996#, #January 8, 1996#)
```

returns 0 for diff1 and 1 for diff2.

The value returned using "ww" will *never* be less than that returned using "w." Use the *First-DayOfWeek* argument to change the definition of the first day of a calendar week.

CONSTANT	VALUE	DESCRIPTION
vbUseSystem	0	Use the application setting if one exists; otherwise use NLS API setting.
vbSunday	1	Sunday (default)
vbMonday	2	Monday
vbTuesday	3	Tuesday
vbWednesday	4	Wednesday
vbThursday	5	Thursday
vbFriday	6	Friday
vbSaturday	7	Saturday

For the previous example,

```
diff = DateDiff("ww", #January 5, 1996#, #January 8, 1996#, vbTuesday
```

returns 0.

 As a companion to DateAddW(), we provide next DateDiffW(), which returns the number of working days between two dates. It's based on Microsoft's Product Support Service (PSS) ID number Q95977.

Example

```
Function DateDiffW(BegDate As Date, EndDate As Date) As Long
    Dim nWeeks As Long

    If BegDate > EndDate Then
        Select Case WeekDay(BegDate)
            Case vbSunday: BegDate = BegDate - 2
            Case vbSaturday: BegDate = BegDate - 1
            Case Else
        End Select
        Select Case WeekDay(EndDate)
            Case vbSunday: EndDate = EndDate + 1
            Case vbSaturday: EndDate = EndDate + 2
            Case Else
        End Select
    Else
        Select Case WeekDay(BegDate)
            Case vbSunday: BegDate = BegDate + 1
            Case vbSaturday: BegDate = BegDate + 2
            Case Else
        End Select
        Select Case WeekDay(EndDate)
```

```
            Case vbSunday: EndDate = EndDate - 2
            Case vbSaturday: EndDate = EndDate - 1
            Case Else
       End Select
    End If
    nWeeks = DateDiff("ww", BegDate, EndDate)
      DateDiffW = nWeeks * 5 + WeekDay(EndDate) -
WeekDay(BegDate)
    End Function
```

The optional last argument for DateDiff(), *FirstWeekOf Year,* is . . . strange . . . to say the least. It doesn't make sense for DateDiff(). For DatePart(), *FirstDayOf Week* can be used with "ww" to determine which week of the year a date is. How you count weeks can be changed as follows. The problem with DateDiff() is that *both* dates will use the same reference for *FirstDayOf Week,* so when you take the difference, the reference cancels itself out and has no effect. For the sake of completeness, we offer the valid values for *FirstWeekOf Year* in the following table.

CONSTANT	VALUE	DESCRIPTION
vbUseSystem	0	Use the application setting if one exists; otherwise use NLS API setting.
vbFirstJan1	1	Start with the week in which January 1 occurs (default).
vbFirstFourDays	2	Start with the first week that has at least four days in the new year.
vbFirstFullWeek	3	Start with the first full week of the year.

DatePart Function

DatePart() returns the specified part of the date (or time).

Usage   *VariantValue* = DatePart(*Interval*:=, *Date*:=[, *FirstDayOf Week*:=[, *FirstWeekOf Year*:=]])

Interval is a string used to specify the part that is returned. It can take on the values given in the following table.

INTERVAL STRING	DESCRIPTION AND RANGE
"yyyy"	Year (100 to 9999)
"q"	Quarter (1 to 4)
"m"	Month (1 to 12)
"y"	Day of year (1 to 366) no typo
"d"	Day of month (1 to 31)
"w"	Day of week (1 to 7)
"ww"	Week of year (1 to 53) no typo
"h"	Hour (0 to 23)
"n"	Minute (0 to 59)
"s"	Second (0 to 59)

You always thought there are 365 days to the year and 52 weeks? Well, DatePart can return some surprising results:

Example
```
part1 = DatePart("d", #12/31/96#)
    part2 = DatePart("ww", #1/6/96#, vbSunday, vbFirstFullWeek)
```

Result
```
part1 = 366
    part 2 = 53
```

All right, the first example isn't too tough—there's an extra day in a leap year. The second one is interesting, though. Because of the vbFirstFullWeek setting (see the next paragraph), the week of the year can return 53, thus indicating that the first few days of the new year belong to the 53rd week of the *previous* year.

The *FirstDayOfWeek* argument matters only when *Interval* is "w" or "ww." For "w," DatePart() returns the day of the week as counted from *FirstDayOfWeek;* the default is vbSunday.

CONSTANT	VALUE	DESCRIPTION
vbUseSystem	0	Use the application setting if one exists; otherwise use NLS API setting.
vbSunday	1	Sunday (default)
vbMonday	2	Monday
vbTuesday	3	Tuesday
vbWednesday	4	Wednesday
vbThursday	5	Thursday
vbFriday	6	Friday
vbSaturday	7	Saturday

The *FirstWeekOfYear* argument has an effect only for "ww." It adjusts which week of the year should be considered 1. The default is vbFirstJan1, which means the week containing January 1 should be week 1. Alternatively, you can choose week 1 to be the week that has at least four days of the new year or the first full week of the year.

CONSTANT	VALUE	DESCRIPTION
vbUseSystem	0	Use the application setting if one exists; otherwise use NLS API setting.
vbFirstJan1	1	Start with the week in which January 1 occurs (default).
vbFirstFourDays	2	Start with the first week that has at least four days in the new year.
vbFirstFullWeek	3	Start with the first full week of the year.

Example

January 1, 1999, falls on a Friday, so there are only two days of the new year in that week. The following calls

```
part1 = DatePart("ww", "1/1/99")
part2 = DatePart("ww", "1/1/99", FirstWeekOfYear:=vbFirstFourDays)
part3 = DatePart("ww", "1/1/99", FirstWeekOfYear:= vbFirstFullWeek)
```

return

```
part1 = 1
part2 = 52
part3 = 52
```

Note that for the last two calls, January 1, 1999, belongs to the 52nd week of the *previous* year. You can also use the *FirstDayOfWeek* argument to change the reference point for vbFirst-FourDays and vbFirstFullWeek.

Example

Using the same January 1, 1999, date example, we use the *FirstDayOfWeek* argument to change the behavior so that

```
part1 = DatePart("ww", "1/1/99", vbTuesday)
part2 = DatePart("ww", "1/1/99", vbTuesday,
part3 = DatePart("ww", "1/1/99", vbTuesday, vbFirstFullWeek)
```

returns

```
part1 = 1
part2 = 1
part3 = 52
```

This is because if the week were to start on Tuesday, then January 1 (Friday) through January 4 (Monday) would belong to the new year, thus satisfying vbFirstFourDays's condition that four days belong to the new year.

DateSerial Function

DateSerial() builds a Date value based on the given arguments.

Usage   *VariantValue* = DateSerial(*Year*:=, *Month*:=, *Day*:=)

The arguments can be any type or expression that can be interpreted as a number. All floating-point values are rounded according to statistical rounding.

PARAMETER	VALUE	MEANING
Year	100 to 9999	The year
	0 to 99	The year of the current century. For instance, 2 is 1902. If you're reading this in the year 2005 (yeah right!), then 2 will mean 2002.
	–1800 to –1	The number of years before 1900. For instance, –1 is (1900 – 1) = 1899.
Month	1 or greater	The month as counted from January of the specified year. If the value is greater than 12, the year is incremented by 1 for each multiple of 12.
	0	December of the previous year.
	Negative	Subtracts months from December of the previous year. The year is adjusted appropriately as the month value decreases.
Day	1 or greater	The day as counted from the specified month and year. Note that if the day is greater than the number of days in the specified month, then the month (and maybe year) is incremented appropriately.
	0	The last day of the previous month as specified by the year and month.
	Negative	Subtracts days from the last day of the previous month as specified by the year and month.

Examples
```
date1 = DateSerial(96, 1, 1)
  date2 = DateSerial(96, 0, 1)
  date3 = DateSerial(96, 1, 0)
  date4 = DateSerial(96, 0, -56)
```

Return
```
date1 = 1/1/96
  date2 = 12/1/95
  date3 = 12/31/95
  date4 = 1/25/96
```

Note that you can use DateSerial() as a poor person's DateAdd(), since you can enter any numbers for *Month* and *Day*. But you'll find that DateAdd() is much more flexible.

DateValue Function

DateValue() converts into a Date value any expression that can be interpreted as a date and time.

Usage   *VariantValue* = DateValue(*Date*:=)

If the expression is not a valid date or time, an error occurs. The date must be between "January 1, 100, 12:00:00 AM" and "December 31, 9999, 11:59:59 PM." Although the *Date* expression can include a time, the return value *does not* include the time. If the year is omitted, then the current year is used.

This function is really useful only for converting a String value to a Date value.

Example   d = DateValue("July 4, 1996")

returns the Date value #July 4, 1996#. Not too exciting, eh? If *Date* is Null, DateValue returns Null.

Day Function

Day() returns the day of month for the specified *Date* expression.

Usage   *VariantValue* = Day(*Date*:=)

The return value ranges from 1 to 31. The *Date* expression can be any number or string that can be interpreted as a valid date. If *Date* is Null, Day also returns Null.

Example   d = Day(Date)

returns the day of the month for today's date.

Hour Function

Hour() returns the hour of day specified by the *Time* expression.

Usage   *VariantValue* = Hour(*Time*:=)

The return value ranges from 0 to 23. If *Time* is Null, Hour also returns Null. The *Time* expression can be any valid date and time expression; if the expression lacks a time, then 0 is returned (for 12:00:00 A.M.).

Example   h = Hour(Time)

returns the current hour of day.

Minute Function

Minute() returns the minute of the hour specified by the *Time* expression.

Usage   *VariantValue* = Minute(*Time*:=)

The return value ranges from 0 to 59. If *Time* is Null, Minute also returns Null. The *Time* expression can be any valid date and time expression; if it lacks a time, then 0 is returned (for 12:00:00 A.M.).

Example   m = Minute(Time)

returns the minute of the current hour.

Month Function

Month() returns the month of the year specified by the *Date* expression.

Usage   *VariantValue* = Month(*Date*:=)

The return value ranges from 1 to 12. The *Date* expression can be any number or string that can be interpreted as a valid date. If *Date* is Null, Month() also returns Null.

Example   `m = Month(Date)`

returns the month of the current date.

Now Function

Now() returns the current system date and time as a Variant value.

Usage   *VariantValue* = Now

It's essentially the same as

`Date & " " & Time`

Second Function

Second() returns the second of the minute specified by the *Time* expression.

Usage   *VariantValue* = Second(*Time*:=)

The return value ranges from 0 to 59. If *Time* is Null, Second() also returns Null. The *Time* expression can be any valid date and time expression; if it lacks a time, then 0 is returned (for 12:00:00 A.M.).

Example   `s = Second(Time)`

returns the second elapsed for the current minute.

Time Function

Time() returns a Variant value representing the current system time.

Usage   *VariantValue* = Time

It is displayed in the time format set for your system.

Time Statement

The Time statement sets the system time.

Usage   Time = *Time*

The *Time* expression can be either a literal date and time (enclosed in a pair of # characters) or a string that can be interpreted as a time. If the expression contains both a date and time, then the date is ignored. If it contains only a date, then the time gets set to 12:00:00 A.M.

Timer Function

Timer() returns the number of seconds elapsed since midnight of the current day (with two decimal places of precision).

Usage   *SingleValue* = Timer

It can be used to perform some relative timing functions.

Example
```
StartTime = Timer
MyFunction()
StopTime = Timer
Elapsed = StopTime - StartTime
If Elapsed < 0 Then Elapsed = Elapsed + 86400!
MsgBox "MyFuction took " & Elapsed & " seconds to run"
```

You have to watch out when running this function near midnight. If the example started at "11:59:59 PM" and stopped at "12:00:01 AM," a straight difference of StopTime and StartTime would return –86,398 instead of 2. Thus we check that the difference is less than zero and then add back a day's worth of seconds (86,400). Note that you cannot use the previous example to time something that lasts over a day.

 We're not sure why you'd want to use Timer() rather than the GetTickCount API function. GetTickCount() returns the time elapsed since Windows was started. It does this in millisecond resolution (ten times better than Timer()). Also, it doesn't wrap until the system has been up about 49.7 days, so you're less likely to run into problems.

Example
```
Declare Function GetTickCount Lib "Kernel32" () As Long
StartTime = GetTickCount
MyFunction()
StopTime = GetTickCount
Elapsed = StopTime - StartTime
If Elapsed < 0 Then Elapsed = Elapsed + 4294967296#
MsgBox "MyFuction took " & Elapsed & " ms to run"
```

TimeSerial Function

TimeSerial() builds a Date and Time value based on the given arguments.

Usage   *VariantValue* = TimeSerial(*Hour*:=, *Minute*:=, *Second*:=)

The arguments can be any type or expression that can be interpreted as a number from –32,768 to 32,767. All floating-point values are rounded according to statistical rounding.

PARAMETER	VALUE	MEANING
Hour	0 to 23 –23 to –1	The hour of the day. Treat negative values as if they were positive.
	–32,768 to –24	–24 corresponds to #12/29/1899 12:00:00 AM#, and each –24 hours bumps the date down by one. *But,* within each 24-hour division, each decrement in the Hour value corresponds to an increment in the date/time result as follows: –24 corresponds to #12/29/1899 12:00:00 AM# –25 corresponds to #12/29/1899 1:00:00 AM# ... –47 corresponds to #12/29/1899 11:00:00 PM# –48 corresponds to #12/28/1899 12:00:00 AM# ... –32,768 corresponds to #4/4/1896 8:00:00 AM#
	24 to 32,767	24 corresponds to #12/31/1899 12:00:00 AM#. Each increment in the Hour value bumps up the time, and the date adjusts appropriately (every 24 hours) until 32,767, which corresponds to #9/26/1903 7:00:00 AM#.
Minute	0 to 32,767	Adds minutes to the specified hour to arrive at a time. For each 60 minutes, the Hour value is incremented appropriately. If Minute causes the Hour value to increment beyond 23, then a date shows up (see above).
	–32,768 to –1	Subtracts minutes from the specified hour to arrive at a time. Each –60 minutes bumps the hour down by 1, *except that* within each 1,440-minute division that represents a day, each decrement in the Minute value corresponds to an increment in the date/time result.
Second	0 to 32,767	Adds seconds to the specified hour and minutes. Each 60 seconds increments the minutes by 1.
	–32,768 to –1	Subtracts seconds from the specified hour and minutes. Each –60 seconds bumps the Minute value down by 1. But if the Second value causes the result to change the date (depends on the hour and minute), then decrements in seconds could correspond to increments in the date/time result.

Are you confused about how negative values work? They're not so bad if you remember that the internal representation of a date is a double-precision floating-point value, where the integer part represents the date and the *absolute value* of the fractional part represents the time. For instance, whereas –1.5 (#12/29/1899 12:00:00 PM#) is a larger number than –1.8 (#12/29/1899 7:12:00 PM#), when you look at just the fractional part, 0.5 (#12:00:00 PM#) is *less* than 0.8 (#7:12:00 PM#).

Examples
```
time1 = TimeSerial(9, -90, 0)
  time2 = TimeSerial(1, -90, 0)
  time3 = TimeSerial(1, -100, 0)
```

Returns
```
time1 = 7:30:00 AM
  time2 = 12:30:00 AM
  time3 = 12:40:00 AM
```

The first example shows how you can use TimeSerial() to determine the time that is 90 minutes before 9 A.M. The last two show that you get unexpected results when subtracting minutes causes you to cross day boundaries; 90 minutes before 1 A.M. is *not* 12:30 A.M., and 100 minutes before 1 A.M. is *not* supposed to be *later* than 90 minutes before 1 A.M.

Note that you can use TimeSerial() as a poor-person's DateAdd(), since you can enter any numbers for *Minute* and *Second*. But you'll find that DateAdd() is much more flexible *and* much more predictable:

Examples
```
time1 = DateAdd("n", -90, #1 AM#)
  time2 = DateAdd("n", -100, #1 AM#)
```

Returns
```
time1 = 11:30:00 PM
  time2 = 11:20:00 PM
```

TimeValue Function

TimeValue() converts any expression that can be interpreted as a date and time into a Time value.

Usage   *VariantValue* = TimeValue(*Time*:=)

If the *Time* expression is not a valid date or time, an error occurs. The time must be between #0:00:00# and #23:59:59#. If it's a string, it can be entered in 12-hour or 24-hour format. Although the *Time* expression can include a date, the return value *does not* include the date.

This function is really useful only for converting a string value to a Time value.

Example   ```t = TimeValue("22:46:55")```

returns the value, #10:46:55 PM#. Actually, how that value is displayed depends on your system settings.

If *Time* is Null, TimeValue() returns Null.

WeekDay Function

WeekDay() returns the day of the week for the given date.

Usage   *ReturnValue* = WeekDay(*Date*:=[, *FirstDayOfWeek*:=])

The *Date* argument can be any expression that can be interpreted as a date. If it is Null, WeekDay returns Null.

The day that starts the week can be adjusted with the optional *FirstDayOfWeek* argument. This argument can take on the values shown in the following table.

CONSTANT	VALUE	DESCRIPTION
vbUseSystem	0	Use the application setting if one exists; otherwise use NLS API setting.
vbSunday	1	Sunday (default)
vbMonday	2	Monday
vbTuesday	3	Tuesday
vbWednesday	4	Wednesday
vbThursday	5	Thursday
vbFriday	6	Friday
vbSaturday	7	Saturday

WeekDay() returns an integer that represents the day of the week, starting the count from the value given by *FirstDayOfWeek*. Note that the Help file on WeekDay() (typical of many Windows Help files) is *confusing* about the return value.

Example
```
w  = WeekDay(#1/1/96#)
w1 = WeekDay(#1/1/96#, vbSunday)
w2 = WeekDay(#1/1/96#, vbMonday)
w3 = WeekDay(#1/1/96#, vbTuesday)
w4 = WeekDay(#1/1/96#, vbWednesday)
w5 = WeekDay(#1/1/96#, vbThursday)
w6 = WeekDay(#1/1/96#, vbFriday)
w7 = WeekDay(#1/1/96#, vbSaturday)
```

Return
```
w  = 2
w1 = 2
w2 = 1
w3 = 7
w4 = 6
w5 = 5
w6 = 4
w7 = 3
```

Year Function

Year() returns the year part of the *Date* expression.

Usage   *VariantValue* = Year(*Date*:=)

The return value ranges from 100 to 9999. The *Date* expression can be any number or string that can be interpreted as a valid date. If *Date* is Null, Year() also returns Null.

Example   `y = Year(Date)`

returns the current year.

The FileSystem Module

The commands and functions in the FileSystem module deal with files and folders (directories). All strings that represent file and directory names are case-insensitive.

For all file operations that require a file number as input, VB will first use statistical rounding on floating-point values to rid them of fractional parts. The input variable can even be a string, as long as VB can interpret it as a number.

ChDir Statement

The ChDir statement changes the default directory.

Usage   ChDir *Path*:=

Path is any String expression. If the path does not exist or is a file, an error occurs. If *Path* includes a drive letter that isn't the default (i.e., current) drive, the default directory on the specified drive is changed, but neither the default drive nor the default directory on the *current* drive is changed.

Example   `ChDir "\"`
                `ChDir "D:\TMP"`

The first statement changes the default directory of the default drive to its root directory. The second statement changes the default directory of D: to \TMP but does not set the default drive to D:.

ChDrive Statement

The ChDrive statement changes the default drive.

Usage   ChDrive *Drive*:=

The new default drive is specified by the *Drive* string. If *Drive* is an empty string, the current drive is not changed. Only the first character of *Drive* is used. If the specified drive does not exist or if the first character is not a letter, then an error occurs.

Example `ChDrv "D"`

Note that changing drives does not affect the default directories of any drives.

CurDir Function

CurDir() returns the current directory of the current drive or a specified drive.

Usage   *VariantValue* = CurDir[(*Drive*:=)]

If no drive is specified or if *Drive* is an empty string, then the current drive is used. Only the first letter of *Drive* is used. If the drive does not exist or the first character is not a letter, then an error occurs.

Example `d1$ = CurDir`
       `d2$ = CurDir("G")`

The first call returns the current directory on the current drive. The second example returns the current directory on drive G:.

Dir Function

Dir() finds files and directories that match the specified name pattern and file attributes.

Usage   *StringValue* = Dir[(*PathName*:=[, *Attributes*:=])]

PathName can include the * wildcard character to match any number of characters or the ? wildcard character to match any one character. The wildcards will also match periods. If the attributes are not given, Dir() finds only normal and read-only files.

You cannot exclude read-only files! Even if you explicitly use the vbNormal attribute, read-only files are returned.

  If no matches are found, Dir returns an empty string (""), not Null, as indicated in the Help file.

If there is at least one match, Dir() returns the first one it finds. To retrieve the other matches, you have to call Dir() repeatedly *without* any arguments until it returns an empty string (""). The search is case-*insensitive*. Note that Dir() returns only the filename, not the full path information, even though *PathName* may contain a full directory path.

PARAMETER	VALUE	MEANING
PathName	"" "*"	Finds everything that matches the attributes.
	drive name only	Finds everything in the current directory of the specified drive that matches the attributes.
	"anydir\"	Finds everything in the string that matches the attributes. The last character must be a backslash.
	any other string	Finds files and directories that match the string. Use * and ? wildcards.

Example
```
d1$ = Dir("")

d2$ = Dir("*")
d3$ = Dir("C:")
d4$ = Dir("G:tmp\")
d5$ = Dir("*.ini")
```

Return
```
d1$ is first file found in current directory
d2$ is first file found in current directory
d3$ is the first file found in the current directory of C:
d4$ is the first file found in the G:tmp\ directory
d5$ is the first file in the current directory with .ini extension
```

You can expand the search by using the *Attributes* argument. You cannot limit your search to files matching only those attributes. In other words, you can find all normal and hidden files, but you cannot find *only* hidden files. The only exception to the rule is finding the volume label, in which case that's all you will find. See the following table for a list of valid attribute values.

PARAMETER	VALUE	MEANING
Attributes	vbNormal	Normal file (does not work).
	vbReadOnly	Read-only file. May be added to other attributes.
	VbHidden	Hidden file. May be added to other attributes.
	VbSystem	System file. May be added to other attributes.
	VbVolume	Volume label. Cannot be combined with other attributes. Pathname ignored!
	vbDirectory	Directory. May be added to other attributes.

Note that if vbVolume is combined with other attributes, it will be ignored. If you select vb-Directory and *PathName* is not a root directory, you might get both "." and ".." as the returned values!

Example
```
d1$ = Dir("", vbDirectory)
    d2$ = Dir("*.sys", vbSystem Or vbHidden)
    v$ = Dir("any junk here is ignored", vbVolume)
```

Return
```
d1$ is the first file or subdirectory in the current directory
    d2$ is first .sys file. The search includes system and hidden
    files
    v$ is the volume label of the current drive.
```

EOF Function

EOF() returns True if the end of file has been reached for the file associated with *FileNumber;* otherwise, it returns False.

Usage   *IntegerValue* = EOF(*FileNumber:=*)

You would typically use EOF () to check on a file before attempting to access the file to prevent errors.

Example
```
Open "file" For Binary As #1

Do While Not EOF(1)
    Get 1,, Variable
    vCollection.Add Variable
Loop
Close 1
```

If *FileNumber* is not a valid file number, an error occurs.

FileAttr Function

FileAttr() returns the access mode if a file handle for a file opened with the Open statement.

Usage   *LongValue* = FileAttr(*FileNumber:=*, *ReturnType:=*)

If *ReturnType* is 1, the return value represents the access mode; if *ReturnType* is 2, the return value is the operating-system file handle. The access-mode return values can be one of those in the following table.

LongValue	Meaning
1	Input
2	Output
4	Random
8	Append
32	Binary

Example   mode = FileAttr(1, 1)

                   hnd = FileAddr(1, 2)

The first call returns the mode of the file opened as *FileNumber* 1. The second returns the operating-system file handle.

FileCopy Statement

The FileCopy statement makes a copy of a file.

Usage   FileCopy *Source*:=, *Destination*:=

The *Destination* string must be a filename; it cannot be a directory name. If *Destination* exists, FileCopy will overwrite it without warning, *unless* the destination file has the read-only attribute set.

 If the destination file exists and has the system and/or hidden attributes set, FileCopy will overwrite it without warning, *but* the system and/or hidden attributes will remain set *regardless* of the attributes of the source file!

If the source file does not exist or if either file is open, an error occurs.

Example   FileCopy "C:\autoexec.bat", "C:\autoexec.tmp"

FileDateTime Function

FileDateTime() returns a Variant value that represents the date and time the file or directory was created or last modified.

Usage   *VariantValue* = FileDateTime(*PathName*:=)

The *PathName* string cannot contain just a drive or the root directory of any drive.

Example   d$ = FileDateTime("c:\windows")

FileLen Function

FileLen() returns the size in bytes of the file specified by the *PathName* string.

Usage   *LongValue* = FileLen(*PathName*:=)

If the file is already open, FileLen() returns the size of the file immediately before the file was opened. If you opened the file using the Open statement, you can use LOF() to determine the size of the file.

FreeFile Function

FreeFile() returns an unused file number that you can use to open a file.

Usage   *IntegerValue* = FreeFile[(*RangeNumber*:=)]

The *RangeNumber* argument can be used to select between two sets of possible file numbers, as the following table shows.

PARAMETER	VALUE	MEANING
RangeNumber	0	Returns a value from 1 to 255.
	1	Returns a value from 256 to 511.

If all the numbers in a range are in use, FreeFile() returns an error.

GetAttr Function

GetAttr() returns the attributes of the file or directory specified by the *PathName* string.

Usage   *IntegerValue* = GetAttr(*PathName*:=)

The return values consists of a sum of the values given in the following table.

VALUE	CONSTANT	MEANING
0	vbNormal	Normal
1	vbReadOnly	Read-only
2	vbHidden	Hidden
4	vbSystem	System file
16	vbDirectory	Directory
32	vbArchive	File has changed since last backup

To determine if any of the attributes are set, use the And operator with the above constants (except vbNormal).

Example
```
Dim subdirs$(50), nSubDirs As Integer

Dim f$

' Find all entries in the current directory
f$ = Dir("", vbDirectory Or vbReadOnly Or vbHidden Or vbSystem)
Do While f$ <> ""
```

```
        If (GetAttr(f$) And vbDirectory) <> 0 Then
              subdirs$(nSubDirs) = f$
              nSubDirs = nSubDirs + 1
        End If
        f$ = Dir
  Loop
```

This example gets a list of all subdirectories in the current directory. Since the Dir command does not limit its return values to only directories, you need to do it manually using GetAttr() and the vbDirectory flag.

Example

```
sysHid = (vbSystem Or vbHidden)
  isSysHidden = (GetAttr("c:\io.sys") And sysHid) = sysHid
```

The isSysHidden variable in this example will contain True if "c:\io.sys" is a system file and is also hidden.

Kill Statement

The Kill statement deletes files.

Usage   Kill *PathName*:=

The *PathName* string can include the wildcard characters, * and ?. If an error is encountered for one file in a multifile Kill, processing halts. If a file has the read-only attribute, Kill returns a "Path/File access error" and halts processing. If the specified file has the System or Hidden attribute set, Kill returns a "File not found" error and halts processing.

 If a file is opened by another application, Kill may delete the file *with no warning*. This depends on whether the application uses file-sharing features of the operating system. Most simple editors in DOS do not use such features—not even Microsoft's own EDIT.COM! Surprisingly, even Windows NOTEPAD.EXE doesn't use file-sharing.

You cannot remove directories with the Kill command. Use RmDir instead.

Loc Function

Loc() returns the current read/write position in the file opened as *FileNumber*.

Usage   *LongValue* = Loc(*FileNumber*:=)

If *FileNumber* is not a valid number, an error occurs.
The interpretation of the return value depends on the mode in which the file is opened, as shown in the following table.

Mode	Return-value Meaning
Random	Number of the last record read from or written to the file. The start of file returns 0.
Sequential	This value is useless.
Binary	Position of the last byte read or written. The start of file returns 0.

If the file is opened for sequential access, Loc() is essentially useless. Loc() is supposed to return the bytes from the start of the file, divided by 128, but even that function isn't consistent. You should probably use Seek() instead of Loc().

LOF Function

LOF() returns the file size in bytes.

Usage   *LongValue* = LOF(*FileNumber*:=)

The file must have been opened by the Open statement. Use FileLen() to determine the size of a closed file.

MkDir Statement

The MkDir statement makes a directory.

Usage   MkDir *Path*:=

The *Path* string can include the drive name, which may include embedded spaces. Use RmDir to remove directories.

Reset Statement

The Reset statement closes all files that were opened using the Open statement.

Usage   Reset

For output files, all buffered data are written to disk before they are closed.

RmDir Statement

The RmDir statement removes an existing—but *empty*—directory.

Usage   RmDir *Path*:=

If the directory does not exist or is not empty, an error occurs. You can use the Kill statement to remove all files in the directory before using RmDir. The *Path* string can include a drive name.

Seek Function

Seek() returns the current read or write position within a file opened with the Open statement.

Usage   *LongValue* = Seek(*FileNumber:=*)

The interpretation of the return value depends on the Open mode, as the following table shows:

OPEN MODE	MEANING
Random	Record number of the next record to be read or written.
Output	Byte position at which next output is to take place.
Input	Byte position at which next input is to take place.
Binary	Byte position at which next operation is to take place.
Append	Byte position at which next append is to take place.

Because the return number is always defined in terms of the *next* operation, the minimum number it returns is always 1. That is, right after a file is opened in any mode, a call to Seek() will return 1. The maximum return value is $(2^{31} - 1)$, or 2,147,483,647. This means you'll get in trouble when your file sizes become greater than 2GB, so watch out! (Heh, heh.)

This function is preferable to Loc(); it returns more meaningful results. Use the Seek statement (next) to change the position in the file.

Seek Statement

The Seek statement sets the file position at which the next read or write operation will occur.

Usage   Seek *FileNumber, Position*

The file must have been opened using the Open statement.

PARAMETER	VALUE	MEANING
FileNumber	1 through 511	Any valid file number of a file that was opened using the Open statement. If the file was not opened, an error occurs.
	Any other number	Error
Position	1 through 2,147,483,647	If FileNumber was opened in Random mode, this represents the record number; otherwise, it represents the byte position in the file. Statistical rounding is used to convert a number into a Long value. If position is a string, it must be able to be interpreted as a number or an error occurs.
	Any other number	Error

SetAttr Statement

SetAttr() sets the file attributes for a named file.

Usage   SetAttr *PathName*:=, *Attributes*:=

The *PathName* expression represents a file or directory. It can contain drive information, but the file or directory must exist. *Attributes* is any number that can be composed by combining the flags given in the following table (any others generate an error).

CONSTANT	VALUE	MEANING
vbNormal	0	Normal file
vbReadOnly	1	Read-only
vbHidden	2	Hidden
vbSystem	4	System
vbArchive	32	Archive bit is set to indicate that the file should be backed up.

To make your code more readable, use the constant names and combine them using the Or operator.

Example   `SetAttr "f:\Private.doc", vbReadOnly Or vbHidden`

If you change the attributes of a file and you want that change to be backed up the next time you run backup, be sure to include vbArchive in your attributes. If you don't, that file will *not* be backed up when you choose "incremental" backup.
          Note: Valid integer values of attributes can range from 0 to 15 and from 32 to 47.

The Help file says SetAttr will generate an error if the file is already open. We found this to be true only if the file is opened by a Share-aware application. Some DOS editors and even NOTEPAD.EXE can have a file open, but SetAttr will happily change the file attributes.

The Financial Module

This section details the financial-calculation functions of VBA.

DDB Function

DDB() calculates the depreciation for an asset in the specified period.

Usage   *DoubleValue* = DDB(*Cost*:=, *Salvage*:=, *Life*:=, *Period*:=[, *Factor*:=])

If no *Factor* is given, the double-declining balance is used.

PARAMETER	VALUE	MEANING
Cost	Any positive number	Initial cost of the asset.
Salvage	Any positive number	Value of the asset at the end of its useful life.
Life	Any positive number	Length of the useful life expressed as a number of periods.
Period	Range from 1 to *Life*	Specified period for the depreciation calculation. Must be in the same unit as that used for *Life*. Any other value generates an error.
Factor	Any positive number	Rate of decline for the asset value (balance). If omitted, 2 is used for the double-declining method.

Example
```
dep1 = DDB(1500000, "300,000", 10, 4)
    dep2 = DDB("1,5000,000", 300000, 10, 4, 1.5)
```

Return
```
dep1 = 153600
    dep2 = 138178.125
```

The first example finds the double-declining-balance depreciation for the fourth year of an asset that costs $1.5M with a useful life of 10 years and salvage value of $300,000. The second example uses a factor of 1.5 for the same asset. Note that you can use strings as long as they represent valid numbers.

   We're not sure what the Help file is trying to say with its formula for DDB, but it's not even close. Here's the real algorithm:

```
PrevBalance = Cost * (1 - Factor/Life)^(Period - 1)
Balance = Cost * (1 - Factor/Life)^Period
If PrevBalance < Salvage Then
    Depreciation = 0
ElseIf Balance < Salvage Then
    Depreciation = PrevBalance - Salvage
Else
    Depreciation = PrevBalance - Balance
End If
```

That is, the balance keeps decreasing according to a strict formula until the *Salvage* value is met.

FV Function

FV() calculates the future value of a series of constant payments made regularly over a number of periods (an annuity) at a constant interest rate. The annuity can represent a loan or a savings plan.

Usage $DoubleValue$ = FV($Rate$:=, $NPer$:=, Pmt:=[, PV:=[, Due:=]])

 That last-named argument is *Due*, not *type*, as indicated in the Help file.

PARAMETER	VALUE	MEANING
Rate	Any numeric	Interest rate per payment period. If the payments occur monthly, then you must divide the annual percentage rate by 12.
NPer	Any numeric	Total number of payment periods in the annuity. The period must be expressed in the same unit as that used for *Rate*.
Pmt	Any numeric	The amount of payment made each period. If the payment represents cash going out, this number should be negative.
PV	Any numeric	Present value of the annuity. If omitted, 0 is used. If you made an initial deposit for an investment, this value should be negative (cash going out). If you took out a loan, this value should be positive (cash in).
Due	0 or omitted	Payment due at the end of a payment period.
	Any other value	Payment due at the beginning of a payment period.

Example
```
fv1 = FV(.08/12, 360, -733.77, 100000
fv2 = FV(.051/12, 60, -100, -5000)
```

Return
```
fv1 = 8.08687014131965
fv2 = 13266.8111719546
```

The first example can represent a 30-year loan of $100,000 with payments of $733.77 at an annual percentage rate (APR) of 8%. After the final payment, the balance of $8.09 is left. The second example can represent an initial deposit of $5,000 into an account earning 5.1% annually, compounded monthly, and a monthly deposit of $100. After five years, the account is worth $13,266.81.

In case you're interested, here are the formulas. For payment due at the end of the payment period,

```
FV = Pmt * ((1 - (1 + Rate)^Nper) / (Rate)) - PV * (1 + Rate)^Nper
```

For payments due at the beginning of the payment period,

```
FV = Pmt * ((1 + Rate)*(1 - (1 + Rate)^Nper) / (Rate)) - PV * (1 + Rate)^Nper
```

IPmt Function

IPmt() calculates the interest payment for the specified period (*Per*) of an annuity based on a series of regular payments and a constant interest rate (*Rate*).

Usage $DoubleValue$ = IPmt(*Rate*:=, *Per*:=, *NPer*:=, *PV*:=[, *FV*:=][, *Due*:=])

The annuity lasts *NPer* payment periods with an initial value of *PV* and a final value of *FV.* The annuity can represent a loan or a savings plan.

 That last-named argument is *Due,* not *type,* as indicated in the Help file.

PARAMETER	VALUE	MEANING
Rate	Any numeric	Interest rate per payment period. If you make monthly payments, then you must divide the annual percentage rate by 12.
Per	Range from 1 to NPer	The period for which interest payment is to be calculated. Any other value generates an error.
NPer	Any numeric	Total number of payment periods in the annuity. The period must be expressed in the same unit as that used for *Rate.*
PV	Any numeric	Present value of the annuity. If you made an initial deposit for an investment, this value should be negative (cash going out). If you took out a loan, this value should be positive (cash in).
FV	Any numeric	Value of the annuity at the end of *NPer* periods. For a loan, this value is 0. If omitted, 0 is used.
Due	0 or omitted	Payment due at the end of a payment period.
	Any other value	Payment due at the beginning of a payment period.

Example
```
ipmt1 = IPmt(.08/12, 5, 360, 100000, 0, 1)
    ipmt2 = IPmt(.06/12, 10, 18*12, -1000, 50000, 0)
```

Return
```
-660.456374214987
   10.8076670351235
```

The first example calculates the interest payment in the fifth month of a 30-year loan of $100,000 at 8% APR; the payments are due at the beginning of each month. The second example calculates the interest earned for the tenth period of a savings plan earning 6% APR with a target of $50,000 in 18 years; an initial deposit of $1,000 is made.

In case you're interested, here are the formulas. For payments due at the end of the payment period,

```
X = 1 + Rate
IPmt = PV * Rate * (X^NPer - X^(Per - 1)) / (1 - X^Nper)
    + FV * Rate * (1 - X^(Per - 1)) / (1 - X^NPer)
```

For payments due at the beginning of the payment period,

```
X = 1 + Rate
IPmt = PV * Rate * (X^(NPer - 1) - X^(Per - 2)) / (1 - X^Nper)
     + FV * Rate * (1 - X^(Per - 1)) / X / (1 - X^NPer)
```

IRR Function

IRR() calculates the internal rate of return (IRR) for a series of periodic cash flows, as represented in the *ValueArray* Double array.

Usage   *DoubleValue* = IRR(*ValueArray*:=[, *Guess*:=])

The internal rate of return is *equivalent* to the interest rate earned for an investment consisting of a series of cash flows occurring at regular intervals, but the cash flows do not have to remain constant.

IRR() calculates using iteration, starting with *Guess*. If the return value does not converge to within 0.00001% after 20 tries, IRR() fails with an error.

 That first-named argument is *ValueArray,* not *values,* as indicated in the Help file.

PARAMETER	VALUE	MEANING
ValueArray	Array of type Double	Series of cash-flow values. The array must contain at least one negative value (payment) and one positive value (receipt). If the array is not of type Double, IRR() will return an error. The order of entries in the array is important.
Guess	Any numeric	Optional estimate of the return value. If omitted, 0.1 is used.

Example
```
Dim Cflow(6) As Double
   Cflow(0) = -5000
   Cflow(1) = -100: Cflow(2) = -100
   Cflow(3) = -100: Cflow(4) = -100
   Cflow(5) = -100: Cflow(6) = 5960
   r = IRR(Cflow()) * 12
```

Return   `r = 0.169290390448859`

This example represents an initial investment of $5,000 and dollar-cost average of $100 per month for a period of six months, at which time the investment was sold at $5,960. The annualized IRR is the result of the IRR times 12 (twelve months per year), thus yielding roughly 16.9%.

MIRR Function

MIRR() calculates the modified IRR for a series of periodic cash flows, as represented in the *ValueArray* Double array.

Usage $DoubleValue = $ MIRR(*ValueArray*:=, *FinanceRate*:=, *ReinvestRate*:=)

The modified IRR allows you to specify finance rates for payments (*ReinvestRate*) and receipts (*FinanceRate*). The result of MIRR() will be the same as that of IRR() *only* if *FinanceRate* and *ReinvestRate* are the *same* as the return value from IRR().

 That named arguments described in the Help file are wrong.

Parameter	Value	Meaning
ValueArray	Array of type Double	Series of cash-flow values. The array must contain at least one negative value (payment) and one positive value (receipt). If the array is not of type Double, MIRR() will return an error. The order of entries in the array is important.
FinanceRate	Any numeric	The finance rate charged for loans (receipts).
ReinvestRate	Any numeric	The interest rate given for reinvestments (payments).

Example
```
Dim Cflow(6) As Double
    Cflow(0) = -5000
    Cflow(1) = -100: Cflow(2) = -100
    Cflow(3) = -100: Cflow(4) = -100
    Cflow(5) = -100: Cflow(6) = 5960
    r = MIRR(Cflow(), .08 / 12, .06 / 12) * 12
```

Return   0.165357466121415

This example represents an initial investment of $5,000 and dollar-cost average of $100 per month for a period of six months, at which time the investment was sold at $5,960. The annualized modified IRR is the result of the MIRR times 12 (twelve months per year), thus yielding roughly 16.5%. The *FinanceRate* and *ReinvestRate* used are 8% APR and 6% APR, respectively.

NPer Function

NPer() calculates the number of regular payments (annuity) needed to bring the present value (*PV*) to the future value (*FV*) given constant payments (*Pmt*) and interest rate (*Rate*). The annuity can represent a loan or an investment.

Usage $DoubleValue = $ NPer(*Rate*:=, *Pmt*:=, *PV*:=[, *FV*:=][, *Due*:=])

That last-named argument is *Due*, not *type*, as indicated in the Help file.

PARAMETER	VALUE	MEANING
Rate	Any numeric	Interest rate per payment period. If the payments occur monthly, then you must divide the annual percentage rate by 12.
Pmt	Any numeric	The amount of payment made each period. The period must be ex-pressed in the same unit as that used for *Rate*. *Pmt* MUST be enough to cover the interest payment (*PV * Rate*) or an error occurs.
PV	Any numeric	Present value of the annuity. If you make an initial deposit for an invest-ment, this value should be negative (cash going out). If you took out a loan, this value should be positive (cash in).
FV	Any numeric	Value of the annuity at the end. For a loan, this value is 0. If omitted, 0 is used.
Due	0 or omitted	Payment due at the end of a payment period.
	Any other value	Payment due at the beginning of the payment period.

Example
```
n1 = NPer(.08/12, -150, 20000, 0, 0)

   n2 = NPer(0.065/12, -100, -1000, 50000, 1)
```

Return
```
330.681082260616

232.16493067985
```

The first example calculates the number of periods it takes to pay off $20,000 at 8% APR with monthly payments of $150. The second example calculates the number of payments needed to bring an investment at 6.5% APR up to $50,000 with monthly payments of $100 and an initial deposit of $1,000.

In case you're interested, here are the formulas. For payments due at the end of the payment period,

```
NPer = (log(FV * Rate - Pmt) - log(-PV * Rate - Pmt)) / log(1 + Rate)
```

For payments due at the beginning of the payment period,

```
X = 1 + Rate
NPer = (log(FV * Rate - Pmt * X) - log(-PV * Rate - Pmt * X)) / log(X)
```

NPV Function

NPV() calculates the net present value of a series of periodic—but not necessarily constant—payments in the future, using a constant interest rate.

Usage   *DoubleValue* = NPV(*Rate*:=, *ValueArray*:=)

The first value of the *ValueArray* array represents the start of the *second* period of the investment. Simply add the value of the payment at the start of the first period to the result of NPV() to get the net present value of all payments.

 Don't pay attention to the named arguments in the Help file. We also think that the payment of the first period should have been included in the *ValueArray*, rather than its having to be added to the result of NPV().

PARAMETER	VALUE	MEANING
Rate	Any numeric	Discount rate (constant) over the entire payment periods.
ValueArray	Array of type Double	Series of cash-flow values. The array must contain at least one negative value (payment) and one positive value (receipt). If the array is not of type Double, NPV will return an error. The order of entries in the array is important.

Example

```
Dim Cflow(5) As Double

    Cflow(0) = -100
    Cflow(1) = -100: Cflow(2) = -100
    Cflow(3) = -100: Cflow(4) = -100
    Cflow(5) = 5960
    v = NPV(0.03/12, Cflow()) - 5000
```

Return   v = 375.10529807323

This example calculates the net present value of a $5,000 initial investment plus $100 monthly payments for five months and a cash-out value of $5,960 at the end of the payment periods. The assumed inflation rate is 3% APR over the period.

Pmt Function

Pmt() calculates the payments needed for an annuity—based on constant payments and interest rate (*Rate*)—over *NPer* payment periods with present value of *PV* and future value (*FV*) at the end of the payment periods. The annuity can represent a loan or a savings plan.

Usage   *DoubleValue* = Pmt(*Rate*:=, *NPer*:=, *PV*:=[, *FV*:=][, *Due*:=])

 That last-named argument is *Due*, not *type*, as indicated in the Help file.

Parameter	Value	Meaning
Rate	Any numeric	Interest rate per payment period. If you make monthly payments, then you must divide the annual percentage rate by 12.
NPer	Any numeric	Total number of payment periods in the annuity. The period must be expressed in the same unit as that used for *Rate*.
PV	Any numeric	Present value of the annuity. Actually, it's the initial value of the annuity. If you made an initial deposit for an investment, this value should be negative (cash going out). If you took out a loan, this value should be positive (cash in).
FV	Any numeric	Value of the annuity at the end of *NPer* periods. For a loan, this value is 0. If omitted, 0 is used.
Due	0 or omitted	Payment due at the end of a payment period.
	Any other value	Payment due at the beginning of a payment period.

Example
```
pmt1 = Pmt(.08/12, 360, 100000, 0, 1)
    pmt2 = Pmt(.06/12, 18*12, -1000, 50000, 0)
```

Return
```
pmt1 = -728.90520584044
    pmt2 = -121.499537650631
```

The first example calculates the monthly payment for a 30-year loan of $100,000 at an 8% APR; the payments are due at the beginning of each month. The second example calculates the monthly payment needed for a savings plan earning 6% APR with a target of $50,000 in 18 years; an initial deposit of $1,000 is made.

In case you're interested, here are the formulas. For payments due at the end of the payment period,

```
X = 1 + Rate
Pmt = PV * Rate * (X^NPer) / (1 - X^Nper) + FV * Rate / (1 - X^NPer)
```

For payments due at the beginning of the payment period,

```
X = 1 + Rate
Pmt = PV * Rate * (X^(NPer - 1)) / (1 - X^Nper) + FV * Rate / X / (1 - X^NPer)
```

PPmt Function

PPmt() calculates the principal payment for the specified period (*Per*) for an annuity—based on constant payments and interest rate (*Rate*)—over *NPer* payment periods with present value of *PV* and future value (*FV*) at the end of the payment periods. The annuity can represent a loan or a savings plan.

Usage   *DoubleValue* = PPmt(*Rate*:=, *Per*:=, *NPer*:=, *PV*:=[, *FV*:=][, *Due*:=])

That last-named argument is *Due,* not *type,* as indicated in the Help file.

Parameter	Value	Meaning
Rate	Any numeric	Interest rate per payment period. If you make monthly payments, then you must divide the annual percentage rate by 12.
Per	Range from 1 to NPer	The period for which interest payment is to be calculated. Any other value generates an error.
NPer	Any numeric	Total number of payment periods in the annuity. The period must be expressed in the same unit as that used for *Rate.*
PV	Any numeric	Present value of the annuity. If you made an initial deposit for an investment, this value should be negative (cash going out). If you took out a loan, this value should be positive (cash in).
FV	Any numeric	Value of the annuity at the end of *NPer* periods. For a loan, this value is 0. If omitted, 0 is used.
Due	0 or omitted	Payment due at the end of a payment period.
	Any other value	Payment due at the beginning of a payment period.

Example
```
ppmt1 = PPmt(.08/12, 5, 360, 100000, 0, 1)
  pmt2 = PPmt(.06/12, 10, 18*12, -1000, 50000, 0)
```

Return
```
ppmt1 = -68.4488316254535
  ppmt2 = -132.307204685755
```

The first example calculates the principal reduction for the fifth month of a 30-year loan of $100,000 at 8% APR; the payments are due at the beginning of each month. The second example calculates the principal increase for the tenth period of a savings plan earning 6% APR with a target of $50,000 in 18 years; an initial deposit of $1,000 is made.

In case you're interested, here are the formulas. For payments due at the end of the payment period,

```
X = 1 + Rate
PPmt = PV * Rate * (X^(Per - 1)) / (1 - X^Nper)
    + FV * Rate * (X^(Per - 1)) / (1 - X^NPer)
```

For payments due at the beginning of the payment period,

```
X = 1 + Rate
PPmt = PV * Rate * (X^(Per - 2)) / (1 - X^Nper)
    + FV * Rate * (X^(Per - 2)) / (1 - X^NPer)
```

PV Function

PV() calculates the present value of a series of constant payments made regularly over a number of periods (an annuity) at a constant interest rate. The annuity can represent a loan or a savings plan.

Usage   *DoubleValue* = PV(*Rate*:=, *NPer*:=, *Pmt*:=[, *FV*:=][, *Due*:=])

    That last-named argument is *Due,* not *type,* as indicated in the Help file.

PARAMETER	VALUE	MEANING
Rate	Any numeric	Interest rate per payment period. If the payments occur monthly, then you must divide the annual percentage rate by 12.
NPer	Any numeric	Total number of payment periods in the annuity. The period must be expressed in the same unit as that used for *Rate.*
Pmt	Any numeric	The amount of payment made each period. If the payment represents cash going out, this number should be negative.
FV	Any numeric	Value of the annuity at the end of *NPer* periods. For a loan, this value is 0. If omitted, 0 is used.
Due	0 or omitted	Payment due at the end of a payment period.
	Any other value	Payment due at the beginning of the payment period.

Example
```
pv1 = PV(.08/12, 360, -733.77, 0)
  pv2 = PV(.051/12, 60, -100, 5000)
```

Return
```
pv1 = 100000.739490678
  pv2 = 1409.550793073
```

The first example determines the present value of 30 years of monthly payments of $733.77 each at 8% APR. The second example calculates the present value of five years' worth of monthly payments of $100 at 5.1% APR with an end value of $5,000.

In case you're interested, here are the formulas. For payment due at the end of the payment period,

```
PV = Pmt * ((1 - (1 + Rate)^Nper) / Rate / (1 + Rate)^NPer)
   - FV / (1 + Rate)^Nper
```

For payments due at the beginning of the payment period,

```
PV = Pmt * ((1 - (1 + Rate)^Nper) / Rate / (1 + Rate)^(NPer - 1))
   - FV / (1 + Rate)^Nper
```

Rate Function

Rate() calculates by iteration the interest rate for a series of regular, constant payments (*Pmt*) over *NPer* payment periods with an initial value of *PV* and value at the end of the payment periods of *FV*. The annuity can represent either a loan or an investment.

Usage   *DoubleValue* = Rate(*NPer*:=, *Pmt*:=, *PV*:=[, *FV*:=][, *Due*:=][, *Guess*:=])

Starting with *Guess* for the interest rate, Rate() iterates until the change in the return value is less than 0.00001%. If after 20 iterations the values have not converged, an error is generated.

   The last-named argument is *Due*, not *type*, as indicated in the Help file.

PARAMETER	VALUE	MEANING
NPer	Any numeric	Total number of payment periods in the annuity. The return value of Rate() will be expressed in terms of the same unit as that used for *NPer*.
Pmt	Any numeric	The amount of payment made each period. If the payment represents cash going out, this number should be negative.
PV	Any numeric	Present value of the annuity. If you made an initial deposit for an investment, this value should be negative (cash going out). If you took out a loan, this value should be positive (cash in).
FV	Any numeric	Value of the annuity at the end of *NPer* periods. For a loan, this value is 0. If omitted, 0 is used.
Due	0 or omitted	Payment due at the end of a payment period.
	Any other value	Payment due at the beginning of the payment period.
Guess	Any numeric	Estimate of the interest rate. If omitted, 0.1 is used.

Example
```
r1 = Rate(360, -728.91, 100000, 0, 1, .01) * 12
r2 = Rate(18*12, -121.50, -1000, 50000, .01) * 12
```

Return
```
r1 = 8.00006983788256E-02
r2 = 0.059999672206716
```

The first example calculates the APR for monthly payments of $728.91 for a 30-year loan of $100,000 with payments due at the beginning of each month. The return value of Rate() is the monthly rate, so we need to multiply by 12 to get the APR. The second example calculates the APR for a savings plan consisting of monthly payments of $121.50 and an initial deposit of $1,000 with a target of $50,000 in 18 years.

Without supplying an initial guess, these examples fail with an error.

SLN Function

SLN() calculates the per-period straight-line depreciation of an asset acquired at *Cost* with a useful life of *Life* periods and a value at the end of Life of *Salvage.*

Usage   *DoubleValue* = SLN(*Cost*:=, *Salvage*:=, *Life*:=)

PARAMETER	VALUE	MEANING
Cost	Any positive number	Initial cost of asset. .
Salvage	Any positive number	Value of the asset at the end of its useful life.
Life	Any positive number	Length of the useful life expressed as the number of periods.

Example   `dep1 = SLN(1500000, "300,000", 10)`

Return   `dep1 = 120000`

This example finds the straight-line depreciation for each year of an asset that costs $1.5M and has a useful life of 10 years and a salvage value of $300,000. Note that you can use strings as long as they represent valid numbers.

The formula for this one is simple:

```
Depreciation = (Cost - Salvage) / Life
```

SYD Function

SYD() calculates the sum-of-years' digits depreciation of an asset for the specified period.

Usage   *DoubleValue* = SYD(*Cost*:=, *Salvage*:=, *Life*:=, *Period*:=)

 The Help file incorrectly gives the last-named argument as *Per.* It should be *Period.*

PARAMETER	VALUE	MEANING
Cost	Any positive number	Initial cost of the asset.
Salvage	Any positive number	Value of the asset at the end of its useful life.
Life	Any positive number	Length of the useful life expressed as the number of periods.
Period	Range from 1 to Life	Specified period for the depreciation calculation. Must be in the same unit as that used for Life. Any other value generates an error.

Example   `dep1 = SYD(1500000, "300,000", 10, 4)`

Return   `dep1 = 152727.272727273`

This example calculates the sum-of-years' digits depreciation for the fourth year of an asset that costs $1.5M and has a useful life of 10 years and a salvage value of $300,000.

Here's the formula:

```
Dep = 2 * (Cost - Salvage) * (Life - Period + 1) / Life / (Life + 1)
```

The Information Module

This set of functions and statements provides information on status and variables.

Err Function

Err() returns the error object that describes the error that just occurred. It's typically used in error-handling sections of code. See the description of Err Object() for properties and methods.

Usage   *ErrObject* = Err()

Example

```
Sub TestErr()
      On Error GoTo GotErr
      a = 256 * 256
      Exit Sub
   GotErr:
      MsgBox "Your Error is: " & Err() & " " & Err().Description
End Sub
```

Return   `Your Error is: 6 Overflow`

The statement, "a = 256 * 256," generates an error because the result overflows the allowed value for a Byte type.

IMEStatus Function

IMEStatus() is available only in Far East versions of VB. It returns the current Input Method Editor (IME) mode. (This will make sense if you have one of these versions.)

Usage   *IntegerValue* = IMEStatus()

Basically, the Far East languages use 2-byte characters, so there must be some special input modes to allow a (near) standard keyboard to input these 2-byte characters.

The return values also are different for the Japanese, Chinese, and Korean versions. For the Japanese locale, IMEStatus() returns the values given in the following table.

CONSTANT	VALUE	MEANING
vbIMENoOP	0	No IME installed
vbIMEOn	1	IME on
vbIMEOff	2	IME off
vbIMEDisable	3	IME disabled
vbIMEHiragana	4	Hiragana double-byte characters (DBC)
vbIMEKatakanaDbl	5	Katakana DBC
vbIMEKatakanaSng	6	Katakana single-byte characters (SBC)
vbIMEAlphaDbl	7	Alphanumeric DBC
vbIMEAlphaSng	8	Alphanumeric SBC

For the Chinese locale, IMEStatus() returns the values given in this table.

CONSTANT	VALUE	MEANING
vbIMENoOP	0	No IME installed
vbIMEOn	1	IME on
vbIMEOff	2	IME off

For the Korean locale, the return status is bit oriented. You have to look at the five least-significant bits (lsb) of the status. See the following table.

Bit	Value	Meaning
0	0	No IME installed
	1	IME installed
1	0	IME disabled
	1	IME enabled
2	0	IME English mode
	1	Hangeul mode
3	0	Banja mode (SB)
	1	Junja mode (DB)
4	0	Normal mode
	1	Hanja conversion mode

You can test the Korean-locale status by using the And operator with 1, 2, 4, 8, and 16 to test bits 0 through 4. Presumably a combination of bit patterns is allowed, although we have not tested this.

IsArray Function

IsArray() determines if a variable is an array. *VarName cannot* be an instance of a user-defined type.

Usage   *BooleanValue* = IsArray(*VarName*:=)

Example
```
Dim a()
If IsArray(a) Then
    MsgBox "This better be displayed."
Else
    MsgBox "Somethin's fishy"
End If
```

IsDate Function

IsDate() determines if *Expression* is a valid Date value.

Usage   *BooleanValue* = IsDate(*Expression*:=)

Expression can be a literal value, a variable, or any expression. It *cannot* be an instance of a user-defined type.

Example
```
d$ = "Random String"
    b1 = IsDate(Expression:=#11 jan 95# + 3.32)
    b2 = IsDate(d$)
```

Return
```
True
    False
```

Note that the date calculation in the first IsDate() call results in a valid Date value.

IsEmpty Function

IsEmpty() returns True if *Expression* represents an uninitialized variable of Variant type or is a variable explicitly set to Empty.

Usage   *BooleanValue* = IsEmpty(*Expression*:=)

Expression cannot be an instance of a user-defined type.

 The named argument should have been *VarName* rather than *Expression*, since you can determine only if a *variable* is empty, not an expression.

Example
```
Dim a, b, c As Integer
   Debug.Print IsEmpty(a)
   a = 4
   Debug.Print IsEmpty(a)
   a = Empty
   Debug.Print IsEmpty(a)
   Debug.Print IsEmpty(a + b)
   Debug.Print IsEmpty(c)
```

Return
```
True
   False
   True
   False
   False
```

Note from the last example that IsEmpty() is truly useless for expressions. Even when both "a" and "b" are uninitialized, any expression using them has IsEmpty() returning False. Note also that because "c" is explicitly Dim'd to be an Integer, IsEmpty() returns False.

IsError Function

IsError() returns True if *Expression* represents an error value. This means *Expression must* be of an Error data type. That is, TypeName(*Expression*) will return Error or VarType(*Expression*) will return vbError.

Usage   *BooleanValue* = IsError(*Expression*:=)

About the *only* way we've found to get an Error type is by using CVErr(). Even Err() does not return an Error type (it returns an Err Object.) *Expression cannot* be an instance of a user-defined type.

Example
```
Dim e As Error
   b = IsError(e)
```

Return   `False`

Note that even if you explicitly Dim a variable as type Error, IsError() won't return True.

The real usefulness of IsError() comes when it is used in conjunction with CVErr() and user-defined functions. A user-defined function that normally returns Variant values to the caller can also return errors by using CVErr() to generate the error values. The caller can then use IsError() to determine if the result is normal or an error.

Example
```
Sub TestErr()
        result = MyFunc()
        If IsError(result) Then
            MsgBox "MyFunc returned error: " & CStr(result)
        End If
End Sub

Function MyFunc()
        ...
GotErr:
        MyFunc = CVErr(3001)
End Function
```

Note that IsError() does *not* return True when used on Err().

Example
```
Sub TestErr()
        On Error GoTo GotErr
        a = 256 * 256
GotErr:
        Debug.Print IsError(Err)
        Debug.Print Err
End Sub
```

Return   `False`
                `6`

The return shows the two Debug.Print results. IsError() returned False, but clearly Err() returns a valid error number of 6.

IsMissing Function

IsMissing() is used inside user-defined functions and subroutines to determine if Optional and ParamArray arguments have been supplied by the calling routine.

Usage   *BooleanValue* = IsMissing(*ArgName*:=)

Use of IsMissing() allows your procedures to provide "default" values when arguments are not supplied, or even to change the functionality of your procedures. *ArgName cannot* be an instance of a user-defined type.

Example

```
Function EnableOptions(ctrlArrayName As String, _
        Optional iDefault, Optional iOnOff)

    Dim onOff 'Temp variable to indicate ON or OFF

    'If last arg is missing, set onOff to True
    If IsMissing(iOnOff) Then onOff = True Else onOff = iOnOff

    'Turn all controls ON or OFF
    For i = Controls(ctrlArrayName).LBound To _
            Controls(ctrlArrayName).UBound
        Controls(ctrlArrayName)(i).Enabled = onOff
    Next i

    'Set default button if arg is given, and if in range
    If Not IsMissing(iDefault) Then
        If iDefault >= Controls(ctrlArrayName).LBound And _
            iDefault <= Controls(ctrlArrayName).UBound Then
            Controls(ctrlArrayName)(iDefault) = True
        End If
    End If
    EnableOptions = True
End Function

Sub TestOpt()
    EnableOptions("btnOpt") 'Turn options ON
    EnableOptions("btnOpt", 4) 'Turn options ON, activate 4th
    EnableOptions("btnOpt", 3, 0) 'Turn options OFF, activate 3rd
End Sub
```

This example shows how IsMissing() is used to define a function that is versatile. If EnableOptions() is called with only the name of the OptionButton array, then it in turn enables all the buttons. If the second argument is given, then EnableOptions will select that option button. Finally, if the last argument is given, and it is 0, all buttons are disabled.

IsNull Function

IsNull() returns True if *Expression* contains *any* value or variable that is Null.

Usage   *BooleanValue* = IsNull(*Expression*:=)

A variable is Null if it contains no valid value, and an expression evaluates to Null if it contains any value that is Null. The reason for this function is that you cannot use If var = Null Then or If var <> Null Then because those expressions contain Null, so they will always evaluate to Null, and hence False. *Expression cannot* be an instance of a user-defined type.

You need to distinguish between Null and Empty. Empty represents an uninitialized variable, whereas Null is used explicitly to indicate no valid data.

Example
```
Dim a
    Debug.Print IsEmpty(a)
    Debug.Print IsNull(a)
```

```
a = ""
Debug.Print IsNull(a)
a = Null
Debug.Print IsNull(a)
```

Return   True
               False
               False
               True

Note that a zero-length string is also *not* Null.

IsNumeric Function

IsNumeric() returns True if *Expression* can be interpreted as a number.

Usage   *BooleanValue* = IsNumeric(*Expression*:=)

Expression can be a string or number. IsNumeric will return False if *Expression* is a date or time. *Expression cannot* be an instance of a user-defined type.

Example   ```
               Debug.Print IsNumeric(1.3)
               Debug.Print IsNumeric("504,304")
               Debug.Print IsNumeric("543a")
               Debug.Print IsNumeric("11:34")
               ```

*Return*       True
               True
               False
               False

Actually, the second example will depend on the thousands separator for your system.

## IsObject Function

IsObject() returns True if *Expression* is a variable of type Object, a user-defined object, or a control.

*Usage*        *BooleanValue* = IsObject(*Expression*:=)

*Expression cannot* be an instance of a user-defined type.

*Example*      ```
               Dim o As Object, i As Integer
               Debug.Print IsObject(o)
               Debug.Print IsObject(i)
               Debug.Print IsObject(Me.btnOpt)
               Debug.Print IsObject(Me.btnOpt(10))
               ```

Return   True
             False
             True
             True

In this example, btnOpt represents an OptionButton array on the form. There are only six array members. Nevertheless, note that the last statement returns True! Hey Microsoft: Is this a bug?

QBColor Function

QBColor() converts the color code used by other versions of BASIC and MS-DOS applications to the RGB values used by VBA.

Usage   *LongValue* = QBColor(*Color*:=)

The color codes can have the following values.

PARAMETER	VALUE	MEANING
Color	0	Black
	1	Blue
	2	Green
	3	Cyan
	4	Red
	5	Magenta
	6	Yellow
	7	White
	8	Gray
	9	Light Blue
	10	Light Green
	11	Light Cyan
	12	Light Red
	13	Light Magenta
	14	Light Yellow
	15	Bright White
	Any other value	Error

If the *Color* argument is a floating-point value, statistical rounding is applied to convert the value in an Integer first.

RGB Function

RGB() converts individual settings of Red, Green, and Blue values into the RGB color value used by VBA. All floating-point values are statistically rounded before being evaluated by the RGB function.

Usage $LongValue = \text{RGB}(Red:=, Green:=, Blue:=)$

PARAMETER	VALUE	MEANING
Red	0 through 255 256 through 32,767 Any other value	Red intensity value. 0 is lowest. Same as 255 Error
Green	0 through 255 256 through 32,767 Any other value	Green intensity value. 0 is lowest. Same as 255 Error
Blue	0 through 255 256 through 32,767 Any other value	Blue intensity value. 0 is lowest. Same as 255 Error

The formula used is:

```
RGBVal = Red + &H100 * Green + &H10000 * Blue
```

Thus to recover the individual colors from an RGB value, use

```
Red = RGBVal And &HFF
Green = Int(RGBVal / &H100) And &HFF
Blue = Int(RGBVal / &H10000) And &HFF
```

TypeName Function

TypeName() returns a string describing the type of specified variable.

Usage $StringValue = \text{TypeName}(VarName:=)$

If the variable refers to an OLE Automation object, the name of the object type is returned. *VarName cannot* be an instance of a user-defined type. *VarName can* be a literal value.

The return values of TypeName are given in the following table.

VALUE	VARIABLE TYPE
objecttype	An OLE Automation object. The return value is the name of an object.
Byte	Byte value
Integer	Integer value
Long	Long value
Single	Single value
Double	Double value

VALUE	VARIABLE TYPE
Current	Currency value
Date	Date value
String	String value
Boolean	Boolean value
Error	Error value
Empty	Uninitialized variable
Null	Not valid data. A variable that was set explicitly to Null.
Object	An object that supports OLE Automation, but is not a specific object.
Unknown	An OLE automation object whose type cannot be determined.
Nothing	An object variable that doesn't refer to a specific instance of an object or that has not yet been set using the Set keyword.

TypeName() can return reasonable results even if its argument is not a variable name.

Example

```
Debug.Print TypeName(0)
   Debug.Print TypeName(&H1234)
   Debug.Print TypeName(&H12345)
   Debug.Print TypeName(1.5)
   Debug.Print TypeName(#11:00# + .2)
```

Return

```
Integer
Integer
Long
Double
Date
```

In the following example, the form name is Form1 and btnOpt is a OptionButton array.

Example

```
Debug.Print TypeName(Me)
   Debug.Print TypeName(btnOpt)
   Debug.Print TypeName(btnOpt(0))
```

Return

```
Form1
   Object
   OptionButton
```

Note the distinction between Nothing and Empty in the following examples:

Example

```
Dim o As Object, n
   Debug.Print TypeName(n)
   Debug.Print TypeName(o)
   n = 3
   o = btnOpt
   Debug.Print TypeName(n)
   Debug.Print TypeName(o)
```

Return
```
Empty
Nothing
Integer
Object
```

VarType Function

VarType() returns an integer value that represents the data type of the specified variable.

Usage   *IntegerValue* = VarType(*VarName*:=)

    VarName() can be a literal value, but it *cannot* be an instance of a user-defined type. This function does *not* always return the equivalent values as TypeName() in some cases (see examples at the end of this subsection).

    The following table shows return values of VarType().

CONSTANT	VALUE	MEANING
vbEmpty	0	Empty (uninitialized)
vbNull	1	Null (no valid data)
vbInteger	2	Integer
vbLong	3	Long integer
vbSingle	4	Single-precision floating-point number
vbDouble	5	Double-precision floating-point number
vbCurrency	6	Currency
vbDate	7	Date
vbString	8	String
vbObject	9	OLE Automation object
vbError	10	Error
vbBoolean	11	Boolean
vbVariant	12	Variant (used only with arrays of Variants)
vbDataObject	13	Non-OLE Automation object
vbByte	17	Byte
vbArray	8192	Array. This value is added to one of the others to indicate the type of array.

    VarType() does not return vbArray for Control arrays. In the following example, btnOpt is an array of OptionButton arrays:

Example
```
Debug.Print TypeName(btnOpt)
Debug.Print VarType(btnOpt)
Debug.Print TypeName(btnOpt(1))
Debug.Print VarType(btnOpt(1))
```

| *Return* | ```
Object
9
OptionButton
11
``` |

TypeName() returns Object for btnOpt, so it's not too surprising that VarType() cannot tell btnOpt is an array. Its return value of vbObject (9) is at least consistent. Note btnOpt(1) represents the OptionButton with index of 1, and TypeName() properly returns OptionButton, but look at VarType(). It returns vbBoolean (11)! Apparently, it's returning the type information for the *value* of the Option button.

| *Example* | ```
Debug.Print VarType(0)
  Debug.Print TypeName(&H1234)
  Debug.Print VarType(&H12345)
  Debug.Print VarType(1.5)
  Debug.Print VarType(#11:00# + .2)
``` |
| *Return* | ```
2
  2
  3
  5
  7
``` |

The Interaction Module

The following set of commands and functions represent interaction with the user and other applications.

AppActivate Statement

The AppActivate statement activates (changes focus to) the application with the title text or task ID that matches *Title*. If no exact match is found, then an application with title text that begins with *Title* will be selected (arbitrarily if there is more than one).

Usage	AppActivate *Title*:=[, *Wait*:=]

The AppActivate statement does not affect the minimized or maximized state of the application.

PARAMETER	VALUE	MEANING
Title	Any string	The string must match at least the beginning of the title text of a running application. The task ID returned by a Shell statement can also be used. If no match is found, an error occurs.
Wait	False or omitted True	Immediately activates the specified application. Waits until the calling application is activated before changing focus to the specified application.
```

Using the task ID returned by Shell() does not always work! You can get an "Invalid procedure call" error. Try the following:

```
myApp = Shell("Explorer.exe", vbNormalFocus)
AppActivate myApp
```

Now for some examples that work.

As long as the title bar for Microsoft Word has not been changed, the following statement will activate it, regardless of which document is open:

Example   `AppActivate "Microsoft Word"`

If your application explicitly started the other application using Shell(), you can save the task ID for use with AppActivate to ensure that you will get exactly the instance of the application you desire.

Example
```
MyAppID = Shell("C:\WORD\WINWORD.EXE", 1)
    AppActivate MyAppID        ' Activate Microsoft
```

Beep Statement

Beep generates a tone on your computer's speaker or sound system. You can use this statement to warn users of warning or error conditions.

Usage   Beep

Example
```
If MyFunc() = NULL Then
        Beep : MsgBox "MyFunc returned an invalid value"
End If
```

Choose Function

Choose returns a single value from the list of Variant-valued choices.

Usage   *VariantValue* = Choose(*Index, Choice1*[, *Choice2*[, ...[, *ChoiceN*]]])

All the choices are evaluated before a selection is made, so if your choices are expressions, you have to be aware of possible side effects (see the following example).

This function is most useful in converting your OptionButton array choices into more meaningful (possibly String) values.

PARAMETER	VALUE	MEANING
Index	1 through *n*	Specifies the choice. The number is statistically rounded before evaluating.
	< 1 or > *n*	Choose returns Null.
Choice	Any expression	Index selects one from the *n* choices.

Example

```
Function DoubleString(x)
     x = x * 2
     DoubleString = "Value: " & x
End Function
Sub TestChoose()
     Dim ans, n
     n = 1
     ans = Choose(2, DoubleString(n + 2), DoubleString(n + 1), _
     DoubleString(n))
     Debug.Print ans
End Sub
```

Return   6

Note that 6 is not the anticipated result. That's because DoubleString() changes its input argument. Since Choose() evaluates all its choices (from last to first), after DoubleString() is first run, *n* is changed from 1 to 2. This makes the second choice DoubleString(3), which gives 6.

In the following example, assume you have three option buttons of the btnOpt OptionButton array with button text: "Letter", "Fax", and "Memo."

Example

```
Sub btnOpt_Click(Index As Integer)
     ans = Choose(Index + 1, "Letter", "Fax", "Memo")
     MsgBox "You have selected a " & ans
End Sub
```

You can even place filenames in the choices to directly access a file based on the user's button selection.

Command Function

Command() returns command-line arguments used to start VB or an application built from VB. The return value depends on the situations given in the following table.

Usage   *StringValue* = Command

APPLICATION	RETURN VALUE
VB	If VB is started with `vb /cmd cmdoptions` the return value will be cmdoptions. If the command-line arguments are set using the "Tools," "Options," "Advanced" panel, the return value matches those settings.
VB-built Application	If the VB-built application is started with `MyApp cmdoptions` the return value will be cmdoptions.
VB-built DLL	For a VB in-process OLE server (DLL), this function always returns an empty string.

CreateObject Function

CreateObject() creates an OLE Automation object and returns a reference to that object.

Usage   Set *ObjectValue* = CreateObject(*Class*:=)

If the object is capable of having multiple instances running at the same time, a new instance of the server application is started in response to the CreateObject() call. To attach it to an already running instance of an object, use GetObject(). Whether the server application starts up in visible or hidden mode depends on the application.

The *Class* argument has the format *appname.objectType,* where each part is described in the following table.

PART	TYPE	MEANING
appname	String	The name of the server application to which the object belongs. This name is one that is registered in the registration database and does not necessarily have any relation to the executable filename of the application. You'll need to consult the documentation for the server application or look in the registration database.
objectType	String	The name of the object that is registered by the server application. Again, you'll need to consult the documentation for the application for a list of valid object types.

To see a list of possible *appname.objectType* pairs, look in the registration database of Windows 95 or Windows NT for the topic: HKEY_CLASSES_ROOT. However, consult the documentation to be sure.

Example
```
Sub GetStyles()
        'This subroutine files the LstStyles ListBox with all
        ' the styles defined for the current Word document.
        Dim oWord As Object, nStyles As Integer, i As Integer

        LstStyles.Clear      'Clear list before filling

        Set oWord = CreateObject("Word.Basic")
        nStyles = oWord.CountStyles()
        For i = 1 To nStyles
            LstStyles.AddItem oWord.[StyleName$](i)
        Next I
        Set oWord = Nothing
    End Sub
```

See *The Underground Guide to Microsoft Office, OLE 2, and VBA* (Hudspeth and Lee, Addison-Wesley, 1995) for an excellent discussion of all the nuances of interacting with Microsoft Office applications.

Note: Some server applications automatically quit when you set the object reference to Nothing or when the object reference variable goes out of scope. For other server applications (such as EXCEL), you have to explicitly quit the application before setting the reference to Nothing.

DeleteSetting Statement

The DeleteSetting statement deletes an entry from the Windows Registry under

`HKEY_CURRENT_USER\Software\VB and VBA Program Settings`

Usage   DeleteSetting *AppName*:=[, *Section*:=][, *Key*:=]

If only *AppName* is given, the entire set of settings under *AppName* is deleted. If only *AppName* and *Section* are given, then all keys in that section are deleted. If all three arguments are given, then all values for the specified *Key* are deleted. If the specified setting to be deleted does not exist, an error occurs.

PARAMETER	VALUE	MEANING
AppName	Any string	This string typically represents the application name for which you are deleting a setting. If the string contains backslash (\) characters, each part separated by the backslash characters represents a sublevel in the Registry. Spaces are allowed.
Section	Any string	This string typically represents the section name of an application for which you are deleting a setting. If the string contains backslash (\) characters, each part separated by the backslash characters represents a sublevel under that specified by AppName. Spaces are allowed.
Key	Any string	This string typically represents the key name for which you are deleting a setting. If the string contains backslash (\) characters, each part separated by the backslash characters represents a sublevel under that specified by AppName and Section. Spaces are allowed.

 The Windows 95 Registry allows Registry keys to hold any number of named values. If you use REGEDIT.EXE, you'll see that the key is actually a folder that can contain any number of values. The VBA registry commands, however, do not allow you to set or access those values; you can only create and access the key itself. Also, you have access to only the subtree under

`HKEY_CURRENT_USER\Software\VB and VBA Program Settings`

The following examples all represent the same Registry entry:

Example
```
DeleteSetting "MyApp", "MySec", "MyKey"
DeleteSetting "MyApp", "MySec\MyKey"
DeleteSetting "MyApp\MySec\MyKey"
```

Note that because you can use backslash characters in each of the arguments, you can access keys to arbitrarily deep levels.

DoEvents Function

DoEvents() causes your VB application to suspend execution to allow the operating system to process other events. It returns the number of open forms.

Usage   *IntegerValue* = DoEvents

Use this function if you are performing intensive calculations in a loop to allow other applications to run and the user to perform input using the mouse and keyboard.

You do have to be careful, however, that when your application does give up control, another application will not cause the same code to be executed again. This is especially true if you are developing an in-process OLE server (DLL).

Example
```
Do While Not Done
      Done = MyFunc
      If cnt > 1000 Then
            cnt = 0 : DoEvents
      End If
      cnt = cnt + 1
Loop
```

This example yields the processor every 1,000 times it executes MyFunc.

Environ Function

Environ() returns the specified operating-system environment variable. *Expression* can be either a string or a numeric expression.

Usage   *VariantValue* = Environ(*Expression*:=)

Example
```
Debug.Print Environ("winbootdir")
  Debug.Print Environ(Expression:=1)
  Debug.Print Environ("1")
```

Return
```
C:\WINDOWS
  winbootdir=C:\WINDOWS
  ""
```

Note that strings that contain numbers are *not* converted to a number before evaluation. The last example returns an empty string because there is no environment variable named "1."

PARAMETER	VALUE	MEANING
Expression	Any string	The name of an environment variable. If the variable is found, its value is returned. If it is not found, an empty string ("") is returned. Environ() is case-insensitive, so "WINDIR" is the same as "windir."
	Numeric 1 through 255	The numeric position of the variable in the environment table. The return value includes both the environment variable name and its value, separated by an equals sign, as in `windir=C:\WINDOWS` If there are fewer environment variables than the specified number, an empty string ("") is returned. All floating-point values are statistically rounded before the function is evaluated.
	Any other numeric	Error

GetAllSettings Function

GetAllSettings() returns a two-dimensional array that contains all keys and values for the specified *AppName* and *Section* from the Registry.

Usage   *VariantValue* = GetAllSettings(*AppName*:=, *Section*:=)

The first index of the array represents the position number of the key. The second index indicates the key or value: 0 for key, 1 for value. The first index starts at 0. You can determine the number of keys by using UBound().

All Registry entries accessed by the VBA Setting routines are relative to the subtree

`HKEY_CURRENT_USER\Software\VB and VBA Program Settings`

PARAMETER	VALUE	MEANING
AppName	Any string	This string typically represents the application name for which you are getting settings. If the string contains backslash (\) characters, each part separated by the backslash characters represents a sublevel in the Registry. Spaces are allowed.
Section	Any string	This string typically represents the section name of an application for which you are getting settings. If the string contains backslash (\) characters, each part separated by the backslash characters represents a sublevel under that specified by AppName. Spaces are allowed.

Example

```
Sub TestSetting()
    For i = 1 To 10
        SaveSetting "MyApp", "MySec\MySubSec", "MyKey" & i, _
    "MyVal" & i
```

```
        Next i
        arr = GetAllSettings("MyApp\MySec", "MySubSec")
        For i = 0 To UBound(arr)
            Debug.Print arr(i, 0) & " = " & arr(i, 1)
        Next I
    End Sub
```

This example makes a bunch of settings and then prints them out using GetAllSettings().
Note the use of the return array to get the keys and values.

GetObject Function

GetObject() gets a reference to the specified OLE Automation object and optionally specifies a
file to open for the application.

Usage   Set *ObjectValue* = GetObject([*PathName*:=][, *Class*:=])

The *Class* argument has the format *appname.objectType*. If a new instance of the server application is started, whether it is a hidden instance depends on the application.

PARAMETER	VALUE	MEANING
PathName	String	The name of a file to open by the OLE Automation object. If no Class is given, GetObject() uses the extension of the filename to start a registered server application. If the file has multiple parts that can be accessed via OLE Automation, you can specify the part by separating the filename and the part name by an exclamation point, as in `"filename!partname"`
	Empty string	Class is required. GetObject() creates a new instance of the server application with no open documents. If the object is registered as single-instance (such as Word.Basic), the current instance of the server application is used.
	Omitted	Class is required. GetObject() returns a reference to the current document in an existing instance of the Class object. If no current instance of the server application exists, an error occurs.
Class	appname string	The name of the server application to which the object belongs. This name is one that is registered in the registration database and does not necessarily have any relation to the executable filename of the application. You need to consult the application's documentation or look in the registration database.
	ObjectType string	The name of an object that is registered by the application. Again, you'll need to consult the application's documentation for a list of valid object types.

PARAMETER	VALUE	MEANING
Class	Omitted	The PathName argument must be supplied and the filename extension must be registered so that the correct server application may be started. 　　The default object of the application will be used. If the application supports more than one object, you should not leave this blank to ensure you connect to the object you want.

Note: Some server applications automatically quit when you set the object reference to Nothing or when the object reference variable goes out of scope. For other server applications (such as EXCEL), you have to explicitly quit the application before setting the reference to Nothing.

You can't use GetObject() to get a reference to a class created with VB; use CreateObject() instead.

Example
```
Dim oXls As Object, amount
    Set oXls = GetObject("C:\Excel\MySheet.xls", "Excel.Sheet")
    amount = oXls.Range("LoanAmount")
    oXls.Parent.Saved = True
    oXls.Application.Quit
    Set oXls = Nothing
    MsgBox "Loan Amount = " & Format(amount, "Currency")
```

This example retrieves the value of a cell named "LoanAmount" from the MySheet.xls spreadsheet. Note that we explicitly reset the Saved flag before quitting. Although doing this isn't needed for this example, it's good practice in order to prevent accidental changes from being saved.

GetSetting Function

GetSetting() retrieves a key value from the registration database for the specified application, section, and key.

Usage　　　　*StringValue* = GetSetting(*AppName*:=, *Section*:=, *Key*:=[, *Default*:=])

If the specified key does not exist and *Default* is omitted, an empty string is returned. All Registry entries accessed by the VBA Setting routines are relative to the subtree

```
HKEY_CURRENT_USER\Software\VB and VBA Program Settings
```

Example
```
Sub TestSetting()
        SaveSetting "MyApp", "MySec", "MyKey", "MyVal"
        Debug.Print GetSetting("MyApp", "MySec", "MyKey")
        Debug.Print GetSetting("MyApp", "MySec", "MyBadKey", "Bad")
    End Sub
```

Return
```
MyKey
    Bad
```

PARAMETER	VALUE	MEANING
AppName	Any string	This string typically represents the application name for which you are getting settings. If the string contains backslash (\) characters, each part separated by the backslash characters represents a sublevel in the Registry. Spaces are allowed.
Section	Any string	This string typically represents the section name of an application for which you are getting settings. If the string contains backslash (\) characters, each part separated by the backslash characters represents a sublevel under that specified by AppName. Spaces are allowed.
Key	Any string	This string typically represents the key name for which you are getting a setting. If the string contains backslash (\) characters, each part separated by the backslash characters represents a sublevel under that specified by AppName and Section. Spaces are allowed.
Default	Any string	If the specified key does not exist, this value is returned by GetSetting().

Note that you cannot access general Registry settings using GetSetting(). You need to use the Windows Registry API functions.

IIf Function

IIf() evaluates *Expression* and, based on the result, returns one of two values. Both *TruePart* and *FalsePart* expressions are evaluated, but only one of the results is returned. You have to be aware of any side effects.

Usage   *VariantValue* = IIf(*Expression*:=, *TruePart*:=, *FalsePart*:=)

The named arguments in the Help file are wrong.

PARAMETER	VALUE	MEANING
Expression	Any expression	This expression will be evaluated and converted to a Boolean value True or False.
TruePart	Any expression	The result of this expression is returned if Expression evaluates to True.
FalsePart	Any expression	The result of this expression is returned if Expression evaluates to False.

Example
```
Sub TestIIf()
    Dim Score(5)
    Randomize 556
```

```
                    For i = 0 To UBound(Score())
                        Score(i) = Int((101) * Rnd)
                    Next i

                    For i = 0 To UBound(Score())
                        Debug.Print Score(i) & " " & _
                            IIf(Score(i) > 60, "Passed", "Failed")
                    Next i
                End Sub
```

Return
```
65 Passed
91 Passed
85 Passed
30 Failed
78 Passed
82 Passed
```

This example prints a list of Passed and Failed strings for the Score() array.

Example
```
answer = IIf(b <> 0, a / b, Null)
```

This example appears like it will work, since it reads, "If b is not zero, then calculate (a/b); otherwise, return Null." Unfortunately, (a/b) is always evaluated, even if b is zero, thus generating an Overflow error.

InputBox Function

InputBox() displays a dialog box that prompts the user to input text.

Usage   *StringValue* = InputBox(*Prompt*:=[, *Title*:=][, *Default*:=][, *XPos*:=][, *YPos*:=][, *HelpFile*:=, *Context*:=])

InputBox() waits for the user's input before returning the input as a string, but if the user clicks the Cancel button (or the Esc key), it returns an empty string.

If the Help button is displayed, the dialog box dimension is about 5784 twips wide and 2736 twips high for a 1024 × 768 display using Large Fonts. (See note on twips in Section 1.) Other display drivers may have different values. If your *Prompt* string is long, the dialog box may grow in height to accommodate it.

Example
```
nm$ = InputBox("Enter your name, last name first", _
     "MyApp - Name")
id$ = InputBox("Enter your ID", "MyApp - ID", "000-00-0000", _
     0, 0, "C:\WINDOWS\HELP\MyHelp.hlp", 101)
```

The first example displays the dialog box, which is centered in the display; only the OK and Cancel buttons are available. The second example also displays a Help button that, when clicked, will display the topic in "MyHelp.hlp" with the context number of 101.

PARAMETER	VALUE	MEANING
Prompt	Any string	This is the message displayed in the dialog box, typically used to describe to the user what your program wants for user input. You can use vbCr, vbLf, or vbCrLf constants for manual line breaks. A maximum of 1023 characters will be displayed, but no errors will occur if Prompt is longer.
Title	Any string	This string is displayed in the Title Bar. Only one line of text is displayed; that works out to a maximum of around 114 characters.
	Omitted	The application name is displayed in the Title Bar.
Default	Any string	This string represents the default user response. The text box of the dialog box will be filled with this string, thus allowing the user to simply click OK to accept the default string. The entire default string is selected when the dialog box comes up, so any keyboard input will first delete the default string.
	Omitted	The text box comes up blank.
XPos	−32,768 through 32,767	This specifies the position of the left edge of the dialog box in twips. Larger numbers move the dialog box further to the right. Negative values are allowed. These move the dialog box beyond the left edge of the display.
	Other value	This causes an overflow error.
	Omitted	The dialog box is horizontally centered.
YPos	−32,768 through 32,767	This specifies the position of the top edge of the dialog box in twips. Larger numbers move the dialog box further down. Negative values are allowed. These move the dialog box beyond the top edge of the display.
	Other value	This causes an overflow error.
	Omitted	The dialog box is vertically centered.
HelpFile	String	This is the name of a Help file. If used, Context must also be supplied! A Help button will be added to the dialog box.
Context	Numeric expression	This is a Help-context number. You'll need to consult the Help-file designer for valid numbers. If you supply an invalid number, an error occurs.

MsgBox Function

MsgBox() displays a dialog box to inform the user with a message or to ask the user to make a decision by clicking a button.

Usage   *IntegerValue* = MsgBox(*Prompt*:=[, *Buttons*:=][, *Title*:=][, *HelpFile*:=, *Context*:=])

   MsgBox() waits for the user to click a button (or the Esc or Enter key) and returns a value that indicates the button selected by the user.
   The appearance of the dialog box—the icon displayed, how many buttons, and the button text—are specified by the *Buttons* argument (see table on next page). You can also provide context-sensitive help by using the *HelpFile* and *Context* arguments.

Parameter	Value	Meaning
Prompt	Any string	This is the message displayed in the dialog box. The dialog box will be sized to fit your message. You can use vbCr, vbLf, or vbCrLf constants for manual line breaks. A maximum of 1023 characters will be displayed, but no errors will occur if Prompt is longer.
Buttons	–32,768 through 32,767	Not all numbers are valid (see the following table). All invalid numbers are treated like 0 (OK button only). All floating-point values are statistically rounded before being evaluated.
	Other value	This causes an overflow error.
	Omitted	This is the same as 0.
Title	Any string	This string is displayed in the Title Bar. Only one line of text is displayed, so there is a limit to the number of characters displayed.
	Omitted	The application name is displayed in the Title Bar.
HelpFile	String	This is the name of a Help file. If used, Context must also be supplied! The user can use the F1 key to call up the Help file.
Context	Numeric expression	This is a Help-context number. You need to consult the Help-file designer for valid numbers. If you supply an invalid number, an error occurs.

The *Buttons* argument is composed by using the following values to describe the appearance of the dialog box. These constants are separated into four groups, and Buttons is formed by summing a value from each group.

Group	Constant	Value	Meaning
Button Style	vbOKOnly vbOKCancel vbAbortRetryIgnore vbYesNoCancel vbYesNo vbRetryCancel	0 1 2 3 4 5	OK button only OK and Cancel buttons Abort, Retry, and Ignore buttons Yes, No, and Cancel buttons Yes and No buttons Retry and Cancel buttons
Icon Style	? vbCritical vbQuestion vbExclamation vbInformation	0 16 32 48 64	No icon Critical Message icon Warning Query icon Warning Message icon Information Message icon
Default Button	vbDefaultButton1 vbDefaultButton2 vbDefaultButton3	0 256 512	First button is default Second button is default Third button is default
Modal	vbApplicationModal	0	Application modal. The user must respond to the message box before being allowed to interact further with the current application.
	vbSystemModal	4096	System modal. The user must respond to the message box before being allowed to interact further with any application.

The return value of MsgBox() indicates which button the user selected. Use the constants in the following table to make your code more readable.

Constant	Value	Meaning
vbOK	1	OK button
vbCancel	2	Cancel button, or Esc key when Cancel button is displayed
vbAbort	3	Abort button
vbRetry	4	Retry button
vbIgnore	5	Ignore button
vbYes	6	Yes button
vbNo	7	No button

Example

```
If MsgBox("Do you want to continue?", vbYesNo + vbQuestion, _
    "MyApp", "MyHelp.hlp", 1001) = vbNo Then
    Exit Sub
End If
```

This example asks the user if he or she wants to continue. If the user answers no, the subroutine ends. The user can press F1 to call up the help context 1001 of MyHelp.hlp.

Partition Function

Partition() returns a string of the form low:high that describes a range of values enclosing the specified number.

Usage   *VariantValue* = Partition(*Number*:=, *Start*:=, *Stop*:=, *Interval*:=)

This is most useful in database queries. Partition() divides a range of numbers between *Start* and *Stop* into equal divisions (except for the last one)—each division has *Interval* number of values. The return value describes in which of these intervals *Number* lies. All numbers are statistically rounded before evaluating.

Each of the low and high values in the return string is padded with leading spaces to make the number of characters the same as that for *Stop*.

Parameter	Value	Meaning
Number	−2,147,483,648 through 2,147,483,647	The number used to evaluate which interval contains the number.
Start	0 through 2,147,483,647	The first number of the range of values to be divided into intervals.
Stop	1 through 2,147,483,647	The last number of the range of values to be divided into intervals. This number must be greater than Start.
Interval	1 through 2,147,483,647	The size of each interval. The last interval may be smaller than this number.

We got the following to GPF every time:

```
Debug.Print Partition(2^31 - 2, 0, 2^31 - 2, 10)
```

If any input value is Null, Partition() returns Null.

Example
```
Debug.Print Partition(-55, 0, 101, 10)
  Debug.Print Partition(0, 0, 101, 10)
  Debug.Print Partition(52, 0, 101, 10)
  Debug.Print Partition(100, 0, 101, 10)
  Debug.Print Partition(237, 0, 101, 10)
```

Return
```
  : -1
  0: 9
  50: 59
  100:101
  102:
```

SaveSetting Statement

The SaveSetting statement creates or changes a key setting in the registration database for the specified application, section, and key.

Usage   SaveSetting *AppName*:=, *Section*:=, *Key*:=, *Setting*:=

All Registry entries accessed by the VBA Setting routines are relative to the subtree

```
HKEY_CURRENT_USER\Software\VB and VBA Program Settings
```

PARAMETER	VALUE	MEANING
AppName	Any string	This string typically represents the application name for which you are saving settings. If the string contains backslash (\) characters, each part separated by the backslash characters represents a sublevel in the Registry. Spaces are allowed.
Section	Any string	This string typically represents the section name of an application for which you are saving settings. If the string contains backslash (\) characters, each part separated by the backslash characters represents a sublevel under the one specified by AppName. Spaces are allowed.
Key	Any string	This string typically represents the key name for which you are saving a setting. If the string contains backslash (\) characters, each part separated by the backslash characters represents a sublevel under the one specified by AppName and Section. Spaces are allowed.
Setting	Any expression	This is any string that represents the value of the specified key.

Example
```
Sub TestSetting()
    SaveSetting "MyApp", "MySec", "MyKey", "MyVal"
    Debug.Print GetSetting("MyApp", "MySec", "MyKey")
    Debug.Print GetSetting("MyApp", "MySec", "MyBadKey", "Bad")
End Sub
```

Return
```
MyKey
Bad
```

Note that you cannot access general registry settings using SaveSetting. You'll need to use the Windows Registry API functions.

SendKeys Statement

The SendKeys statement simulates keystrokes to the active window of the active application.

Usage   SendKeys *String*:=[, *Wait*:=]

Note that you can use AppActivate to set the active application explicitly. Keystrokes are represented by keycode characters, arranged in order to form the *String* argument. The key codes for most printable keys are simply the character that matches the key (e.g., "A" means the capital A key). The key codes for special keys are represented by keywords enclosed in braces ({ }) (see the following table).

SendKeys is the simplest way to interact with another application, but it may also be the most unreliable. You should use it as a last resort.

PARAMETER	VALUE	MEANING
String	String	The list of characters representing keystrokes to send. See the next table for entry of nonprinting keys.
Wait	False or omitted	Does not wait for the keys to be processed. Control is returned to the caller immediately.
	True	Does not continue execution until all keystrokes have been processed by the active application.

The following table shows the key codes for special nonprinting keys and special keys (capitalization is optional).

KEY	CODE
SHIFT	+
CTRL	^
ALT	%
+	{+}
^	{^}
%	{%}

KEY	CODE
~	{~}
(	{(}
)	{)}
[	{[}
]	{]}
{	{{}
}	{}}
BACKSPACE	{BACKSPACE}, {BS}, or {BKSP}
BREAK	{BREAK}
CAPS LOCK	{CAPSLOCK}
DEL	{DELETE} or {DEL}
DOWN ARROW	{DOWN}
END	{END}
ENTER	{ENTER} or ~
ESC	{ESC}
HELP	{HELP}
HOME	{HOME}
INS	{INSERT}
LEFT ARROW	{LEFT}
NUM LOCK	{NUMLOCK}
PAGE DOWN	{PGDN}
PAGE UP	{PGUP}
PRINT SCREEN	{PRTSC}
RIGHT ARROW	{RIGHT}
SCROLL LOCK	{SCROLLLOCK}
TAB	{TAB}
UP ARROW	{UP}
F1	{F1}
F2	{F2}
F3	{F3}
F4	{F4}
F5	{F5}
F6	{F6}
F7	{F7}
F8	{F8}
F9	{F9}
F10	{F10}
F11	{F11}
F12	{F12}
F13	{F13}
F14	{F14}
F15	{F15}
F16	{F16}

The key modifiers—+, ^, and % (for SHIFT, CTRL, and ALT, respectively)—are used in combination with the keycodes that follow them. For instance, <CTRL>+A is represented by the string "^A." To have a key modifier apply to more than one keystroke, enclose the keystrokes in parentheses. For instance, <ALT>+A, <ALT>+B, <ALT>+C is represented by "%(ABC)."

You can also use the "{*key number*}" syntax to specify the number of times a key should be repeated. For instance, "{UP 4}" represents hitting the <UpArrow> four times.

Example
```
SendKeys "AB"
  SendKeys "+(ab)"
```

Both of these send an uppercase "A" and "B" to the active window.

Example
```
Sub DeleteFiles(path$, pattern$)
        AppActivate "Exploring"           'Activate Explorer Window
        SendKeys "% R%TFF", True          'Find Files
        SendKeys "%N" & pattern$ & "%L" & path$ & "%i", True
        SendKeys "%EA", True              'Select All
        SendKeys "{DEL}Y", True           'Delete All
        SendKeys "%{F4}", True            'Close Find window
        SendKeys "% n", True              'Minimize Explorer
    End Sub

    Sub DeleteTmpFiles
        DeleteFiles "F:\", "*.tmp"
    End Sub
```

This example removes all ".tmp" files on the F: drive using the Windows 95 Explorer. The AppActivate statement assumes that the Explorer is already running. It's not pretty, but it works.

Shell Function

Shell() starts an executable program and returns the task ID if successful. If unsuccessful, an error occurs.

Usage   *DoubleValue* = Shell(*PathName*:=[, *WindowStyle*:=])

The Shell() function does *not* block; it waits for the program to finish. The program you start and your program will run simultaneously, so be careful about any assumptions you make!

You can use the return value from Shell() with the AppActivate statement to activate the new program at any time (well, not always . . . see BUG in AppActivate).

vbNormalNoFocus does not always work. Consider this:

```
myApp = Shell("calc.exe", vbNormalNoFocus)
```

This calculator still has the focus after this command runs.

Parameter	Value	Meaning
PathName	String	The name of a program or a document that has been associated with an executable program. If PathName does not contain the full path, the specified program must be on the system's search PATH. PathName should contain any command-line arguments you wish to use.
WindowStyle	Omitted	Same as vbMinimizedFocus
	vbHide or 0	The application window is activated, but it is supposed to be hidden. We can't see any difference between this and vbMinimizedFocus. It does not behave like GetObject(), which really creates a hidden instance of an application.
	vbNormalFocus or 1	The application window is activated and is restored to its most recent size and position.
	vbMinimizedFocus or 2	The application window is activated and is displayed as an icon.
	vbMaximizedFocus or 3	The application window is activated and is maximized.
	vbNormalNoFocus or 4	The application window is restored to its most recent size and position, but the currently active window remains active. This does not work for all applications.
	vbMinimizedNoFocus or 6	The application window is displayed as an icon, and the currently active window remains active.

Example

```
Sub DeleteFiles(path$, pattern$)
    On Error GoTo NotStarted
    AppActivate "Exploring", True 'Activate Explorer Window
    On Error GoTo 0
    SendKeys "% R%TFF", True      'Find Files
    SendKeys "%N" & pattern$ & "%L" & path$ & "%i", True
    SendKeys "%EA", True          'Select All
    SendKeys "{DEL}Y", True       'Delete All
    SendKeys "%{F4}", True        'Close Find window
    SendKeys "% n", True          'Minimize Explorer
    Exit Sub
NotStarted:
    MyApp = Shell("Explorer.exe", vbMinimizedNoFocus)
    Resume
End Sub

Sub DeleteTmpFiles
    DeleteFiles "F:\", "*.tmp"
End Sub
```

This example tries to activate the Explorer window. If there is no Explorer window, the error-trapping uses Shell() to start up the application before resuming. The DeleteFiles routine uses Explorer to remove all files matching the pattern beneath a starting directory.

Switch Function

Switch() accepts any number of *Expr/Value* pairs of arguments.

Usage   *VariantValue* = Switch(*Expr1*, *Value1*[, *Expr2*, *Value2*,...[, *ExprN*, *ValueN*]])

It evaluates *all* the *Expr* expressions as Boolean values, and it returns the *Value* associated with the first *Expr* expression that evaluates to True. Switch() returns Null if no *Expr* expressions evaluate to True, or if the *Value* corresponding to the first True expression is Null.

Note again that all expressions and values are evaluated before Switch() returns, even if the first expression returns True, so side effects will need to be avoided.

PARAMETER	VALUE	MEANING
Expr	Any expression	The expression is evaluated as a Boolean value. The first one that evaluates to True causes the corresponding value to be returned.
Value	Any expression	This value or the result of this expression is returned if the corresponding Expr expression is the first one that returns True. Each Expr expression must have a corresponding value. Otherwise, the call generates an error.

Example
```
Function GLocks(temp As Double)
    GLocks = Switch(temp > 100, " too hot!", _
        temp < 96, " too cold!", _
        temp >= 96 And temp <= 100, " just right!")
End Function

Sub TestSwitch()
    Dim Temperature As Double
    Temperature 98.6
    Debug.Print "This porridge is" & GLocks(Temperature)
End Sub
```

Return   `This porridge is just right!`

Note that Switch() performs similar functions as the Select...Case statements, but it can be more compact in terms of code. One thing that Switch() is missing is the equivalent of the Case Else statement that will return a default result in case no expressions evaluate to True. You can mimic this behavior by checking for Switch() returning Null. For instance, GLocks() may be written as in the following example:

Example
```
Function GLocks(temp As Double)
    GLocks = Switch(temp > 100, " too hot!", _
        temp < 96, " too cold!")
    If IsNull(GLocks) Then GLocks = " just right!"
End Function
```

The Math Module

This section describes mathematical functions.

Atn Function

Atn() calculates the arctangent of a number and returns the result in radians as a value between –pi/2 and pi/2. The *Number* argument can be any valid numeric expression.

Usage   *DoubleValue* = Atn(*Number*:=)

The arctangent function is the inverse of the tangent function (Tan()), such that *tan*(Atn(*x*)) = *x* for any value *x*.

For a right triangle, the ratio of the lengths of its two perpendicular sides uniquely defines all angles in the right triangle. The arctangent function calculates one of these angles, given a number that is the ratio of the length of the side opposite the angle to that of the side adjacent to the angle.

Example   `Debug.Print Atn(1)`

Return   `0.785398163397448`

This return value is pi/4. To get the return value in degrees, multiply the result by 180/pi. A problem is that pi is not a constant in VBA. Luckily, since we know (OK, some of us know) that Atn(1) is pi/4, we can calculate pi as in this example:

Example   `pi = 4 * Atn(1)`
              `    Debug.Print Atn(1) * (180 /pi)`

Return   `45`

Cos Function

Cos() calculates the cosine of an angle that is expressed in radians. The return value ranges from –1 to 1. The *Number* argument can be any valid numeric expression.

Usage   *DoubleValue* = Cos(*Number*:=)

In terms of a right triangle, the cosine of an angle can be briefly described as the ratio of the length of the side adjacent to the angle to the length of the side opposite the right angle (hypotenuse). This description is valid only if the angle is between 0 and pi/2, but the cosine function is well defined for any angular value.

Example   `pi = 4 * Atn(1)`
              `    Debug.Print Cos(pi / 4)`

Return   `0.707106781186548`

Because of limited numerical precision, the return values will not be exact. For instance, the cosine of pi/2 is 0, but because we cannot represent pi exactly (only by the above calculation), you will get the following:

Example
```
pi = 4 * Atn(1)
     Debug.Print Cos(pi / 2)
```

Return   `6.12303176911189E-17`

Exp Function

Exp() calculates the base of the natural logarithm, *e*, raised to the specified power: e^{Number}.

Usage   *DoubleValue* = Exp(*Number*:=)

This is the inverse function of Log(). That is, $log(Exp(x)) = x$ for any value x. The *Number* argument can be any numeric expression that evaluates to a value less than 709.78271289338402. It can be any negative value.

One use of Exp() is to allow you to perform calculations of large numbers without producing intermediate overflow errors. Consider the following example:

Example
```
Sub TestLog()
        a = 3.4E+307
        b = 2.5E+209
        c = 5.6E+256
        'd = a * b / c
        d = Exp(Log(a) + Log(b) - Log(c))
        Debug.Print d
    End Sub
```

Return   `1.51785714285726E+260`

Note that although the final result and all individual values are within the range of a double-precision number, the intermediate result would cause the calculation to overflow. Using Log() and Exp() ensures that all values remain within range.

The following calculates *e* (within the precision of the machine):

Example   `e = Exp(1)`

Return   `2.71828182845905`

Log Function

Log() calculates the natural logarithm of a number.

Usage   *DoubleValue* = Log(*Number*:=)

The *Number* argument must be a value or a numeric expression that evaluates to a positive number greater than 2.47032822920624E-324.

Log() and Exp() are inverses of each other. That is, *log*(Exp(*x*)) = *x* for any value *x*.

See Exp() for an example of the use of Log() and Exp().

Randomize Statement

The Randomize statement is used in conjunction with the Rnd() function. It initializes the random-number generator.

Usage   Randomize[*Number*:=]

You "seed" the random-number generator with the numeric argument, but the sequence of numbers is *not* repeated if you call Randomize again with the same seed number. This behavior is different from that of other programming languages.

To repeat a sequence of *Number,* call Rnd() with a negative number before calling Randomize.

PARAMETER	VALUE	MEANING
Number	Any numeric expression	A seed for the random-number generator. Used to change the sequence of numbers returned by Rnd(). The number can be in the range of a double-precision number.
	Omitted	Uses as a seed the value returned by the system timer.

We're not sure why Randomize is needed, since Rnd() also is able to provide a seed to the random-number generator by using a negative-valued argument. In fact, if Randomize is never called, Rnd() will seed itself.

Example
```
Sub RandomizeRepeat(Seed)
        Rnd(-1)
        Randomize Seed
    End Sub
```

This routine allows you to repeat a sequence of random numbers corresponding to the specified seed.

Rnd Function

Rnd() returns a random number between 0 and 1. (It's supposed to be able to return 0, but we never got a value less than about 3E-07.)

Usage   *SingleValue* = Rnd([*Number*:=])

The input argument, *Number,* can be any numeric expression that returns a value within the acceptable range for a single-precision number.

PARAMETER	VALUE	MEANING
Number	Negative	Reinitializes the random-number generator using the number as a seed. Calling Rnd() with the same negative number always returns the same value.
	0	Returns the most recently generated random number. It's the number returned by the last Rnd() call, provided Randomize was not called.
	Positive or omitted	Returns the next number in the random-number sequence.

To get random numbers between any two numbers, try one of the following examples:

Example
```
Function Rand(lower, upper)
        Rand = (upper - lower) * Rnd + lower
    End Function
```

Example
```
Function RandInt(lower, upper)
        RandInt = Int((upper - lower + 1) * Rnd) + lower
    End Function
```

Sin Function

Sin() calculates the sine of an angle that is expressed in radians. The return value ranges from –1 to 1.

Usage   *DoubleValue* = Sin(*Number:*=)

The *Number* argument can be any valid numeric expression.

In terms of a right triangle, the sine of an angle can be briefly described as the ratio of the length of the side opposite to the angle to the length of the side opposite the right angle (hypotenuse). This description is valid only if the angle is between 0 and pi/2, but the sine function is well defined for any angular value.

Example
```
pi = 4 * Atn(1)
    Debug.Print Sin(pi / 4)
```

Return   `0.707106781186548`

Because of limited numerical precision, the return values will not be exact. For instance, the sine of pi is 0, but because we cannot represent pi exactly (only by the above calculation), we get the following:

Example
```
pi = 4 * Atn(1)
    Debug.Print Sin(pi)
```

Return   `1.22460635382238E-16`

Sqr Function

Sqr() calculates the square root of a number.

Usage   *DoubleValue* = Sqr(*Number*:=)

The *Number* argument can be any value or numeric expression that evaluates to a number greater than or equal to 0.

Example   `Sqr(65536)`

Return   `256`

Tan Function

Tan() calculates the tangent of an angle expressed in radians.

Usage   *DoubleValue* = Tan(*Number*:=)

The *Number* argument can be any valid numeric expression. The tangent function is the inverse of the arctangent function, Atn(), such that $tan(\text{Atn}(x)) = x$ for any value x.

For a right triangle, the ratio of the lengths of its two perpendicular sides uniquely defines all angles in the right triangle. Given one of the angles, Tan() calculates the ratio of the length of the side opposite the angle to that of the side adjacent to the angle. This description is valid only for angles between 0 and pi/2, but Tan() is well defined for any angular value.

Example
```
pi = 4 * Atn(1)
    Debug.Print Tan(pi / 2)
```

Return   `1.63317787283838E+16`

Because of the limited numeric precision, return values may not be as expected. The previous example should have overflowed (the tangent of pi/2 is infinity), but because we cannot represent pi exactly, the return value is merely a large number.

The Strings Module

The functions in this section perform string manipulation.

Asc Function

Asc() returns the ANSI character code of the first letter of *String*. If *String* is an empty string, an error occurs.

Usage	*IntegerValue* = Asc(String:=)

Example
```
Debug.Print Asc("Zebra")
    Debug.Print Asc("Z")
    Debug.Print Asc("z")
```

Return
```
90
    90
    122
```

If the language version on your system uses wide characters, it may be safer to use AscB() and AscW() to make sure you're getting the values (byte or character) you want.

AscB Function

AscB() returns the value of the first byte of *String*. If *String* is an empty string, an error occurs.

Usage	*IntegerValue* = AscB(*String*:=)

This function becomes important if the language on your system uses double-byte (wide) characters.

AscW Function

AscW() returns the native character code of the first letter of *String*. If *String* is an empty string, an error occurs.

Usage	*IntegerValue* = AscW(*String*:=)

This function becomes important if the language on your system uses double-byte (wide) characters.

Chr Function

Chr() returns as a Variant value the character corresponding to the specified ANSI character code. Character codes from 0 to 31 are equivalent to the ASCII character codes.

Usage	*VariantValue* = Chr(*CharCode*:=)

Depending on the language version on your system, characters may be 2 bytes, so you can use ChrB() and ChrW() to specify explicitly byte or double-byte codes. *CharCode* must evaluate to a value ranging from 0 to 255.

Example
```
Sub ShowChr(Str)
    For i = 1 To Len(Str)
        c = Asc(Mid(Str, i, 1))
        Debug.Print Chr(c) & ", " & c
    Next i
End Sub
Sub TestChr(Str)
    ShowChr "String"
End Sub
```

Return
```
S, 83
t, 116
r, 114
i, 105
n, 110
g, 103
```

ChrB Function

ChrB() returns as a Variant value specified byte.

Usage   *VariantValue* = ChrB(*CharCode*:=)

Depending on the language version on your system, characters may be 2 bytes, so you can use ChrB() return values that correspond to single bytes. *CharCode* must evaluate to a value ranging from 0 to 255.

ChrW Function

ChrW() returns as a Variant value the character corresponding to the specified native character code.

Usage   *VariantValue* = ChrW(*CharCode*:=)

Depending on the language version on your system, characters may be 2 bytes, so you can use ChrW() to specify explicitly double-byte codes. *CharCode* must evaluate to a value ranging from 0 to 65,535.

Format Function

Format() formats an expression for display and returns the result as a string Variant value. With no optional arguments specified, this function is equivalent to the CStr() function.

Usage   *VariantValue* = Format(*Expression*:=[, *Format*:=][, *FirstDayOfWeek*:=]
             [, *FirstWeekOfYear*:=])

The *FirstDayOfWeek* and *FirstWeekOfYear* arguments make sense only for dates you want to display as the weekday or week number in a year.

PARAMETER	VALUE	MEANING
Expression	Any expression	The expression whose value you want to present in a particular format.
Format	String	Any valid named format or a string describing the user-defined format.
FirstDayOfWeek	vbUseSystem or 0	Uses NLS API setting.
	vbSunday or 1 or Omitted	Sunday
	vbMonday or 2	Monday
	vbTuesday or 3	Tuesday
	vbWednesday or 4	Wednesday
	vbThursday or 5	Thursday
	vbFriday or 6	Friday
	vbSaturday or 7	Saturday
	Other value	Error
FirstWeekOfYear	vbUseSystem or 0	Uses NLS API setting.
	vbFirstJan1 or 1 or Omitted	Starts with the week in which January 1 occurs.
	VbFirstFourDays or 2	Starts with the first week that has at least 4 days in the year.
	vbFirstFullWeek or 3	Starts with the first full week of the year.
	Other value	Error

Number Formats

A number-format string can consist of four sections, each of which is separated by semi-colons. The following table gives the interpretation of the sections.

SECTION	MEANING
First	Used for all positive numbers. If only one section is given, it applies to all numbers. If only two sections are given, it also applies to zero values.
Second	Used for all negative numbers.
Third	Used for all zero values.
Fourth	Used if Expression is Null.

Each format section consists of a string with characters that represent placeholders for specific parts of a number. The following table describes the valid formatting characters. All other characters will be displayed literally and use a backslash to display literally one of the special characters.

FORMAT CHARACTER(S)	MEANING	DESCRIPTION
None	No formatting	Displays the expression with no formatting.

0	Digits placeholder	Displays a digit or a zero.
		    The number of zeros to the right of the decimal in the format string specifies the exact number of digits that are to be displayed to the right of the decimal. Rounding is to the specified number of digits. An expression that has fewer digits is padded with zeros.
		    The number of zeros to the left of the decimal in the format string specifies the minimum number of digits to display and pads zeros from the left if the expression has fewer digits.
		    If the expression has more digits to the left of the decimal than the format string has, the additional digits are displayed as is.

#	Digits placeholder	Displays a digit or nothing.
		    The number of # placeholders to the right of the decimal in the format string controls rounding but does not pad with zeros if the expression result has fewer digits.
		    The number of # placeholders to the left of the decimal of the format string is useful only when used in conjunction with the thousands separator.

.	Decimal separator	In some locales, a comma is used as the decimal separator.
		    If you want the fractional part of a number displayed, you have to include the decimal-separator character in the format string.
		    Without the decimal separator, the fractional part is not displayed. You need a digits placeholder (0 or #) to the right of the decimal to display any digits.

%	Percentage placeholder	The expression is multiplied by 100. The percent character (%) is inserted in the position in which it appears in the format string.

,	Thousands separator	In some locales, a period is used as a thousands separator.
		    If you want a thousands separator to be displayed, you have to include the separator character in the format string surrounded by digits placeholders (0 or #). Thousands separators appear to the left of the decimal and separate every 3 digits.
		    All right, here's an interesting twist. If the right-most thousands separator in the format string does not have a digits placeholder to its right, no thousands separators will be displayed, but the number will be divided by 1,000. Each additional thousands separator immediately to the left of the right-most one causes an additional division of 1,000. If you choose to use this scaling method, you'll need another thousands separator in the format string that is surrounded by digit placeholders in order to have thousands separators appear in the result.

FORMAT CHARACTER(S)	MEANING	DESCRIPTION
E– E+ e– e+	Scientific format	The E–, E+, e–, or e+ scientific-format placeholders must have a digits placeholder (0 or #) immediately to the right of it and another one to the left, although not necessarily adjacent to it. Scientific format is simply shorthand for "multiply the number to the left of the placeholder (mantissa) by 10 raised to the power of the number to the right of the placeholder (exponent)." Thus 1.234e+3 = 1.234 * 10^3 = 1234. Accordingly, the digits placeholders to the left of the scientific-format placeholder specify formatting for the mantissa and those to the right specify formatting for the exponent. E– and e– place minus signs next to negative exponents and nothing for positive exponents. E+ and e+ place plus signs next to positive exponents and minus signs next to negative exponents.
– + $ ( ) space	Literal character	These characters are displayed literally in the location indicated in the format string. Any other characters must be preceded by a backslash (\).
\	Quote character	The character following the \ is displayed literally. To display a backslash, use two of them (\\). To display a double quote, use two of them ("").
"" Chr(34)	Literal string	Displays the characters between a pair of double-quotes literally as a string. To specify this formatting from code, you need to use either Chr(34) for the double-quote characters or two double-quotes.

Example

```
a = 24.135
    Debug.Print Format(a, ".00")
    Debug.Print Format(a, ".0000")
    Debug.Print Format(a, "0.0000")
    Debug.Print Format(a, "000")
```

Return

```
24.14
    24.1350
    24.1350
    024
```

Example

```
a = 24.135
    Debug.Print Format(a, ".##")
    Debug.Print Format(a, ".####")
    Debug.Print Format(a, "#.####")
    Debug.Print Format(a, "###")
```

Return

```
24.14
    24.135
    24.135
    24
```

Example

```
a = 0.35
```

```
                    Debug.Print Format(a, "%")
                    Debug.Print Format(a, "#.000%")
                    Debug.Print Format(a, "#.###%")
```

Return   35%
                   35.000%
                   35.%

Example   a = 1234567890.12
                    Debug.Print Format(a, "#,#")
                    Debug.Print Format(a, "#,#.0")
                    Debug.Print Format(a, "#,") & " K"
                    Debug.Print Format(a, "#,#,") & " K"
                    Debug.Print Format(a, "#,,.000") & " M"

Return   1,234,567,890
                   1,234,567,890.1
                   1234568 K
                   1,234,568 K
                   1235.6 M

Example   a = 1234567890.12
                    Debug.Print Format(a, "0e-000")
                    Debug.Print Format(a, "#.000e+###")
                    Debug.Print Format(a, "#,000E+###")

Return   1e009
                   1.235e+9
                   1,235E+6

Example   a = 12345678.12
                    DQ$ = Chr(34)
                    Debug.Print Format(a, DQ$ & "You have just won " & DQ$ & _
                        "$#,#,,\M\!")
                    Debug.Print Format(a, """You have just won """ & _
                        "$#,#,,\M\!")

Return   You have just won $12M!
                   You have just won $12M!

Example   fmt$ = "#,#.##;(#,#.##);-0-;-NULL-"
                    Debug.Print Format(12.3, fmt$)
                    Debug.Print Format(-12.3, fmt$)
                    Debug.Print Format(0, fmt$)
                    Debug.Print Format(Null, fmt$)

Return   12.3
                   (12.3)
                   -0-
                   -NULL-
```
```

As a convenience, VBA defines some *named* number formats that represent predefined formats for specific classes of numbers. Using these named formats can make your formatting independent of the locale settings for systems running your code.

Format Name	Equiv. Format String	Description
General Number	0.############	Displays the number as is, with no thousands separators.
Currency	$#,0.00;$(#,0.00)	Displays the number with the thousands separator, if appropriate; displays 2 digits to the right of the decimal separator. The currency symbol in the output depends on the system locale settings.
Fixed	0.00	Displays at least 1 digit to the left and 2 to the right of the decimal separator.
Standard	#,0.00	Displays the number with the thousands separator—at least 1 digit to the left and 2 to the right of the decimal separator.
Percent	0.00%	Displays the number multiplied by 100 with a percent sign (%) appended to the right. Always displays 2 digits to the right of the decimal separator.
Scientific	0.00E+00	Uses standard scientific notation.
Yes/No	""Yes"";""Yes""; ""No""	Displays No if number is 0; otherwise, displays Yes.
True/False	""True"";""True""; ""False""	Displays False if number is 0; otherwise, displays True.
On/Off	""On"";""On""; ""Off""	Displays Off if number is 0; otherwise, displays On.

Date and Time Formats

The formatting for short and long dates is specified using the formatting characters described in the following table.

Format Character(s)	Meaning	Description
:	Time separator	Represents the time separator. In some locales, other characters may be used to represent the time separator. The time separator separates hours, minutes, and seconds for time values.
/	Date separator	Represents the date separator. In some locales, other characters may be used to represent the date separator. The date separator separates the day, month, and year for short-date formats.

FORMAT CHARACTER(S)	MEANING	DESCRIPTION
c	Date and time	Displays the date in short-date format and then the time. If either the time or date part is missing, that part is not displayed. The date part of the format is equivalent to ddddd, and the time part of the format is equivalent to ttttt.
d	Simple day	Displays the day of the month without a leading zero.
dd	Day	Displays the day of the month with a leading zero (if needed).
ddd	Abbrev. weekday	Displays the weekday name as an abbreviation.
dddd	Weekday	Displays the full weekday name.
ddddd	Short date	Displays complete date in the short-date format for your system. The default setting is equivalent to m/d/yy.
dddddd	Long date	Displays the complete date in the long-date format for your system. The default setting is equivalent to dddd, mmmm dd, yyyy.
w	Week day number	Displays the day of the week as a number (1 for Sunday through 7 for Saturday). This number is affected by the FirstDayOfWeek argument.
ww	Week	Displays the week of the year as a number. This number is affected by the FirstDayOfWeek and FirstWeekOfYear arguments.
m	Simple month or simple minute	Displays the month of the year as a number without a leading zero. If m immediately follows h or hh, then it displays minutes without a leading zero.
mm	Month or minute	Displays the month of the year as a number with a leading zero (if needed). If mm immediately follows h or hh, then it displays minutes with a leading zero (if needed).
mmm	Abbrev. month	Displays the month name as an abbreviation.
mmmm	Month	Displays the full month name.
q	q	Displays the quarter of the year as a number.
y	Day of year	Displays the day of the year as a number without a leading zero.
yy	Simple year	Displays the year as a 2-digit number (with a leading zero when needed).
yyyy	Year	Displays the year as the full 4-digit number.
h	Simple hour	Displays the hour of the day without a leading zero.
hh	Hour	Displays the hour of the day with a leading zero when needed.
n	Simple minute	Displays the minute of the hour without a leading zero.
nn	Minute	Displays the minute of the hour with a leading zero when needed.
s	Simple second	Displays the second of the minute without a leading zero.
ss	Second	Displays the second of the minute with a leading zero when needed.
ttttt	Time	Displays the time in the system time format. The default is equivalent to h:mm:ss AMPM.

Format Character(s)	Meaning	Description
AM/PM	12-hour format	Displays the time in the 12-hour format. Time before noon is displayed using uppercase AM and after noon using uppercase PM.
am/pm	12-hour format	Displays the time in the 12-hour format. Time before noon is displayed using lowercase am and after noon using lowercase pm.
A/P	12-hour format	Displays the time in the 12-hour format. Time before noon is displayed using uppercase A and after noon using uppercase P.
a/p	12-hour format	Displays the time in the 12-hour format. Time before noon is displayed using lowercase a and after noon using lowercase p.
AMPM	12-hour format	Displays the time in the 12-hour format. The AM and PM strings defined in your system settings are used.

As a convenience, VBA defines some *named* date and time. Using these named formats can make your formatting independent of the locale settings for systems running your code, since it's already taken care of for you.

Format Name	Equiv. Format String	Description
General Date	c	Displays a date and/or time. The date is in the short-date format for your system, and the time uses the time format for your system.
Long Date	dddddd	Displays a date according to your system's long-date format.
Medium Date	dd-mmm-yy	Displays a date using the medium-date format of your system. (The equivalent format string may not match that on your system.)
Short Date	ddddd	Displays a date using your system's short-date format.
Long Time	ttttt	Displays a time using your system's long-time format. Includes hours, minutes, seconds, and, possibly, AM/PM.
Medium Time	hh:mm AM/PM	Displays a time in the 12-hour format using hours and minutes and AM/PM.
Short Time	hh:mm	Displays a time using the 24-hour format, but without seconds.

String Formats

A String-format string can consist of two sections, each of which is separated by semi-colons. The interpretation of the sections are in this table:

Section	Meaning
First	Used for non-Null and non-empty strings.
Second	Used if Expression is Null and strings are zero-length.

Each format section consists of a string of formatting characters. The following table describes the valid formatting characters.

FORMAT	MEANING	DESCRIPTION
@	Character placeholder	Displays a string or a space. Each placeholder (@ or &) in the format string (not necessarily adjacent to each other) corresponds to a character in the input expression. The right-most placeholder corresponds to the right-most character in the expression (unless the ! format character is used). If there are fewer characters in Expression than the number of placeholders, the left-most @ placeholders in the format string are replaced with spaces. If there are more characters in Expression than the number of placeholders, the left-most characters of Expression that did not match a placeholder are displayed first as the left-most characters of the result (unless the ! format character is used).
&	Character placeholder	Displays a string or nothing. Each placeholder (@ or &) in the format string (not necessarily adjacent to each other) corresponds to a character in the input expression. The right-most placeholder corresponds to the right-most character in the expression (unless the ! format character is used). If there are fewer characters in Expression than the number of placeholders, the left-most & placeholders in the format string are ignored. If there are more characters in Expression than the number of placeholders, the left-most characters of Expression that did not match a placeholder are displayed first as the left-most characters of the result (unless the ! format character is used).
<	Force lowercase	Displays all characters from Expression in lowercase.
>	Force uppercase	Displays all characters from Expression in uppercase.
!	Left justification	Forces left-to-right fill of placeholders. That is, the left-most placeholder matches the left-most character of Expression. If there are more characters in Expression than the number of placeholders, the right-most characters of Expression that did not match a placeholder are displayed last as the right-most characters of the result.

Example

```
Sub FormatAnswers(answers)
    fmt = ""
    For i = 1 To Len(answers)
        fmt = fmt & """Answer " & i & ": ""@" & vbCr
    Next i
    Debug.Print Format(answers, fmt)
End Sub

Sub TestFormat()
    FormatAnswers("dbabdc")
End Sub
```

Result

```
Answer 1: d
    Answer 2: b
```

```
Answer 3: a
Answer 4: b
Answer 5: d
Answer 6: c
```

LCase Function

LCase() converts all characters of *String* to lowercase and returns the result.

Usage   *VariantValue* = LCase(*String*:=)

If *String* is Null, LCase() returns Null. LCase() can be useful when performing case-insensitive compares.

Example
```
fname$ = Dir("*.ini")
   Do While LCase(fname$) <> LCase(myini$)
       fname$ = Dir()
   Loop
   If LCase(fname$) = LCase(myini$) Then Found = True
```

Left Function

Left retrieves the specified number of characters from the beginning of *String*.

Usage   *VariantValue* = Left(*String*:=, *Length*:=)

If *String* contains Null, Left() returns Null.

PARAMETER	VALUE	MEANING
String	Any string	The input string, whose left-most characters you want.
Length	0	Returns a zero-length string.
	Positive	Specifies the number of characters to get. If the number is greater than the string length, the entire string is returned. The maximum value is $2^{30} - 1 = 1073741823$.
	Negative	Error

LeftB Function

LeftB() returns the specified number of bytes from the beginning of *String*.

Usage   *VariantValue* = LeftB(*String*:=, *Length*:=)

The distinction from Left() is important on systems using double-byte (wide) character sets. If *String* contains Null, LeftB() returns Null.

PARAMETER	VALUE	MEANING
String	Any string	The input string, whose left-most bytes you want.
Length	0	Returns a zero-length string.
	Positive	Specifies the number of bytes to get. If the number is greater than the string length, the entire string is returned. The maximum value is $2^{31} - 1 = 2147483647$.
	Negative	Error

LTrim Function

LTrim() removes leading spaces from *String* and returns the result.

Usage   *VariantValue* = LTrim(*String*:=)

It does *not* remove other white-space characters, such as the tab (Chr(9)), carriage-return (Chr(13)), and newline (Chr(11)). If *String* contains Null, then LTrim() returns Null.

Mid Function

Mid() retrieves the specified number of characters from the middle of *String*. If *String* contains Null, Left() returns Null.

Usage   *ReturnValue* = Mid(*String*:=, *Start*:=[, *Length*:=])

PARAMETER	VALUE	MEANING
String	Any string	The input string containing the characters you want to get.
Start	Greater than 0	The character position of the first character to retrieve. If it is greater than the length of String, Mid() returns a zero-length string. The first character position of String is 1. The maximum value can be $2^{30} = 1073741824$.
	0 or less	Error
Length	0 or Greater	The number of characters to retrieve, starting with the character position specified by Start. If the number is greater than the length of String, all characters from Start to the end of String are returned. The maximum value can be $2^{30} - 1 = 1073741823$.
	Omitted	All characters from the Start position to the end of the String are returned.
	Negative	Error

Mid Statement

The Mid statement replaces the specified characters in a string variable with *String*. The length of *StringVar* is never changed. *String* cannot contain Null.

Usage   Mid(*StringVar*, *Start*[, *Length*]) = *String*

PARAMETER	VALUE	MEANING
StringVar	String variable	The string variable whose contents you wish to change.
Start	Number from 1 through Len(StringVar)	The character position of the first character of StringVar to be replaced.

Length	Positive	The maximum number of characters to replace.
		    The length of the string in StringVar is never changed by the replacement. If Start + Length is greater than Len(StringVar), then all characters from Start to the end of StringVar are replaced.
		    If the length of String is less than Length, then only Len(String) characters are replaced.
		    The maximum value can be $2^{30} - 1 = 1073741823$.

String	Any valid string expression	Only the first Length characters of String are used for replacement. Start + Length is larger than the length of the StringVar. Only the first (Len(StringVar) – Start + 1) characters of String are used.

MidB Function

MidB() returns the specified number of bytes from the middle of *String*.

Usage   *VariantValue* = MidB(*String*:=, *Start*:=[, *Length*:=])

PARAMETER	VALUE	MEANING
String	Any string	The input string containing the bytes you want to get.
Start	Greater than 0	The byte position of the first byte to retrieve. If it is greater than the length of String, MidB() returns a zero-length string. The first byte position of String is 1. The maximum value can be $2^{31} - 1 = 2147483647$.
	0 or less	Error
Length	0 or greater	The number of bytes to retrieve, starting with the byte position specified by Start. If the number is greater than the length of String, all bytes from Start to the end of String are returned. The maximum value can be $2^{31} - 1 = 2147483647$.
	Omitted	All bytes from the Start position to the end of the String are returned.
	Negative	Error

The distinction from Mid() is important on systems using double-byte (wide) character sets. If *String* contains Null, MidB() returns Null.

MidB Statement

The MidB statement replaces the specified bytes in a string variable with *String*.

Usage   MidB(*StringVar*, *Start*[, *Length*]) = *String*

The length of *StringVar* is never changed. *String* cannot contain Null.

PARAMETER	VALUE	MEANING
StringVar	String variable	The string variable whose contents you wish to change.
Start	Number from 1 through Len(StringVar)	The byte position of the first byte of StringVar to be replaced.
Length	Positive	The maximum number of bytes to replace. The length of the string in StringVar is never changed by the replacement. If Start + Length is greater than the length of StringVar, then all characters from Start to the end of StringVar are replaced. If the length of String is less than Length, then only the number of bytes of String characters are replaced. The maximum value can be 2^31 − 1 = 2147483647.
String	Any valid string expression	Only the first Length bytes of String are used for replacement. Start + Length is larger than the length of the StringVar. Only the first (Len(StringVar) − Start + 1) bytes of String are used.

Right Function

Right() retrieves the specified number of characters from the end of *String*.

Usage   *VariantValue* = Right(*String*:=, *Length*:=)

If *String* contains Null, Right() returns Null.

PARAMETER	VALUE	MEANING
String	Any string	The input string, whose right-most characters you want.
Length	0	Returns a zero-length string.
	Positive	Specifies the number of characters to get. If the number is greater than the string length, the entire string is returned. The maximum value is 2^30 − 1 = 1073741823.
	Negative	Error

RightB Function

RightB() returns the specified number of bytes from the end of *String*.

Usage   *VariantValue* = RightB(*String*:=, *Length*:=)

The distinction from Right() is important on systems using double-byte (wide) character sets. If *String* contains Null, RightB() returns Null.

PARAMETER	VALUE	MEANING
String	Any string	The input string, whose right-most bytes you want.
Length	0	Returns a zero-length string.
	Positive	Specifies the number of bytes to get. If the number is greater than the string length, the entire string is returned. The maximum value is $2^{31} - 1 = 2147483647$.
	Negative	Error

RTrim Function

RTrim() removes trailing spaces from *String* and returns the result.

Usage   *VariantValue* = RTrim(*String*:=)

It does *not* remove other white-space characters, such as the tab (Chr(9)), carriage-return (Chr(13)), and newline (Chr(11)). If *String* contains Null, then LTrim() returns Null.

Space Function

Space() returns a string containing the specified number of spaces.

Usage   *VariantValue* = Space(*Number*:=)

StrConv Function

StrConv() is a generic string-conversion function.

Usage   *VariantValue* = StrConv(*String*:=, *Conversion*:=)

PARAMETER	VALUE	MEANING
String	Any string	The string for which conversion will apply.
Conversion	vbUpperCase or 1	Converts the string to uppercase characters.
	vbLowerCase or 2	Converts the string to lowercase characters.
	vbProperCase or 3	Converts the first letter of every word in String to uppercase.
	vbWide or 4	Converts narrow (single-byte) characters in String to wide (double-byte) characters (Far East locales).
	vbNarrow or 8	Converts wide (double-byte) characters in String to narrow (single-byte) characters (Far East locales).
	vbKatakana or 16	Converts Hiragana characters in String to Katakana characters (Japan only).
	vbHiragana or 32	Converts Katakana characters in String to Hiragana characters (Japan only).
	vbUnicode or 64	Converts the string to Unicode using the default code page of the system. (An error on 16-bit systems.)
	vbFromUnicode or 128	Converts the string from Unicode to the default code page of the system. (An error on 16-bit systems.)

String Function

String() returns a string composed of the specified number of the specified character.

Usage   *VariantValue* = String(*Number*:=, *Character*:=)

PARAMETER	VALUE	MEANING
Number	0 or greater	The number of characters to return.
Character	String	Only the first character is used. It is repeated Number of times to form the output string.
	Number	Represents an ANSI character code from 0 to 255. If the value is outside the range, Character Mod 256 is used.

Example   `Debug.Print "'" & String(62, "_") & "'"`

Return   '_____

Trim Function

Trim() removes beginning *and* trailing spaces from *String* and returns the result.

Usage   *VariantValue* = Trim(*String*:=)

It does *not* remove other white-space characters, such as the tab (Chr(9)), carriage-return (Chr(13)), and newline (Chr(11)). If *String* contains Null, then LTrim() returns Null.

UCase Function

UCase() converts all characters of *String* to uppercase and returns the result.

Usage   *VariantValue* = UCase(*String*:=)

If *String* is Null, UCase() returns Null. UCase() can be useful when performing case-insensitive compares.

Example
```
fname$ = Dir("*.ini")
  Do While UCase(fname$) <> UCase(myini$)
      fname$ = Dir()
  Loop
  If UCase(fname$) = UCase(myini$) Then Found = True
```

SECTION 3: VB OBJECTS AND COLLECTIONS

I may be drunk, but you, madam, are ugly. At least when I wake in the morning, I'll be sober.

—Winston Churchill

This section describes Visual Basic objects. It also includes some constants and functions that do not fit elsewhere.

App Object

The App object is a global object that specifies information about the running VB application, including its title, the pathname of its executable and Help files, and whether a previous instance of the application is running.

Example

```
Private Sub Form_Load()
    'Recover all settings from registry
    If App.StartMode = vbSModeStandalone Then InitDialogs
End Sub
```

If your VB application can be run as either a standalone application or an OLE Automation OLE server, you can use the StartMode property of the App object to determine which mode is being run. You can check this in the Form_Load event, for instance, to determine whether you have to initialize the graphical-user-interface portions of your application.

Following are the properties of the App object. See the individual properties for more details.

Properties

Comments	CompanyName	EXEName
FileDescription	HelpFile	hInstance
LegalCopyright	LegalTrademarks	Major
Minor	OLERequestPendingMsgText	OLERequestPendingMsgTitle
OLERequestPendingTimeout	OLEServerBusyMsgText	OLEServerBusyMsgTitle
OLEServerBusyRaiseError	OLEServerBusyTimeout	Path
PrevInstance	ProductName	Revision
StartMode	TaskVisible	Title

Button Object

To create a toolbar, you need buttons. The Button object describes individual buttons, including the image a button will show and the tool tip that will appear when you hold your cursor over a button for a couple of seconds. At design time, right-click a Toolbar control and select Properties. Then select the Buttons pane to add, change, or remove buttons. At runtime, you can access a particular button—and add or remove buttons—via the Buttons collection of the Toolbar.

The one catch is that the Button object works only with Windows 95 and NT 3.51. Those of you left with Windows 3.11 or earlier are out of luck.

Button objects have no event procedures of their own. You need to use the ButtonClick event of the Toolbar to define what happens when a button is clicked. Button objects also have no methods.

Following are the properties of the Button object.

Properties

Caption	Description	Enabled
Height	Image	Index
Key	Left	MixedState
Style	Tag	ToolTipText
Top	Value	Visible
Width		

Buttons Collection

The Buttons collection is a bunch of Button objects grouped conveniently so that you can manipulate them for a toolbar.

 There's always a catch, though. Here's the one for the Buttons collection. This collection is what Microsoft calls a "1-based collection," which is a fancy way of saying it's nonstandard because it starts numbering its elements at 1 rather than 0. This means that if you want to get to the fifth button in a collection, you don't write

```
Toolbar1.Buttons(4)
```

Instead you write

```
Toolbar1.Buttons(5)
```

Use the Buttons collection's methods to manage the buttons of a Toolbar. Following are the property and methods of the Buttons collection.

Property

Count

Methods

Add	Clear	Item
Remove		

ClassModule Object

A ClassModule object defines a class that can contain both properties and methods for the class. Use a ClassModule object to define the code for the methods and for the setting and getting of its properties. Each ClassModule object defines a single class, named by its Name property. A project can include multiple ClassModule objects.

Create a ClassModule object at design time by selecting Insert/ClassModule. Create instances of a class in code by using the New keyword, such as

```
Dim MyInstance As New MyClass
```
where MyClass is the name of a ClassModule object.

Public Functions and Subs in a ClassModule object become its methods. Property Get, Property Let, and Property Set procedures in the ClassModule object define the custom properties of the class and the access methods for the properties.

A ClassModule object also has the following predefined properties and events.

Properties (Predefined)

Instancing   Name   Public

Events

Initialize   Terminate

Clipboard Object

The Clipboard object allows you to access the Window's Clipboard. It does not have any properties or event routines. It has only a set of methods you can use to manipulate text and graphics on the Clipboard so that you can copy, cut, or paste the text and graphics into your application.

The Clipboard can contain simultaneously one piece of data for each supported data type. Placing a set of data on the Clipboard will overwrite any data of the same type. Use the GetData and SetData commands to get data of different formats and use GetText and SetText to access regular text on the Clipboard.

See the documentation for the individual methods for more details.

Following are the methods of the Clipboard object.

Methods

Clear   GetData   GetFormat
GetText   SetData   SetText

Column Object/Columns Collection

The Column object is part of the DBGrid control; it represents a column in that control. With its properties and methods, you can set captions as well as lock and generally adjust a DBGrid's columns.

The Columns collection is a bunch of Column objects. You can use it to add, remove, and count columns in DBGrid.

Following are the properties and methods of the Column object.

Properties

Alignment	AllowSizing	BackColor, ForeColor
Caption	ColIndex	DataField
DefaultValue	DividerStyle	Font
HeadBackColor	HeadForeColor	Height, Width
Left, Top	Locked	NumberFormat
ScrollBars	Text	Value
Visible		

Methods

CellText   CellValue

Following are the property and methods of the columns collection.

Property

Count

Methods

Add(DBGrid)   Item   Remove

ColumnHeader Object/ColumnHeaders Collection

Windows 95 introduced a new way of looking at files; for example, in the Explorer. It's called the ListView. ListView enables you to view the items in a list as large icons, small icons, or a straightforward list. The ColumnHeader object contains text that describes the heading in the Report-style view of a ListView.

The column headers will appear only at runtime *and* when ListView control's View property is IvwReport (3).

The ColumnHeader object works only with Windows 95 and NT 3.51. (Those of you left with Windows 3.11 or earlier are out of luck.)

The ColumnHeaders collection contains a group of ColumnHeader objects. At design time, right-click a ListView control and select Properties. Then select the ColumnHeaders pane to add, remove, and define column headers. At runtime, you can access the ColumnHeader objects via ListView's ColumnHeaders collection.

Following are the properties of a ColumnHeader object.

Properties

Alignment	Index	Key
Left	SubItemIndex	Tag
Text	Width	

Following are the property and methods of the ColumnHeaders collection.

Property

Count

Methods

Add	Clear	Item
Remove		

Container Object/Containers Collection

The concept of the Container object is a little difficult to grasp at first. It's kind of like an object that consists of collections, but not quite. Each Database object has a Containers collection that consists of built-in Container objects. The built-in Container objects are Databases, Tables, and Relationships. Don't confuse these built-in Container *objects* with the collections by the same names. The difference is subtle but important: The Container objects refer to *all* the saved objects of that type, whereas the collections refer only to the *open* objects of that type. Applications may also define their own Container objects, but you can't define your own.

To make matters even more confusing, each Container object has a Documents collection that itself contains Document objects for each instance of the type of object it is describing. In other words, a Databases Container contains Document objects for each database object instance.

A Containers Collection is a group of Container objects.

So why should you care? Well, a Container object's properties enable you to find out an object's name, to find out who owns an object, and to control access permissions. To refer to a Container object, you can either call it as an index in the Containers collection—for example, Containers(1)—or by its Name property—for example, Containers(Databases).

Note: Security won't work if you don't have a SYSTEM.MDW file.

Following are the collections and properties of the Container object.

Collections

Documents	Properties

Properties

AllPermissions	Inherit	Name
Owner	Permissions	UserName

Following are the property and method of the Containers collection.

Property

Count

Method

Refresh

Control Object

A Control object is a type of object that you place on Form objects for interaction with the user. It accepts user input and displays information and output. Control objects have properties that specify their appearances and behavior. They may have methods that allow their manipulation via code. They also may have event procedures that allow you to customize their responses to user input. Use the Toolbox and the Menu Editor to add Control objects to your Forms. Use the Properties window to set Control properties at design time; many of these are also changeable at runtime.

Following are the standard Control objects:

CheckBox	HScrollBar
ComboBox	Image
CommandButton	Label
CommonDialog	Line
Data	ListBox
DBCombo	Menu
DBGrid	OLE Container
DBList	OptionButton
DirListBox	PictureBox
DriveListBox	Shape
FileListBox	TextBox
Frame	Timer
Grid	VScrollBar

Control is a well-known type in VB, so you can declare variables or procedure parameters As Control.

Example

```
Sub PrintTypeAndName(ByVal ctl As Control)
    Debug.Print TypeName(ctl) & ", " & ctl.name
End Sub
```

Controls Collection

The Controls collection enumerates all controls of a Form or MDIForm object. It is a form-level variable available only at runtime. Use the Controls collection to iterate through all controls on a form to perform some actions.

Usage

```
Control = [object.]Controls(Index)
Control = object(Index)
IntegerValue = [object.]Controls.Count
IntegerValue = object.Count
```

Applies To   Form Object
                  MDIForm Object

If you omit *object,* then the active form is used. You can also omit the Controls keyword if you provide the *object* name:

Example

```
For i = 0 To Form1.Count - 1
     Form1(i).Enabled = True
Next i
```

Omitting the Controls keyword may be confusing for people reading your code, since without it the code looks like it is manipulating Form arrays, and Form arrays do not exist in VB.

Following is the only property of the Controls collection.

Property

Count

Example

```
Sub PrintTypeAndName(ByVal ctl As Control)
    Debug.Print TypeName(ctl) & ", " & ctl.name
End Sub

Private Sub Form_DblClick()
    For i = 0 To Controls.Count - 1
         PrintTypeAndName (Controls(i))
    Next i
End Sub
```

Data Access Objects

It's howdy-data time. Typically, you'll access databases through controls such as the Data control. Sometimes you may find yourself accessing data directly through the Data Access Objects.

The following table lists the collections and objects that are part of the Data Access Objects (DAO) framework.

In addition, the Dynaset, Snapshot, and Table objects are replaced by the Recordset object with appropriate settings for its Type property. The Dynaset, Snapshot, and Table objects, however, still exist for backwards compatibility.

COLLECTION	OBJECT	MEANING
Columns	Column	Used to store column information for the DBGrid control.
Containers	Container	Stores information about a predefined object type.
Databases	Database	Refers to an open database.
None	DBEngine	Refers to the Microsoft Jet database engine.
Documents	Document	Stores information about a saved, predefined object.
Errors	Error	Stores information about any errors associated with this object.
Fields	Field	Refers to a column that is part of a table, query, index, relation, or recordset.
Groups	Group	Refers to a group of user accounts.
Indexes	Index	Refers to a predefined ordering and uniqueness of values in a table.
Parameters	Parameter	Stores a parameter for a parameter query.
Properties	Property	Refers to a built-in or user-defined property.
QueryDefs	QueryDef	Contains a saved query definition.
Recordsets	Recordset	Refers to the records in a base table or query.
Relations	Relation	Refers to a relationship between fields in tables and queries.
SelBookmarks	Bookmark	Refers to a set of selected rows in the DBGrid object.
TableDefs	TableDef	Contains a saved table definition.
Users	User	Refers to a user account.
Workspaces	Workspace	Refers to a session of the Jet database engine.

Database Object/Databases Collection

A Database object represents an open database. This object gives you a lot of power to really mess up your database. Trust us. Before you try any serious coding, play around with the methods and properties you think you'll need to see how they work. Words can't quite describe it.

At its simplest, the Database object enables you to examine a database—its tables, queries, and so on. But you can also create tables, queries, recordsets, whatever you feel like. You can even execute stored QueryDefs or pass along a SQL string. (Doing this is how we once "severely altered" [read: really messed up] a database; but that's a different story.)

This object requires you to have added a reference to the Data Access (DA) object library in the Object Browser. This means you have to have added the DAO Component Object Library in the References dialog.

A Databases collection represents all open Database objects in a given Workspace object. To use it, select Tools/References to add the DAO Component Object Library and then use the Object Browser to add a reference to the Data Access object library.

Following are the collections, properties, and methods of the Database object.

Collections

Containers	QueryDefs	Recordsets
Relations	TableDefs (default)	

Properties

CollatingOrder	Connect	Name
QueryTimeout	RecordsAffected	Transactions
Updatable	Version	V1xNullBehavior

Methods

Close	CreateProperty	CreateQueryDef
CreateRelation	CreateTableDef	Execute
ExecuteSQL	MakeReplica	OpenRecordset
Synchronize		

Following are the property and method of the Databases collection.

Property

Count

Method

Refresh

DBEngine Object

The mother of all database objects, the DBEngine object represents the Jet database engine. It is the top-level object. Consequently, it has no corresponding collection (how, after all, could you have a collection of top-level objects?). Similarly, you can't create more DBEngines. You use it to manipulate the Jet engine itself, as well as to work with temporary objects that don't belong to any collection.

For example, you can use the RepairDatabase method to fix a corrupted database or set DBEngine to nothing in order to initialize the Jet engine.

To use it, select Tools/References to add the DAO Component Object Library and then use the Object Browser to add a reference to the Data Access object library.

Following are the properties and methods of the DBEngine object.

Properties

DefaultPassword	DefaultUser	IniPath
LoginTimeout	Version	

Methods

CompactDatabase	CreateWorkspace	Idle
RegisterDatabase	RepairDatabase	

Document Object/Documents Collection

The Document object works with the Container object through the Documents collection in order to provide access to one instance of a type of object, for example a database, query, relationship, or table.

A Documents collection contains all the Document objects for a specific type of object.

As with the Container object, don't confuse these objects with the collections that have the same names. The Document objects refer to *all* instances of an object; the collections refer to *active* instances only.

Document objects correspond to existing database objects, so you can't create or delete them. You can, however, check Name properties to figure out which objects are named, figure out or set the owner of an object, and so on. You refer to a Document object by its Name property like this:

```
MyContainer.Documents("documentobjectname")
```

Following are the properties of the Document object.

Properties

AllPermissions	Container	Count
DateCreated	LastUpdated	Name
Owner	Permissions	UserName

Following are the property and method of the Documents collection.

Property

Count

Method

Refresh

Error Object/Errors Collection

An Error object contains information about a data access error. Any DAO operation can generate an error. All these errors get logged into the Errors collection of the DBEngine object. The Errors collection, however, gets cleared every time a new DAO operation generates an error, so watch for errors closely. Worse, this collection isn't in a logical order. Rather than errors being ordered by time or something else useful, they are ordered by the amount of detail regarding the error. In other words, the most detailed errors go at index 0 and the most general go at the end of the collection.

It's not so bad, however, because you know that the Errors collection contains only the information about one action's error, with the detail level decreasing as you go away from index 0. Well, maybe it still isn't a really great way to log errors, but it's all we have. All this error information is also available in the Err object.

Following are the properties of the Error object.

Properties

Description	HelpContext	HelpFile
Number	Source	

Following are the property and method of the Errors collection.

Property

Count

Method

Refresh

Field Object/Fields Collection

The Field object represents a column of data. The column has a common data type and properties. You'll find Field objects in the Index, QueryDef, Recordset, Relation, and TableDef objects. In the Recordset object, the Field object represents one row of data, just as you'd expect. Every time you read in a new row, the data in that row goes into the fields of the Fields collection.

The Field object enables you to manipulate rows of data, as well as other aspects of the data. For example, you can find out where the data came from and change validation rules.

The Value property of a Field enables you to add members to a Fields collection. The Fields collection contains all the Field objects of the active Index, QueryDef, Recordset, Relation, and TableDef objects. The syntax is as you'd expect for databases: Fields(*"field name"*). As a general rule, enclose the name of the field in brackets ([]), single quotes, or double quotes; you *must* do this if the field name has a space.

Following are the properties and methods of the Field object.

Properties

AllowZeroLength	Attributes	CollatingOrder
DataUpdatable	DefaultValue	ForeignName
Name	OrdinalPosition	Required

Size	SourceField	SourceTable
Type	ValidateOnSet	ValidationRule
ValidationText	Value	

Methods

| AppendChunk | CreateProperty | FieldSize |
| GetChunk | | |

Following are the property and methods of the Fields collection.

Property

Count

Methods

| Append | Delete | Refresh |

Font Object

The Font object sets and returns attributes of display fonts. It's more versatile than the old font properties (such as FontBold and FontItalic). In particular, there's a new Weight property that, unfortunately, isn't yet supported by Windows. If it were, you'd be able to futz with just how bold bold is. You'd no longer have only the choice of either normal *or* bold; you'd have a whole range of boldness.

The Font object is derived from the StdFont base class but behaves a little differently. You may use the Font object to modify the font properties of objects that support it (such as the TextBox control). You may not, however, use the Font object to create a new font type. For that, you need to use StdFont. In other words, this works:

```
Private Sub Command1_Click()
    Text1.Font.Bold = True
    Text1.Font.Name = "Times New Roman"
End Sub
```

but this doesn't:

```
Private Sub Command1_Click()
    Dim X As New Font
    X.Bold = True
    X.Name = "Arial"
    Set Text1.Font = X
End Sub
```

Instead, if you wanted the second example to work, you'd do this:

```
Private Sub Command1_Click()
              Dim X As New StdFont
              X.Bold = True
              X.Name = "Arial"
              Set Text1.Font = X
        End Sub
```

StdFont is typically used to create new font types when you want to use a simple variable (like X in the previous example) to modify a font's properties many times. You'd probably use the Font object when you want to modify the font only once. In other words, it's typing economy.

Following are the properties of the Font object.

Properties

Bold	Italic	Name
Size	StrikeThrough	Underline
Weight		

Form Object

A Form object is a window in your application. As a designer, you place controls on a Form object to interact with the user. You can also draw directly on the Form using the Form object's graphics methods. As with most other objects in VB, a Form object has properties that specify its appearance and behavior, methods that allow its manipulation by code, and event procedures to have it respond to user input.

You can have multiple instances of a Form object by using the New keyword in Dim, Set, or Static statements. These Form objects will all appear separately on the Windows desktop. You can also choose to implement the multiple-document interface (MDI) style of application, where a main MDIForm contains multiple instances of an MDI child form, which is just a regular Form object with its MDIChild property set to True. Which style you choose depends on the type of application. For a document-centric application, such as a word processor or spreadsheet application, using MDIForms might make sense, since each document window is essentially the same object. But in applications like VB, where all windows are different, it doesn't make sense to use MDIForms.

A Form object can act as a source in a DDE conversation, where the data is supplied by Label, PictureBox, or TextBox controls on the form. You must set the LinkMode to vbLinkSource (1) and the LinkTopic to the topic name to which the Form will respond. Form is a well-known type in VB, so you can declare variables or procedure parameters "As Form."

The Caption property of a Form is the text displayed in its Title Bar. Use the BorderStyle property to set the type of window your Form object will display, such as a sizable window, dialog box, or a toolbar. To display a window with a border, but no other embellishments, set the ControlBox, MaxButton, and MinButton properties to False and use an empty string for the Caption property.

To show and hide your forms at runtime, use either the Hide and Show methods or the Load and Unload statements. Hide keeps the Form loaded in memory, but hidden, so Showing it will be quick. Unload saves memory, but Loading the form again may take longer.

Following are the properties, methods, and events for the Form object. See them for more details.

Properties

ActiveControl	ActiveForm	AutoRedraw
Appearance	BackColor	BorderStyle
Caption	ClipControls	ControlBox
Count	CurrentX	CurrentY
DrawMode	DrawStyle	DrawWidth
Enabled	FillColor	FillStyle
Font	FontBold	FontItalic
FontName	FontSize	FontStrikethru
FontTransparent	FontUnderline	ForeColor
hDC	Height	HelpContextID
hWnd	Icon	Image
KeyPreview	Left	LinkMode
LinkTopic	MaxButton	MDIChild
MinButton	MouseIcon	MousePointer
Name	NegotiateMenus	Picture
ScaleHeight	ScaleLeft	ScaleMode
ScaleTop	ScaleWidth	ShowInTaskbar
Tag	Top	Visible
WhatsThisButton	WhatsThisHelp	Width
WindowState		

Methods

Circle	Cls	Hide
Item	Line	Move
PaintPicture	Point	PopupMenu
Print	PrintForm	PSet
Refresh	Scale	ScaleX
ScaleY	SetFocus	Show
TextHeight	TextWidth	WhatsThisMode
ZOrder		

Events

Activate	Click	DblClick
Deactivate	DragDrop	DragOver
GotFocus	Initialize	KeyDown
KeyPress	KeyUp	LinkClose
LinkError	LinkExecute	LinkOpen
Load	LostFocus	MouseDown

MouseMove	MouseUp	Paint
QueryUnload	Resize	Terminate
Unload		

Forms Collection

A Forms collection is an array of Form objects loaded for an application. The collection includes both the MDIForm (if applicable), all MDI child forms, and normal Forms. There's only a single property, Count, that returns the number of Form objects.

Forms is an intrinsic global variable, so you can always access it. You also can use it to iterate through all the forms to perform an action.

Example

```
Sub HideAllChildForms()
    For Each frm In Forms
        If Not TypeOf frm Is MDIForm Then
            If frm.MDIChild Then
                frm.Hide
            End If
        End If
    Next frm
End Sub
```

Following is the Forms collection's only property.

Property

Count

Group Object/Groups Collection

It's a security thing. The Group object represents a group of user accounts. These accounts have common rights when using a particular Workspace object. You create the groups using the CreateGroup method of a User or Workspace object. You can limit access to databases, tables, and even queries by using Document objects.

Jet comes with three predefined Group objects: Admins, Users, and Guests. Admins have all rights, Users have read and write rights, and Guests have read-only rights.

The Groups collection represents all the Group objects of a Workspace object or User object.

Following are the properties and method of the Group object.

Properties

Name	PID

Method

CreateUser

Following are the property and methods of the Groups collection.

Property

Count

Methods

Append   Delete   Refresh

Index Object/Indexes Collection

The Index object enables you to control how tables are indexed; for example, their sort order or result sets and uniqueness. Just remember that indexes grow with every update and row addition, but they don't shrink when you remove rows. You have to use CompactDatabase to recover the space that results from removing rows.

By default, when you create a table, it probably won't have an index. When you set a primary key, Jet automatically makes it the primary index, too. This means your primary key column will have to contain unique values.

To create new Indexes, use the CreateIndex method of the TableDef object and then the CreateField method on the Index object (to create a Field object for each field in the Index). Next, set the Index object's properties as you want them, add the Field object to the Fields collection, and add the Index object to the Indexes collection.

An Indexes collection contains the Index objects of a TableDef object. (Isn't the plural of Index Indices?)

 Jet doesn't support clustered indexes.

Following are the properties and methods of the Index object.

Properties

Clustered   Foreign   IgnoreNulls
Name   Primary   Required
Unique

Methods

CreateField   CreateProperty

Following are the property and methods of the Indexes collection.

Property

Count

Methods

Append   Delete   Refresh

ListImage Object/ListImages Collection

The name of this object and collection thrusts us into the territory of confusion, what with ImageList, ListItem, and ListImage. However, a ListImage object is just a bitmap that you use in other controls, while the ListImages collection is (ho-hum) just a collection of ListImage objects.

To keep things confusing: The ListImages collection is a 1-based collection, that is, it starts numbering at 1 rather than 0.

Example   Create a form and place on it an ImageList control and a TreeView control. Then add the following code to the Form_Load event:

```
Sub Form_Load()
    Dim imgSmallIcons As ListImage
    Set imgSmallIcons = ImageList1.ListImages. _
        Add(, "No", LoadPicture("bitmaps\tlbr_w95\back.bmp"))
    Set imgSmallIcons = ImageList1.ListImages. _
        Add(, , LoadPicture("bitmaps\tlbr_w95\discnet.bmp"))
    Set imgSmallIcons = ImageList1.ListImages. _
        Add(, , LoadPicture("bitmaps\tlbr_w95\camera.bmp"))
    Set imgSmallIcons = ImageList1.ListImages. _
        Add(, , LoadPicture("bitmaps\tlbr_w95\arc.bmp"))
    Set imgSmallIcons = ImageList1.ListImages. _
        Add(, , LoadPicture("bitmaps\tlbr_w95\arc.bmp"))
    ImageList1.MaskColor = vbGreen

    Dim nodSmallIconsDemo As Node
    Set nodSmallIconsDemo = _
        TreeView1.Nodes.Add(, , "R", "Root")
    Set nodSmallIconsDemo = _
        TreeView1.Nodes.Add("R", tvwChild, "C1", "Child 1")
    Set nodSmallIconsDemo = _
        TreeView1.Nodes.Add("R", tvwChild, "C2", "Child 2")
    Set nodSmallIconsDemo = _
        TreeView1.Nodes.Add("R", tvwChild, "C3", "Child 3")
    nodSmallIconsDemo.EnsureVisible

    Set TreeView1.ImageList = ImageList1
    For i = 1 To TreeView1.Nodes.Count
        TreeView1.Nodes(i).Image = i
    Next i
End Sub
```

This example associates icons with the nodes in a TreeView.
Following are the properties and methods of the ListImage object.

Properties

Index	Key	Picture

Methods

Draw	ExtractIcon

Following are the property and methods of the ListImages collection.

Property

Count

Methods

Add	Clear	Item
Remove		

ListItem Object/ListItems Collection

The ListView control enables you to view files in four different ways: as a list, large icons, small icons, and a report. The ListItem object is the text and index of a subitem (in Report view, it includes an array of strings). ListItem objects can contain both text and pictures, but to use pictures you have to use an ImageList control, too. The ListItems collection is a bunch of ListItem objects.

Note: This stuff works only with Windows 95 and NT 3.51 and later.
Following are the properties and methods of the ListItem object.

Properties

Ghosted	Height	Icon
Index	Key	Left
Selected	SmallIcon	SubItems
Tag	Text	Top
Width		

Methods

CreateDragImage	EnsureVisible

Following are the property and methods of the ListItems collection.

Property

Count

Methods

Add   Clear   Item
Remove

MDIForm Object

A multiple-document interface (MDI) may be useful for document-based applications where each document is displayed in a separate window within a container window. Each document window is free to move within the boundaries of the container window and even may be minimized within the container window.

This container window may be implemented in VB using an MDIForm object. Each document window is implemented as a Form object with its MDIChild property set to True.

Create an MDIForm object for your project by using the Insert menu. Only one MDIForm object may be created for a single project. An MDIForm object can contain only Menu controls, PictureBox controls, and custom controls that have an Align property. To include other types of controls, place them inside a PictureBox. The space used by PictureBox controls within an MDIForm object may not be used to display MDI child forms.

MDI child forms appear inside the MDIForm object only at runtime (not at design time). You can create menus for the MDI child forms, but at runtime, the active MDI child form's menus replace the parent MDIForm's menus and are not displayed in the child form's window.

Like the Form object, an MDIForm object can access its controls using the Controls collection and Count property. Both of the following examples achieve the same result:

Example
```
For Each ctrl In MDIForm1.Controls
    ctrl.Visible = True
Next ctrl
```

Example
```
For i = 0 To MDIForm1.Count - 1
    MDIForm1.Controls(i).Visible = True
Next ctrl
```

Unlike the Form object, however, an MDIForm object cannot be shown modally.

Caution: If you use TypeOf...Is syntax to perform runtime type checking, you'll find that an MDIForm object returns True when you check it against the Form type. Since there are operations that apply to Forms but not to MDIForms, you also should check against MDIForm before proceeding.

Example
```
Private Sub ShowModal(obj As Object)
    If TypeOf obj Is Form Then
        If Not TypeOf obj Is MDIForm Then
```

```
            obj.Show vbModal
        End If
    End If
End Sub
```

Following are the properties, methods, and events of an MDIForm object.

Properties

ActiveControl	ActiveForm	Appearance
AutoShowChildren	BackColor	Caption
Count	Enabled	Height
HelpContextID	hWnd	Icon
Left	LinkMode	LinkTopic
MouseIcon	MousePointer	Name
NegotiateToolbars	Picture	ScaleHeight
ScaleWidth	ScrollBars	Tag
Top	Visible	WhatsThisHelp
Width	WindowState	

Methods

Arrange	Hide	Move
PopupMenu	SetFocus	Show
WhatsThisMode	ZOrder	

Events

Activate	Click	DblClick
Deactivate	DragDrop	DragOver
Initialize	LinkClose	LinkError
LinkExecute	LinkOpen	Load
MouseDown	MouseMove	MouseUp
QueryUnload	Resize	Terminate
Unload		

Node Object/Nodes Collection

Look at the Windows 95 Explorer. Okay, now look at the left pane. See all those little folders, the little disk drive, and the little desktop all with their names? Those are nodes. More specifically, Node objects. Technically, a Node object is an item in a TreeView control that can contain images and text. The Nodes collection holds Node objects. And needless to say, this is a Windows 95 and Windows NT 3.51 (and later) thing. Only. Windows 3.1 ain't got it.

Your plain-vanilla Node object is just text—in the case of the Explorer, the name of the folder or I/O device. You can add pictures by associating an ImageList control with the Node object's ImageList property. The neat thing here is that you can have the pictures change as the state

of the Node object changes; for example, you can make the Node look different when it's selected. You do this little trick with the SelectedImage property. Create a form and place on it an ImageList control and a TreeView control. Then add the following code to the Form_Load event:

Example

```
Sub Form_Load()
    Dim imgSmallIcons As ListImage
    Set imgSmallIcons = ImageList1.ListImages. _
        Add(, "No", LoadPicture("bitmaps\tlbr_w95\back.bmp"))
    Set imgSmallIcons = ImageList1.ListImages. _
        Add(, , LoadPicture("bitmaps\tlbr_w95\discnet.bmp"))
    Set imgSmallIcons = ImageList1.ListImages. _
        Add(, , LoadPicture("bitmaps\tlbr_w95\camera.bmp"))
    Set imgSmallIcons = ImageList1.ListImages. _
        Add(, , LoadPicture("bitmaps\tlbr_w95\arc.bmp"))
    Set imgSmallIcons = ImageList1.ListImages. _
        Add(, , LoadPicture("bitmaps\tlbr_w95\arc.bmp"))
    ImageList1.MaskColor = vbGreen

    Dim nodSmallIconsDemo As Node
    Set nodSmallIconsDemo = _
        TreeView1.Nodes.Add(, , "R", "Root")
    Set nodSmallIconsDemo = _
        TreeView1.Nodes.Add("R", tvwChild, "C1", "Child 1")
    Set nodSmallIconsDemo = _
        TreeView1.Nodes.Add("R", tvwChild, "C2", "Child 2")
    Set nodSmallIconsDemo = _
        TreeView1.Nodes.Add("R", tvwChild, "C3", "Child 3")
    nodSmallIconsDemo.EnsureVisible

    Set TreeView1.ImageList = ImageList1
    For i = 1 To TreeView1.Nodes.Count
        TreeView1.Nodes(i).Image = i
    Next i
End Sub
```

This example associates icons with the nodes in a TreeView.
Following are the properties and methods of the Node object.

Properties

Child	Children	Enabled
Expanded	ExpandedImage	FirstSibling
FullPath	Image	Index
Key	LastSibling	Next
Parent	Previous	Root
Selected	SelectedImage	Sorted
Tag	Text	Visible

Methods

CreateDragImage   Ensure Visible

Following are the property and methods of the Nodes collection.

Property

Count

Methods

Add   Clear   Item
Remove

Panel Object/Panels Collection

The Panel object is a part of the StatusBar control. Look at the bottom of Microsoft Word for Windows's main screen. The Status Bar down there has your current page number, section, and a whole bunch of other stuff. The Status Bar at the bottom of Windows 95's desktop shows the time and which applications you're running. Each subsection of a Status Bar is a Panel object. Panel objects can contain text or a picture.

The Panels collection is a bunch of Panel objects. The Panels collection is another 1-based collection, meaning it starts numbering at 1, not 0. When you add a StatusBar control to your Form, StatusBar1.Panels(1) is there already by default, so remember to subtract 1 from the total number of panels you want.

Following are the properties and events of the Panel object.

Properties

Alignment	Autosize	Bevel
Enabled	Index	Left
MinWidth	Picture	Style
Tag	Text	Visible
Width		

Events

PanelClick   PanelDblClick

Following are the property and methods of the Panels collection.

Property

Count

Methods

Add	Clear	Item
Remove		

Parameter Object/Parameters Collection

QueryDefs can have parameters, like a Name, a Type, or a Value. The Parameter object represents one of these properties.

The Parameters collection contains the Parameter objects of a QueryDef object.

Following are the properties of the Parameter object.

Properties

Name	Type	Value

Following are the property and method of the Parameters collection.

Property

Count

Method

Refresh

Picture Object

The Picture object enables you to manipulate bitmaps, icons, and metafiles without actually using a PictureBox control or even a Form object. It supports two different handles: one to the picture and one to the palette of that picture. (A handle is a unique identifier that Windows can use to talk to objects.) The handles make the Picture object an ideal choice when you are dealing with Windows APIs, since the Graphics Device Interface (GDI) often requires handles in order to do its thing.

You work with Picture objects like you do any other object. You set one object's Picture property equal to the Picture object. You can, for example, manipulate a picture using the Picture object and then just drop the finished picture into a PictureBox. Or you can create an array of Picture objects and manipulate them together (rather than creating an array of PictureBox controls).

This object is derived from the StdPicture object and supports the same properties and methods. The two objects differ in that if you want to create a new Picture object, you must use the StdPicture object. In other words, this won't work:

```
Dim X As New Picture
```

but this will:

```
Dim X As New StdPicture
```

and so will this:

```
Dim X As Picture
Set X = LoadPicture("PICTURE.BMP")
Picture1.Picture = X
```

Following are the properties and method of the Picture object.

Properties

Handle	Height	hPal
Type	Width	

Method

Render

Printer Object

The Printer object enables you to access a printer attached to your system. Use the Printer object's properties to determine or set the printer attributes, such as PrintQuality, PaperBin, and PaperSize. Use graphics methods to draw text and graphics and then use the EndDoc method to send them to the printer for printing. Graphics that do not fit on a page are clipped at the bottom, but text will be pushed onto a new page.

Drawing directly on the Printer object takes careful planning and lots of paper during the development stages, but doing this could produce better results than just using the Form object's PrintForm method to print a bitmap of the Form.

The intrinsic global variable, Printer, is an object that represents the currently active printer for the application. To change the printer, use "Set Printer = Printers(i)" to switch to a printer in the Printers collection.

Following are the properties and methods of the Printer object.

Properties

ColorMode	Copies	CurrentX
CurrentY	DeviceName	DrawMode
DrawStyle	DrawWidth	DriverName
Duplex	FillColor	FillStyle
Font	FontBold	FontCount
FontItalic	FontName	Fonts
FontSize	FontStrikethru	FontTransparent

FontUnderline	ForeColor	hDC
Height	Orientation	Page
PaperBin	PaperSize	Port
PrintQuality	ScaleHeight	ScaleLeft
ScaleMode	ScaleTop	ScaleWidth
TrackDefault	TwipsPerPixelX	TwipsPerPixelY
Width	Zoom	

Methods

Circle	EndDoc	KillDoc
Line	NewPage	PaintPicture
Print	PSet	Scale
ScaleX	ScaleY	TextHeight
TextWidth		

Printers Collection

The Printers collection gives you read-only access to all available printers on your system. It is an array of Printer objects, each corresponding to a printer installed on your system. There's only a single property, Count, that returns the number of Printer objects.

Printers is an intrinsic global variable, so you can always access it. You also can use it to iterate through all the printers to perform an action.

Example
```
Sub ListPrinters(lst As ListBox)
    lst.Clear
    For Each prn In Printers
        lst.AddItem prn.DeviceName & " on " & prn.Port
    Next prn
End Sub
```

To gain write access to the properties of a printer, you must first use the Set statement to make the printer the default printer. The following example makes the third printer the default:

Example
```
Set Printer = Printers(2)
```

Note that Printers is a zero-based array, so the maximum index value is Printers.Count − 1. Following is the single property of the Printers collection.

Property

Count

Property Object/Properties Collection

A Property object is a property of all DAOs that uniquely identifies a particular instance of the DAO; for example, a Name, a Value, or a Type. These Property objects are stored in a Properties collection. In addition to the built-in properties, you can create your own for instances of some objects, including Database, Index, QueryDef, and TableDef objects, as well as Field objects in Fields collections of QueryDef and TableDef objects.

Here's how. Use the CreateProperty method to create a Property object with a unique Name property. Then set the Type and Value properties of this property and append it to the Properties collection.

Following are the properties of the Property object.

Properties

Inherited	Name	Type
Value		

Following are the property and methods of the Properties collection.

Property

Count

Methods

Append	Delete	Refresh

QueryDef Object/QueryDefs Collection

The QueryDef object is a query definition stored in a Jet database, much like a stored procedure. It's basically a compiled SQL statement and has all the capabilities that SQL enables, plus a few more, such as timeout information. Because the queries are precompiled, they run faster than a raw SQL query runs.

A QueryDefs collection is a collection of QueryDef objects.

Following are the properties and methods of the QueryDef object.

Properties

Connect	DateCreated	LastUpdated
LogMessages	Name	ODBCTimeout
RecordsAffected	ReturnsRecords	SQL
Type	Updatable	

Methods

CreateProperty	Execute	OpenRecordset

Following are the property and methods of the QueryDefs collection.

Property

Count

Methods

Append	Delete	Refresh

Recordset Object/Recordsets Collection

A Recordset object represents the records in a table or those resulting from a query. There are three kinds of Recordsets, all of which consist of records and fields: Table-type Recordset, Dynaset-type Recordset, and Snapshot-type Recordset. The Table-type Recordset basically represents a single table. The Dynaset-type Recordset represents the result of a query that has updatable records. And a Snapshot-type Recordset is a static copy of a set of records from either a single table or a query. You set the type of Recordset when you use the OpenRecordset method. By default, the type is Table-type; if that doesn't work, Jet tries Dynaset-type.

Note that the Recordset object's Table-type, Dynaset-type, and Snapshot-type objects are different from the Table, Dynaset, and Snapshot DAOs in previous versions of the Jet engine. Although you can use the older DAO types, please use the Recordset object's types because there's no guarantee that future versions of VB will support the older types.

The Recordsets collection contains all open Recordset objects in a Database object.

Following are the properties and methods of the Recordset object.

Properties

AbsolutePosition	BOF	Bookmark
Bookmarkable	CacheSize	CacheStart
DateCreated	EditMode	EOF
Filter	Index	LastModified
LastUpdated	LockEdits	Name
NoMatch	PercentPosition	RecordCount
Restartable	Sort	Transactions
Type	Updatable	ValidationRule
ValidationTex		

Methods

AddNew	CancelUpdate	Clone
Close	CopyQueryDef	Delete

Edit	FillCache	FindFirst
FindLast	FindNext	FindPrevious
GetRows	Move	MoveFirst
MoveLast	MoveNext	MovePrevious
OpenRecordset	Requery	Seek
Update		

Following are the property and method of the Recordsets collection.

Property

Count

Method

Refresh

Relation Object/Relations Collection

Sometimes you want to set up relationships between tables or queries in a database, for example, to limit input in one table based on a field in a second. The Relation object represents such a relationship between fields in tables or queries. It can also turn on referential integrity checking. To create a new Relation object, use the CreateRelation method.

A Relations collection contains stored Relation objects.

Following are the properties and method of the Relation object.

Properties

Attributes	ForeignTable	Name
Table		

Method

CreateField

Following are the property and methods of the Relations collection.

Property

Count

Methods

Append	Delete	Refresh

RowBufferObject

The RowBuffer object holds rows of data that you've retrieved. Contained in the DBGrid control, RowBuffer transfers that data between your application and an unbound DBGrid control. Row-Buffer works only with an unbound DBGrid.

More specifically, here's how it works. When an UnboundReadData event occurs, Row-Buffer gets the data. DBGrid then fills its cache with that data. When DBGrid changes that data, it sends an UnboundWriteData event and passes RowBuffer as an argument. Similarly, when you create a new row, the UnboundAddData event gets RowBuffer to play with. This means that RowBuffer isn't going to do you any good when it comes to updating your database. You still have to use the standard methods to commit your data to the database.

Following are the properties of the RowBuffer object.

Properties

Bookmark	ColumnCount	ColumnName
RowCount	Value	

Screen Object

The Screen object represents the video display. Use it to manipulate display-level settings, such as Form-window positions and mouse pointer attributes when the mouse is outside any of your Form windows, and to determine the active form or control for your application. The intrinsic global variable, Screen, is always available.

In the following example, the Menu command causes the active control to update its link information. No error checking is performed.

Example

```
Private Sub mnuUpdateLink_Click()
    With Screen.ActiveControl
        .LinkMode = vbLinkManual
        .LinkRequest
        .LinkMode = vbLinkNone
    End With
End Sub
```

Following are the properties of the Screen object.

Properties

ActiveControl	ActiveForm	FontCount
Fonts	Height	MouseIcon
MousePointer	TwipsPerPixelX	TwipsPerPixelY
Width		

SelBookmarks Collection

The SelBookmarks collection contains bookmarks for each selected row in a DBGrid control. You control it with the DBGrid's SelBookmarks property. You use the Add method to add bookmarks to the SelBookmarks collection and then move to a particular bookmark using the bookmark property of the DBGrid control. Bookmarked rows appear highlighted in the DBGrid control.

Following are the property and methods of the SelBookmarks collection.

Property

Count

Methods

Add(DBGrid)   Item   Remove

StdFont Object

You use the StdFont object to create new font classes and set and return attributes of display fonts. It's more versatile than the old font properties (such as FontBold and FontItalic). In particular, there's a new Weight property that, unfortunately, isn't yet supported by Windows. But if it were, you'd be able to futz with just how bold bold is. You'd no longer have only the choice of either normal *or* bold; you'd have a whole range of boldnesses.

Note the difference between the StdFont object and the Font object. You may use the Font object to modify the font properties of objects that support it (such as the TextBox control). You may not, however, use it to create a new font type. For that, you use StdFont. In other words, this works:

```
Private Sub Command1_Click()
     Text1.Font.Bold = True
     Text1.Font.Name = "Times New Roman"
End Sub
```

but this doesn't:

```
Private Sub Command1_Click()
     Dim X As New Font
     X.Bold = True
     X.Name = "Arial"
     Set Text1.Font = X
End Sub
```

Instead, if you wanted the second example to work, you'd do this:

```
Private Sub Command1_Click()
```

```
      Dim X As New StdFont
      X.Bold = True
      X.Name = "Arial"
      Set Text1.Font = X
End Sub
```

Typically, you'll use StdFont to create new font types when you want to use a simple vari-able (like X in the previous example) to modify a font's properties many times. You'll probably use the Font object when you want to modify the font only once. In other words, it's typing econ-omy.

Following are the properties of the StdFont object.

Properties

Bold	Italic	Name
Size	StrikeThrough	Underline
Weight		

StdPicture Object

The StdPicture object enables you to create new picture classes and manipulate bitmaps, icons, and metafiles without actually using a PictureBox control or even a Form object. It supports two different handles: one to the picture and one to the palette of that picture. (A handle is a unique identifier that Windows can use to talk to objects.) The handles make the Picture object an ideal choice when dealing with Windows APIs, since the Graphics Device Interface (GDI) often re-quires handles in order to do its thing.

You work with StdPicture objects just like you do any other object. You set one object's Pic-ture property equal to the StdPicture object. You can, for example, manipulate a picture using the Picture object and then just drop the finished picture into a PictureBox. Or you can create an ar-ray of Picture objects and manipulate them together (rather than creating an array of PictureBox controls).

Note how the StdPicture object and the Picture object differ. To create a new Picture object, you must use the StdPicture object. In other words, this won't work:

```
Dim X As New Picture
```

but this will:

```
Dim X As New StdPicture
```

and so will this:

```
Dim X As Picture
Set X = LoadPicture("PICTURE.BMP")
Picture1.Picture = X
```

Following are the properties and method of the StdPicture object.

Properties

Handle	Height	hPal
Type	Width	

Method

Render

Tab Object/Tabs Collection

Tabbed dialog boxes are a big thing in Windows 95. The Tab object represents one of the Tabs on a tabbed dialog box, and the Tabs collection is a bunch of Tab objects. You use them with a TabStrip control. To see how the TabStrip works, put an ImageList and a TabStrip control on your Form and then paste the following code under the Form_Load section:

```
Private Sub Form_Load()
    'You'll need this later
    Dim Counter As Integer

    'Set up ImageList control
    Dim imgTest As ListImage
    Set imgTest = ImageList1. _
    ListImages.Add(, "Note", LoadPicture("bitmaps\assorted\note.bmp"))
    Set imgTest = ImageList1. _
    ListImages.Add(, "Cup", LoadPicture("bitmaps\assorted\cup.bmp"))
    Set imgTest = ImageList1. _
    ListImages.Add(, "Balloon", LoadPicture("bitmaps\assorted\balloon.bmp"))

    'Set the MaskColor so that the pictures look right
    ImageList1.MaskColor = vbGreen

    'Now set up the TabStrip
    'First, point it to the ImageList
    Set TabStrip1.ImageList = ImageList1
    'Second, create the tabs and set their captions and their Tool Tip Text
    TabStrip1.Tabs(1).Caption = "Music"
    TabStrip1.Tabs.Add 2, , "Drinks"
    TabStrip1.Tabs.Add 3, , "Conversation"
    TabStrip1.Tabs(1).ToolTipText = "Click here to see stuff about music"
    TabStrip1.Tabs(2).ToolTipText = "Click here to see information about
drinks"
    TabStrip1.Tabs(3).ToolTipText = "Click here to have a conversation"
    'Now, use Counter to point the tabs to images
    For Counter = 1 To TabStrip1.Tabs.Count
        TabStrip1.Tabs(Counter).Image = Counter
    Next Counter
End Sub
```

As you can see, Tab objects and the Tab collection work like the other objects and collections in VB. Key properties of the Tab object are Caption, Image, and ToolTipText. You also can attach images to the TabStrip by using an ImageList control. You can use the SelectedItem property to get a reference to the tab a user has selected and use the Selected property to see if a specific tab is selected. Use these properties with the BeforeClick event to write whatever values the user has set on a specific tab before going to the next one.

Following are the properties of the Tab object.

Properties

Caption	Height	Image
Index	Left	Key
Selected	Tag	ToolTipText
Top	Width	

Following are the property and methods of the Tabs collection.

Property

Count

Methods

Add	Clear	Item
Remove		

TableDef Object/TableDefs Collection

The TableDef object represents the stored definition of a base table or attached table. It represents only the definition, not the data. Consequently you can examine and change the table's structure and where it gets data from and so on, but you can't actually access the data using this object.

The VB Help file lists the default collections and properties of various objects and collections around the TableDef object. However, we recommend that in order to keep your code easily legible, you spell out everything, even though doing so means you'll have to type more. If the default properties change in a future version of VB, you'll be glad you did. To create a new TableDef object, use the CreateTableDef method.

A TableDefs collection contains all stored TableDef objects.

Following are the properties and methods of the TableDef object.

Properties

Attributes	ConflictTable	Connect
DateCreated	LastUpdated	Name
RecordCount	SourceTableName	Updatable
ValidationRule	ValidationText	

Methods

CreateField   CreateIndex   CreateProperty
OpenRecordset   RefreshLink

Following are the property and methods of the TableDefs collection.

Property

Count

Methods

Append   Delete   Refresh

UserObject/Users Collection

If you have security enabled, a User object represents a user account and its access permissions. User objects can belong to a Group object. Jet comes with two user objects predefined: Admin (all powers) and Guest (read only).

To create a new User object, use the CreateUser method.

A Users collection contains all stored User objects of a Workspace or group account.

Following are the properties and methods of the User object.

Properties

Name   Password   PID

Methods

CreateGroup   NewPassword

Following are the property and methods of the Users collection.

Property

Count

Methods

Append   Delete   Refresh

Workspace Object/Workspaces Collection

The Workspace concept is simple: A Workspace is all the tables, queries, databases, and transactions a user has open at once. Basically, it's a user's session. You use the Workspace to manage transactions and security, for example, rolling back a transaction or setting a password on a session. Every user has at least one open Workspace object (DBEngine.Workspaces(0) is the default).

You create extra Workspace objects usually when you want to perform special transaction-oriented tasks. Separate Workspace objects enable you to track different, unrelated transactions simultaneously but separately. In that way, you can roll back a particular transaction without rolling back events you want to stay committed. You create extra Workspace objects with DBEngine's CreateWorkspace method.

The Workspaces collection contains all active, unhidden Workspace objects of DBEngine. Following are the properties and methods of the Workspace object.

Properties

IsolateODBCTrans	Name	UserName

Methods

BeginTrans	Close	CommitTrans
CreateDatabase	CreateGroup	CreateUser
OpenDatabase	Rollback	

Following are the property and methods of the Workspaces collection.

Property

Count

Methods

Append	Delete	Refresh

SECTION 4: VB CONTROLS

"And now here's something we hope you'll really like."

—Rocky the Squirrel

Controls are VB's prefab chunks of code that enable you to write apps quickly. Here are the ones included in VB's standard edition.

CheckBox Control

The CheckBox control displays a check mark in a box when that box is selected (e.g., ☑); the check mark disappears when the check box is cleared. Use this control to give the user a True/False or Yes/No option. You can use CheckBox controls in groups to display multiple choices from which the user can select one or more. It also has the option of giving a third, "don't care" or unavailable, choice, but this is not well supported. See the example for the Value property in the Methods and Properties section of this book for how to implement the "don't care" option.

CheckBox and OptionButton controls function similarly, but CheckBox controls can be used to select multiple items from a set of choices, whereas OptionButton controls are used to select only one of many choices.

Use the Caption property to display text next to a CheckBox Control and the Value property to set or determine the state of the control.

See the references for the individual properties, methods, and events for more details.

Properties

Alignment	Appearance	BackColor
Caption	Container	DataChanged
DataField	DataSource	DragIcon
DragMode	Enabled	Font
FontBold	FontItalic	FontName
FontSize	FontStrikethru	FontUnderline
ForeColor	Height	HelpContextID
hWnd	Index	Left
MousePointer	Name	Parent
TabIndex	TabStop	Tag
Top	Value	Visible
WhatsThisHelpID	Width	

Methods

Drag	Move	Refresh
SetFocus	ShowWhatsThis	ZOrder

Events

Click	DragDrop	DragOver
GotFocus	KeyDown	KeyPress
KeyUp	LostFocus	MouseDown
MouseMove	MouseUp	

ComboBox Control

The ComboBox control is a combination of a ListBox control and a TextBox control. When the user selects an item from the list, the ComboBox control fills the text box with the selection. The user can also type directly into the text box to enter a string that is not part of the list at all. The current value of a ComboBox control is its Text property that just returns the string in the TextBox part of the ComboBox control.

Use a ComboBox control when you need to provide the user with a convenient list of options from which to choose, but also with the option of entering any other values. To save space on your forms, you can set its Style property to vbComboDropdown (0) to create a drop-down list. But be aware that for the user, the drop-down list represents an extra mouse click before he or she can select an item from the list.

There is one quirk of the ComboBox control. You can set its Style property to vbCombo-DropdownList (2), in which case the control loses its TextBox part and presents only a drop-down list. Why this is not a style of the ListBox control instead of the ComboBox control is beyond us.

To bind a ComboBox to a Data control, use a DBCombo control instead. See the individual properties, methods, and events for more details.

Properties

Appearance	BackColor	Container
DataChanged	DataField	DataSource
DragIcon	DragMode	Enabled
Font	FontBold	FontItalic
FontName	FontSize	FontStrikethru
FontUnderline	ForeColor	Height
HelpContextID	hWnd	Index
IntegralHeight	ItemData	Left
List	ListCount	ListIndex
MouseIcon	MousePointer	Name
NewIndex	Parent	SelLength
SelStart	SelText	Sorted
Style	TabIndex	TabStop
Tag	Text	Top
Visible	WhatsThisHelpID	Width

Methods

AddItem	Clear	Drag
Move	Refresh	RemoveItem
SetFocus	ShowWhatsThis	ZOrder

Events

Change	Click	DblClick
DragDrop	DragOver	DropDown
GotFocus	KeyDown	KeyPress
KeyUp	LostFocus	

CommandButton Control

A CommandButton control is used to execute a command. When you press the left mouse button over a CommandButton control, it appears to be pushed in. Pressing the right mouse button has no such effect. A CommandButton control can display only text. To have a button that displays a picture, you must create your own using an Image control.

Typically, a CommandButton control "runs" the command when it gets a Click event. This can occur when a user clicks it using the left mouse button, but *only* if its DragMode property is set to vbManual (0). The Click event is also triggered if the CommandButton control's Value property is set to 1. If you want the command to execute whenever the user presses the Enter key, then set the control's Default property to True. If you want the command to execute whenever the user presses the Esc key, then set the control's Cancel property to True.

If you set a CommandButton control's DragMode property to vbAutomatic (1), then its Click event cannot be triggered by a click with a mouse button.

See the individual properties, methods, and events for more details.

Properties

Appearance	BackColor	Cancel
Caption	Container	Default
DragIcon	DragMode	Enabled
Font	FontBold	FontItalic
FontName	FontSize	FontSrikethru
FontUnderline	Height	HelpContextID
hWnd	Index	Left
MouseIcon	MousePointer	Name
Parent	TabIndex	TabStop
Tag	Top	Value
Visible	WhatsThisHelpID	Width

Methods

Drag	Move	Refresh
SetFocus	ShowWhatsThis	ZOrder

Events

Click	DragDrop	DragOver
GotFocus	KeyDown	KeyPress
KeyUp	LostFocus	MouseDown
MouseMove	MouseUp	

CommonDialog Control

Don't design your own dialog boxes—at least not for the Open, Save, or Print commands or for color or font choices. Not only will doing so take time, but the end result will very likely be a nonstandard dialog box that magazine editors will comment on when they see your app, making you feel stupid. Instead use the Microsoft CommonDialog control. It provides consistent dialog boxes based on COMMDLG.DLL. And it's pretty easy to use. Just include COMDLG16.OCX or COMDLG32.OCX (for 16-bit and 32-bit apps, respectively) in your project. Typically, your code is no more complex than this:

```
Private Sub Open_Click(Index As Integer)
    CommonDialog1.ShowOpen
End Sub
```

You need to include only one CommonDialog control in your form in order to access the different types of dialog boxes. Display the dialog boxes using its methods, such as ShowOpen and ShowFont, but first set the properties of a CommonDialog control according to which type of dialog is to be shown. Also use the properties to retrieve the values selected by the user when a call to a ShowXX methods returns.

Properties

COLOR DIALOG

Action	CancelError	Color
Flags	HelpCommand	HelpContext
HelpFile	HelpKey	Object

FILE DIALOG

Action	CancelError	DefaultExt
DialogTitle	FileName	FileTitle
Filter	FilterIndex	Flags
HelpCommand	HelpContext	HelpFile
HelpKey	InitDir	MaxFileSize
Object		

FONT DIALOG

Action	CancelError	Flags
FontBold	FontItalic	FontName
FontSize	FontStrikethru	FontUnderline
HelpCommand	HelpContext	HelpFile
HelpKey	Max	Min
Object		

PRINT DIALOG

Action	CancelError	Copies

Flags	FromPage	hDC
HelpCommand	HelpContext	HelpFile
HelpKey	Max	MaxFileSize
ToPage		

Methods

ShowColor	ShowFont	ShowHelp
ShowOpen	ShowPrinter	ShowSave

Data Control

You can't say too much about this, the premier of VB data access. We aren't even going to try. Instead, we're going to talk about some of its most important properties and how it works.

The basic workings of the Data control are simple. You connect it to a recordset through (surprise) the Recordset property. The Data control provides four basic maneuvering controls for getting through your recordset: forward and backward one record and beginning and end of the recordset.

The Data control knows about three kinds of recordsets: tables, dynasets, and snapshots. You set the kind of recordset you're dealing with through the (surprise, again) RecordsetType property.

But wait, there's a catch. Under VB3, the Data control knows about dynasets. In VB4, it doesn't—not according to the documentation, anyway. Seems nobody could figure out what the heck a dynaset was, so Microsoft just did away with it. (Just kidding.) In truth, you can still set your RecordsetType property to be a dynaset, but some of the methods that VB3 had to operate on a dynaset are gone (like CreateDynaset).

A table is just that. A Dynaset object is the result of a query. A snapshot is a one-time glance at either a query or a table; it's not updated dynamically as tables and dynasets are. You can use snapshots to create pick lists.

Properties

Align	Appearance	BackColor
BOFAction	Caption	Connect
Database	DatabaseName	DragIcon
DragMode	EditMode	Enabled
EOFAction	Exclusive	Font
FontBold	FontItalic	FontName
FontSize	FontStrikethru	FontUnderline
ForeColor	Height	Index
Left	MouseIcon	MousePointer
Name	Options	ReadOnly
Recordset	RecordsetType	RecordSource
WhatsThisHelpID	Width	

Methods

Drag	Move	Refresh
ShowWhatsThis	UpdateControls	UpdateRecord
ZOrder		

Events

DragDrop	DragOver	Error
MouseDown	MouseMove	MouseUp
Reposition	Resize	Validate

DBGrid Control (Apex Data Bound Grid Library)

The DBGrid control makes its debut in VB4. It provides a spreadsheet-like view of a recordset, showing multiple columns and rows simultaneously. Because it can show columns and rows at once, you bind it to a Data control on the DataSource property and don't have to set anything like the RecordSource property.

Properties

Align	AllowAddNew	AllowDelete
AllowRowSizing	AllowUpdate	BackColor
Bookmark	BorderStyle	Caption
ColumnHeaders	Columns	Container
DataMode	DataSource	DefColWidth
DragIcon	DragMode	Enabled
Font	ForeColor	HeadFont
HeadLines	Height	HelpContextID
Index	Left	LeftCol
Name	Negotiate	Object
RowHeight	ScrollBars	SelBookmarks
SelEndCol	SelStartCol	TabIndex

Methods

ColContaining	Drag	GetBookmark
Move	Rebind	Refresh
RowBookmark	RowContaining	RowTop
Scroll	SetFocus	ShowWhatsThis
ZOrder		

Events

AfterColUpdate	AfterDelete	AfterInsert
AfterUpdate	BeforeColUpdate	BeforeDelete
BeforeInsert	BeforeUpdate	Change

Click	ColResize	DblClick
DragDrop	DragOver	GotFocus
HeadClick	KeyDown	KeyPress
KeyUp	LostFocus	MouseDown
MouseMove	MouseUp	RowColChange
RowLoaded	RowResize	Scroll
SelChange	UnboundAddData	UnboundDeleteRow
UnboundReadData	UnboundWriteData	

DBList and DBCombo Controls

The DBList and DBCombo controls are like the List and Combo controls, except that they have properties that bind them to a Data control. Consequently, they're really easy to populate with the information in recordsets, and they make great navigation tools.

There are five important properties you have to deal with when you use these two controls, given in the following table. They don't always behave as they should, but they all seem to need to be filled.

PROPERTY	DESCRIPTION
RowSource	Specifies the Data control that you want to use for the list part of the control.
ListField	The name of the field from RowSource that's going to fill the list.
BoundColumn	Specifies the field in the recordset (the one specified by RowSource) that's passed to DataField once you make a selection.
DataSource	The name of the Data control to update when a user chooses something from the list. You can point it back at the Data control in RowSource if there's only one Data control on the form.
DataField	The name of the field from DataSource to update when a user chooses something from the list. You can point it to the same field as BoundColumn if there's nothing else to point it to.

Following are the properties, methods, and events of the DBList control.

Properties

Appearance	BackColor	BoundColumn
BoundText	DataChanged	DataField
DataSource	DragIcon	DragMode
Enabled	Font	ForeColor
Height	HelpContextID	Index
IntegralHeight	Left	ListField
Locked	MatchedWithList	MatchEntry
MouseIcon	MousePointer	Name
Parent	RowSource	SelectedItem
TabIndex	TabStop	Tag

Text	Top	Visible
VisibleCount	VisibleItems	WhatsThisHelpID
Width		

Methods

Drag	Move	Refill
Refresh	SetFocus	ShowWhatsThis
ZOrder		

Events

Click	DblClick	DragDrop
DragOver	GotFocus	KeyDown
KeyPress	KeyUp	LostFocus
MouseDown	MouseMove	MouseUp

Following are the properties, methods, and events of the DBCombo control.

Properties

Appearance	BackColor	BoundColumn
BoundText	Container	DataChanged
DataField	DataSource	DragIcon
DragMode	Enabled	Font
ForeColor	Height	HelpContextID
Index	IntegralHeight	Left
ListField	Locked	MatchedWithList
MatchEntry	MouseIcon	MousePointer
Name	Object	Parent
RowSource	SelectedItem	SelLength
SelStart	SelText	Style
TabIndex	TabStop	Tag
Text	Top	Visible
VisibleCount	VisibleItems	WhatsThisHelpID
Width		

Methods

Drag	Move	Refill
Refresh	SetFocus	ShowWhatsThis
ZOrder		

Events

Change	Click	DblClick
DragDrop	DragOver	GotFocus
KeyDown	KeyPress	KeyUp
LostFocus	MouseDown	MouseMove
MouseUp		

DirListBox Control

The DirListBox control displays a tree view of directories. For a directory specified by its Path property, the list contains all the parent directories of Path and all subdirectories within Path. Used in conjunction with the DriveListBox and FileListBox controls, it allows you to provide an interface that enables your user to browse the file system. Before you use these controls, however, check out the CommonDialog control. It already provides FileOpen and FileSaveAs file-selection capabilities. Also, using it will make your application have a more standard look and feel.

 See the individual properties, methods, and events for more details.

Properties

Appearance	BackColor	Container
DragIcon	DragMode	Enabled
Font	FontBold	FontItalic
FontName	FontSize	FontStrikethru
FontUnderline	ForeColor	Height
HelpContextID	hWnd	Index
Left	List	ListCount
ListIndex	MouseIcon	MousePointer
Name	Parent	Path
TabIndex	TabStop	Tag
Top	Visible	WhatsThisHelpID
Width		

Methods

Drag	Move	Refresh
SetFocus	ShowWhatsThis	ZOrder

Events

Change	Click	DragDrop
DragOver	GotFocus	KeyDown
KeyPress	KeyUp	LostFocus
MouseDown	MouseMove	MouseUp

DriveListBox Control

The DriveListBox control displays a list of available drives at runtime. Used in conjunction with the DirListBox and FileListBox controls, this control lets you provide an interface that allows your user to browse the file system. Before you use these controls, however, check out the CommonDialog control. It already provides FileOpen and FileSaveAs file-selection capabilities. Plus using it will make your application have a more standard look and feel.

 See the individual properties, methods, and events for more details.

Properties

Appearance	BackColor	Container
DragIcon	DragMode	Drive
Enabled	Font	FontBold
FontItalic	FontName	FontSize
FontStrikethru	FontUnderline	ForeColor
Height	HelpContextID	hWnd
Index	Left	List
ListCount	ListIndex	MouseIcon
MousePointer	Name	Parent
TabIndex	TabStop	Tag
Top	Visible	WhatsThisHelpID
Width		

Methods

Drag	Move	Refresh
SetFocus	ShowWhatsThis	ZOrder

Events

Change	DragDrop	DragOver
GotFocus	KeyDown	KeyPress
KeyUp	LostFocus	

FileListBox Control

The FileListBox control lists all files in the directory specified by its Path property that match the pattern specified by its Pattern property. Used in conjunction with the DirListBox and Drive-ListBox controls, it enables you to provide an interface that allows your user to browse the file system to select a file or group of files. Before you use these controls, however, check out the CommonDialog control. It already provides FileOpen and FileSaveAs file-selection capabilities. Also, using it will make your application have a more standard look and feel.

See the individual properties, methods, and events for more details.

Properties

Appearance	Archive	BackColor
Container	DragIcon	DragMode
Enabled	FileName	Font
FontBold	FontItalic	FontName
FontSize	FontStrikethru	FontUnderline
ForeColor	Height	HelpContextID
Hidden	hWnd	Index
Left	List	ListCount

ListIndex	MouseIcon	MousePointer
MultiSelect	Name	Normal
Parent	Path	Pattern
ReadOnly	Selected	System
TabIndex	TabStop	Tag
Top	TopIndex	Visible
WhatsThisHelpID	Width	

Methods

Drag	Move	Refresh
SetFocus	ShowWhatsThis	ZOrder

Events

Click	DblClick	DragDrop
DragOver	GotFocus	KeyDown
KeyPress	KeyUp	LostFocus
MouseDown	MouseMove	MouseUp
PathChange	PatternChange	

Frame Control

A Frame control lets you physically—and visually—group a set of controls. This is especially important when using OptionButton controls because a Frame control automatically manages all of its OptionButtons such that only one is active at any one time. OptionButtons within different Frame controls do not affect each other. However, you do not have to use Frame controls only for OptionButtons. A Frame control also provides a nice way to visually separate groups of controls, especially if you assign meaningful captions to the Frames.

To group controls, you first must draw the Frame control. Then draw controls inside the Frame. You cannot double-click the control icons in the Toolbox window; doing that places the controls only on the Form, not inside the Frame. The dimensions and locations of all controls inside a frame are specified in twips and are relative to the top-left corner of the Frame control. Thus when you move a Frame control, all controls inside the Frame move with it.

To select multiple controls inside a Frame control at design time, hold down the Ctrl key and then use the mouse to draw a selection rectangle around the controls. Be sure to start the selection rectangle *inside* the Frame.

Properties

Appearance	BackColor	Caption
ClipControls	Container	DragIcon
DragMode	Enabled	Font
FontBold	FontItalic	FontName
FontSize	FontStrikethru	FontUnderline

ForeColor	Height	HelpContextID
hWnd	Index	Left
MouseIcon	MousePointer	Name
Parent	TabIndex	Tag
Top	Visible	WhatsThisHelpID
Width		

Methods

| Drag | Move | Refresh |
| ShowWhatsThis | ZOrder | |

Events

Click	DblClick	DragDrop
DragOver	MouseDown	MouseMove
MouseUp		

Grid Control

For an easy way to display rows and columns of information (à la a spreadsheet), use the Grid control. Think of it as the grid of your dreams. Or don't. Anyway, the Grid control works pretty much like a spreadsheet in many ways: rows and columns intersect to form cells and you can put text, numbers, and even pictures into the cells, and so on.

Note: The Grid control is a custom control and isn't included in your VB environment by default. To add it, select Tools/Custom Controls and click Microsoft Grid Control. The control will then appear in the Object Browser as MSGrid. To make it available to users of your application, you must install it to the Windows System directory when you install your application.

When you want to specify a particular cell, use the Row and Col properties and then use the Text property to access any text in that cell or the Picture property to access a picture in the cell. Text wraps as you'd expect, to the width specified in ColWidth, and displays until you run out of height (as specified by RowHeight).

You're limited to 16,352 rows and 5,450 columns.

Properties

BackColor	BorderStyle	CellSelected
Clip	Col	ColAlignment
ColIsVisible	ColPos	Cols
ColWidth	Container	DragIcon
DragMode	Enabled	FillStyle
FixedAlignment	FixedCols	FixedRows
Font	FontBold	FontItalic
FontName	FontSize	FontStrikethru
FontUnderline	ForeColor	GridLines

GridLineWidth	Height	HelpContextID
HighLight	hWnd	Index
Left	LeftCol	MouseIcon
MousePointer	Name	Object
Parent	Picture	Row
RowHeight	RowIsVisible	RowPos
Rows	ScrollBars	SelEndCol
SelEndRow	SelStartCol	SelStartRow
TabIndex	TabStop	Tag
Text	Top	TopRow
Visible	WhatsThisHelpID	Width

Methods

AddItem	Drag	Move
Refresh	RemoveItem	SetFocus
ShowWhatsThis	ZOrder	

Events

Click	DblClick	DragDrop
DragOver	GotFocus	KeyDown
KeyPress	KeyUp	LostFocus
MouseDown	MouseMove	MouseUp
RowColChange	SelChange	

HScrollBar, VScrollBar Controls

Scroll bars allow a user to adjust the value of a variable graphically by using the mouse. When tied to a long list of items or long text, they allow the user to specify which part of the list or text to view. Used separately, they may be used to adjust a single variable, such as the red, green, and blue components of RGB color; the scale and offset of a graph; or even the speed and volume for playback of a recording.

The Value property of a scroll bar also determines where the scroll box—the draggable part of the scroll bar—is displayed. To limit the range of values that a user may choose from when using a scroll bar, set the Max and Min properties to correspond to the values at both ends of the bar.

Use the LargeChange property to set how much the value changes when the user clicks the mouse to either side of the scroll box. Use the SmallChange property to set how much the value changes when the user clicks the mouse on the arrow boxes at the ends of the scroll bar.

The properties, methods, and events for the HScrollBar and VScrollBar Controls are the same.

Properties

Appearance	Container	DragIcon
DragMode	Enabled	Height

HelpContextID	hWnd	Index
LargeChange	Left	Max
Min	MouseIcon	MousePointer
Name	Parent	SmallChange
TabIndex	TabStop	Tag
Top	Value	Visible
WhatsThisHelpID	Width	

Methods

Drag	Move	Refresh
SetFocus	ShowWhatsThis	ZOrder

Events

Change	DragDrop	DragOver
GotFocus	KeyDown	KeyPress
KeyUp	LostFocus	Scroll

Image Control

An Image control displays a graphic either from a file or from the graphics of another control or Form (using the Picture, Image, Icon, DragIcon, or MouseIcon properties). To conserve resources, use the Image control to display a graphic when you do not need the additional features provided by a PictureBox.

Because an Image control uses fewer system resources than a PictureBox, it repaints faster. By default, an Image control has no borders. You can add a border, however, by changing its BorderStyle property. You can use the Stretch property to specify whether the graphic will be automatically scaled to fit the control. You cannot place other controls inside an Image control.

Properties

Appearance	BorderStyle	Container
DataChanged	DataField	DataSource
DragIcon	DragMode	Enabled
Height	Index	Left
MouseIcon	MousePointer	Name
Parent	Picture	Stretch
Tag	Top	Visible
WhatsThisHelpID	Width	

Methods

Drag	Move	Refresh
ShowWhatsThis	ZOrder	

Events

Click	DblClick	DragDrop
DragOver	MouseDown	MouseMove
MouseUp		

ImageList Control

The ImageList control is basically an array that holds lots of images—either bitmaps or icons. Technically, it contains a collection of ListImage objects. As with an array, you can get at any element in the ImageList array by referring to its index. Why would you want to? The ImageList control is a great way to load, set up, and store a bunch of images so that they're ready at the drop of a key to be sucked into another control's Picture property (for example).

So, say you have a form with a PictureBox and an ImageList control. You could use the one line

```
Set PictureBox1.Picture = ImageList1.ListImages(1).Picture
```

to pull the contents of the first picture in the ImageList control into the PictureBox. Note the use of the ListImage object to identify which picture. For more information on ListImage, see the ListImage object section earlier in Section 3.

There are some catches to the ImageList control. First, although it can load bitmaps and icons (or even both at the same time), all must be the same size. Second, it loads images into memory, so you'll find that loading a lot of images is a drain on system resources. It's possible to get around this problem by using the ImageList control with the ListView, ToolBar, TabStrip, and TreeView controls and hooking them together through an image-related property (for example, setting the ImageList property to point to an ImageList control).

Note: The ImageList control works only with Windows 95 and NT 3.51 and higher.

Example

```
Private Sub Form_Load()
        Dim imgTest As ListImage
        Set imgTest = ImageList1. _
        ListImages.Add(,"butterfly",LoadPicture("butterfly.ico"))
        Set imgTest = ImageList1. _
        ListImages.Add(,"toad",LoadPicture("toad.ico"))
        Set imgTest = ImageList1. _
        ListImages.Add(,"house",LoadPicture("house.ico"))

        ListView1.Icons = ImageList1

        Dim itmTest as ListItem
        Set itmTest = ListView1.ListItems.Add()
        itmTest.Icon = 1
End Sub
```

Or, for another kind of example, create a Form and place on it an ImageList control and a TreeView control. Then add the following code to the Form_Load event:

Example

```
Sub Form_Load()
    Dim imgSmallIcons As ListImage
    Set imgSmallIcons = ImageList1.ListImages. _
        Add(, "No", LoadPicture("bitmaps\tlbr_w95\back.bmp"))
    Set imgSmallIcons = ImageList1.ListImages. _
        Add(, , LoadPicture("bitmaps\tlbr_w95\discnet.bmp"))
    Set imgSmallIcons = ImageList1.ListImages. _
        Add(, , LoadPicture("bitmaps\tlbr_w95\camera.bmp"))
    Set imgSmallIcons = ImageList1.ListImages. _
        Add(, , LoadPicture("bitmaps\tlbr_w95\arc.bmp"))
    Set imgSmallIcons = ImageList1.ListImages. _
        Add(, , LoadPicture("bitmaps\tlbr_w95\arc.bmp"))
    ImageList1.MaskColor = vbGreen

    Dim nodSmallIconsDemo As Node
    Set nodSmallIconsDemo = _
        TreeView1.Nodes.Add(, , "R", "Root")
    Set nodSmallIconsDemo = _
        TreeView1.Nodes.Add("R", tvwChild, "C1", "Child 1")
    Set nodSmallIconsDemo = _
        TreeView1.Nodes.Add("R", tvwChild, "C2", "Child 2")
    Set nodSmallIconsDemo = _
        TreeView1.Nodes.Add("R", tvwChild, "C3", "Child 3")
    nodSmallIconsDemo.EnsureVisible

    Set TreeView1.ImageList = ImageList1
    For i = 1 To TreeView1.Nodes.Count
        TreeView1.Nodes(i).Image = i
    Next i
End Sub
```

What, you ask, does this do? Paste it and find out. Basically it associates icons with the nodes in a TreeView.

An ImageList control has no events. Following are its properties and method.

Properties

BackColor	ImageHeight	ImageWidth
Index	ListImages	MaskColor
Name	Object	Parent
Tag		

Method

Overlay

Label Control

A Label control displays text that cannot be edited by the user. Use a Label control to identify a control that does not have a Caption property of is own, such as a TextBox control, or to display status messages.

If you use a Label control to identify another control, make sure the Label control appears immediately before the other control in Tab Order. Then you can set the UseMnemonic property to True and precede a character in the Label text with an ampersand (&) to make it an access key. At runtime, the user can use the access key with the Alt key to jump focus to the control identified by the label.

When used for status messages, this control can have its AutoSize and WordWrap properties set to display multiple lines.

A Label control can be the destination (client) in a DDE conversation. You just need to set its LinkTopic, LinkItem, and LinkMode properties appropriately. If you set these properties at design time, VB will attempt to connect as soon as the application starts running.

Properties

Alignment	Appearance	AutoSize
BackColor	BackStyle	BorderStyle
Caption	Container	DataChanged
DataSource	DataField	DragIcon
DragMode	Enabled	Font
FontBold	FontItalic	FontName
FontSize	FontStrikethru	FontUnderline
ForeColor	Height	Index
Left	LinkItem	LinkMode
LinkTimeout	LinkTopic	MouseIcon
MousePointer	Name	Parent
TabIndex	Tag	Top
UseMnemonic	Visible	WhatsThisHelpID
Width	WordWrap	

Methods

Drag	LinkExecute	LinkPoke
LinkRequest	Move	Refresh
ShowWhatsThis	ZOrder	

Events

Change	Click	DblClick
DragDrop	DragOver	LinkClose
LinkError	LinkNotify	LinkOpen
MouseDown	MouseMove	MouseUp

Line Control

A Line control is a graphical object that displays a line in a Form object, PictureBox control, or Frame control. Line controls are automatically redrawn when uncovered by another window, so you do not have to set the AutoRedraw property or implement redrawing in a Paint event procedure.

Unlike the Line method, you can use Line controls at design time to draw lines. A line control does not have any Move methods, but you can change its X1, Y1, X2, and Y2 properties to move the endpoints of the line. Also, you can change how the line is displayed by setting its BorderStyle, BorderWidth, and BorderColor properties.

 The same bug exists for Line controls as for other controls regarding the BorderStyle property. If BorderWidth is not set to 1, then you cannot display dashed or dotted lines by setting the BorderStyle property.

The Line control has no event procedures. Following are its properties and methods.

Properties

BorderColor	BorderStyle	BorderWidth
Container	DrawMode	Index
Name	Parent	Tag
Visible	X1	X2
Y1	Y2	

Methods

Refresh	ZOrder

 The Help file incorrectly lists Appearance as a property of the Line control.

ListBox Control

A ListBox control presents a list of text items from which the user can select one or more items, depending on the setting of the MultiSelect property. A vertical scroll bar is automatically added to the ListBox control when the number of items cannot all be displayed in the control simultaneously.

The ListIndex property returns the index of the selected item or the item with focus if multiple selection is enabled. The first item has a ListIndex of 0. If no items are selected, ListIndex returns –1. The ListCount property gives the total number of items in the list. Since ListIndex starts at 0, ListCount is always 1 greater than the maximum value of ListIndex.

Use the AddItem and RemoveItem methods to add and remove items from the list at runtime. You can also add items at design time by typing entries into the Properties window. Access the list items by using the List and ListIndex properties.

Properties

Appearance	BackColor	Columns
Container	DataChanged	DataField
DataSource	DragIcon	DragMode
Enabled	Font	FontBold
FontItalic	FontName	FontSize
FontStrikethru	FontUnderline	ForeColor
Height	HelpContextID	hWnd
Index	IntegralHeight	ItemData
Left	List	ListCount
ListIndex	MouseIcon	MousePointer
MultiSelect	Name	NewIndex
Parent	SelCount	Selected
Sorted	TabIndex	TabStop
Tag	Text	Top
TopIndex	Visible	WhatsThisHelpID
Width		

Methods

AddItem	Clear	Drag
Move	Refresh	RemoveItem
SetFocus	ShowWhatsThis	ZOrder

Events

Click	DblClick	DragDrop
DragOver	GotFocus	KeyDown
KeyPress	KeyUp	LostFocus
MouseDown	MouseMove	MouseUp

ListView Control

Open Windows 95's Explorer. That way of viewing items is what the ListView control does. You can view items (with the View property) four ways: as big icons, small icons, a list, and "details," or what the ListView control calls a report.

The ListView control contains two important collections of objects: ListItems and Column-Headers. The ListItem object controls all sorts of miscellany of how you view the items, such as how the description will read, what icons will show up, and what subitems will show up (see the

SubItem property). The ColumnHeader object controls the column headers you see in Report view.

The Windows Help file comes with a good example of how to use the ListView control.

Note: This control is available only with Windows 95 or NT 3.51 or later.

Properties

Arrange	BackColor	BorderStyle
ColumnHeaders	Container	DragIcon
DragMode	DropHighLight	Enabled
Font	ForeColor	Height
HelpContextID	HideColumnHeaders	HideSelection
hWnd	Icons	Index
LabelEdit	LabelWrap	Left
ListItems	MouseIcon	MousePointer
MultiSelect	Name	Object
Parent	SelectedItem	SmallIcons
Sorted	SortKey	SortOrder
TabIndex	TabStop	Tag
Top	View	Visible
WhatsThisHelpID	Width	

Methods

Drag	FindItem	GetFirstVisible
HitTest	Move	Refresh
SetFocus	ShowWhatsThis	StartLabelEdit
ZOrder		

Events

AfterLabelEdit	BeforeLabelEdit	Click
ColumnClick	DblClick	DragDrop
DragOver	GotFocus	ItemClick
KeyDown	KeyPress	KeyUp
LostFocus	MouseDown	MouseMove
MouseUp		

Menu Control

A Menu control allows you to create custom menus for your Form windows. Each menu can contain commands, submenus, and separator bars. A maximum of four levels of submenus is allowed. You do not have to display menus in a menu bar at the top of a window. You can pop up menus using the PopupMenu method at runtime to provide context-sensitive immediate menus.

Create Menu controls at design time using the Menu Editor, which is available from the Tools menu. Enter in the Caption box the text to display in the menu; include an ampersand (&) in front of the access character. To create a separator bar, use a single hyphen (-) in the Caption. Enter the name of the Menu control in the Name box. Using the Menu Editor, you can define additional properties, such as whether the menu displays a check mark, shortcut keys, the HelpContextID value, and so on. Other properties are available from the Properties window directly by selecting the Menu controls from the drop-down Objects list.

Use the arrows button and Next, Insert, and Delete buttons to position, insert, and delete menu entries and to create submenus.

By convention, if your Menu command pops up other dialog boxes or windows, you should put ellipses (...) at the end of the Caption text.

If you create a menu for an MDI child form, its Menu Bar will replace that of the parent MDIForm object when the child form becomes active.

Menu controls have no methods. Following are its properties and event.

Properties

The properties of a Menu control that are exposed, or supplied by VB, to add-ins are read-only at runtime.

Caption	Checked	Enabled
HelpContextID	Index	Name
NegotiatePosition	Parent	ShortCut
Tag	Visible	WindowList

Event

Click

The Help file incorrectly lists Appearance as a property of the Menu control.

OLE Container Control

The OLE Container control is a placeholder for adding "insertable objects" to your Forms. These objects may be linked to existing files or embedded directly in your application. At runtime, your VB application becomes an OLE client that can negotiate menus and toolbars, with the server application supplying the object for full in-place editing.

The object contained in an OLE Container control may be created at design time or at runtime. When you first create an OLE Container control, the Insert Object dialog box will appear to ask you to select an object to insert. If you click Cancel, no object will be inserted at that time. Subsequently, you can use the Insert Object, Paste Special, and other commands from the popup menu to embed or link an object. Only one object may be placed in an OLE Container control at any one time. At runtime, you can use the appropriate methods to create a link or embed an object.

To find an appropriate class name to use for an insertable object, select an OLE Container control at design time. Then find the Class property in the Properties window and click on the "..." button of the Class property.

You can also bind an OLE Container control to a database through a Data control.

Clicking the right mouse button over an OLE Container control at design time or runtime displays a popup menu. The available commands may depend on the state of the OLE Container control.

POPUP MENU COMMAND	OLE CONTAINER CONTROL STATE
Insert Object	Design time; always enabled.
Paste Special	Design time; when the Clipboard object contains a valid object.
Delete Embedded Object	Design time; when the OLE Container control contains an embedded object.
Delete Linked Object	Design time; when the OLE Container control contains a linked object.
Create Link	Design time; when the SourceDoc property is edited, but the file has not been linked yet.
Create Embedded Object	Design time; when the SourceDoc property is edited, but the file has not been embedded yet.

At runtime, the popup menu may contain the verbs supported by the object, depending on the setting of the AutoVerbMenu property. Most objects support the verbs listed in the following table.

POPUP MENU COMMAND	MEANING
Edit	Tries to perform in-place editing, if the source application allows.
Open	Opens the source application in a separate window to edit the object.

Properties

Action	Appearance	AppIsRunning
AutoActivate	AutoVerbMenu	BackColor
BackStyle	BorderStyle	Class
Container	Data	DataChanged
DataField	DataSource	DataText
DisplayType	DragIcon	DragMode
Enabled	FileNumber	Format
Height	HelpContextID	HostName
hWnd	Index	Left
lpOleObject	MiscFlags	MouseIcon
MousePointer	Name	Object
ObjectAcceptFormats	ObjectAcceptFormatsCount	ObjectGetFormats

ObjectGetFormatsCount	ObjectVerbFlags	ObjectVerbs
ObjectVerbsCount	OLEDropAllowed	OLEType
OLETypeAllowed	Parent	PasteOK
Picture	SizeMode	SourceDoc
SourceItem	TabIndex	TabStop
Tag	Top	UpdateOptions
Verb	Visible	WhatsThisHelpID
Width		

Methods

Close	Copy	CreateEmbed
CreateLink	Delete	DoVerb
Drag	FetchVerbs	InsertObjDlg
Move	Paste	PasteSpecialDlg
ReadFromFile	Refresh	SaveToFile
SaveToOle1File	SetFocus	ShowWhatsThis
Update	ZOrder	

Events

Click	DblClick	DragDrop
DragOver	GotFocus	KeyDown
KeyPress	KeyUp	LostFocus
MouseDown	MouseMove	MouseUp
ObjectMove	Resize	Updated

OptionButton Control

A group of OptionButton controls is typically used to present the user with a set of choices, only one of which may be selected. When they are grouped together inside a Frame or PictureBox control, VB automatically manages the OptionButtons to turn off all other options within the Frame or PictureBox when one option is selected.

To place OptionButton controls inside a Frame or PictureBox, you must manually draw the OptionButton controls inside the Frame or PictureBox. If you simply highlight the Frame or PictureBox and then double-click the OptionButton in the Toolbox window, the newly created OptionButton will not be in the Frame or PictureBox.

To provide the user with a set of choices, several of which may be selected, use CheckBox controls instead.

Properties

Alignment	Appearance	BackColor
Caption	Container	DragIcon
DragMode	Enabled	Font

FontBold	FontItalic	FontName
FontSize	FontStrikethru	FontUnderline
ForeColor	Height	HelpContextID
hWnd	Index	Left
MouseIcon	MousePointer	Name
Parent	TabIndex	TabStop
Tag	Top	Value
Visible	WhatsThisHelpID	Width

Methods

Drag	Move	Refresh
SetFocus	ShowWhatsThis	ZOrder

Events

Click	DblClick	DragDrop
DragOver	GotFocus	KeyDown
KeyPress	KeyUp	LostFocus
MouseDown	MouseMove	MouseUp

PictureBox Control

A PictureBox control may be used to display graphics from a file, from graphics controls, and from graphics and text methods. It can even hold other controls. When placed in an MDIForm object, it can serve as a toolbar or status bar. Large graphics are clipped at the edges of the PictureBox control, unless its AutoSize property is set to True.

You can use a Frame or PictureBox control to group OptionButton controls. The PictureBox control is the only standard VB control that can be placed in an MDIForm object, but you can place other controls on the PictureBox control. To create animation effects, you must use graphics properties and methods in code to execute at runtime.

You can also use a PictureBox control as a destination control in a DDE conversation.

Properties

Align	Appearance	AutoRedraw
AutoSize	BackColor	BorderStyle
ClipControls	Container	CurrentX
CurrentY	DataChanged	DataField
DataSource	DragIcon	DragMode
DrawMode	DrawStyle	DrawWidth
Enabled	FillColor	FillStyle
Font	FontBold	FontItalic
FontName	FontSize	FontStrikethru
FontTransparent	FontUnderline	ForeColor

hDC   Height   HelpContextID
hWnd   Image   Index
Left   LinkItem   LinkMode
LinkTimeout   LinkTopic   MouseIcon
MousePointer   Name   Negotiate
Parent   Picture   ScaleHeight
ScaleLeft   ScaleMode   ScaleTop
ScaleWidth   TabIndex   TabStop
Tag   Top   Visible
WhatsThisHelpID Width

Methods

Circle   Cls   Drag
Line   LinkExecute   LinkPoke
LinkRequest   LinkSend   Move
PaintPicture   Point   Print
PSet   Refresh   Scale
ScaleX   ScaleY   SetFocus
ShowWhatsThis   TextHeight   TextWidth
ZOrder

Events

Change   Click   DblClick
DragDrop   DragOver   GotFocus
KeyDown   KeyPress   KeyUp
LinkClose   LinkError   LinkNotify
LinkOpen   LostFocus   MouseDown
MouseMove   MouseUp   Paint
Resize

ProgressBar Control

As your fingers drum on the table, you watch as the Progress Bar gradually edges its way to completion. (That's a fancy way of saying the ProgressBar control shows the progress of a lengthy operation by filling a rectangle with chunks from left to right.) It's a little like the Gauge control, but less precise.

When you write the code that makes a ProgressBar control work, keep a few things in mind. First, you need to know the minimum and maximum boundaries of whatever is taking place—for example, how many files you're copying. Second, you have to manually increment the Progress-Bar control's Value property to move the little blocks along. The Width property controls how precise the ProgressBar control will be (larger numbers are more precise).

```
Private Sub Form_Click()
    Dim Counter As Integer
```

```
    ProgressBar1.Min = 1
    ProgressBar1.Max = 50
    ProgressBar1.Visible = True

    ProgressBar1.Value = ProgressBar1.Min

    For Counter = 1 To 50
        ProgressBar1.Value = Counter
    Next Counter
    ProgressBar1.Value = ProgressBar1.Min
End Sub
```

The ProgressBar control is a Windows 95 and NT 3.51 thing only.

Properties

Align	Appearance	BorderStyle
Container	DragIcon	DragMode
Enabled	Height	hWnd
Index	Left	Max
Min	MouseIcon	MousePointer
Name	Negotiate	Object
Parent	TabIndex	Tag
Top	Value	Visible
WhatsThisHelpID	Width	

Methods

Drag	Move	ShowWhatsThis
ZOrder		

Events

Click	DragDrop	DragOver
MouseDown	MouseMove	MouseUp

RichTextBox Control

If the plain, old-fashioned TextBox control isn't what you need, why not indulge in the Rich-TextBox control, which does everything the TextBox does, but it

1. doesn't have a 64,000-character limit,

2. supports multiple fonts for different selections,

3. supports all sorts of weird formatting, and

4. supports drag-and-drop of rich-text-format files.

In case you're wondering, rich text format (or RTF) is a pretty sophisticated formatting style. Windows 95's WordPad editor is actually an RTF editor. Rich text even seems to be able to do so-phisticated things like save WinWord 6's annotations, revisions, and footnotes.

The RichTextBox does all that, and it's at your disposal. The catch is that you can perform character and paragraph formatting only to selected text. This is unlike the TextBox control, which allows you to define *all* the text as italic, bold, or a different font. It's not really much of a limitation, but you need to know about it.

Probably the neatest thing about the RichTextBox control is that it has methods (LoadFile and SaveFile) to read and write rich text (and ASCII) files directly. Or, as we mentioned earlier, you can drag-and-drop a file (from the Explorer, for example) or a selection (from WordPad, for example) directly into the box.

Note that, like so many other controls, RichTextBox is a 32-bit OCX that will run only on Windows 95 and Windows NT 3.51 and later. Also, to use it you need to add RICHTX32.OCX to your project.

Properties

Appearance	BackColor	BorderStyle
BulletIndent	Container	DataChanged
DataField	DataSource	DisableNoScroll
DragIcon	DragMode	Enabled
FileName	Font	Height
HelpContextID	HideSelection	hWnd
Index	Left	Locked
MaxLength	MouseIcon	MousePointer
MultiLine	Name	Object
Parent	ScrollBars	SelAlignment
SelBold	SelBullet	SelCharOffset
SelColor	SelFontName	SelFontSize
SelHangingIndent	SelIndent	SelItalic
SelLength	SelRightIndent	SelRTF
SelStart	SelStrikethru	SelTabCount
SelTabs	SelText	SelUnderline
TabIndex	TabStop	Tag
Text	TextRTF	Top
Visible	WhatsThisHelpID	Width

Methods

Drag	Find	GetLineFromChar
LoadFile	Move	Refresh
SaveFile	SelPrint	SetFocus
ShowWhatsThis	Span	UpTo
ZOrder		

Events

Change	Click	DblClick
DragDrop	DragOver	GotFocus

KeyDown	KeyPress	KeyUp
LostFocus	MouseDown	MouseMove
MouseUp	SelChange	

Shape Control

A Shape control is a graphical object that displays a rectangle, square, oval, circle, rounded rectangle, or rounded square in a Form object, PictureBox control, or Frame control. Shape controls are automatically redrawn when uncovered by another window, so you do not have to set the AutoRedraw property or implement redrawing in a Paint event procedure. Unlike the graphics methods, you can use Shape controls at design time to draw graphics.

You can change how the border of a shape is displayed using the BorderStyle, BorderWidth, and BorderColor properties.

 The same bug exists for Shape controls as for other controls regarding the BorderStyle property. If BorderWidth is not set to 1, then you cannot display dashed or dotted lines by setting the BorderStyle property.

The Shape control has no event procedure. Following are its properties and methods.

Properties

BackColor	BackStyle	BorderColor
BorderStyle	BorderWidth	Container
DrawMode	FillColor	FillStyle
Height	Index	Left
Name	Parent	Shape
Tag	Top	Visible
Width		

Methods

Move	Refresh	ZOrder

 The Help file incorrectly lists Appearance as a property of the Shape control.

Sheridan Tabbed Dialog Control

The Sheridan Tabbed Dialog (SSTab) is, in general, superior to the TabStrip control, especially for creating tabbed dialog boxes. Why? It's easier to use—you don't have to worry about using Picture controls to group icons, for example. Each tab on an SSTab control is a container for other controls. The tabs behave just as they do in most Windows applications, with one and only one becoming active when you click it. You set the name, the graphic to display by the name, and so on.

To use it, figure out how many tabs you want and set them using the Tabs and TabsPerRow properties. Then simply add the controls you want to the tabs on which you want them.

SSTab also has a distribution advantage over the TabStrip. It comes in 16-bit (TABCTL16.OCX) and 32-bit (TABCTL32.OCX) versions, so you can use it under Windows 3.1 in addition to Windows 95 and Windows NT 3.51 and later. Add it in the usual way.

Properties

BackColor	Caption	Container
DragIcon	DragMode	Enabled
Font	ForeColor	Height
HelpContextID	hWnd	Index
Left	MouseIcon	MousePointer
Name	Object	Parent
Picture	Rows	ShowFocusRect
Style	Tab	TabCaption
TabEnabled	TabHeight	TabIndex
TabMaxWidth	TabOrientation	TabPicture
Tabs	TabsPerRow	TabStop
TabVisible	Tag	Top
Visible	WhatsThisHelpID	Width
WordWrap		

Methods

Drag	Move	SetFocus
ShowWhatsThis	ZOrder	

Events

Click	DblClick	DragDrop
DragOver	GotFocus	KeyDown
KeyPress	KeyUp	LostFocus
MouseDown	MouseMove	MouseUp

Slider Control

A Slider control works like a lever that you push to change values. It contains the slider itself and probably tick marks (depending on its size). You move it by clicking and dragging, clicking to one side, or using the keyboard. It is a Windows 95 and Windows NT 3.51 thing only.

Properties

BorderStyle	Container	DragIcon
DragMode	Enabled	Height
HelpContextID	hWnd	Index
LargeChange	Left	Max
Min	MouseIcon	MousePointer
Name	Orientation	Parent
SelectRange	SelLength	SelStart
SmallChange	TabIndex	TabStop
Tag	TickFrequency	TickStyle
Top	Value	Visible
WhatsThisHelpID	Width	

Methods

ClearSel	Drag	GetNumTicks
Move	Refresh	SetFocus
ShowWhatsThis	ZOrder	

Events

Change	Click	DragDrop
DragOver	GotFocus	KeyDown
KeyPress	KeyUp	LostFocus
MouseDown	MouseMove	MouseUp
Scroll		

StatusBar Control

A status bar runs across the bottom (usually) of an application and provides useful information such as (in a word processor) what page you're on. The StatusBar control creates a status bar, by default with one Panel object—the pane in which information is actually displayed. Panel objects may hold text or even pictures. Look at the bottom of the Word 7 for Windows 95 screen, you'll see that its status bar contains a little book with a pencil in the right side showing that it's doing on-the-fly spell checking. You can add Panel objects (to the Panels collection), with up to 16 per StatusBar control. See the Panel object reference section for more information on how to display things like the status of the Caps Lock key.

Note: The StatusBar control is a Windows 95 and Windows NT 3.51 and later thing.

Properties

Align	Container	DragIcon
DragMode	Enabled	Font
Height	hWnd	Index
Left	MouseIcon	MousePointer

Name	Negotiate	Panels
Parent	SimpleText	Style
Tag	Top	Visible
WhatsThisHelpID	Width	

Methods

| Move | Refresh | ShowWhatsThis |
| ZOrder | | |

Events

Click	DblClick	DragDrop
DragOver	MouseDown	MouseMove
MouseUp	PanelClick	PanelDblClick

TabStrip Control

Tabbed dialog boxes are a big thing in Windows 95. The Tab object represents one of these Tabs and the Tabs collection is a bunch of Tab objects. You use them with a TabStrip control.

To get an idea about how the TabStrip works, put an ImageList and a TabStrip control on your Form. Then paste the following code under the Form_Load section:

```
Private Sub Form_Load()
    'You'll need this later
    Dim Counter As Integer

    'Set up ImageList control
    Dim imgTest As ListImage
    Set imgTest = ImageList1. _
    ListImages.Add(, "Note", LoadPicture("bitmaps\assorted\note.bmp"))
    Set imgTest = ImageList1. _
    ListImages.Add(, "Cup", LoadPicture("bitmaps\assorted\cup.bmp"))
    Set imgTest = ImageList1. _
    ListImages.Add(, "Balloon", LoadPicture("bitmaps\assorted\balloon.bmp"))

    'Set the MaskColor so that the pictures look right
    ImageList1.MaskColor = vbGreen

    'Now set up the TabStrip
    'First, point it to the ImageList
    Set TabStrip1.ImageList = ImageList1
    'Second, create the tabs and set their captions and their Tool Tip Text
    TabStrip1.Tabs(1).Caption = "Music"
    TabStrip1.Tabs.Add 2, , "Drinks"
    TabStrip1.Tabs.Add 3, , "Conversation"
    TabStrip1.Tabs(1).ToolTipText = "Click here to see stuff about music"
    TabStrip1.Tabs(2).ToolTipText = "Click here to see information about
drinks"
```

```
     TabStrip1.Tabs(3).ToolTipText = "Click here to have a conversation"
     'Now, use Counter to point the tabs to images
     For Counter = 1 To TabStrip1.Tabs.Count
         TabStrip1.Tabs(Counter).Image = Counter
     Next Counter
End Sub
```

As you can see, Tab objects and the Tabs collection work like the other objects and collections in VB. Key properties of the Tab object are Caption, Image, and ToolTipText. You can attach images to the TabStrip by using an ImageList control. You can use the SelectedItem property to get a reference to the tab a user has selected and use the selected property to see if a specific tab is selected. Use these properties with the BeforeClick event to write whatever values the user has set on a specific tab before going to the next one.

Use the Style property to set whether the TabStrip control looks like push buttons (Buttons) or notebook tabs (Tabs). By default, a TabStrip has one notebook tab. You can add more by adding elements to a Tabs collection.

Note: The TabStrip control is for Windows 95 and Windows NT 3.51 and later.

Properties

ClientHeight	ClientLeft	ClientTop
ClientWidth	Container	DragIcon
DragMode	Enabled	Font
Height	HelpContextID	hWnd
ImageList	Index	Left
MouseIcon	MousePointer	MultiRow
Name	Object	Parent
SelectedItem	ShowTips	Style
TabFixedHeight	TabFixedWidth	TabIndex
Tabs	TabStop	TabWidthStyle
Tag	Top	Visible
WhatsThisHelpID	Width	

Methods

Drag	Move	Refresh
SetFocus	ShowWhatsThis	ZOrder

Events

BeforeClick	Click	DblClick
DragDrop	DragOver	GotFocus
KeyDown	KeyPress	KeyUp
LostFocus	MouseDown	MouseMove
MouseUp		

TextBox Control

The TextBox control presents text that may be entered or changed by the user at runtime. For this reason, it is often called an "edit field" or "edit control." When the application starts, a TextBox control displays the string entered for its Text property at design time, or the text set by the Form_Load event procedure.

A TextBox control will not display multiple lines—even if the text has embedded carriage return characters (Chr(13))—unless the MultiLine property is set to True. With MultiLine set to True, and with the ScrollBars property set to vbSBNone (0) or vbVertical (2) so that no horizontal scroll bars are displayed, text within the TextBox control will automatically wrap at word boundaries.

You can set the text alignment in a TextBox control using the Alignment property, but only if MultiLine is set to True.

A TextBox control can also be the destination or source in a DDE conversation.

Properties

Alignment	Appearance	BackColor
BorderStyle	Container	DataChanged
DataField	DataSource	DragIcon
DragMode	Enabled	Font
FontBold	FontItalic	FontName
FontSize	FontStrikethru	FontUnderline
ForeColor	Height	HelpContextID
HideSelection	hWnd	Index
Left	LinkItem	LinkMode
LinkTimeout	LinkTopic	Locked
MaxLength	MouseIcon	MousePointer
MultiLine	Name	Parent
PasswordChar	ScrollBars	SelLength
SelStart	SelText	TabIndex
TabStop	Tag	Text
Top	Visible	WhatsThisHelpID
Width		

Methods

Drag	LinkExecute	LinkPoke
LinkRequest	Move	Refresh
SetFocus	ShowWhatsThis	ZOrder

Events

Change	Click	DblClick
DragDrop	DragOver	GotFocus
KeyDown	KeyPress	KeyUp
LinkClose	LinkError	LinkNotify

LinkOpen   LostFocus   MouseDown
MouseMove   MouseUp

Timer Control

A Timer control may be used to execute code at regular intervals—as when implementing animation or background processing—or only once at a later time—as when implementing a timer alarm. The code to run is usually in or run from the Timer control's Timer event. The Timer control appears as a small button with a stop watch at design time but is invisible at runtime, so it doesn't really matter where you place it.

Use the Interval property to set the elapsed time between repeated triggers of the Timer event and the elapsed time between the time the control is Enabled and the first Timer event.

For Windows, a maximum of 16 timers may be running at any one time. Trying to start another one causes an error.

The Timer control has no methods. Following are the properties and event.

Properties

Enabled   Index   Interval
Left   Name   Parent
Tag   Top

Event

Timer

Toolbar Control

A toolbar is a group of Button objects. Typically, these buttons correspond to menu selections or macros. But a toolbar can also be just a handy place to stash tools, rather like the VB Tool-Box.

The Toolbar control enables you to create toolbars. First you create some Button objects (complete with pictures and text) and then add them to a ToolBar control using the ToolBar1.Buttons. Add collection syntax. As you're creating your button objects, you can associate images using an ImageList control and syntax like Toolbar1.ImageList = ImageList1. Set the Caption property and the ToolTipText property of each Button object. Use the ButtonClick event to get each button to work right. Use the ButtonGroup style to group buttons so that, for example, if one is active none of the others can be. The AllowCustomize property enables users to create their own toolbars. If you enable it, you'll need to write code under the SaveToolbar and RestoreToolbar methods. Finally, the Toolbar control is 32-bit and will only work with Windows 95 and NT 3.51 and later.

Properties

Align	AllowCustomize	ButtonHeight
Buttons	ButtonWidth	Container
DragIcon	DragMode	Enabled
Font	Height	hWnd
ImageList	Index	Left
MouseIcon	MousePointer	Name
Negotiate	Object	Parent
ShowTips	TabIndex	Tag
Top	Visible	WhatsThisHelpID
Width	Wrappable	

Methods

Customize	Drag	Move
Refresh	RestoreToolbar	SaveToolbar
ShowWhatsThis	ZOrder	

Events

ButtonClick	Change	Click
DblClick	DragDrop	DragOver
MouseDown	MouseMove	MouseUp

TreeView Control

Use the TreeView control to navigate hierarchical information such as directory structures, database structures, and document structures. Look at the left side of the Windows 95 Explorer; that's a TreeView.

Here's how it works. Create a form and place on it an ImageList control and a TreeView control. Then add the following code to the Form_Load event:

```
Sub Form_Load()
    Dim imgSmallIcons As ListImage
    Set imgSmallIcons = ImageList1.ListImages. _
        Add(, "No", LoadPicture("bitmaps\tlbr_w95\back.bmp"))
    Set imgSmallIcons = ImageList1.ListImages. _
        Add(, , LoadPicture("bitmaps\tlbr_w95\discnet.bmp"))
    Set imgSmallIcons = ImageList1.ListImages. _
        Add(, , LoadPicture("bitmaps\tlbr_w95\camera.bmp"))
    Set imgSmallIcons = ImageList1.ListImages. _
        Add(, , LoadPicture("bitmaps\tlbr_w95\arc.bmp"))
    Set imgSmallIcons = ImageList1.ListImages. _
        Add(, , LoadPicture("bitmaps\tlbr_w95\arc.bmp"))
    ImageList1.MaskColor = vbGreen

    Dim nodSmallIconsDemo As Node
```

```
    Set nodSmallIconsDemo = _
        TreeView1.Nodes.Add(, , "R", "Root")
    Set nodSmallIconsDemo = _
        TreeView1.Nodes.Add("R", tvwChild, "C1", "Child 1")
    Set nodSmallIconsDemo = _
        TreeView1.Nodes.Add("R", tvwChild, "C2", "Child 2")
    Set nodSmallIconsDemo = _
        TreeView1.Nodes.Add("R", tvwChild, "C3", "Child 3")
    nodSmallIconsDemo.EnsureVisible

    Set TreeView1.ImageList = ImageList1
    For i = 1 To TreeView1.Nodes.Count
        TreeView1.Nodes(i).Image = i
    Next i
End Sub
```

This example associates icons with the nodes in a TreeView.

Note: The TreeView control is 32-bit and available only for Windows 95 and NT 3.51 and later.

Properties

BorderStyle	Container	DragIcon
DragMode	DropHighlight	Enabled
Font	Height	HelpContextID
HideSelection	hWnd	ImageList
Indentation	Index	LabelEdit
Left	LineStyle	MouseIcon
MousePointer	Name	Nodes
PathSeparator	Parent	Scrollbars
SelectedItem	Sorted	Style
TabIndex	TabStop	Tag
Top	Visible	WhatsThisHelpID
Width		

Methods

Clear	GetVisibleCount	HitTest
Move	Refresh	Remove
SetFocus	StartLabelEdit	ShowWhatsThis
ZOrder		

Events

AfterLabelEdit	BeforeLabelEdit	Click
Collapse	DblClick	DragDrop
DragOver	Expand	GotFocus
KeyDown	KeyPress	KeyUp
LostFocus	MouseDown	MouseMove
MouseUp	NodeClick	

SECTION 5: MISCELLANEOUS VB CONSTANTS

Egress this way.

—P. T. Barnum

Rather than relying on obscure numeric values for your statements, please use these slightly-less-obscure constants.

Color Constants

You usually select colors at design time using the drop-down palette or in code by using the RGB() and QBColor() functions. There are, however several predefined color constants you can use in your code to improve readability of your code. You'll also find these constants using the Object Browser at design time. Look under the VB libraries for the ColorConstants module.

Applies To   BackColor Property
                     BorderColor Property
                     Color Property
                     FillColor Property
                     ForeColor Property

The second set of color constants come in useful when you are designing a well-behaved user interface. Instead of choosing specific colors, you use these constants to specify colors that match those set for particular elements in the Window manager—such as button face, button shadow, and scroll bar. That way, if your user changes the Windows color scheme, your VB app will automatically pick up those changes. Unfortunately, you cannot select these constants from a palette at design time. You just have to know the constant values.

CONSTANT	VALUE	MEANING
vbBlack	&H0&	Black
vbRed	&HFF&	Red
vbGreen	&HFF00&	Green
vbYellow	&HFFFF&	Yellow
vbBlue	&HFF0000&	Blue
vbMagenta	&HFF00FF&	Magenta
vbCyan	&HFFFF00&	Cyan
vbWhite	&HFFFFFF&	White
SYSTEM COLORS		
vbScrollBars	&H80000000&	Scroll bar color
vbDesktop	&H80000001&	Desktop color
vbActiveTitleBar	&H80000002&	Color of the title bar for the active window
vbInactiveTitleBar	&H80000003&	Color of the title bar for the inactive window
vbMenuBar	&H80000004&	Menu background color
vbWindowBackground	&H80000005&	Window background color
vbWindowFrame	&H80000006&	Window frame color
vbMenuText	&H80000007&	Color of text on menus

CONSTANT	VALUE	MEANING
vbWindowText	&H80000008&	Color of text in windows
vbTitleBarText	&H80000009&	Color of text in captions, size boxes, and scroll arrows
vbActiveBorder	&H8000000A&	Border color of active window
vbInactiveBorder	&H8000000B&	Border color of inactive window
vbApplicationWorkspace	&H8000000C&	Background color of multiple-document interface (MDI) applications
vbHighlight	&H8000000D&	Background color of items selected in a control
vbHighlightText	&H8000000E&	Text color of items selected in a control
vbButtonFace	&H8000000F&	Color of shading on the face of Command buttons
vbButtonShadow	&H80000010&	Color of shading on the edge of Command buttons
vbGrayText	&H80000011&	Grayed (disabled) text
vbButtonText	&H80000012&	Text color on push buttons
vbInactiveCaptionText	&H80000013&	Color of text in an inactive caption
vb3DHighlight	&H80000014&	Highlight color for 3D display elements
vb3DDKShadow	&H80000015&	Darkest shadow color for 3D display elements
vb3DLight	&H80000016&	Second lightest of the 3D colors after vb3DHighlight
vbInfoText or vbMsgBox	&H80000017&	Color of text in ToolTips
vbInfoBackground or vbMsgBoxText	&H80000018&	Background color of ToolTips

KeyCode Constants

These constants are useful whenever you need to process key codes, such as in the keyboard-event procedures: KeyPress, KeyDown, and KeyUp.

CONSTANT	VALUE	MEANING
vbKeyLButton	&H1	Left mouse button
vbKeyRButton	&H2	Right mouse button
vbKeyCancel	&H3	Cancel key
vbKeyMButton	&H4	Middle mouse button
vbKeyBack	&H8	Backspace key
vbKeyTab	&H9	Tab key
vbKeyClear	&HC	Clear key
vbKeyReturn	&HD	Enter key

Constant	Value	Meaning
vbKeyShift	&H10	Shift key
vbKeyControl	&H11	Ctrl key
vbKeyMenu	&H12	Menu key
vbKeyPause	&H13	Pause key
vbKeyCapital	&H14	Caps Lock key
vbKeyEscape	&H1B	Esc key
vbKeySpace	&H20	Spacebar
vbKeyPageUp	&H21	Page Up key
vbKeyPageDown	&H22	Page Down key
vbKeyEnd	&H23	End key
vbKeyHome	&H24	Home key
vbKeyLeft	&H25	Left arrow key
vbKeyUp	&H26	Up arrow key
vbKeyRight	&H27	Right arrow key
vbKeyDown	&H28	Down arrow key
vbKeySelect	&H29	Select key
vbKeyPrint	&H2A	Print Screen key
vbKeyExecute	&H2B	Execute key
vbKeySnapshot	&H2C	Snapshot key
vbKeyInsert	&H2D	Insert key
vbKeyDelete	&H2E	Delete key
vbKeyHelp	&H2F	Help key
vbKeyNumlock	&H90	Num Lock key
vbKeyA	65	A key
vbKeyB	66	B key
vbKeyC	67	C key
vbKeyD	68	D key
vbKeyE	69	E key
vbKeyF	70	F key
vbKeyG	71	G key
vbKeyH	72	H key
vbKeyI	73	I key
vbKeyJ	74	J key
vbKeyK	75	K key
vbKeyL	76	L key
bKeyM	77	M key
vbKeyN	78	N key
vbKeyO	79	O key
vbKeyP	80	P key
vbKeyQ	81	Q key
vbKeyR	82	R key
vbKeyS	83	S key
vbKeyT	84	T key
vbKeyU	85	U key
vbKeyV	86	V key

Constant	Value	Meaning
vbKeyW	87	W key
vbKeyX	88	X key
vbKeyY	89	Y key
vbKeyZ	90	Z key
vbKey0	48	0 key
vbKey1	49	1 key
vbKey2	50	2 key
vbKey3	51	3 key
vbKey4	52	4 key
vbKey5	53	5 key
vbKey6	54	6 key
vbKey7	55	7 key
vbKey8	56	8 key
vbKey9	57	9 key
vbKeyNumpad0	&H60	0 key
vbKeyNumpad1	&H61	1 key
vbKeyNumpad2	&H62	2 key
vbKeyNumpad3	&H63	3 key
vbKeyNumpad4	&H64	4 key
vbKeyNumpad5	&H65	5 key
vbKeyNumpad6	&H66	6 key
vbKeyNumpad7	&H67	7 key
vbKeyNumpad8	&H68	8 key
vbKeyNumpad9	&H69	9 key
vbKeyMultiply	&H6A	Multiplication sign (*) key
vbKeyAdd	&H6B	Plus sign (+) key
vbKeySeparator	&H6C	Enter key
vbKeySubtract	&H6D	Minus sign (–) key
vbKeyDecimal	&H6E	Decimal point (.) key
vbKeyDivide	&H6F	Division sign (/) key
vbKeyF1	&H70	F1 key
vbKeyF2	&H71	F2 key
vbKeyF3	&H72	F3 key
vbKeyF4	&H73	F4 key
vbKeyF5	&H74	F5 key
vbKeyF6	&H75	F6 key
vbKeyF7	&H76	F7 key
vbKeyF8	&H77	F8 key
vbKeyF9	&H78	F9 key
vbKeyF10	&H79	F10 key
vbKeyF11	&H7A	F11 key
vbKeyF12	&H7B	F12 key
vbKeyF13	&H7C	F13 key
vbKeyF14	&H7D	F14 key
vbKeyF15	&H7E	F15 key
vbKeyF16	&H7F	F16 key

MouseButton Constants

Use the following constants to refer to mouse buttons in your code—such as in the MouseDown, MouseMove, and MouseUp events—in order to clarify the code.

CONSTANT	VALUE	MEANING
vbLeftButton	1	Left mouse button
vbRightButton	2	Right mouse button
vbMiddleButton	4	Middle mouse button

Example

```
Private Sub Form_MouseDown(Button As Integer, Shift As Integer, _
    X As Single, Y As Single)
    If Button = vbRightButton Then 'Right button
        PopupMenu mnuPopup, vbPopupMenuRightButton
    End If
End Sub
```

This example displays a popup menu when the right mouse button is clicked on a Form.

Shift Constants

Use the following constants to refer to Shift, Control, and Alt keys in the Mouse and Key events such as MouseDown, MouseUp, MouseMove, KeyUp, and KeyDown.

CONSTANT	VALUE	MEANING
vbShiftMask	1	Shift key bit mask
vbCtrlMask	2	Ctrl key bit mask
vbAltMask	4	Alt key bit mask

Example

```
Private Sub Form_MouseDown(Button As Integer, Shift As Integer, _
    X As Single, Y As Single)
    If Button = vbRightButton And \
        (Shift And vbCtrlMask) <> 0 Then '<Ctrl>+<Right button>
        PopupMenu mnuPopup, vbPopupMenuRightButton
    End If
End Sub
```

This example displays a popup menu when the right mouse button is clicked on a Form *and* the Ctrl key is down.

SECTION 6: VB METHODS AND PROPERTIES

The ways of the lord are dark but seldom pleasant.

—Unknown

This section contains the methodological properties of VB's main objects.

Action Property

This Action property is provided for backwards compatibility with VB 3.0. Use the equivalent methods of an OLE Container control listed in the following table instead.

Usage   *object*.Action = *IntegerValue*

Applies To   OLE Container Control

Setting the Action property to a value causes an action to be performed. These actions now have equivalent methods, so use the methods instead of the Action property.

VALUE	DESCRIPTION	EQUIVALENT METHOD
0	Creates an embedded object.	CreateEmbed
1	Creates a linked object from the contents of a file.	CreateLink
4	Copies the object to the Clipboard object.	Copy
5	Copies data from the Clipboard object to the OLE Container control.	Paste
6	Gets the most current data from the server application that supplied the object for display.	Update
7	Opens the object for an operation, such as editing.	DoVerb
9	Closes the object and terminates the connection to the server application.	Close
10	Deletes the object and releases the memory used by the object.	Delete
11	Saves the object to a data file.	SaveToFile
12	Loads an object from a file.	ReadFromFile
14	Pops up the Insert Object dialog box.	InsertObjDlg
15	Pops up the Paste Special dialog box.	PasteSpecialDlg
17	Updates the list of verbs supported by the object.	FetchVerbs
18	Saves the object to the OLE file format.	SaveToOle1File

Action Property (CommonDialog Control)

This Action property controls the type of dialog box to be displayed. It is now outdated. You're better off using the ShowColor, ShowFont, ShowHelp, ShowOpen, ShowPrinter, and ShowSave methods.

Usage   object.Action = *IntegerValue*
                       IntegerValue = object.Action

Applies To   CommonDialog Control

PARAMETER	VALUE	MEANING
IntegerValue	0	No action.
	1	Shows the Open dialog box (equivalent to the ShowOpen method).
	2	Shows the Save As dialog box (similar to the ShowSave method).
	3	Shows the Color dialog box (equivalent to the ShowColor method).
	4	Shows the Font dialog box (like the ShowFont method).
	5	Shows the Printer dialog box (like the ShowPrinter method).
	6	Runs WINHELP.EXE (like ShowHelp).

ActiveControl Property

The ActiveControl property is a read-only property that returns the control that either has input focus or would have focus if its parent form were active. It is not available at design time. Use it at runtime to invoke the methods or access the properties of the active control.

Usage   *Control* = object.ActiveControl

Applies To   Form Object
                       MDIForm Object
                       Screen Object

   If you attempt to get the ActiveControl property of a form that has disabled or hidden all its controls, you will get an error. If you pass Screen.ActiveControl to a procedure, the procedure's parameters must be declared "As Control," rather than as a specific type of control, such as "As TextBox."
   The following example implements a Tool button in an MDIForm object that copies selected text from a TextBox control to the Clipboard object.

Example
```
Private Sub CmdCopy_Click()
    If TypeOf ActiveForm.ActiveControl Is TextBox Then
        Clipboard.SetText ActiveForm.ActiveControl.SelText
    End If
End Sub
```

ActiveForm Property

The ActiveForm property returns the Form object that either is the active window or would be the active window if the running application were to become active. If this property is referenced from an MDIForm object, then it specifies the active MDI child form. Use the ActiveForm property at runtime to invoke the methods or access the properties of the active form.

Usage   *Form = object*.ActiveForm

Applies To   MDIForm Object
                   Screen Object

   Screen.ActiveForm returns the active form for your application—even if your application is not the active one. If the active form is an MDIForm object, then Screen.ActiveForm will return the active MDI *child* form of that MDIForm, *not* the MDIForm object itself. If the active form is not an MDIForm object, then Screen.ActiveForm will return that form. MDIForm1.ActiveForm, however, will return its MDI child form that would be active were the MDIForm to become active.

   When an MDI child form is active but not maximized, then both it and its parent MDIForm's Title Bar appear active.

   If you pass Screen.ActiveForm or MDIForm.ActiveForm as a procedure parameter, the parameter must be declared "As Form," rather than as the name of your form, such as "Form1."

   The following example activates the MDIForm if the Form's active child form is not the active form for the Screen.

Example
```
If Screen.ActiveForm <> MDIForm1.ActiveForm Then
    AppActivate MDIForm1.Name
End If
```

Add Method (Buttons Collection)

This Add method adds a Button object to the Buttons collection and returns a reference to the newly created object.

Usage   Set *ButtonObject = object*.Add([*Index*][, *Key*][, *Caption*][, *Style*][, *Image*])

Applies To   Buttons Collection

   The parameters to the Add method have the meanings given in the following table.

PARAMETER	VALUE	MEANING
Index	Omitted	The Button object is added to the end of the collection.
	1 to Count	An integer value specifying the position at which the Button object will appear in the collection.
Key	Omitted	No key associated with this Button object.
	String expression	Associates a unique string with the Button object so that it can be retrieved later from the collection using this string. Since the position of the button may change, the Key string is the only sure way to indicate which Button you want.
Caption	Omitted	No caption for the Button.
	String expression	The Caption string appears below the image of a Button object.
Style	Omitted	Uses tbrDefault (0) as the style.
	Integer	Sees the Style Property (Button object) for the available styles of a Button object.
Image	Omitted	No graphic is displayed on the Button object.
	Integer	Specifies the ListImage object in the associated ImageList control for displaying a graphic on the Button object.

The following example adds a button with caption "MyBtn," to the end of the Toolbar:

Example
```
Set btn = Toolbar1.Buttons.Add(,,"MyBtn")
```

Add Method (ColumnHeaders Collection)

This Add method adds a ColumnHeader object to the ColumnHeaders collection and returns a reference to the newly created object.

Usage   Set *ColumnHeaderObject* = *object*.Add([*Index*][, *Key*][, *Text*][, *Width*][, *Alignment*])

Applies To   ColumnHeaders Collection

The parameters of the Add method have the meanings given in the following table.

PARAMETER	VALUE	MEANING
Index	Omitted	The ColumnHeader object is added to the end of the collection.
	1 to Count	An integer value specifying the position at which the ColumnHeader object will appear in the collection.
Key	Omitted	No key associated with this ColumnHeader object.

PARAMETER	VALUE	MEANING
Key	String expression	Associates a unique string with the ColumnHeader object so that it can be retrieved later from the collection using this string. Since the position of the ColumnHeader may change, the Key string is the only sure way to indicate which ColumnHeader you want.
Text	Omitted	The ColumnHeader will display no text.
	String expression	The string will be displayed in the ColumnHeader at runtime.
Width	Omitted	On our system, the default width is 1444.536 twips, or just a hair above 1 inch.
	Single-precision value	Specifies the width of the ColumnHeader in the unit used by the container of the ListView control.
Alignment	Omitted	Uses lvwColumnLeft (0).
	Integer	See the Alignment Property (ColumnHeader Object) for valid values.

Add Method (ListImages Collection)

This Add method adds a ListImage object to the ListImages collection and returns a reference to the newly created object.

Usage   Set *ListImageObject = object*.Add([*Index*][, *Key*], *Picture*)

Applies To   ListImages Collection

Note that the Picture argument is required. The parameters for this method have the meanings given in the following table.

PARAMETER	VALUE	MEANING
Index	Omitted	The ListImage object is added to the end of the collection.
	1 to Count	An integer value specifying the position at which the ListImage object will appear in the collection.
Key	Omitted	No key associated with this ListImage object.
	String expression	Associates a unique string with the ListImage object so that it can be retrieved later from the collection using this string. Since the position of the ListImage may change, the Key string is the only sure way to indicate which ListImage you want.
Picture	Picture object	Specifies the Picture object to add to the collection. This is typically done using the LoadPicture function.

Add Method (ListItems Collection)

This Add method adds a ListItem object to the ListItems collection and returns a reference to the newly created object.

Usage   Set *ListItemObject* = *object*.Add([*Index*][, *Key*][, *Text*][, *Icon*][, *SmallIcon*])

Applies To   ListItems Collection

The parameters for this method have the meanings given in the following table.

PARAMETER	VALUE	MEANING
Index	Omitted	The ListItem object is added to the end of the collection.
	1 to Count	An integer value specifying the position at which the ListItem object will appear in the collection.
Key	Omitted	No key associated with this ListItem object.
	String expression	Associates a unique string with the ListItem object so that it can be retrieved later from the collection using this string. Since the position of the ListItem may change, the Key string is the only sure way to indicate which ListItem you want.
Text	Omitted	No string is displayed for the ListItem object.
	String expression	Specifies the string to display for the ListItem object in a ListView control.
Icon	Omitted	No icon will be displayed for the ListItem object in the Icon view.
	Integer	Specifies the index of a ListImage object in an ImageList control associated with the ListView control to display for the ListItem object when in Icon view.
SmallIcon	Omitted	No icon will be displayed for the ListItem object in the SmallIcon view.
	Integer	Specifies the index of an ListImage object in an ImageList control associated with the ListView control to display for the ListItem object when in SmallIcon view.

Add Method (Nodes Collection)

This Add method adds a Node object to the Nodes collection and returns a reference to the newly created object.

Usage   Set *NodeObject* = *object*.Add([*Relative*][, *Relationship*][, *Key*], *Text*[, *Image*][, *SelectedImage*])

Applies To   Nodes Collection

Note that the Text argument is required. The parameters for this method have the meanings given in the following table.

PARAMETER	VALUE	MEANING
Relative	Omitted	The new node will be placed relative to the last node.
	Integer or String expression	This could be the Index number or Key string of an existing Node object in the collection. The new Node object is placed relative to the specified node, and the relationship is specified by the second argument.
Relationship	Omitted	Same as tvwNext (2). The new node is placed immediately after the Node specified by the Relative argument and at the same level.
	tvwLast or 1	The new node is placed as the last node at the same level as the Node object specified by the Relative argument.
	tvwNext or 2	The default. The new node is placed immediately after the Node specified by the Relative argument and at the same level.
	tvwPrevious or 3	The new node is placed immediately before the Node specified by the Relative argument and at the same level.
	tvwChild or 4	The new node is placed as the last child of the Node specified by the Relative argument.
Key	Omitted	No key is associated with the new Node.
	String expression	Associates a unique string with the Node object so that it can be retrieved later from the collection using this string.
Text	String expression	The text to display for the Node.
Image	Omitted	No picture is displayed for the Node.
	Integer	Specifies the index of a ListImage object in an ImageList control associated with the TreeView control to display for the Node object when the node is not selected.
SelectedImage	Omitted	Displays the image specified by the Image parameter even when the Node is selected.
	Integer	Specifies the index of a ListImage object in an ImageList control associated with the TreeView control to display for the Node object when the node is selected.

Add Method (Panels Collection)

This Add method adds a Panel object to the Panels collection and returns a reference to the newly created object.

Usage   Set *PanelObject* = *object*.Add([*Index*][, *Key*][, *Text*][, *Style*][, Picture])

Applies To   Panels Collection

PARAMETER	VALUE	MEANING
Index	Omitted	The Panel object is added to the end of the collection.
	1 to Count	An integer value specifying the position at which the Panel object will appear in the collection.
Key	Omitted	No key associated with this Panel object.
	String expression	Associates a unique string with the Panel object so that it can be retrieved later from the collection using this string. Since the position of the Panel may change, the Key string is the only sure way to indicate which Panel you want.
Text	Omitted	No text will be displayed in the Panel object.
	String expression	Specifies the string to be displayed in the Panel object.
Style	Omitted	Same as sbrText (0); accepts either text or bitmap.
	Integer	See Style Property (Panel Object) for details.
Picture	Omitted	No picture will be displayed in the Panel object.
	Picture object	Specifies the Picture object to display in the newly created Panel. You'll probably use the LoadPicture function to load one from file.

Add Method (Tabs Collection)

This Add method adds a Tab object to the Tabs collection and returns a reference to the newly created object.

Usage   Set *TabObject* = *object*.Add([*Index*][, *Key*][, *Caption*][, *Image*])

Applies To   Tabs Collection

PARAMETER	VALUE	MEANING
Index	Omitted	The Tab object is added to the end of the collection.
	1 to Count	An integer value specifying the position at which the Tab object will appear in the collection.
Key	Omitted	No key associated with this Tab object.

PARAMETER	VALUE	MEANING
Key	String expression	Associates a unique string with the Tab object so that it can be retrieved later from the collection using this string. Since the position of the Tab may change, the Key string is the only sure way to indicate which Tab you want.
Caption	Omitted	No text will be displayed on the Tab.
	String expression	Specifies the text to display on the new Tab object.
Image	Omitted	No graphic will be displayed on the new Tab.
	Integer	Specifies the index of a ListImage object in an ImageList control associated with the TabStrip control to display on the Tab object.

AddItem Method

The AddItem method adds an item to a ListBox or ComboBox control or a row to a Grid control.

Usage   *object*.AddItem *Item*[, *Index*]

Applies To   ComboBox Control
                     Grid Control
                     ListBox Control

The parameters to the AddItem method have the meanings given in the following table.

PARAMETER	VALUE	MEANING
Item	Any string	For the ComboBox and ListBox controls, only the first 1024 characters of the string will be used. For a Grid control, only the first 255 characters will be used for the text of each cell. Separate the text for each cell of the new row using a Tab (Chr(9)) character.
Index	Omitted	Adds the new item or row at the end if the Sorted property is False or in alphabetical order if Sorted is True.
	0	Adds the new item or row at the beginning.
	Positive integer	Adds the new item or row at the indicated position. If the Index is greater than the number of items in the control, an error occurs.
	Negative integer	Error

A ListBox or ComboBox control that is bound to a Data control does not support the AddItem method.

Example
```
For i = LBound(MyArray$) To UBound(MyArray$)
    List1.AddItem MyArray$(i)
Next i
```

Align Property

This Align property specifies the positioning of the control on a form. It is typically used for Pic-tureBox Controls that are used as toolbars and for Data Controls that provide access to databases. The settings allow you to "snap" the control to any of the four sides of the form.

Usage   *control*.Align = *IntegerValue*
                   IntegerValue = *control*.Align

Applies To   Data Control
                   DBGrid Control
                   PictureBox Control

Valid values for the Align property are given in the following table.

CONSTANT	VALUE	MEANING
vbAlignNone	0	The location and size of the control set at design time or in code. The control is not locked to any side of the form. You cannot use this value if the control is inside an MDIForm object.
vbAlignTop	1	The top of the control is locked either to the top of the form or to the bottom edge of the lowest control that is also using the vbAlignTop setting. The width of the control is automatically set to the width of the form. With this setting, you cannot manually change the Width property of the control. Assigning the Align property to this value will not change the height of the control.
vbAlignBottom	2	The bottom of the control is locked either to the bottom of the form or to the top edge of the highest control that is also using the vbAlignBottom setting. The width of the control is automatically set to the width of the form. With this setting, you cannot manually change the Width property of the control. Assigning the Align property to this value will not change the height of the control.
vbAlignLeft	3	The left side of the control is locked either to the left side of the form or to the right edge of the right-most control that is also using the vbAlignLeft setting. The height of the control is automatically set to the height of the form *unless* there are controls using the vbAlignTop or vbAlignBottom settings. In these cases, the height is adjusted to make room for the heights of those controls. With this setting, you cannot manually change the Height property of the control. Assigning the Align property to this value will not change the width of the control.

CONSTANT	VALUE	MEANING
vbAlignRight	4	The right side of the control is locked either to the right side of the form or to the left edge of the left-most control that is also using the vbAlignRight setting. The height of the control is automatically set to the height of the form *unless* there are controls using the vbAlignTop or vbAlignBottom settings. In these cases, the height is adjusted to make room for the heights of those controls. With this setting, you cannot manually change the Height property of the control. Assigning the Align property to this value will not change the width of the control.

 If you are changing the Align property from the vbAlignTop or vbAlignBottom value to vbAlignLeft or vbAlignRight (or vice versa), you have to manually adjust the width and height of the control. Otherwise, you'll end up with a control that fills the *entire* form.

Align Property (DBGrid)

This Align property controls where the DBGrid will be aligned on the form.

Usage   *object*.Align = *IntegerValue*
                    IntegerValue = *object*.Align

Applies To   DBGrid Control

PARAMETER	VALUE	MEANING
IntegerValue	dbgLeft or 0	Aligns the control on the left of your form.
	dbgRight or 1	Aligns the control on the right of your form.
	dbgCenter or 2	Centers the control on your form.
	dbgGeneral or 3	Aligns the control wherever you put it.

Alignment Property

This Alignment property specifies the text justification of controls that contain text or the appearance of the CheckBox and OptionButton Controls.

Usage   *control*.Alignment = *IntegerValue*
                    IntegerValue = *control*.Alignment

Applies To   CheckBox Control
                      Column Object
                      Label Control
                      OptionButton Control
                      TextBox Control

Valid values for the Alignment property are given in the following table.

CONSTANT	VALUE	MEANING
vbLeftJustify	0	Left justifies text for Label and TextBox in MultiLine mode. For CheckBox and OptionButton, this places the control to the left of the Caption. Caption is left-justified immediately following the control.
vbRightJustify	1	Right justifies text for Label and TextBox in MultiLine mode. For CheckBox and OptionButton, this places the control to the right of the Caption. Caption is left-justified at the left edge of the bounding box; the control is at the right edge of the bounding box.
vbCenter	2	Centers text for Label and TextBox in MultiLine mode. Does not apply to CheckBox or OptionButton.
dbgLeft	0	Left justifies text in Column.
dbgRight	1	Right justifies text in Column.
dbgCenter	2	Centers text in Column.
dbgGeneral	3	Left justifies text and right justifies numbers in Column.

Note: If a TextBox does not have MultiLine mode enabled, all text is left justified.

Alignment Property (ColumnHeader)

This Alignment property specifies the alignment of text that appears in a ColumnHeader object.

Usage   object.Alignment = *IntegerValue*
                 IntegerValue = object.Alignment

Applies To   ColumnHeader Control

PARAMETER	VALUE	MEANING
IntegerValue	lvwColumnLeft or 0	Default. Left-justified text.
	lvwColumnRight or 1	Right-justified text.
	lvwColumnCenter or 2	Centered text.

Alignment Property (Panel Object)

This Alignment property controls where and how text will be aligned in a StatusBar's Panel objects.

Usage   *object*.Alignment = *IntegerValue*
             IntegerValue = *object*.Alignment

Applies To   Panel Object

PARAMETER	VALUE	MEANING
IntegerValue	sbrLeft or 0	Text is left-justified to the right of the picture.
	sbrCenter or 1	Text is centered and to the right of the picture.
	sbrRight or 2	Text is right-justified and to the left of the picture.

AllowAddNew Property

The AllowAddNew property determines whether users may add new elements to a recordset through a DBGrid control.

Usage   *object*.AllowAddNew = *BooleanValue*
             BooleanValue = *object*.AllowAddNew

Applies To   DBGrid Control

PARAMETER	VALUE	MEANING
BooleanValue	True	Users may add new record.
	False	Users may not add new records.

Here's how it works. If you enable AllowAddNew, the last row of a DBGrid is blank. Users may type in new information there. When they move off the row, the information in the new row is (by default) committed to the database. If the value's False, users can't get to this row.

Note that if the recordset doesn't allow additions, enabling AllowAddNew and trying to add a new row will generate an error.

AllowCustomize Property

The AllowCustomize property specifies whether a Toolbar control may be customized by the user at run time using the Customize Toolbar dialog box.

Usage *BooleanValue = object*.AllowCustomize
object.AllowCustomize = *BooleanValue*

Applies To Toolbar Control

PARAMETER	VALUE	MEANING
BooleanValue	True	The end user can customize the toolbar. Double-clicking the Toolbar control or calling the Customize method at runtime brings up the Customize Toolbar dialog box.
	False	The end user cannot customize the toolbar.

AllowDelete Property

The AllowDelete property determines whether users may delete elements from a recordset through a DBGrid control.

Usage *BooleanValue = object*.AllowDelete
object.AllowDelete = *BooleanValue*

Applies To DBGrid Control

PARAMETER	VALUE	MEANING
BooleanValue	True	Users may delete records.
	False	Users may not delete records.

If you enable AllowDelete, then when a user selects a row in a DBGrid and presses delete, that record is deleted from the database. If the value's False, pressing delete will delete the information in the first column.

Note that if the recordset doesn't allow deletions, enabling AllowDelete and trying to delete a row will generate an error.

AllowRowSizing Property

The AllowRowSizing property determines whether a user may resize rows in a DBGrid control.

Usage   *BooleanValue* = *object*.AllowRowSizing
                     object.AllowRowSizing = *BooleanValue*

Applies To   DBGrid Control

PARAMETER	VALUE	MEANING
BooleanValue	True	Users may resize rows.
	False	Users may not resize rows.

If you set this value to True, the mouse pointer changes to a double-headed arrow when you move it over a row divider. Changing the row size causes a RowResize event. If you change one row, you change them all.

AllowUpdate Property

The AllowUpdate property determines whether users may update elements in a recordset through a DBGrid control.

Usage   *BooleanValue* = *object*.AllowUpdate
                     object.AllowUpdate = *BooleanValue*

Applies To   DBGrid Control

PARAMETER	VALUE	MEANING
BooleanValue	True	Users may update records.
	False	Users may not update records.

If you enable AllowUpdate, users may change the values in cells in the DBGrid. If the value's False, users may not.

Note that if the recordset doesn't allow updates, enabling AllowUpdate and trying to update a row will generate an error.

Appearance Property

This Appearance property specifies whether the control has a three-dimensional appearance. This property can be set only at design time; it is read-only at runtime. Setting this property may change the BackColor and ForeColor properties of the form or control.

This property does not exist for 16-bit versions of the controls.

Usage   *IntegerValue = object*.Appearance

Applies To   CheckBox Control
                 ComboBox Control
                 CommandButton Control
                 Data Control
                 DBCombo Control
                 DBList Control
                 DirListBox Control
                 DriveListBox Control
                 FileListBox Control
                 Form Object
                 Frame Control
                 Image Control
                 Label Control
                 ListBox Control
                 MDIForm Object
                 OLE Container Control
                 OptionButton Control
                 PictureBox Control
                 TextBox Control

The possible settings for this property are listed in the following table.

VALUE	MEANING
0	Flat. The controls and forms have the old flat look. Don't know why you'd want this setting. It causes BackColor property to be set to vbWindowBackground (&H80000005&), the Windows background color.
1	3D. This is the default. The controls and forms are colored in shades of gray that provide a three-dimensional look. It causes BackColor property to be set to vbButtonFace (&H8000000F&), the color of button faces.

The Appearance property of an MDIForm object does not affect the appearance of its child forms.

Appearance Property (Custom Controls)

This Appearance property controls whether a control looks "flat" or 3D.

Usage   *IntegerValue = object*.Appearance
                     object.Appearance = *IntegerValue*

Applies To   ListView Control
                     ProgressBar Control
                     RichTextBox Control
                     TreeView Control

PARAMETER	VALUE	DESCRIPTION
IntegerValue	0	Tells a control to have a "flat" appearance.
	1	Tells a control to have a 3D appearance.

Appearance Property (DBCombo, DBList)

This Appearance property controls whether a DBList or DBCombo looks "flat" or 3D.

Usage   *IntegerValue = object*.Appearance
                     object.Appearance = *IntegerValue*

Applies To   DBCombo Control
                     DBList Control

PARAMETER	VALUE	DESCRIPTION
IntegerValue	dblFlat or 0	Tells a DBList of DBCombo to have a "flat" appearance.
	dbl3D or 1	Tells a DBList or DBCombo to have a 3D appearance.

AppIsRunning Property

The AppIsRunning property specifies whether the server application that supplies the object contained in an OLE Container control is running. You can set the property to True to start the application. This property is not available at design time.

Usage   *BooleanValue = object*.AppIsRunning
                     object.AppIsRunning = *BooleanValue*

Applies To   OLE Container Control

The values of the AppIsRunning property have the meanings given in the following table.

VALUE	MEANING
True	The server application that supplied the object is running. Set the property to True to start the application.
False	The server application that supplied the object is not running. Set the property to False to cause the application to close as soon as the object loses focus.

Archive Property

The Archive property specifies whether a file with its Archive attribute set is displayed in a FileListBox control. When the contents of a file is changed, its Archive bit is set so that a backup program can easily determine which files need to be backed up. See also the Hidden, Normal, ReadOnly, and System properties.

Usage   *BooleanValue = object*.Archive
              object.Archive = *BooleanValue*

Applies To   FileListBox Control

The values for the Archive property have the following meanings for files *without* Hidden *or* System attributes set.

VALUE	MEANING
True	The default. Displays all files with their Archive attribute set, regardless of the setting for Normal and ReadOnly properties.
False	Do not display files with their Archive attributes set *unless* the Normal property is set to True or the ReadOnly property applies.

For a file with either the Hidden or System attribute set, the Archive property has no effect on whether it is displayed in the FileListBox. See the sections for Hidden and System properties for files that have Hidden or System attributes set.

Setting the Archive property at runtime will refresh the list of files.

To display all files, you must set the Normal, Hidden, and System properties to True.

Arrange Method

The Arrange method arranges the MDI child forms or icons in an MDIForm object. This method may be invoked even when the MDIForm itself is minimized.

Usage   *object*.Arrange = *Arrangement*

Applies To   MDIForm Object

PARAMETER	VALUE	MEANING
Arrangement	vbCascade or 0	Cascades all nonminimized MDI child forms.
	vbTileHorizontal or 1	Horizontally tiles all nonminimized MDI child forms.
	vbTileVertical or 2	Vertically tiles all nonminimized MDI child forms.
	vbArrangeIcons or 3	Arranges icons for minimized MDI child forms.

 vbTileHorizontal actually places the child windows one above another, each filling the width of the MDI parent form. vbTileVertical places the windows side-by-side, with heights that fill the MDI parent. It's supposed to be the other way around!

In the following example, assume your MDIForm object has four menu buttons that read "Cascade," "Tile Horizontal," "Tile Vertical," and "Icons" as indexes 0, 1, 2, and 3 of a control array called "mnuArrange." The code for these menu buttons can be as simple as this:

Example
```
Private Sub mnuArrange_Click(Index As Integer)
        Arrange Index
End Sub
```

Arrange Property

The Arrange property controls the alignment of the icons in SmallIcon view.

Usage   *object*.Arrange = *IntegerValue*
              IntegerValue = *object*.Arrange

Applies To   ListView Control

PARAMETER	VALUE	MEANING
IntegerValue	lvwNoArrange or 0	No alignment.
	lvwAutoLeft or 1	Aligns icons on the left side of the control.
	lvwAutoTop or 2	Aligns icons along the top of the control.

AutoActivate Property

The AutoActivate property specifies how an OLE object in an OLE Container control is activated.

Usage   *IntegerValue = object*.AutoActivate
                 object.AutoActivate = *IntegerValue*

Applies To   OLE Container Control

It can take on one of the values given in the following table.

CONSTANT	VALUE	MEANING
vbOLEActivateManual	0	The OLE object cannot be automatically activated through any user action, but it can be activated via code using the DoVerb method.
vbOLEActivateGetFocus	1	The OLE object is activated when the OLE Container control gets the focus, typically as a result of a single mouse click. This doesn't have any effect.
vbOLEActivateDoubleclick	2	The OLE object is activated when the OLE Container control is double-clicked or if the Enter key is pressed when the control has the focus. This is the default. The setting disables the DblClick event for the OLE Container control.
vbOLEActivateAuto	3	The OLE object is activated based on the object's default method of activation (focus or double-click).

Click. Clickclick. Clickclickclickclick. Wham! Using this setting, we could not activate the object no matter how many clicks we used. We could not get the vbOLEActivateGetFocus setting to work at all.

AutoRedraw Property

The AutoRedraw property specifies whether or not graphics methods draw persistent graphics. Set the AutoRedraw property to True to draw persistent graphics, such as grid lines, and then set the AutoRedraw property to False to draw the temporary graphics. Persistent graphics will be redrawn if you resize your object or cover and then cover it with another window. Temporary graphics will need to be redrawn.

Usage   *BooleanValue = object*.AutoRedraw
                 object.AutoRedraw = *BooleanValue*

Applies To   Form Object
                      PictureBox Control

The values for the AutoRedraw property has the meanings given in the following table.

VALUE	MEANING
True	Enables automatic repainting of a Form object of PictureBox control for the graphics that are drawn when AutoRedraw is True. While it is True, the object does not receive Paint events.
False	The default. Disables automatic repainting of an object for the graphics that are drawn when AutoRedraw is False. Those objects drawn when it was True are *still* redrawn. While AutoRedraw is False, the object will receive Paint events to repaint any temporary graphics.

The affected graphics methods include Circle, Cls, Line, Point, Print, and PSet. The graphics drawn when AutoRedraw was True and before AutoRedraw is set to False become the background. When you use Cls, this background will *not* be cleared unless you first reset AutoRedraw to True. If, however, you set the BackColor property, all graphics and text will be erased, regardless of the setting for AutoRedraw.

You can retrieve the persistent graphic of an object by using the Image property. It will not include any temporary graphics drawn when AutoRedraw is set to False. You can also pass the persistent graphic to a Windows API function by using the object's hDC property.

When a form's AutoRedraw property is set to False, minimizing a form causes the form's ScaleHeight and ScaleWidth properties to be set to the icon size. If AutoRedraw is True, Scale-Height and ScaleWidth will not change.

The following example draws a circle as the background graphic. Clicking the PictureBox draws a temporary X from corner to corner. Cover the PictureBox and uncover it to force a redraw. Observe that the circle is automatically redrawn, but the X may be removed. Now double-click PictureBox and observe that the circle is copied to Image1, but the temporary X is not.

Example
```
Private Sub Form_Load()
    Picture1.AutoRedraw = True   ' Turn on AutoRedraw.
    Picture1.Circle (Picture1.ScaleWidth / 2, _
        Picture1.ScaleHeight / 2), _
        Picture1.ScaleHeight * 0.3    ' Draw a circle.
    Picture1.AutoRedraw = False ' Turn off AutoRedraw.
End Sub

Private Sub Picture1_Click()
    ' Select random color
    Picture1.ForeColor = RGB(Rnd * 255, 0, 0)
    ' Draw X
    Picture1.Line (0, 0)-(Picture1.ScaleWidth, _
        Picture1.ScaleHeight)
    Picture1.Line (0, Picture1.ScaleHeight)- _
        (Picture1.ScaleWidth, 0)
```

```
        End Sub

        Private Sub Picture1_DblClick()
            Image1 = Picture1.Image
        End Sub
```

AutoShowChildren Property

The AutoShowChildren property specifies whether MDI child forms of the MDIForm object will be automatically displayed when they are loaded.

Usage   *BooleanValue = object*.AutoShowChildren
                   object.AutoShowChildren = *BooleanValue*

Applies To   MDIForm Object

The values of the AutoShowChildren property have the meanings given in the following table.

VALUE	MEANING
True	The default. MDI child forms will be displayed when loaded.
False	MDI children will not be displayed until explicitly shown using the Show method or the setting of its Visible property to True.

The AutoShowChildren property allows you to load MDI child forms into memory so that they can be displayed quickly when you invoke their Show methods.

AutoSize Property

This AutoSize property specifies whether a control is resized automatically to make all its contents visible. If the new size makes the control larger than its Form object, the contents will be clipped by the boundaries of the control.

Usage   *BooleanValue = object*.AutoSize
                   object.AutoSize = *BooleanValue*

Applies To   Label Control
                   PictureBox Control

The values of the AutoSize property have the meanings given in the following table.

VALUE	MEANING
True	The control is automatically resized to display its contents.
False	The default. The size of the control will change only if explicitly resized by changing its Width and Height properties. Its contents will be clipped by the boundaries of the control.

 When displaying multiple lines of messages in a Label control, you may want to set its AutoSize to True.

The following table summarizes the behavior for combinations of WordWrap and AutoSize properties.

AUTOSIZE	WORDWRAP	BEHAVIOR
False	Don't Care	Label control does not resize. Text automatically wraps at word boundaries to create new lines.
True	False	Text does not automatically wrap at word boundaries, but Label control sizes automatically both horizontally and vertically to display all text.
True	True	Label control does not resize horizontally, so text automatically wraps at word boundaries to create new lines. Label control sizes vertically automatically to display all text.

AutoSize Property (Panel Object)

This AutoSize property controls whether a Panel object will be automatically sized when the contents change or the parent form changes size.

Usage   *object*.AutoSize = *IntegerValue*
IntegerValue = *object*.AutoSize

Applies To   Panel Object

PARAMETER	VALUE	MEANING
IntegerValue	sbrNoAutosize or 0	No autosizing. The panel's width is fixed.
	sbrSpring or 1	The panel's width changes when there is extra space available but never goes below MinWidth.
	sbrContents or 2	The panel's width changes to fit its contents.

AutoVerbMenu Property

The AutoVerbMenu property specifies whether a popup menu is displayed that contains the OLE object's verbs when the user right clicks the OLE Container control that contains the object.

Usage	*BooleanValue = object*.AutoVerbMenu *object*.AutoVerbMenu = *BooleanValue*
Applies To	OLE Container Control

The values for the AutoVerbMenu property have the meanings given in the following table.

VALUE	MEANING
True	The default. When the user right-clicks the OLE Container control, a popup menu appears that displays the verbs supported by the object. This setting disables the Click and MouseDown events for the right mouse button.
False	No popup menu is displayed.

BackColor Property

The BackColor property specifies the background color of an object.

Usage	*LongValue = object*.BackColor *object*.BackColor = *LongValue*
***Applies* To**	CheckBox Control Column Object ComboBox Control CommandButton Control Data Control DBCombo Control DBGrid Control DBList Control DirListBox Control DriveListBox Control FileListBox Control Form Object Frame Control Grid Control Label Control ListBox Control MDIForm Object

OLE Container Control
OptionButton Control
PictureBox Control
Shape Control
TextBox Control

You can use the RGB or QBColor functions to generate RGB colors for this property.

 Even though you may set BackColor to any color, it will display only in the nearest solid, not dithered, color.

For a Label or Shape control, the BackColor property is ignored if the control's BackStyle property is set to 0 (Transparent).

For a Form object or PictureBox control, all text and graphics will be erased when you set its BackColor at runtime.

The default BackColor is vbWindowBackground (&H80000005&).

VALUE	MEANING
0 to &H00FFFFFF&	This specifies the color in RGB. The lower three bytes, from least significant to most, specifies color intensity of red, green, and blue. Each color component can range from 0 to 255.
&H80000000& to &H80000018&	These specify a system color. See the table in the "Color Constants" section or use the VB Object Browser.
&H01000000& to &H02FFFFFF&	This does not generate an error, but the effect of the high byte is not documented. It seems that if the high byte is 1, then the color always results in black. If the high byte is 2, then the effect is possible lightening of the RGB color indicated by the lower 3 bytes, the result always being a solid (not dithered) color.
Other	Error

BackStyle Property

The BackStyle property specifies whether the background of a Label, OLE Container, or Shape control is opaque or transparent. If transparent, the background or graphics of the control's parent—and any other control beneath it—will show through.

Usage   *IntegerValue = object*.BackStyle
                 object.BackStyle = *IntegerValue*

Applies To   Label Control
                 OLE Container Control
                 Shape Control

The values for the BackStyle property have the meanings given in the following table.

VALUE	MEANING
0	Transparent. Default for Shape controls. The background of the control is transparent, thereby allowing the parent's background and graphics to show through. For Label and OLE Container controls, you'll probably want to set the BorderStyle to vbBSNone (0). The control's BackColor is ignored.
1	Opaque. Default for Label and OLE Container controls. The control's BackColor fills the control, thereby obscuring the parent's background and graphics and any other controls behind it.

The FillStyle of a Shape control must not be set to vbFSSolid (0); otherwise BackStyle has no effect.

Bevel Property

The Bevel property controls the bevel style of a StatusBar control's Panel object.

Usage   *object*.Bevel = *IntegerValue*
                 IntegerValue = *object*.Bevel

Applies To   Panel Object

PARAMETER	VALUE	MEANING
IntegerValue	sbrNoBevel or 0	The panel isn't beveled.
	sbrrInset or 1	Panels appear sunk into the Status Bar.
	sbrRaised or 2	Panels appear raised.

BOFAction Property

The BOFAction property specifies the action that the Data control takes when the user selects the MovePrevious button of the Data control to move backwards beyond the first record.

Usage   *object*.BOFAction = *IntegerValue*
                 IntegerValue = *object*.BOFAction

Applies To   Data Control

The property can take on the values given in the following table.

CONSTANT	VALUE	MEANING
vbMoveFirst	0	The default action. It keeps the first record as the current record.
vbBOF	1	Moving past the beginning of a Recordset triggers the Data control Validate event on the first record, followed by a Reposition event on the invalid (BOF) record. The MovePrevious button on the Data control is disabled.

 The Help file lists the constant names incorrectly as vbBOFActionMoveFirst and vb-BOFActionBOF.

The BOFAction Property has no effect when records are selected via code.

Bold Property

The Bold property works with the Font and StdFont objects to make a font bold or not bold.

Usage   *Font*.Bold = *BooleanValue*
               BooleanValue = *Font*.Bold

Applies To   Font Object
               StdFont Object

PARAMETER	VALUE	MEANING
BooleanValue	True	The font is bold.
	False	The font is not bold.

Bookmark Property (Data Access)

The Bookmark property contains the current record in a recordset. You may set it or read it.

Usage   *object*.Bookmark = *StringValue*
               StringValue = *object*.Bookmark

Applies To   Recordset Object

PARAMETER	VALUE	MEANING
StringValue	String or Variant	The value evaluates to a valid bookmark.

Internally, bookmarks are Byte arrays. You need to convert them to String or Variant before performing such functions as compare one bookmark to another (you can't compare arrays).

When you open a recordset (or create one), every member gets a unique bookmark. You can save the bookmark of the current record or set the Bookmark property to a particular value and thereby move to that location.

The catch is that not all objects support bookmarks. All Jet database engine tables do, as do Dynaset, Snapshot, and Table objects. But some external database types (e.g., Paradox tables without a primary key) don't.

Example

1. Create a form.

2. Add a DBCombo box (DBCombo1), a DBGrid (DBGrid1), and a Data control (Data1).

3. Set Data1's DatabaseName property to BIBLIO.MDB and its RecordSource to Authors.

4. Point DBCombo1's RowSource and DataSource properties at Data1, set ListField to Author, and set BoundColumn and DataField to Au_ID.

5. Now set DBGrid1's DataSource to Data1.

6. Add the following code to DBCombo1's Click event:

```
Private Sub DBCombo1_Click(Area As Integer)
    Data1.Recordset.Bookmark = DBCombo1.SelectedItem
End Sub
```

Now run it. When you click a row in DBGrid1, DBCombo1's value changes *and* when you select an item from DBCombo1, DBGrid1's value changes.

Note: This property also applies to the Dynaset, Snapshot, and Table objects, but the use of these objects is now discouraged. You can do everything using the Recordset object.

Bookmark Property (DBGrid)

This Bookmark property specifies a bookmark for the indicated row of a RowBuffer object in an unbound DBGrid control.

| *Usage* | *VariantValue* = *object*.Bookmark(*Row*) |
| | *object*.Bookmark(*Row*) = *VariantValue* |

| *Applies To* | DBGrid Control |

The parameters and values of the Bookmark property have the meanings given in the following table.

Parameter	Value	Meaning
Row	0 to RowCount– 1	This integer specifies the row in which to place the bookmark. RowCount is a property of the RowBuffer object.
VariantValue	Variant	This is a user-defined value to use for the bookmark. It must be unique for each row.

The Bookmark is passed to the UnboundXX event procedures that require you to update from or to your database. Following are issues associated with each of these events:

- UnboundAddData: The bookmark identifies the row of data to be added.

- UnboundReadData: The bookmark specifies the starting row that is to be updated with data from the database.

- UnboundWriteData: The bookmark identifies the row of data to be updated.

BorderColor Property

The BorderColor property specifies the color of a graphic object's border.

Usage   *LongValue* = *object*.BorderColor
                 object.BorderColor = *LongValue*

Applies To   Line Control
                 Shape Control

VB constants that may be used for the BorderColor property are listed in the Color Constants section. Additionally, you can use the RGB or QBColor functions to generate RGB colors for this property. Even though you may set BorderColor to any color, it will display only in the nearest solid, not dithered, color.

The default value for the BorderColor property is vbWindowText (&H80000008&).

BorderStyle Property

The BorderStyle property allows you to set or get the style used for the border of the object or control.

Usage   *object*.BorderStyle = *IntegerValue*
                 IntegerValue = *object*.BorderStyle

Applies To   Form Object
                 DBGrid Control

Image Control
Label Control
OLE Container Control
PictureBox Control
TextBox Control
Line Control
Shape Control

There are two sets of constants you can use for the specifying values for BorderStyle: one for Forms, DBGrid, Image, Label, OLE Container, PictureBox, and TextBox controls and the other set for Line and Shape controls.

Form and TextBox BorderStyles *cannot* be set at runtime. Moreover, you cannot see the results of BorderStyle for Forms until runtime.

FORM, DBGRID, IMAGE, LABEL, OLE, PICTUREBOX, TEXTBOX		
CONSTANT	VALUE	MEANING
vbBSNone	0	No border. This is the default for Label and Image controls. When this constant is applied to Forms, the Form window cannot be moved or sized at runtime.
vbFixedSingle	1	Fixed single. This is the default for DBGrid, OLE Container, PictureBox, and TextBox controls. This constant, when applied to Forms, prevents the Form from being sized at runtime. Selecting this setting automatically sets the MaxButton and MinButton settings to False and ShowInTaskbar to True, but you can change these manually.
vbSizable	2	Sizable (Forms only). This is the default for Forms. Selecting this setting automatically sets the MaxButton, MinButton, and ShowInTaskbar settings to True, but you can set these to False manually.
vbFixedDouble	3	Fixed Dialog style (Forms only). We're not sure why the constant name has not been changed yet, but it is confusing. At runtime, the Form is not sizable, and Maximize and Minimize buttons will not show regardless of their settings. The ShowInTaskbar setting is automatically set to False, but you can change it manually. If the form has a menu, the setting is equivalent to vbFixedSingle.
	4	Fixed ToolWindow style (Forms only). This is useful for creating nonsizable floating toolbar windows on Windows 95 systems. On other systems, it's the same as vbFixedSingle. No Maximize or Minimize buttons are displayed, and ShowInTaskbar setting is automatically set to False (it can be changed). The title text and Title Bar are supposed to be reduced in size, but all we get is the title text displayed in a nonboldface font. There doesn't seem to be a registered constant name as of this writing.
	5	Sizable ToolWindow style (Forms only). This is useful for creating sizable floating toolbar windows on Windows 95 systems. On other systems, it's the same as vbSizable.

FORM, DBGRID, IMAGE, LABEL, OLE, PICTUREBOX, TEXTBOX		
CONSTANT	VALUE	MEANING
vb FixedDouble	5 (*cont.*)	No Maximize or Minimize buttons are displayed, and ShowInTaskbar setting is automatically set to False (it can be changed). The title text and Title Bar are supposed to be reduced in size, but all we get is the title text displayed in a nonboldface font. There doesn't seem to be a registered constant name as of this writing.

The Line and Shape controls also have a BorderStyle property that probably should have been named LineStyle to avoid confusion. It determines how the Line or border of a Shape should be drawn.

 For the Dash and Dot styles, BorderWidth *must* be 1! Otherwise, vbBSSolid is used.

LINE, SHAPE		
CONSTANT	VALUE	MEANING
vbTransparent	0	Transparent
vbBSSolid	1	Solid. For a Shape control, the border extends beyond the shape edge by half the BorderWidth.
vbBSDash	2	Dash
vbBSDot	3	Dot
vbBSDashDot	4	Dash-dot
vbBSDashDotDot	5	Dash-dot-dot
vbBSInsideSolid	6	Inside solid. Has no effect on Line control. For a Shape control, the outer edge of the border is at the shape edge.

BorderStyle Property (Custom Controls)

This BorderStyle property specifies the border style for an object.

Usage   *IntegerValue* = *object*.BorderStyle
              object.BorderStyle = *IntegerValue*

Applies To   ListView Control
              ProgressBar Control
              RichTextBox Control

Slider Control
Toolbar Control
TreeView Control

The values for the BorderStyle property have the meanings given in the following table.

CONSTANT	VALUE	MEANING
ccNone	0	Default. No border.
ccFixedSingle	1	Fixed single.

Setting BorderStyle for a ProgressBar control decreases the size of the progress blocks being displayed.

BorderStyle Property (DBGrid)

This Border Style property controls the border around a DBGrid.

Usage   *object*.BorderStyle = *IntegerValue*
                 IntegerValue = *object*.BorderStyle

Applies To   DBGrid Control

PARAMETER	VALUE	MEANING
IntegerValue	dbgNone or 0	Gives the DBGrid no border.
	dbgFixedSingle or 1	Gives the control a fixed single-line border.

BorderWidth Property

The BorderWidth property specifies in pixels the width of a control's border.

Usage   *IntegerValue* = *object*.BorderWidth
                 object.BorderWidth = *IntegerValue*

Applies To   Line Control
                 Shape Control

The value of the BorderWidth property should be able to range from 1 to 32,767, but the Help file indicates that the maximum value is 8,192. We have no way of verifying either maximum figure, since we don't have a monitor with enough pixels—yet. Maybe next year.

When the BorderWidth is 1, then all the BorderStyle properties can be used to create solid, dashed, or dotted lines. If the BorderWidth is greater than 1, then only BorderStyles of vbBS-Solid (1) or vbBSInsideSolid (6) have any effect.

BORDERSTYLE	BORDERWIDTH	MEANING
vbTransparent	Don't care	No border is displayed.
vbBSSolid	1 through 32,767	The "location" of the border is measured from the center of the border. That is, for a Shape control, its Width and Height are measured from the center of the borders. Similarly for a Line control, the X1, Y1, X2, and Y2 coordinates specify locations in the center of the line width.
vbBSInsideSolid	1 through 32,767	The "location" of the border is measured from the outside edge of the border. For a Shape control, its Width and Height are measured from the outer edge of the borders. For a Line control, the X1, Y1, X2, and Y2 coordinates still specify the points in the center of the line width.
vbBSDash, vbBSDot, vbBSDashDot, vbBSDashDotDot	1	The border is drawn in the indicated style.
	2 through 32,767	Same as vbBSSolid—no dash or dot effects.

BoundColumn Property

The BoundColumn property is used as part of the setup to have the selection in a DBCombo or DBList control change to reflect selections you make in other bound data controls.

Usage   *object*.BoundColumn = *StringValue*
                    StringValue = *object*.BoundColumn

Applies To   DBCombo Control
                    DBList Control

PARAMETER	VALUE	MEANING
StringValue	A string	Specifies (or returns) the name of the field in the recordset specified by RowSource that will update the DataField property in a Data control.

This property works with the DataField property to help pass information between two Data controls. It applies to the DBCombo and DBList controls. It requires that you specify a value for the RowSource property.

Example

You want a form that shows, in a DBGrid, the title information from BIBLIO.MDB, and a DB-List box that shows the publisher information about the currently selected title. Create a form (Form1) with two Data controls (Data1 and Data2), a DBGrid control (DBGrid1), and a DBList control (DBList1). Set the following properties while you're designing the form (VB won't let you set these properties at runtime, alas, so you can't do them under Form_Load):

```
DBList1.DataSource = Data1
DBList1.RowSource = Data2
DBGrid1.DataSource = Data1
```

Next, enter the following code under the Form_Load() event:

```
Private Sub Form_Load()
    Dim SQL As String
    SQL = "SELECT PubID, Name FROM Publishers ORDER BY PubID "

    Data1.DatabaseName = "BIBLIO.MDB"
    Data1.RecordSource = "Titles"
    Data1.RecordsetType = Table

    Data2.Visible = False
    Data2.DatabaseName = "BIBLIO.MDB"
    Data2.RecordSource = SQL
    Data2.Refresh
    'Order is important: set ReocordsetType after Refresh
    Data2.RecordsetType = Snapshot

    'Information from Data1
    DBList1.DataField = "PubID"
    'Information from Data2
    DBList1.BoundColumn = "PubID"
    DBList1.ListField = "Name"
End Sub
```

So, DBGrid1 is linked to Data1, which is just pulling the information from the Titles table of BIBLIO.MDB. Data2 is also pulling its information from BIBLIO.MDB, but it's basing its RecordSource on a SQL query that is pulling PubID and Name from the Publishers table.

Note that there are PubID fields in both RecordSources. This is key because this is the field on which you're going to be linking with DBList1. DBList1 pulls the selected record from Data1 through the field specified in DataField (PubID) and then funnels it to Data2 through the Bound-Column property. Data2 runs the SQL query and returns the name of the publisher to DBList1, which highlights it.

In other words, when a user selects a title from the grid, the publisher of that title will be highlighted in DBList1. (Note, however, that when the user selects a publisher, VB won't display that publisher's titles in DBGrid1. For how to do that, see DBCombo's SelectedItem property.)

The Help file seemingly incorrectly states that, "If the ListField property is not provided, the field specified by the BoundColumn property is also used to fill the control's list." When we ran out tests, we found that if you don't specify ListField, you don't get a list.

 If you're setting BoundColumn or ListField in your DBList or DBCombo box and see the error message, "Object variable or With block variable not set," it seems that you can safely ignore it. There seems to be no good reason for it to appear. It just does.

BoundText Property

The BoundText property contains whatever is in the field specified by the BoundColumn property after you've made a selection.

Usage   *object*.BoundText =*StringValue*
                StringValue = *object*.BoundText

Applies To   DBCombo Control
                DBList Control

PARAMETER	VALUE	MEANING
StringValue	A string	The data where BoundColumn intersects with the selection you've made.

Remember that the value in BoundColumn isn't necessarily the same as the value in ListField. *Note:* When a user types something into a DBList or DBCombo control, but there's no match; the value is going to be null.

BulletIndent Property

Dodge those bullets, or at least indent them, with the BulletIndent property. When SetBullet is set to True, this property controls by how much bullets will be indented.

Usage   *object*.BulletIndent = *SingleValue*
                SingleValue = *object*.BulletIndent

Applies To   RichTextBox Control

PARAMETER	VALUE	MEANING
IntegerValue	Single-precision value	The amount of indentation, in the scale of the Form that holds the RichTextBox.

If what you've selected spans multiple paragraphs that have different margin settings, this property won't work; it returns Null.

 The Help file incorrectly states that the BulletIndent property uses Integer values.

ButtonHeight, ButtonWidth Properties

The ButtonHeight and ButtonWidth properties specify the size of a Toolbar control's Button objects. All Button objects have the same size. If the caption of a Button object is longer than ButtonWidth allows, the ButtonWidth will be automatically adjusted to fit the string.

Usage   *SingleValue* = *object*.ButtonHeight
object.ButtonHeight = *SingleValue*

SingleValue = *object*.ButtonWidth
object.ButtonWidth = *SingleValue*

Applies To   Toolbar Control

These properties specify sizes expressed in the same units as the container of the Toolbar control.

Buttons Property

The Buttons property returns a reference to the Buttons collection of a Toolbar control.

Usage   *ObjectValue* = *object*.Buttons

Applies To   Toolbar Control

PARAMETER	VALUE	MEANING
ObjectValue	A Buttons collection	The Buttons collection you're referencing.

Cancel Property

The Cancel property specifies whether a CommandButton—or an OLE Container control containing an object that acts like a CommandButton—will be activated when the user presses the Esc key.

Usage   *BooleanValue* = *object*.Cancel
                     object.Cancel = *BooleanValue*

Applies To   CommandButton Control
                     OLE Container Control

The values for the Cancel property have the meanings given in the following table.

VALUE	MEANING
True	The CommandButton's Click event will run when the user presses the Esc key. When you set the Cancel property of one CommandButton to True, VB sets the Cancel property of *all* other CommandButtons to False. In this way, only one Command Button will be the Cancel button at any one time.
False	The default. The CommandButton will not respond to the Esc key.

A CommandButton with its Cancel property set to True should execute commands that cancel any uncommitted changes and either reverts the form back to its previous state or hides the form. If it is important that the user not accidentally commit changes, also set the CommandButton's Default property to True so that the Enter key also activates it. As with any other CommandButton, you can still activate it by clicking it or by pressing the Enter key when it has focus.

CancelError Property

The CancelError property controls whether an error is generated when the user chooses the Cancel button.

Usage   *object*.CancelError = *BooleanValue*
                     BooleanValue = *object*.CancelError

Applies To   CommonDialog Control

PARAMETER	VALUE	MEANING
BooleanValue	True	Generates error 32,755 (cdlCancel).
	False	Doesn't generate error (the default).

Caption Property

The Caption property specifies the text to be displayed for a control or Form. For a control, the text may be inside or next to the control, depending on the type of control. For a Form or MDI-Form, the caption represents the text in the Title Bar and next to its icon.

Usage   *StringValue* = [*object.*]Caption
                    [*object.*]Caption = *StringValue*

If *object* is omitted, the property applies to the active Form object.

Applies To   CheckBox Control
                    CommandButton Control
                    Data Control
                    DBGrid Control
                    Form Object
                    Frame Control
                    Label Control
                    MDIForm Object
                    Menu Control
                    MenuLine Object
                    OptionButton Control

For a MenuLine object that exposes menus to VB Add-Ins, this property is read-only. By default, the caption is set to the Name property of the control or object. You should change it to be more descriptive for your users.

Quick-Access Keys

You can make your application more usable by providing quick-access keys for your controls. To define a quick-access key, precede a character in the caption text with an ampersand (&). The character will now be underlined, and the user can hold the ALT key while pressing the underlined character to move focus to that control and activate the control, if applicable. To display an ampersand in your caption text, use a pair of ampersand characters (&&).

Length Limits

Although Label controls can display up to 1,024 characters, each line can be only 256 characters long. Set the AutoSize property to True so that the label can automatically size itself to fit the caption string. Other controls can display 255 characters. If the input string is longer than these limits (frankly, we can't see why it would be), the string will be clipped; no errors. If a string is too long for the control, it will still be clipped, regardless of the maximum character limit. For a CheckBox, CommandButton, and OptionButton control, the lines will wrap to form multiple lines, but these additional lines won't be very useful because only the bottom half of the first line will be displayed in the control. You can insert Chr$(13) into your Label captions to form multiple lines.

The VB Help file incorrectly states that Label controls can handle 2,048 characters.

Captions in Forms and MDIForms

If you select none for BorderStyle, no title bar will be displayed, so the caption will not be displayed. If an MDI child form is maximized, its caption will be combined with that of the parent MDIForm and will be displayed in the MDIForm Title Bar.

CellText Method

The CellText pulls formatted text from a cell in a DBGrid control.

Usage   *StringValue = object*.CellText(*Bookmark*)

Applies To   Column Object

PARAMETER	VALUE	MEANING
Bookmark	String	A string that represents a row in the DBGrid control.

If you feed CellText a column number (probably through the Columns collection) and a bookmark (which specifies a row), it will return the cell at which the two intersect.

 CellText works great, but the example in the Help page has a typo. It should read more like this:

```
Private Sub DBGrid1_Click()
    Dim TopRow, BottomRow
    TopRow = DBGrid1.Columns(0).CellText(DBGrid1.FirstRow)
    BottomRow = _
    DBGrid1.Columns(0).CellText(DBGrid1.RowBookmark(DBGrid1.VisibleRows - 1))
    Label1.Text = _
    "Records " & TopRow & " to " & BottomRow & " are currently displayed."
End Sub
```

CellValue Method

The CellValue method does for raw data pretty much what CellText does for text: It pulls the value.

Usage   *VariantValue = object*.CellValue(*Bookmark*)

Applies To   Column Object

PARAMETER	VALUE	MEANING
Bookmark	String	A string that represents a row in the DBGrid control.

Checked Property

The Checked property specifies whether a check mark is displayed next to a menu entry. Use this property to indicate to the user a toggle condition for the pertinent menu entry.

Usage   *BooleanValue = object*.Checked
object.Checked = *BooleanValue*

Applies To   Menu Control
MenuLine Object

The values of the Checked property have the meanings given in the following table.

VALUE	MEANING
True	A check mark is displayed next to the menu entry. Use this to indicate that a mode is in effect and that selecting the same menu entry again will turn that off mode and remove the check mark.
False	The default. Does not display a check mark for the menu item.

The check mark is not automatically toggled on and off when you select a menu entry. You have to manage the toggling explicitly in the Menu control's Click event. You can set its initial condition in the Menu editor.

Example
```
Private Sub mnuViewToolbars_Click()
    If mnuViewToolbars.Checked Then
        picToolbar.Visible = False
        mnuViewToolbars.Checked = False
    Else
        picToolbar.Visible = True
        mnuViewToolbars.Checked = True
    End If
End Sub
```

Another way to do the same thing uses a trick that takes into account that True is equivalent to the value −1:

Example

```
Private Sub mnuViewToolbars_Click()
    'Toggle value between 0 and -1
    mnuViewToolbars.Checked = - (mnuViewToolbars.Checked + 1)
    picToolbar.Visible = mnuViewToolbars.Checked
End Sub
```

Child Property

The Child property references the first child of a Node object in a TreeView control.

Usage   Set *NodeObject* = *object*.Child

Applies To   Node Object

This property gets the big "huh?" Yes, it really just returns a reference to the first and only the first child of a Node object. We're sure it's useful; we're just not quite sure for what. You're probably not going to bother placing this on your "most frequently used" list. The Help page points out that because the Child, FirstSibling, LastSibling, Previous, Parent, Next, and Root properties all reference Node objects other than the currently selected one, you can do stuff to them behind the scenes, like this:

```
With TreeView1.Nodes(x).Child
    .Text = "New text"
    .Key = "New key"
    .SelectedImage = 3
End With
```

Children Property

The Children property returns the number of children a Node object has.

Usage   *IntegerValue* = *object*.Children

Applies To   Node Object

PARAMETER	VALUE	MEANING
IntegerValue	An integer	The number of children a Node object has.

You use the Children property as a safety check before doing something to a Node's children (make sure there are some first) with a construct like If Node.Children > 0 Then (whatever).

Circle Method

The Circle graphics method draws a circle, ellipse, or arc on an object.

Usage   *object*.Circle [Step] (X, Y), *Radius*[, *Color*][, *Start*][, *End*][, *Aspect*]

Applies To   Form Object
PictureBox Control
Printer Object

The parameters for the Circle method have the meanings given in the following table.

PARAMETER	VALUE	MEANING
Step	Omitted	The coordinates of the center, (X, Y), are specified in terms of the coordinate system of the object.
	Step	The coordinates of the center, (X, Y), are specified as an offset relative to the current location, (CurrentX, CurrentY).
(X, Y)	Single-precision values	The coordinates for the center of the circle, ellipse, or arc. The Scale properties of the object determine the units of measure.
Radius	Single value	The radius of the circle, ellipse, or arc. The Scale properties of the object determine the units of measure. If Aspect is less than 1, Radius is the width of the ellipse or arc; if Aspect is greater than 1, Radius is the height of the ellipse or arc.
Color	Omitted	Use the ForeColor property.
	Long value	Use one of the Color constants or the return values of the RGB or QBColor functions to specify a color.
Start	Omitted	Start the arc at 0 radians.
	Single value from 0 to 2π	Starting angle of the arc specified in radians.
	Negative single value from 0 to -2π	The absolute value of Start specifies the starting angle of a partial circle or ellipse. The negative sign causes a radius line to be drawn from the center of the circle or ellipse to the starting point along the radius. If both Start and End are negative, it creates a closed partial circle or ellipse that can be filled. You cannot draw a radius at zero because of the required negative sign, but you can approximate it by using a small negative value.
	Other values	Error
End	Omitted	End of arc at 2π radians.
	Single value from 0 to 2π	Ending angle of the arc specified in radians.
	Negative single value from 0 to -2π	The absolute value of End specifies the ending angle of a partial circle or ellipse. The negative sign causes a radius line to be drawn from the center of the circle or ellipse to the ending point

PARAMETER	VALUE	MEANING
End	Negative single value from 0 to –2π *(cont.)*	along the radius. If both Start and End are negative, it creates a closed partial circle or ellipse that can be filled.
	Other values	Error
Aspect	Omitted	Aspect is 1.0, which specifes a perfect circle.
	Single value less than 1	Specifies the aspect ratio of an ellipse or elliptical arc. The horizontal dimension is Radius. Twice the Radius multiplied by the Aspect ratio gives the height of the ellipse or arc.
	Single value greater than 1	Specifies the Aspect ratio of an ellipse or elliptical arc. The vertical dimension is Radius. Twice the Radius divided by the Aspect ratio gives the width of the ellipse or arc.

The Circle method always draws in a counter-clockwise, or positive, direction, regardless of the relative magnitude of the Start and End arguments. The CurrentX and CurrentY properties will be set to X and Y after the call to Circle.

Use the object's FillColor and FillStyle properties to fill the circle or ellipse. Use the object's DrawWidth, DrawMode, and DrawStyle properties to change the way the outline of the circle, ellipse, or arc is drawn.

When you want to include arguments at the end of the syntax but omit some arguments in the middle, leave in the commas that separate the arguments. The following example specifies an Aspect ratio but leaves out the Color, Start, and End arguments.

Example   `Picture1.Circle (100, 100), 50,,,,0.5`

Class Property

The Class property specifies the class name of an insertable object in the OLE Container control. You can get a list of valid class names by selecting the OLE Container control at design time. Then find the Class property in the Properties window and click the "..." button of the Class property.

Usage   *StringValue = object*.Class
             object.Class = *StringValue*

Applies To   OLE Container Control

The class name supplied by applications that support OLE or OLE Automation uses the following syntax:

`[Application.]ObjectType.Version`

The parts of the class name have the meanings given in the following table.

PART	MEANING
Application	The name of the server application that supplies the object.
ObjectType	The object's type as defined in the object library.
Version	The version number of the object format or the server application that supplies the object.

Examples of class names:

```
Excel.Sheet.5
Excel.Chart.5
MSGraph.Chart.5
MSWordArt.2
PowerPoint.Show.7
PowerPoint.Slide.7
Visio.Drawing.4
Word.Document.6
Word.Picture.6
Wordpad.Document.1
```

To automatically set the Class property for the OLE Container control, create an object using the Insert Object or Paste Special dialog boxes or paste from the Clipboard object.

Clear Method

This Clear method clears the contents of the associated object.

Usage   *object*.Clear

Applies To   Clipboard Object
                   ComboBox Control
                   ListBox Control

For the Clipboard object, Clear will clear all data of all formats.

Clear Method (Custom Controls)

This Clear method clears the objects from a collection.

Usage   *object*.Clear

Applies To   Buttons Collection
                   ColumnHeaders Collection

> ListImages Collection
> ListItems Collection
> Nodes Collection
> Panels Collection
> Tabs Collection

ClearSel Method

The ClearSel method clears the current selection of a Slider control, setting it back to 0.

Usage   *object*.ClearSel

Applies To   Slider Control

ClientHeight, ClientWidth, ClientLeft, ClientTop Properties

These four properties work together to tell you the coordinates of the display part of a TabStrip control. They are read-only and are available only at runtime.

Usage   *IntegerValue* = *object*.ClientHeight
                 IntegerValue = *object*.ClientWidth
                 IntegerValue = *object*.ClientLeft
                 IntegerValue = *object*.ClientTop

Applies To   TabStrip Control

PARAMETER	VALUE	MEANING
IntegerValue	An integer	The coordinate of the parameter you use.

The TabStrip control is a little brain-dead. Consequently, if you just put controls on a specific tab, it's not too great about knowing when to show them and when to hide them as users click through different tabs. The workaround for this problem involves the ClientHeight, ClientWidth, ClientLeft, and ClientTop properties. Typically, what you'll do is place a PictureBox control and match the PictureBox's size to these four properties; for example:

```
Picture1.Left = TabStrip1.ClientLeft
Picture1.Top = TabStrip1.ClientTop
Picture1.Width = TabStrip1.ClientWidth
Picture1.Height = TabStrip1.ClientHeight
```

Then create a PictureBox control array and associate it with a specific Tab object. You then either toggle the PictureBox's Visible property depending on whether the correct Tab object is selected or play with the PictureBox's ZOrder method.

ClipControls Property

The ClipControls property determines how graphics methods in Paint events are applied to the object—either to the entire object or to only the newly exposed areas. This property is read-only at runtime.

Usage   *BooleanValue* = *object*.ClipControls

Applies To   Form Object
                   Frame Control
                   PictureBox Control

The values of the ClipControls property have the meanings given in the following table.

VALUE	MEANING
True	The default. The entire object is repainted by graphics methods executed in the Paint event.
False	Only the newly exposed areas are repainted by graphics methods executed in the Paint event. This allows complex forms to repaint faster.

Setting the ClipControls property to True also causes outlines of the object and its controls to be created in memory such that Windows can paint the object without affecting its controls. The exceptions to this are the Image, Label, Line, and Shape controls. In practice, we don't see any difference between clipping or no clipping on the Child controls.

In the following example, run the application twice—once with ClipControls set to True and once to False—and cover and expose regions of the Form object. When ClipControls is set to True, the Form background will always be a single color, since the entire form is repainted. With it set to False, only the exposed regions will be painted in the new color.

Example
```
Private Sub Form_Paint()
    BackColor = &HFFFFFF * Rnd
End Sub
```

Close Method

The Close method shuts down the editing of an OLE object contained in an OLE Container control. It also shuts down the connection to the server application that supplied the object.

Usage   *object*.Close

Applies To   OLE Container Control

When the object is linked, this method may not close the file that was opened in the server application when the object was activated. Nor will it necessarily shut down the server application.

When the object is embedded, this method works correctly by closing the object and ending any editing sessions.

Cls Method

The Cls method clears graphics and text from a Form or PictureBox that were drawn at runtime. If the AutoRedraw property is True, then all drawn graphics and text are cleared. If it is False, then only the temporary graphics and text—drawn when AutoRedraw is False—are cleared. The graphics set by the Picture property are not cleared by Cls.

Usage   *object*.Cls

Applies To   Form Object
                 PictureBox Control

After Cls is called, the object's CurrentX and CurrentY properties are set to 0.

Col, Row Properties

The Col and Row properties specify the active cell in a grid. They are not available at design time.

Usage   *IntegerValue = object*.Col
                 object.Col = *IntegerValue*

                 IntegerValue = object.Row
                 object.Row = *IntegerValue*

Applies To   DBGrid Control
                 Grid Control

Columns and rows are numbered from zero. Changing these properties at runtime does *not* change the selected cells; those cells are changed using the SelEndCol, SelStartCol, SelEndRow, and SelStartRow properties.

ColContaining Method

The ColContaining method returns the ColIndex of the DBGrid column that contains the coordinate (X) value you specify.

Usage   *IntegerValue = object*.ColContaining(*CoordinateValue*)

Applies To   DBGrid Control

PARAMETER	VALUE	MEANING
CoordinateValue	Single-precision value Numeric expression	The horizontal coordinate, specified in the scale unit used for the DBGrid control.

You use this method when you're letting users drag and drop stuff into a DBGrid control. It returns a number that corresponds to a column index, ranging from 0 to Columns.Count –1. If the coordinate you feed it is outside the DBGrid's coordinate system, you get a trappable error.

ColIndex Property

The ColIndex property enables you to locate or reorder columns in a DBGrid control.

Usage   *object*.ColIndex = *IntegerValue*
                     IntegerValue = object.ColIndex

Applies To   Column Control

PARAMETER	VALUE	MEANING
IntegerValue	An integer	Columns in DBGrid start numbering at 0 (far left) and end with the value of the Column object's Count property.

If you set IntegerValue to 0, you'll move the column over to the far left. Columns formerly to the left of the column have ColIndex incremented. Set it to Count, and you move it to the far right and columns formerly to the right are decremented. Set it to something in between and the columns between where it was and where you moved will either be decremented (if you moved it to the right) or incremented (if you moved it to the left).

If you want to create a button that promotes the current column (wherever the cursor is) to be the one on the far left, you can write this:

```
Private Sub Command1_Click()
    Dim I As Integer
```

```
    I = DBGrid1.Col
    Debug.Print DBGrid1.Columns(I).ColIndex
    DBGrid1.Columns(I).ColIndex = 0
End Sub
```

Color Property

The Color property sets or returns the selected color for the Color or Font dialog of a Common-Dialog control.

Usage   *LongValue = object*.Color
                 object.Color = *LongValue*

Applies To   CommonDialog Control

The value of the Color property may be set using the RGB or QBColor functions or one of the color constants listed in the Color Constants section.

- Color dialog: To set a color in the dialog box, set the cdlCCRGBInit (&H1&) flag.

- Font Dialog: To return a color from the dialog box, set the cdlCFEffects (&H100&) flag.

ColorMode Property

The ColorMode property indicates whether the printer prints in color or monochrome. This is available only at runtime.

Usage   *IntegerValue = object*.ColorMode
                 object.ColorMode = *IntegerValue*

Applies To   Printer Object

The return value can be one of the those in the following table.

CONSTANT	VALUE	MEANING
vbPRCMMonochrome	1	Printer output is monochrome, usually in shades of black and white.
vbPRCMColor	2	Printer output is color.

Note: You can change the Printer property only for the default printer. Set it by using the Set Printer = command.

Note: Not all printers support this property or all possible values of this property. You might get an error for your printer.

Cols, Rows Properties

The Cols and Rows properties specify the number of columns and rows in a Grid control.

Usage	*IntegerValue = object*.Cols
	object.Cols *= IntegerValue*
	IntegerValue = object.Rows
	object.Rows *= IntegerValue*
Applies To	Grid Control

ColumnCount Property

The ColumnCount property tells you the number of columns that a RowBuffer object holds in an unbound DBGrid.

Usage	*object*.ColumnCount
Applies To	RowBuffer Object

The RowBuffer object is where you put rows of retrieved data when you're transferring it between your application and an unbound DBGrid. It's available only with unbound DBGrids. Your application must make sure to take the information from a RowBuffer and update the actual database.

The syntax for a RowBuffer object is simply

```
DBGrid.RowBuffer
```

RowBuffer works with UnboundReadData, UnboundWriteData, and UnboundAddData to manipulate data into and out of unbound DBGrids.

ColumnHeaders Property (DBGrid)

This ColumnHeaders property specifies whether column headers are displayed in a DBGrid control.

Usage	*BooleanValue = object*.ColumnHeaders
	object.ColumnHeaders *= BooleanValue*

Applies To   DBGrid Control

The values of the DBGrid's ColumnHeaders property have the meanings given in the following table.

PARAMETER	VALUE	MEANING
BooleanValue	True	Column headers are displayed.
	False	Column headers are not displayed.

ColumnHeaders Property (ListView)

This ColumnHeaders property returns a reference to a collection of ColumnHeader objects in a ListView control.

Usage   *ObjectValue = object*.ColumnHeaders

Applies To   ListView Control

PARAMETER	VALUE	MEANING
ObjectValue	A ColumnHeader collection	The ColumnHeader collection you're referencing.

ColumnName Property

The ColumnName property tells you the name of a column within a RowBuffer object in an unbound DBGrid.

Usage   *StringValue = object*.ColumnName (*ColumnValue*)

Applies To   RowBuffer Object

PARAMETER	VALUE	MEANING
StringValue	A string	The name of the column returned.
ColumnValue	A string	Tells ColumnName for which column you want the name.

Columns Property (ListBox)

This Columns property specifies the number of columns to be displayed in a ListBox control at any one time. It divides the width of the ListBox into equal-sized columns; if you increase the width of the ListBox, the column widths also will increase. If the Columns property is nonzero, the ListBox will fit as many items as it can vertically—limited by the Height property—and then create a new column for additional items. It continues to create new columns until all items are listed. If the total number of columns created becomes greater than the value of the Columns property, a horizontal scroll bar will be created to allow scrolling through the list.

Usage   *IntegerValue = object*.Columns
                   object.Columns = *IntegerValue*

Applies To   ListBox Control

The values of the Columns property have the meanings given in the following table.

VALUE	MEANING
0	The default. Only one column is displayed and the list scrolls vertically. When set at design time, this value cannot be changed to a nonzero value at runtime.
1 through 32,767	The number of equal-sized columns to be displayed within the width of the ListBox. Multiple columns are created automatically to list all the data; each column lists as many items as will fit within the height of the ListBox control. The ListBox scrolls horizontally through the columns. When this value is set at design time to a nonzero value, you cannot change it to zero at runtime, although you can set it to a different nonzero value.
Other values	Error

Note that if you set Columns to 1, only one column is visible, just as when Columns is set to 0. But for Columns set to 1, the scroll bar will appear horizontally along the bottom of the List-Box control when needed.

Columns Property (DBGrid)

This Columns property returns a reference to a collection of Column objects in a DBGrid control.

Usage   *ObjectValue = object*.Columns

Applies To   DBGrid Control

PARAMETER	VALUE	MEANING
ObjectValue	A Column object	The Column object(s) you're referencing.

Comments Property

At runtime, the Comments property is read-only, returning a string that contains comments about the running application. To set the comments, select the File/Make EXE File... menu and then click the Options button. In the "Version Information" section, select "Comments" from the list and enter the value in the text box.

Usage   *String Value = object.*Comments

Applies To   App Object

CompanyName Property

At runtime, the CompanyName property is read-only, returning a string that contains the name of the company or person that created the application. To set the CompanyName property, select the File/Make EXE File... menu and then click the Options button. In the "Version Information" section, select "Company Name" from the list and enter the value in the text box.

Usage   *String Value = object.*CompanyName

Applies To   App Object

Connect Property

The Connect property tells you (and lets you set) the application format of the database you're dealing with. In other words, you can create a database and make it a Paradox database instead of the default Access-compatible database.

Usage   *Databasetype*; *Parameters = object.*Connect
                  *object.*Connect = *Databasetype*; *Parameters*

Applies To   Data Control
                  Database Object
                  QueryDef Object
                  TableDef Object

PARAMETER	VALUE	MEANING
Databasetype	"dBASE III;"	Creates a dBASE III database.
	"dBASE IV;"	Creates a dBASE IV database.
	"Paradox 3.x;"	And so on...
	"Paradox 4.x;"	
	"Btrieve;"	
	"FoxPro 2.0;"	
	"FoxPro 2.5;"	
	"FoxPro 2.6;"	
	"Excel 3.0;"	
	"Excel 4.0;"	
	"Excel 5.0;"	
	"Text;"	
	"ODBC; DATABASE=dbname; UID=username; PWD=password; DSN=datasourcename; LOGINTIMEOUT= seconds"	It's a mess, but this is how you create an ODBC database. Notice that each parameter gets its own semicolon to separate it from the others.
Parameters	"drive:\path"	Specifies the drive and pathname of the file you're dealing with.

Container Property

Controls may be placed in a container, such as a Frame or PictureBox control. The Container property specifies to which container this control belongs. You can use it at runtime to move controls around on your form.

When a control belongs to a container, its coordinates (top and left) are expressed relative to the container and its dimensions (width, height, and so on) are expressed in the units used by the container.

Usage   *ObjectValue* = *object*.Container
            Set *object*.Container = *ObjectValue*

Applies To   CheckBox Control

ComboBox Control
CommandButton Control
DBCombo Control
DBGrid Control
DBList Control
DirListBox Control
DriveListBox Control
FileListBox Control
Frame Control
Grid Control
HScrollBar Control
Image Control
Label Control
Line Control
ListBox Control
OLE Container Control
OptionButton Control
PictureBox Control
Shape Control
TextBox Control
VScrollBar Control

If a control is not in a container (Frame or PictureBox), then trying to retrieve the Container property generates an error. You can, however, set the Container property to a Form or MDIForm to move it out of a container. You cannot move a control to a different form.

Example
```
Set Command1.Container = Picture1
        Command1.Top = 10 : Command1.Left = 10
```

This example moves the CommandButton to the Picture control. To move it back to the form, use this:

Example
```
Set Command1.Container = Form1
```

 It's an oversight that the Container property is invalid when the container is a Form or MDIForm rather than a Frame or a PictureBox, especially since they can all hold other controls.

ControlBox Property

The ControlBox property specifies whether the Control menu icon is displayed at the left of the title bar of a Form window at runtime. You click the icon to access the Restore, Move, Size, Minimize, Maximize, Close, and other commands that manipulate the window. This property can be set only at design time and read only at runtime.

Usage   *BooleanValue = object*.ControlBox

Applies To   Form Object

The values of the ControlBox property can have the meanings given in the following table.

VALUE	MEANING
True	The default. Displays the Control menu icon. The form's BorderStyle property must be vbFixedSingle (1), vbSizable (2), or vbFixedDouble (3).
False	Removes the Control menu icon.

Note: If you set the Form object's MaxButton and MinButton properties to False, then the Maximize and Minimize choices, respectively, of the Control menu will be disabled.

Copies Property

The Copies property specifies the number of copies of a document to print. It is not available at design time for the Printer object.

Usage   *IntegerValue = object*.Copies
                     object.Copies = *IntegerValue*

Applies To   CommonDialog Control
                     Printer Object

The values for the Copies property for a Printer object have the meanings given in the following table.

VALUE	MEANING
1 through 999	The number of copies to print. Actually, the valid range may depend on your printer driver. If the Copies property is greater than 1, whether printed output will be collated depends on the printer driver. If you must have collating, set Copies to 1 and then use a For loop to print multiple copies.
Other integer	Error

The Copies property for a Print CommonDialog control returns the number of copies requested by the user. If the UseDevModeCopies flag for the CommonDialog control is set, Copies always returns 1.

Note: You can change the Copies property only for the default printer. Set it by using the Set Printer = command.

Note: Not all printers support this property or all possible values of this property. You might get an error for your printer.

Copy Method

The Copy method copies an object in the OLE Container control to the system Clipboard. Use this method to support an Edit/Copy menu command for your applications.

Usage   *object*.Copy

Applies To   OLE Container Control

The object can be linked or embedded. All object data and link information are copied to the system Clipboard.

Example
```
Private Sub mnuEditCopy_Click()
    OLE1.Copy
End Sub
```

Count Property

The Count property returns the number of objects in a collection.

Usage   *IntegerValue = object*.Count

Applies To   Controls Collection
                   Form Object
                   Forms Collection
                   MDIForm Object
                   Printers Collection

Use the Count property to cycle through all elements in a collection using For...Next.

Example
```
For i = 0 To MDIForm1.Controls.Count - 1
    If TypeOf MDIForm1.Controls(i) Is Label Then
        MDIForm1.Controls(i).Enabled = False
    End If
Next i
```

In VB4, only one component can be selected at any one time for a project, so the Count property of the SelectedComponents collection (exposed by VB to Add-Ins) is never greater than 1.

Form and MDIForm Objects

Because the Controls collection is the default intrinsic global variable of a Form or MDIForm object, when you use Form1.Count or MDIForm1.Count, you actually get Form1.Controls.Count or MDIForm1.Controls.Count, respectively, that returns the number of controls on the Form.

CreateDragImage Method

The CreateDragImage method dithers an object's icon (not its label, as the Help file says) to create a "drag image"—the image that you'll see in drag-and-drop operations.

Usage   *object*.CreateDragImage

Applies To   ListItem Control
                 Node Object

CreateEmbed Method

The CreateEmbed method creates an embedded object in an OLE Container control.

Usage   *object*.CreateEmbed *SourceDoc*[, *Class*]

Applies To   OLE Container Control

The parameters to the CreateEmbed method have the meanings given in the following table.

PARAMETER	VALUE	MEANING
SourceDoc	String expression	The name of a file used as a template for the embedded object. If you do not wish to specify a file, use a zero-length string (" ").
Class	String expression	The name of the class of the embedded object to create. The SourceDoc has to be a zero-length string (" "). If SourceDoc specifies a filename, then this parameter is checked for validity, but not used. To see a list of valid class names, select the Class property from the Properties window for the OLE Container control and click the "..." button.

A class name for a server application must be registered with the operating system.

Example   `OLE1.CreateEmbed "e:\prj\office.vsd"`

CreateLink Method

The CreateLink method creates a lined object in an OLE Container control.

Usage   *object*.CreateLink *SourceDoc*[, *SourceItem*]

Applies To   OLE Container Control

The parameters to the CreateEmbed method have the meanings given in the following table.

PARAMETER	VALUE	MEANING
SourceDoc	String expression	The name of a file used for the linked object. This value will replace the SourceDoc property of the OLE Container control.
SourceItem	String expression	The name of a piece of data within the document to be linked to the object. This value will replace the SourceItem property of the OLE Container control.

For a linked object created by this method, the OLE Container control contains only link references to the linked item and displays a metafile image of the item; it does not contain the actual data. As a result, saving the object will save only the link references.

A class name for a server application must be registered with the operating system.

Example   ```
OLE1.CreateLink "C:\MyDoc.doc", "OLE_LINK1"
```

# CurrentX, CurrentY Properties

The CurrentX and CurrentY properties specify the horizontal (CurrentX) and vertical (CurrentY) coordinates for the next printing or drawing method. These are available only at runtime and are set to zero initially when the object is first created.

*Usage*          *SingleValue* = *object*.CurrentX
                 *object*.CurrentX = *SingleValue*

                 *SingleValue* = *object*.CurrentY
                 *object*.CurrentY = *SingleValue*

*Applies To*      Form Object
                 PictureBox Control
                 Printer Object
```

The coordinate system specified by CurrentX and CurrentY originates from the top-left corner of the object, unless it is changed by the ScaleLeft and ScaleTop properties. The units of measurement are determined by the ScaleHeight, ScaleWidth, and ScaleMode properties.

The CurrentX and CurrentY properties may be changed directly or by the graphics methods.

METHOD	RESULTING CURRENTX AND CURRENTY
Circle	The center of the circle.
Cls	Reset to 0, 0.
EndDoc	Reset to 0, 0.
Line	The last end point of the line.
NewPage	Reset to 0, 0.
Print	The position where the next Print would start.
Pset	The location of the point drawn by PSet.

The following examples are identical:

Example
```
Line -(1000, 1000)
       Line (CurrentX, CurrentY)-(1000, 1000)
```

Customize Method

The Customize method brings up the Customize Toolbar dialog box, which allows the end user to rearrange or hide Button objects on a Toolbar control.

Usage   *object*.Customize

Applies To   Toolbar Control

The dialog box that enables users to customize a Toolbar control is built into the control, so you might as well take advantage of it. Set the AllowCustomize property to True. Use the SaveToolbar and RestoreToolbar methods to save a toolbar configuration and to restore the configuration to the default.

With some severe coding, you can even enable users to create their own toolbars.

Data Property

The Data property specifies the handle to a memory object or graphical device interface (GDI) object that represents the data in a specified format (Format property) for an OLE Container control. Avoid using this property if the object supports OLE Automation. This property is not available at design time.

Usage   *LongValue = object*.Data
                     object.Data = *LongValue*

Applies To   OLE Container Control

Setting the Data property sends data to the server application that supplied the object in the OLE Container control. You must set the Format property first to specify the type of data contained in the memory object or GDI object referenced by the Data property. The ObjectAccept-Formats and ObjectGetFormats properties return lists of acceptable object formats. Setting the Data property to 0 frees the memory associated with the object handle.

For objects supporting OLE Automation, you can access the object through the Object property or using the CreateObject and GetObject functions.

Database Property

The Database property enables you to look at the database underlying a recordset.

Usage   *object*.Database
                     Set *databaseobject = object*.Database (Professional Edition only)

Applies To   Data Control

Database objects themselves have methods and properties that you can use, like Close. You can also look at the structure of a database by looking at the properties of the TableDefs, Fields, and Indexes collections.

DatabaseName Property

The DatabaseName contains the name and location of the data source for a Data control.

Usage   *object*.DatabaseName = *StringValue*
                     StringValue = object.DatabaseName

Applies To   Data Control

PARAMETER	VALUE	MEANING
StringValue	A legal path name	Points to the system, directory, and file of the database you want to access.

DataChanged Property

The DataChanged property indicates whether the value of the control has changed. If, however, the control is bound to a Data object and its value changes because it's being updated with data from the current record, the DataChanged property will *not* be set to True.

Usage   *BooleanValue* = *object*.DataChanged
                 object.DataChanged = *BooleanValue*

Applies To   CheckBox Control
                 ComboBox Control
                 DBCombo Control
                 DBList Control
                 Image Control
                 Label Control
                 List Control
                 PictureBox Control
                 TextBox Control

The values of the DatabaseName property can be interpreted as given in the following table.

VALUE	MEANING
True	The value in the control has changed, but not because of an update from a Data control for the current record.
False	The data has not changed. This is the initial value of all controls when the application is first run. For a bound control, the property is set to False every time a new record is selected.

You might want to check the DataChanged property in the control's Change event to prevent cascading an event from one control to another.

Data Bound Controls

When a Data control moves to a new record, it updates the data in its bound controls and sets the DataChanged property of those controls to False. If the user or your code subsequently changes the value of the control, VB sets the DataChanged property to True. Just before the data control moves to another record, the Data control invokes the Edit and Update methods if any bound controls have DataChanged set to True. If any errors occur during the update, the Data control will remain in the same record.

If you do not wish to save any changes to the database, you can use the control's Validate event to set the DataChanged property to False.

DataField Property

If a Data control is bound to a Data object using the DataSource property, the DataField property specifies the name of a field in the current record that is bound to the control. That is, the control will display the value of a field of the current record.

Usage   *StringValue = object*.DataField
                   object.DataField = *StringValue*

Applies To   CheckBox Control
                   ComboBox Control
                   DBCombo Control
                   DBGrid Control
                   DBList Control
                   Image Control
                   Label Control
                   ListBox Control
                   OLE Container Control
                   PictureBox Control
                   TextBox Control

If the specified field is not valid or the field and the control have different data types, you will get an error when the Data object updates the control.

Note that the Data control uses its DatabaseName and RecordSource properties to specify a Recordset object. The DataField property of the bound control must specify a valid field in that Recordset.

If the Recordset is a QueryDef object or a SQL statement that returns results of an expression, the Microsoft Jet database engine automatically generates a field name that is the string "Expr1" followed by a three-character number starting at "000." As a consequence, you should use an AS clause in your SQL statements to provide a more-friendly field name that can be used to set the DataField property.

Example
```
Data1.RecordSource = "SELECT SUM(Sales) AS TotalSales " _
        & "FROM SalesTable"
    Text1.DataField = "TotalSales"
Data1.Refresh
```

Assuming Text1's DataSource property is set to Data1, this example will place the total sales figure in Text1.

DataMode Property

The DataMode property determines whether a DBGrid control is going to be bound or unbound (available at design time only).

Usage   *object*.DataMode = *IntegerValue*
                        IntegerValue = *object*.DataMode

Applies To   DBGrid Control

PARAMETER	VALUE	MEANING
IntegerValue	dbgBound or 0	Makes it so that you can bind this DBGrid to a Data control.
	dbgUnbound or 1	Makes it so that you don't have to bind this control to a Data control.

Setting DataMode to 1 when DBGrid is bound to a data source (e.g., Data1) generates an error.

DataSource Property

The DataSource property specifies the Data control to which the control is bound. The bound control accesses fields in the Recordset managed by the Data control. This property can be set only at design time using the Properties window and *cannot be accessed* at runtime. You must still set the DataField property of the control to connect it to a field in the Recordset managed by the Data control.

Usage   *StringValue* = *object*.DataSource
                        object.DataSource = *StringValue*

Applies To   CheckBox Control
                    ComboBox Control
                    DBCombo Control
                    DBGrid Control
                    DBList Control
                    OLE Container Control
                    Image Control
                    Label Control
                    ListBox Control
                    PictureBox Control
                    TextBox Control

PARAMETER	VALUE	MEANING
StringValue	A string	The name of a valid Data control.

DataText Property

The DataText property specifies a string to retrieve or set for the object contained in an OLE Container control. Avoid using this property if the object supports OLE Automation. This property is not available at design time.

Usage   *StringValue* = *object*.DataText
                  object.DataText = *StringValue*

Applies To   OLE Container Control

Setting the DataText property sends a string to the server application that supplied the object in the OLE Container control. You must first set the Format property to a format supported by the object. The ObjectAcceptFormats and ObjectGetFormats properties return lists of acceptable object formats.

When getting data, the string sent by the object is contained in the DataText property and ends at the first null character. For 16-bit versions of VB, the DataText string is limited to 64K characters. For 32-bit, it is unlimited.

For objects supporting OLE Automation, you can access the object through the Object property or using the CreateObject and GetObject functions.

Default Property

The Default property specifies whether a CommandButton is activated when the user presses the Enter key *and* the focus is not on another CommandButton or OLE Container control. This applies also to an OLE Container control containing an object that acts like a CommandButton.

Usage   *BooleanValue* = *object*.Default
                  object.Default = *BooleanValue*

Applies To   CommandButton Control
                  OLE Container Control

The values for the Default property have the meanings given in the following table.

VALUE	MEANING
True	The CommandButton's Click event will run when the user presses the Enter key (*and* the focus is not on another CommandButton or OLE Container control). When you set the Default property of one CommandButton to True, VB sets the Default property of *all* other CommandButtons to False. As a result, only one CommandButton will be the Default button at any one time.
False	The default. The CommandButton will not respond to the Enter key unless it has focus.

A CommandButton with its Default property True should be the last control that the user interacts with to commit changes or to start some process. If, however, it is important that the user not accidentally commit changes, also set the Cancel button's Default property to True so that pressing the Enter key also cancels any changes.

DefaultExt Property

The DefaultExt property controls default filename extension for the dialog box.

Usage   *object*.DefaultExt = *StringValue*
                     StringValue = *object*.DefaultExt

Applies To   CommonDialog Control

PARAMETER	VALUE	MEANING
StringValue	A string	The file extension that will be appended when a user doesn't specify one of his/her own.

DefaultValue Property

The DefaultValue property sets or shows the default value for a field (more specifically, a Field object) in a DBGrid.

Usage   *object*.DefaultValue = *StringValue*
                     StringValue = *object*.DefaultValue

Applies To   DBGrid Control
                     Field Object

PARAMETER	VALUE	MEANING
StringValue	A string	A string with up to 255 characters.

When you create a new record, the default value of the field you chose will be DefaultValue. But the DefaultValue property doesn't work with all the different ways of looking at data. This property works great if you opened your data as a TableDef. With QueryDefs and Recordsets, you can read the value but not set it. You can't use this property to do anything at all to an Index or a Relation.

Example
```
Dim DBSample As Database
Dim TableTemp As TableDef
Dim FieldTest As Field
Dim I As Integer
Set DBSample = Workspaces(0).OpenDatabase("TEST.MDB")
Set TableTemp = DBSample.CreateTableDef("MyTable2")
Set FieldTest = TableTemp.CreateField("Blah", dbDate)
TableTemp.Fields.Append MyField
DBSample.TableDefs.Append MyTableDef
FieldTest.DefaultValue = "No"
```

DefColWidth Property

The DefColWidth property determines the default column width for all columns in the DBGrid control.

Usage
> *object*.DefColWidth = *SingleValue*
> *SingleValue* = *object*.DefColWidth

Applies To   DBGrid Control

PARAMETER	VALUE	MEANING
SingleValue	Single-precision value	The default column width in the units of measure for the DBGrid control.

If you set Value to 0, the columns autosize to the width of the column heading or the Size property setting of the underlying field, whichever is larger.

Example
```
Private Sub Form_Load()
    DBGrid1.DefColWidth = 0
End Sub
```

Delete Method

The Delete method deletes the object from an OLE Container control and releases the memory associated with the object.

Usage   *object*.Delete

Applies To   OLE Container Control

Use the Delete method to explicitly delete OLE objects. You do not need to explicitly use Delete when you close forms or replace objects with new ones.

Description Property (Button Object)

The Description property for the Button object controls the text that you (or a user) will see when you use the Customize Toolbar dialog box.

Usage   *object*.Description = *StringValue*
                   StringValue = *object*.Description

Applies To   Button Object

PARAMETER	VALUE	MEANING
StringValue	A string	The words that will show up when you use the Customize Toolbar dialog box.

Note: This property works only with Windows 95 NT 3.51 and higher.
You can set the Description text when you add a Button object, as follows:

Example
```
Dim btnOpen As Button
Set btnOpen = Toolbar1.Buttons.Add(,"open")
btnOpen.Description = "Open a file or files"
```

DeviceName Property

The DeviceName property returns the name of the printer represented by the Printer object. The name matches one of the entries in your Windows Printers utility.

Usage   *StringValue* = *object*.DeviceName

Applies To   Printer Object

The printer names are those that have been set up by you or your system administrator. More than one printer may use the same printer driver.

Example
```
MsgBox "The current printer is: " & Printer.DeviceName & _
       " on " & Printer.Port
```

DialogTitle Property

The DialogTitle property controls the string displayed in the Title Bar of the dialog box.

Usage   *object*.DialogTitle = *StringValue*
                     StringValue = *object*.DialogTitle

Applies To   CommonDialog Control

PARAMETER	VALUE	MEANING
StringValue	A string	The string that will appear in the Title Bar of the dialog box. It is ignored by the Color and Font dialog boxes. Probably best to leave the default value.

DisableNoScroll Property

The DisableNoScroll property controls whether scroll bars in the RichTextBox control are disabled.

Usage   *object*.DisableNoScroll = *BooleanValue*
                     BooleanValue = *object*.DisableNoScroll

Applies To   RichTextBox Control

PARAMETER	VALUE	MEANING
BooleanValue	True	Scroll bars are disabled (dimmed).
	False	Scroll bars appear normal and are enabled.

DisplayType Property

The DisplayType property specifies whether an OLE Container control displays its object's data or its object's icon.

Usage   *IntegerValue* = *object*.DisplayType
                     object.DisplayType = *IntegerValue*

Applies To   OLE Container Control

The DisplayType property can take on one of the values given in the following table.

CONSTANT	VALUE	MEANING
vbOLEDisplayContent	0	The OLE Container control displays its object's data. This is the default.
vbOLEDisplayIcon	1	The OLE Container control displays its object's icon. Using this setting checks the Display As Icon check box in the Insert Object and Paste Special dialog boxes.

 The Help file is *wrong* when it states that this property cannot be changed after the OLE object has been created.

DividerStyle Property

The DividerStyle property determines what the right edge of a column in the DBGrid control is going to look like.

Usage   *object*.DividerStyle = *IntegerValue*
                 IntegerValue = *object*.DividerStyle

Applies To   Column Object

PARAMETER	VALUE	MEANING
IntegerValue	dbgNoDividers or 0	Gives the control no dividers between columns.
	dbgBlackLine or 1	Makes the divider between columns or rows a black line.
	dbgDarkGrayLine or 2	Makes the divider between columns or rows a dark gray line.
	dbgRaised or 3	Makes the divider between columns or rows raised.
	dbgInset or 4	Makes the divider between columns or rows inset.
	dbgUseForeColor or 5	Uses the foreground color in the divider between columns or rows.

DividerStyle works exactly as you'd expect; there seem to be no surprises. The example in the Windows Help file isn't great because it changes the border of the currently selected column, so you can't really see what's going on. The property does work, however.

DoVerb Method

The DoVerb method opens an OLE object for an operation, such as editing. Each OLE object supports its own set of verbs, usually with positive integer values and available from the ObjectVerbs property of the OLE Container control. However, each OLE object should support the standard set of verbs. At runtime, right-clicking over the OLE object should pop up a menu listing the custom verbs it supports.

Usage   *object*.DoVerb [*Verb*]

Applies To   OLE Container Control

PARAMETER	VALUE	MEANING
Verb	vbOLEPrimary or 0 or omitted	Executes the default verb of the OLE object.
	vbOLEShow or –1	Activates the OLE object for editing. If the server application supports in-place activation *and* the object is embedded (not linked), the object is activated within the OLE Container control rather than a separate window. If the object is linked, this linkage opens the object in a separate application window. *Note:* In-place activation makes each toolbar of the OLE server application appear in a separate window.
	vbOLEOpen or –2	Opens the object in a separate application window, even if the application supports in-place activation.
	vbOLEHide or –3	For embedded objects, hides the application that created the object. This applies only to in-place editing; otherwise, you'll get "Runtime error '31027': Unable to activate object." This verb does *not* hide the toolbars of the OLE application!
	vbOLEInPlaceUIActivate or –4	An error if the OLE server application does not support in-place activation and if the object is linked. Otherwise, in-place editing is activated, and all user-interface tools associated with the application are enabled.
	vbOLEInPlaceActivate or –5	The object waits for the user to click inside for editing. If the OLE server application does not support activation on a single mouse-click, an error occurs. *Note:* The OLE server application does not always wait! In-place activation may occur immediately.
	vbOLEDiscardUndoState or –6	Discards all record of changes that the OLE object's server application can undo. *Note:* Not all OLE server applications support this verb. You'll need to test this for your applications.
	Other integer value	Custom verbs defined for the OLE object.

If you set the AutoActivate property to 2 (Double-Click), the OLE Container control automatically activates the current object when the user double-clicks the control.

Use the following code to test the vbOLEDiscardUndoState verb for your OLE server application. Place an OLE Container control called "OLE1" on a form and link it to an OLE object. Run your VB application and activate the OLE object for editing. Make some changes. Check the

Edit menu of your server application to make sure Undo is enabled. Then right-click the form to send the verb and look in the Edit menu again. If you cannot select Undo, then the verb worked.

Example

```
Private Sub Form_MouseDown(Button As Integer, Shift As Integer, \
    X As Single, Y As Single)
    If Button = 2 Then  'Right Button
        OLE1.DoVerb vbOLEDiscardUndoState
    End If
End Sub
```

Drag Method

The Drag method controls the drag-and-drop action of a control. VB4 changed the behavior of the Drag method! Previously, statements following the Drag method in the code were executed before the Drag operation was complete. Now, no statements are executed until Drag is complete.

Usage   *object*.Drag [*Action*]

Applies To   CheckBox Control
                 ComboBox Control
                 CommandButton Control
                 Data Control
                 DBGrid Control
                 DirListBox Control
                 DriveListBox Control
                 FileListBox Control
                 Frame Control
                 Grid Control
                 HScrollBar Control
                 Image Control
                 Label Control
                 ListBox Control
                 OLE Container Control
                 OptionButton Control
                 PictureBox Control
                 TextBox Control
                 VScrollBar Control

PARAMETER	VALUE	MEANING
Action	vbCancel or 0	Cancels the drag operation.
	vbBeginDrag or 1	Begins the drag operation by "picking up" the control. No MouseUp events for the source control will be generated during drag-and-drop.
	vbEndDrag or 2	Ends the drag operation by "dropping" the control.

The following example demonstrates dragging a Label control (using a control array called "Label1") within a PictureBox control.

Example

```
Private DeltaX As Single, DeltaY As Single

Private Sub Label1_MouseDown(Index As Integer, Button As _
    Integer, Shift As Integer, X As Single, Y As Single)
        DeltaX = X: DeltaY = Y
        Label1(Index).Drag vbBeginDrag
    End Sub

Private Sub Picture1_DragDrop(Source As Control, X As Single, _
    Y As Single)
    If Source.Name = "Label1" Then
        Source.Move X - DeltaX, Y - DeltaY
    End If
End Sub
```

DragIcon Property

The DragIcon property specifies the icon to use as the cursor when performing a drag-and-drop operation for the control. Use this property to provide visual feedback during a drag-and-drop operation to indicate valid and invalid drop targets.

Usage

PictureObject = *object*.DragIcon
object.DragIcon = *PictureObject*

Applies To

CheckBox Control
ComboBox Control
CommandButton Control
Data Control
DBCombo Control
DBGrid Control
DBList Control
DirListBox Control
DriveListBox Control
FileListBox Control
Frame Control
Grid Control
HScrollBar, VScrollBar Controls
Image Control
Label Control
ListBox Control
OLE Container Control
OptionButton Control
PictureBox Control
TextBox Control

The DragIcon value may be set to an icon file at design time via the Properties window or at runtime by assigning it to the result of a LoadPicture function. The file must have the .ICO filename extension and file format. It may also be set to another control's or object's DragIcon or Icon properties.

If this property is not set, the icon will be a rectangle that is the bounding box of the control and the normal arrow cursor.

You can reset the DragIcon property in the drag source control's MouseDown event. Then use the DragOver event of target controls to change the drag source's DragIcon property to indicate valid or invalid drop targets.

DragMode Property

The DragMode property determines how drag-and-drop is initiated for a control.

Usage	*object*.DragMode = *IntegerValue*
	IntegerValue = *object*.DragMode

Applies To	CheckBox Control
	ComboBox Control
	CommandButton Control
	Data Control
	DBCombo Control
	DBGrid Control
	DBList Control
	DirListBox Control
	DriveListBox Control
	FileListBox Control
	Frame Control
	Grid Control
	HScrollBar, VScrollBar Controls
	Image Control
	Label Control
	ListBox Control
	OLE Container Control
	OptionButton Control
	PictureBox Control
	TextBox Control

Applies To	All controls except Line, Menu, Shape, Timer, or CommonDialog

The DragMode property can accept the constants given in the following table.

Constant	Value	Meaning
vbManual	0	The default. It requires using the source control's Drag method to initiate a drag-and-drop operation.
vbAutomatic	1	Clicking the source control automatically initiates a drag-and-drop operation. OLE Container controls are automatically dragged only when they don't have focus. Using this mode, the source control does not respond normally to MouseDown and MouseUp events.

For either mode, during a drag, no keyboard or mouse events for the source control are generated.

Note: If you set DragMode property to vbAutomatic, the control will not respond to the Click or DblClick events. You won't even get MouseDown and MouseUp events for the left mouse button.

Draw Method

The Draw method draws an image from a ListImage object into a specified device context, such as a PictureBox control. You can perform an optional graphical operation on the image before drawing to the destination.

Usage   *object*.Draw (*hDC*[, X, Y][, *Style*])

Applies To   ListImage Object

The parameters to the Draw method have the meanings given in the following table.

Parameter	Value	Meaning
hDC	Handle	The handle to a device context. For a PictureBox control, Form object, or Printer object, you can use its hDC property.
X, Y	Single-precision values	The coordinates, specified in the units of measure for the destination, of the location for the image.
	Omitted	Places the image at the origin of the destination.
Style	imlNormal or 0 or Omitted	Normal. Copies the image with no changes.
	imlTransparent or 1	Transparent. The MaskColor property determines which color will be transparent.
	imlSelected or 2	Selected. Dithers the image with the system highlight color.
	imlFocus or 3	Focus. Dithers and stripes the image with the system highlight color, thus creating a hatched effect. You can use this to indicate that the image has focus.

Because an object's hDC value may change, use the hDC property of the destination directly, such as:

```
ImageList1.ListImages(2).Draw Picture1.hDC
```

DrawMode Property

The DrawMode property determines how graphics are rendered for Line or Shape controls or the graphics methods of the Form, Printer, and PictureBox objects.

DrawMode specifies the bit-wise operation to use in combining the pixels of the drawing pattern with the *existing* background pixels in arriving at the final pattern. The "pen color" of the foreground pixels used in the bit-wise operation is specified by the current or specified drawing color: BorderColor, ForeColor, FillColor, FillStyle, or that specified by the drawing methods.

Usage   *object*.DrawMode = *IntegerValue*
            IntegerValue = *object*.DrawMode

Applies To   Form Object
            Line Control
            PictureBox Control
            Printer Object
            Shape Control

This bit-wise operation is *not* performed using the RGB value of the colors. It is probably performed using the *index* number of the color in your hardware color palette, so the results can be unpredictable unless you're using one of the 20 standard VGA colors (these "static" colors are defined in the color palette to give the correct results).

The DrawMode can be one of the values given in the following table.

CONSTANT	VALUE	MEANING
vbBlackness	1	Uses Black, regardless of the pen color.
vbNotMergePen	2	Not Merge pen. The inverse of vbMergePen, where the pen and background colors are combined using the Or operator.
vbMaskNotPen	3	Mask Not pen. The combination of the background color and the inverse of the pen using the And operator.
vbNotCopyPen	4	Not Copy pen. Uses the inverse of the pen color.
vbMaskPenNot	5	Mask pen Not. The combination of the pen color and the inverse of the background color using the And operator.
vbInvert	6	Invert. Uses the inverse of the background color.
vbXorPen	7	Xor pen. The combination of the pen color and the background color using the XOR operator.

Constant	Value	Meaning
vbNotMaskPen	8	Not Mask pen. The inverse of vbMaskPen, where pen and background colors are combined using the And operator.
vbMaskPen	9	Mask pen. The combination of the pen and background colors using the And operator.
vbNotXorPen	10	Not Xor pen. The inverse of vbXorPen, where pen and background colors are combined using the XOR operator.
vbNop	11	No operation. No drawing is performed.
vbMergeNotPen	12	Merge Not pen. The combination of the background color and the inverse of the pen color using the Or operator.
vbCopyPen	13	Copy pen. Uses the pen color.
vbMergePenNot	14	Merge pen Not. The combination of the pen color and the inverse of the background color using the Or operator.
vbMergePen	15	Merge pen. The combination of the pen color and the background color using the Or operator.
vbWhiteness	16	Uses White, regardless of the pen color.

The following example creates polka dots in a PictureBox:

Example

```
Private Sub Picture1_MouseDown(Button As Integer, _
    Shift As Integer, X As Single, Y As Single)
If Button = 1 Then
    Picture1.FillColor = QBColor(Int(Rnd * 16))
    Picture1.DrawMode = ((Picture1.DrawMode + 1) Mod 16) + 1
    Picture1.Circle (X, Y), 120
End If
End Sub
```

DrawStyle Property

The DrawStyle property specifies the line style for the graphics methods of the Form, Printer, and PictureBox objects.

Usage

object.DrawStyle = *IntegerValue*
IntegerValue = *object*.DrawStyle

Applies To

Form Object
PictureBox Control
Printer Object

This property can take on the values given in the following table.

Constant	Value	Meaning
vbSolid	0	Solid line. The drawn line will be centered on the boundaries of the shapes drawn using the Circle and Line methods.
vbDash	1	Dashed line. Solid if DrawWidth is *not* 1!
vbDot	2	Dotted line. Solid if DrawWidth is *not* 1!
vbDashDot	3	Dash-dot line. Solid if DrawWidth is *not* 1!
vbDashDotDot	4	Dash-dot-dot line. Solid if DrawWidth is *not* 1!
vbInvisible	5	Invisible (transparent) line.
vbInsideSolid	6	Inside solid. In shapes drawn using the Circle and Line methods, the outer edges of the lines will match the boundaries of the shapes.

Here's an example of how you can let users draw lines in a PictureBox. The line is started on MouseDown, and a preview of the line is drawn to follow the mouse as it moves. The line is drawn finally on MouseUp. Note that we use the vbXorPen and vbDash to draw the preview lines.

Example

```
Private OrigX As Single, OrigY As Single
Private SaveX As Single, SaveY As Single

Private Sub Picture1_MouseDown(Button As Integer, _
    Shift As Integer, X As Single, Y As Single)
    If Button = 1 Then
        OrigX = X: SaveX = X
        OrigY = Y: SaveY = Y
        Picture1.DrawMode = vbXorPen
        Picture1.DrawStyle = vbDot
    End If
End Sub

Private Sub Picture1_MouseMove(Button As Integer, _
    Shift As Integer, X As Single, Y As Single)
    If Button = 1 Then
        Picture1.Line (OrigX, OrigY)-(SaveX, SaveY), vbRed
        Picture1.Line (OrigX, OrigY)-(X, Y), vbRed
        SaveX = X: SaveY = Y
    End If
End Sub

Private Sub Picture1_MouseUp(Button As Integer, _
    Shift As Integer, X As Single, Y As Single)
    If Button = 1 Then
        Picture1.Line (OrigX, OrigY)-(SaveX, SaveY), vbRed
        Picture1.DrawMode = vbCopyPen
        Picture1.DrawStyle = vbSolid
        Picture1.Line (OrigX, OrigY)-(X, Y), vbRed
    End If
End Sub
```

DrawWidth Property

The DrawWidth property specifies the line width—in pixels—drawn by the graphics methods.

Usage	*IntegerValue = object*.DrawWidth
	object.DrawWidth = *IntegerValue*

Applies To	Form Object
	PictureBox Control
	Printer Object

The value for the DrawWidth property can range from 1 to 32,767. Any other value results in an error.

 If the DrawWidth property is set larger than 1, then DrawStyle cannot be used to produce any of the dashed-line styles (vbDash (1), vbDot (2), vbDashDot (3), and vbDashDotDot (4)).

Drive Property

The Drive property specifies the current drive of a DriveListBox control at runtime. It is not available at design time.

Usage	*StringValue = object*.Drive
	object.Drive = *StringValue*

Applies To	DriveListBox Control

The values for the Drive property differ depending on if you're reading or setting the property. For reading, it will return one of the values given in the following table, depending on the drive type.

DRIVE TYPE	VALUE
Floppy disks	The drive letter plus a colon, such as "a:" and "b:".
Local fixed drives	The drive letter, colon, and volume label, as in "c: [USERS]."
Network connections	The drive letter, colon, and UNC name, as in "k: \\server\share."

Only the first character of the Drive property is used. It is case insensitive. If the drive letter is invalid, an error occurs. Setting the Drive property causes

- the Change event of the DriveListBox control to run and
- the list to refresh so that new network connections will be added.

DriverName Property

The DriverName property returns the name of the printer driver used by the Printer object. More than one printer—each with a different DeviceName—may share the same printer driver.

Usage   *StringValue = object*.DriverName

Applies To   Printer Object

The DriverName is typically the name of the printer-driver file without the extension.

Note: Whether or not the setting of a Printer-object property has any effect depends on the printer driver, as does whether or not errors are generated when settings are not acceptable.

DropHighlight Property

The DropHighlight property works with the HitTest method to correctly highlight items as you drag over them.

Usage   *object*.DropHighlight = *ObjectValue*
                 ObjectValue = object.DropHighlight

Applies To   ListView Control
                 TreeView Object

PARAMETER	VALUE	MEANING
ObjectValue	A Node or ListItem object	The object to be highlighted.

Example
```
Private Sub TreeView1_DragOver(Source As Control, X As Single,
Y As Single, State As Integer)
      Set TreeView1.DropHighlight = TreeView1.HitTest(X,Y)
      ...
      Set TreeView1.DropHighlight = Nothing
End Sub
```

To release the highlight, we had to set DropHighlight = Nothing.

Duplex Property

The Duplex property specifies the duplex printing mode for a printer that can print on both sides of a page. This property is available only at runtime.

Usage   *IntegerValue* = object.Duplex
               object.Duplex = *IntegerValue*

Applies To   Printer Object

The possible values of this property are given in the following table.

CONSTANT	VALUE	MEANING
vbPRDPSimplex	1	Single-sided printing.
vbPRDPHorizontal	2	Double-sided printing. Flips the paper horizontally such that the top of the page for both sides of a sheet of paper are on the same end of the paper.
vbPRDPVertical	3	Double-sided printing. Flips the paper vertically such that the top of the page on one side coincides with the bottom of the page of the other side.

Note: You can change the printer property only for the default printer. Set it by using the Set Printer = command.

Note: Not all printers support this property or all possible values of this property. You might get an error for your printer.

EditMode Property

The EditMode property returns the editing state for the current record.

Usage   *IntegerValue* = *object*.EditMode

Applies To   Data Control

The values of the EditMode property have the meanings given in the following table.

PARAMETER	VALUE	MEANING
IntegerValue	dbEditNone or 0	The current record is not being edited.
	dbEditInProgress or 1	The current record in the copy buffer is being modified.
	dbEditAdd or 2	The current record in the copy buffer is a new record that has not been saved to the database yet.

Check the EditMode property in the Validate event to determine if the Update method should be called.

Enabled Property

The Enabled property specifies whether the form or control can respond to the user. You can use this to enable or disable parts of the interface, depending on the current state of the application. For a Timer control, setting Enabled to False stops the countdown.

Usage	*BooleanValue = object*.Enabled
	object.Enabled = *BooleanValue*

Applies To	CheckBox Control
	ComboBox Control
	CommandButton Control
	Data Control
	DBCombo Control
	DBGrid Control
	DBList Control
	DirListBox Control
	DriveListBox Control
	FileListBox Control
	Form Object
	Frame Control
	Grid Control
	HScrollBar, VScrollBar Controls
	Image Control
	Label Control
	ListBox Control
	MDIForm Object
	Menu Control
	MenuLine Object
	OLE Container Control
	OptionButton Control
	PictureBox Control
	TextBox Control
	Timer Control

VALUE	MEANING
True	The default. Allows the object to respond to events.
False	Prevents the object from responding to events.

For menu items that are exposed or supplied by VB to Add-Ins, the Enabled property is read-only.

EndDoc Method

The EndDoc method ends the print operation for the current document being sent to the Printer object. It also releases the document to the print device or spooler.

Usage   *object*.EndDoc

Applies To   Printer Object

If EndDoc is called immediately after the NewPage method, no additional blank page is printed in order to conserve paper.

EnsureVisible Method

The EnsureVisible method ensures that a specified ListItem object is visible by scrolling or expanding a ListView (or TreeView) as needed.

Usage   *BooleanValue* = *object*.EnsureVisible

Applies To   ListItem Control
                    Node Object

PARAMETER	VALUE	MEANING
BooleanValue	True	The ListView or TreeView control must scroll or expand to expose the object.
	False	The object is already in plain view.

EOFAction Property

The EOFAction property specifies the action that the Data control takes when the user selects the MoveNext button of the Data control to move forward beyond the last record.

Usage   *object*.EOFAction = *IntegerValue*
                    IntegerValue = *object*.EOFAction

Applies To   Data Control

The EOFAction property can take on the values given in the following table.

CONSTANT	VALUE	MEANING
vbMoveLast	0	The default action. It keeps the last record as the current record.
vbEOF	1	Moving past the end of a recordset triggers the Data control's Validate event on the last record, followed by a Reposition event on the invalid (EOF) record. The MoveNext button on the Data control is disabled.
vbAddNew	2	Moving past the last record triggers the Data control's Validation event on the last record, followed by an automatic AddNew, and then by a Reposition event on the new record.

 The Help file lists the constant names incorrectly as vbEOFActionMoveLast, vbEOFActionEOF, and vbEOFActionAddNew.

The EOFAction Property has no effect when records are selected via code.

Exclusive Property

The Exclusive property determines whether the Data control's database is opened for single-use access.

Usage   *BooleanValue = object*.Exclusive
                 object.Exclusive = *BooleanValue*

Applies To   Data Control

The values of the Exclusive property have the meanings given in the following table.

PARAMETER	VALUE	MEANING
BooleanValue	True	Single-user access. No other applications can open the database until this instance is closed. This setting makes database operations run faster.
	False	The default. Other applications can open and access the database.

If you change the value of the Exclusive property at runtime, you must use the Refresh method to apply the changes. If you try to set Exclusive to True and other users or applications already have the database open, you will get an error.

When the ODBC is used, the Exclusive property is ignored.

EXEName Property

The EXEName property is read-only and returns the name of the executable file for running an application without the path names or file extension. If the application is run from the VB development environment, it returns the name of the VB project.

Usage	*StringValue = object*.EXEName
Applies To	App Object

Expanded Property

Use the Expanded property to expand and collapse a Node object in a TreeView (and to check to see if a Node is expanded).

Usage	*object*.Expanded = *BooleanValue* *BooleanValue = object*.Expanded
Applies To	Node Object

PARAMETER	VALUE	MEANING
BooleanValue	True	It's expanded.
	False	It's not expanded.

ExpandedImage Property

The ExpandedImage property controls the image that will appear by a Node when it's expanded.

Usage	*object*.ExpandedImage = *VariantValue* *VariantValue = object*.ExpandedImage
Applies To	Node Object

PARAMETER	VALUE	MEANING
VariantValue	Numeric or string expression	The index or key of the ListImage object in an ImageList control to display.

ExtractIcon Method

The ExractIcon method turns a bitmap stored in a ListImage object into an icon and returns the reference to the newly created icon.

Usage   *object*.ExtractIcon

Applies To   ListImage Object

FetchVerbs Method

The FetchVerbs method updates the ObjectVerbs property with the most current list of verbs supported by the object in an OLE Container control. Because the supported verbs can change depending on the object's state, it is important to call FetchVerbs before trying to access the ObjectVerbs list.

Usage   *object*.FetchVerbs

Applies To   OLE Container Control

FileDescription Property

At runtime, the FileDescription property is read-only. It returns a string that contains the description of the running application. To set the description, select the File/Make EXE File... menu and then click the Options... button. In the "Version Information" section, select "File Description" from the list and enter the value in the text box.

Usage   *StringValue = object*.FileDescription

Applies To   App Object

FileName Property

The FileName property specifies the filename—possibly including the full path—of a file selected from the control. It is unavailable at design time for the FileListBox control and ProjectTemplate object.

Usage   *StringValue = object*.FileName
                    object.FileName = *StringValue*

Applies To   CommonDialog Control
                      FileListBox Control

When a control is first created or when no file has been selected, its FileName property returns an empty string (" ").

CommonDialog

The CommonDialog control returns the full path name of the currently selected file. You can set the FileName property only before displaying the dialog box. If the string used to set the FileName property includes full path information, then the CommonDialog control will change to the specified directory first and display just the filename in the File name: text box. If the filename part of the string is really a pattern, then that pattern will be applied before the list of choices is displayed.

FileListBox

The FileListBox control returns only the filename part of the selected file; it is the same as using List(File1.ListIndex). You must use the Path property to get the directory name. If the MultiSelect property is True, the FileName property returns the file that has the focus rectangle, which may *not* be selected.

When you set the FileName property and the string contains full path information, it will change the Path property of the FileListBox and invoke the PathChange event. If in addition, the filename part of the string is really a pattern, it will change the Pattern property and trigger the PatternChange event. If the string is an exact match for the name of an existing file, it will select the file and trigger the DblClick event.

The FileName property setting can be in the form of a network path and filename:

```
\\server\share\pathname
```

FileName Property (RichTextBox Control)

The FileName property, available at design-time, controls the filename of the .RTF file loaded into the RichTextBox control.

Usage   *object*.FileName

Applies To   RichTextBox Control

FileNumber Property

The FileNumber property specifies the file number last used or to be used when saving or loading an OLE object contained in an OLE Container control. This property is not available at design time. It is provided *only* for backwards compatibility to use with the Action property. You should use the SaveToFile and ReadFromFile methods instead.

Usage   *IntegerValue* = *object*.FileNumber
           object.FileNumber = *IntegerValue*

Applies To   OLE Container Control

The file number must reference an open, binary file.

FileTitle Property

The FileTitle property returns the name (without the path) of the file to open or save. Use the FileName property to get the full path name.

Usage   *object*.FileTitle

Applies To   CommonDialog Control

You use this property to find out which file a user selected in the File dialog box so that you can save or open a specific file.

FillColor Property

The FillColor property specifies the color used to fill in Shape controls and the circles and boxes drawn by the Circle and Line graphics methods. This property is ignored if the FillStyle property is set to vbFSTransparent (1).

Usage   *LongValue* = *object*.FillColor
           object.FillColor = *LongValue*

Applies To   Form Object
               PictureBox Control
               Printer Object
               Shape Control

By default, FillColor is set to vbBlack (0).

Example
```
Picture1.FillStyle = vbFSSolid
    Picture1.FillColor = vbRed
    Picture1.Circle (100, 100), 100
```

FillStyle Property

The FillStyle property determines the pattern used to fill the Shape control or drawings created by the Circle and Line methods.

Usage   *object*.FillStyle = *IntegerValue*
                     IntegerValue = *object*.FillStyle

Applies To   Form Object
                     PictureBox Control
                     Printer Object
                     Shape Control

The possible values of the FillStyle property are given in the following table.

CONSTANT	VALUE	MEANING
vbFSSolid	0	Solid color.
vbFSTransparent	1	Transparent.
vbHorizontalLine	2	Horizontal lines.
vbVerticalLine	3	Vertical lines.
vbUpwardDiagonal	4	Upward diagonal lines: upper left to lower right.
vbDownwardDiagonal	5	Downward diagonal lines: lower left to upper right.
vbCross	6	Cross. Both horizontal and vertical lines.
vbDiagonalCross	7	Diagonal cross. Both upward and downward diagonal lines.

The color of the lines of the fill pattern are determined by the FillColor property.

Filter Property

The Filter property controls the filters that the Type list box displays.

Usage   *object*.Filter = "*description1\filter1\description2\filter2...*"

Applies To   CommonDialog Control

PARAMETER	VALUE	MEANING
Description	A string	A description of the type of file.
Filter	A string	The file extension.

Use this property to control the types of files a dialog box displays. But beware: The Help page is wrong on a few counts. First, its Syntax line has spaces around the vertical bar. You don't want 'em—they'll appear in the dialog box and confuse matters. Second, it neglects to mention that you tend to need quotes around the description and filter. Otherwise, you get a syntax error:

```
Private Sub Open_Click(Index As Integer)
    CommonDialog1.Filter = "Text|*.txt|Bitmap|*.bmp"
    CommonDialog1.ShowOpen
End Sub
```

Also, note that stringing together a bunch of filters creates a drop-down list in the Files of Type textbox on the dialog. By default, the default extension is the first filter in the list. To change that, use the FilterIndex property. There doesn't seem to be a way to show simultaneously files with different extensions.

FilterIndex Property

The FilterIndex property controls which filter (set by the Filter property) will be the default for an Open or Save As dialog box.

Usage	*object*.FilterIndex = *IntegerValue*
	IntegerValue = *object*.FilterIndex

Applies To   CommonDialog Control

PARAMETER	VALUE	MEANING
IntegerValue	An integer	The index of the filter to use. The default = 1, the first filter.

Find Method

The Find method searches the text in a RichTextBox control for a given string.

Usage   *object*.Find(*String*[, *Start*][, *End*][, *Options*])

Applies To   RichTextBox Control

This method doesn't support named arguments.

PARAMETER	VALUE	MEANING
String	A string	This required parameter is the string you want to find.
Start	An integer	This optional parameter determines where to start, measured by the character index of the character. Every character has a unique integer index; the first character has an index of 0.
End	An integer	This optional parameter determines where to end the search.
Options	rtfWholeWord or 2	This optional parameter determines whether a match will be based on a whole word or a partial word.
	rtfMatchCase or 4	This optional parameter determines whether to match case in the search.
	rtfNoHighlight or 8	This optional parameter determines whether a match should be highlighted.

Note: You can combine multiple options by either adding their values or constants together or by combining the values by using the Or operator.

If Find finds something, it highlights it (by default) and returns the index of the first character. If it doesn't find anything, it returns –1. Also note that if you don't specify a start parameter, but do specify an end parameter, the Find method searches from the current insertion point to the end. If, however, you omit both start and end parameters, Find searches the whole document from the beginning (not from wherever the insertion point is).

Also, there is some odd behavior regarding highlighting in special circumstances. In particular, if you use Find without the rtfNoHighlight option, but HideSelection is True for the Rich-TextBox, but the RichTextBox doesn't have the focus, the control highlights whatever it finds anyway. (Yikes!)

FindItem Method

The FindItem method finds a ListItem object in a ListView control.

Usage   *object*.FindItem (*String*[, *IntegerValue*][, *Index*][, *Match*])

Applies To   ListView Control

PARAMETER	VALUE	MEANING
String	A string	Asks what value you are trying to find.
IntegerValue	lvwText or 0	Matches with a ListItem's Text property.
	lvwSubitem or 1	Matches with a ListItem's SubItems property.

PARAMETER	VALUE	MEANING
IntegerValue	lvwTag or 2	Matches with the object's Tag property.
Index	An integer or key	Indicates from where to start the search. This value must be either a unique integer or key (e.g., "First") value. The index value can range from 1 to the number of ListItems in the ListView control.
	Omitted	Use 1.
Match	lvwWholeWord or 0 or omitted	The search string must be the whole first word in the Text property (no partial matches).
	lvwPartial or 1	Match partial words.

Note: Don't even think of using named arguments. They won't work.

FirstRow Property

The FirstRow property determines the bookmark for the first visible row in a DBGrid control.

Usage   object.FirstRow = *StringValue*
                   StringValue = object.FirstRow

Applies To   DBGrid Control

PARAMETER	VALUE	MEANING
StringValue	A string	Contains a bookmark that corresponds to the first visible row in a DBGrid control.

If you set this property, the DBGrid will scroll to make the bookmarked row the top visible row in the control.

Example

Create a form. Add a DBCombo box (DBCombo1), a DBGrid (DBGrid1), and a Data control (Data1). Set Data1's DatabaseName property to BIBLIO.MDB and RecordSource to Authors. Point DBCombo1's RowSource and DataSource properties at Data1. Then set ListField to Author and set BoundColumn and DataField to Au_ID. Next, set DBGrid1's DataSource to Data1. Add the following code to DBCombo1's Click event:

```
Private Sub DBCombo1_Click(Area As Integer)
    Dim BM As String
```

```
    BM = DBCombo1.SelectedItem
    Data1.Recordset.Bookmark = BM
    DBGrid1.FirstRow = BM
End Sub
```

This code will select in DBGrid1 the row you select in DBCombo1 *and* scroll so that the row is at the top of DBGrid1.

Notice that we Dim BM As String. If we tried something like

```
DBGrid1.FirstRow = DBCombo1.SelectedItem
```

we'd get an invalid bookmark error because FirstRow expects a String.

FirstSibling Property

The FirstSibling property is kind of like the Child property, only it works on the first sibling—the Node that appears first in the same hierarchy level—of a Node object in a TreeView control.

Usage   Set *NodeObject* = *object*.FirstSibling

Applies To   Node Object

Exactly *which* Node you get back depends on how the objects are sorted. The Help page points out that because the Child, FirstSibling, LastSibling, Previous, Parent, Next, and Root properties all reference Node objects other than the currently selected one, you can do stuff to them behind the scenes, like this:

Example
```
With TreeView1.Nodes(x).FirstSibling
      .Text = "New text"
      .Key = "New key"
      .SelectedImage = 3
End With
```

Flags Property (Color Dialog)

This Flags property controls the options for a Color dialog box.

Usage   *object*.Flags = *IntegerValue*
                       IntegerValue = *object*.Flags

Applies To   CommonDialog Control

You can set more than one flag with the Or operator (e.g., CommonDialog1.Flags = cdC-ClFullOpen Or cdlCCRGBInit), or you can add together the constant values (yuck).

PARAMETER	VALUE	MEANING
IntegerValue	cdCClFullOpen or &H2&	Shows the entire dialog box, including the part for creating custom colors.
	cdlCCPreventFullOpen or &H4&	Disables the part of the Colors dialog box that enables you to create custom colors.
	cdlCCRGBInit or &H1&	Sets the initial color value for the dialog box.
	cdlCCShowHelp or &H8&	Puts a Help button onto the Colors dialog box.

Flags Property (File Dialog)

This Flags property controls the options for the Open and Save As dialog boxes.

Usage   *object*.Flags = *IntegerValue*
               IntegerValue = *object*.Flags

Applies To   CommonDialog Control

PARAMETER	VALUE	MEANING
IntegerValue	cdlOFNAllowMultiselect or &H200&	Makes the dialog box allow multiple selections via the Shift and Ctrl keys. FileName returns the filenames delimited by spaces.
	cdlOFNCreatePrompt or &H2000&	If the file the user specifies doesn't exist, he or she will be prompted to create it. This value automatically sets cdlOFNPathMustExist and cdlOFNFileMustExist.
	cdlOFNExtensionDifferent or &H400&	Gets set automatically if the filename extension the user typed in differs from DefaultExt.
	cdlOFNFileMustExist or &H1000&	The user may enter only names of existing files.
	cdlOFNHideReadOnly or &H4&	Hides the read-only check box.
	cdlOFNNoChangeDir or &H8&	Forces the dialog box to set the current directory to what it was when the user opened the dialog box.
	cdlOFNNoReadOnlyReturn or &H8000&	The returned file won't be read only, nor will it be in a write-protected directory.
	cdlOFNNoValidate or &H100&	The dialog allows invalid characters.
	cdlOFNOverwritePrompt or &H2&	Generates a confirmation dialog if the file in a Save dialog box already exists.
	cdlOFNPathMustExist or &H800&	The user may use only existing paths.

PARAMETER	VALUE	MEANING
IntegerValue	cdlOFNReadOnly or &H1&	The read-only check box will be checked by default.
	cdlOFNShareAware or &H4000&	Ignores sharing violations.
	cdlOFNHelpButton or &H10&	Shows the Help button.
	cdlOFNExplorer or &H8000&	Uses the Windows 95 Explorer-like Open dialog box (Windows 95 only).
	cdlOFNNoDereferenceLinks or &H100000&	Does not de-reference shortcuts (Windows 95 only).
	cdOFNLongNames or &H200000&	Allows long filenames (Windows 95 only).

You can set more than one flag with the Or operator (e.g., CommonDialog1.Flags = cdlOFN-HideReadOnly Or cdlOFNPathMustExist), or you can add together the constant values (yuck).

Flags Property (Font Dialog)

This Flags property controls the options for the Font dialog box.

Usage   object.Flags = *IntegerValue*
                   IntegerValue = object.Flags

Applies To   CommonDialog Control

PARAMETER	VALUE	MEANING
IntegerValue	cdlCFANSIOnly or &H400&	The dialog box allows only the fonts that use the Windows character set (i.e., roman characters).
	cdlCFBoth or &H3&	The dialog box lists printer and screen fonts.
	cdlCFEffects or &H100&	The dialog box enables strikethrough, underline, and color effects.
	cdlCFFixedPitchOnly or &H4000&	The dialog box selects only fixed-pitch fonts.
	cdlCFForceFontExist or &H10000&	An error message box is displayed if the user selects a font or style that doesn't exist.
	cdlCFLimitSize or &H2000&	The dialog box selects font sizes within the range specified by the Min and Max properties.
	cdlCFNoSimulations or &H1000&	The dialog box doesn't allow graphics device interface (GDI) font simulations.

PARAMETER	VALUE	MEANING
IntegerValue	cdlCFNoVectorFonts or &H800&	The dialog box doesn't allow vector-font selections.
	cdlCFPrinterFonts or &H2&	The dialog box lists only the fonts supported by the printer, as specified by the hDC property.
	cdlCFScalableOnly or &H20000&	The dialog box allows only fonts that can be scaled.
	cdlCFScreenFonts or &H1&	The dialog box lists only the screen fonts supported by the system.
	cdlCFHelpButton or &H4&	The dialog box displays a Help button.
	cdlCFTTOnly or &H40000&	The dialog box allows only the selection of TrueType fonts.
	cdlCFWYSIWYG or &H8000&	The dialog box allows only the selection of fonts that are available on both the printer and on-screen. If this flag is set, the cdlCFBoth and cdlCFScalableOnly flags should also be set.

For some reason, you must set the Flags property to cdlCFScreenFonts, cdlCFPrinterFonts, or cdlCFBoth before displaying the Fonts dialog box. Otherwise, you get the error "No Fonts Exist."

You can set more than one flag with the Or operator (e.g., CommonDialog1.Flags = cdlCFANSIOnly Or cdlCFFixedPitchOnly), or you can add together the constant values (yuck).

Flags Property (Print Dialog)

This Flags property controls the options for the Print dialog box.

Usage   object.Flags = IntegerValue
               IntegerValue = object.Flags

Applies To   CommonDialog Control

PARAMETER	VALUE	MEANING
IntegerValue	cdlPDAllPages or &H0&	Controls the All Pages option button.
	cdlPDCollate or &H10&	Returns or sets the Collate check box.
	cdlPDDisablePrintToFile or &H80000&	Disables the Print To File check box.
	cdlPDHidePrintToFile or &H100000&	Hides the Print To File check box.
	cdlPDNoPageNums or &H8&	Disables the Pages option button and the associated edit control.

PARAMETER	VALUE	MEANING
IntegerValue	cdlPDNoSelection or &H4&	Disables the Selection option button.
	cdlPDNoWarning or &H80&	Suppresses a warning message when there is no default printer.
	cdlPDPageNums or &H2&	Controls the Pages option button.
	cdlPDPrintSetup or &H40&	Displays the Print Setup dialog box rather than the Print dialog box.
	cdlPDPrintToFile or &H20&	Controls the Print To File check box.
	cdlPDReturnDC or &H100&	Returns a device context for the printer selection.
	cdlPDReturnIC or &H200&	Returns an information context for the printer selection made in the dialog box. An information context provides a fast way to get information about the device without creating a device context. The information context is returned in the dialog box's hDC property.
	cdlPDReturnDefault or &H400&	Returns the default printer name.
	cdlPDSelection or &H1&	Controls the Selection option button.
	cdlPDHelpButton or &H800&	Displays the Help button.
	cdlPDUseDevModeCopies or &H40000&	If a printer driver doesn't support multiple copies, setting this flag disables the Copies Edit control. If a driver does support multiple copies, setting this flag indicates that the dialog box stores the requested number of copies in the Copies property.

You can set more than one flag with the Or operator (e.g., CommonDialog1.Flags = cdlPDDisablePrintToFile Or cdlPDNoPageNums), or you can add together the constant values (yuck).

Font Property

The Font property specifies the Font object used by the control to display text.

Usage   *FontObject* = *object*.Font
                object.Font = *FontObject*

Applies To   CheckBox Control
                ComboBox Control
                CommandButton Control
                Data Control
                DBCombo Control

        DBGrid Control
        DBList Control
        DirListBox Control
        DriveListBox Control
        FileListBox Control
        Form Object
        Frame Control
        Grid Control
        Label Control
        ListBox Control
        OptionButton Control
        PictureBox Control
        Printer Object
        TextBox Control

To set the font, you can use a string that is the name of the font:

Example
```
Text1.Font = "Times New Roman"
Text1.Font.Bold = 1
Text1.Font.Italic = 1
```

If the requested font does not exist, a font that is similar will be used.

For PictureBox controls and Form and Printer objects, changing this property does not change the appearance of text already drawn. For other controls, the change is reflected immediately.

FontBold, FontItalic, FontStrikethru, FontUnderline Properties

These properties turn on or off font attributes for the selected font of the control. The attributes are **Bold**, *Italic*, ~~Strikethru~~, and <u>Underline</u>. These properties are included for backwards compatibility and for the CommonDialog control. New code should change the font properties of a Font object, rather than using these control properties.

Usage
        BooleanValue = object.FontBold
        object.FontBold = *BooleanValue*

        BooleanValue = object.FontItalic
        object.FontItalic = *BooleanValue*

        BooleanValue = object.FontStrikethru
        object.FontStrikethru = *BooleanValue*

        BooleanValue = object.FontUnderline
        object.FontUnderline = *BooleanValue*

Applies To   CheckBox Control
                    ComboBox Control
                    CommandButton Control
                    CommonDialog Control
                    Data Control
                    DirListBox Control
                    DriveListBox Control
                    FileListBox Control
                    Form Object
                    Frame Control
                    Grid Control
                    Label Control
                    ListBox Control
                    OptionButton Control
                    PictureBox Control
                    Printer Object
                    TextBox Control

Value	Meaning
True	The font attribute specified by the property is turned on. The FontBold property may be True by default on Windows 3.1 systems.
False	The font attribute specified by the property is turned off. This is the default for Windows 95.

To use these properties with the CommonDialog control, you must set its cdlCFEffects flag (&H100&).

You should change the FontName property of a control before you change the font size and attributes. For TrueType fonts smaller than 8 points, set the FontSize first, then the FontName, and then the FontSize again. As we said, it might be easier to use the Font object and its properties instead.

FontCount Property

The FontCount property returns the number of fonts available for a display device or the active printer. The actual font names may be retrieved using the Fonts property that returns an array of font names. The list of fonts may change depending on the display, printer driver, or system configuration, so you should retrieve values of the Fonts and FontCount properties right before you need them.

Usage   *IntegerValue* = *object*.FontCount

Applies To   Printer Object
                    Screen Object

The Fonts array is a zero-based array, so the maximum index of the array is FontCount −1.

Example
```
For i = 0 To Printer.FontCount - 1
    List1.AddItem Printer.Fonts(i)
Next i
```

FontItalic Property

See the FontBold property.

FontName Property

The FontName property specifies the name of the font used to display text in a control or object. This property is included for backwards compatibility and for the CommonDialog control. New code should change the font properties of a Font object, rather than using this control property.

Usage   *StringValue* = *object*.FontName
                   object.FontName = *StringValue*

Applies To   CheckBox Control
                   ComboBox Control
                   CommandButton Control
                   CommonDialog Control
                   Data Control
                   DirListBox Control
                   DriveListBox Control
                   FileListBox Control
                   Form Object
                   Frame Control
                   Grid Control
                   Label Control
                   ListBox Control
                   OptionButton Control
                   PictureBox Control
                   Printer Object
                   TextBox Control

The default font for a control is determined by the operating system. It is typically "MS Sans Serif" at 8 points. You should change the FontName property of a control before you change the font size and attributes. For TrueType fonts smaller than 8 points, set the FontSize first, then the FontName, and then the FontSize again. As we said, it might be easier to use the Font object and its properties instead. At runtime, you can obtain a list of available fonts from the FontCount and Fonts properties of the Screen and Printer objects.

Fonts Property

The Fonts property returns all the font names available for the specified display (Screen object) or printer (Printer object) as a string array. Use the FontCount property to determine the size of the Fonts array.

Usage   *StringValue = object*.Fonts(*Index*)

Applies To   Printer Object
                 Screen Object

The parameters of the Fonts property have the meanings given in the following table.

PARAMETER	VALUE	MEANING
Index	0 through (FontCount − 1)	Index into the Fonts array. Specifies the element of the array to retrieve.
	Other values	Error

The list of fonts may change depending on the display, printer driver, or the system configuration, so you should retrieve values of the Fonts and FontCount properties right before you need them.

FontSize Property

The FontSize property specifies the size of the font used to display text in a control or object. This property is included for backwards compatibility and for the CommonDialog control. New code should change the font properties of a Font object, rather than using this control property.

Usage   *SingleValue = object*.FontSize
                 object.FontSize = *SingleValue*

Applies To   CheckBox Control
                 ComboBox Control
                 CommandButton Control
                 CommonDialog Control
                 Data Control
                 DirListBox Control
                 DriveListBox Control
                 FileListBox Control
                 Form Object
                 Frame Control
                 Grid Control

> Label Control
> ListBox Control
> OptionButton Control
> PictureBox Control
> Printer Object
> TextBox Control

The FontSize value is expressed in points. The maximum allowed value is 2,160. The default font and font size for a control is determined by the operating system. It is typically "MS Sans Serif" at 8 points. You should change the FontName property of a control before you change the font size and attributes. For TrueType fonts smaller than 8 points, set the FontSize first, then the FontName, and then the FontSize again. It might be easier to use the Font object and its properties instead.

FontStrikethru Property

See the FontBold property.

FontTransparent Property

The FontTransparent property specifies whether the background graphics and text are displayed around the lines that make up the characters.

Usage	*BooleanValue* = *object*.FontTransparent
	object.FontTransparent = *BooleanValue*

Applies To	Form Object
	PictureBox Control
	Printer Object

The values for the FontTransparent property have the meanings given in the following table.

VALUE	MEANING
True	The default. Only the lines that make up the characters are drawn, thereby allowing the background graphics and text to show through.
False	The interior of the bounding box for each character is filled with a solid gray color, overwriting any background graphics or text.

Changing the FontTransparent property at runtime does not change the appearance of text already drawn.

Example

```
Private Sub Form_Click()
    Form1.BackColor = vbRed
    Form1.FontTransparent = True
    Form1.Print "ABCD"
    Form1.FontTransparent = False
    Form1.Print "ABCD"
End Sub
```

Run this example to see the effects of the FontTransparent property.

FontUnderline Property

See the FontBold property.

ForeColor Property

The ForeColor property specifies the foreground color used to display text and graphics in a control or object.

Usage

LongValue = *object*.ForeColor
object.ForeColor = *LongValue*

Applies To

CheckBox Control
Column Object
ComboBox Control
Data Control
DBCombo Control
DBGrid Control
DBList Control
DirListBox Control
DriveListBox Control
FileListBox Control
Form Object
Frame Control
Grid Control
Label Control
ListBox Control
OptionButton Control
PictureBox Control
Printer Object
TextBox Control

VB constants that may be used for the ForeColor property are listed in the Color Constants section. Additionally, you can use the RGB or QBColor functions to generate RGB colors for this property. Even though you may set ForeColor to any color, it will display only in the nearest solid, not dithered, color.

For a Form or Printer object or PictureBox control, setting the ForeColor property doesn't affect graphics output already drawn. On all other controls, the screen color changes immediately. The default ForeColor for all except the Printer object is vbWindowText (&H80000008&).

VALUE	MEANING
0 to &H00FFFFFF&	Specifies the color in RGB. The lower three bytes, from least significant to most, specifies color intensity of red, green, and blue. Each color component can range from 0 to 255.
&H80000000& to &H80000018&	Specifies a system color. See the table in the Color Constants section or use the VB Object Browser.
&H01000000& to &H02FFFFFF&	Does not generate an error, but the effect of the high byte is not documented. It seems that if the high byte is 1, then the color always results in black. If the high byte is 2, then it has the effect of possibly lightening the RGB color indicated by the lower 3 bytes. The result is always a solid (not dithered) color.
Other	Error

Format Property

The Format property specifies the name of a data format for sending or retrieving data from a server application that supplied the object for an OLE Container control. This property is used in conjunction with the Data and DataText properties. It is not available at design time.

Usage   *StringValue = object*.Format
          object.Format = *StringValue*

Applies To   OLE Container Control

To find valid data formats for a class of object, use the ObjectAcceptFormats, ObjectAcceptFormatsCount, ObjectGetFormats, and ObjectGetFormatsCount properties. Most applications support only one or two formats.

FromPage Property

The FromPage property controls the From box on the Printer dialog box.

Usage   *object*.FromPage = *IntegerValue*
          IntegerValue = object.FromPage

Applies To   CommonDialog Control

PARAMETER	VALUE	MEANING
IntegerValue	An integer	The page to start printing on.

Note: This property is valid only when cdlPDPageNums is set.

FullPath Property

The FullPath property is kind of a cool property. It returns the "fully qualified" path to the Node you've selected in a TreeView. In other words, it'll look kind of like "Root.Child1.Child2. Child3."

Usage   *StringValue = object*.FullPath

Applies To   Node Object

PARAMETER	VALUE	MEANING
StringValue	A string	The path.

The value of the PathSeparator property determines the delimiter.

GetBookmark Method

The GetBookmark method retrieves the bookmark value of a row relative to the current DBGrid row.

Usage   *VariantValue = object*.GetBookmark(*IntegerValue*)

Applies To   DBGrid Control

PARAMETER	VALUE	MEANING
IntegerValue	0	The bookmark of the current row (same as DBGrid1.Bookmark).
	1	The bookmark of the row after the current row.
	−1	The bookmark of the row before the current row.
	N	The bookmark of row N rows away from the current row (positive or negative allowed). N should be an integer.

GetData Method

The GetData method retrieves graphics data from the Clipboard object. To retrieve text, use GetText.

Usage   *PictureValue* = *object*.GetData([*Format*])

Applies To   Clipboard Object

The Format argument can take on the values given in the following table.

PARAMETER	VALUE	MEANING
Format	0 or omitted	Automatically uses data of the correct format, depending on the destination for the result.
	vbCFBitmap or 2	Windows bitmap files (.BMP).
	vbCFMetafile or 3	Windows metafiles (.WMF).
	vbCFDIB or 8	Device-independent bitmap (.DIB).
	vbCFPalette or 9	Color palette.
	Otherwise	Returns nothing, but no errors.

Example   `Picture1 = Clipboard.GetData(vbCFDIB)`

This example displays the DIB contents of the Clipboard object in the Picture1 PictureBox control. If no data of the requested format is on the Clipboard, then nothing is returned.

GetFirstVisible Method

The GetFirstVisible method tells you the first ListItem object at the top of the ListView control.

Usage   Set *ListItemObject* = *object*.GetFirstVisible()

Applies To   ListView Control

'Nuff said.

GetFormat Method

The GetFormat method determines whether data of the specified format is stored in the Clipboard object. If there is, GetFormat() returns True. Otherwise, it returns False.

Usage   *BooleanValue = object*.GetFormat(*Format*)

Applies To   Clipboard Object

PARAMETER	VALUE	MEANING
Format	vbCFLink or &HBF00	DDE conversation information.
	vbCFRTF or &HBF01	Rich Text Format (.RTF file).
	vbCFText or 1	Text (.TXT file).
	vbCFBitmap or 2	Bitmap (.BMP file).
	vbCFMetafile or 3	Metafile (.WMF file).
	vbCFDIB or 8	Device-independent bitmap.
	vbCFPalette or 9	Color palette.
	Any other value from 0 to &HFFFF	Reserved for future use. Will return False.
	Other value	Error

After determining the type of data, you can use the GetData() or GetText() methods to retrieve the Clipboard data.

GetLineFromChar Method

The GetLineFromChar method returns the number of the line that contains a specified character position in a RichTextBox control.

Usage   *LineNumber = object*.GetLineFromChar(*LongValue*)

Applies To   RichTextBox Control

This method doesn't support named arguments. The return value is also a Long integer.

PARAMETER	VALUE	MEANING
LongValue	Long integer	The index of the character whose line you want. See the note on the RichTextBox's Find method for more information on character indexes.

Get this. The first character has index of 1, but the first line number is 0!

GetNumTicks Method

The GetNumTicks method returns the number of ticks between the Min and Max properties of the Slider control.

Usage   *LongValue* = *object*.GetNumTicks

Applies To   Slider Control

GetText Method

The GetText method retrieves a text string from the Clipboard object. To retrieve graphics data, use the GetData method.

Usage   *TextValue* = *object*.GetText([*Format*])

Applies To   Clipboard Object

The Format argument can take on the values given in the following table.

PARAMETER	VALUE	MEANING
Format	vbCFText or 1 or omitted	The default. Gets text from the Clipboard.
	vbCFLink or &HBF00	Gets DDE conversation information.

GetText returns an empty string (" ") if there are no text strings on the Clipboard object that match the requested format.

DDE server (source) applications supposedly should place vbCFLink information on the Clipboard of the form:

```
application|topic!item
```

but in practice, we haven't found that to be so. After copying WinWord or Excel data to the Clipboard, both applications recognize that there is data on the Clipboard that can be pasted as a link. Using the GetText method with vbCFLink format, however, *always* returns an empty string. A bug in VB? maybe.

Anyway, you should be able to implement a PasteLink command in your VB application using something like the following example:

Example
```
Private Sub EditPasteLink_Click()
    Dim linkItem$, idxExcl As Integer, idxPipe As Integer
    'Active control must be PictureBox or TextBox
    If Not (TypeOf Screen.ActiveControl is PictureBox _
        Or TypeOf Screen.ActiveControl is TextBox) Then
```

```
                     Exit Sub
               End If

      'If linkItem$ is empty, then no link info on Clipboard
          linkItem$ = Clipboard.GetText(vbCFLink)
          If linkItem$ = "" Then Exit Sub

      'Parse link string
          idxExcl = InStr(linkItem$, "!")
          idxPipe = InStr(linkItem$, "|")
          If idxExcl <> 0 Then
          With Screen.ActiveControl
             .LinkMode = vbLinkNone
             .LinkTopic = Left(linkItem$, idxExcl - 1)
             .LinkItem = Mid(linkItem$, idxExcl + 1)
             .LinkMode = vbLinkAutomatic
          End With
          ElseIf idxPipe <> 0 Then
          With Screen.ActiveControl
             .LinkMode = vbLinkNone
             .LinkTopic = linkItem$
             .LinkItem = ""
          .LinkMode = vbLinkAutomatic
          End With
          End If
      End Sub
```

Ghosted Property

Is a ListItem object dimmed? Do you want it to be? Then use the Ghosted property.

Usage   *object*.Ghosted = *BooleanValue*
                BooleanValue = *object*.Ghosted

Applies To   ListItem Object

PARAMETER	VALUE	MEANING
BooleanValue	True	The item is dimmed (ghosted).
	False	The item isn't ghosted.

Handle Property

The Handle property returns the handle value of a Picture or StdPicture object based on the Type property. The return value is either an Integer or a Long integer depending on whether you're running on a 16-bit or 32-bit system.

Usage   *LongValue = object*.Handle

Applies To   Picture Object

The value returned depends on the setting of the Picture's Type property as given in the following table.

PROPERTY	VALUE	MEANING
Type	HBITMAP or 1	The image is a bitmap.
	HMETAFILE or 2	The image is a Windows metafile.
	HICON or HCURSOR or 3	The image is an icon.

Use the Handle property when you need to pass a graphic's handle to a DLL or the Windows API.

hDC Property

A *device context* contains the attributes of graphics and text that are to be drawn in a client area. All drawing operations in Microsoft Windows require the handle to a device context. The hDC property returns the handle of the device context for the object. You can pass this handle to any Windows API functions that require an hDC argument.

Usage   *LongValue = object*.hDC

Applies To   CommonDialog Control
Form Object
PictureBox Control
Printer Object

Because the hDC property can change while your program is running, never save the value of the hDC property in another variable. Directly call the hDC property every time you need to use it.

If the AutoRedraw property of the object is True, hDC refers to the device context of the persistent (background) graphics—returned by the Image property—of the object. If AutoRedraw is False, then hDC refers to the actual device context of the object.

For a CommonDialog control, the hDC property makes sense only when using the Print dialog box. If its Flag property includes cdlPDReturnDC (&H100), hDC returns the device context of the selected printer. If Flag includes cdlPDReturnIC, hDC returns the information context of the selected printer.

The following example directly uses the GetDeviceCaps API to ask for the size of the display. The ratios between

- HORZSIZE and VERTSIZE,

- HORZRES and VERTRES, and

- Screen.Width and Screen.Height

should all be the same.

Example

```
Private Declare Function GetDeviceCaps Lib "Gdi32" ( _
    ByVal hDC As Long, ByVal index As Long) As Long
Private Const HORZSIZE = 4
Private Const VERTSIZE = 6
Private Const HORZRES = 8
Private Const VERTRES = 10
Private Const LOGPIXELSX = 88
Private Const LOGPIXELSY = 90

Private Sub Form_DblClick()
    Debug.Print "HORZSIZE = " & GetDeviceCaps(hDC, HORZSIZE) _
        / 25.4 & " inches"
    Debug.Print "VERTSIZE = " & GetDeviceCaps(hDC, VERTSIZE) _
        / 25.4 & " inches"
    Debug.Print "HORZRES = " & GetDeviceCaps(hDC, HORZRES) _
        & " dots"
    Debug.Print "VERTRES = " & GetDeviceCaps(hDC, VERTRES) _
        & " dots"
    Debug.Print "LOGPIXELSX = " & GetDeviceCaps(hDC, LOGPIXELSX) _
        & " dpi"
    Debug.Print "LOGPIXELSY = " & GetDeviceCaps(hDC, LOGPIXELSY) _
        & " dpi"
    Debug.Print "Screen.Width = " & Screen.Width & " twips"
    Debug.Print "Screen.Height = " & Screen.Height & " twips"
End Sub
```

HeadFont Property

The HeadFont property determines the font that a DBGrid will use in its headers.

Usage   *object*.HeadFont = *ObjectValue*
                 ObjectValue = *object*.HeadFont

Applies To   DBGrid Control

PARAMETER	VALUE	MEANING
ObjectValue	Object expression	This expression evaluates to a Font object.

Changing HeadFont may resize the headers.

Example
```
Private Sub Command1_Click()
     Dim X As New StdFont
     X.Bold = True
     X.Name = "Arial"
     Set DBGrid1.HeadFont = X
End Sub
```

Note that you can't just Set DBGrid1.HeadFont = "Arial". You have to Dim a new StdFont. This is how Font objects work.

 The Help file has an incorrect syntax. It substitutes Type for HeadFont on two occasions.

HeadLines Property

The HeadLines property controls the number of lines a DBGrid will show in its header.

Usage   *object*.HeadLines = *SingleValue*
                 SingleValue = *object*.HeadLines

Applies To   DBGrid Control

PARAMETER	VALUE	MEANING
SingleValue	A single-precision value 1–10	The number of lines in a header. The default is 1 and the range is 0–10; 0 shows no headings.

Height, Width Properties

The Height and Width properties specify the dimensions of the control. For a Columns object or DBGrid control, only the Width property applies. For the Printer and Screen objects, these properties are available only at runtime.

Usage   *SingleValue* = *object*.Height
                  object.Height = *SingleValue*

                  SingleValue = *object*.Height
                  object.Height = *SingleValue*

Applies To   CheckBox Control
                  Columns Object
                  ComboBox Control
                  CommandButton Control
                  Data Control
                  DBCombo Control
                  DBGrid Control
                  DBList Control
                  DirListBox Control
                  DriveListBox Control
                  FileListBox Control
                  Form Object
                  Frame Control
                  Grid Control
                  HScrollBar, VScrollBar Controls
                  Image Control
                  Label Control
                  ListBox Control
                  MDIForm Object
                  OLE Container Control
                  OptionButton Control
                  Picture Object
                  PictureBox Control
                  Printer Object
                  Screen Object
                  Shape Control
                  TextBox Control

These properties are measured according to the following rules:

- Form and MDIForm objects: measured from the outside edge of the window, including the borders and title bar. The unit of measure is always the twip (1,440 twips = 1 inch).

- Control: measured from the center of the control's border, thereby allowing controls to align correctly regardless of their border widths. The units are expressed in the scale unit of its container (Form, Frame, MDIForm, PictureBox, or Printer). The unit of measure for the inside of a Frame control is the twip.

- Printer object: measures the physical dimensions of the paper size set for the printer. These properties override the PaperSize property. The unit of measure is always the twip. If the printer driver allows only a fixed number of sizes, the Width and Height properties will be adjusted to match the nearest supported size.

- Screen object: measures the screen size and are read-only at runtime. The unit of measure is always the twip.

- Picture object: measures the dimensions of the object in HiMetric units. Use its ScaleX and ScaleY methods to convert the HiMetric units into an appropriate scale.

The maximum limits of the Width and Height properties are system-dependent. Use the ScaleLeft, ScaleTop, ScaleHeight, and ScaleWidth properties of a Form, MDIForm, PictureBox, or Printer to set its internal coordinates for placing controls or drawing objects.

If a DriveListBox or ComboBox control has its Style property set for a drop-down box (vb-ComboDropdown or vbComboDropdownList), the Height property cannot be changed.The height of the drop-down list will be adjusted automatically to fit the number of lines up to a maximum of eight lines. For more than eight items in the list, a vertical scroll bar will be displayed to allow the user to scroll for additional choices.

For the Columns object of the DBGrid control, the default value for Width is the value of the DefColWidth property of DBGrid.

HelpCommand Property

The HelpCommand property controls the type of online help requested.

Usage   *object*.HelpCommand = *IntegerValue*
                IntegerValue = *object*.HelpCommand

Applies To   CommonDialog Control

PARAMETER	VALUE	MEANING
IntegerValue	cdlHelpCommand or &H102	Executes a Help macro.
	cdlHelpContents or &H3	Displays the Help contents topic, set by the Contents option in the [OPTION] section of the .HPJ file.
	cdlHelpContext or &H1	Displays Help for a context (works with HelpContext property).
	cdlHelpContextPopup or &H8	Displays popup Help.
	cdlHelpForceFile or &H9	Ensures that WinHelp displays the correct Help file.
	cdlHelpHelpOnHelp or &H4	Displays Help for Help.
	cdlHelpIndex or &H3	Displays the index of the specified Help file.
	cdlHelpKey or &H101	Help for a particular keyword (works with the HelpKey property).
	cdlHelpPartialKey or &H105	Displays the topic found in the keyword list that matches the keyword passed in the dwData parameter if there is one exact match.

PARAMETER	VALUE	MEANING
IntegerValue	cdlHelpQuit or &H2	Quits WinHelp.
	cdlHelpSetContents or &H5	Determines which contents topic to show when a user presses the F1 key.
	cdlHelpSetIndex or &H5	Sets the context specified by the HelpContext property as the current index for the Help file specified by the HelpFile property.

HelpContext Property

The HelpContext property controls the context ID of the requested Help topic.

Usage   *object*.HelpContext = *StringValue*
             StringValue = *object*.HelpContext

Applies To   CommonDialog Control

PARAMETER	VALUE	MEANING
StringValue	A string	The context ID of the requested Help topic.

HelpContextID Property

The HelpContextID property specifies a context number of a topic in a Help file, thereby allowing you to provide context-sensitive help for your application. When the user hits the F1 key and the HelpContextID of the control with focus is nonzero, then Help will be started and jump to the specified topic. If the HelpContextID is zero, then the HelpContextID of the container object or control is checked until a nonzero one is found. If no nonzero HelpContextID properties are found, Help is not started. If the context number does not exist, you will get an error. Use the HelpFile property of the parent form to specify the full path name of the Help file.

Usage   *LongValue* = *object*.HelpContextID
             object.HelpContextID = *LongValue*

Applies To   CheckBox Control
             ComboBox Control
             CommandButton Control
             DBCombo Control
             DBGrid Control
             DBList Control
             DirListBox Control

DriveListBox Control
FileListBox Control
Form Object
Frame Control
Grid Control
HScrollBar, VScrollBar Controls
ListBox Control
MDIForm Object
Menu Control
MenuLine Object
OLE Container Control
OptionButton Control
PictureBox Control
TextBox Control

The possible values of this property are given in the following table.

VALUE	MEANING
0	The default. No context number is used.
Positive Long integer	A valid context number for a topic in a Help file. The context number must be specified when the Help file is compiled.

For a Menu control that is exposed to Add-Ins, the HelpContextID property is read-only at runtime. Otherwise, the property can be read and written.

To build a Help file, use the Microsoft Windows Help Compiler that is included with the VB Professional Edition. You'll also need a word processor, such as Microsoft Word, that can generate RTF (Rich-Text Format) files to feed the Help Compiler.

HelpFile Property

The HelpFile property specifies the name of a Microsoft Windows Help file that the object uses to display help and online documentation. To set this property for the application at design time, use the Tools/Options... menu and then select the Project tab.

Usage   *StringValue = object*.HelpFile
object.HelpFile = *StringValue*

Applies To   App Object
CommonDialog Control
Err Object
Error Object
MenuLine Object (Add-In)

The value of the property is a string expression specifying the full path name of the Windows Help file.

To hook up a Help file to your application, set the HelpFile property for your App object and then specify HelpContextID for all applicable forms and controls that match topics in the Help file. When the user runs your application, he can hit the F1 key to obtain help from the specified Help file on the active control or form. If no HelpContextID applies, then the main contents screen is shown.

This property has no effect for the CommonDialog Control running under Windows 95. By default, the Err object's HelpFile property is set to the main VB Help file, and the Error object's HelpFile property is set to the Microsoft Jet database-engine error-message Help file. Although you can set this property for the Err and Error objects, your settings will be overwritten every time VB encounters an error.

Example

```
Sub TestHelp
    On Error Goto ErrHandler
    a% = 65536
    Exit Sub
ErrHandler:
    msg$ = "Press F1 to see the Help file " & _
        "topic for this error"
    msgTitle$ = "Error: " & Err.Description
    MsgBox msg$, vbOKOnly, msgTitle$, Err.HelpFile, _
        Err.HelpContext
End Sub
```

HelpFile Property (CommonDialog Control)

The HelpFile property controls the path and filename of a Microsoft Windows Help file.

Usage

object.HelpFile = *StringValue*
StringValue = object.HelpFile

Applies To   CommonDialog Control

PARAMETER	VALUE	MEANING
StringValue	A String	The filename and path of a valid Windows Help file.

HelpKey Property

The HelpKey property controls the keyword that identifies the requested Help topic.

Usage   *object*.HelpKey = *StringValue*
                   StringValue = *object*.HelpKey

Applies To   CommonDialog Control

PARAMETER	VALUE	MEANING
StringValue	A string	The keyword that identifies the Help topic.

Hidden Property

The Hidden property specifies whether a file with its Hidden attribute set is displayed in a FileListBox control. This property overrides the settings for Archive, Normal, ReadOnly, and System properties for any file with its Hidden attribute set.

Usage   *BooleanValue* = *object*.Hidden
                   object.Hidden = *BooleanValue*

Applies To   FileListBox Control

The values for the Hidden property have the meanings given in the following table.

VALUE	MEANING
True	Displays files that have their Hidden attribute set, but their System attribute is *not* set, regardless of the settings for the Archive, Normal, and ReadOnly properties. If a file has *both* its Hidden and System attributes set, then *both* the Hidden and System properties must be set to True—regardless of the settings for the Archive, Normal, and ReadOnly properties—before the filename is displayed in the FileListBox.
False	The default. Does not display files that have their Hidden attribute set.

Setting the Hidden property at runtime will refresh the list of files.
To display all files, set the Normal, Hidden, and System properties to True.

Hide Method

The Hide method hides an MDIForm or Form object but doesn't unload it from memory. Using Hide can use more memory, but your forms may redisplay much quicker when the Show method is called.

Usage   *object*.Hide

Applies To   Form Object
              MDIForm Object

If the Form object is not loaded when its Hide method is invoked, the Form will be loaded but won't be displayed.

Hiding a form sets its Visible property to False, but its controls are still available to the running application via code, to other processes communicating with the form via DDE, and to Timer events.

The following example implements a CommandButton that closes its Form window:

Example
```
Private Sub cmdClose_Click()
        Hide
End Sub
```

HideColumnHeaders Property

The HideColumnHeaders property controls whether you can see column headers in List view.

Usage   *object*.HideColumnHeaders = *BooleanValue*
              BooleanValue = *object*.HideColumnHeaders

Applies To   ListView Control

PARAMETER	VALUE	MEANING
BooleanValue	True	The column headers are invisible.
	False	The column headers are visible.

Note that you can see the subitems even if you can't see the column headers. Don't ask why. Just because.

HideSelection Property

The HideSelection property specifies whether selected text in a control remains highlighted when the control loses focus. Set this property to False if another active form must display the selected text in this control for the user. Examples include a spell-checking form. This property is read-only at runtime.

Usage   *BooleanValue = object*.HideSelection

Applies To   TextBox Control

The values for the HideSelection property have the meanings given in the following table.

VALUE	MEANING
True	The default. The selected text is not highlighted if the control does not have focus.
False	The selected text remains highlighted when the control loses focus.

hInstance Property

The hInstance property is supposed to return the handle to the instance of the running application. If run from the VB development environment, it returns VB's instance handle.

Usage   *IntOrLongValue = object*.hInstance

Applies To   App Object

The return-value type is Integer for applications created by 16-bit VB and Long for those created by 32-bit VB.

 In practice, this property always returns the *same* value on our system (32-bit VB running under Windows 95): &H400000&. If we create an .EXE standalone application and run multiple copies of it, each returns the same &H400000&.

HitTest Method

The HitTest method identifies the ListItem object or Node under the mouse (you use it with drag-and-drop ops).

Usage   Set *obj* = *object*.HitTest (*XValue As Single, YValue As Single*)

Applies To   ListView Control
                   TreeView Control

PARAMETER	VALUE	MEANING
XValue	Single-precision value	The X value under the mouse.
YValue	Single-precision value	The Y value under the mouse.

If there's no valid object under the mouse, HitTest returns Nothing.

HostName Property

The HostName property specifies the name of your VB application. During editing of an OLE object in a separate window (not in-place editing), this name is displayed in the object's window title.

Usage   *StringValue* = *object*.HostName
                   object.HostName = *StringValue*

Applies To   OLE Container Control

Setting the HostName property makes editing objects more friendly for the user, since the user can tell which application initiated the editing and which application to return to when editing is done.

hPal Property

The hPal property returns or sets a handle to the palette of a picture in a Picture or StdPicture object.

Usage   *object*.hPal = *HandleValue*
                   HandleValue = *object*.hPal

Applies To   Picture Object

PARAMETER	VALUE	MEANING
HandleValue	A handle	A handle to the palette of a picture.

---

hWnd Property

The hWnd property returns the Window handle to the form or control. It may be used in calls to the Windows API functions that require a Window handle.

Usage   *LongValue* = *object*.hWnd

Applies To   CheckBox Control
                 ComboBox Control
                 CommandButton Control
                 DirListBox Control
                 DriveListBox Control
                 FileListBox Control
                 Form Object
                 Frame Control
                 Grid Control
                 HScrollBar, VScrollBar Controls
                 ListBox Control
                 MDIForm Object
                 OptionButton Control
                 OLE Container Control
                 PictureBox Control
                 TextBox Control

The Windows operating environment identifies each form and control in an application by assigning it a handle, or hWnd. The hWnd property is used with Windows API calls. Many Windows operating environment functions require the hWnd of the active window as an argument.

Note: Because the value of this property can change while a program is running, never store the hWnd value in a variable.

The following example creates a form that "floats" on top of all other windows. The Declare statement and the Public constants may be placed in a global code Module.

Example
```
Declare Function SetWindowPos Lib "User32" (ByVal hwnd&, _
    ByVal hb&, ByVal x&, ByVal y&, ByVal cx&, ByVal cy&, _
    ByVal f&) As Long

'Values from the Windows header files or WINAPI.TXT
Public Const SWP_NOMOVE& = 2
Public Const SWP_NOSIZE& = 1
```

```
    Public Const FLAGS& = SWP_NOMOVE Or SWP_NOSIZE
    Public Const HWND_TOPMOST& = -1
    Public Const HWND_NOTOPMOST& = -2

    Private Sub Form_Load()
        Dim success&
        'Make it the top-most window
        success& = SetWindowPos(Me.hwnd, HWND_TOPMOST, 0, _
            0, 0, 0, FLAGS)
    End Sub
```

Icon, SmallIcon Properties (ListItem object)

This Icon property is a little different from the others. It controls the index (or key) value of an icon (or small icon) attached to a ListItem object. The icon is selected from an ImageList control associated with the ListView control containing the ListItem object.

Usage   *object*.Icon = *VariantValue*
                  object.SmallIcon = *VariantValue*
                  VariantValue = *object*.Icon
                  VariantValue = *object*.SmallIcon

Applies To   ListItem Object

PARAMETER	VALUE	MEANING
VariantValue	An integer (or key)	The index (or key, e.g., "First") for the icon.

    The syntax for this particular property isn't exactly straightforward. It will probably look like this:

```
ListView1.ListItems(1).Icons = 1
```

or like this:

```
ListView1.ListItems(1).SmallIcon = "First"
```

Icon Property

This Icon property specifies the icon displayed in the Title Bar of the Form object (Windows 95) and when the Form is minimized at runtime. If the Form's ControlBox property is False, no icons will be displayed.

Usage	*IconValue = object*.Icon
	object.Icon = *IconValue*

Applies To	Form Object
	MDIForm Object

Using an icon that communicates the functionality of a form is very useful for a user when minimizing the form. The file loaded for the Icon property must have the .ICO filename extension and be in the icon format. The default icon for Form objects is the VB icon for forms.

 VB ships with a library of icons, located in the ICONS subdirectory. If you are not on a Windows 95 system, then you must minimize the Form before you can see the icon. And the Form cannot be minimized unless its BorderStyle property is vbFixedSingle (1) or vbSizable (2) and its MinButton property is True.

If you are on Windows 95, then the icon is also displayed at the left of the Form's Title Bar. Clicking the icon brings up the ControlBox menu. So the ControlBox property must be set to True for the icon to be displayed.

At runtime, you can assign the Icon property to other object's Icon or DragIcon properties or use the LoadPicture and LoadResPicture functions. You can use LoadPicture without any arguments to clear the icon altogether.

In the following example, a timer is used to cycle through 10 icons stored in a resource file attached to the project:

Example	```Private Sub Timer1_Timer()```

```
Private Sub Timer1_Timer()
    Static index
    index = (index Mod 10) + 1
    Form1.Icon = LoadResPicture(index, vbResIcon)
End Sub
```

Icons, SmallIcons Properties

The Icons and SmallIcons properties specify the ImageList controls to associate with the Icon and SmallIcon views for a ListView control.

Usage	*ImageListObject = object*.Icons
	object.Icons = *ImageListObject*
	ImageListObject = object.SmallIcons
	object.SmallIcons = *ImageListObject*

Use the Icon and SmallIcon properties of the ListView's ListItem objects to set the individual icons by indexing the corresponding ImageList controls.

Image Property

The Image property returns a handle to a persistent graphic that, when exposed, will be redrawn automatically by the Windows operating system—*not* by the object's Paint events. It is read-only at runtime.

Usage   *PictureValue = object*.Image

Applies To   Form Object
                     PictureBox Control

   The Image property may be assigned to the Picture property of other controls or passed to Windows API calls, but you cannot assign it to a temporary variable to be used later. The persistent graphic of an object is created by setting the object's AutoRedraw property to True before drawing with the graphics methods. By default, the persistent graphic is simply a rectangle the size of the object filled with the color specified by its BackColor property. Note that changing the AutoRedraw property to change the persistent graphic can also cause the value of the Image property to change. Use the hDC property to retrieve the handle of the device context for the Image.

Example
```
Picture2.Picture = Picture1.Image'Copy image
```

Image Property (Custom Controls)

This Image property is an index number or key that specifies a ListImage object in an ImageList control associated with the custom control. Since this property is associated with the ImageList control, it is available only for Windows 95 and NT 3.51 or newer systems.

Usage   *VariantValue = object*.Image
                     object.Image = *VariantValue*

Applies To   Button Object
                     Node Object
                     Tab Object

   A Toolbar control holds Button objects; a TreeView control holds Node objects; a Tab-Strip control holds Tab objects. The ImageList property of these container controls must be assigned to an ImageList control before the Image property of a Button, Node, or Tab object can be set.

   Use the key of an Image whenever possible to make the code more self-documenting and to make it immune to changes in the order of ListImage objects in the ImageList control.

ImageHeight Property

Use the ImageHeight property to set (or return) the height of the objects in an ImageList control.

Usage   *object*.ImageHeight = *IntegerValue*
                  IntegerValue = *object*.ImageHeight

Applies To   ImageListControl

PARAMETER	VALUE	MEANING
IntegerValue	Integer	The height of the image in pixels.

Note that all images in the ImageList control must be the same height, which is determined by the height of the first object you put into it. If you then try to put in an object of a different height, you get an error.

ImageList Property

The ImageList property specifies the ImageList control to associate with the custom control.

Usage   *ImageListObject* = *object*.ImageList
                  object.ImageList = *ImageListObject*

Applies To   TabStrip Control
                  Toolbar Control
                  TreeView Control

ImageWidth Property

Use the ImageWidth property to set (or return) the Width of the objects in an ImageList control.

Usage   *object*.ImageWidth = *IntegerValue*
                  IntegerValue = *object*.ImageWidth

Applies To   ImageListControl

PARAMETER	VALUE	MEANING
IntegerValue	Integer	The width of the image in pixels.

Note that all images in the ImageList control must be the same width, which is determined by the width of the first object you put into it. If you then try to put in an object of a different width, you get an error.

Indentation Property

The Indentation property controls how much indentation each new child Node object gets in a TreeView control.

Usage   *object*.Indentation = *SingleValue*
                 SingleValue = *object*.Indentation

Applies To   TreeView Control

PARAMETER	VALUE	MEANING
SingleValue	Single-precision value	The width (in whatever scale the container is using) by which each Node is indented.

Index Property

The Index property is available *only* if the control is part of a control array. It returns the number that uniquely identifies the control within the control array. This property is read-only at runtime.

Usage   *IntegerValue* = *object*[(*number*)].Index

Of course, if you already know *number* then you should know the Index. They are the same number.

Applies To   CheckBox Control
                 ComboBox Control
                 CommandButton Control
                 CommonDialog Control
                 Data Control
                 DBCombo Control
                 DBGrid Control
                 DBList Control
                 DirListBox Control
                 DriveListBox Control
                 FileListBox Control
                 Frame Control
                 Grid Control

> HScrollBar, VScrollBar Controls
> Image Control
> Label Control
> Line Control
> ListBox Control
> Menu Control
> OLE Container Control
> OptionButton Control
> PictureBox Control
> Shape Control
> TextBox Control
> Timer Control

The Index property returns the values given in the following table.

VALUE	MEANING
0	The default. The control is not part of a control array.
0 to 32,767	The control is part of a control array, and the number uniquely identifies the control within the control array. VB automatically assigns an integer when you create a control within a control array. You can manually set it to any positive value less than 32,768 at design time. You can also use the Load statement at runtime to create a new control in a control array with any Index number that does not already exist.

InitDir Property

The InitDir property controls the initial directory in which a CommonDialog will look.

Usage   *object*.InitDir = *StringValue*
                     StringValue = *object*.InitDir

Applies To   CommonDialog Control

PARAMETER	VALUE	MEANING
StringValue	A string	The path to the initial directory. (The default is the current directory.)

InsertObjDlg Method

The InsertObjDlg method displays the Insert Object dialog box so that the user can select an object to insert into the OLE Container control. Using this dialog box, the user can choose to insert the object as an embedded or linked object.

Usage   *object*.InsertObjDlg

Applies To   OLE Container Control

You can set the OLETypeAllowed property before invoking the InsertObjDlg method to limit the type of objects the user can select.

Example
```
Private Sub mnuInsert_Click()
        OLE1.OLETypeAllowed = vbOLEEither
        OLE1.InsertObjDlg
End Sub
```

Instancing Property

The Instancing property specifies whether an instance of the class may be created outside the project. It can be set at design time only and is not available at runtime. An instance of a class may be created outside the project when the project implements an OLE server.

Applies To   ClassModule Object

The possible values for the Instancing property are described in the following table.

VALUE	MEANING
0	The default. Private. An instance of the class may be created only within the project.
1	Public Single Use. An instance of the class may be created both inside and outside the project. When created outside the project by OLE clients, each instance causes a separate copy of the OLE server to be started. The Public property must be set to True, or this setting is ignored.
2	Public Multiple Use. An instance of the class may be created both inside and outside the project. When created outside the project by OLE clients, each instance will be created by an already running instance of the OLE server. If an OLE server is not running, one will be started to provide an instance of the class. The Public property must be set to True, or this setting is ignored.

When the Public property of the class is True, this class module is visible to other applications. They can then create instances of this class in order to access its methods and properties. The instances may be created using the CreateObject function or the New keyword:

Example
```
Set newInstance = CreateObject("MyApp.MyClass")
```
or
```
Dim newInstance As New MyClass
```

IntegralHeight Property

The IntegralHeight property specifies whether the vertical height of the list-box part of the control is adjusted to display only complete lines. This property is read-only at runtime and is ignored if the list box is a drop-down style box.

Usage   *BooleanValue* = *object*.IntegralHeight

Applies To   ComboBox Control
                 DBCombo Control
                 DBList Control
                 ListBox Control

The possible values of IntegralHeight are given in the following table.

VALUE	MEANING
True	The default. The list-box part of the control automatically resizes so that only complete lines are displayed. The resulting size is never greater than the requested height and is almost always adjusted downward to prevent partial lines.
False	The height of the control will be the requested height. Only part of the last line may be displayed if the list box is not tall enough.

When you adjust the height of the control at design time, the Properties box will enforce the IntegralHeight property by adjusting the height.

The following example works only for ComboBox controls using the vbComboSimple (1) style and the default "MS Sans Serif" 8-point font.

Example   ```
                 'Combo1's IntegralHeight is True
                 Combo1.Height = 1380
                 Debug.Print Combo1.Height

                 'Combo2's IntegralHeight is False
                 Combo2.Height = 1380
                 Debug.Print Combo2.Height
                 ```

*Result*         ```
                 1296
                 1380
                 ```

Interval Property

The Interval property specifies the elapsed time between repeated triggers of a Timer control's Timer event. The unit of measure is the millisecond.

Usage   *LongValue* = *object*.Interval
                   object.Interval = *LongValue*

Applies To   Timer Control

The values for the Interval Property have the meanings given in the following table.

VALUE	MEANING
0	The default. The Timer control is disabled. You can also use the Enabled property to disable the control.
1 through 65,535	If the Enabled property is True, the value specifies in milliseconds the elapsed time between Timer events. Setting the Enabled property to True resets the countdown to this value. The maximum value of 65,535 sets the timer to just over 1 minute.
Other values	Error

You cannot determine the current value of the countdown.

To use the Timer control as an alarm, set the Enabled property to False in the Timer event to disable the control.

The following example uses an HScrollBar to set the Interval property of a Timer control:

Example

```
Private Sub Form_Load()
     HScroll1.Min = 0
     HScroll1.Max = 32767
End Sub

Private Sub HScroll1_Change ()
    ' Interval will range from 0 to 65534
    Timer1.Interval = HScroll1.Value * 2
End Sub
```

Italic Property

The Italic property works with the Font and StdFont objects to make a font italic or not italic.

Usage   *Font*.Italic = *BooleanValue*
                   BooleanValue = *Font*.Italic

Applies To   Font Object
                   StdFont Object

PARAMETER	VALUE	MEANING
BooleanValue	True	The font is italic.
	False	The font is not italic.

Item Method (Custom Controls)

The Item method retrieves an object from a collection. The Item keyword is optional.

Usage   *object*.Item(*Index*)
             object(*Index*)

Applies To   Buttons Collection
             ColumnHeaders Collection
             ListImages Collection
             ListItems Collection
             Nodes Collection
             Panels Collection
             Tabs Collection

ItemData Property

The ItemData property refers to an array of Long integers in a ComboBox or ListBox control that parallels the array referenced by the List property. Each item in the List array may be assigned a value in a ItemData array, thereby allowing you to store some private data or identification number with each list element. At design time, you can set values for the array by using the ItemData drop-down list box in the Properties window.

Usage   *LongValue* = *object*.ItemData(*Index*)
             object.ItemData(*Index*) = *LongValue*

Applies To   ComboBox Control
             ListBox Control

Use the Index argument to specify the element in the ItemData array.

When you add an item to the List array of the ComboBox or ListBox control, its associated ItemData value is set to 0. You need to change the ItemData explicitly.

The ItemData property may be useful if you are using a sorted list to present an array of data structures that may *not* be sorted. You can use ItemData to keep track of the index into the unsorted array. In the following example, assume that GetBookList grabs a list of books (unsorted) and places them in the MyBooks array. Then List1 is used to display all the Titles, sorted alphabetically.

Example

```
Public Type BookType
    Title As String
    Year As Integer
    ISBN As String
    Publisher As String
    Subject As String
End Type

Private MyBooks(100) As BookType

Private Sub FillBookList()
    GetBookList(MyBooks)
    For i = LBound(MyArray) To UBound(MyArray)
        List1.AddItem MyArray(i).Title
        List1.ItemData(List1.NewIndex) = i
    Next i
End Sub
```

 The VB Help file indicates *incorrectly* that when you insert items into the middle of a ComboBox or ListBox using the AddItem method, the ItemData array will not be adjusted to keep the proper association. In our test, the array adjusted just fine. You do not have to manually adjust ItemData when you insert items into the controls, and the ItemData associated with the new item is zero.

Key Property

The Key property returns or sets a string that uniquely identifies a member in a collection.

Usage   *object*.Key = *StringValue*
                 StringValue = *object*.Key

Applies To   Button Object
                 ColumnHeader Object
                 ListImage Object
                 ListItem Object
                 Node Object
                 Panel Object
                 Tab Object

PARAMETER	VALUE	MEANING
StringValue	Any string	The string that will identify the member.

Note: If the string is not unique within a collection, you'll get an error.

KeyPreview Property

The KeyPreview property specifies whether keyboard events (KeyDown, KeyUp, and KeyPress) for Form objects are invoked before keyboard events for controls on the Form.

Set the KeyPreview property of the Form object to True to create keyboard-handling routines that apply to all controls on the form.

Usage	*BooleanValue* = *object*.KeyPreview
	object.KeyPreview = *BooleanValue*

Applies To   Form Object

The settings for the KeyPreview property are given in the following table.

VALUE	MEANING
True	The Form object receives keyboard events first, before the control with focus does.
False	The default. The control with focus receives keyboard events; the Form object does not.

With this property set to True, pressing and releasing a key when a control has focus generates the following sequence of events:

- Form_KeyDown

- control_KeyDown

- Form_KeyPress

- control_KeyPress

- Form_KeyUp

- control_KeyUp

If you don't want the keyboard events at the Form level to pass the keystroke to the control that has focus, then the Form's KeyPress event must set its KeyAscii argument to 0 and the Form's KeyDown event must set its KeyCode argument to 0.

Some controls can intercept keyboard events even if the Form's KeyPreview property is True. These include the following:

- A CommandButton with focus intercepts the Enter key.

- A CommandButton with the Default property set to True intercepts the Enter key regardless of the current focus.

- A CommandButton with the Cancel property set to True intercepts the Esc key regardless of the current focus.

- The Tab key cannot be detected by the Form object. The Tab key always changes the focus according to the tab order set with the TabIndex properties of the controls on the Form.

- A ComboBox, ListBox, DBCombo, or DBList intercepts the navigation keys.

If a Form object does not contain a control that can receive focus, the keyboard events of the Form will be triggered regardless of the setting of the KeyPreview property.

KillDoc Method

The KillDoc method requests that the current print job for the Printer object be terminated.

Usage   *object*.KillDoc

Applies To   Printer Object

If background printing is being provided by the Print Manager, KillDoc deletes the print job from the queue. If the job is deleted before the Print Manager has a chance to process it, then the printer will receive nothing of the cancelled job.

If background printing is not enabled, then the KillDoc method directly requests the printer to abort the print job. Some data may have printed already, and the printer may not get a chance to abort before the entire document is printed. The KillDoc method causes the printer to reset after the print job terminates.

LabelEdit Property

The LabelEdit property controls whether users may edit labels of ListItem or Node objects.

Usage   *object*.LabelEdit = *IntegerValue*
                     IntegerValue = *object*.LabelEdit

Applies To   TreeView Control
                     ListView Control

PARAMETER	VALUE	MEANING
IntegerValue	lvwAutomatic for ListView (tvwAutomatic for TreeView) or 0	The label may be edited (the BeforeLabelEdit event gets generated when you click a label).
	lvwManual for ListView (tvwManual for TreeView) or 1	You can edit labels only by using the StartLabelEdit method.

LabelWrap Property

The LabelWrap property tells you if labels are wrapped when a ListView is in icon view.

Usage   *object*.LabelWrap = *BooleanValue*
                 BooleanValue = *object*.LabelWrap

Applies To   TreeView Control
                 ListView Control

PARAMETER	VALUE	MEANING
BooleanValue	True	Yes
	False	No

LargeChange Property

This LargeChange property specifies the amount by which to change the Value of an HScrollBar or VScrollBar control when the user clicks the mouse in the area between the scroll box and the scroll arrows. Depending on which side of the scroll box is clicked, the value of the LargeChange property will be added or subtracted from the Value property.

Usage   *IntegerValue* = *object*.LargeChange
                 object.LargeChange = *IntegerValue*

Applies To   HScrollBar Control
                 VScrollBar Control

The values for the LargeChange property have the meanings given in the following table.

VALUE	MEANING
1 to 32,767	The value that will be added or subtracted from the Value property. By default, LargeChange is set to 1.
Other values	Error

Note that the increments for scroll bars on a ComboBox or ListBox control are set automatically.

Set LargeChange to be larger than SmallChange to make your scroll bars easier to use.

LargeChange Property (Slider Control)

This LargeChange property controls how many ticks a Slider control will move when you press PageUp or PageDown or click the mouse to one side of a slider.

Usage   *object*.LargeChange = *LongValue*
                 LongValue = *object*.LargeChange

Applies To   Slider Control

PARAMETER	VALUE	MEANING
LongValue	A long integer	How many ticks the slider moves (default is 5).

LastSibling Property

The LastSibling property is kind of like the Child property, only it works on the last sibling—the Node that appears last in whatever hierarchy you have selected—of a Node in a TreeView.

Usage   *object*.LastSibling

Applies To   Node Object

Exactly which Node you get back depends on how the objects are sorted. The Help page points out that because the Child, FirstSibling, LastSibling, Previous, Parent, Next, and Root properties all reference Node objects other than the currently selected one, you can do stuff to them behind the scenes, like this:

Example
```
With TreeView1.Nodes(x).LastSibling
     .Text = "New text"
     .Key = "New key"
     .SelectedImage = 3
End With
```

Left, Top Properties

The Left and Top properties specify the coordinates of the top, left corner of a control or object, with respect to the top, left corner its Container control or object. The unit of measure depends on the scale unit of the Container control or object. For a Timer control, these properties are read-only at runtime.

Usage   *SingleValue* = *object*.Left
                       object.Left = *SingleValue*

                       SingleValue = *object*.Top
                       object.Top = *SingleValue*

Applies To   CheckBox Control
                       Column Object
                       ComboBox Control
                       CommandButton Control
                       CommonDialog Control
                       Data Control
                       DBCombo Control
                       DBGrid Control
                       DBList Control
                       DirListBox Control
                       DriveListBox Control
                       FileListBox Control
                       Form Object
                       Frame Control
                       Grid Control
                       HScrollBar, VScrollBar Controls
                       Image Control
                       Label Control
                       ListBox Control
                       MDIForm Object
                       OLE Container Control
                       OptionButton Control
                       PictureBox Control
                       Shape Control
                       TextBox Control
                       Timer Control

The coordinates specified by these properties are measured according to the following rules:

- Form and MDIForm objects: measured from the outside edge of the window, including the borders and title bar. The unit of measure is always the twip.

- Controls: The Left property specifies the location of the *center* of the left border of the control, and the Top property specifies the location of the *center* of the top border of the control. This arrangement allows controls using the same coordinates to line up correctly regardless of their border widths. The units are expressed in the scale unit of their container (Form, Frame, MDIForm, PictureBox, or Printer). The unit of measure inside a Frame control is the twip.

The limits of the Left and Top properties are system-dependent. Use the ScaleLeft, ScaleTop, ScaleHeight, and ScaleWidth properties of a Form, MDIForm, PictureBox, or Printer to set its internal coordinates for placing controls or drawing objects.

LeftCol Property

The LeftCol property specifies the leftmost, non-fixed column that is visible in a grid. This property is available only at runtime.

Usage	*IntegerValue* = *object*.LeftCol *object*.LeftCol = *IntegerValue*
Applies To	DBGrid Control Grid Control

The values of the LeftCol property have the meanings given in the following table.

PARAMETER	VALUE	MEANING
IntegerValue	0 to Columns.Count − 1	The column index of the column in a DBGrid control to place at the leftmost position. The default is 0.
	0 to Cols − 1	The column index of the column in a Grid control to place at the leftmost position. The default is 0.

Use the LeftCol and TopRow properties to scroll a Grid or DBGrid control via code.

LegalCopyright Property

At runtime, the LegalCopyright property is read-only. It returns a string that contains the legal copyright notice for the running application. To set this notice, select the File/Make EXE File... menu and then click the Options... button. In the "Version Information" section, select "Legal Copyright" from the list. Enter the value in the text box.

Usage	*StringValue* = *object*.LegalCopyright
Applies To	App Object

LegalTrademarks Property

At runtime, the LegalTrademarks property is read-only. It returns a string that contains legal trademark information for the running application. To enter this information, select the File/Make EXE File... menu and then click the Options... button. In the "Version Information" section, select "Legal Trademarks" from the list. Enter the value in the text box.

Usage   *StringValue = object*.LegalTrademarks

Applies To   App Object

Line Method

The Line method draws lines and rectangles on an object.

Usage   *object*.Line [Step] [(*X1, Y1*)] - [Step] (*X2, Y2*)[, *Color*][, B[F]]

Applies To   Form Object
PictureBox Control
Printer Object

The parameters for the Line method have the meanings given in the following table.

PARAMETER	VALUE	MEANING
Step	Omitted	The coordinates (X1, Y1) are specified in terms of the coordinate system of the object.
	Step	The coordinates (X1, Y1) are specified as an offset relative to the current location (CurrentX, CurrentY).
(X1, Y1)	Omitted	The start of the line or rectangle will be (CurrentX, CurrentY).
	Single-precision values	The coordinates of the start of the line or the first corner of the rectangle. The Scale properties of the object determine the unit of measure.
Step	Omitted	The coordinates (X2, Y2) are specified in terms of the coordinate system of the object.
	Step	The coordinates (X2, Y2) are specified as an offset relative to (X1, Y1).
(X2, Y2)	Single-precision values	The coordinates of the end of the line or the second corner of the rectangle. The Scale properties of the object determine the unit of measure.
Color	Omitted	Uses the ForeColor property.
	Long value	Uses one of the Color Constants or the return values of the RGB or QBColor functions to specify a color.
B	Omitted	A line is drawn.
	B	A rectangle is drawn using the provided coordinates as opposite corners of the rectangle.
F	Omitted	The rectangle fill is determined by the FillColor and FillStyle properties.
	F	The rectangle is filled with the same color as the outline of the rectangle.

After the call to Line, the CurrentX and CurrentY properties are set to X2 and Y2. Use the DrawWidth, DrawMode, and DrawStyle properties to change the way the line or outline of the rectangle is drawn.

The following example draws connected lines through all the points specified by a two-dimensional array:

Example

```
Private Sub DrawLines(points())
    Dim i As Integer, l As Integer, u As Integer
    l = LBound(points, 1)
    u = UBound(points, 1)
    PSet (points(l, 0), points(l, 1))
    For i = l + 1 To u
        Line -(points(i, 0), points(i, 1))
    Next i
End Sub
```

LineStyle Property

The LineStyle property controls the style of lines displayed between Node objects.

Usage   *object*.LineStyle = *IntegerValue*
        IntegerValue = *object*.LineStyle

Applies To   TreeView Control

PARAMETER	VALUE	MEANING
IntegerValue	tvwTreeLines or 0	Standard tree lines between Node siblings and their parents.
	tvwRootLines or 1	In addition to the standard lines, adds lines between root nodes.

LinkExecute Method

The LinkExecute method lets a DDE destination control send a command string to the source application in a DDE conversation. The command string must be formatted according to the requirements of the source application. The LinkTopic and LinkMode properties must be set before using LinkExecute. The LinkItem property is not used.

Usage   *object*.LinkExecute *Command*

Applies To   Label Control
        PictureBox Control
        TextBox Control

The DDE specifications place no restrictions on the commands you send in a LinkExecute method. But it is standard practice to enclose source-application commands in square brackets ([ ]). That way, you can send multiple commands in a single string. You need to consult the documentation for the source application for valid commands.

The following example sends text to a WinWord document at a bookmark named "bkmk." It makes sure that the inserted text is again covered by the same bookmark so that the command may be used again. The double double-quotes (" ") are used to send a double-quote character to the source application. You could use Chr(34) instead of two double-quotes.

Example

```
Private Sub Command1_Click()
    Dim cmd$
        Text1.LinkTopic = "WinWord|MyDoc.doc"
        Text1.LinkMode = 2
        cmd$ = "[Activate ""MyDoc.doc""]"
        cmd$ = cmd$ & "[EditGoto ""bkmk""]"
        cmd$ = cmd$ & "[SetStartOfBookmark ""bkmk""]"
        cmd$ = cmd$ & "[Insert """ & Text1.Text & """]"
        cmd$ = cmd$ & "[ExtendSelection]"
        cmd$ = cmd$ & "[EditGoto ""bkmk""]"
        cmd$ = cmd$ & "[InsertBookmark .Name = ""bkmk""]"
        cmd$ = cmd$ & "[AppActivate ""Form1""]"
        Text1.LinkExecute cmd$
        Text1.LinkMode = 0
    End Sub
```

LinkItem Property

Together with the LinkTopic property, the LinkItem property specifies the "name" of a piece of data to be passed in a DDE conversation. This name depends on the source (server) application. For example, when conversing with WinWord, the LinkItem property can be set to the name of a bookmark; when conversing with Microsoft Excel, it could be a cell reference.

Usage   *StringValue = object*.LinkItem
               object.LinkItem = *StringValue*

Applies To   Label Control
               PictureBox Control
               TextBox Control

The LinkItem property is set for a control acting as the destination of a DDE link. When a Form object is acting as the DDE source, the destination application uses the name of a Label, PictureBox, or TextBox control on the form as the item name; the control's LinkItem property is not used.

Avoid using a control as both the destination and source to the same item in another application. This can cause an infinite loop where both items are continually updating each other. For this reason, if you implement Paste Link commands in your application, you should document the application|topic pairs that you establish so that the user does not create these infinite loops inadvertently.

You can set permanent data links at design time by using the Paste Link command from the Edit menu. This command also automatically sets the control's LinkMode, LinkTopic, and LinkItem properties. When these properties are set at design time, VB will try to establish the conversation every time the form is loaded at runtime.

Most DDE server applications support the "System" topic with the "Topics" item that returns a tab-delimited list of available items in a string. The following example gets a list of topics from Microsoft Excel and places it in a list box. Note that it hides the Label control that receives the raw "Topics" string.

Example

```
Private Sub cmdTopics_Click()
        lblTopics.Visible = False
        lblTopics.LinkTopic = "Excel|System"
        lblTopics.LinkItem = "Topics"
        lblTopics.LinkMode = vbLinkManual
        lblTopics.LinkRequest
        lblTopics.LinkMode = vbLinkNone

        If lblTopics.Caption = "" Then Exit Sub
        topics$ = lblTopics.Caption
        lstTopics.Clear
        i1 = 1
        Do
            i2 = InStr(i1, topics$, Chr(9))
            If i2 <> 0 Then
                lstTopics.AddItem Mid(topics$, i1, i2 - i1)
            Else
                lstTopics.AddItem Mid(topics$, i1)
            End If
            i1 = i2 + 1
        Loop While i2 <> 0
End Sub
```

LinkMode Property

The LinkMode property determines whether and how data for a control or form are updated via DDE conversations (or Links).

Usage   *object*.LinkMode = *IntegerValue*
                 IntegerValue = *object*.LinkMode

Applies To   Form Object
                 Label Control
                 MDIForm Object

PictureBox Control
TextBox Control

For the controls that support DDE, the LinkMode property allows the control to become a DDE "client." It does this by using the control's LinkTopic and LinkItem properties to specify the DDE conversation. VB will try to initiate a conversation as soon as the LinkMode property is set to a nonzero value.

For Forms or MDIForms, the LinkMode property allows the form to become a DDE "server," thereby letting other DDE clients request information or services from the Form. Whenever a client terminates a conversation with a control on the Form, the control's LinkMode property will be set to vbLinkNone, regardless of its initial setting.

The property can take on the values given in the following table.

CONSTANT	VALUE	MEANING
vbLinkNone	0	None. LinkExecute, LinkPoke, LinkRequest, or LinkSend will generate errors, and forms will not allow DDE clients to initiate a conversation. If a form uses vbLinkNone at design time, vbLinkNone cannot be changed to vbLinkSource at runtime.
vbLinkSource	1	Source (forms only). This setting lets a form become a DDE server, with the form name as the DDE "topic." Clients can request and poke data into Label, TextBox, and PictureBox controls on the form as well as trigger the LinkExecute event for the form. The form must set LinkMode to vbLinkSource to 1 at design time. Then at runtime, it can toggle the setting between vbLinkNone and vbLinkSource.
vbLinkAutomatic	1	Automatic (controls only). Any changes to the linked data will update the control. As a result, the Change event of the control will be triggered for each update, even if the actual data did not change.
vbLinkManual	2	Manual (controls only). The control is updated only when its LinkRequest method is executed.
vbLinkNotify	3	Notify (controls only). Any changes to the linked data triggers the control's LinkNotify event, but the control is not updated until the LinkRequest method is executed.

In the following table are LinkMode constants for compatibility with VB1. You should avoid using them.

CONSTANT	VALUE	MEANING
vbHot	1	Hot link. Same as vbLinkAutomatic. Controls only.
vbServer	1	Server. Same as vbLinkSource. Forms only.
vbCold	2	Cold link. Same as vbLinkManual. Controls only.

Example
```
Private Sub Text1_DblClick()
        Text1.LinkTopic = "Winword|System"
        Text1.LinkItem = "Topics"
        Text1.LinkMode = vbLinkManual
        Text1.LinkRequest
        Text1.LinkMode = vbLinkNone
End Sub
```

This example gets a list of topics from WinWord. Most DDE-aware servers provide the "System" topic and "Topics" item to return a tab-delimited list of valid topics. For WinWord, the valid topics are the "System" and the list of open documents and templates.

Example
```
Private Sub Text1_DblClick()
        Text1.LinkTopic = "Winword|C:\Mydoc.doc"
        Text1.LinkItem = "MyBookmark"
        Text1.LinkMode = vbLinkManual
        Text1.LinkRequest
        Text1.LinkMode = vbLinkNone
End Sub
```

This example grabs the contents of the "MyBookmark" bookmark from the C:\Mydoc.doc file. WinWord must be running, and the document must already be open.

LinkPoke Method

The LinkPoke method sends the contents of a control to the source application in a DDE conversation. It is the opposite of the LinkRequest method, which gets data from the source application. The LinkTopic, LinkItem, and LinkMode properties must be set and a conversation established before LinkPoke may be used.

Usage　　　　　*object*.LinkPoke

Applies To　　　Label Control
　　　　　　　　PictureBox Control
　　　　　　　　TextBox Control

Since most DDE conversation involves data flowing from a source application to a destination client, the source application may not accept LinkPoke data. In these cases, there will be an error.

The LinkMode property should be set to vbLinkManual (2). It makes no sense to set it to vbLinkAutomatic (1), since that would allow the source to update the destination control automatically. Doing this would destroy the data you want to send to the source application.

The following table summarizes the data transferred to the source application for each type of control.

CONTROL	DATA SENT
Label	Text value of the Caption property.
PictureBox	Graphic value of the Picture property.
TextBox	Text value of the Text property.

Example

```
Private Sub Text1_DblClick()
    Text1.LinkTopic = "Winword|C:\Mydoc.doc"
    Text1.LinkItem = "MyBookmark"
    Text1.LinkMode = vbLinkManual
    Text1.LinkPoke
    Text1.LinkMode = vbLinkNone
End Sub
```

LinkRequest Method

The LinkRequest method transfers the most recent data from the source application in a DDE conversation to a destination control. It is the opposite of the LinkPoke method that sends data to the source application. The LinkTopic, LinkItem, and LinkMode properties must be set and a conversation established before LinkRequest may be used.

Usage   *object*.LinkRequest

Applies To   Label Control
                 PictureBox Control
                 TextBox Control

The following table summarizes which properties are updated with the data transferred from the source application for each type of control.

CONTROL	DATA SENT
Label	Text value of the Caption property.
PictureBox	Graphic value of the Picture property.
TextBox	Text value of the Text property.

LinkRequest is not needed if LinkMode is set to vbLinkAutomatic (1), since the control will be updated automatically. With LinkMode set to vbLinkManual (2), you need LinkRequest to initiate data transfer. With LinkMode set to vbLinkNotify (3), the control's LinkNotify event will be triggered with the source data changes. You need to execute the LinkRequest method in the event procedure to actually transfer the data to the control.

Example
```
Private Sub Text1_DblClick()
    Text1.LinkTopic = "Excel|C:\[MySheet.xls]Sheet1"
    Text1.LinkItem = "R1C1"
    Text1.LinkMode = vbLinkManual
    Text1.LinkRequest
    Text1.LinkMode = vbLinkNone
End Sub
```

LinkSend Method

The LinkSend method transfers the contents of a PictureBox control on a source Form object to a destination application in a DDE conversation.

Usage   *object*.LinkSend

Applies To   PictureBox Control

    The Form object containing the PictureBox control must have its LinkMode property set to vbLinkSource (1). For performance reasons, the source Form will not automatically update the destination application when the graphic in a PictureBox changes. You must explicitly issue a LinkSend to update the destination.

LinkTimeout Property

The LinkTimeout property specifies how long a destination control waits for a response to a DDE message before generating an error. Use this property to increase the wait time if your server application takes a long time to respond.

Usage   *IntegerValue* = *object*.LinkTimeout
              object.LinkTimeout = *IntegerValue*

Applies To   Label Control
              PictureBox Control
              TextBox Control

    The values of the LinkTimeout property have the meanings given in the following table.

VALUE	MEANING
−32,768 to −1	Forces the system to wait for the maximum amount of time for the server to respond. The wait may be canceled by the user using the Esc key. So what's this maximum timeout value? A long time. Let's put it this way. We started the request. When we looked at it 2½ hours later, it had timed out. It's probably the same as setting it to 65,535.

VALUE	MEANING
1 to 65,535	Specifies the amount of time to wait in tenths of seconds. The default value is 50 (5 seconds). The maximum wait time you can specify is about 6,553.5 seconds, or 1 hour 49 minutes.
0	Useless. It always gives the timeout error.
Other values	Overflow error.

At design time, you cannot set LinkTimeout to a value greater than 32,767 even though valid values can range to 65,535.

LinkTopic Property

To establish a DDE conversation, the client needs to indicate both a "topic" of interest and perhaps an "item" within the topic to use for the conversation. The available topic names and item names are completely up to the server application to define, but most support the "System" topic and "Topics" item that returns a tab-separated list of valid topic names.

In VB, the Label, PictureBox, and TextBox controls are clients (the destination) of DDE conversations, thus their LinkTopic properties specify the server (source) application name and topics in the server from which they want to retrieve or set data. Their LinkItem properties must also be set to complete the DDE-conversation specification.

A Form or MDIForm object can be a server (source) of DDE conversation. Setting its LinkTopic property specifies the topic name to which it will respond. The DDE client needs to further specify the name of a Label, PictureBox, or TextBox control as the link item from which to grab or set data.

Usage   *StringValue* = *object*.LinkTopic
                  object.LinkTopic = *StringValue*

Applies To   Form Object
                  Label Control
                  MDIForm Object
                  PictureBox Control
                  TextBox Control

Destination Control

For a destination control, the LinkTopic string uses the format *ApplicationName|Topic*. The application name is *usually* (but not always) the name of the source application without the .EXE extension.

Example   `Text1.LinkTopic = "Winword|System"`

You'll need to consult the source application for the exact syntax. Usually, the topics correspond to the filenames of open documents or worksheets in the source application. And the link items correspond to bookmarks or cell names in those documents or worksheets; a cell reference may be the name assigned to a cell or an R1C1-type reference.

Example
```
Text1.LinkTopic = "Winword|c:\My Documents\FormLetter.doc"
Text1.LinkItem = "Addressee"          'Name of a bookmark

Text2.LinkTopic = "Excel|c:\Worksheets\[mortgage.xls]Sheet1"
Text2.LinkTopic = "Amount"            'Name of a cell
```

Before you establish the link, however, you'll need to make sure the source application is running and that the file you need is opened. Use the Shell command to start the application if it is not running yet.

Setting the LinkTopic property will break existing links. So it is recommended that you always set the LinkMode property to vbLinkNone (0) before changing the LinkTopic property.

If you use the Edit/PasteLink command at design time to establish a link, it automatically sets the LinkMode, LinkTopic, and LinkItem properties for the control and the settings are saved with the project. The link becomes permanent such that VB will try to reestablish the conversation every time the Form containing the control is loaded.

Source Form

A DDE destination application can link to information contained in a Label, PictureBox, or TextBox control on a source Form object. The destination application must specify the information in the following table to establish a conversation.

PARAMETER	MEANING
Application	The name of the project or application that contains your source form. If the application is run from the development environment, this name is the name of the VB project (without the .VBP extension) that contains your source form. If the application is run as a standalone, it is the name that you specified when you chose "Make EXE File" (without the .EXE extension). If the user renames the application, the application will *not* respond to the new name.
Topic	The LinkTopic property you set for your source form. It can be any string, but you should not use the 'l' or '!' characters.
Item	The name of a Label, PictureBox, or TextBox control on the source form.

The syntax of how to use the Application, Topic, and Item strings to establish a conversation will depend on your source application.

Changing the LinkTopic property breaks all existing destination links to the old topic. So you should set the LinkMode property to vbLinkNone (0) before changing the LinkTopic property.

List Property

The List property refers to a string array that is the content of the control's list box. At design time, you can add items to the ComboBox and ListBox controls by using the Properties window. This property is read-only at runtime for DirListBox, DriveListBox, and FileListBox controls.

Usage	*StringValue = object*.List(*Index*) *object*.List(*Index*) = *StringValue*
Applies To	ComboBox Control DirListBox Control DriveListBox Control FileListBox Control ListBox Control

The Index argument selects an item from the List array. To select the first item in the list, the index starts at 0 for all but the DirListBox. The maximum value for Index is (ListCount − 1). For a DirListBox, an index of −1 refers to the current directory for the control as specified by its Path property. An index of −2 refers to the parent directory, −3 to one more directory up, and so on until the root directory of the drive is reached. These indexes are not affected by the Option Base statement.

Trying to set the value of an item using an index outside the range of valid entries in a list generates an error. Trying to get the value using the same index returns an empty string with no errors.

The initial entries in the list are given in the following table.

CONTROL	INITIAL ENTRIES
ComboBox and ListBox	Empty
DirListBox	A list of all subdirectories within the directory specified by the Path property and the directories above Path. Each item contains full path information.
DriveListBox	A list of all valid drives for the system. Each item contains the volume label for the drive enclosed in square brackets, such as "d: [USER]."
FileListBox	A list of all files in the directory specified by the Path property that match the setting of the Pattern property. Each item contains only the filename without path information.

Use the AddItem and RemoveItem methods at runtime to add and remove items from the ComboBox and ListBox controls. Set the Sorted property to keep the list sorted in alphabetical order. Use the ListIndex property to determine the currently selected item and the NewIndex property to determine the index of the most recently added item.

Example

```
For i = 0 To Combo1.ListCount - 1
    Debug.Print Combo1.List(i)
Next i
```

ListCount Property

The ListCount property returns the number of items in the list box part of a control. Because the items in a list box are indexed from zero (regardless of the Option Base setting for the module), ListCount is always one more than the maximum value for ListIndex. This is a read-only property available only at runtime.

Usage   *IntegerValue* = *object*.ListCount

Applies To   ComboBox Control
                   DirListBox Control
                   DriveListBox Control
                   FileListBox Control
                   ListBox Control

The ListCount property has more specific meanings for each type of control as given in the following table.

CONTROL	MEANING
ComboBox and ListBox	The number of items in the list.
DirListBox	The number of subdirectories in the directory specified by the Path property. Actually, the number of items in the list box is more than ListCount because it displays all the folders above Path.
DriveListBox	The number of available drives on the system.
FileListBox	The number of files in the directory specified by the Path property that match the Pattern property setting.

The following example shows a typical way of traversing a list:

Example

```
For i = 0 To File1.ListCount - 1
    Debug.Print File1.List(i)
Next i
```

Note that the DBCombo and DBList controls do not have the ListCount property.

ListField Property

Part of the holy trinity of data-bound control obfuscation, the ListField property returns or sets the name of the field that a DBCombo or DBList box will display.

Usage   *object*.ListField = *StringValue*
                  StringValue = *object*.ListField

Applies To   DBCombo Control
                  DBList Control

PARAMETER	VALUE	MEANING
StringValue	A string	The name of the field to display (or the one being displayed) in the list portion of a DBList or DBCombo control from the recordset specified by BoundColumn.

If you're hungry for an example, look under the BoundColumn property.

 The Help file states—incorrectly, it would seem—that "If the ListField property is not provided, the field specified by the BoundColumn property is also used to fill the control's list." When we ran out tests, we found that if you don't specify ListField, you don't get a list. If ListField can't find the field it's looking for, you get a trapable error, typically Error 380, the invalid property value error.

ListIndex Property

The ListIndex property allows you to get or set the currently selected item in the list box portion of the control. When multiple selection is allowed and multiple items are selected, ListIndex indicates the item that has focus, although that item is not necessarily selected.

Usage   *IntegerValue* = *object*.ListIndex
                  object.ListIndex = *IntegerValue*

Applies To   ComboBox Control
                  DirListBox Control
                  DriveListBox Control

FileListBox Control
ListBox Control

The values of the ListIndex property are given in the following table.

VALUE	MEANING
Less than –1	Possible only for the DirListBox. The DirListBox displays all folders from the root of the current drive to the current path as specified by the Path property plus all subdirectories under Path. Selecting a directory above the current path will return negative numbers for the ListIndex property. The immediate-parent directory will return –2, the one above it –3, and so on.

–1	The default for all but the DriveListBox. It indicates that no item is selected. It has additional meanings for the following controls:
	    ComboBox: If the user enters a value into the text box portion, even if it matches one of the items exactly, ListIndex will return –1.
	    DirListBox: Using –1 will return the same value as the Path property, the current path of the DirListBox control.

0 to (ListCount – 1)	These select an item from the list. The maximum value of ListIndex is ListCount – 1, because the index starts at zero (regardless of the Option Base setting for the module). The default ListIndex for a DriveListBox control is the index of the drive that contains the directory specified by the Path property.

To get the string for the selected item, you may use List1.List(List1.ListIndex).

 The Help file incorrectly states that a ListIndex of –1 for DriveListBox will return the current drive. It also incorrectly states that the default value of ListIndex for FileList-Box and ListBox is not –1.

The LBound and UBound functions may not be used on the List property of a control to determine the minimum and maximum values of ListIndex. This means there is no way to determine the actual number of items displayed in a DirListBox without having to manually parse the Path property to ascertain the number of parent folders that are also displayed.

Note: The DBCombo and DBList controls do not have the ListIndex property.

ListItems Property

Not to be confused with the ListItem object, the ListItems property returns a reference to a collection of ListItem objects in a ListView.

Usage   *object*.ListItems

Applies To   ListView Control

Load Statement

The Load statement loads a Form, MDIForm, or control-array element into memory. Use the Load statement for forms that you do not want to display immediately. Also use it for control arrays to create additional array items at runtime.

Usage   Load *object*[(*Index*)]

Applies To: Form Object
                     MDIForm Object

The object argument is the name of a Form or MDIForm object or a placeholder for the name of a Form object, a MDIForm object, or an element of a control array. Use the parentheses and Index to load a new control-array element; the Index must not be the same as an existing array element.

Loading a form initializes its properties to their initial values set at design time. Then the Load event procedure is called. Also, for MDI child forms—Form objects with their MDIChild properties set to True—loading will cause their parent MDIForm objects to load first (if they are not yet loaded). Moreover, if the MDIForm object's AutoShowChildren property is set to True, both the MDIForm object and the loaded MDI child form will be displayed.

Note that you do not need to explicitly load your forms; any reference to a property or method of a form will cause the form to be loaded. Once a form is loaded, you can access its properties and controls, even if the form is not visible.

If a Form or MDIForm object is set as the Startup Form for the project using the Tools/Options menu at design time, then it will be loaded automatically as soon as the application starts to run.

When you load a new element of a control array, all of the new element's property settings—except Visible, Index, and TabIndex—are copied from the element in the array with the lowest index number. The Visible property is always False after loading. After creating the new element, you typically have to move it, size it, and change its caption before making it visible; otherwise, it will overlap the existing element.

In the following example, the Startup form is a simple "splash screen" that can be loaded and displayed quickly. It then loads the main application forms that may take a long time to load. Once loaded, the main forms may be displayed and hidden quickly to provide snappier response for your users.

Example
```
Private Sub frmStart_Load()
        Load frmMain
        Load frmProperties
        frmMain.Show
        Hide
End Sub
```

The following example loads a new OptionButton control as a new element of a control array. All buttons are stacked vertically, so the example just performs a simple calculation to place the control.

Example

```
Private Sub NewOpt(Index As Integer, strCaption As String)
    Load btnOpt(Index)
    btnOpt(Index).Caption = strCaption
    btnOpt(Index).Top = Index * btnOpt(Index).Height
    btnOpt(Index).Visible = True
End Sub
```

 The Help file incorrectly states that MDI child forms cannot be hidden.

LoadFile Method

The LoadFile method replaces the contents of a RichTextBox control with an .RTF or text file.

Usage   *object*.LoadFile *Path*[, *FileType*]

Applies To   RichTextBox Control

This method doesn't support named arguments.

PARAMETER	VALUE	MEANING
Path	A string	The path and filename of the file to load.
FileType	rtfRTF or 0	Optional. Says that the file must be a .RTF file.
	rtfText or 1	Optional. Says that you can load any text file.

LoadFile blows away whatever is in the RichTextBox.

LoadPicture Function

The LoadPicture function loads a graphic from a file at runtime. Use LoadPicture to set the Picture, DragIcon, Icon, and MouseIcon properties of forms and controls. You can also assign its result to a variable of type Picture.

Usage   *GraphicProperty* = LoadPicture([*Filename*])
                   Set *PictureVariable* = LoadPicture([*Filename*])

The first form is used to set the Picture, DragIcon, Icon, and MouseIcon properties of a form or control. The second is used to assign the loaded graphic to a variable.

The parameters of the LoadPicture function have the meanings given in the following table.

PARAMETER	VALUE	MEANING
Filename	Omitted	Clears the graphics of the form or control.
	String expression	The filename that contains the graphic to be loaded. The file format may be bitmap (.BMP), icon (.ICO), run-length encoded (.RLE), or metafile (.WMF) files. 　　Note that the icon properties can accept only icon (.ICO) files, so you will get an error if you use LoadPicture to load other types of files.

The following example loads a graphic into a PictureBox control:

Example
```
Picture1.Picture = LoadPicture("scenes.bmp")
```

The next example changes a PictureBox's DragIcon property during a drag-and-drop operation. It changes the DragIcon of the source to the "Do Not Enter" sign when it's dragged over another PictureBox control. It uses the PictureBox's DragIcon property to save the original Source's DragIcon picture.

Example
```
Private Sub Picture1_DragOver(Source As Control, X As Single, _
    Y As Single, State As Integer)
    Dim IconFile$
    IconFile$ = "icons\misc\Misc06.ico"
    Select Case State
      Case vbEnter
        Picture1.DragIcon = Source.DragIcon
        Source.DragIcon = LoadPicture(IconFile$)
      Case vbLeave
        Source.DragIcon = Picture1.DragIcon
      Case Else
    End Select
End Sub
```

The Clipboard object, too, can use the LoadPicture function to directly load a graphic from a file:

Example
```
Clipboard.SetData LoadPicture("bitmaps\assorted\balloon.bmp")
```

LoadResData Function

The LoadResData function loads a resource from the resource (.RES) file attached to the current project (via the File/Add File menu). A Byte array is returned.

Usage　　　　*ByteArray* = LoadResData(*Index, Format*)

PARAMETER	VALUE	MEANING
Index	Integer or string	The ID value or string that identifies the resource for the specified Format in the .RES resource file. The ID 1 is reserved for the application icon. Resources of different Formats can share the same Index.
Format	1	Cursor resource (.CUR).
	2	Bitmap resource (.BMP).
	3	Icon resource (.ICO).
	4	Menu resource.
	5	Dialog box.
	6	String resource. In this case, the return value is a String value.
	7	Font directory resource.
	8	Font resource.
	9	Accelerator table.
	10	User-defined resource.
	12	Group cursor.
	14	Group icon.

Use the LoadResPicture() function to retrieve cursor, bitmap, and icon resources as pictures rather than as a Byte array.

Resource files allow you to load data on demand, thus reducing the load size of your forms and modules and making them load faster. By your isolating the resources that need to be translated between locales into one resource file per locale, you can localize your VB application without having to change the source code. Only one resource file can be added to a project at any one time.

Example   ```
Dim b() As Byte
b() = LoadResData(3, 2)
```

This example loads a bitmap with resource ID of 3 into a Byte array.

 Although the Index argument could be a string, we could not get it to work. Part of the problem is that string IDs in a resource file (.RES) are stored in Unicode (2-byte character) format and LoadResData may not be translating the string before trying to access the resource. We keep getting "Runtime error 326: Resource with identifier 'PRJBMP' not found."
```

LoadResPicture Function

The LoadResPicture function loads a bitmap, icon, or cursor from the resource (.RES) file attached to the current project (via the File/Add File menu). A picture value is returned and can be assigned to the Picture property of a control or form.

Usage   *Picture* = LoadResPicture(*Index*, *Format*)

PARAMETER	VALUE	MEANING
Index	Integer or string	The ID value or string that identifies the picture in the .RES resource file. The ID 1 is reserved for the application icon.
Format	vbResBitmap or 0	Bitmap resource (.BMP).
	vbResIcon or 1	Icon resource (.ICO).
	vbResCursor or 2	Cursor resource (.CUR).

Resource files allow you to load data on demand, thus reducing the load size of your forms and modules and making them load faster. By your isolating the resources that need to be translated between locales into one resource file per locale, you can localize your VB application without having to change the source code. Only one resource file can be added to a project at any one time.

Example   `Picture1.Picture = LoadResPicture(3, vbResBitmap)`

This example loads a bitmap with resource ID of 3 and puts it in Picture1 control.

The next example allows you to display some animation in the Image1 control, using 10 bitmaps stored in the resource file with indices ranging from 2 to 11. You can adjust the update rate by changing the Interval property of the Timer1 control.

Example
```
Private Sub Timer1_Timer()
    Static index
    index = (index Mod 10) + 2
    Image1 = LoadResPicture(index, vbResBitmap)
    index = index + 1
End Sub
```

Although the Index argument could be a string, we could not get it to work. Part of the problem is that string IDs in a resource file (.RES) are stored in Unicode (2-byte character) format and LoadResPicture may not be translating the string before trying to access the resource. We keep getting "Runtime error 326: Resource with identifier 'PRJBMP' not found."

LoadResString Function

The LoadResString function loads and returns a string from the resource (.RES) file attached to the current project (via the File/Add File menu).

Usage   *StringValue* = LoadResString(*Index*)

PARAMETER	VALUE	MEANING
Index	Integer	The ID value that identifies the string in the .RES resource file. The ID 1 is reserved for the application icon.

Resource files allow you to load data on demand, thus reducing the load size of your forms and modules and making them load faster. By your isolating the resources that need to be translated between locales into one resource file per locale, you can localize your VB application without having to change the source code. Only one resource file can be added to a project at any one time. This is especially true for strings used as labels on your forms.

Example   `Label1.Caption = LoadResString(22)`

This example loads a string with resource ID of 22 and uses it as the label caption.

Locked Property

This Locked property specifies whether a control may be edited by the user at runtime. Set this property to True to allow the user to select, but not change, text or values.

Usage   *BooleanValue* = *object*.Locked
                 object.Locked = *BooleanValue*

Applies To   Column Object
                 DBCombo Control
                 DBList Control
                 TextBox Control

The values for the Locked property have the meanings given in the following table.

VALUE	MEANING
True	The default for TextBox. At runtime, the user can select text in the control or object and copy it to the system Clipboard but cannot change any text. The program can still change the text in a TextBox control via code by changing the Text property.

VALUE	MEANING
True (*cont.*)	For a Column object, if the underlying field's DataUpdatable property is False and the user changes the value, an error occurs when the control tries to update the database. If the Column object is unbound or the underlying data source does not support DataUpdatable, the default setting for Locked is True. Otherwise, the default is the same as the DataUpdatable property of the underlying data field.
False	The user can edit the text or values in the control or object at runtime.

Locked Property (RichTextBox Control)

The Locked property controls whether the contents in a RichTextBox control can be edited.

Usage   *object*.Locked = *BooleanValue*
                      BooleanValue = *object*.Locked

Applies To   RichTextBox Control

PARAMETER	VALUE	MEANING
BooleanValue	True	A user can view but not edit the contents of the control. You can change the contents using the Text property.
	False	The user may edit the contents of the control.

lpOleObject Property

The lpOleObject property returns the address (far pointer) of the object contained in an OLE Container object. This property is read-only at runtime.

Usage   *LongValue* = *object*.lpOleObject

Applies To   OLE Container Control

Use this property with OLE DLLs or API functions that require the address on an object as argument. The value of the lpOleObject property is 0 if no object is contained in the OLE Container object.

Major Property

The Major property is read-only at runtime. It returns an integer that is the major release number of the running application. To enter this number, select the File/Make EXE File... menu and then click the Options... button. In the "Version Number" section, find the "Major" text box and enter the value.

Usage   *IntegerValue* = *object*.Major

Applies To   App Object

The valid range of the Major property is from 0 to 9,999. The VB development environment will not allow you to enter values outside this range.

MaskColor Property

The MaskColor property controls the color that VB will mask out during operations such as an overlay.

Usage   *object*.MaskColor = *ColorValue*
                         ColorValue = *object*.MaskColor

Applies To   ImageList Control

PARAMETER	VALUE	MEANING
ColorValue	Any valid color	The color that VB will mask, that is, make transparent during operations such as overlays.

Note: You may specify the color using either the RGB function, the QBColor function, or the VB color constants. So you don't have to look them up in the Windows Help file, here they are.

CONSTANT	VALUE	DESCRIPTION
vbBlack	0x0	Black.
vbRed	0xFF	Red.
vbGreen	0xFF00	Green.
vbYellow	0xFFFF	Yellow.
vbBlue	0xFF0000	Blue.
vbMagenta	0xFF00FF	Magenta.
vbCyan	0xFFFF00	Cyan.

Constant	Value	Description
vbWhite	0xFFFFFF	White.
vbScrollBars	0x80000000	Scroll bar color.
vbDesktop	0x80000001	Desktop color.
vbActiveTitleBar	0x80000002	Color of the title bar for the active window.
vbInactiveTitleBar	0x80000003	Color of the title bar for the inactive window.
vbMenuBar	0x80000004	Menu background color.
vbWindowBackground	0x80000005	Window background color.
vbWindowFrame	0x80000006	Window frame color.
vbMenuText	0x80000007	Color of text on menus.
vbWindowText	0x80000008	Color of text in windows.
vbTitleBarText	0x80000009	Color·of text in captions and size boxes and of scroll arrows.
vbActiveBorder	0x8000000A	Border color of active window.
vbInactiveBorder	0x8000000B	Border color of inactive window.
vbApplicationWorkspace	0x8000000C	Background color of multiple-document interface (MDI) applications.
vbHighlight	0x8000000D	Background color of items selected in a control.
vbHighlightText	0x8000000E	Text color of items selected in a control.
vbButtonFace	0x8000000F	Color of shading on the face of command buttons.
vbButtonShadow	0x80000010	Color of shading on the edge of command buttons.
vbGrayText	0x80000011	Grayed (disabled) text.
vbButtonText	0x80000012	Text color on push buttons.
vbInactiveCaptionText	0x80000013	Color of text in an inactive caption.
vb3DHighlight	0x80000014	Highlight color for 3D display elements.
vb3DDKShadow	0x80000015	Darkest shadow color for 3D display elements.
vb3DLight	0x80000016	Second lightest of the 3D colors after vb3DHighlight.
vbInfoText	0x80000017	Color of text in ToolTips.
vbInfoBackground	0x80000018	Background color of ToolTips.

MatchedWithList Property

The MatchedWithList property is a Boolean property that is True when whatever is in BoundText matches a record in the list portion of DBList or DBCombo.

Usage   *BooleanValue* = *object*.MatchedWithList

Applies To   DBList Control
                     DBCombo Control

PARAMETER	VALUE	MEANING
BooleanValue	True	Whatever is in BoundText matches a record in the list portion of DBList or DBCombo.
	False	It doesn't match.

Use the MatchedWithList property when you're allowing users to enter values into a DB-Combo box. You can check the value and trap entries that aren't in your drop-down list. Then you can either write code to tell the users that they entered an incorrect value or run some kind of code to add the entry to the source table.

Remember, however, that the value in BoundText isn't necessarily the value in ListField. You may be looking at nice English words, and BoundText could be a numeric index.

Example
```
Private Sub DBCombo1_KeyPress(KeyAscii As Integer)
    If KeyAscii = vbKeySpace Then
        If DBCombo1.MatchedWithList = False Then
            Debug.Print "Not in list"
        End If
    Debug.Print DBCombo1.BoundText
    End If
End Sub
```

MatchEntry Property

The MatchEntry property determines whether a DBCombo or DBList box will use Basic Matching or Extended Matching. With Basic Matching, the control matches the next character entered based on the first letter of the entries in your list. Extended Matching narrows the search as you type more letters.

Usage   *object*.MatchEntry = *IntegerValue*
                     IntegerValue = *object*.MatchEntry

Applies To   DBCombo Control
                     DBList Control

PARAMETER	VALUE	MEANING
IntegerValue	vbMatchEntrySimple or 0	Basic Matching, which checks whatever you're typing against the first letter of the entries in the list. (Typing the same letter over and over cycles you through elements in the list that start with that letter.)
	vbMatchEntryExtended or 1	Extended Matching, which checks the list using all the letters you've typed, so typing more letters narrows the search.

You may get some odd behavior when you try to do anything with this property on a DBCombo box. VB may (not very politely) tell you that this property is read-only. It's not. Or at least, it wouldn't be if any of the manuals told you that in order to enable Extended Matching, you have to set your DBCombo box Style to be a dropdown list not the default dropdown combo. (But beware: You can't set the Style property of a DBCombo box at runtime, only at design time.)

Max Property

This Max property specifies the maximum value of the Value property for an HScrollBar or VScrollBar control. Set this appropriately if you are using a scroll bar to allow the user to change the value of a variable.

Usage   *IntegerValue = object*.Max
                 object.Max = *IntegerValue*

Applies To   HScrollBar Control
                 VScrollBar Control

The values of the Max property have the meanings given in the following table.

VALUE	MEANING
–32,768 to 32,767	The maximum value allowed for the Value property of a scroll bar control. The default value is 32,767.
Other values	Error

If Max is greater than Min, the maximum value is at the right or bottom of a scroll bar. If Max is less than Min, then the maximum value is at the left or top of a scroll bar.

The size of the scroll box cannot be set manually. If you change the Max property to anything other than the default 32,767, the scroll box changes from a near square box to a small thin box.

Max Property (CommonDialog Control)

This Max property controls two things: the maximum font size in the Font dialog and the maximum page number for a print range in the Printer dialog.

Usage   *object*.Max = *IntegerValue*
              IntegerValue = *object*.Max

Applies To   CommonDialog Control

PARAMETER	VALUE	MEANING
IntegerValue	A point size	With the Font dialog, the maximum allowable font size.
	An integer	With the Printer dialog, the maximum page for the To box.

Max Property (ProgressBar, Slider Control)

This Max property specifies the maximum value for the control.

Usage   *object*.Max = *SingleOrLongValue*
              SingleOrLongValue = *object*.Max

Applies To   ProgressBar Control
              Slider Control

The ProgressBar's Max property is a single-precision value, while the Slider's is a long-integer value. For a ProgressBar, the Max property defaults to 100, and its Min property cannot be less than zero. For a Slider control, the Max property defaults to 10.

MaxButton Property

The MaxButton property specifies whether a Form object has a Maximize button in its Title Bar at runtime. It is setable only at design time (but you won't see the change until runtime) and read-only at runtime. This property is ignored and no Maximize button will be displayed if the BorderStyle property is not vbFixedSingle (1) or vbSizable (2).

Usage   *BooleanValue* = *object*.MaxButton

Applies To   Form Object

The values of the MaxButton property have the meanings given in the following table.

VALUE	MEANING
True	The default. The form has a Maximize button, provided the BorderStyle is vbFixedSingle or vbSizable.
False	The form does not have a Maximize button.

The Maximize button allows a user to make the Form window fill the entire screen. Once the Form window is maximized, the Maximize button becomes a Restore button that will restore the window to its previous size and placement. Once the window is restored, the button becomes the Maximize button once again.

Maximizing or restoring a Form window at runtime generates a Resize event and sets the WindowState property to reflect the new window state. Setting the WindowState property directly at runtime to vbMaximized (2) will always maximize the window, regardless of the settings of the MaxButton and BorderStyle properties.

MaxFileSize Property

The MaxFileSize property controls the maximum size of the filename you can open with the CommonDialog control.

Usage   *object*.MaxFileSize = *IntegerValue*
                    IntegerValue = *object*.MaxFileSize

Applies To   CommonDialog Control

PARAMETER	VALUE	MEANING
IntegerValue	An integer from 1 to 32K	The maximum filename size in bytes. The default is 256.

MaxLength Property (TextBox Control)

This MaxLength property specifies the maximum number of characters that may be entered into a TextBox control.

Usage   *LongValue* = *object*.MaxLength
                    object.MaxLength = *LongValue*

Applies To   TextBox Control

The values of the MaxLength property have the meanings given in the following table.

VALUE	MEANING
0	The default. Limits set to inherent limits of the control that may be set by the control or memory constraints. For a TextBox, the maximum is 32,766.
1 through 32,766	The maximum number of characters allowed in the TextBox.
Greater than 32,766	No errors, but only the first 32,766 characters of a string are saved in the Text property.
Negative value	Error

At runtime, the user cannot enter more characters than allowed by the MaxLength property or the inherent maximum of 32,766. The code may still set the Text property to a string longer than the maximum length, but the string will be truncated at the maximum length.

Changing the MaxLength property does not affect the existing text in the TextBox control. If the new MaxLength value is smaller than the length of the existing text, the user will be able to erase characters in the existing text but won't be able to add more characters if doing so will make the string length greater than MaxLength.

MaxLength Property (RichTextbox Control)

This MaxLength property controls whether there is a maximum number of characters in a Rich-TextBox control and, if so, specifies it.

Usage   *object*.MaxLength = *IntegerValue*
              IntegerValue = *object*.MaxLength

Applies To   RichTextBox Control

PARAMETER	VALUE	MEANING
IntegerValue	An integer	The maximum number of characters. The default is 0, meaning the limit is determined by the amount of memory in the system.

Setting this property will result in truncation of the characters in a RichTextBox, should the number of characters exceed Value.

MDIChild Property

The MDIChild property specifies whether the form will appear as an MDI child form inside the application's MDIForm object at runtime. MDI child forms cannot be moved outside its parent MDIForm. The MDIChild property is read-only at runtime.

Usage   *BooleanValue = object*.MDIChild

Applies To   Form Object

The values of the MDIChild property have the meanings given in the following table.

VALUE	MEANING
True	The Form object is an MDI child form and at runtime will be displayed inside the application's MDIForm object. If multiple instances of the Form are created, each will appear inside the MDIForm. If no MDIForm has been defined for the application, this setting will generate an error at runtime.
False	The default. The Form object will be displayed as a separate top-level window, not inside an MDIForm.

The multiple-document interface (MDI) is useful for document-based applications, where each document can be represented by a single Form window. You simply create a new instance of the Form inside a parent MDI form for each document.

MDI child forms have the following characteristics:

- An MDI child form may be moved to within its parent MDI form but cannot be moved outside it. When the parent MDI form is minimized, you cannot access any of its child forms.

- When an MDI child form is maximized at runtime, its caption is combined with that of the parent MDIForm and displayed in the parent MDIForm's Title Bar.

- At design time, an MDI child form is *not* displayed inside the MDIForm object, but its icon in the Project window is changed to reflect the setting of its MDIChild property.

- An MDI child form may not be modal. Attempting to make it so using the Show method will generate a runtime error.

- The size and placement of the MDI child form set at design time in the Properties window are ignored. You must set these explicitly in the Form's Load event. Otherwise, the Windows operating system controls the initial size and placement of MDI child forms.

- If an MDI child form is referenced—by reading or setting its properties—or loaded before the parent MDIForm, the MDIForm is automatically loaded.

 The VB Help file indicates that MDIChild forms ignore the settings of the Border-Style, ControlBox, MinButton, and MaxButton properties for Windows 3.0 or later. This turns out to be *not* true when running Windows 95.

Min Property (HScrollBar, VScrollBar Control)

This Min property specifies the minimum value of the Value property for an HScrollBar or VScrollBar control. Set this appropriately if you are using a scroll bar to allow the user to change the value of a variable.

Usage   *IntegerValue = object*.Min
               object.Min = *IntegerValue*

Applies To   HScrollBar Control
               VScrollBar Control

The values of the Min property have the meanings given in the following table.

VALUE	MEANING
−32,768 to 32,767	The minimum value allowed for the Value property of a scroll bar control. The default value is 0.
Other values	Error

If Max is greater than Min, the maximum value is at the right or bottom of a scroll bar. If Max is less than Min, then the maximum value is at the left or top of a scroll bar.

Min Property (CommonDialog Control)

This Min property controls two things: the minimum font size in the Font dialog and the minimum page number for a print range in the Printer dialog.

Usage   *object*.Min = *IntegerValue*
               IntegerValue = object.Min

Applies To   CommonDialog Control

PARAMETER	VALUE	MEANING
IntegerValue	A point size	With the Font dialog, the minimum allowable font size.
	An integer	With the Printer dialog, the minimum page for the From box.

Min Property (ProgressBar, Slider Control)

This Min property specifies the minimum value for the control.

Usage   *object*.Min = *SingleOrLongValue*
                SingleOrLongValue = *object*.Min

Applies To   ProgressBar Control
                Slider Control

The ProgressBar's Min property is a single-precision value, while the Slider's Min property is a long-integer value. For a ProgressBar, the Min property defaults to 0, and it cannot be less than 0. For a Slider control, the Min property defaults to 0.

MinButton Property

The MinButton property specifies whether a Form object has a Minimize button in its Title Bar at runtime. It is setable only at design time (but you won't see the change until runtime) and read-only at runtime. If the BorderStyle property is not vbFixedSingle (1) or vbSizable (2), this property is ignored and no Minimize button will be displayed.

Usage   *BooleanValue* = *object*.MinButton

Applies To   Form Object

The values of the MinButton property have the meanings given in the following table.

VALUE	MEANING
True	The default. The form has a Minimize button, provided the BorderStyle is vbFixedSingle or vbSizable.
False	The form does not have a Minimize button.

The Minimize button allows a user to "close" the Form window into an icon displayed on the Task Bar (for Windows 95) or on the desktop. Once minimized, the user can double-click the icon to restore the window to its previous size and placement.

Minimizing or restoring a Form window at runtime generates a Resize event and sets the WindowState property to reflect the new window state. Setting the WindowState property directly at runtime to vbMinimized (1) will always minimize the window, regardless of the settings of the MinButton and BorderStyle properties.

Minor Property

The Minor property is read-only at runtime. It returns an integer that is the minor release number of the running application. To enter this number, select the File/Make EXE File... menu and then, click the Options... button. In the "Version Number" section, find the "Minor" text box and enter the value.

Usage   *IntegerValue = object*.Minor

Applies To   App Object

The valid range of the Minor property is from 0 to 9,999. The VB development environment will not allow you to enter values outside this range.

MinWidth Property

The MinWidth property controls the minimum width of a StatusBar control's Panel object.

Usage   *object*.MinWidth = *SingleValue*
                   SingleValue = object.MinWidth

Applies To   Panel Object

PARAMETER	VALUE	MEANING
SingleValue	Single-precision value	The minimum width of a panel, measured in the same units as whatever contains the StatusBar control.

MiscFlags Property

The MiscFlags property specifies the value that determines access to one or more additional features of the OLE Container control.

Usage   *IntegerValue = object*.MiscFlags
                   object.MiscFlags = *IntegerValue*

Applies To   OLE Container Control

This property is composed of one or more of the values, combined using the Or operator, given in the following table.

CONSTANT	VALUE	MEANING
vbOLEMiscFlagMemStorage	1	Makes the OLE Container control use memory—rather than disk—to store the object while it's loaded to speed up performance. Be careful! This can use a lot of memory, especially for bitmap graphics objects.
vbOLEMiscFlagDisableInPlace	2	Overrides the control's default behavior of allowing in-place activation for objects that support it. A separate window will be opened for the OLE object.

MixedState Property

The MixedState property determines whether a Button object in a Toolbar control appears in an indeterminate state.

Usage   *object*.MixedState = *BooleanValue*
              BooleanValue = *object*.MixedState

Applies To   Button Object

PARAMETER	VALUE	MEANING
BooleanValue	True	The Button object is confused and is dimmed.
	False	The Button object is in a known state and is normal.

Note: MixedState works only with Windows 95 or NT 3.51 and higher.

You'll typically see buttons in a MixedState when you're working with something that has a variety of attributes, for example, a text block that contains both italic and bold text.

MouseIcon Property

The MouseIcon property specifies the icon that is displayed when the mouse pointer moves over the control and the MousePointer property is set to vbCustom (99).

Usage   *Picture = object*.MouseIcon
              object.MouseIcon = *Picture*
              object.MouseIcon = LoadPicture(*Pathname*)

Applies To   CheckBox Control
                 ComboBox Control
                 CommandButton Control

Data Control
DBCombo Control
DBList Control
DirListBox Control
DriveListBox Control
FileListBox Control
Form Object
Frame Control
Grid Control
HScrollBar, VScrollBar Controls
Image Control
Label Control
ListBox Control
MDIForm Object
OLE Container Control
OptionButton Control
PictureBox Control
Screen Object
TextBox Control

The MouseIcon is a Picture object that may be set from the Picture property of another control or object (Form, PictureBox, Image, and so on) or the MouseIcon property of another control. You can also set it using the LoadPicture function by giving it the path name of a cursor (.CUR) or icon (.ICO) file. You cannot use animated cursors (.ANI).

MousePointer Property

The MousePointer property specifies the type of mouse pointer that is displayed at runtime when the mouse is over a control. Use it to indicate changes in functionality as the mouse moves over your forms and controls.

Usage   *object*.MousePointer = *IntegerValue*
                 IntegerValue = *object*.MousePointer

Applies To   CheckBox Control
                 ComboBox Control
                 CommandButton Control
                 Data Control
                 DBCombo Control
                 DBList Control
                 DirListBox Control
                 DriveListBox Control
                 FileListBox Control
                 Form Object
                 Frame Control

Grid Control
HScrollBar, VScrollBar Controls
Image Control
Label Control
ListBox Control
MDIForm Object
OLE Container Control
OptionButton Control
PictureBox Control
Screen Object
TextBox Control

CONSTANT	VALUE	MEANING
vbDefault	0	The default shape determined by the object.
vbArrow	1	Arrow.
vbCrosshair	2	Crosshair.
vbIbeam	3	I beam.
vbIconPointer	4	Icon. This is supposed to be a small square within a square, but we can't get it to work!
vbSizePointer	5	Sizing cursor (four-pointed arrow pointing north, south, east, and west).
vbSizeNESW	6	Sizing NE, SW (double arrow pointing northeast and southwest).
vbSizeNS	7	Sizing N, S (double arrow pointing north and south).
vbSizeNWSE	8	Sizing NW, SE (double arrow pointing northwest and southeast).
vbSizeWE	9	Sizing W, E (double arrow pointing west and east).
vbUpArrow	10	Up arrow.
vbHourglass	11	Hourglass. This is especially useful to indicate intensive computation and for asking the user to wait.
vbNoDrop	12	No drop.
vbArrowHourglass	13	Arrow and hourglass. (Available only in 32-bit VB4.)
vbArrowQuestion	14	Arrow and question mark. (Available only in 32-bit VB4.)
vbSizeAll	15	Size all. (Available only in 32-bit VB4.) This looks the same as vbSizePointer.
vbCustom	99	Custom icon specified by the MouseIcon property.

The MousePointer property can be set for the entire screen using the Screen object. If the application is not 32-bit and does not call the DoEvents function to release the CPU, then the MousePointer setting overrides all other applications. If it does call DoEvents, the mouse pointer may temporarily change when it is moved over a custom control.

Example   Form1.MousePointer = vbCustom
                    Form1.MouseIcon = LoadPicture("icons\computer\mouse01.ico")

This example loads a custom icon as the mouse pointer.

  We could not get vbIcon setting to do anything. It's supposed to be a square within a square, but on our system, it was just the plain, normal arrow cursor.

Move Method

This Move method moves the associated object to the specified coordinates. You can optionally resize the object along the way.

Usage   *object*.Move *Left*[, *Top*[, *Width*[, *Height*]]]

Applies To   CheckBox Control
                    ComboBox Control
                    CommandButton Control
                    Data Control
                    DBCombo Control
                    DBGrid Control
                    DBList Control
                    DirListBox Control
                    DriveListBox Control
                    FileListBox Control
                    Form Object
                    Frame Control
                    Grid Control
                    HScrollBar Control
                    Image Control
                    Label Control
                    Line Control
                    ListBox Control
                    MDIForm Object
                    OLE Container Control
                    OptionButton Control
                    PictureBox Control
                    Shape Control
                    TextBox Control
                    VScrollBar Control

The Move method parameters have the meanings given in the following table.

PARAMETER	VALUE	MEANING
Left	Single value	The horizontal coordinate (x-axis) of the left of the object. For a control, this is the coordinate of the center of the left border of the object.
Top	Single value	The vertical coordinate (y-axis) of the top of the object. For a control, this is the coordinate of the center of the top border of the object.
Width	Single value	The new width for the object. For a control, this is measured between the centers of the left and right borders.
Height	Single value	The new height of the object. For a control, this is measured between the centers of the top and bottom borders.

If any parameter is omitted, that property of the object is not changed.

Units of Measure

The unit of measure for the inside of a Frame control is always the twip, as is the unit used by a Frame (to move the frame on the Screen). Also, the coordinates are specified with respect to the top-left of the object's container, where the corner's coordinates are (0, 0). The Scale properties of Form objects, PictureBox controls, and Printer objects may be used to change the unit of measure and origin for their child objects.

Move Method (Recordset Object)

This Move method moves around a recordset.

Usage   recordset.Move *LongRowValue*[, *StartString*]

Applies To   Recordset Object

PARAMETER	VALUE	MEANING
LongRowValue	Long	The number of rows to move. Numbers greater than 0 move forward; those less than 0 move backward (toward the beginning of the file). Required.
StartString	String	A bookmark from which to start the move (optional).

MultiLine Property (TextBox Control)

This MultiLine property specifies whether a TextBox control will display multiple lines. This property is read-only at runtime.

Usage   *BooleanValue* = *object*.MultiLine

Applies To   TextBox Control

The values for this MultiLine property have the meanings given in the following table.

VALUE	MEANING
True	Allows multiple lines in a TextBox control. The text automatically wraps at word boundaries, provided a horizontal scroll bar is not displayed (see the Scrollbar property). Manual line breaks may be inserted by embedding carriage-return characters (Chr(13)).
False	The default. Only a single line is displayed regardless of the height of the text box. Carriage-return characters are displayed as unprintable characters (shown as a thick vertical bar).

When using a multiple-line TextBox control, you may not want to set a default Command-Button. Otherwise, when the user presses the Enter key, he or she will activate the default CommandButton rather than adding a new line to the text. The user can still use Ctrl+Enter to insert new lines, but doing this may be cumbersome.

MultiLine Property (RichTextBox Control)

This MultiLine property controls whether a RichTextBox control can accept and display multiple lines of text.

Usage   *object*.MultiLine = *BooleanValue*
                     BooleanValue = *object*.MultiLine

Applies To   RichTextBox Control

The MultiLine property is read-only at runtime.

PARAMETER	VALUE	MEANING
BooleanValue	True	A RichTextBox can have multiple lines of text.
	False	Ignore carriage returns; allow only one line. This is the default (!).

MultiRow Property

The MultiRow property controls whether a TabStrip control can display multiple rows of tabs.

Usage　　　　*object*.MultiRow = *BooleanValue*
　　　　　　　BooleanValue = *object*.MultiRow

Applies To　　TabStrip Control

PARAMETER	VALUE	MEANING
BooleanValue	True	It can.
	False	You get only one row of tabs.

MultiSelect Property (FileListBox, ListBox Control)

This MultiSelect property specifies whether to allow multiple selection in a FileListBox or List-Box control and how the multiple selection is made. It can be set only at design time.

Usage　　　　*IntegerValue* = *object*.MultiSelect

Applies To　　FileListBox Control
　　　　　　　ListBox Control

The possible values for the MultiSelect property are given in the following table.

CONSTANT	VALUE	MEANING
vbMultiSelectNone	0	Single selection only. No multiple selections allowed.
vbMultiSelectSimple	1	Simple multiple selection. Clicking the left mouse button or pressing the spacebar when a list item has focus toggles its selection on or off. The arrow keys move the focus.
vbMultiSelectExtended	2	Extended multiple selection. This is the most common behavior for list boxes that allow multiple selection. With this setting, pressing the Shift key and clicking the mouse on a list item selects *all* items from the previously selected item to the current items. Pressing the Shift key and one of the arrow keys includes the new item in the selection. Pressing the Ctrl key and clicking the mouse on an item toggles its selection on or off without affecting the other selected items.

To process multiple selections, run through all items in the list using the list's Selected method.

MultiSelect Property (ListView Control)

This MultiSelect property specifies whether multiple ListItems may be selected in a ListView control.

Usage	*BooleanValue* = *object*.MultiSelect
	object.MultiSelect = *BooleanValue*

Applies To	ListView Control

The values of the MultiSelect property have the meanings given in the following table.

PARAMETER	VALUE	MEANING
BooleanValue	False	The default. Single selection only.
	True	Multiple Selection. The Shift key extends selection from the previously selected ListItem to the selected ListItem by including all other ListItem objects between the two. The Ctrl key toggles the inclusion of only the selected ListItem into the selection.

Name Property

The Name property specifies the name of a control or object. It is read-only at runtime.

Usage	*StringValue* = *object*.Name

Applies To	Application Object
	CheckBox Control
	ClassModule Object
	ComboBox Control
	CommandButton Control
	CommonDialog Control
	Component Object (Add-In)
	Data Control
	Database Object
	DBCombo Control
	DBGrid Control
	DBList Control
	DirListBox Control
	DriveListBox Control
	FileListBox Control
	Font Object
	Form Object

> Frame Control
> Grid Control
> HScrollBar, VScrollBar Controls
> Image Control
> Label Control
> Line Control
> ListBox Control
> MDIForm Object
> Menu Control
> OLE Container Control
> OptionButton Control
> PictureBox Control
> Property Object
> Shape Control
> TextBox Control
> Timer Control

A valid Name property must begin with a letter and contain numbers and the underline characters; no spaces or punctuation characters are allowed. Maximum string length is 40. Form names are global, so it cannot be named the same as another public object, such as Clipboard, Screen, or App. You should also try to avoid using a built-in keyword or property name for the name of your controls or objects.

At design time, you cannot have two Forms with the same name. But at runtime, you can create new instances of the same form, each of which will have the same name.

When you create a new control or object at design time, VB assigns a name that is the type of the object plus a unique integer, for example, Text1, Text2, and Text3. It might also set the Caption, Text, or LinkTopic of the control to the same value. You should change these values to meaningful names.

To create a control array, assign the same Name property to more than one control of the same type. VB will assign a unique Index property value to each control to distinguish them from each other. (You can manually change the Index properties to meet your needs.)

Negotiate Property

The Negotiate property is used by controls in an MDIForm object that can be aligned using their Align properties. If the MDIForm object's NegotiateToolbars property is set to True, then those controls with their Negotiate properties set to True are displayed along with the toolbars of an active OLE object. This property is not available at runtime.

Usage	*BooleanValue* = *object*.Negotiate
	object.Negotiate = *BooleanValue*
Applies To	Data Control
	DBGrid Control
	PictureBox Control

The values for the Negotiate property have the meanings given in the following table.

VALUE	MEANING
True	The control remains visible when an OLE object on the same form becomes active and displays its toolbars. The control and toolbars will negotiate for space within the MDIForm object.
False	The default. The control is hidden when an OLE object on the same form becomes active and displays its toolbars.

If the NegotiateToolbars property of the MDIForm object is False, then the toolbars of the active OLE object will not be displayed within the MDIForm. The Negotiate property of the control is ignored.

NegotiateMenus Property

The NegotiateMenus property specifies whether a form will merge menus from an active OLE object into its Menu Bar. This property is not available at runtime.

Usage   *BooleanValue* = *object*.NegotiateMenus
                    object.NegotiateMenus = *BooleanValue*

Applies To   Form Object, Forms Collection

The values of the NegotiateMenus property have the meanings given in the following table.

VALUE	MEANING
True	The default. When an OLE object on the form is activated for editing, the menus of the object are displayed on the Form's Menu Bar, subject to the settings of the NegotiatePosition property for the menu controls. The Form's Menu Bar must be defined but does not have to be visible.
False	The menus of the active OLE object are not displayed on the Form's Menu Bar.

If the Form's MDIChild property is set to True, the menus of the active object are displayed on the parent MDIForm's Menu Bar instead.

NegotiatePosition Property

The Negotiate Position property specifies whether and how the top-level Menu control defined for the form is displayed in the form's Menu Bar while an OLE object is active and displaying its menus. This property is not available at runtime. The NegotiateMenus property of the Form object must be set to True for NegotiatePosition to have any effect.

| *Usage* | *IntegerValue* = *object*.NegotiatePosition |
| | *object*.NegotiatePosition = *IntegerValue* |

| *Applies To* | Menu Control |

The values of the NegotiatePosition property have the meanings given in the following table.

VALUE	MEANING
0	The default. The Menu control is not displayed in the Menu Bar when the OLE object is active.
1	Left. The Menu control is displayed at the left end of the Menu Bar when the OLE object is active.
2	Middle. The Menu control is displayed in the middle of the Menu Bar when the OLE object is active.
3	Right. The Menu control is displayed at the right end of the Menu Bar when the OLE object is active.

The NegotiatePosition property allows you to specify on an individual basis which of a Form's menus will appear in the Menu Bar along with those of the active OLE object.

NegotiateToolbars Property

The NegotiateToolbars property specifies whether the Toolbars of the active OLE object on an MDI child form are displayed inside the MDIForm object. This property is not available at runtime.

| *Usage* | *BooleanValue* = *object*.NegotiateToolbars |
| | *object*.NegotiateToolbars = *BooleanValue* |

| *Applies To* | MDIForm Object |

The values for the NegotiateToolbars property have the meanings given in the following table.

VALUE	MEANING
True	The default. The MDIForm object displays the Toolbars of the active OLE object at the top or bottom of the MDIForm, where the position is specified by the object.
False	The Toolbars of the active OLE object are either displayed as separate floating Toolbar windows or not displayed at all, as specified by the object.

Setting NegotiateToolbars to True may give a more integrated feel between your application and the OLE server application used to edit the OLE object. If you do not have enough room inside the MDIForm, however, set the property to False to allow the Toolbars to be displayed as separate Toolbar windows.

NewIndex Property

The NewIndex property returns the index of the most recently added item in a ComboBox or ListBox control. This becomes useful for a sorted list if you need to add an ItemData value for each item you add to the list using AddItem.

Usage   *IntegerValue = object*.NewIndex

Applies To   ComboBox Control
                   ListBox Control

The NewIndex property returns –1 if the list is empty or an item was removed since an item was added.

Example   ```
List1.AddItem userName$
List1.ItemData(List1.NewIndex) = userID%
```

# NewPage Method

The NewPage method causes the Printer object to terminate the current page and start on a new page at the upper-left corner of the printable area.

*Usage*            *object*.NewPage

*Applies To*       Printer Object

NewPage causes the Page property to increment by 1. Calling EndDoc immediately after NewPage prevents the printing of a final blank page.

# Next Property

The Next property returns a reference to the next sibling of a Node object.

*Usage*            *object*.Next

*Applies To*       Node Object

The Help page points out that because the Child, FirstSibling, LastSibling, Previous, Parent, Next, and Root properties all reference Node objects other than the currently selected one, you can do stuff to them behind the scenes, like this:

*Example*          ```
With TreeView1.Nodes(x).Next
        .Text = "New text"
```

```
            .Key = "New key"
            .SelectedImage = 3
    End With
```

Nodes Property

The Nodes property references a collection of TreeView control Node objects.

Usage   *NodeValue = object*.Nodes

Applies To   TreeView Control

PARAMETER	VALUE	MEANING
NodeValue	Node	The node being referenced.

If you need to manipulate a specific Node object, use a key or index (for example, Tree-View1.Nodes(1)).

Normal Property

A *Normal* file is a file that has neither its Hidden nor its System attribute set. The Normal property specifies whether a Normal file is displayed in a FileListBox control. This property overrides the settings for the Archive and ReadOnly properties for Normal files. See also the Hidden, Normal, ReadOnly, and System properties.

Usage   *BooleanValue = object*.Normal
                   object.Normal = *BooleanValue*

Applies To   FileListBox Control

The values for the Normal property have the meanings for "Normal" files given in the following table.

VALUE	MEANING
True	The default. Displays *Normal* files—those files without Hidden or System attributes set—regardless of the settings for the Archive and ReadOnly properties.
False	Does not display files with *none* of its file attributes set. You must explicitly set the Archive or ReadOnly properties to True to display files with those attributes set.

For a file with either its Hidden or System attribute set, the Normal property has no effect on whether it is displayed in the FileListBox. See the sections on Hidden and System properties for files that have their Hidden or System attributes set.

Setting the Archive property at runtime will refresh the list of files.

To display all files, set the Normal, Hidden, and System properties to True.

NumberFormat Property

The NumberFormat property controls the format string for columns in a DBGrid control.

Usage *object*.NumberFormat = *StringValue*
StringValue = object.NumberFormat

Applies To Column Object

PARAMETER	VALUE	MEANING
StringValue	General number	The generic number format with no thousands separators.
	Currency	Shows two digits to the right of the decimal point (or other separator, depending on your locale setting) and uses thousands separators.
	Fixed	Shows at least one digit to the left (zero if necessary) and two to the right of the decimal separator.
	Standard	Same as Fixed, but uses thousands separators.
	Percent	Multiplies the value by 100 and shows the percent sign (%) after the number. This format always has two digits to the right of the decimal separator.
	Scientific	Standard scientific notation (exponents and so on).
	Yes/No	Translates 0 into the word No; everything else is Yes.
	True/False	Translates 0 into the word False; everything else is True.
	On/Off	Translates 0 into the word Off; everything else is On.

If these don't tickle your fancy, you can use the custom formatting. For example, VB is missing a constant to display a typical US-style phone number.

VALUE	BRIEF MEANING	LENGTHY MEANING
None	No formatting	Display the number with no formatting.
0	Digits placeholder	Display a digit or a zero according to the following rules. If the number has a digit where the 0 appears in the format string, show it; otherwise, show a zero. If the number has fewer digits than there are zeros (on either side of the decimal) in the format expression, show leading or trailing zeros. If the

VALUE	BRIEF MEANING	LENGTHY MEANING
0		number has more digits to the right of the decimal separator, round the number to as many decimal places as there are zeros. If the number has more digits to the left of the decimal separator, display them unchanged.
#	Digits placeholder	Display a digit or nothing. # works like 0, except leading and trailing zeros aren't displayed if the number has the same or fewer digits than there are # characters on either side of the decimal separator in the format expression.
. (or ,)	Decimal placeholder	If you're in a locale where , is the decimal separator, use that instead. This symbol determines how many digits to display to the left and right of the decimal separator.
%	Percent placeholder	Multiply the number by 100 and shows the % sign where it appears in the format string.
, (or .)	Thousands separator	If you're in a locale where . is the thousands separator, use that. This symbol works as expected. Place two side-by-side or immediately to the left of the decimal separator, and the number will be divided by 1,000 and scaled.
:	Time separator	Separates hours from minutes and seconds. You may be in a locale where another symbol is used.
/	Date separator	Like the time separator, but for day, month, and year.
E- E+ e- e+	Scientific format	Put at least one digits placeholder (either 0 or #) to the right of one of these symbols, and the number shows up in scientific format with an e or E between the number and exponent. The number of placeholders to the right determines the number of digits in the exponent. E- and e- place minus signs next to negative exponents; E+ and e+ use plus signs next to positive exponents and minus signs next to negative ones.
- + $ ( ) space	Display a literal character	These characters appear as typed. If you want another, "quote" it with either a backslash (\) or double quotes (" ").
\	Display the next character in the format string	The "quote" character protects the next character from interpretation and displays it literally, just like enclosing it in double-quotes (" "). Use two to display a backslash (\\). Many letters and symbols fall into this category. When in doubt, quote it.
"ABC"	Display the string inside the double quotation marks	Enclose all formatted text in double-quotes (use Chr(34) if a straight " doesn't work).

Generally you'll use NumberFormat when you create a new column, although it is possible to apply it to a column that already exists. In this case, make sure the underlying database structure will store the format you specify. For example, say you place the following code into your grid:

Example

```
Private Sub DBGrid1_AfterUpdate()
    DBGrid1.Columns(2).NumberFormat = "(###) ###-####"
End SubText
```

And assume that the underlying data format for that column in the database is just an integer. When you arrow off a new entry, the grid will automatically format it to adhere to the phone number format. But when you exit your application, that formatting is lost; the database can't store it. So when you reenter your application, you'll find that the phone number format doesn't appear.

Object Property (OLE Container Control)

This Object property allows you to access the object contained in an OLE Container control, its properties, and its methods.

Usage   *object*.Object[*.Property* | *.Method*]

Applies To   OLE Container Control

Use this property with a server application that supports OLE Automation. Using the object returned by the Object property, you can use the properties and methods of the object. You will need to consult the documentation of the server application for a list of valid properties and methods.

If your OLE Container control contains a drawing created by the Visio program, then to find the number of shapes in the container use

Example   `n = OLE1.Object.Shapes.Count`

Object Property

VB automatically supplies a standard set of properties and methods to all custom controls. When there is a naming conflict between a custom control's custom property or method and one of the standard ones, the standard ones take precedence. To access the custom version of the property or method, use the reference returned by this Object property of the custom control.

Usage   *object*.Object[*.Property* | *.Method*]

Applies To   CommonDialog Control
                 Custom Controls
                 DBCombo Control
                 DBGrid Control
                 DBList Control
                 Grid Control

The parts of this Object property syntax have the meanings given in the following table.

PARAMETER	VALUE	MEANING
Property	Property name	The property that you want to access for the control.
Method	Method name	The method that you want to access for the control.

The following properties may be automatically extended to custom controls:

Align	Cancel	Container
DataChanged	DataField	DataSource
Default	DragIcon	DragMode
Enabled	Height	HelpContextID
Index	Left	LinkMode
LinkItem	LinkTimeout	LinkTopic
Name	Negotiate	Parent
TabIndex	TabStop	Tag
Top	Visible	WhatsThisHelpID
Width		

The following methods may be automatically extended to custom controls:

Drag	LinkExecute	LinkPoke
LinkRequest	LinkSend	Move
SetFocus	ShowWhatsThis	ZOrder

ObjectAcceptFormats Property

The ObjectAcceptFormats property returns an array of names of formats that an object in an OLE Container control can accept. When data is sent to the object using the Data or DataText properties, it must be in one of these formats. Set the Format property to one of the strings in the ObjectAcceptFormats array. Use the ObjectAcceptFormatsCount property to get the number of items in the ObjectAcceptFormats array.

Usage   *StringValue* = *object*.ObjectAcceptFormats(*Number*)

Applies To   OLE Container Control

The parameters for the ObjectAcceptFormats property have the meanings given in the following table.

PARAMETER	VALUE	MEANING
Number	Integer from 0 through ObjectAcceptFormatsCount − 1	The index number specifying an element of the array of format strings.
	Other values	Error

If the OLE Container control does not contain an object, using ObjectAcceptFormats generates an error.

Example

```
For i = 0 To OLE1.ObjectAcceptFormatsCount - 1
    List1.AddItem OLE1.ObjectAcceptFormats(i)
Next i
```

ObjectAcceptFormatsCount Property

The ObjectAcceptFormatsCount property returns the number of formats that an object contained in an OLE Container control can accept. The actual format names can be retrieved from the array given by the ObjectAcceptFormats property.

Usage   *IntegerValue* = *object*.ObjectAcceptFormatsCount

Applies To   OLE Container Control

The ObjectAcceptFormats array is zero based, so valid index numbers range from 0 to (ObjectAcceptFormatsCount – 1).

ObjectGetFormats Property

The ObjectGetFormats property returns an array of names of formats that an object in an OLE Container control can provide. Data from the object obtained using the Data or DataText properties must be in one of these formats. Set the Format property to one of the strings in the ObjectGetFormats array. Use the ObjectGetFormatsCount property to get the number of items in the ObjectGetFormats array.

Usage   *StringValue* = *object*.ObjectGetFormats(*Number*)

Applies To   OLE Container Control

The parameters for the ObjectGetFormats property have the meanings given in the following table.

PARAMETER	VALUE	MEANING
Number	Integer from 0 through ObjectGetFormatsCount – 1	The index number specifying an element of the array of format strings.
	Other values	Error

If the OLE Container control does not contain an object, using ObjectGetFormats generates an error.

Example

```
For i = 0 To OLE1.ObjectGetFormatsCount - 1
    List1.AddItem OLE1.ObjectGetFormats(i)
Next i
```

ObjectGetFormatsCount Property

The ObjectGetFormatsCount property returns the number of formats that an object contained in an OLE Container control can provide. The actual format names can be retrieved from the array given by the ObjectGetFormats property.

Usage   *IntegerValue* = *object*.ObjectGetFormatsCount

Applies To   OLE Container Control

The ObjectGetFormats array is zero based, so valid index numbers range from 0 through (ObjectGetFormatsCount − 1).

ObjectVerbFlags Property

At runtime, right-clicking the mouse over an OLE object inside an OLE Container control pops up a menu listing all the verbs in the ObjectVerbs array of the OLE Container control. The ObjectVerbFlags property returns the menu state for each verb.

Usage   *IntegerValue* = *object*.ObjectVerbFlags(*Number*)

Applies To   OLE Container Control

PARAMETER	VALUE	MEANING
Number	Any numeric expression	The number specifies the array index of the ObjectVerbs array of the OLE Container control. The value must be between 0 and the value of the ObjectVerbsCount property. Using 0 returns the flags for the default verb, but this verb appears again in the ObjectVerbs array.
IntegerValue	vbOLEFlagEnabled or &H0000	The menu item is enabled.
	vbOLEFlagGrayed or &H0001	The menu item is dimmed and disabled.

PARAMETER	VALUE	MEANING
IntegerValue	vbOLEFlagDisabled or &H0002	The menu item is disabled, but not dimmed.
	vbOLEFlagChecked or &H0008	The menu item is checked.
	vbOLEFlagSeparator or &H0800	The menu item is a separator bar.

ObjectVerbs Property

The ObjectVerbs property returns an array of verbs (command names) supported by the object in an OLE Container control. The number of items in the array is given by the ObjectVerbsCount property. Use this property to create an Edit/Object menu for your application that lists all valid verbs for the object.

Usage   *StringValue* = *object*.ObjectVerbs(*Number*)

Applies To   OLE Container Control

The parameters for the ObjectVerbs property have the meanings given in the following table.

PARAMETER	VALUE	MEANING
Number	Integer from 0 through ObjectVerbsCount – 1	The index number specifying an element of the array of verb strings. The verb at index 0 is the default verb that typically activates the object.
	Other values	Error

Each verb specifies an action that an object is to perform when activated with the DoVerb method. If the AutoVerbMenu property is set to True and the user right-clicks the OLE Container control, the list of verbs may be displayed at runtime. ObjectVerbs (0) is the default verb and is not displayed in the menu. This same verb, however, may be repeated in the ObjectVerbs array so that it is displayed in the popup menu.

Every object supports a standard set of verbs, where the verb names are given by constants. See the table in the DoVerbs method.

To update the list of verbs, use the FetchVerbs method. Updating is especially important when building Edit/Object menus because the list of verbs may change depending on the state of the object.

Example
```
For i = 0 To OLE1.ObjectVerbsCount - 1
    List1.AddItem OLE1.ObjectVerbs(i)
Next i
```

ObjectVerbsCount Property

The ObjectVerbsCount property returns the number of verbs supported by an object contained in an OLE Container control. The actual verb names can be retrieved from the array given by the ObjectVerbs property.

Usage   *IntegerValue* = *object*.ObjectVerbsCount

Applies To   OLE Container Control

The ObjectVerbs array is zero based, so valid index numbers range from 0 through (ObjectVerbsCount – 1).

OLEDropAllowed Property

The OLEDropAllowed property specifies whether an OLE Container control be the target for an OLE drag-and-drop operation.

Usage   *BooleanValue* = *object*.OLEDropAllowed
                 object.OLEDropAllowed = *BooleanValue*

Applies To   OLE Container Control

The values for the OLEDropAllowed property have the meanings given in the following table.

VALUE	MEANING
True	The OLE Container control can be a drop target for an object that can be linked or embedded. The drop icon appears when the mouse pointer moves over the OLE Container control, provided the MousePointer property is set to vbDefault (0). The result of the drop is the same as that from using the Paste method. It also changes the Class, SourceDoc, and SourceItem properties. The OLE Container control does not receive DragDrop or DragOver events. The DragMode property is also ignored.
False	The default. The OLE Container control cannot be a drop target. No drop icon appears when the mouse pointer is moved over the control, and dropping the object has no effect on the control.

If the MousePointer property is not set to vbDefault (0), the mouse pointer will not automatically change to the drop icon when it is moved over the OLE Container control.

The OLETypeAllowed property must be set correctly to link or embed the dropped object.

OLERequestPendingMsgText Property

Once an OLE Automation request has been accepted by the OLE server, it cannot be canceled. All mouse and keyboard input to your application will be rejected by a busy dialog box that allows you to retry or switch to the server application. If you do not wish to give the user the option to retry or switch, use the OLERequestPendingMsgText property to provide an alternative message. When you use this property, the dialog box will contain only the message and an OK button. This property is available *only* at runtime.

Usage   *StringValue* = *object*.OLERequestPendingMsgText
                object.OLERequestPendingMsgText = *StringValue*

Applies To   App Object

PARAMETER	VALUE	MEANING
StringValue	Nonempty string	Displays this string, along with an OK button in place of the default busy dialog box.
	Empty string	Causes the default busy message and dialog box with the Switch To and Retry buttons to be displayed.

If you are using an OLE server that is hidden or runs on a remote machine (Remote Automation) and your OLE Automation request may take a long time, then you should set an appropriate message using the OLERequestPendingMsgText property, since Switch To doesn't make sense in these situations. In fact, we recommend that if you use Remote Automation, you *always* use this property, since network traffic may delay the response from the server.

Example
```
Sub TestOLE()
    Dim oTest As Object
    Set oTest = CreateObject("ServerTest.ServTest")

    App.OleRequestPendingMsgTitle = "Testing Server"
    App.OleRequestPendingMsgText = "What do you want? I'm BUSY!"
    r = oTest.Calc("This is a Test")
    MsgBox r & ""
End Sub
```

Assuming the Calc method takes a long time to complete and you click the form, you'll get a very rude message.

OLERequestPendingMsgTitle Property

Once an OLE Automation request has been accepted by the OLE server, it cannot be canceled. All mouse and keyboard input to your application will be rejected by a busy dialog box that allows you to retry or switch to the server application. If you use the OLERequestPendingMsgText property to provide an alternative message box, you can use the OLERequestPendingMsgTitle to provide a replacement title for that message box. This property is ignored if the OLERequestPendingMsgText property is an empty string. This property is available *only* at runtime.

Usage   *StringValue* = *object*.OLERequestPendingMsgTitle
                 object.OLERequestPendingMsgTitle = *StringValue*

Applies To   App Object

PARAMETER	VALUE	MEANING
StringValue	Nonempty string	This string will be displayed in the title bar of the replacement dialog box.
	Empty string	The title of the replacement dialog box will be the value of the App.Title property.

OLERequestPendingTimeout Property

The OLERequestPendingTimeout property specifies the time in milliseconds that must elapse before a busy message can be triggered by mouse or keyboard input while an OLE Automation request is in progress. This property is available *only* at runtime. The default value is 5,000 milliseconds (5 seconds).

Usage   *LongValue* = *object*.OLERequestPendingTimeout
                 object.OLERequestPendingTimeout = *LongValue*

Applies To   App Object

It is a good idea to set this property immediately before an OLE Automation request—or set of requests—and then to reset it after the request(s) has completed.

OLEServerBusyMsgText Property

If the OLE server is busy when your application makes an OLE Automation request, a busy message box will be displayed that allows the user to retry or switch to the server application. If you do not wish to give the user the option to switch, use the OLEServerBusyMsgText property to provide an alternative message. When you use this property, the dialog box will contain only the message, a Retry button, and a Cancel button. This property is available *only* at runtime.

Usage   *StringValue* = *object*.OLEServerBusyMsgText
                 object.OLEServerBusyMsgText = *StringValue*

Applies To   App Object

Parameter	Value	Meaning
StringValue	Nonempty string	Displays this string, along with the Retry and Cancel buttons in place of the default busy dialog box.
	Empty string	Causes the default busy message and dialog box with the Switch To and Retry buttons to be displayed.

If you click the Retry button, your OLE Automation request will be attempted immediately and the busy dialog may be displayed once again. If instead you click the Cancel button, you will get the error "Runtime error: –2147418111 (80010001), OLE Automation error."

If you are using an OLE server that is hidden or runs on a remote machine (Remote Automation) and your OLE Automation server may be busy, then you should set an appropriate message using the OLEServerBusyMsgText property, since Switch To doesn't make sense in these situations. In fact, we recommend that if you use Remote Automation, you *always* use this property, since network traffic may delay the response from the server.

Example
```
Sub TestOLE()
    Dim oTest As Object
    Set oTest = CreateObject("ServerTest.ServTest")

    App.OLEServerBusyMsgTitle = "Testing Server"
    App.OLEServerBusyMsgText = "Wait a sec! I'm BUSY!"
    r = oTest.Calc("This is a Test")
    MsgBox r & ""
End Sub
```

Assuming the *ServerTest.ServTest* OLE server is busy, you'll get a very rude message.

OLEServerBusyMsgTitle Property

If the OLE server is busy when your application makes an OLE Automation request, a busy message box will be displayed that allows the user to retry or switch to the server application. If you use the OLEServerBusyMsgText property to provide an alternative message box, you can use the OLEServerBusyMsgTitle to provide a replacement title for that message box. This property is ignored if the OLEServerBusyMsgText property is an empty string. This property is available *only* at runtime.

| *Usage* | *StringValue* = *object*.OLEServerBusyMsgTitle |
| | *object*.OLEServerBusyMsgTitle = *StringValue* |

Applies To   App Object

PARAMETER	VALUE	MEANING
StringValue	Nonempty string	This string will be displayed in the title bar of the replacement dialog box.
	Empty string	The title of the replacement dialog box will be the value of the App.Title property.

OLEServerBusyRaiseError Property

The OLEServerBusyRaiseError property determines whether an error is generated instead of a busy dialog box when an OLE Automation server fails to respond to a request within the time specified by the value of the OLEServerBusyTimeout property. Setting this property to True allows you to provide a custom error handler.

| *Usage* | *BooleanValue* = *object*.OLEServerBusyRaiseError |
| | *object*.OLEServerBusyRaiseError = *BooleanValue* |

Applies To   App Object

PARAMETER	VALUE	MEANING
BooleanValue	False	The default. This allows either the default busy dialog box or the message provided by the OLEServerBusyMsgText property to be displayed.
	True	This causes error number &H80010001& (−2147418111) to be raised when the OLE Automation server is busy.

OLEServerBusyTimeout Property

The OLEServerBusyTimeout property specifies the time in milliseconds that must elapse before a busy message or error can be triggered while waiting for an OLE Automation server to respond to a request. This property is available *only* at runtime. The default value is 10,000 milliseconds (10 seconds).

Usage   *LongValue = object*.OLEServerBusyTimeout
                   object.OLEServerBusyTimeout = *LongValue*

Applies To   App Object

It is a good idea to set this property immediately before an OLE Automation request—or set of requests—and then to reset it after the request(s) has completed.

OLEType Property

The OLEType property returns the status of the OLE object in a OLE Container control.

Usage   *IntegerValue = object*.OLEType

Applies To   OLE Container Control

The OLEType property can return one of the values given in the following table.

CONSTANT	VALUE	MEANING
vbOLELinked	0	The OLE Container control contains a linked object. VB does not manage the object's data; it manages only link information such as SourceDoc and SourceItem. Links are useful when the object may be shared by many applications. Changes to the source are reflected by the linked Container controls. One drawback of this mode is that you cannot use in-place activation to edit your OLE object.
vbOLEEmbedded	1	The OLE Container control contains an embedded object. VB manages all the object's data. Embedded objects are useful when the object is needed only by VB, but you need to use the capabilities provided by the server application.
vbOLENone	3	The OLE Container control doesn't contain an object.

OLETypeAllowed Property

The OLETypeAllowed property determines the type of OLE object an OLE Container control can contain.

Usage   *IntegerValue = object*.OLETypeAllowed
                   object.OLETypeAllowed = *IntegerValue*

Applies To   OLE Container Control

CONSTANT	VALUE	MEANING
vbOLELinked	0	The OLE Container control can contain only linked objects.
vbOLEEmbedded	1	The OLE Container control can contain only embedded objects.
vbOLEEither	2	The OLE Container control can contain either a linked or an embedded object.

Changing this setting from the default value of vbOLEEither prevents the Link check box from being displayed in the Insert Object dialog box that is displayed when you create or link an object to the OLE Container control at design time.

Options Property

The Options property specifies characteristics of the Recordset object referenced by a Data control's Recordset property.

Usage   *IntegerValue = object.*Options
            *object.*Options *= IntegerValue*

Applies To   Data Control

The Options property may be set to more than one of the values given in the following table by using the Or operator.

CONSTANT	VALUE	MEANING
dbDenyWrite	1	Other users or applications that have opened the same database cannot make changes to records in the recordset.
dbDenyRead	2	For Table-type Recordset objects. Other users or applications cannot read the records.
dbReadOnly	4	You cannot modify the records in the recordset.
dbAppendOnly	8	You can add new records to the recordset but cannot access existing records.
dbInconsistent	16	Updates are applied even to fields of a record that violate the join condition. If dbConsistent is also set, this value is ignored.
dbConsistent	32	The default. Updates apply only to those fields that do not violate the join condition. If dbInconsistent is also set, dbConsistent is used.
dbSQLPassThrough	64	Passes the SQL statement in the RecordSource property to the ODBC database (SQL server or Oracle database) for processing.

CONSTANT	VALUE	MEANING
dbSQLPassThrough	64 (*cont.*)	This applies only to dynaset-type and snapshot-type Recordset objects. But for better performance, you might want to use a SQL PassThrough QueryDef object instead by setting the Recordset property to a Recordset object created from this QueryDef.
dbForwardOnly	256	Does not apply for a Data control, since it can move both forward and backward.
dbSeeChanges	512	Generates a trapable error if another user or application changes data that you are editing.

You must use the Refresh method to apply runtime changes to the Options property.

Orientation Property (Printer Object)

This Orientation property specifies whether the printer prints in portrait or landscape mode. This property is available only at runtime.

Usage   *IntegerValue* = *object*.Orientation
                    object.Orientation = *IntegerValue*

Applies To   Printer Object

The possible values of this property are given in the following table.

CONSTANT	VALUE	MEANING
vbPRORPortrait	1	Portrait mode. The top of the page is the narrow end of the paper.
vbPRORLandscape	2	Landscape mode. The top of the page is the long end of the paper.

Note: You can change the printer property only for the default printer. Set it by using the Set Printer = command.

Note: Not all printers support this property or all possible values of this property. You might get an error for your printer.

Orientation Property (Slider Control)

This Orientation property specifies the orientation of a Slider control.

Usage   *IntegerValue = object*.Orientation
                     object.Orientation = *IntegerValue*

Applies To   Slider Control

CONSTANT	VALUE	MEANING
sldHorizontal	0	The default. Horizontal. Tick marks appear at the top or bottom of the slider.
sldVertical	1	Vertical. Tick marks appear at the left or right of the slider.

Overlay Method

The Overlay method overlays one image in a ListImages collection over another.

Usage   *object*.Overlay (*Index1*, *Index2*)

Applies To   ImageList Control

PARAMETER	VALUE	MEANING
Index1	An integer	The index of the image that will be on top.
Index2	An integer	The index of the image that will be on the bottom.

You'll probably have to use the MaskColor property in order to get the overlay to work right. Otherwise the image on top likely will completely obliterate the one on the bottom.

Note: You aren't limited to using numeric indexes. You also can use a key value (e.g., First, Second, and so on). Just remember to put it between quotes.

Page Property

The Page property returns the current page number for the current document being printed. The Page property is reset to 1 after the EndDoc method is executed.

Usage   *IntegerValue = object*.Page

Applies To   Printer Object

The Page property is automatically incremented by 1 if

• the NewPage method is called and

• the Print method causes text to be pushed onto a new page.

The following example displays the current page number being printed in a PictureBox used as a status bar:

Example
```
picStatus.Cls
picStatus.Print "Printing Page " & Printer.Page & "..."
```

Note: Graphics methods do not cause new pages. Graphics that do not fit on the page are clipped to the printable area of the page.

PaintPicture Method

The PaintPicture method transfers the graphic from a source picture (created from .BMP, .WMF, .EMF, .ICO, or .DIB) to a destination Form, PictureBox, or Printer. You can scale the image, limit the transfer to only a portion of the source picture, or even use a raster-op operation to combine the graphic with the existing graphics of the destination. The resulting graphic does *not* become a permanent attribute of the destination object or control. In particular, the graphic will not be automatically redrawn if it is covered and then uncovered by another window.

Usage
[*object.*]PaintPicture *Picture, X1, Y1*[, *Width1*][, *Height1*][, *X2, Y2*][, *Width2*][, *Height2*][, *Opcode*]

Applies To
Form Object
PictureBox Control
Printer Object

The arguments for the PaintPicture method are described in the following table.

PARAMETER	VALUE	MEANING
Picture	Picture object	The source of the graphic to be drawn onto the specified *object*. It could be the Picture property of a Form or PictureBox or the result of a LoadPicture call.
X1, Y1	Single-precision values	The coordinates for the top-left corner of the destination of the graphic. The coordinates are specified relative to the top-left corner of *object,* and the unit of measure is specified by the ScaleMode property of *object.*
Width1	Omitted	The destination width is the width of the source picture.

PARAMETER	VALUE	MEANING
Width1	Single-precision value	Indicates the destination width of the source picture. The ScaleMode property of *object* specifies the unit of measure. The picture is stretched or compressed to fit the destination width. Use a negative value to flip it horizontally.
Height1	Omitted	The destination height is the height of the source picture.
	Single-precision value	Indicates the destination height of the source picture. The ScaleMode property of *object* specifies the unit of measure. The picture is stretched or compressed to fit the destination height. Use a negative value to flip it vertically.
X2, Y2	Single-precision values	Limits the transfer region of the source picture to a rectangular area whose top-left corner is specified by (X2, Y2). The coordinates uses the unit of measure specified by the ScaleMode property of *object*.
	Omitted	0 is used for a missing coordinate.
Width2	Single-precision value	Specifies the width of the source region to transfer to the destination. The unit of measure is specified by the ScaleMode property of *object*.
	Omitted	The full width of the source picture, minus the X2 value, is used for Width2.
Height2	Single-precision value	Specifies the height of the source region to transfer to the destination. The unit of measure is specified by the ScaleMode property of *object*.
	Omitted	The full height of the source picture, minus the Y2 value, is used for Height2.
Opcode	Omitted	Same as vbSrcCopy.
	&H00000042	(Blackness) Ignores the source picture and fills the destination rectangle using the color associated with index 0 in the physical palette (usually black).
	vbDstInvert or &H00550009	Ignores the source bitmap and just inverts the color values (using the Not operator) of the destination bitmap.
	vbMergeCopy or &H00C000CA	Combines the destination and source bitmaps using the And operator.
	vbMergePaint or &H00BB0226	Inverts the source bitmap, and then combines the result with the destination bitmap by using the Or operator.
	vbNotSrcCopy or &H00330008	Copies the inverted source bitmap to the destination.
	vbNotSrcErase or &H001100A6	Combines the destination and source bitmaps by using the Or operator and then inverts the result.

PARAMETER	VALUE	MEANING
Opcode	vbPatCopy or 0x00F00021L	Copies the pattern specified by FillColor and FillStyle of *object* to the destination bitmap.
	vbPatInvert or 0x005A0049L	Combines the destination bitmap with the pattern by using the Xor operator.
	vbPatPaint or 0x00FB0A09L	Combines the inverted source bitmap with the pattern by using the Or operator. Combines the result with the destination bitmap by using the Or operator.
	vbSrcAnd or 0x008800C6	Combines the destination and source bitmaps by using the And operator.
	vbSrcCopy or 0x00CC0020	Copies the source bitmap to the destination.
	vbSrcErase or 0x00440328	Inverts the destination bitmap and then combines the result with the source bitmap by using the And operator.
	vbSrcInvert or 0x00660046	Combines the destination and source bitmaps by using the Xor operator.
	vbSrcPaint or 0x00EE0086	Combines the destination and source bitmaps by using the Or operator.
	&H00FF0062	(Whiteness) Ignores the source picture and fills the destination rectangle using the color associated with index 1 in the physical palette (usually white).

The source picture width is scaled by (Width1/Width2), and the height is scaled by (Height1/Height2). You can omit any parameter by leaving a space between commas, but the command line cannot end in a comma.

Example
```
Dim p As Picture
Set p = LoadPicture("my.bmp")
Picture1.PaintPicture p, 100, 100, , , 50, 50, , , vbSrcCopy
```

This example copies the source bitmap—starting at the coordinate (50, 50)—to the destination, starting at (100, 100). The widths and heights are omitted, so we get all of the source image starting at (50, 50). No scaling occurs.

Example
```
Dim p As Picture
Set p = LoadPicture("my.bmp")
w = Picture1.ScaleX(p.Width, 8) * 2      'Convert to Picture1 units
h = Picture1.ScaleY(p.Height, 8) * 2
Picture1.PaintPicture p, 100, 100, w, h, 0, 0, , , vbSrcCopy
```

Picture object width and height are specified in HiMetric units. We use the ScaleX and ScaleY methods of the Picture1 object to convert to the ScaleMode units used by Picture1. Then we double the size of the source picture before displaying it.

Panels Property

The Panels property returns a reference to a collection of Panel objects in a StatusBar control.

Usage   *ObjectValue* = *object*.Panels

Applies To   StatusBar Control

PARAMETER	VALUE	MEANING
ObjectValue	A Panel collection	The panel object(s) you're referencing.

PaperBin Property

The PaperBin property specifies the paper bin on the printer to use for printing. This property is available only at runtime.

Usage   *IntegerValue* = *object*.PaperBin
                 object.PaperBin = *IntegerValue*

Applies To   Printer Object

The possible values of the PaperBin property are given in the following table.

CONSTANT	VALUE	MEANING
vbPRBNUpper	1	Upper bin.
vbPRBNLower	2	Lower bin.
vbPRBNMiddle	3	Middle bin.
vbPRBNManual	4	Manual feed. Waits for the paper from the manual-feed tray.
vbPRBNEnvelope	5	Envelope feeder.
vbPRBNEnvManual	6	Manually feeds the envelope.
vbPRBNAuto	7	Uses paper from the current default bin for the printer.
vbPRBNTractor	8	Tractor feeder.
vbPRBNSmallFmt	9	Small-format paper bin.
vbPRBNLargeFmt	10	Large-format paper bin.
vbPRBNLargeCapacity	11	Large capacity bin.
vbPRBNCassette	14	Cassette cartridge.

Note: You can change the printer property only for the default printer. Set it by using the Set Printer = command.

Note: Not all printers support this property or all possible values of this property. You might get an error for your printer.

PaperSize Property

The PaperSize property specifies the paper size to use for printing. This property is available only at runtime.

Usage   *IntegerValue = object*.PaperSize
                object.PaperSize = *IntegerValue*

Applies To   Printer Object

The possible values of the PaperSize property are given in the following table. If you manually set the Width and Height properties of the printer, the PaperSize property is set to vbPRPS-User.

CONSTANT	VALUE	MEANING
vbPRPSLetter	1	Letter (8½ × 11 in.)
vbPRPSLetterSmall	2	Letter-Small (8½ × 11 in.)
vbPRPSTabloid	3	Tabloid (11 × 17 in.)
vbPRPSLedger	4	Ledger (17 × 11 in.)
vbPRPSLegal	5	Legal (8½ × 14 in.)
vbPRPSStatement	6	Statement (5½ × 8½ in.)
vbPRPSExecutive	7	Executive (7½ × 10½ in.)
vbPRPSA3	8	A3 (297 × 420 mm)
vbPRPSA4	9	A4 (210 × 297 mm)
vbPRPSA4Small	10	A4 Small (210 × 297 mm)
vbPRPSA5	11	A5 (148 × 210 mm)
vbPRPSB4	12	B4 (250 × 354 mm)
vbPRPSB5	13	B5 (182 × 257 mm)
vbPRPSFolio	14	Folio (8½ × 13 in.)
vbPRPSQuarto	15	Quarto (215 × 275 mm)
vbPRPS10x14	16	10 × 14 in.
vbPRPS11x17	17	11 × 17 in.

Constant	Value	Meaning
vbPRPSNote	18	Note (8½ × 11 in.)
vbPRPSEnv9	19	Envelope #9 (3⅞ × 8⅞ in.)
vbPRPSEnv10	20	Envelope #10 (4⅛ × 9½ in.)
vbPRPSEnv11	21	Envelope #11 (4½ × 10⅜ in.)
vbPRPSEnv12	22	Envelope #12 (4½ × 11 in.)
vbPRPSEnv14	23	Envelope #14 (5 × 11½ in.)
vbPRPSCSheet	24	C-size sheet
vbPRPSDSheet	25	D-size sheet
vbPRPSESheet	26	E-size sheet
vbPRPSEnvDL	27	Envelope DL (110 × 220 mm)
vbPRPSEnvC5	28	Envelope C5 (162 × 229 mm)
vbPRPSEnvC3	29	Envelope C3 (324 × 458 mm)
vbPRPSEnvC4	30	Envelope C4 (229 × 324 mm)
vbPRPSEnvC6	31	Envelope C6 (114 × 162 mm)
vbPRPSEnvC65	32	Envelope C65 (114 × 229 mm)
vbPRPSEnvB4	33	Envelope B4 (250 × 353 mm)
vbPRPSEnvB5	34	Envelope B5 (176 × 250 mm)
vbPRPSEnvB6	35	Envelope B6 (176 × 125 mm)
vbPRPSEnvItaly	36	Envelope (110 × 230 mm)
vbPRPSEnvMonarch	37	Envelope-Monarch (3⅞ × 7½ in.)
vbPRPSEnvPersonal	38	Envelope (3⅝ × 6½ in.)
vbPRPSFanfoldUS	39	U.S. Standard Fanfold (14⅞ × 11 in.)
vbPRPSFanfoldStdGerman	40	German Standard Fanfold (8½ × 12 in.)
vbPRPSFanfoldLglGerman	41	German Legal Fanfold (8½ × 13 in.)
vbPRPSUser	256	User-defined

Note: You can change the printer property only for the default printer. Set it by using the Set Printer = command.

Note: Not all printers support this property or all possible values of this property. You might get an error for your printer.

Parent Property

A parent-child relationship can exist between a form, object, or collection and controls or other objects and collections. The Parent property returns the parent of the specified object.

Usage   *objectValue = object*.Parent

Applies To   Application Object
                      CheckBox Control
                      ComboBox Control
                      CommandButton Control
                      CommonDialog Control
                      Component Object
                      ControlTemplate Object, ControlTemplates Collection
                      Data Control
                      DBCombo Control
                      DBList Control
                      DirListBox Control
                      DriveListBox Control
                      FileControl Object
                      FileListBox Control
                      FormTemplate Object
                      Frame Control
                      Grid Control
                      HScrollBar, VScrollBar Controls
                      Image Control
                      Label Control
                      Line Control
                      ListBox Control
                      Menu Control
                      MenuItems Collection
                      MenuLine Object
                      OLE Container Control
                      OptionButton Control
                      PictureBox Control
                      ProjectTemplate Object
                      Property Object, Properties Collection
                      SelectedComponents Collection
                      SelectedControlTemplates Collection
                      Shape Control
                      TextBox Control
                      Timer Control

Use the Parent property to access the properties, methods, or controls of an object's parent. Being able to do this is useful if you pass controls or objects as arguments to functions or subroutines.

Interestingly, a Container and Parent are not the same thing. For instance, if in Form1, Frame1 contains an Option1 OptionButton, Option1's Container is Frame1, but Option1's Parent is Form1! The following sets the mouse pointer for a control and its parent:

Example

```
Sub ProcessControl(source As Control)
     source.MousePointer = vbHourglass
     source.Parent.MousePointer = vbHourglass
End Sub
```

 An MDI child form has a parent-child relationship with its container MDIForm, but Forms have no Parent property!

Parent Property (Node Object)

The Parent property returns or sets the parent object of a Node object and is available only at run-time.

Usage

object.Parent = *NodeValue*
NodeValue = *object*.Parent

Applies To   Node Object

PARAMETER	VALUE	MEANING
NodeValue	A Node object	The parent of the current Node.

Note that you can't set a Node to be a child of its own descendants.

The Help page points out that because the Child, FirstSibling, LastSibling, Previous, Parent, Next, and Root properties all reference Node objects other than the currently selected one, you can do stuff to them behind the scenes, like this:

Example

```
With TreeView1.Nodes (x) .Parent
     .Text = "New text"
     .Key = "New key"
     .SelectedImage = 3
End With
```

PasswordChar Property

The PasswordChar property specifies the character that is displayed for each character of the Text property but does not change the Text property. This property allows you to use the TextBox control for a password-entry box. The MultiLine property of the TextBox must be False.

Usage   *StringValue* = *object*.PasswordChar
                 object.PasswordChar = *StringValue*

Applies To   TextBox Control

The values of the PasswordChar property have the meanings given in the following table.

VALUE	MEANING
Empty string (" ")	The default. No replacement. The Text property is displayed as is.
Any string	Only the first character is used as the display character for all characters of the Text property. By convention, password-entry boxes use the asterisk (*) character (Chr(42)). The Text property is never affected and always contains the characters typed by the user or set from code.

Changing the PasswordChar property at runtime affects existing text immediately.

Paste Method

The Paste method pastes the data from the system Clipboard into an OLE Container control. Use this method to support an Edit/Paste menu command for your application. With it, the user does not get to select whether the object will be embedded or linked. Set the OLETypeAllowed property before calling the Paste method to select the type to paste, and check the PasteOK property to make sure there is valid data on the Clipboard.

Usage   *object*.Paste

Applies To   OLE Container Control

Once the Paste method is run, you can use the OLEType property to check the type of object created. If the Paste method was not successful, OLEType will be set to vbOLENone (3) and the object that was in the OLE Container control will be deleted.

Example
```
Private Sub mnuEditPaste_Click()
      If OLE1.PasteOK Then
            OLE1.OLETypeAllowed = vbOLELinked 'Create a linked object
            OLE1.Paste
      End If
End Sub
```

PasteOK Property

Use the PasteOK property to determine whether the contents of the system Clipboard may be pasted into the OLE Container control. This property is read-only at runtime.

Usage   *BooleanValue = object*.PasteOK

Applies To   OLE Container Control

Before attempting to paste from the system Clipboard with the Paste method, check the PasteOK property to make sure it's True. The OLETypeAllowed property specifies whether the pasted object is embedded or linked. The OLEType property may be checked after pasting to determine the type of object that was created.

You can also use the PasteSpecialDlg to display the Paste Special dialog box with which the user can specify the type of object to paste.

Example
```
Private Sub mnuEditPaste_Click()
    If OLE1.PasteOK Then
        OLE1.OLETypeAllowed = vbOLEEither
        OLE1.PasteSpecialDlg
    End If
End Sub
```

PasteSpecialDlg Method

The PasteSpecialDlg method displays the Paste Special dialog box so that the user can select whether to paste an object from the system Clipboard into an OLE Container control as embedded or linked.

Usage   *object*.PasteSpecialDlg

Applies To   OLE Container Control

You can set the OLETypeAllowed property before invoking the PasteSpecialDlg method to limit the type of paste the user can select. You should also check the PasteOK property first to make sure the contents of the Clipboard can be pasted. If the paste fails, the original contents of the OLE Container control will be deleted and the OLEType will be set to vbOLENone (3).

Path Property

The Path property specifies the directory or current directory of the object. This property is available only at runtime and is read-only for the App object.

Usage   *StringValue* = *object*.Path
           object.Path = *StringValue*

Applies To   App Object
           DirListBox Object
           FileListBox Control

The property value is a string that represents the directory (or path) of the object without the trailing backslash. If the string is empty (" "), then the Path property is not changed. For the App object, Path specifies the directory of the project file (.VBP) when the application is running from the VB development environment or the directory of the executable file (.EXE) when the application is running as a standalone.

For a DirListBox or FileListBox control, the default value of the Path property is the current path when the control is created at runtime. However, setting the property changes the contents of the DirListBox and FileListBox controls to reflect the contents of the new path. Relative path names are allowed, and specifying only a drive letter with a colon (:) selects the current directory on that drive. The Path property can also be set to a network path name without a drive specification:

```
\\ServerName\ShareName\Path
```

A change to the Path property generates the Change event for a DirListBox control or the PathChange event for a FileListBox control. Use the Path property, rather than List(ListIndex) to retrieve full path names from a DirListBox control.

If you decide to manage your own DriveListBox, DirListBox, and FileListBox controls rather than using the CommonDialog control, you'll need to use the Path property to link up the controls so that they behave as expected. The following example shows some of this interaction:

Example
```
Private Sub DriveDropDown_Change()
    On Error Resume Next' Delay error handling
    ' If new drive was chosen, this causes the Dirs box
    ' to update itself.
    DirsBox.Path = DriveDropDown.Drive
    If Err Then          ' If an error occurred, tell user what
        MsgBox (Error$) ' it was, then reset Drive1.Drive.
        ' DirsBox.Path was not changed, therefore it
        ' still has old drive spec.
        DriveDropDown.Drive = DirsBox.Path
    End If
End Sub

Private Sub DirsBox_Change()
    FileListBox.Path = DirsBox.Path
End Sub

Private Sub FileListBox_PathChange()
    ' Change DirsBox.Path and DriveDropDown.Drive to reflect
    ' the new path.
    DirsBox.Path = FileListBox.Path
    DriveDropDown.Drive = FileListBox.Path
End Sub
```

PathSeparator Property

The PathSeparator property controls the delimiter string used for the path returned by the Full-Path property.

Usage   *object*.PathSeparator = *StringValue*
                 StringValue = *object*.PathSeparator

Applies To   TreeView Control

PARAMETER	VALUE	MEANING
StringValue	A string	The string you'll see between Nodes. By default, it's a period.

Pattern Property

The Pattern property specifies a filename pattern to use to limit the files displayed in a FileList-Box control. Changing the Pattern property triggers the PatternChange event.

Use the Pattern property to help your users locate the type of files needed by your application.

Usage   *StringValue* = *object*.Pattern
                 object.Pattern = *StringValue*

Applies To   FileListBox Control

This property is case insensitive. It uses the * and ? characters as wildcards for a pattern. The * matches any number of any characters, and the ? matches any one character. The default pattern is *.* for finding all files. You can use semicolons (;) to provide multiple patterns. If the string is empty (" "), then the Pattern property is not changed.

Example   `File1.Pattern = "*.exe;*.com;*.bat"'Find all executable files`

If the FileName property of the FileListBox control is set and it contains a pattern, then the Pattern property will be updated automatically to match, thereby triggering the PatternChange event.

 You cannot set the pattern to * to find all files. The wildcard characters do not match the dot (.) character, but only the first one! For instance, if you have a file named "a.b.c.d," then the pattern *.* will find it but will not find * or *.*.*. Surprisingly, *.b *will* match, but *.b.c.d will *not!* That's because VB is still using the DOS file system rather than the new long filenames of Win95. Windows NT systems may behave differently.

The file-pattern matching of DOS is pretty weak. The * wildcard can be used only twice in a pattern, once before the dot and once after. For the * before the dot, all characters between it and the dot character are ignored; for the * after the dot, all characters after the * are ignored. So you can't use *95.* to try to find all filenames that have 95 right before the dot.

Picture Property

The Picture property specifies the graphics to display in an object. For the OLE Container control, the Picture property is not available at design time and is read-only at runtime.

Usage   *PictureValue* = *object*.Picture
                   object.Picture = *PictureValue*

Applies To   Form Object
                   Image Control
                   MDIForm Object
                   OLE Container Control
                   PictureBox Control

By default, the Picture property is empty, representing no picture. You can set and use the Picture property in the following ways:

- At design time, use the browser to assign Picture to a bitmap (.BMP), icon (.ICO), or metafile (.WMF) graphics file. The graphics becomes permanent and will be saved with the project, built into the executable generated by the Make EXE file... command.

- At design time, paste a graphic from the Clipboard or copy or cut a graphic to the Clipboard.

- At runtime, use the LoadPicture function to load a bitmap, icon, or metafile graphics file.

- At runtime, use the Clipboard methods GetData and SetData with the vbCFBitmap, vbCFMetafile, or vbCFDIB formats to retrieve or copy graphics from or to the Clipboard.

- At runtime, set the Picture property to any other object's DragIcon, Icon, Image, or Picture property.

Use the SavePicture statement to save a graphic from an object into a file at runtime. The following example uses the Form's Click event to cycle through a list of 10 bitmaps stored in a resource file:

Example
```
Private Sub Form1_Click()
    Static index
    index = (index Mod 10) + 1
    Picture1.Picture = LoadResPicture(index, vbResBitmap)
End Sub
```

Point Method

The Point method returns the red-green-blue (RGB) color of the specified point on an object. The return value may be used either to set color properties or as color arguments to graphics methods.

Usage $LongValue = object.Point(X, Y)$

Applies To   Form Object
                    PictureBox Control

The arguments of the Point method have the meanings given in the following table.

PARAMETER	VALUE	MEANING
(X, Y)	Single-precision values	The coordinates of the point to analyze for color. The Scale properties of the object specify the units of measure. If the point lies outside the object, Point returns –1.

The following example creates a random color palette in Picture1. Then when you click a color on the palette, that color will be used to draw a circle on the form.

Example
```
Private Sub Form_Load()
    Picture1.AutoRedraw = True
    Picture1.Scale (0, 0)-(5, 5)
    For i = 1 To 5
        For j = 1 To 5
            c = RGB(Rnd * 255, Rnd * 255, Rnd * 255)
            Picture1.Line (i - 1, j - 1)-(i, j), c, BF
        Next j
    Next i
    Picture1.AutoRedraw = False
End Sub

Private Sub Picture1_MouseDown(Button As Integer, _
    Shift As Integer, x As Single, y As Single)
    If Button = vbLeftButton Then
        FillStyle = vbSolid
        FillColor = Picture1.Point(x, y)
        Circle (ScaleWidth / 2, ScaleHeight / 2), _
            ScaleWidth / 2
    End If
End Sub
```

PopupMenu Method

The PopupMenu method displays a popup menu (or immediate menu) at the current mouse location or at the optional specified location. This method works *only* for the 32-bit version of VB running on Windows 95 systems. It is usually implemented for right-mouse-button clicks on a Form or MDIForm

Usage   [*object.*]PopupMenu *MenuName*[, *Flags*][, *X*][, *Y*][, *BoldCommand*]

Applies To   Form Object
                   MDIFormObject

PARAMETER	VALUE	MEANING
MenuName	Control name	The name of the menu to be displayed. The menu must have at least one submenu. If you're using a Menu control array, include the array index of the control.
Flags	vbPopupMenuLeftAlign or 0 or omitted	The left side of the menu is located at the current mouse location or at *X*, if specified.
	vbPopupMenuCenterAlign or 4	The menu is centered on the current mouse location or at *X*, if specified.
	vbPopupMenuRightAlign or 8	The right side of the menu is located at the current mouse location or at *X*, if specified.
	vbPopupMenuLeftButton or 0	The default. Forces a left-click on a Menu control to activate it.
	vbPopupMenuRightButton or 2	Add this value to the menu position flags to allow either the left or right mouse button to activate a Menu control. This is by far the more natural motion: Right-click and hold to bring up the menu. Then move over to the Menu control and release the mouse button to activate it.
X	Omitted	The popup menu is displayed at the *x*-coordinate of the mouse cursor.
	Any numeric value	Specifies the *x*-coordinate at which the menu is displayed. The unit of measure is specified by the ScaleMode property of the form and is relative to the form.
Y	Omitted	The popup menu is displayed at the *y*-coordinate of the mouse cursor.
	Any numeric value	Specifies the *y*-coordinate at which the menu is displayed. The unit of measure is specified by the ScaleMode property of the form and is relative to the form.
BoldCommand	Omitted	No controls on the popup menu appear in bold.
	Control name	Specifies the name of a Menu control in the popup menu to display in bold text. If you're using a Menu control array, include the array index of the control.

VB will wait for the user's response before executing code that follows the call to the PopupMenu method. This means the code for the Click event of the selected Menu control will execute before the code following the call to PopupMenu.

Only one popup or pull-down menu can be displayed at a time, so if one is already displayed, PopupMenu will be ignored *and the code that follows will be executed immediately!* This may generate unexpected results. You may want to make the code following the PopupMenu statement check to see if it (the code) was processed before proceeding.

Use the Menu Editor to design your popup menus. Set its Visible property to False. Then, the menu will not be in the menu bar of your forms but will pop up when you call PopupMenu.

Example

```
Private Sub Form_MouseDown(Button As Integer, Shift As Integer, _
    X As Single, Y As Single)
    If Button = vbRightButton Then 'Right button
        PopupMenu mnuPopup, vbPopupMenuRightButton
    End If
End Sub
```

This example displays a popup menu in response to a right click on the form. You can easily make all the controls on the form to pop up different menus so as to create context-sensitive "immediate" menus.

The following example illustrates very simply a potential problem:

Example

```
Private Sub Form_MouseDown(Button As Integer, Shift As Integer, _
    X As Single, Y As Single)
    If Button = vbRightButton Then 'Right button
        PopupMenu mnuPopup, vbPopupMenuRightButton
        MsgBox "After Popup"
    End If
End Sub
```

On the first right click, the popup menu is displayed, but the MsgBox statement is not executed yet. If the user again right-clicks, the PopupMenu statement is *ignored,* because a popup menu is displayed already, and the MsgBox statement executes immediately. In fact the display of the MsgBox *removes* the popup menu!

Port Property

The Port property returns the name of the printer port through which documents print.

Usage   *StringValue = object*.Port

Applies To   Printer Object

The port names are determined by your system and include the familiar DOS ports: LPT1:, COM1:, and so on. If you've installed the Microsoft Fax for Windows 95, you'll get a FAX: port. The string returned by the Port property always includes the final colon (:).

Note: Not all printers support this property. You might get an error for yours.

Example

```
Sub ListPrinters(lst As ListBox)
    lst.Clear
    For Each prn In Printers
        lst.AddItem prn.DeviceName & " on " & prn.Port
    Next prn
End Sub
```

PrevInstance Property

The PrevInstance property specifies whether another instance of the application is already running. This property does not detect a previous instance if it was run from the VB development environment.

Usage   *BooleanValue = object*.PrevInstance

Applies To   App Object

If only one instance of your application can run at any one time, use this property to determine whether another instance is already running and quit if PrevInstance returns True.

Previous Property

The Previous property returns a reference to the previous sibling of a Node object.

Usage   *object*.Previous

Applies To   Node Object

The Help page points out that because the Child, FirstSibling, LastSibling, Previous, Parent, Next, and Root properties all reference Node objects other than the currently selected one, you can do stuff to them behind the scenes, like this:

Example

```
With TreeView1.Nodes(x).Previous
    .Text = "New text"
    .Key = "New key"
    .SelectedImage = 3
End With
```

Print Method

The Print method prints the specified text on the object.

Usage	*object*.Print [*OutputList*]

Applies To	Debug Object
	Form Object
	PictureBox Control
	Printer Object

This method of the Debug object prints text in the Immediate pane of the Debug window. For the Printer object, it sends text to the printer. For a Form and a PictureBox, it prints text on the object.

If OutputList is omitted, the Print method sends an empty line to the object. Otherwise, it has the following syntax:

`[Spc(n) | Tab[(n)]] [Expression] [CharPos] ...`

and the parts discussed in the following table.

PART	VALUE	MEANING
Spc(*n*)		Inserts space characters, where n is the number of characters.
Tab(*n*)		Positions the insertion point at the *n*th column. Each column has the same width, but width of column is not necessarily the same as the width of a character, since the font used may be a proportionally spaced font. If you use Tab(*n*) to align data, make sure *n* is large enough to hold printed data. If no argument is given, the insertion point is set to the beginning of the next print zone.
Expression	Numeric or string expression	Does automatic conversion to strings. You do not have to use the Str or CStr function. The conversion depends on the data type: • Number: string equivalent of the number. It uses the international settings for the decimal separator. • Boolean: the string "True" or "False." • Date: short date and time format. If the date is missing, only the time is printed. Similarly, if the time is missing, only the date is printed. • Null: the string "Null." • Error: the string "Error *errorcode*," where errorcode is a number. • Nothing: an empty string. Multiple expressions may appear in the OutputList.
CharPos	Semicolon (;) or space	The insertion point immediately follows the last character that was printed.

For the Printer object, when you reach the bottom of the page, additional printed text is carried over to the next page. For other objects, the text is clipped.

Example   `Debug.Print "This is the date: " Date`

PrinterDefault Property

The PrinterDefault property controls whether the setup in the Print dialog box changes the system default printer settings.

Usage   *object*.PrinterDefault = *BooleanValue*
                 BooleanValue = *object*.PrinterDefault

Applies To   CommonDialog Control

PARAMETER	VALUE	MEANING
BooleanValue	True	Changes become the default settings.
	False	Changes are one-time only.

PrintForm Method

The PrintForm method prints an image of the Form object on the current printer as a bitmap.

Usage   *object*.PrintForm

Applies To   Form Object

PrintForm prints all visible objects and bitmaps of the Form object, but no temporary graphics drawn on the Form or PictureBox controls when the AutoRedraw property is set to False. The current printer is set via Windows's Control Panel settings.

 Watch out on this one. We got PrintForm to consistently cause a GPF in the Post-Script printer driver if there were any permanent graphics on the Form or in a PictureBox that were drawn when AutoRedraw was set to True.

PrintQuality Property

The PrintQuality property specifies the printer resolution. This property is available only at run-time.

Usage   *IntegerValue = object*.PrintQuality
              object.PrintQuality = *IntegerValue*

Applies To   Printer Object

The possible values of the PrintQuality property are given in the following table.

CONSTANT	VALUE	MEANING
vbPRPQDraft	−1	Draft resolution.
vbPRPQLow	−2	Low resolution.
vbPRPQMedium	−3	Medium resolution.
vbPRPQHigh	−4	High resolution.
	Any positive integer	The integer represents a valid resolution in dots per inch, such as 300 or 600. If your printer does not support the requested resolution, it may return an error.

You can use the constants to try to set the print quality, but the property always returns the DPI resolution.

Note: You can change the printer property only for the default printer. Set it by using the Set Printer = command.

Another Note: Not all printers support this property or all possible values of this property. You might get an error for yours.

ProductName Property

The ProductName property is read-only at runtime. It returns a string that contains the product name of the running application. To set the product name, select the File/Make EXE File... menu and then click the Options... button. In the "Version Information" section, select "Product Name" from the list and enter the value in the text box.

Usage   *StringValue = object*.ProductName

Applies To   App Object

PSet Method

The PSet method draws a point on the object in the specified color.

Usage   *object*.PSet [*Step*] (*X*, *Y*)[, *Color*]

Applies To   Form Object
                 PictureBox Control
                 Printer Object

The arguments of the PSet method have the meanings given in the following table.

PARAMETER	VALUE	MEANING
Step	Omitted	The coordinates (X, Y) are specified in terms of the coordinate system of the object.
	Step	The coordinates (X, Y) are specified as an offset relative to the current location (CurrentX, CurrentY).
(X, Y)	Single-precision values	These are the coordinates of the center of the point to draw on the object. The Scale properties of the object determine the units of measure.
Color	Omitted	Uses the ForeColor property.
	Long value	Uses one of the Color Constants or the return values of the RGB or QBColor functions to specify a color.

The CurrentX and CurrentY properties will be set to X and Y after the call to PSet. Use the DrawWidth, DrawMode, and DrawStyle properties to change the way the point is drawn. A DrawWidth of 1 draws a single pixel.

The following example "erases" a point by setting it to the background color.

Example   `Picture1.PSet (150, 230), Picture1.BackColor`

Public Property

The Public property specifies whether the ClassModule is available outside the project. It is setable at design time and not available at runtime. When creating OLE servers, set the Public property of classes to True to allow OLE client applications to create instances of the class.

Usage   *object*.Public = BooleanValue

Applies To   ClassModule Object

The values of the Public property have the meanings given in the following table.

VALUE	MEANING
True	The Class is available to other modules in the project and to other applications.
False	The default. The Class is available only to other modules in the project.

In addition to setting the Public property, you need to set the Instancing property to determine how instances of your classes may be created. See the description of the Instancing property for more details.

ReadFromFile Method

The ReadFromFile method loads an object from a data file that was created using the SaveToFile or SaveToOle1File method. The object is loaded into an OLE Container control.

Usage   *object*.ReadFromFile *FileNumber*

Applies To   OLE Container Control

The parameters of the ReadFromFile method have the meaning given in the following table.

PARAMETER	VALUE	MEANING
FileNumber	Integer	The file number of a file opened for binary input using the Open statement.

Example
```
Open "d:\OLEObjs\FloorPlan.ole" for binary as 1
OLE1.ReadFromFile 1
Close 1
```

ReadOnly Property

For a FileListBox control, this ReadOnly property specifies whether a file with its ReadOnly attribute set is displayed in the control. See also the Archive, Hidden, Normal, and System properties.
     For a Data control, the ReadOnly property specifies whether the control can be changed.

Usage   *BooleanValue* = *object*.ReadOnly
                   object.ReadOnly = *BooleanValue*

Applies To   Data Control
                   FileListBox Control

Data Control

The values for the ReadOnly property have the meanings given in the following table.

VALUE	MEANING
True	Changes to the control's Database object are not allowed.
False	Changes to the control's Database object are allowed.

FileListBox Control

For files *without* their Hidden *or* System attributes set, the values for the ReadOnly property have the meanings given in the following table.

VALUE	MEANING
True	The default. Displays all files with their ReadOnly attribute set, regardless of the setting for the Normal and Archive properties.
False	Does not display a file with its ReadOnly attribute set *unless* the Normal property is set to True or the Archive property applies.

For a file with either its Hidden or System attribute set, the ReadOnly property has no effect on whether the filename is displayed in the FileListBox. See the entries for Hidden and System properties for files that have Hidden or System attributes set.

Setting the ReadOnly property at runtime will refresh the list of files.

To display all files, set the Normal, Hidden, and System properties to True.

ReadOnly Property (Data Control)

This ReadOnly property determines whether a Data control opens a recordset with read/write access (the default) or read-only access.

Usage   *object*.ReadOnly = *BooleanValue*
                BooleanValue = *object*.ReadOnly

Applies To   Data Control
                FileListBox Control

PARAMETER	VALUE	MEANING
BooleanValue	True	The recordset is opened as read-only.
	False	The recordset is opened as read/write.

Rebind Method

The Rebind method refreshes the DBGrid control's properties and columns, just as when you set the DataSource property.

Usage   *object*.Rebind

Applies To   DBGrid Control

RecordSelectors Property

The RecordSelectors property determines whether a DBGrid displays record selectors. A record selector is a gray column to the left of the first column that enables users to select an entire row at once.

Usage   *object*.RecordSelectors = *BooleanValue*
                   BooleanValue = *object*.RecordSelectors

Applies To   DBGrid Control

PARAMETER	VALUE	MEANING
BooleanValue	True	DBGrid displays record selectors.
	False	DBGrid doesn't display record selectors.

Recordset Property

The Recordset property controls the recordset that a Data control opens.

Usage   *object*.Recordset = *StringValue*
                   StringValue = *object*.Recordset

Applies To   Data Control

PARAMETER	VALUE	MEANING
StringValue	String	The path to the recordset to open.

RecordsetType Property

The RecordsetType property controls the kind of recordset a Data control is dealing with.

Usage   *object*.RecordsetType = *IntegerValue*
                 IntegerValue = *object*.RecordsetType

Applies To   Data Control

PARAMETER	VALUE	MEANING
IntegerValue	vbRSTypeTable or 0	A table.
	vbRSTypeDynaset or 1	A dynaset.
	vbRSTypeSnapshot or 2	A snapshot.

RecordSource Property

The RecordSource property controls the table, SQL query, or QueryDef object underlying a Data control.

Usage   *object*.RecordSource = *StringValue*
                 StringValue = *object*.RecordSource

Applies To   Data Control

PARAMETER	VALUE	MEANING
StringValue	String	This string can be either a table name, a SQL query, or a QueryDef object that's in the database object's QueryDefs collection.

The RecordSource is what makes bound controls work. It's what they connect to.

Refill Method

The Refill method forces a DBCombo or DBList to recreate its list.

Usage   *object*.Refill

Applies To   DBCombo Control
                 DBList Control

Note that Refill is more powerful than the Refresh method, which just repaints the object.

Refresh Method

Normally, forms and controls are redrawn—if necessary—only when the application is not busy handling events. This Refresh method causes the associated object to be redrawn immediately. You can also use the Refresh method to update the contents of a file-system list box (DirListBox, DriveListBox, and FileListBox) or a Data control.

Usage	*object*.Refresh
Applies To	CheckBox Control
	ComboBox Control
	CommandButton Control
	Data Control
	DBCombo Control
	DBGrid Control
	DBList Control
	DirListBox Control
	DriveListBox Control
	FileListBox Control
	Form Object
	Frame Control
	HScrollBar, VScrollBar Controls
	Image Control
	Label Control
	Line Control
	ListBox Control
	Menu Control
	OLE Container Control
	OptionButton Control
	PictureBox Control
	Shape Control
	TextBox Control

For some reason, MDIForm objects do not have the Refresh method. But you can use Refresh for the MDI child Form object. Since menus are normally displayed only in response to a user-generated event, they will be redrawn at those times. Similarly, since a Timer control is not displayed at all, it has no Refresh method.

If you change the DatabaseName, ReadOnly, Exclusive, or Connect properties of a Data control, use the Refresh method to reopen the database and rebuild the dynaset referenced by the Data control's Recordset property.

Note: Although the Refresh method causes a file-system list box to update its content, the list box's Change event will not be called even if the content of the list box has changed to reflect changes to the file system. This is because the Change event for a DirListBox, for instance, is called if the current directory is changed either by the user or via code, not if the content of the directory has changed.

Refresh Method (DAO)

This Refresh method pulls fresh data out of the recordset.

Usage   *recordset*.Refresh

Applies To   Containers Collection
                     Documents Collection
                     Fields Collection
                     Groups Collection
                     Indexes Collection
                     Parameters Collection
                     Properties Collection
                     QueryDefs Collection
                     Relations Collection
                     TableDefs Collection
                     Users Collection

Remove Method (Custom Controls)

The Remove method removes an object from a collection.

Usage   *object*.Remove *Index*

Applies To   Buttons Collection
                     ColumnHeaders Collection
                     ListImages Collection
                     ListItems Collection
                     Nodes Collection
                     Panels Collection
                     Tabs Collection

RemoveItem Method

The RemoveItem method removes an item from a ListBox or ComboBox control or a row from a Grid control.

Usage   *object*.RemoveItem *Index*

Applies To   ComboBox Control
                   Grid Control
                   ListBox Control

The argument to the RemoveItem method has the meanings given in the following table.

PARAMETER	VALUE	MEANING
Item	0 or positive integer	Indicates the item or row to remove. The first item or row has Index = 0. If the Index is greater than or equal to the number of items or rows in the control, an error occurs.
	Negative integer	Error

A ListBox or ComboBox control bound to a Data control does not support the RemoveItem method.

The following example removes all items from the list that include a colon (:):

Example
```
For i = Combo1.ListCount - 1 To 0 Step -1
    If InStr(Combo1.List(i), ":") <> 0 Then
        Combo1.RemoveItem i
    End If
Next i
```

Render Method

The Render method draws all or part of an image into a Picture or StdPicture object.

Usage   *object*.Render(*hdc, xdest, ydest, destwid, desthgt, xsrc, ysrc, srcwid, srchgt, wbounds*)

Applies To   Picture Object

Note: All parameters are required. It's probably easier to use PaintPicture instead.

PARAMETER	VALUE	MEANING
hdc	Handle	The handle to the destination object's device context.
xdest	Integer	The x-coordinate of the upper-left corner of the drawing region in the destination object. This coordinate is measured in the same unit as the destination object.
ydest	Integer	The y-coordinate of the upper-left corner of the drawing region in the destination object. This coordinate is measured in the same unit as the destination object.

PARAMETER	VALUE	MEANING
destwid	Integer	The width of the drawing region in the destination object. This is measured in the same unit as the destination object.
desthgt	Integer	The height of the drawing region in the destination object. This is measured in the same unit as the destination object.
xsrc	Integer	The x-coordinate of the upper-left corner of the drawing region in the source object. This coordinate is in HIMETRIC units.
ysrc	Integer	The y-coordinate of the upper-left corner of the drawing region in the source object. This coordinate is in HIMETRIC units.
srcwid	Integer	The width of the drawing region in the source object, in HIMETRIC units.
srchgt	Integer	The height of the drawing region in the source object, in HIMETRIC units.
wbounds	Integer	The world bounds of a metafile. This argument should be passed a value of Null unless drawing to a metafile, in which case the argument is passed a user-defined type corresponding to a RECTL structure.

RestoreToolbar Method

The RestoreToolbar method restores a toolbar, created with a Toolbar control, to its original state after being customized. *Note:* This method doesn't support named arguments.

Usage   *object*.RestoreToolbar(*Key As String*, *Subkey As String*, *StringValue As String*)

Applies To   Toolbar Control

PARAMETER	VALUE	MEANING
Key	String	The key in the Windows Registry—such as HKEY_CURRENT_USER and HKEY_LOCAL_MACHINE—from which the method is going to retrieve information about the toolbar.
Subkey	String	The location under the key.
StringValue	String	The toolbar information stored in the subkey.

For an example, look in the Windows Help pages under "Toolbar control."

 No matter *what* key we use, the entry is taken from the HKEY_CURRENT_USER tree. Key can even be a random number.

Revision Property

The Revision property is read-only at runtime. It returns an integer that is the revision version number of the running application. To enter this number, select the File/Make EXE File... menu and then click the Options... button. In the "Version Number" section, go to the "Revision" text box and enter the value.

Usage	*IntegerValue = object*.Revision
Applies To	App Object

The valid range of the Revision property is from 0 to 9,999. The VB development environment will not allow you to enter values outside this range.

RightMargin Property

The RightMargin property controls the right margin for the text in a RichTextBox control.

Usage	*object*.RightMargin = *SingleValue*
	SingleValue = object.RightMargin
Applies To	RichTextBox Control

PARAMETER	VALUE	MEANING
SingleValue	Single-precision value	The indentation from the right edge of the text box. It is expressed in the unit of measure used by the RichTextBox control's container. The RichTextBox uses this value to determine where to wrap words.

Root Property

The Root property returns a reference to the root Node object of a selected Node.

Usage	*object*.Root
Applies To	Node Object

The Help page points out that because the Child, FirstSibling, LastSibling, Previous, Parent, Next, and Root properties all reference Node objects other than the currently selected one, you can do stuff to them behind the scenes, like this:

Example
```
With TreeView1.Nodes(x).Root
    .Text = "New text"
    .Key = "New key"
    .SelectedImage = 3
End With
```

RowBookmark Property

The RowBookmark property contains a value for a visible row in a DBGrid control.

Usage   *VariantValue = object*.RowBookmark(*RowNum*)

Applies To   DBGrid Control

PARAMETER	VALUE	MEANING
RowNum	Integer	The integer enables RowBookmark to create a bookmark. It ranges from 0 to VisibleRows −1.

You use this property if, for some reason, you want to perform an operation on a specific visible row. It's not one we used until we tested it. FYI: RowBookmark (0) is the same as FirstRow.

 Do not save RowBookmark values. They change as the visible values change.

RowContaining Method

The RowContaining method returns a value that corresponds to the row number of a DBGrid row that contains the vertical coordinate (Y value) you specify.

Usage   *IntegerValue = object*.RowContaining(*Coordinate*)

Applies To   DBGrid Control

PARAMETER	VALUE	MEANING
Coordinate	Single-precision value	The vertical coordinate, expressed in the unit of measure of the DBGrid control's container.

You use this method when you let users drag and drop stuff into a DBGrid control. It returns a number that corresponds to a column index, ranging from 0 to VisibleRows − 1. If the coordinate you feed it is outside the DBGrid's coordinate system, you get a trappable error.

RowCount Property

The RowCount property returns or sets the number of rows contained in a RowBuffer object in an unbound DBGrid.

Usage   object.RowCount = *LongValue*
                LongValue = object.RowCount

Applies To   RowBuffer Object

PARAMETER	VALUE	MEANING
LongValue	Long integer	The number of rows.

RowDividerStyle Property

The RowDividerStyle property determines the style of the border between rows of a DBGrid.

Usage   object.RowDividerStyle = *IntegerValue*
                IntegerValue = object.RowDividerStyle

Applies To   DBGrid Control

PARAMETER	VALUE	MEANING
IntegerValue	dbgNoDividers or 0	Gives the control no dividers between columns.
	dbgBlackLine or 1	Makes the divider between columns or rows a black line.
	dbgDarkGrayLine or 2	Makes the divider between columns or rows a dark gray line.
	dbgRaised or 3	Makes the divider between columns or rows raised.
	dbgInset or 4	Makes the divider between columns or rows inset.
	dbgUseForeColor or 5	Uses the foreground color in the divider between columns or rows.

RowHeight Property

The RowHeight property specifies the height of rows in a DBGrid or Grid control.

- DBGrid: RowHeight is a single-precision value specifying the height of all rows in the control, expressed in the unit of measure of the container for the DBGrid control.

- Grid: RowHeight is specified for individual rows, expressed in twips as a long integer value. It is not available at design time.

Usage   *SingleOrLongValue = object*.RowHeight[(*Row*)]
                 object.RowHeight[(*Row*)] = *SingleOrLongValue*

Applies To   DBGrid Control
                 Grid Control

The parts of the syntax for the RowHeight property have the meaning given in the following table.

PARAMETER	VALUE	MEANING
Row	Integer	Specifies the row number in a Grid control.

Rows Property

The Rows property tells you how many rows of tabs are in an SSTab control.

Usage   *IntegerValue = object*.Rows

Applies To   SSTab Control

PARAMETER	VALUE	MEANING
IntegerValue	Integer	The number of rows in the SSTab.

When you design an SSTab control, you set the number of tabs using the Tabs property and you set the number of tabs in each row using TabsPerRow.

RowSource Property

The RowSource property specifies the Data control that will fill a DBList or DBCombo's List-Field and BoundColumn properties. This property is available only at design time.

Usage   *object*.RowSource = *StringValue*
                 StringValue = *object*.RowSource

Applies To   DBList Control
                 DBCombo Control

PARAMETER	VALUE	MEANING
StringValue	String	The Data control to fill a DBList or DBCombo box's Listfield and BoundColumn.

There seems to be nothing at all special about this property. Thank goodness.

RowTop Method

The RowTop method returns the *y*-coordinate of the top of a specified row in a DBGrid, expressed in the unit of measure used by the container of the DBGrid control.

Usage   *SingleValue* = *object*.RowTop(*RowNum*)

Applies To   DBGrid Control

PARAMETER	VALUE	MEANING
RowNum	Integer	Specifies a row. Range is from 1 to Visible Rows −1.

Use RowTop with the RowHeight, Left, and Width properties to figure out the location and dimensions of a specific cell.

SaveFile Method

The SaveFile method saves the content of a RichTextBox control to a file.

Usage   *object*.SaveFile(*PathValue*[, *IntegerValue*])

Applies To   RichTextBox Control

This method doesn't support named arguments.

PARAMETER	VALUE	MEANING
PathValue	String	Required. Specifies the path and file to receive the content of the control.
IntegerValue	rtfRTF or 0 or omitted	Optional. Says the file will be a .RTF file.
	rtfText or 1	Optional. Says the file will be text only.

SavePicture Statement

The SavePicture statement saves the graphics from a Form object or control to a file. You can save the graphics accessed by the Picture, Image, Icon, DragIcon, and MouseIcon properties of a Form or control. In addition, you can save the graphics referenced by a variable of the Picture type.

Usage   SavePicture *PictureValue, Filename*

The parameters of the SavePicture statement have the meanings given in the following table.

PARAMETER	VALUE	MEANING
PictureValue	Picture, Icon, DragIcon MouseIcon properties	The graphics loaded into these properties will be saved in the same file format as the original file. These properties must have been loaded with a valid picture, or you will get a runtime error when you try to save.
	Image property	You can always save the Image property of a Form object or PictureBox control. When you save the Image property, it will be saved as a bitmap (.BMP) file containing graphics from the Picture property and any other graphics drawn when the AutoRedraw property was set to True. Temporary graphics drawn when AutoRedraw was False are not saved.
	Picture variable	A variable loaded with a picture may be saved into another file. If the variable does not contain a valid picture, an error occurs.
Filename	String expression	The name of the file for saving the graphics.

The following example saves the graphics referenced by the Image property of a form. Only the "permanent" text is saved.

Example
```
Private Sub SaveImage
    Form1.AutoRedraw = True
    Form1.Print "Permanent"
    Form1.AutoRedraw = False
    Form1.Print "Temporary"
    SavePicture Form1.Image, "mypic.bmp"
End Sub
```

SaveToFile Method

The SaveToFile method saves an object within an OLE Container control to a binary data file. The file may be read in again using the ReadFromFile method.

Usage   *object*.SaveToFile *FileNumber*

Applies To   OLE Container Control

The parameters of the SaveToFile method have the meaning given in the following table.

PARAMETER	VALUE	MEANING
FileNumber	Integer	The file number of a file opened for binary output using the Open statement.

If the object being saved is linked, only the link references and a metafile image are saved to the file. If the object is embedded, then the actual data is saved.

Example
```
Open "d:\OLEObjs\FloorPlan.ole" for binary as 1
OLE1.SaveToFile 1
Close 1
```

SaveToolbar Method

The SaveToolbar method works with the Customize method; it saves the state of a user-customized toolbar.

Usage   *object*.SaveToolbar(*Key As String*, *Subkey As String*, *StringValue As String*)

Applies To   Toolbar Control

This method doesn't support named arguments.

PARAMETER	VALUE	MEANING
Key	String	The key in the Windows Registry—such as HKEY_CURRENT_USER and HKEY_LOCAL_MACHINE—from which the method is going to retrieve information about the toolbar.
Subkey	String	The location under the key.
StringValue	String	The toolbar information stored in the subkey.

No matter *what* key we use, the entry is made in the HKEY_CURRENT_USER tree. Key can even be a random number.

SaveToOle1File Method

The SaveToOle1File method saves an object contained in an OLE Container control in the OLE file format. Use the SaveToFile method instead whenever possible.

Usage   *object*.SaveToOle1File *FileNumber*

Applies To   OLE Container Control

The parameters of the SaveToOle1File method have the meaning given in the following table.

PARAMETER	VALUE	MEANING
FileNumber	Integer	The file number of a file opened for binary output using the Open statement.

If the object being saved is linked, only the link references and a metafile image are saved to the file. If the object is embedded, then the actual data is saved.

Scale Method

The Scale method defines the coordinate system for the interior of a Form, PictureBox, or Printer object for use by graphics methods and for the placement of controls. You supply the coordinates of the upper-left and lower-right corners of the object, and the Scale method will automatically set the ScaleHeight, ScaleWidth, ScaleLeft, and ScaleTop properties. It will also set ScaleMode to vbUser (0).

Usage   *object*.Scale [(*X1*, *Y1*)–(*X2*, *Y2*)]

Applies To   Form Object
                         PictureBox Control
                         Printer Object

The arguments to the Scale method have the meanings given in the following table.

PARAMETER	VALUE	MEANING
(X1, Y1)	Omitted	Resets Scale to using twips. The upper-left corner has coordinates (0, 0). (X2,Y2) also must be omitted.
	Single-precision values	Specifies the coordinates to use for the upper-left corner of the object.
(X2, Y2)	Omitted	Resets Scale to using twips. The upper-left corner has coordinates (0, 0). (X1,Y1) also must be omitted.
	Single-precision values	Specifies the coordinates to use for the lower-right corner of the object.

The Scale method will not affect existing graphics or controls. In fact, the left, top, width, and height of all controls on the object will be adjusted to match the new coordinate system.

Note that in the following example, the Scale method causes the ScaleHeight property to be set to a negative number, indicating that the vertical coordinate increases from bottom to top.

Example

```
Scale (0, 100)-(100,0)
Debug.Print "ScaleLeft: " & ScaleLeft
Debug.Print "ScaleTop: " & ScaleTop
Debug.Print "ScaleWidth: " & ScaleWidth
Debug.Print "ScaleHeight: " & ScaleHeight
```

Result

```
ScaleLeft: 0
ScaleTop: 100
ScaleWidth: 100
ScaleHeight: -100
```

ScaleHeight, ScaleWidth Properties

The ScaleHeight and ScaleWidth properties may be used to change the unit of measure to a completely arbitary unit for the *interior* of an object when drawing or placing controls in the object. They do not affect existing graphics or controls. When these properties are used in conjunction with the ScaleLeft and ScaleTop properties, you can define a custom coordinate system for the object. The absolute value of the ScaleHeight property (it can be negative) specifies the total number of vertical units, and the absolute value of the ScaleWidth property specifies the total number of horizontal units.

For MDIForm objects, the ScaleHeight and ScaleWidth properties are not available at design time and are read-only at runtime.

Usage

SingleValue = *object*.ScaleHeight
object.ScaleHeight = *SingleValue*

SingleValue = *object*.ScaleWidth
object.ScaleWidth = *SingleValue*

Applies To   Form Object
                 MDIForm Object
                 PictureBox Control
                 Printer Object

If your application plots data collected from surveys or experiments, you can draw the plot using the actual data points. By first setting the ScaleLeft, ScaleTop, ScaleWidth, and Scale-Height properties of the destination object, you can move and scale the plotted data to fill the entire plot area. Use the Scale method to set all the Scale properties at the same time.

Setting ScaleHeight and ScaleWidth to positive values makes coordinates increase from top to bottom and left to right, respectively. Setting them to negative values makes coordinates increase from bottom to top and right to left, respectively. You cannot set them to 0.

To use a scale based on a standard unit of measure, use the ScaleMode property. This property will automatically adjust ScaleHeight and ScaleWidth to the new unit and reset ScaleLeft and Scale-Top to zero. On the other hand, setting ScaleHeight or ScaleWidth resets ScaleMode to vbUser (0).

For MDIForm objects, you can use PictureBox controls as toolbars, so the ScaleHeight and ScaleWidth properties apply only to areas not covered by PictureBox controls. So, you should avoid using these properties in the Resize event of an MDIForm to resize PictureBoxes.

Example
```
'Draw a circle in the center of the PictureBox, filling
' 60% of the height
Picture1.Circle (Picture1.ScaleWidth / 2, _
    Picture1.ScaleHeight / 2), Picture1.ScaleHeight * 0.3
```

The ScaleHeight and ScaleWidth properties are *not* the same as the Height and Width properties that specify the object's size in the units of *its* parent form or control.

ScaleLeft, ScaleTop Properties

The ScaleLeft and ScaleTop properties specify the coordinates of the interior of an object that coincide with the object's top-left corner. These properties affect the placement of controls in the object and the graphics drawn using graphics methods. They do not affect existing graphics or controls. When these properties are used in conjunction with the ScaleHeight and ScaleWidth properties, you can define a custom coordinate system for the interior of an object.

Usage   *SingleValue* = *object*.ScaleLeft
                 object.ScaleLeft = *SingleValue*

                 SingleValue = *object*.ScaleTop
                 object.ScaleTop = *SingleValue*

Applies To   Form Object
                 PictureBox Control
                 Printer Object

If your application plots data collected from surveys or experiments, you can draw the plot using the actual data points. By first setting the ScaleLeft, ScaleTop, ScaleWidth, and Scale-Height properties of the destination object, you can move and scale the plotted data to fill the entire plot area. Use the Scale method to set all the Scale properties at the same time.

To use a scale based on a standard unit of measure, use the ScaleMode property. This property will automatically adjust ScaleHeight and ScaleWidth to the new unit and reset ScaleLeft and ScaleTop to zero. On the other hand, setting ScaleLeft or ScaleTop resets ScaleMode to vbUser (0).

The following may be used to plot an array of values in a PictureBox control:

Example
```
Private Sub PlotPrices(Prices())
        Dim i As Integer, l As Integer, u As Integer
        l = LBound(Prices()) : u = UBound(Prices())
        Picture1.ScaleHeight = -100'Maximum Price
        Picture1.ScaleWidth = u - l'All data
        Picture1.ScaleTop = 100
        Picture1.ScaleLeft = 0
        Picture1.PSet (l, Prices(0))
        For i = l + 1 to u
            Picture1.Line -(i, Prices(i))
    Next i
End Sub
```

The ScaleLeft and ScaleTop properties are *not* the same as the Left and Top properties that specify the coordinates of the object's top-left corner in the units of *its* parent form or control.

ScaleMode Property

The ScaleMode property specifies the unit of measure for an object when using graphics methods or when positioning child controls.

Usage   *IntegerValue* = *object*.ScaleMode
                 object.ScaleMode = *IntegerValue*

Applies To   Form Object
                 PictureBox Control
                 Printer Object

The possible values for this property are given in the following table.

CONSTANT	VALUE	MEANING
vbUser	0	User defined. This value occurs when one or more of the object's ScaleHeight, ScaleWidth, ScaleLeft, or ScaleTop properties have been changed to custom values.

CONSTANT	VALUE	MEANING
vbTwips	1	Twips. The default. 20 twips per point; 1,440 twips per logical inch; 567 twips per logical centimeter.
vbPoints	2	Points. 72 points per logical inch; 28.3 points per logical centimeter.
vbPixels	3	Pixels. The smallest unit of resolution for a monitor or printer. For a printer, this is commonly known as the "dots" in dots per inch (DPI).
vbCharacters	4	Characters. 120 twips per character horizontally; 240 twips per character vertically.
vbInches	5	Inches.
vbMillimeters	6	Millimeters.
vbCentimeters	7	Centimeters.

Setting any one of the ScaleHeight, ScaleWidth, ScaleLeft, and ScaleTop properties of the object will automatically change ScaleMode to vbUser (0). Conversely, changing ScaleMode to any other value resets ScaleHeight and ScaleWidth to the new unit of measure and resets both ScaleLeft and ScaleTop to 0. The CurrentX and CurrentY values are also changed to reflect the new coordinate system.

Use the ScaleX and ScaleY method to convert between two units of measure.

ScaleTop Property

See the ScaleLeft Property.

ScaleWidth Property

See the ScaleHeight Property.

ScaleX, ScaleY Methods

The ScaleX and ScaleY methods are used to convert the coordinates in the interior of a Form, PictureBox, or Printer object from one unit of measure to another.

Usage

ScaleWidth = object.ScaleX(*Width*[, *FromScale*, *ToScale*])
ScaleHeight = object.ScaleY(*Height*[, *FromScale*, *ToScale*])

Applies To   Form Object
                      PictureBox Control
                      Printer Object

The parameters of the ScaleX and ScaleY methods have the meanings given in the following table.

PARAMETER	VALUE	MEANING
ScaleWidth	Single-precision value	The result of ScaleX is the number of units in the horizontal direction, where the ToScale argument specifies the unit of measure.
ScaleHeight	Single-precision value	The result of ScaleY is the number of units in the vertical direction, where the ToScale argument specifies the unit of measure.
Width	Single-precision value	The number of units in the horizontal direction to convert, where the FromScale argument specifies the unit of measure.
Height	Single-precision value	The number of units in the vertical direction to convert, where the FromScale argument specifies the unit of measure.
FromScale	Omitted	Same as 8, meaning HiMetric units. HiMetric is the unit of measure for Picture objects. ToScale must be omitted.
	vbUser or 0	Use the custom unit of measure defined by the object. If the object's ScaleMode is not vbUser (0), an error is generated.
	vbTwips or 1	Twips. 1,440 twips = 1 logical inch; 567 twips = 1 logical centimeter.
	vbPoints or 2	Points. 72 points = 1 logical inch.
	vbPixels or 3	Pixels. A pixel is the smallest unit for the object. This is a pixel for something displayed on a monitor and a dot (as in dots per inch, DPI) for something to be printed.
	vbCharacters or 4	Characters. These are units for fixed-width characters: 1 character width = 120 twips; 1 character height = 240 twips.
	vbInches or 5	Inches.
	vbMillimeters or 6	Millimeters.
	vbCentimeters or 7	Centimeters.
	8	HiMetric. This is the unit of measure used by Picture objects.
ToScale	Omitted	Use the value of the ScaleMode property. This converts Width or Height into the unit used by the object's graphics methods.
	See FromScale values	

The ScaleX and ScaleY properties are handy when used with the PaintPicture method to display a graphic undistorted in a Form, PictureBox, or Printer object that is using an arbitrary coordinate system.

Note that you can use ScaleX and ScaleY to convert between two units of measure unrelated to the current coordinate system used by the object. For example, to convert between inches and centimeters, use the following example:

Example   `Debug.Print ScaleX(1, vbInches, vbCentimeters)`

Result   `2.540003`

Scroll Method

The Scroll method scrolls a DBGrid horizontally and vertically at the same time.

Usage   *object*.Scroll *Colvalue, Rowvalue*

Applies To   DBGrid Control

PARAMETER	VALUE	MEANING
Colvalue	Long value	Required. Specifies a column.
Rowvalue	Long value or numeric expression	Required. Specifies a row.

This method is like using TopRow and Left, but it achieves the same result in one event.

ScrollBars Property

This ScrollBars property specifies whether an object uses horizontal or vertical scroll bars. The scroll bars are not enabled (and may not appear) unless the content of the object or control extends beyond the object's borders. This property is read-only at runtime.

Usage   *IntegerValue = object*.ScrollBars

Applies To   Column Object
                    Grid Control
                    MDIForm Object
                    TextBox Control

The possible return values for this property are given in the following table.

CONSTANT	VALUE	MEANING
GRID, COLUMN, TEXTBOX		
vbSBNone	0	None, even if the object's content extends beyond its borders.
vbHorizontal	1	Horizontal.
vbVertical	2	Vertical.
vbBoth	3	Both.
MDIFORM		
True	Nonzero	The MDIForm has one or both horizontal and vertical scroll bars.
False	0	The MDIForm has no scroll bars, even if the object's content extends beyond its borders.

If the MultiLine property is False for a Textbox control, no scroll bars will be displayed regardless of the setting of the control's ScrollBars property.

ScrollBars Property (DBGrid)

This ScrollBars property controls whether (and what kind of) scroll bars are on a DBGrid control.

Usage   *object*.ScrollBars = *IntegerValue*
             IntegerValue = *object*.ScrollBars

Applies To   DBGrid Control

PARAMETER	VALUE	MEANING
IntegerValue	dbgNone or 0	Gives the DBGrid no scroll bars.
	dbgHorizontal or 1	Gives the DBGrid a horizontal scroll bar.
	dbgVertical or 2	Gives the DBGrid a vertical scroll bar.
	dbgBoth or 3	Gives the DBGrid both scroll bars.
	dbgAutomatic or 4	Lets the DBGrid automatically choose which scroll bars to display.

ScrollBars Property (RichTextBox Control)

This ScrollBars property controls whether a RichTextBox control has horizontal or vertical scroll bars.

Usage

object.ScrollBars = *IntegerValue*
IntegerValue = *object*.ScrollBars

Applies To

RichTextBox Control

This property is read-only at runtime.

PARAMETER	VALUE	MEANING
IntegerValue	rtfNone or 0	No scroll bars.
	rtfHorizontal or 1	A horizontal scroll bar only.
	rtfVertical or 2	A vertical scroll bar only.
	rtfBoth or 3	Both scroll bars.

If you set this property to anything but 0, you must set MultiLine to True.

SelAlignment Property

The SelAlignment property controls the alignment of the selected paragraphs in a RichTextBox control.

Usage

object.SelAlignment = *IntegerValue*
IntegerValue = *object*.SelAlignment

Applies To

RichTextBox Control

This property is not available at design time.

PARAMETER	VALUE	MEANING
IntegerValue	Null	The current selection holds more than one paragraph and the paragraphs have different alignments.
	rftLeft or 0	Left alignment.
	rtfRight or 1	Right alignment.
	rtfCenter or 2	Centers the stuff.

Use the IsNull function to figure out whether you can change the alignment; for example:

Example   `If IsNull(RichTextBox1.SelAlignment) = True Then...`

SelBold Property

The SelBold property controls whether the selected text in a RichTextBox control will appear in bold format.

Usage   *object*.SelBold = *BooleanValue*
                 BooleanValue = *object*.SelBold

Applies To   RichTextBox Control

This property is not available at design time.

PARAMETER	VALUE	MEANING
BooleanValue	True	All the characters in the selection or the characters after the insertion point will be bold.
	False	None of the characters in the selection or the characters after the insertion point will be bold.
	Null	The current selection holds more than one character and the characters have multiple styles.

SelBookmarks Property

The SelBookmarks property returns a collection of bookmarks for all selected records in a DBGrid.

Usage   *object*.SelBookmarks

Applies To   DBGrid Control

The SelBookmarks property often works hand-in-hand with the SelBookmarks collection, which contains pointers to all the selected rows in yourDBGrid.

Example
```
Sub  SelectAllVisible_Click ()
     Dim I
     For I = 0 To DataGrid1.VisibleRows - 1
          DataGrid1.SelBookmarks.Add
          DataGrid1.RowBookmark(I)
```

```
            Next I
        End Sub
```

This example selects all visible rows in your DBGrid.

SelBullet Property

The SelBullet property controls whether a paragraph in the RichTextBox control has the bullet style.

Usage   *object*.SelBullet = *BooleanValue*
                  BooleanValue = *object*.SelBullet

Applies To   RichTextBox Control

This property is not available at design time.

PARAMETER	VALUE	MEANING
BooleanValue	True	All the paragraphs in the selection are bulleted.
	False	None of the paragraphs in the selection are bulleted.
	Null	The current selection holds more than one paragraph and the paragraphs have multiple styles.

SelCharOffset Property

The SelCharOffset property controls whether text will appear normal, superscripted, or subscripted.

Usage   *object*.SelCharOffset = *IntegerValue*
                  IntegerValue = *object*.SelCharOffset

Applies To   RichTextBox Control

This property is not available at design time.

PARAMETER	VALUE	MEANING
IntegerValue	Null	The current selection has multiple styles.
	A positive integer	The distance from the baseline in twips that the characters will be superscripted.
	A negative integer	The distance from the baseline in twips that the characters will be subscripted.

SelColor Property

The SelColor property controls the color of text in the RichTextBox control.

Usage	*object*.SelColor = *IntegerValue*
	IntegerValue = *object*.SelColor

Applies To   RichTextBox Control

This property is not available at design time.

PARAMETER	VALUE	MEANING
Value	Null	The selection has a mixture of colors.
	RGB colors	Colors are specified with the RGB or QBColor functions.
	Color constants	Colors are specified with the system's color constants.

Common constants are given in the following table.

CONSTANT	VALUE	MEANING
vbBlack	0x0	Black
vbRed	0xFF	Red
vbGreen	0xFF00	Green
vbYellow	0xFFFF	Yellow
vbBlue	0xFF0000	Blue
vbMagenta	0xFF00FF	Magenta
vbCyan	0xFFFF00	Cyan
vbWhite	0xFFFFFF	White

Also see the Color Constants section for more constants.

SelCount Property

The SelCount property returns the number of items selected in a ListBox control. It is not available at design time and is read-only at runtime. Use this property when MultiSelect is True to determine how many items the user has selected.

Usage   *IntegerValue = object*.SelCount

Applies To   ListBox Control

   If no items are selected, SelCount returns 0.
   To allocate arrays to process the selected items in a list, use the SelCount property to perform the allocation before going through the list with the Selected property to find the selected items.

Selected Property

This Selected property refers to a Boolean array that provides the selection status of each item in a FileListBox or ListBox control. Use of this property is essential when determining the selected items in a list whose MultiSelect property is set to True.

Usage   *BooleanValue = object*.Selected(*Index*)
                     object.Selected(*Index*) = *BooleanValue*

Applies To   FileListBox Control
                     ListBox Control

   The values of the Selected property have the meanings given in the following table.

VALUE	MEANING
True	The item indicated by the Index argument is selected.
False	The default. The item is not selected.

   In a control that allows multiple selection, the ListIndex property returns the index of the item that has focus, but that item is not necessarily selected. You *must* use the Selected property to determine which items are selected.
   If Index is out of range, an error occurs.

Selected Property (Custom Controls)

This Selected property specifies whether the object is selected.

Usage   *BooleanValue = object*.Selected
                     object.Selected = *BooleanValue*

Applies To   ListItem Object
                     Node Object
                     Tab Object

If multiple ListItems are selected in a ListView control, you may need to loop through all items to check their Selected items.

SelectedImage Property

The SelectedImage property controls which ListImage object from an ImageList control will be displayed when you select a Node.

| *Usage* | *object*.SelectedImage = *IntegerValue* |
| | *IntegerValue* = *object*.SelectedImage |

Applies To   Node Object

PARAMETER	VALUE	MEANING
IntegerValue	Integer or key	The index or key of a ListImage object in an ImageList control.

Note: You'll probably want to set the ImageMask property before you use any images.

SelectedItem Property (DBCombo, DBList Control)

This SelectedItem property returns a value with a bookmark that points to the record you selected in a DBCombo or DBList control.

Usage   *StringValue* = *object*.SelectedItem

Applies To   DBCombo Control
DBList Control

PARAMETER	VALUE	MEANING
StringValue	String	The bookmark of the record in the DBCombo control.

Whenever you pick something from a DBCombo control's list, SelectedItem contains a bookmark. You can use this bookmark to move the selected record in the recordset specified by the RowSource property.

Here's an example that should work. Create a form. Add a DBCombo box (DBCombo1), a DBGrid (DBGrid1), and a Data control (Data1). Set Data1's DatabaseName property to BIB-

LIO.MDB and RecordSource to Authors. Point DBCombo1's RowSource and DataSource properties at Data1, set ListField to Author, and set BoundColumn and DataField to Au_ID. Then set DBGrid1's DataSource to Data1 and add the following code to DBCombo1's Click event:

Example
```
Private Sub DBCombo1_Click(Area As Integer)
    Data1.Recordset.Bookmark = DBCombo1.SelectedItem
End Sub
```

Now run it. When you click a row in DBGrid1, DBCombo1's value changes *and* when you select an item from DBCombo1, DBGrid1's value changes.

 It doesn't always work this way. If you try to do this with the Publishers table in BIB-LIO.MDB and set DBCombo1's BoundColumn and DataField to PubID, for example, it will consistently return "This action was cancelled by an associated object." This error not only has a misspelling (canceled has one "l") and is in the passive voice, it also doesn't tell you much. Looking it up on the Help page doesn't help much either. You can solve this problem by setting Data1's ReadOnly property to True. However, then, of course, you can't alter the data. There are some other oddities with this passing of data between the two controls, where sometimes moving around with DBCombo1 will alter data. In all, we're not so sure that this works really well.

SelectedItem Property

This SelectedItem property references a selected ListItem, Node, or Tab object.

Usage   *object*.SelectedItem

Applies To   DBCombo Control
               ListView Control
               TabStrip Control
               TreeView Control

SelectRange Property

The SelectRange property specifies whether the user can select a range on the Slider control.

Usage   *BooleanValue* = *object*.SelectRange
               object.SelectRange = *BooleanValue*

Applies To   Slider Control

PARAMETER	VALUE	MEANING
BooleanValue	True	The Slider can select a range of values. Use the SelStart and SelLength properties in event procedures to allow the user to select a range.
	False	The default. The Slider can be used to select only a single value. The SelStart and Value properties will always be the same; changing one will automatically change the other. The SelLength property is ignored.

SelEndCol, SelStartCol Properties

The SelEndCol and SelStartCol properties specify the range of selected cells in a DBGrid or Grid control. They are not available at design time.

- SelEndCol: The rightmost selected column

- SelStartCol: The leftmost selected column

Usage   *IntegerValue* = *object*.SelEndCol
                object.SelEndCol = *IntegerValue*

                IntegerValue = *object*.SelStartCol
                object.SelStartCol = *IntegerValue*

Applies To   DBGrid Control
                Grid Control

For a Grid control, also use the SelStartRow and SelEndRow properties to specify multiple rows in a selection.

 We couldn't select more than one cell except by clicking the column headers or row headers (the leftmost gray column). Then no matter what we set SelEndCol to, both SelEndCol and SelStartCol ended up being −1. If we set SelStartCol multiple times, we eventually ended up selecting multiple columns. To select columns 1 and 2, for instance, try this example:

Example
```
DBGrid1.SelStartCol = 1
DBGrid1.SelStartCol = 1
DBGrid1.SelStartCol = 2
```

SelEndRow, SelStartRow Properties

The SelEndRow and SelStartRow properties specify the range of selected cells in a Grid control. They are not available at design time.

- SelEndRow: The bottom selected row
- SelStartRow: The top selected row

Usage   *IntegerValue* = *object*.SelEndRow
                   object.SelEndRow = *IntegerValue*

                   IntegerValue = *object*.SelStartRow
                   object.SelStartRow = *IntegerValue*

Applies To   Grid Control

Also use the SelStartCol and SelEndCol properties to specify multiple columns in a selection.

SelFontName Property

The SelFontName property controls the font that the currently selected text or the characters immediately following the insertion point will be in in the RichTextBox control.

Usage   *object*.SelFontName = *StringValue*
                   StringValue = *object*.SelFontName

Applies To   RichTextBox Control

This property is not available at design time.

PARAMETER	VALUE	MEANING
StringValue	String	The name of a font installed on the system.
	Null	Means you've selected text that contains multiple fonts.

SelFontSize Property

The SelFontSize property controls the size of the font in a RichTextBox control.

Usage   *object*.SelFontSize = *IntegerValue*
                   IntegerValue = *object*.SelFontSize

Applies To   RichTextBox Control

This property is not available at design time.

PARAMETER	VALUE	MEANING
IntegerValue	Integer	The size of the font in points. The max is 2,160.
	Null	Means you've selected text that contains multiple font sizes.

 Choose your font name (SelFontName) before setting the size and style of the font, except when using TrueType fonts with a size below 8 points. In this latter case, you have to set the point size with SelFontSize first, then set the font name with SelFont-Name, and then set the size again. Why? Must be a BUG.

SelHangingIndent Property

The SelHangingIndent property controls the hanging indentation settings for paragraphs in a RichTextBox control.

Usage   *object*.SelHangingIndent = *IntegerValue*
                    IntegerValue = *object*.SelHangingIndent

Applies To   RichTextBox Control

A hanging indent in VB is the distance between the left edge of the first line of text and the left edge of the rest of the paragraph. This property works either on paragraphs that contain what's se-lected or on paragraphs that you add at the current insertion point. It is not available at design time.

PARAMETER	VALUE	MEANING
IntegerValue	Integer	Controls how much text will be indented. It uses the scale of the form on which the RichTextBox control resides.
	0	The selection contains multiple paragraphs with different margin settings.

SelIndent Property

The SelIndent property controls how much the left side of the body of a paragraph in a Rich-TextBox control will be indented from the left edge of the RichTextBox.

Usage   *object*.SelIndent = *IntegerValue*
                   IntegerValue = *object*.SelIndent

Applies To   RichTextBox Control

This property works either on paragraphs that contain what's selected or on paragraphs that you add at the current insertion point. It is not available at design time.

PARAMETER	VALUE	MEANING
IntegerValue	Integer	Controls how much text will be indented. It uses the scale of the form on which the RichTextBox control resides.
	0	The selection contains multiple paragraphs with different margin settings.

SelItalic Property

The SelItalic property controls whether the selected text in a RichTextBox control will appear in italic format.

Usage   *object*.SelItalic = *BooleanValue*
                   BooleanValue = *object*.SelItalic

Applies To   RichTextBox Control

This property is not available at design time.

PARAMETER	VALUE	MEANING
BooleanValue	True	All the characters in the selection or the characters after the insertion point will be italic.
	False	None of the characters in the selection or the characters after the insertion point will be italic.
	Null	The current selection holds more than one paragraph, and the paragraphs have multiple styles.

SelLength Property

This SelLength property specifies the number of characters selected in the text-box portion of the control. It is not available at design time.

Usage	*LongValue = object*.SelLength
	object.SelLength = *LongValue*

Applies To	ComboBox Control
	DBCombo Control
	TextBox Control

The return value of SelLength ranges from 0 to the number of characters in the text-box portion of the control. Setting SelLength to a value has the meanings given in the following table.

VALUE	MEANING
0	Deselects all characters.
Positive number	Selects the indicated number of characters, starting from the character specified by the SelStart property. If the value is greater than the number of characters in the existing text, then all characters from SelStart to the end of the existing text are selected. No error occurs.
Negative number	Error

Use this property with SelStart and SelText properties to manipulate text in controls. The following example selects a substring from the second through the fifth character:

Example
```
Combo1.SelStart = 2
Combo1.SelLength = 4
```

SelLength Property (RichTextBox, Slider Control)

This SelLength property controls how many characters (for the RichTextBox) or how much space (for a Slider) is selected. It's not available at design time.

Usage	*object*.SelLength = *IntegerValue*
	IntegerValue = object.SelLength

Applies To	RichTextBox Control
	Slider Control

PARAMETER	VALUE	MEANING
IntegerValue	Numeric expression	The number of characters that are selected in a RichTextBox control or the number of characters you want to select after the insertion mark. For the Slider control, it's the length of the selected range.

SelPrint Method

The SelPrint method prints formatted text in a RichTextBox control.

Usage   *object*.SelPrint(*hdc*)

Applies To   RichTextBox Control

PARAMETER	VALUE	MEANING
hdc	A Windows device context	The device context of the printer you want to use.

The SelPrint method prints what you select in a RichTextBox, not the whole form. If you select nothing, SelPrint prints the entire contents.

SelRightIndent Property

The SelRightIndent property controls how much the text in a RichTextBox control will be indented from the right side of the control.

Usage   *object*.SelRightIndent = *IntegerValue*
                  IntegerValue = *object*.SelRightIndent

Applies To   RichTextBox Control

This property is not available at design time.

PARAMETER	VALUE	MEANING
IntegerValue	Integer	The indentation measured in the unit of measure of the form on which the RichTextBox resides.
	0	You've selected multiple paragraphs with different margin settings.

SelRTF Property

The SelRTF property controls what text is in the current selection of a RichTextBox control.

Usage   *object*.SelRTF = *StringValue*
                  StringValue = *object*.SelRTF

Applies To   RichTextBox Control

This property is not available at design time.

PARAMETER	VALUE	MEANING
StringValue	String	The selected string.

SelStart Property

This SelStart property specifies the start of the selection in the text-box portion of the control. If no text is selected, it returns the insertion point. It is not available at design time.

Usage   *LongValue* = *object*.SelStart
            object.SelStart = *LongValue*

Applies To   Column Object
            ComboBox Control
            DBCombo Control
            Grid Control
            MDIForm Object
            TextBox Control

The return value of SelStart ranges from 0 to the number of characters in the text-box portion of the control. Setting SelStart to a value has the meanings given in the following table.

VALUE	MEANING
0	Sets the insertion point to before the first character in the text box. It resets SelLength to 0, thereby indicating that no text is selected.
Positive number	Sets the insertion point to just after the indicated character. If SelStart is greater than the number of characters, it is set to the number of characters, placing the insertion point at the end of the existing text. It resets SelLength to 0, thereby indicating that no text is selected.
Negative number	Error

Use this property with the SelLength and SelText properties to manipulate text in controls.

The following example sets the insertion point to the end of the existing text of a TextBox control:

Example   `Text1.SelStart = Len(Text1.Text)`

SelStart Property (RichTextBox, Slider Control)

This SelStart property controls where the insertion point is. It sets the starting point of the text to be selected, if appropriate.

Usage   *object*.SelStart = *IntegerValue*
                     IntegerValue = *object*.SelStart

Applies To   RichTextBox Control
                     Slider Control

This property is not available at design time.

PARAMETER	VALUE	MEANING
IntegerValue	Numeric expression	The starting point of selected text in a RichTextBox control. For a Slider control, it is the start of the selected range.

SelStrikeThrough Property

The SelStrikeThrough property controls whether the selected text in a RichTextBox control will appear in strikethrough format.

Usage   *object*.SelStrikeThrough = *BooleanValue*
                     BooleanValue = *object*.SelStrikeThrough

Applies To   RichTextBox Control

This property is not available at design time.

PARAMETER	VALUE	MEANING
BooleanValue	True	All the characters in the selection or the characters after the insertion point will be strikethrough.
	False	None of the characters in the selection or the characters after the insertion point will be strikethrough.
	Null	The current selection holds more than one paragraph, and the paragraphs have multiple styles.

SelTabCount Property

The SelTabCount property controls how many tabs a RichTextBox has.

Usage   *object*.SelTabCount = *IntegerValue*
              IntegerValue = *object*.SelTabCount

Applies To   RichTextBox Control

This property is not available at design time.

PARAMETER	VALUE	MEANING
IntegerValue	Integer	How many tabs stops will be in the selected paragraphs or following paragraphs.

Normally, pressing Tab when typing in a VB application moves focus to the next control in the Tab order. But that's not so great in a word-processor-like application. So, when the RichTextBox has focus, disable the TabStop property of everything else, like this:

Example

```
Private Sub RichTextBox1_GotFocus()
      For Each Control In Controls
            Control.TabStop = False
      Next Control
End Sub
```

Turn it on when the RichTextBox loses focus.

SelTabs Property

The SelTabs property sets absolute tab positions in a RichTextBox control.

Usage   *object*.SelTabs(*Index*) = *IntegerValue*
              IntegerValue = *object*.SelTabs(*Index*)

Applies To   RichTextBox Control

This property is not available at design time.

PARAMETER	VALUE	MEANING
Index	Integer	An index specifying a tab. The first tab has an index of 0; the last one is equal to SelTabCount – 1.
IntegerValue	Integer	The location at which a tab is to go, specified in the unit of the measure of the form that holds the RichTextBox.

Normally, pressing Tab when typing in a VB application moves focus to the next control in the Tab order. But that's not so great in a word-processor-like application. So, when the RichTextBox has focus, disable the TabStop property of everything else, like this:

Example
```
Private Sub RichTextBox1_GotFocus()
        For Each Control In Controls
                Control.TabStop = False
        Next Control
End Sub
```

Turn it on when the RichTextBox loses focus.

SelText Property

This SelText property either returns the text that is selected in the text-box portion of a control or allows you to replace the selected text. It is not available at design time.

Usage   *StringValue* = *object*.SelText
             object.SelText = *StringValue*

Applies To   Column Object
                  ComboBox Control
                  DBCombo Control
                  Grid Control
                  MDIForm Object
                  TextBox Control

If the return value is an empty string, then no text is selected. Setting SelText either replaces the selected text, if any, with the StringValue or inserts text at the insertion point if no characters are selected. Setting SelText also resets SelLength to 0, thereby indicating that no characters are selected after text has been inserted into the text-box portion of the control.

Use this property with the SelLength and SelStart properties to manipulate text in controls.

The following example replaces a substring with a new string:

Example
```
Text1.SelStart = 5
Text1.SelLength = Len(newString$)
Text1.SelText = newString$
```

SelText Property (RichTextBox Control)

This SelText property controls the string containing the currently selected text.

Usage   *object*.SelText = *StringValue*
             StringValue = *object*.SelText

Applies To   RichTextBox Control

PARAMETER	VALUE	MEANING
StringValue	String	The selected text.

SelUnderline Property

The SelUnderline property controls whether the selected text in a RichTextBox control will appear in underlined format.

Usage   *object*.SelUnderline = *BooleanValue*
                    BooleanValue = *object*.SelUnderline

Applies To   RichTextBox Control

This property is not available at design time.

PARAMETER	VALUE	MEANING
BooleanValue	True	All the characters in the selection or the characters after the insertion point will be underlined.
	False	None of the characters in the selection or the characters after the insertion point will be underlined.
	Null	The current selection holds more than one paragraph, and the paragraphs have multiple styles.

SetData Method

The SetData method places graphics data onto the Clipboard object. To set text, use SetText.

Usage   *object*.SetData Data, [*Format*]

Applies To   Clipboard Object

The Format argument can take on the values given in the following table.

PARAMETER	VALUE	MEANING
Data	Picture value	The data to be placed onto the Clipboard.
Format	0 or omitted	Automatically uses data of the correct format, depending on the destination for the result.
	vbCFBitmap or 2	Windows bitmap files (.BMP).
	vbCFMetafile or 3	Windows metafiles (.WMF).
	vbCFDIB or 8	Device-independent bitmap (.DIB).
	vbCFPalette or 9	Color palette.
	Otherwise	Nothing.

Example   `Clipboard.SetData Picture1, vbCFDIB`

This example displays the DIB contents of the Clipboard object in the Picture1 PictureBox control. If no data of the requested format is on the Clipboard, then nothing is returned.

SetFocus Method

The SetFocus method moves the focus to the associated form or control. Calling this method causes the LostFocus event of the control losing focus, followed by GotFocus of the new control to be run.

Usage   *object*.SetFocus

Applies To   CheckBox Control
ComboBox Control
CommandButton Control
DBCombo Control
DBGrid Control
DBList Control
DirListBox Control
DriveListBox Control
FileListBox Control
Form Object
HScrollBar, VScrollBar Controls
ListBox Control
MDIForm Object
OLE Container Control
OptionButton Control
PictureBox Control
TextBox Control

The specified object must be able to receive focus, which means its Enabled and Visible properties must be True. Moreover, you can use the SetFocus method in the Load event of a form to move focus to one of its controls *only* after you have used the Show method to show the form.

SetText Method

The SetText method for the Clipboard object places a text string on the Clipboard using the specified data format.

Usage   *object*.SetText *Data*[, *Format*]

Applies To   Clipboard Object

The arguments to the SetText property have the meanings given in the following table.

PARAMETER	VALUE	MEANING
Data	String expression	The string data to place on the Clipboard.
Format	vbCFText, 1, or omitted	Data is text.
	vbCFLink or &HBF00	Data is DDE conversation information.
	vbCFRTF or &HBF01	Data is in rich-text format.

For the vbCFLink format, the text must be of the form

```
application|topic!item
```

In addition, you should use the SetData method or the SetText method with the vbCFText format to place text or data associated with the link item on the Clipboard. The following example implements an EditCopy command for a DDE source form, thereby allowing a destination application to use PasteLink from a source control on the form:

Example
```
Private Sub EditCopy_Click()
    Dim linkItem$
    Clipboard.Clear
    linkItem$ = App.EXEName & "|" & LinkTopic _
        & "!" & Screen.ActiveControl.Name
    If TypeOf Screen.ActiveControl is PictureBox Then
        Clipboard.SetText linkItem$, vbCFLink
        Clipboard.SetData Screen.ActiveControl.Picture
    ElseIf TypeOf Screen.ActiveControl is TextBox Then
        Clipboard.SetText linkItem$, vbCFLink
        Clipboard.SetText Screen.ActiveControl.Text, vbCFText
    Else
        Clipboard.SetText Screen.ActiveControl, vbCFText
    End If
End Sub
```

The vbCFRTF format doesn't really work. When we try to use the constant, we get an overflow error. If we use &HBF01, nothing gets placed on the Clipboard.

Shape Property

The Shape property specifies the appearance of a Shape control.

Usage   *IntegerValue = object*.Shape
               object.Shape = *IntegerValue*

Applies To   Shape Control

This property can take on the values given in the following table.

Constant	Value	Meaning
vbShapeRectangle	0	Rectangle
vbShapeSquare	1	Square
vbShapeOval	2	Oval
vbShapeCircle	3	Circle
vbShapeRoundedRectangle	4	Rounded rectangle
vbShapeRoundedSquare	5	Rounded square

ShortCut Property

The Shortcut property specifies the short-cut key that selects a menu item. It is also known as the *menu accelerator.*

Usage   *object*.ShortCut = *Value*

Applies To   Menu Control

To tell you the truth, we're not sure how to use the constants given in the following table, since the ShortCut property is selectable only at design time in the Menu Editor from a drop-down list. This property is *not* available at runtime. The following constants all denote user-defined shortcut keystrokes.

Constant	Value	Constant	Value
vbMenuAccelCtrlA	1	vbMenuAccelF6	32
vbMenuAccelCtrlB	2	vbMenuAccelF7	33
vbMenuAccelCtrlC	3	vbMenuAccelF8	34
vbMenuAccelCtrlD	4	vbMenuAccelF9	35
vbMenuAccelCtrlE	5	vbMenuAccelF11	36
vbMenuAccelCtrlF	6	vbMenuAccelF12	37
vbMenuAccelCtrlG	7	vbMenuAccelCtrlF1	38
vbMenuAccelCtrlH	8	vbMenuAccelCtrlF2	39
vbMenuAccelCtrlI	9	vbMenuAccelCtrlF3	40
vbMenuAccelCtrlJ	10	vbMenuAccelCtrlF4	41
vbMenuAccelCtrlK	11	vbMenuAccelCtrlF5	42
vbMenuAccelCtrlL	12	vbMenuAccelCtrlF6	43
vbMenuAccelCtrlM	13	vbMenuAccelCtrlF7	44
vbMenuAccelCtrlN	14	vbMenuAccelCtrlF8	45
vbMenuAccelCtrlO	15	vbMenuAccelCtrlF9	46
vbMenuAccelCtrlP	16	vbMenuAccelCtrlF11	47
vbMenuAccelCtrlQ	17	vbMenuAccelCtrlF12	48
vbMenuAccelCtrlR	18	vbMenuAccelShiftF1	49
vbMenuAccelCtrlS	19	vbMenuAccelShiftF2	50
vbMenuAccelCtrlT	20	vbMenuAccelShiftF3	51
vbMenuAccelCtrlU	21	vbMenuAccelShiftF4	52
vbMenuAccelCtrlV	22	vbMenuAccelShiftF5	53
vbMenuAccelCtrlW	23	vbMenuAccelShiftF6	54
vbMenuAccelCtrlX	24	vbMenuAccelShiftF7	55
vbMenuAccelCtrlY	25	vbMenuAccelShiftF8	56
vbMenuAccelCtrlZ	26	vbMenuAccelShiftF9	57
vbMenuAccelF1	27	vbMenuAccelShiftF11	58
vbMenuAccelF2	28	vbMenuAccelShiftF12	59
vbMenuAccelF3	29	vbMenuAccelShiftCtrlF1	60
vbMenuAccelF4	30	vbMenuAccelShiftCtrlF2	61
vbMenuAccelF5	31	vbMenuAccelShiftCtrlF3	62

CONSTANT	VALUE	CONSTANT	VALUE
vbMenuAccelShiftCtrlF4	63	vbMenuAccelShiftCtrlF12	70
vbMenuAccelShiftCtrlF5	64	vbMenuAccelCtrlIns	71
vbMenuAccelShiftCtrlF6	65	vbMenuAccelShiftIns	72
vbMenuAccelShiftCtrlF7	66	vbMenuAccelDel	73
vbMenuAccelShiftCtrlF8	67	vbMenuAccelShiftDel	74
vbMenuAccelShiftCtrlF9	68	vbMenuAccelAltBksp	75
vbMenuAccelShiftCtrlF11	69		

Show Method

The Show method displays a form. If the form is not yet loaded, it is automatically loaded with this method. Non-MDI child forms can specify a Style argument.

Usage   *object*.Show [*Style*]

Applies To   Form Object
                 MDIFormObject

PARAMETER	VALUE	MEANING
Style	vbModeless or 0	Modeless form. Subsequent lines of code are executed when the form is displayed.
	vbModal or 1	Modal form. Subsequent lines of code are *not* executed until the form is hidden or unloaded. Moreover, keyboard and mouse input to the application are allowed *only* in the displayed form. An MDIForm object may not be shown modally.

To display an About form modally, use the following:

Example   `frmAbout.Show vbModal`

Showing an MDI child form will cause its parent MDIForm object to be loaded and displayed.

ShowColor Method

The ShowColor method shows the CommonDialog control's Color dialog box.

Usage	*object*.ShowColor
Applies To	CommonDialog Control

ShowFocusRect Property

The ShowFocusRect property controls whether the focus rectangle (a dotted rectangle) is visible on a tab on an SSTab control when the tab gets focus.

Usage	*object*.ShowFocusRect = *BooleanValue* *BooleanValue* = *object*.ShowFocusRect
Applies To	SSTab Control

PARAMETER	VALUE	MEANING
BooleanValue	True	The default. The focus rectangle is visible.
	False	The focus rectangle is not visible.

ShowFont Method

The ShowFont method shows the CommonDialog control's Font dialog box.

Usage	*object*.ShowFont
Applies To	CommonDialog Control

 Note that before you use ShowFont, you must set the Flags property of the CommonDialog to either cdlCFBoth, &H3, cdlCFPrinterFonts, &H2, cdlCFScreenFonts, or &H1. Otherwise, you get a specious "There are no fonts installed" error.

ShowHelp Method

The ShowHelp method runs WINHELP.EXE on the file set in the HelpFile property.

Usage	*object*.ShowHelp
Applies To	CommonDialog Control

ShowInTaskbar Property

The ShowInTaskbar property specifies whether a Form window is listed in the Windows 95 Taskbar. This property is available only when run on a system using the Windows 95 interface. It is read-only at runtime.

Usage   *BooleanValue* = *object*.ShowInTaskbar

Applies To   Form Object

The values for the ShowInTaskbar property have the meanings given in the following table.

VALUE	MEANING
True	The default if BorderStyle is vbFixedSingle (1) or vbSizable (2). The Form window is listed in the Taskbar.
False	The default if BorderStyle is *not* vbFixedSingle (1) or vbSizable (2). The Form window is not listed in the Taskbar.

When a window is listed in the Taskbar, the user can quickly activate it by clicking the window's icon. You may not want to list temporary or auxiliary windows—such as a properties box or dialog window—in the Taskbar so as to avoid clutter. In these cases, make sure the ShowInTaskbar property of the Form object is set to False.

ShowOpen Method

The ShowOpen method shows the CommonDialog control's File/Open dialog box.

Usage   *object*.ShowOpen

Applies To   CommonDialog Control

ShowPrinter Method

The ShowPrinter method shows the CommonDialog control's Printer dialog box.

Usage   *object*.ShowPrinter

Applies To   CommonDialog Control

ShowSave Method

The ShowSave method shows the CommonDialog control's File/Save dialog box.

Usage   *object*.ShowSave

Applies To   CommonDialog Control

ShowTips Property

The ShowTips property specifies whether to display ToolTips for an object in a custom control.

Usage   *BooleanValue* = *object*.ShowTips
                 object.ShowTips = *BooleanValue*

Applies To   TabStrip Control
                 Toolbar Control

PARAMETER	VALUE	MEANING
BooleanValue	True	The default. Allows VB to display the text specified by the ToolTipText property of an object when the mouse cursor is held over the object for about a second or so.
	False	ToolTips will not be displayed.

ShowWhatsThis Method

The ShowWhatsThis method is available only for the Windows 95 or Windows NT 3.51 platforms. It displays a "What's This" popup help topic that is specified by the WhatsThisHelpID and HelpFile properties.

Usage   *object*.ShowWhatsThis

Applies To   CheckBox Control
                 ComboBox Control
                 CommandButton Control
                 Data Control
                 DBCombo Control
                 DBGrid Control
                 DBList Control
                 DirListBox Control

DriveListBox Control
FileListBox Control
Frame Control
Grid Control
HScrollBar, VScrollBar Controls
Image Control
Label Control
ListBox Control
OLE Container Control
OptionButton Control
PictureBox Control
TextBox Control

You can use the ShowWhatsThis method to build your own context-sensitive Help button. The WhatsThisHelp property of the parent form *must* be set to True before this method will have any effect.

Example

```
Private LastControl As Control

Private Sub Text1_MouseDown(Button As Integer, Shift As Integer, _
    X As Single, Y As Single)
    If Button = vbRightButton Then
        Set LastControl = Text1
        PopupMenu mnuPopup
    End If
    Set LastControl = Nothing
End Sub

Private Sub mnuPopupWhatsThis_Click()
    LastControl.ShowWhatsThis
End Sub
```

For this example, mnuPopupWhatsThis is a menu item of the mnuPopup popup menu. Context-sensitive help is provided for the Text1 control when the right mouse button is clicked over Text1 and the user selects the mnuPopupWhatsThis menu from the popup menu. By using the MouseDown event of other controls on the form, you can provide context-sensitive help via a click of the right mouse button.

SimpleText Property

The SimpleText property controls what text a StatusBar control will show when its Style property is Simple.

Usage   *object*.SimpleText = *StringValue*

Applies To   StatusBar Control

PARAMETER	VALUE	MEANING
StringValue	String	The text you want the StatusBar to show (typically when a user pulls down a menu, this text will explain what the menu does).

Size Property

The Size property works with the Font and StdFont objects to change the size of a font.

Usage   *Font*.Size = *IntegerValue*
                 IntegerValue = *Font*.Size

Applies To   Font Object
                 StdFont Object

PARAMETER	VALUE	MEANING
IntegerValue	0 – 2,048	The size of your font in points.

SizeMode Property

The SizeMode property specifies how an OLE Container control displays its object.

Usage   *IntegerValue* = *object*.SizeMode
                 object.SizeMode = *IntegerValue*

Applies To   OLE Container Control

The SizeMode property can take on one of the values given in the following table.

CONSTANT	VALUE	MEANING
vbOLESizeClip	0	The default. The object is displayed in its actual size, and its image is clipped by the OLE Container control's borders.
vbOLESizeStretch	1	The object's image is sized to just fill the OLE Container control and will not maintain its original proportions.
vbOLESizeAutoSize	2	The OLE Container control is automatically resized to display the entire object in its actual size and proportions. When the OLE Container control is updated after the object's size has changed, it invokes the Container control's Resize event with the recommended size in the HeightNew

CONSTANT	VALUE	MEANING
vbOLESizeAutoSize	2 (cont.)	and WidthNew arguments to the Resize event. You can intercept and change these values in the Resize event for the Container control. Only after the Resize event runs will the Container control's size change.
vbOLESizeZoom	3	The object's image is sized to fill the OLE Container control while maintaining its original proportions.

SmallChange Property (HScrollbar, VScrollBar Control)

This SmallChange property specifies the amount by which to change the value of an HScrollBar or VScrollBar control when the user clicks the mouse on the scroll arrows. Depending on which arrow is clicked, the value of the SmallChange property will be added or subtracted from the Value property.

Usage
    IntegerValue = object.SmallChange
    object.SmallChange = *IntegerValue*

Applies To   HScrollBar Control
    VScrollBar Control

The values for the SmallChange property have the meanings given in the following table.

VALUE	MEANING
1 to 32,767	The value that will be added or subtracted from the Value property. By default, SmallChange is set to 1.
Other values	Error

Note that the increments for scroll bars on a ComboBox or ListBox control are set automatically.

Set SmallChange to be smaller than LargeChange to make your scroll bars easier to use.

SmallChange Property (Slider Control)

This SmallChange property sets the number of ticks the slider will move when you press the left or right arrow keys.

Usage
    object.SmallChange = *LongValue*
    LongValue = object.SmallChange

Applies To   Slider Control

PARAMETER	VALUE	MEANING
LongValue	Long integer	How many ticks the slider moves (the default is 1).

Sorted Property (ComboBox, ListBox Control)

This Sorted property specifies that the items in the list portion of the control are automatically sorted alphabetically. It can be set only at design time and is read-only at runtime.

Usage   *BooleanValue* = *object*.Sorted

Applies To   ComboBox Control
                   ListBox Control

The possible values of this Sorted property are given in the following table.

VALUE	MEANING
True	The list is sorted alphabetically as items are added.
False	The default. The list is not sorted.

All punctuation is sorted before digits and letters, and digits are sorted before letters. Sorting between letters is alphabetical, regardless of case, but uppercase versions of a letter are sorted before lowercase versions. That is, a, b, A, B are sorted as A, a, B, b.

Note: With this Sorted property set to True, the list will remain sorted only if you use the AddItem method to add items, *without* using the optional Index argument to manually place items in the list.

Sorted Property (ListView Control, Node Object)

This Sorted property answers the question, "Are the ListItem objects in a ListView or Node object sorted?"

Usage   *object*.Sorted = *BooleanValue*
                   BooleanValue = *object*.Sorted

Applies To   ListView Control
                   Node Object

PARAMETER	VALUE	MEANING
BooleanValue	True	The ListItem objects in a ListView or Node are sorted alphabetically, according to SortOrder.
	False	The ListItem objects are not sorted.

Note: When the content of the view changes (e.g., you add a file), the view won't be resorted.

Sorted Property (TreeView)

This Sorted property controls whether Nodes are sorted alphabetically.

Usage   *object*.Sorted = *BooleanValue*
                      BooleanValue = *object*.Sorted

Applies To   TreeView Control

PARAMETER	VALUE	MEANING
BooleanValue	True	Nodes are sorted alphabetically.
	False	Nodes are not sorted.

You can use this Sorted property either with a whole TreeView control to sort the root Nodes (TreeView1.Sorted = True) or on individual Nodes (nodNewNode.Sorted = True).

SortKey Property

The SortKey property tells you how the items in a ListView are sorted.

Usage   *object*.SortKey = *IntegerValue*
                      IntegerValue = *object*.SortKey

Applies To   ListView Control

PARAMETER	VALUE	MEANING
IntegerValue	0	Sorts on the object's Text property.
	1	Sorts using subitem 1.
	2	Sorts using subitem 2.
	...	And so on.

Two comments: First, you have to set Sorted = True before SortKey will work, and second, you should add code like the following to the ColumnClick event of your ListView:

```
Private Sub ListView1_ColumnClick (ByVal ColumnHeader as ColumnHeader)
     ListView1.SortKey=ColumnHeader.Index-1
End Sub
```

This code will automatically sort the view based on a column when the user clicks the column header.

SortOrder Property

The SortOrder property tells you if the ListItem objects are sorted in ascending or descending order.

Usage   *object*.SortOrder = *IntegerValue*
                 IntegerValue = *object*.SortOrder

Applies To   ListView Control

PARAMETER	VALUE	MEANING
IntegerValue	lvwAscending or 0	Sorts ListItem objects in ascending alphabetical, numeric, or date order.
	LvwDescending or 1	Sorts ListItem objects in descending order.

SourceDoc Property

The SourceDoc property specifies the name of a file to use to create an object in an OLE Container control. This property is provided for compatibility with the Action property. However, it should be avoided in new implementations; use the CreateEmbed and CreateLink methods instead.

Usage   *StringValue* = *object*.SourceDoc
                 object.SourceDoc = *StringValue*

Applies To   OLE Container Control

The StringValue specifies a filename.

To link an object using the Action property, use the SourceDoc property to specify the file and the SourceItem property to specify the data within the file for linking.

To embed an object using the Action property, use the SourceDoc property to specify a file to use as a template.

After data has been linked, the SourceItem property is set to a zero-length string (" "). Also, the SourceDoc property is set to the full path of the link and the source item, separated by an exclamation point (!) or a backslash (\):

Example   `"E:\USER\prj\OLE.doc!OLE_LINK1"`

Whether the separator is an exclamation point or backslash depends on the source application.

SourceItem Property

The SourceItem property specifies the data within a file to be linked when creating a linked object in an OLE Container control. The item specifies a unit of data that can correspond to a bookmark, a range of cells, and so on and depends on the source application.

Usage   *StringValue* = *object*.SourceItem
                 object.SourceItem = *StringValue*

Applies To   OLE Container Control

The OLETypeAllowed property must be set to vbOLELinked (0) or vbOLEEither (2), and the SourceDoc property must point to a valid file.

Consult the documentation for the source application that supplies the object in order to determine the proper syntax for specifying the SourceItem property. You can often guess at the proper syntax by using the Paste Special command to link an object and then examining the SourceDoc property for the syntax. In most cases, this property consists of the full path of a file and the source item reference, separated by an exclamation point (!) or backslash (\):

Example   `"C:\Worksheets\Mortgage.xls!R2C1:R3C5"`

Span Method

The Span method selects text in a RichTextBox control based on a set of specified characters. In other words, use Span to select words or sentences.

Usage   *object*.Span *Characterset*[, *Forward*][, *Negate*]

Applies To   RichTextBox Control

This method does not support named arguments.

PARAMETER	VALUE	MEANING
Characterset	String	Required. The set of characters to look for.
Forward	True or omitted	Optional. Selects text from the insertion point toward the end of the text.
	False	Optional. Selects text from the insertion point toward the beginning of the text.
Negate	True	Optional. The selection stops at the first character specified in Characterset.
	False or omitted	Optional. The selection stops at the first character that does not appear in Characterset.

StartLabelEdit Method

The StartLabelEdit method enables a user to edit a label.

Usage   *object*.StartLabelEdit

Applies To   ListView Control
                TreeView Control

When you set LabelEdit to Manual, you must use this method to start a label editing operation. It also triggers the BeforeLabelEdit event.

StartMode Property

The StartMode property is read-only at runtime. It tells you whether the application was started as a stand-alone application or as an OLE Automation server via OLE calls.

Usage   *IntegerValue = object*.StartMode

Applies To   App Object

Valid values for the StartMode property are given in the following table.

CONSTANT	VALUE	MEANING
vbSModeStandalone	0	Stand-alone application.
vbSModeAutomation	1	OLE Automation server.

For debugging, you can set the StartMode to "OLE Server" at design time using the Tools/Options/Project dialog box to pretend the application was started as an OLE Automation server. It has no effect on the generated .EXE or .DLL file.

Example

```
Sub MAIN()
    If App.StartMode = vbSModeStandalone Then
        Form1.Show
    Else
        Load Form1
    End If
End Sub
```

This example displays the form only if the application was started stand-alone. Otherwise, it just loads the form without making it visible.

Stretch Property

The Stretch property specifies whether a graphic is automatically resized to fit an Image control; the original proportions of the graphic are not preserved. If set to True, resizing the Image control also resizes the graphic to fit.

Usage

BooleanValue = object.Stretch
object.Stretch = *BooleanValue*

Applies To   Image Control

The values of the Stretch property have the meanings given in the following table.

VALUE	MEANING
True	The graphics in an Image control are resized to fit the control. Proportions are not preserved, so the image may be distorted.
False	The default. The Image control resizes to fit the graphic. If you subsequently change the size of the control, the graphic will remain unchanged.

StrikeThrough Property

The StrikeThrough property works with the Font and StdFont objects to make a font strikethrough or not strikethrough.

Usage

Font.StrikeThrough = *BooleanValue*
BooleanValue = Font.StrikeThrough

Applies To   Font Object
                    StdFont Object

PARAMETER	VALUE	MEANING
BooleanValue	True	The font is strikethrough.
	False	The font is not strikethrough.

Style Property (ComboBox, DBCombo Control)

This Style property is set at design time to determine the appearance and behavior of the list-box portion of the ComboBox control. It is read-only at runtime.

Usage   *IntegerValue = object*.Style

Applies To   ComboBox Control
                  DBCombo Control

The possible styles of the Style property are given in the following table.

CONSTANT	VALUE	MEANING
vbComboDropdown	0	The default when you first create a ComboBox. It consists of a text box with a drop-down list. The user can select from the list or type in the text box.
vbComboSimple	1	A text box and a list box. The size of the ComboBox includes both the text box and the list.
vbComboDropdownList	2	Includes only the drop-down list. The user can make selections only from the list.

Style Property (Button Object)

This Style property controls the appearance and behavior of a Button object in a Toolbar control.

Usage   *object*.Style = *IntegerValue*
                 IntegerValue = object.Style

Applies To   Button Object

The Style property syntax has the parts given in the following table.

PARAMETER	VALUE	MEANING
IntegerValue	tbrDefault or 0	The Button is normal.
	tbrCheck or 1	The Button is a check button.
	tbrButtonGroup or 2	The Button is part of a group and remains pressed until another button in the group is pressed.
	tbrSeparator or 3	An 8-pixel-wide separator.
	tbrPlaceholder or 4	Like tbrSeparator, but you can set the width.

Note: This Style property works only with Windows 95 and Windows NT 3.51 or higher.

Style Property (DBCombo Control)

This Style property controls what a DBCombo box looks like.

Usage   *object*.Style = *IntegerValue*
               IntegerValue = *object*.Style

Applies To   DBCombo Control

PARAMETER	VALUE	DESCRIPTION
IntegerValue	dbcDropdownCombo or 0	Tells a DBCombo to be a drop-down combo box. Note that the Style property is read-only at runtime. Also note that the Help file says that this constant is called dblDropdownCombo.
	dbcSimpleCombo or 1	Tells a DBCombo to be a simple combo box. Note that the Style property is read-only at runtime. Also note that the Help file says that this constant is called dblSimpleCombo.
	dbcDropdownList or 2	Tells a DBCombo to be a drop-down list. Note that the Style property is read-only at runtime. Also note that the Help file says that this constant is called dblDropdownList.

Style Property (Panel Object)

This Style property controls the style of a StatusBar control's Panel object.

Usage   *object*.Style = *IntegerValue*
                    IntegerValue = *object*.Style

Applies To   Panel Object

PARAMETER	VALUE	MEANING
IntegerValue	sbrText or 0	Either text or a bitmap.
	sbrCaps or 1	The status of the Caps Lock key.
	sbrNum or 2	The status of the NumLock key.
	sbrIns or 3	The status of the Insert key.
	sbrScrl or 4	The status of the Scroll Lock key.
	sbrTime or 5	The current time.
	sbrDate or 6	The current date.

Style Property (SSTab Control)

This Style property specifies the style of the tabs in a SSTab control.

Usage   *IntegerValue* = *object*.Style
                    object.Style = *IntegerValue*

Applies To   SSTab Control

PARAMETER	VALUE	MEANING
IntegerValue	ssStyleTabbedDialog or 0	The default. Uses the Windows 3.1 style of tabs. The tab's font will be bold.
	ssStylePropertyPage or 1	Uses Windows 95-style tabs. The TabMaxWidth property is ignored, thereby allowing the tab widths to adjust to text length. The font is not bold.

Style Property (StatusBar Control)

This Style property specifies the style of a StatusBar control.

Usage   *IntegerValue* = *object*.Style
                    object.Style = *IntegerValue*

Applies To   StatusBar Control

PARAMETER	VALUE	MEANING
IntegerValue	sbrNormal or 0	The default. Normal. The StatusBar shows all its Panel objects.
	sbrSimple or 1	Only one large Panel is displayed. Use the SimpleText property to set the displayed text when using this style.

Style Property (TabStrip Control)

This Style property specifies the appearance of Tab objects in a TabStrip control.

Usage   *object*.Style = *IntegerValue*
                   IntegerValue = *object*.Style

Applies To   TabStrip Control

PARAMETER	VALUE	MEANING
IntegerValue	tabTabs or 0	The default. The tabs look like raised notebook tabs.
	tabButtons or 1	The tabs look like Command buttons.

Style Property (TreeView Control)

This Style property controls the type of graphics and text that appear for each Node object in a TreeView control.

Usage   *object*.Style = *IntegerValue*
                   IntegerValue = *object*.Style

Applies To   TreeView Control

PARAMETER	VALUE	MEANING
IntegerValue	0	Text only.
	1	Images and text.
	2	Plus and minus signs and text.
	3	Like 2, but with images.

PARAMETER	VALUE	MEANING
IntegerValue	4	Lines and text only.
	5	Lines, images, and text.
	6	Lines, plus and minus signs, and text.
	7	Everything.

SubItemIndex Property

The SubItemIndex property controls the index of the subitem (an array of strings describing the ListItem object) associated with a ColumnHeader object.

Usage   *object*.SubItemIndex = *IntegerValue*
              IntegerValue = *object*.SubItemIndex

Applies To   ColumnHeader Object

PARAMETER	VALUE	MEANING
IntegerValue	Integer	The index for a subitem.

Note: This property applies only to Windows 95 and Windows NT 3.51 or higher.

A subitem is an array of strings that contains the information describing a ListItem object. The first ColumnHeader's SubItemIndex property is 0—the small icon and ListItem object's name.

SubItems Property (ListItem Object)

The SubItems property controls a ListItem's subitem text.

Usage   *object*.SubItems(Index) = *StringValue*
              StringValue = *object*.SubItems(Index)

Applies To   ListItem Object

PARAMETER	VALUE	MEANING
StringValue	String	The text that describes the subitem.
Index	Integer	Keys don't seem to work here, but this is the index of the subitem.

A subitem is just VB's way of saying "an array of strings associated with a ListItem object in Report view." Aren't you glad it says subitem instead? To see how it looks, open Windows 95's Explorer and select View/Details. Then look in the right window pane. Those are subitems. Simple, eh? Just remember that (1) subitems are invisible in anything but report (Details) mode, and (2) you have to create a ColumnHeader for each subitem.

System Property

The System property specifies whether a file with its System attribute set is displayed in a FileListBox control. This property overrides the settings for Archive, Hidden, Normal, and Read-Only properties for any file with its System attribute set.

Usage   *BooleanValue = object*.System
                 object.System = *BooleanValue*

Applies To   FileListBox Control

The values for the System property have the meanings given in the following table.

VALUE	MEANING
True	Displays files that have their System attribute set, but their Hidden attribute *not* set, regardless of the settings for the Archive, Normal, and ReadOnly properties. If a file has *both* Hidden and System attributes set, then *both* the Hidden and System properties must be set to True—regardless of the settings for the Archive, Normal, and ReadOnly properties—before the file is displayed in the FileListBox.
False	The default. Does not display files that have their System attribute set.

Setting the System property at runtime will refresh the list of files.
To display all files, set the Normal, Hidden, and System properties to True.

Tab Property (SSTab Control)

The Tab property specifies the current tab for an SSTab control. The current tab is the topmost tab.

Usage   *IntegerValue = object*.Tab
                 object.Tab = *IntegerValue*

Applies To   SSTab Control

The first tab in the control is 0.

TabCaption Property

The TabCaption property sets the caption (title) of a tab in an SSTab control.

Usage   *object*.TabCaption(*Tab*) = *StringValue*
                     StringValue = *object*.TabCaption(*Tab*)

Applies To   SSTab Control

PARAMETER	VALUE	MEANING
Tab	Numeric expression	The number of the tab you want to modify.
StringValue	String	The caption you want to display.

This property works only at runtime. To change things at design time, click the tab you want to alter and modify the Caption property in the Properties window. Alternatively, you can use the general Caption property to change the caption of the currently selected tab.

When you're creating your caption, remember to use access keys. Do this by inserting an ampersand (&) just before the character you want to have work with the Alt key to activate the tab. Double ampersands (&&) enable you to include an ampersand in a tab's caption.

TabEnabled Property

The TabEnabled property controls whether a tab in an SSTab control will respond to being clicked.

Usage   *object*.TabEnabled(*Tab*) = *BooleanValue*
                     BooleanValue = *object*.TabEnabled(*Tab*)

Applies To   SSTab Control

PARAMETER	VALUE	MEANING
Tab	Numeric expression	The number of the tab you want to modify.
BooleanValue	True	The tab is enabled.
	False	The tab is disabled (grayed out).

TabFixedHeight, TabFixedWidth Properties

If TabWidthStyle is set to tabFixed, the TabFixedHeight and TabFixedWidth properties control the height and width of the tabs, respectively.

Usage   *object*.TabFixedHeight = *IntegerValue*
                     IntegerValue = *object*.TabFixedHeight
                     object.TabFixedWidth = *IntegerValue*
                     IntegerValue = *object*.TabFixedWidth

Applies To   TabStrip Control

PARAMETER	VALUE	MEANING
IntegerValue	Integer	The number of pixels (or twips) of the height or width.

TabHeight Property

The TabHeight property controls the height of all tabs on an SSTab control.

Usage   *object*.TabHeight = *SingleValue*
                     SingleValue = *object*.TabHeight

Applies To   SSTab Control

PARAMETER	VALUE	MEANING
SingleValue	Single-precision value	The height of the tabs, in the same scale as whatever form (or container) holds the SSTab control.

TabIndex Property

The tab order lets a user use the Tab key to navigate focus through the objects on a form. Use the TabIndex property of the objects to specify the order in which the objects receive focus. When focus is at the final control in the tab order, tabbing again jumps focus to the first control in the tab order.

Usage   *IntegerValue* = *object*.TabIndex
                     object.TabIndex = *IntegerValue*

Applies To   CheckBox Control
                     ComboBox Control
                     CommandButton Control
                     DBCombo Control
                     DBGrid Control
                     DBList Control

DirListBox Control
DriveListBox Control
FileListBox Control
Frame Control
Grid Control
HScrollBar, VScrollBar Controls
Label Control
ListBox Control
OLE Container Control
OptionButton Control
PictureBox Control
TextBox Control

The TabIndex value must range from 0 to the number of controls on the form that have the TabIndex property. Using a negative value causes an error. By default, VB sets tab ordering to be the order in which you created the objects. You will want to change the tab order to make your application more usable. When you set the TabIndex property of one control, VB readjusts the TabIndex property of other controls to make sure that they remain in order (except for the one you just changed) and that their values remain unique.

All controls except menus and timers have the TabIndex property. However, because Label and Frame controls cannot receive focus, these will always be skipped in the tab order. Also, controls that are hidden or disabled or that have TabStop properties set to False at runtime will be skipped during tabbing.

When forms saved as ASCII text are loaded and the TabIndex of a control conflicts with an already-assigned value, VB will assign the TabIndex a new value. The TabIndex property isn't affected by the ZOrder method.

Many controls do not have the Caption property, so you cannot define access keys for them directly. You can, however, use a Label control to provide the access key. However, you have to ensure that the TabIndex value of your control immediately follows that of the Label control. For instance, to provide an access key for your TextBox control that has a TabIndex of 8, add a Label control and set its TabIndex to 7. Then change its Caption to precede the access key with an ampersand (&).

TabMaxWidth Property

The TabMaxWidth property controls the maximum width of each tab on an SSTab control.

Usage   *object*.TabMaxWidth = *SingleValue*
                     SingleValue = *object*.TabMaxWidth

Applies To   SSTab Control

PARAMETER	VALUE	MEANING
SingleValue	Single-precision	The maximum width of the tabs, in the same scale as whatever form (or container) holds the SSTab control. If the value is 0, the tabs are autosized.

TabOrientation Property

The TabOrientation property controls the location of the tabs on the SSTab control.

Usage   *object*.TabOrientation = *IntegerValue*
                  IntegerValue = *object*.TabOrientation

Applies To   SSTab Control

PARAMETER	VALUE	MEANING
IntegerValue	ssTabOrientationTop or 0	The tabs are at the top of the SSTab.
	ssTabOrientationBottom or 1	The tabs are at the bottom of the SSTab.
	ssTabOrientationLeft or 2	The tabs are at the left of the SSTab.
	ssTabOrientationRight or 3	The tabs are at the right of the SSTab.

TabPicture Property

The TabPicture property controls the image that displays on the specified tab of an SSTab control.

Usage   *object*.TabPicture(*Tab*) = *StringValue*
                  StringValue = *object*.TabPicture(*Tab*)

Applies To   SSTab Control

PARAMETER	VALUE	MEANING
Tab	Numeric expression	The number of the tab to modify.
StringValue	Null	No picture.
	Filename	The name of a bitmap, icon, or metafile file, including a path, to load.

Tabs Property

The Tabs property points to a specific tab in a Tabs collection.

Usage   *object*.Tabs(*IndexValue*)

Applies To   SSTab Control
                 Tabs Control

PARAMETER	VALUE	MEANING
IndexValue	Index	A pointer to one of the tabs in a Tabs collection (which starts numbering at 1).

TabsPerRow Property

The TabsPerRow property controls the number of tabs for each row of an SSTab control.

Usage   *object*.TabsPerRow = *IntegerValue*
                IntegerValue = *object*.TabsPerRow

Applies To   SSTab Control

PARAMETER	VALUE	MEANING
IntegerValue	Numeric expression	The number of tabs on each row.

TabStop Property

This TabStop property is a Boolean that specifies whether the control will be included in the tab order. Hidden or disabled controls will also be skipped in the tab order. The default value is True.

Usage   *BooleanValue* = *object*.TabStop
                object.TabStop = *BooleanValue*

Applies To   CheckBox Control
                 ComboBox Control
                 CommandButton Control
                 Data Control
                 DBCombo Control
                 DBGrid Control

> DBList Control
> DirListBox Control
> DriveListBox Control
> FileListBox Control
> Grid Control
> HScrollBar, VScrollBar Controls
> ListBox Control
> OLE Container Control
> OptionButton Control
> PictureBox Control
> TextBox Control

Set the TabStop property to True to include the control in the tab order. Setting TabStop to False will not affect the object'sTabIndex value, so you can turn TabStop back on without disturbing the original tab order.

TabStop Property

This TabStop property controls whether users can use the Tab key to give focus to an object.

Usage   *object*.TabStop = *BooleanValue*
               BooleanValue = *object*.TabStop

Applies To   Outline Control
               RichTextBox Control
               Slider Control
               SSTab Control
               TabStrip Control
               TreeView Control

PARAMETER	VALUE	MEANING
BooleanValue	True	The object will get focus if the user presses the Tab key.
	False	The object won't get focus from the pressing of the Tab key.

TabVisible Property

The TabVisible property controls whether a tab in an SSTab control is visible or hidden.

Usage   *object*.TabVisible(*Tab*) = *BooleanValue*
               BooleanValue = *object*.TabVisible(*Tab*)

Applies To   SSTab Control

PARAMETER	VALUE	MEANING
Tab	Numeric expression	The number of the tab to modify.
BooleanValue	True	The tab is visible.
	False	The tab is invisible.

TabWidthStyle Property

The TabWidthStyle property determines whether the Tab objects in a TabStrip will be justified, not justified, or fixed.

Usage   *object*.TabWidthStyle = *IntegerValue*
                 IntegerValue = *object*.TabWidthStyle

Applies To   TabStrip Control

PARAMETER	VALUE	MEANING
IntegerValue	tabJustified or 0	Each tab is at least wide enough to accommodate its content; tabs will expand to fill a row if necessary. When MultiRow is False, this setting does nothing.
	tabNonJustified or 1	Each tab is just wide enough to hold its content, and rows generally look messy.
	tabFixed or 2	All tabs are the same width, set by the TabFixed Width property.

Tag Property

The Tag property provides the programmer with a parameter to use as he or she sees fit to attach private information to a control. It is not used by VB. When you create a new instance of a Form object at runtime, for example, it is not created like a Control array, in which you can supply an explicit index number. You can, however, set its Tag property so that you can identify it later.

Usage   *StringValue* = *object*.Tag
                 object.Tag = *StringValue*

Applies To   CheckBox Control
                     ComboBox Control

CommandButton Control
CommonDialog Control
DBCombo Control
DBGrid Control
DBList Control
DirListBox Control
DriveListBox Control
FileListBox Control
Form Object
Frame Control
Grid Control
HScrollBar, VScrollBar Controls
Image Control
Label Control
Line Control
ListBox Control
MDIForm Object
Menu Object
OLE Container Control
OptionButton Control
PictureBox Control
Shape Control
TextBox Control
Timer Control

The default for the Tag property is an empty string (" ").

Example

```
Private Function CreateNewDoc()
     Static nDocs As Integer
     Dim NewDoc As New DocForm' Declare new form.
     nDocs = nDocs + 1
     NewDoc.Tag = "Document" & nDocs
     NewDoc.Caption = NewDoc.Tag
     NewDoc.Show' Show new form.
     Set CreateNewDoc = NewDoc
End Function
```

This example represents a utility function that creates new MDI documents and automatically assigns a Tag and Caption that is "Document" plus the number of documents that have been created since the application started.

TaskVisible Property

The TaskVisible property specifies whether the application appears in the Windows Task List. It applies only if your application, such as an OLE server, does not display any forms.

Usage   *BooleanValue = object*.TaskVisible
        object.TaskVisible = *BooleanValue*

Applies To   App Object

This property can take on the values given in the following table.

CONSTANT	VALUE	MEANING
True	not 0	The default. The running application is listed in the Windows Task List.
False	0	The application is not listed in the Windows Task List.

If your application does display a form and you set TaskVisible to False, you will not get an error, but TaskVisible will remain True.

Text Property

The Text property specifies the text that appears in the edit area of a control. It also can return the selected item of the list part of a control.

Usage   *StringValue = object*.Text
        object.Text = *StringValue*

Applies To   Column Object
        ComboBox Control
        DBCombo Control
        DBList Control
        Grid Control
        ListBox Control
        TextBox Control

More specifically, the Text property has for the controls the meanings given in the following table.

CONTROL	MEANING
ComboBox (Style is vbComboDropdown (0)), ComboBox (Style is vbComboSimple (1)), DBCombo (Style is vbComboDropdown (0)), DBCombo (Style is vbComboSimple (1)), TextBox	Allows read and write and specifies the text in the edit area of the control.
ComboBox (Style is vbComboDropdownList (2)), DBCombo (Style is vbComboDropdownList (2)), DBList, ListBox	Read-only. The property returns the selected item in the list box. If none is selected, it returns an empty string.
Column, Grid	Allows read and write and specifies the text in a single cell or range of cells.

For a TextBox, you can display a maximum of 32,766 characters. This holds true regardless of the setting for its MultiLine property. Of course, if the MultiLine property is False, you can see only one line.

Now things get weird. Each item in a ComboBox (and ListBox) may have a maximum of 1,024 characters. If you do select a long string from the list, ComboBox's Text property will return the long string. If you try to set the Text property to a long string, only the first 255 characters will be accepted. A Grid control's cell also can only hold a maximum string length of 255 characters.

For a Grid control, if its FillStyle property is set to 1, then setting its Text property fills all selected cells with the same text. A cell is selected if its CellSelected property is True. If FillStyle is 0, then only the cell specified by the Row and Col properties is set.

 The DBGrid has no Text property. The Help file is incorrect when it states that the TextBox can display 2,048 characters in single-line mode. We can get only 255 characters.

In the following example, the RstDlgText$ and StoreDlgText$ functions are used to restore and save the values of TextBox controls in the Registry using the built-in SaveSetting and GetSetting functions. The Text properties are saved as control-name/Text property pairs in the key:

```
HKEY_CURRENT_USER\Software\VB and VBA Program Settings\MyApp 2.0\Modem
```

(There is no checking in the routines to see if the object has a Text property.)

Example
```
Public Const APPNAME$ = "MyApp 2.0"
Public Const SECNAME$ = "Modem"

Sub xStorePref(ByVal id$, ByVal val$)
    SaveSetting APPNAME$, SECNAME$, id$, val$
End Sub

Function xFetchPref$(ByVal id$, ByVal default$)
    xFetchPref$ = GetSetting(APPNAME$, SECNAME$, id$, default$)
End Function

Function RstDlgText$(ByVal ctl As Control, ByVal def$)
Dim v$
    v$ = xFetchPref$(ctl.Name, def$)
    ctl.Text = v$
    RstDlgText$ = v$
End Function

Function StoreDlgText$(ByVal ctl As Control)
Dim v$, tmp$
    v$ = CStr(ctl.Text)
    xStorePref ctl.Name, v$
    StoreDlgText$ = v$
End Function
```

TextHeight Method

The TextHeight method returns the height of the text string if it were to be printed on the object using the current font of the object. The unit of measure is specified by the Scale properties of the object.

Usage   *SingleValue = object*.TextHeight(*String*)

Applies To   Form Object
                   PictureBox Control
                   Printer Object

The arguments of the TextHeight method have the meaning given in the following table.

PARAMETER	VALUE	MEANING
String	String expression	The string for which to calculate the text height. If the string includes carriage returns (Chr(13)), then the height is calculated for all lines.

Use the TextHeight method to place text vertically on a Form, PictureBox, or Printer object. The calculated height is a normal line height that includes the proper amount of space above and below the text (leading). The following example places our logo in the center of the form.

Example

```
Private Sub Form_Resize()
    AutoRedraw = True
    Cls
    logo$ = "Hacker's Guide"
    Font.name = "Times New Roman"
    Font.Italic = True
    Font.size = 128
    sw = ScaleWidth : sh = ScaleHeight
    Do
        Font.size = 0.8 * Font.size
        w = TextWidth(logo$)
    Loop While w > sw
    h = TextHeight(logo$)
    CurrentX = (sw - w) / 2 : CurrentY = (sh - h) / 2
    Print logo$
    AutoRedraw = False
End Sub
```

TextRTF Property

The TextRTF property controls the text of a RichTextBox control, including all .RTF code. It blows away whatever is currently in the RichTextBox.

Usage   *object*.TextRTF = *StringValue*
                    StringValue = *object*.TextRTF

Applies To   RichTextBox Control

PARAMETER	VALUE	MEANING
StringValue	String	An expression in .RTF format.

TextWidth Method

The TextWidth method returns the width of the text string if it were to be printed on the object using the current font of the object. The unit of measure is specified by the Scale properties of the object.

Usage   *SingleValue* = *object*.TextWidth(*String*)

Applies To   Form Object
                    PictureBox Control
                    Printer Object

The arguments of the TextWidth method have the meaning given in the following table.

PARAMETER	VALUE	MEANING
String	String expression	The string for which to calculate the text width. If the string includes carriage returns (Chr(13)), then the width is calculated for the longest line.

Use the TextWidth method to place text horizontally on a Form, PictureBox, or Printer object. The following example centers all lines in a message:

Example
```
Private Sub DisplayMsg(p As PictureBox, msg$)
    p.CurrentY = 0
    sw = p.ScaleWidth
    idx1 = 1
    Do
        idx2 = InStr(idx1, msg$, Chr(13))
```

```
            If idx2 <> 0 Then
                tmp$ = Mid(msg$, idx1, idx2 - idx1)
            Else
                tmp$ = Mid(msg$, idx1)
            End If
            w = p.TextWidth(tmp$)
            p.CurrentX = (sw - w) / 2
            p.Print tmp$
            idx1 = idx2 + 1
        Loop While idx2 <> 0
    End Sub
```

TickFrequency Property

The TickFrequency property controls how many ticks will appear on the Slider control. If the TickFrequency property is 2, there will be one tick for every two increments in the range.

Usage   *object*.TickFrequency = *LongValue*
                  LongValue = *object*.TickFrequency

Applies To   Slider Control

PARAMETER	VALUE	MEANING
LongValue	Long integer	Indicates how many integer values per tick are on the Slider. The first and last values of a Slider always have ticks.

TickStyle Property

The TickStyle property controls the style and positioning of the tick marks on the Slider control.

Usage   *object*.TickStyle = *IntegerValue*
                  IntegerValue = *object*.TickStyle

Applies To   Slider Control

PARAMETER	VALUE	MEANING
IntegerValue	sldBottomRight or 0	Tick marks are on the bottom of the Slider (if it's horizontal) or the right of it (if it's vertical).
	sldTopLeft or 1	Tick marks are on the top (horizontal) or left (vertical).
	sldBoth or 2	There are tick marks all over the darn thing.
	sldNoTicks or 3	The Slider is tick-free.

Title Property

The Title property is read-only at runtime. It returns a string that contains the title of the running application. To set the product name, select the File/Make EXE File... menu and then click the Options... button. In the "Application" section, enter the value into the Title text box.

Usage   *StringValue = object*.Title

Applies To   App Object

The maximum length of the Title property is 40 characters.

ToolTipText Property

The ToolTipText property controls the text that will pop up when you hold your cursor over a button for a few seconds.

Usage   *object*.ToolTipText = *StringValue*
                   StringValue = object.ToolTipText

Applies To   Button Object
                   Tab Object

PARAMETER	VALUE	MEANING
StringValue	String	The text that will pop up.

Top Property

See the Left Property.

ToPage Property

The ToPage property controls the To box on the Printer dialog box.

Usage   *object*.ToPage = *IntegerValue*
                   IntegerValue = object.ToPage

Applies To   CommonDialog Control

PARAMETER	VALUE	MEANING
IntegerValue	Integer	The page on which to end printing.

Note: This property is valid only when cdlPDPageNums is set.

TopIndex Property

The TopIndex property specifies which item in a FileListBox or ListBox control is displayed as the first visible item of the list. It is not available at design time.

Usage
$IntegerValue = object$.TopIndex
$object$.TopIndex = $IntegerValue$

Applies To
FileListBox Control
ListBox Control

The values of the TopIndex property have the meanings given in the following table.

VALUE	MEANING
0 through ListCount − 1	The index of the item displayed at the top of the viewable portion of the control. When the TopIndex property is set with the Columns property set to 0, the FileListBox and ListBox control will not force the specified item to the top if doing so would leave blank entries at the bottom of the list box. Thus if index is ListCount − 1, it likely will not be displayed as the top item unless (1) there is only one item in the list or (2) the Height of the control is only enough to display one item at a time. When Columns is nonzero, setting the TopIndex property moves the indicated item to the leftmost column of the visible portion of the control without changing the item's vertical position within its column.
Other values	Error

TopRow Property

The TopRow property specifies the topmost, non-fixed row that is visible in a grid. This property is available only at runtime.

Usage
$IntegerValue = object$.TopRow
$object$.TopRow = $IntegerValue$

Applies To   Grid Control

The values of the TopRow property have the meaning given in the following table.

PARAMETER	VALUE	MEANING
IntegerValue	0 to Rows − 1	The row index of the row to place at the topmost position. The default is 0.

Use the LeftCol and TopRow properties to scroll a Grid control via code.

TrackDefault Property

The TrackDefault property specifies whether the Printer object is changed automatically when you change the default printer for your system via the Control Panel.

Usage   *BooleanValue* = *object*.TrackDefault
                     object.TrackDefault = *BooleanValue*

Applies To   Printer Object

The values for the TrackDefault property have the meanings given in the following table.

VALUE	MEANING
True	When you change the system's default printer from the system's Control Panel, the Printer object is automatically changed to point to the new printer.
False	The default. The Printer object does not change when the system's default printer is changed.

You can change the TrackDefault property while a print job is in progress, but doing so causes the EndPage method of the Printer object to execute.

TwipsPerPixelX, TwipsPerPixelY Properties

These properties return the number of twips per pixel for an object in the horizontal (TwipsPerPixelX) and vertical (TwipsPerPixelY) directions.

Usage   *SingleValue* = *object*.TwipsPerPixelX
                     SingleValue = *object*.TwipsPerPixelY

Applies To   Printer Object
                    Screen Object

To access Windows APIs or other routines that require measurements in pixels, use the TwipsPerPixelX and TwipsPerPixelY properties to convert measurements to pixels without having to change the object's ScaleMode property.

Example
```
pixelsWidth = Printer.ScaleWidth / TwipsPerPixelX
pixelsHeight = Printer.ScaleHeight / TwipsPerPixelY
```

Type Property

This Type property indicates the graphics format of a Picture object. It is read-only at runtime.

Usage   *IntegerValue = object*.Type

Applies To   Picture Object

The possible return values of the Type property are given in the following table.

CONSTANT	VALUE	MEANING
vbPicTypeBitmap	1	Bitmap format (.BMP).
vbPicTypeMetafile	2	Metafile format (.WMF).
vbPicTypeIcon	3	Icon format (.ICO).

The following example shows how to create a Picture object and examine its type:

Example
```
Dim p(2) As Picture
Set p(0) = LoadPicture("my.bmp")
Set p(1) = LoadPicture("my.wmf")
Set p(2) = LoadPicture("my.ico")
Debug.Print p(0).Type & ", " & p(1).Type & ", " & p(2).Type
```

 This Type property seems to return its value based not on what the file actually is but on the graphics file's extension. In other words, a bitmap file with the extension .ICO will confuse Type into thinking the file is an icon.

Underline Property

The Underline property works with the Font and StdFont objects to make a font underlined or not underlined.

Usage   *object*.Underline = *BooleanValue*
                   BooleanValue = *object*.Underline

Applies To   Font Object
                   StdFont Object

PARAMETER	VALUE	MEANING
BooleanValue	True	The font is underlined.
	False	The font is not underlined.

Unload Statement

The Unload statement unloads a Form, MDIForm, or control-array element from memory. Use the Unload statement to remove forms that are no longer needed to conserve memory or to Load again to reset properties and controls to their initial values. Also use Load and Unload to add and remove control-array elements at runtime.

Usage   Unload *object*[(*Index*)]

Applies To   Form Object
                   MDIForm Object
                   Control Array

The object argument is the name of a Form object, MDIForm object, or placeholder for the name of a Form object, MDIForm object, or an element of a control array. Use the parentheses and Index to load a new control-array element; the Index must not be the same as an existing array element.

The Unload statement triggers the QueryUnload event and then the Unload event. Setting the Cancel argument to nonzero in either of these event procedures cancels the Unload. For an MDIForm object, the MDIForm's QueryUnload event occurs, followed by the QueryUnload events for all its MDI child forms, followed by the Unload events for all its MDI child forms, and finally the MDIForm's Unload event.

When a form is unloaded, its properties and controls are not available, but the code for the form module remains in memory. If you subsequently call the Show method for the form, the form will be automatically loaded again before being displayed.

For control arrays, only elements added to a form at runtime may be unloaded at runtime using the Unload statement.

Update Method

The Update method grabs the current data from the source application that supplied the object in an OLE Container control. It displays the data as a graphic in the control.

Usage   *object*.Update

Applies To   OLE Container Control

UpdateControls Method

The UpdateControls method updates controls bound to a Data control with the current record from the Data control's Recordset object. It triggers no events.

Usage   *object*.UpdateControls

Applies To   Data Control

This method is used when a user cancels changes in order to restore the values of the bound controls. This is the same as making the current record current again, but it does not generate any events.

UpdateOptions Property

The UpdateOptions property specifies how a linked OLE object in an OLE Container control is updated when the linked data is changed.

Usage   *IntegerValue* = *object*.UpdateOptions
                 object.UpdateOptions = *IntegerValue*

Applies To   OLE Container Control

The UpdateOptions property can be one of the values given in the following table.

CONSTANT	VALUE	MEANING
vbOLEAutomatic	0	The default. Object is updated any time the linked data changes.
vbOLEFrozen	1	Object is updated whenever the OLE server application saves the linked document.
vbOLEManual	2	Object is updated only when the OLE Container control's Update method is called or when its Action property is set to 6 (Update).

For either the vbOLEAutomatic or vbOLEFrozen settings, the server application invokes the OLE Container control's Update method to update the linked object. For obvious reasons, this property has no effect when the OLE object is embedded.

UpdateRecord Method

The UpdateRecord method saves values in bound controls to the database during a Validate event.

Usage   *recordset*.UpdateRecord

Applies To   Data Control

This method won't trigger a Validate event itself, so UpdateRecord is a neat way to keep the performance of your application decent while still maintaining referential integrity.

UpTo Method

The UpTo method moves the insertion point up to the first character that is a member of the specified character set in a RichTextBox control.

Usage   *object*.UpTo(*Characterset*[, *Forward*][, *Negate*])

Applies To   RichTextBox Control

This method does not support named arguments.

PARAMETER	VALUE	MEANING
Characterset	String	Required. The set of characters to look for.
Forward	True or omitted	Optional. Selects text from the insertion point toward the end of the text.
	False	Optional. Selects text from the insertion point toward the beginning of the text.
Negate	True	Optional. The characters not specified in Characterset are used to move the insertion point.
	False or omitted	Optional. The characters in Characterset are used to move the insertion point.

UseMnemonic Property

The UseMnemonic property specifies whether a Label control can define an access key using an ampersand (&) in its Caption property. The character following the ampersand defines the access key. At runtime, holding down the Alt key while pressing the access key sets focus to the control immediately following the Label control in tab order.

Usage
BooleanValue = *object*.UseMnemonic
object.UseMnemonic = *BooleanValue*

Applies To Label Control

The values for the UseMnemonic property have the meanings given in the following table.

VALUE	MEANING
True	The default. A character following the *last* ampersand (&) of the Caption property becomes the access key. The ampersand is not displayed, and the character for the access key is underlined. To display an ampersand in the Caption, use two ampersands. All other ampersands that are not part of a double-ampersand are not displayed.
False	No access keys will be defined for the Label control. All ampersand characters are displayed as ampersands.

If two controls on a form have defined the same access keys, only the first one in tab order *following* the current control with focus will be triggered. This means that using the Alt+access key repeatedly will swap focus between the two controls that use the same access key.

Value Property

This Value property specifies the state of a control or the contents of an object. This property is the default property of all listed objects—except for the Column object—so the .Value keyword is optional for those objects.

Usage	*object*[.Value] = *IntegerValue*
	IntegerValue = *object*[.Value]

Applies To	CheckBox Control
	Column Object
	CommandButton Control
	Field Object
	HScrollBar, VScrollBar Controls
	OptionButton Control

The following sections describe the Value property in more detail for each control or object.

CheckBox Control

Valid values for the CheckBox control's Value property are given in the following table.

CONSTANT	VALUE	MEANING
vbUnchecked	0	Unchecked. Clears the CheckBox or indicates that the CheckBox is cleared.
vbChecked	1	Checked. Places a check mark in the CheckBox or indicates that the box is checked.
vbGrayed	2	Grayed. Places a check mark in the CheckBox but changes the box to gray or indicates that the box is in the "grayed" state.

Normally, Checkbox toggles between the Checked and Unchecked states to let you ask the user True/False or On/Off questions. CheckBoxes, however, can have a third state, called the "grayed" state whereby the box itself is a light gray and the check mark is a dark gray. In most Windows applications, the grayed state is used to indicate either "don't care" or "disabled." Unfortunately, VB's CheckBox does not have very good support for either of these cases.

 Set CheckBox to the grayed state and run the application. Click the check box. It clears the box! Click it again, and it checks it. So far so good. We'd expect the next click to change the CheckBox back into the grayed state (to indicate "don't care"). Not So! The next click clears the CheckBox again. No matter how you click, you won't get the grayed state again. So what good is it?

The following example shows how to manually implement the Tri-State On/Off/DontCare behavior. We think it should have been built in. Assume we have a CheckBox called Check1.

Example
```
Private Check1State As Integer 'Place in Declarations section

Private Sub Check1_Click()
    Check1 = (CheckedState + 1) Mod 3
End Sub
Private Sub Check1_KeyDown(KeyCode As Integer, Shift As Integer)
    CheckedState = Check1
End Sub

Private Sub Check1_MouseDown(Button As Integer, Shift As _
    Integer, X As Single, Y As Single)
    If Button = 1 Then CheckedState = Check1
End Sub
```

This example uses a Private variable called Check1State available to all routines in the Form to keep track of the state when a key or left mouse button is pressed. When the Click event is called, we manually set the state of the CheckBox based on the previous state.

You'll need a Private variable for each CheckBox.

Column Object

Since the Column object has no default property, the .Value keyword is needed to set or retrieve the content of the object. Because a Column object represents a column for the selected record in a DBGrid control, its Value property refers to the content of a grid in the selected record.

The Value property is not available at design time.

Example
```
Debug.Print DBGrid1.Columns(1).Value
```

This example prints the content of the second column of the selected record.

CommandButton Control

When a CommandButton control is selected either by a mouse click or as a result of pressing the Enter key when the button has focus, its Value property is set to True. If you set a CommandButton control's Value property to True, it selects the button and causes its Click event to execute.

Example
```
'Activate the Command1 CommandButton
Command1 = True
```

This example activates the Command1 CommandButton control, causing its Click event to run.

Interestingly, the Value property is *not* True when the MouseDown and MouseUp events run but *is* True when the Click event executes.

Field Object

For an Index, QueryDef, Recordset, Relation, or TableDef object, the Field object represents a column in the selected record. So, the Field's Value property refers to the content of the specified column of the selected record. This property is available only at runtime.

HScrollBar, VScrollBar Controls

The Value property for HScrollBar and VScrollbar specifies the current position of the scrollbars. The numeric value must be between those for the Min and Max properties that in turn must be in the range from –32,768 to 32,767. Setting this property at runtime causes the scrollbar's Change event to run.

OptionButton Control

The Value property of the OptionButton control specifies the current state of a button as a Boolean value. If it is False, then the button is not selected; if True, it is selected. If at runtime you set the value to True, the OptionButton's Click event will run.

Value Property (Button Object)

This Value property specifies the pressed state of a Button object.

Usage   *IntegerValue* = *object*.Value
                 object.Value = *IntegerValue*

Applies To   Button Object

The values of the Value property are given in the following table.

PARAMETER	VALUE	MEANING
IntegerValue	tbrUnpressed or 0	The default. The button is unpressed.
	tbrPressed or 1	The button is pressed.

Value Property (ProgressBar, Slider Controls)

This Value property controls where the slider part of a Slider control or the boxes of a Progress-Bar control are.

Usage   *object*.Value = *IntegerValue*
                 IntegerValue = *object*.Value

Applies To   ProgressBar Control
                 Slider Control

PARAMETER	VALUE	MEANING
IntegerValue	Integer	How far along the Slider or ProgressBar is.

Note that changing ProgressBar.Value doesn't guarantee that the control will get more (or less) full of progress boxes. ProgressBar approximates how far along things are.

Value Property (RowBuffer)

This Value property determines the value of an item within RowBuffer in an unbound DBGrid.

Usage   *VariantValue = object*.Value (*Row*, *Column*)
                  object.Value (*Row*, *Column*) = *VariantValue*

Applies To   RowBuffer Object

PARAMETER	VALUE	MEANING
VariantValue	Variant	The value in the cell specified by row and column.
Row	Integer	Specifies the row number, ranging from 0 to RowCount – 1.
Column	Integer	Specifies the number of the column of the item, ranging from 0 to ColumnCount –1.

Verb Property

The Verb property specifies the command to perform when an object in an OLE Container control is activated by the Action property. This property is available for compatibility with the Action property and should not be used in new implementations. Use the DoVerb method instead.

Usage   *IntegerValue = object*.Verb
                  object.Verb = *IntegerValue*

Applies To   OLE Container Control

The Verb is specified as an index number of a verb defined in the array given by the ObjectVerbs property. There is also a set of standard verbs supported by all objects. See the full list at the DoVerbs method.

View Property

The View property specifies how the ListItem objects in a ListView control are displayed.

Usage   *IntegerValue = object*.View
                     object.View = *IntegerValue*

Applies To   ListView Control

The values of the View property have the meanings given in the following table.

CONSTANT	VALUE	MEANING
IvwIcon	0	The default. Each ListItem object is displayed using a text label and the image specified by its Icon property. Use the LabelWrap property to specify whether the text labels automatically wrap at word boundaries.
IvwSmallIcon	1	Each ListItem object is displayed using a text label and the image specified by its SmallIcon property.
IvwList	2	The ListItem objects are displayed as a vertical list, one per line. Each ListItem object is displayed using a text label and the image specified by its SmallIcon property. The text is displayed to the right of the icon.
IvwReport	3	The ListItem objects are displayed as a vertical list, one per line. In the first column, each ListItem object is displayed using a text label and the image specified by its SmallIcon property. The text is displayed to the right of the icon. Additional columns of text may be added using each ListItem's SubItem property.

Visible Property

The Visible property specifies whether an object is visible. If you set this property to False at design time, the object will not be hidden until runtime.

Usage   *BooleanValue = object*.Visible
                     object.Visible = *BooleanValue*

Applies To   CheckBox Control
                     Column Object
                     ComboBox Control
                     CommandButton Control
                     Data Control
                     DBCombo Control
                     DBGrid Control
                     DBList Control
                     DirListBox Control

DriveListBox Control
FileListBox Control
Form Object
Frame Control
Grid Control
HScrollBar, VScrollBar Controls
Image Control
Label Control
Line Control
ListBox Control
MDIForm Object
Menu Object
OLE Container Control
OptionButton Control
PictureBox Control
Shape Control
TextBox Control

VALUE	MEANING
True	The default. The object is visible.
False	The object is hidden.

You can use this property to hide and display controls at runtime to create wizard-like applications, where the same window remains displayed, but the content of the window changes when the user clicks, for example, the Next>> or <<Back button.

For Form objects, setting the Visible property is the *same* as using the Show or Hide methods.

VisibleCols Property

The VisibleCols property returns or sets the number of visible columns in a DBGrid control and is available only at runtime.

Usage   *IntegerValue* = *object*.VisibleCols
                 object.VisibleCols = *IntegerValue*

Applies To   DBGrid Control

PARAMETER	VALUE	MEANING
IntegerValue	Integer	Ranges from 0 to the setting of Cols.

This property includes both fully and partially visible columns.

VisibleCount Property

The VisibleCount property returns the number of visible items in a DBCombo or DBList control.

Usage   *IntegerValue = object*.VisibleCount

Applies To   DBCombo Control
                   DBList Control

The VisibleCount value ranges from 0 to the number of items in the control. If the control's IntegralHeight property is set to False, any partially showing item is included in the Visible-Count.

VisibleItems Property

The VisibleItems property returns an array of bookmarks corresponding to the visible items in a DBCombo or DBList control's list box.

Usage   *object*.VisibleItems(*Item*)

Applies To   DBCombo Control
                   DBList Control

The parameter to the VisibleItems property specifies an array index that can range from 0 to VisibleCount – 1.

VisibleRows Property

The VisibleRows property returns the number of visible rows in a DBGrid control.

Usage   *object*.VisibleRows

Applies To   DBGrid Control

This property returns an integer ranging from 0 to the setting of the Rows property and includes fully and partially visible rows.

Weight Property

The Weight property works with the Font and StdFont objects to change the weight (i.e., bold-ness) of a font.

Usage   *Font*.Weight = *IntegerValue*
                        IntegerValue = *Font*.Weight

Applies To   Font Object
                      StdFont Object

PARAMETER	VALUE	MEANING
IntegerValue	Integer	The weight of the font, with 400 being "normal" and 700 being bold.

 There's a catch: VB supports only two weights: 400 and 700. Any number less than 551 converts to 400; any number greater than or equal to 551 converts to 700. You're probably better off using the Bold property.

WhatsThisButton Property

The WhatsThisButton property specifies whether the "What's This" button appears on the right of a Form's Title Bar. This property must be set to True before the WhatsThisHelpID property has any effect. WhatsThisButton is read-only at runtime. This property is available only if you're running Windows 95 or Windows NT 3.51.

Usage   *BooleanValue* = *object*.WhatsThisButton

Applies To   Form Object

The values for the WhatsThisButton property have the meanings given in the following table.

VALUE	MEANING
True	Displays the "What's This" button on the Form's Title Bar provided • the Form's ControlBox property is True, or • the Form's BorderStyle property is vbFixedSingle (1) or vbSizable (2), or • the Form's MinButton and MaxButton properties are False, or • the Form's BorderStyle property is vbFixedDouble (3).
False	The default. The "What's This" button is not displayed.

It's a nice touch to provide the "What's This" button for your forms, but you sacrifice the ability to minimize or maximize your forms.

WhatsThisHelp Property

The WhatsThisHelp property is available only for the Windows 95 or Windows NT 3.51 platforms. It specifies whether the What's This pop up will appear for context-sensitive help. The property is read-only at runtime.

Usage   *BooleanValue* = *object*.WhatsThisHelp

Applies To   Form Object
                     MDIForm Object

The values of the WhatsThisHelp property have the meanings given in the following table.

VALUE	MEANING
True	The application can display the What'sThisHelp pop up to display the help topic specified by the control's WhatsThisHelpID property. The pop up is invoked by any of these three methods: 1. The user's clicking the What's This button in the Form's Title Bar and then using the resulting What's This mouse pointer—an arrow with a question mark—to click a control. The control or one of its ancestors must have its WhatsThisHelpID property defined. 2. Invoking the WhatsThisMode method of a Form object from code. Doing this will change the mouse pointer to the What's This pointer that the user clicks on a control in question. 3. Invoking the ShowWhatsThis method of a control from code. The WhatsThisHelpID of the control or one of its ancestors must be defined.
False	The default. The user must use the F1 key to start the Windows Help utility to load the help topic specified by the HelpContextID property of the active control or its parent.

WhatsThisHelpID Property

The WhatsThisHelpID property is available only for the Windows 95 or Windows NT 3.51 platforms. It specifies the context number of the help topic for the object. When this property is set, it allows the user to click the What's This button—the question mark at the right of the title bar of the parent form—and then use the resulting question-mark cursor to click the object to display its help topic. Use the HelpFile property of the parent form to specify the full path name of the Help file.

See the WhatsThisButton property for restrictions on when the button will be displayed for your forms.

Usage	*LongValue* = *object*.WhatsThisHelpID
	object.WhatsThisHelpID = *LongValue*

Applies To   CheckBox Control
ComboBox Control
CommandButton Control
Data Control
DBCombo Control
DBGrid Control
DBList Control
DirListBox Control
DriveListBox Control
FileListBox Control
Frame Control
Grid Control
HScrollBar, VScrollBar Controls
Image Control
Label Control
ListBox Control
OLE Container Control
OptionButton Control
PictureBox Control
TextBox Control

The possible values of the WhatsThisHelpID property are given in the following table.

VALUE	MEANING
0	The default. No context number is used.
Positive Long integer	A valid context number for a topic in a Help file. The context number must be specified when the Help file is compiled.

In Windows 3.*x,* the standard way of getting context-sensitive help was to give focus to the object in question and then hit the F1 key. In Windows 95, the user can instead use the What's This button. VB allows you to provide both options: set HelpContextID for the F1 key and the WhatsThisHelpID property for the What's This button.

WhatsThisMode Method

The WhatsThisMode method is available only for the Windows 95 or Windows NT 3.51 platforms. This method changes the mouse pointer to the What's This pointer to let the user click a control for displaying the What's This Help pop up for the control. The WhatsThisHelpID property for the control or one of its ancestors must be defined.

Usage   *object*.WhatsThisMode

Applies To   Form Object
                 MDIForm Object

Invoking this method has the same effect as when the user clicks the Whats This button in the Form's Title Bar. Use this method to provide context-sensitive help from the menu.

Width Property (Most Objects)

See the Height Property.

Width Property (Panel Object)

This Width property specifies the width of a StatusBar control's Panel object, expressed in the unit of measure of the StatusBar control's container.

Since this property deals with StatusBar controls, it applies only when you're using the Windows 95 or Windows NT 3.51 system.

Usage   *SingleValue* = *object*.Width
                 object.Width = *SingleValue*

Applies To   Panel Object

If the Panel object's AutoSize property is set to sbrSpring (1) or sbrContents (2), then the Width property will change automatically. The width cannot be smaller than the value of the MinWidth property.

Width Property (Picture Object)

This Width property returns or sets the dimensions of a Picture or StdPicture object.

Usage   *IntegerValue* = *object*.Width

Applies To   Picture Object
                 StdPicture Object

PARAMETER	VALUE	MEANING
IntegerValue	Integer	The width of the picture in himetrics.

Use ScaleX and ScaleY to convert himetric units into whatever scale you need.

WindowList Property

The WindowList property specifies whether the Menu control maintains a list of the current MDI child windows in an MDIForm object. The list appears at the bottom of the Menu control, separated by a separator bar from the other menu items defined at design time. This property is read-only at runtime.

Usage   *BooleanValue = object*.WindowList

Applies To   Menu Object

The values of the WindowList property have the meanings given in the following table.

VALUE	MEANING
True	The Menu control displays a numbered list of window captions for the existing MDI child windows and places a check mark next to the active one. Selecting a window name from the list activates that window. Only one Menu control per form may have its WindowList property set to True.
False	The default. The Menu control does not maintain a list of MDI child windows.

By convention, in an MDI application a top-level Menu control with the caption &Window should be created and its WindowList property set to True to display a list of child windows at runtime. Since the active MDI child window's menus are displayed in the MDIForm's Menu Bar, this &Window Menu control must be defined for the MDI *child* Form object, *not* the MDIForm object.

WindowState Property

The WindowState property determines the display state of the Form or MDIForm object.

Usage   *object*.WindowState = *IntegerValue*
                   IntegerValue = object.WindowState

Applies To   Form Object
                    MDIFormObject

The possible values of the WindowState property are given in the following table.

Constant	Value	Meaning
vbNormal	0	Normal. This is the default before a form is displayed for the first time.
vbMinimized	1	Minimized to an icon.
vbMaximized	2	Maximized to fill the entire screen.

If a form is hidden after it's been shown, this property reflects the previous state until the form is shown again, regardless of any changes made to the WindowState property in the meantime. But if the WindowState property *was* changed, the window will be sized appropriately after it is shown.

Setting the WindowState property directly will always work, regardless of the settings for the MaxButton, MinButton, and BorderStyle properties.

WordWrap Property

The WordWrap property specifies whether a Label control automatically breaks text into multiple lines to make its Caption text fit in the control when the AutoSize property is set to True. If AutoSize is False, then regardless of the setting for WordWrap, text will always wrap to fit horizontally. However, the Label control will not expand vertically to display all lines.

Usage   *BooleanValue = object*.WordWrap
                object.WordWrap = *BooleanValue*

Applies To   Label Control

The values of the WordWrap property have the meanings given in the following table.

Value	Meaning
True	The horizontal size of the Label control does not change, so text will be broken into new lines at word boundaries to make them fit the horizontal size. Because AutoSize is True, the Label control will expand vertically to make sure all lines are displayed.
False	The Label control will expand horizontally to make the text fit, so the text will not be broken automatically into new lines. Carriage-return characters, however, may be embedded in the text for manual line breaks. The vertical size of the Label control will expand automatically to display all manually created lines and to accommodate the selected font size.

The following table summarizes the behavior for combinations of the WordWrap and Auto-Size properties.

AUTOSIZE	WORDWRAP	BEHAVIOR
False	Don't care	The Label control does not resize. Text automatically wraps at word boundaries to create new lines.
True	False	Text does not automatically wrap at word boundaries, but the Label control resizes automatically both horizontally and vertically to display all text.
True	True	The Label control does not resize horizontally, so text automatically wraps at word boundaries to create new lines. The Label control resizes vertically automatically to display all text.

Wrappable Property

The Wrappable property controls whether Toolbar control buttons will automatically wrap when the window is resized. (It has nothing to do with Christmas presents.)

Usage   *object*.Wrappable = *BooleanValue*
            BooleanValue = *object*.Wrappable

Applies To   Toolbar Control

PARAMETER	VALUE	MEANING
BooleanValue	True	The Toolbar control buttons will wrap.
	False	The Toolbar control buttons won't wrap.

Unless you have a really good reason (and one doesn't come to mind), leave this set to True. Otherwise, resizing the control will hide the buttons.

X1, Y1, X2, Y2 Properties

These properties specify the coordinates of the starting point $(X1, Y1)$ and ending point $(X2, Y1)$ of a Line control. The units of measure used are determined by the Scale properties of the parent Form or control.

Usage   *SingleValue* = *object*.X1
            object.X1 = *SingleValue*

> *SingleValue = object.*Y1
> *object.*Y1 *= SingleValue*
>
> *SingleValue = object.*X2
> *object.*X2 *= SingleValue*
>
> *SingleValue = object.*Y2
> *object.*Y2*= SingleValue*

Applies To   Line Control

The horizontal coordinates are given by X1 and Y1; the vertical coordinates are given by Y1 and Y2.

Use Line controls as separators on forms to visually separate different parts of the form. You can also use them to indicate a relationship between two points.

Example
```
Private Sub Form_Resize()
      Line1.X1 = ScaleLeft
      Line1.Y1 = (ScaleHeight - ScaleTop) / 2
      Line1.X2 = ScaleLeft + ScaleWidth
      Line1.Y2 = (ScaleHeight - ScaleTop) / 2
End Sub
```

Zoom Property

The Zoom property specifies the percentage by which to scale printed output. This property is not available at design time.

Usage   *LongValue = object.*Zoom
              *object.*Zoom *= LongValue*

Applies To   Printer Object

The values for the Zoom property have the meanings given in the following table.

VALUE	MEANING
1 through 2,147,483,647	The default is 100 (no scaling). Zoom/100 specifies the scaling factor to use to scale printed output. Both horizontal and vertical dimensions are scaled using the same Zoom value.
Other values	Error

Note: Not all printers support this property or all possible values of this property. You might get an error for your printer.

ZOrder Method

The ZOrder method places a specified object or control at the front or back of the z-order within its graphical level. If placed at the front, the entire object or control is visible, possibly covering all other objects or controls within the same graphical level. If placed at the back, it will be covered by any other objects or controls that overlap it.

Usage	*object*.ZOrder Position
Applies To	CheckBox Control
	ComboBox Control
	CommandButton Control
	Data Control
	DBCombo Control
	DBGrid Control
	DBList Control
	DirListBox Control
	DriveListBox Control
	FileListBox Control
	Form Object
	Frame Control
	Grid Control
	HScrollBar, VScrollBar Controls
	Image Control
	Label Control
	Line Control
	ListBox Control
	MDIForm Object
	OLE Container Control
	OptionButton Control
	PictureBox Control
	Screen Object
	Shape Control
	TextBox Control

The Position argument can take on the values given in the following table.

PARAMETER	VALUE	MEANING
Position	Omitted, vbBringToFront, or 0	Object is positioned at the front.
	vbSendToBack or 1	Object is positioned at the back.

The ZOrder can be set at design time using the Bring To Front or Send To Back command from the Edit menu.

Within an MDIForm object, ZOrder affects MDI child forms only within the MDI client area. For MDIForm or Form objects, ZOrder places the forms in front or behind all other running applications.

Within a form or container, there are three graphical layers. The ZOrder of objects in one layer does not affect those in another. The back layer is used as drawing space on which the results of the graphics methods are displayed.The middle layer is reserved for graphical objects and Label controls.The front layer is used for all nongraphical controls like CommandButton, Check-Box, and ListBox controls. If objects in two layers overlap, the object in the upper layer covers the one in the lower layer.

The VB Help file incorrectly lists the App object as having the ZOrder method. Use the ZOrder method of your Form or MDIForm to make it pop to the front of other windows. BUT this property will not force it to stay on top.

To make your form remain in front of other applications, you must use the SetWin-dowPos Windows API.

Example

```
'In the declarations section of a global module
Declare Function SetWindowPos Lib "User32" (ByVal hwnd&, _
    ByVal hb&, ByVal x&, ByVal y&, ByVal cx&, ByVal cy&, _
    ByVal f&) As Long
Public Const SWP_NOMOVE& = 2
Public Const SWP_NOSIZE& = 1
Public Const FLAGS& = SWP_NOMOVE Or SWP_NOSIZE
Public Const HWND_TOPMOST& = -1

'In your code.
success& = SetWindowPos(Me.hwnd, HWND_TOPMOST, 0, _
    0, 0, 0, FLAGS)
```

SECTION 7: VB EVENTS

This section describes all the basic Visual Basic events.

Activate Event

The Activate event is triggered when a Form or MDIForm becomes the active window of the application. Use this event, for instance, when you want always to display the name of the active window in your application. A Form object cannot receive the GotFocus event unless no control on the Form can receive focus, so you can use the Activate event as a substitute for the GotFocus event that will always work as expected.

Usage   Private Sub *object*_Activate( )

Applies To   Form Object
                 MDIForm Object

An inactive Form can become active by a user's clicking on any part of the Form or by code using the Show or SetFocus methods. The Activate event, however, is triggered only if the focus is moved within the same application. For instance, if a Form is the active window *for the application*—but it is not active because another application is active—clicking the Form will *not* trigger the Activate event.

The Activate event for MDI child forms occurs only when the focus changes *between* child forms. If there is a single MDI child form in a parent MDIForm, switching focus to the MDI child form from a non-MDI form will trigger the Activate event for the MDIForm, *not* the MDI child form. If there are multiple MDI child forms, however, switching focus to an MDI child form will trigger the Activate events of both the MDIForm and the MDI child form (in that order), provided the MDI child form was not the active child form. For a Form object, the Activate event occurs before the GotFocus event. But the GotFocus event will not occur if *any* control on the Form can receive focus.

AfterColUpdate Event

The AfterColUpdate event occurs after data from a cell of a DBGrid control is moved to the control's copy buffer but before it is committed to the underlying recordset. You can use the After-ColUpdate event to update or clean up other tables and controls.

Usage   Private Sub *object*_AfterColUpdate ([Index As Integer,] ByVal ColIndex As Integer)

Applies To   DBGrid Control

The parameters to the AfterColUpdate event have the meanings given in the following table.

PARAMETER	VALUE	MEANING
Index	Integer	Uniquely identifies the control in a control array. This parameter is omitted if the DBGrid control is not part of a control array.
ColIndex	Integer	Identifies the column in the DBGrid control being updated.

When the editing of a cell in a DBGrid control is complete (the cell loses focus or the user hits the Enter key), the BeforeColUpdate event is triggered. If that event procedure does not cancel the action, then data from the cell is moved to the DBGrid control's copy buffer. After the move, the AfterColUpdate event is triggered, but it can no longer cancel the update.

AfterDelete Event

The AfterDelete event is triggered after the user deletes a record from a DBGrid control. You can use the AfterDelete event to update or clean up other tables and controls.

Usage   Private Sub *object*_AfterDelete ([Index As Integer])

Applies To   DBGrid Control

The Index parameter appears only if the DBGrid control is a member of a control array. It identifies which member of the array received the event.

The BeforeDelete event is triggered before a record is deleted (by using Del or Ctrl+X). If that event procedure does not cancel the action, the record is deleted and then the AfterDelete event is triggered. The code may determine which row is being deleted in the BeforeDelete event procedure using the SelBookmarks property. VB does not allow the user to delete multiple records at the same time.

AfterInsert Event

The AfterInsert event is triggered after a new record is inserted into a DBGrid control. Use the AfterInsert event to update or clean up other tables and controls.

Usage   Private Sub *object*_AfterInsert ([Index As Integer])

Applies To   DBGrid Control

The Index parameter appears only if the DBGrid control is a member of a control array. It identifies which member of the array received the event.

When the user enters the first character for a new record, that action triggers the BeforeInsert event and then the BeforeUpdate, AfterUpdate, and AfterInsert events, provided neither BeforeXX event cancels the action. The AfterXX events cannot cancel the action. Use the Bookmark property to access the new record.

After the AfterInsert event is finished, the new record becomes the last row in the DBGrid control, and the new-record row is then reinitialized.

AfterLabelEdit Event

The AfterLabelEdit event occurs after a user edits the label of the currently selected Node or ListItem object.

Usage   Sub *object*_AfterLabelEdit(*Cancel* As Integer, *Newstring* As String)

Applies To   Node Object
                    ListItem Object

PARAMETER	VALUE	MEANING
Cancel	An integer	Anything that's not 0 will cancel the editing operation.
Newstring	A string	This is the string the user entered.

AfterUpdate Event

The AfterUpdate event is triggered after changed data in a DBGrid control has been committed to the underlying database. Use the AfterUpdate event to update or clean up other tables and controls.

Usage   Private Sub *object*_AfterUpdate ([Index As Integer])

Applies To   DBGrid Control

The Index parameter appears only if the DBGrid control is a member of a control array. It identifies which member of the array received the event.

When the user changes data in the current record and moves to another row (record) or the Recordset's Update method is invoked, the data is moved from the DBGrid control's copy buffer to the bound Data control's copy buffer and then committed to the underlying database. The AfterUpdate event is triggered after the update completes.

You can access the updated record using the Bookmark property of the DBGrid control. This is because AfterUpdate occurs before the control moves to the next record. AfterUpdate will also occur before the LostFocus event if the focus is moved to another control.

Note: Changing the data via code does not trigger this event!

BeforeClick Event

The BeforeClick event is triggered for a TabStrip control when one of its Tab objects is clicked or when the Selected property is changed via code. Use this event to validate data in the old Tab object before generating the Click event to change to the new Tab.

Usage　　Private Sub *object*_BeforeClick([Index As Integer,]Cancel As Integer)

Applies To　　TabStrip Control

The parameters to the BeforeClick event have the meanings given in the following table.

PARAMETER	VALUE	MEANING
Index	Integer	Uniquely identifies the control in a control array. This parameter is omitted if the TabStrip control is not part of a control array.
Cancel	Integer	Set to nonzero, cancels the action, restoring the previous tab to be the current one and cancelling the pending Click event. Default is 0.

Note: If you use a MsgBox or InputBox function in this event procedure, the TabStrip control will not receive a Click event.

BeforeColUpdate Event

A user completes editing in a cell by moving focus from the cell or hitting the Enter key. This action triggers the BeforeColUpdate event. If the event procedure does not cancel the action, the data from the cell is moved to the DBGrid control's copy buffer. Use this event to verify changes before committing data to the database.

Usage　　Private Sub *object*_BeforeColUpdate ([Index As Integer,] ByVal ColIndex As Integer, OldValue As Variant, Cancel As Integer)

Applies To　　DBGrid Control

The parameters to the BeforeColUpdate event have the meanings given in the following table.

PARAMETER	VALUE	MEANING
Index	Integer	Uniquely identifies the control in a control array. This parameter is omitted if the DBGrid control is not part of a control array.
ColIndex PARAMETER	Integer VALUE	Identifies the column in the DBGrid control being updated. MEANING

OldValue	Variant value	The contents of the cell before the change.
Cancel	Integer	Set to nonzero, cancels the action, restoring the contents of the cell to OldValue and restoring focus to the DBGrid control. Default is 0.

To restore OldValue to the cell without forcing focus back onto the cell, set Cancel to 0 and manually set the cell contents to OldValue:

```
Cancel = False
DBGrid1.Columns(ColIndex).Value = OldValue
```

BeforeDelete Event

The BeforeDelete event is triggered before the selected record is deleted from a DBGrid control. Use the event to verify deletions.

Usage   Private Sub *object*_BeforeDelete ([Index As Integer,] Cancel As Integer)

Applies To   DBGrid Control

The parameters to the BeforeDelete event have the meanings given in the following table.

PARAMETER	VALUE	MEANING
Index	Integer	Uniquely identifies the control in a control array. This parameter is omitted if the DBGrid control is not part of a control array.
Cancel	Integer	Set to nonzero, cancels the action, leaving focus in the DBGrid control. Default is 0.

Before a record is deleted (by using Del or Ctrl+X), the BeforeDelete event is triggered. If that event procedure does not cancel the action, the record is deleted and then the AfterDelete event is triggered. The BeforeDelete event procedure may determine which row is being deleted by using the SelBookmarks property. VB does not allow the user to delete multiple records at the same time.

BeforeInsert Event

The BeforeInsert event is triggered right before a new record is inserted into a DBGrid control.

Usage   Private Sub *object*_BeforeInsert ([Index As Integer,] Cancel As Integer)

Applies To   DBGrid Control

The parameters to the BeforeInsert event have the meanings given in the following table.

PARAMETER	VALUE	MEANING
Index	Integer	Uniquely identifies the control in a control array. This parameter is omitted if the DBGrid control is not part of a control array.
Cancel	Integer	Set to nonzero, cancels the action, clearing the cell, but leaving focus in the DBGrid control. Default is 0.

When the user enters the first character for a new record, that action triggers the BeforeInsert event. At this point, the record is still in the DBGrid control's copy buffer and has not been added to the underlying database.

If the BeforeInsert event does not cancel the action, then when the action ends, it triggers the BeforeUpdate and then AfterUpdate and AfterInsert events, provided BeforeUpdate does not cancel the action. The AfterXX events cannot cancel the action. Use the Bookmark property to access the new record.

After the AfterInsert event is finished, the new record becomes the last row in the DBGrid control and the new-record row is reinitialized.

BeforeLabelEdit Event

The BeforeLabelEdit event happens when a user attempts to edit the label of the currently selected ListItem or Node object.

Usage   Sub *object*_BeforeLabelEdit(*Cancel* As Integer)

Applies To   Node Object
                            ListItem Object

PARAMETER	VALUE	MEANING
Cancel	An integer	Anything that's not 0 will cancel the editing operation.

BeforeUpdate Event

The BeforeUpdate event is triggered after data is changed in a DBGrid control but before the data is moved to the control's copy buffer. Use the BeforeUpdate event to verify changes.

Usage   Private Sub *object*_BeforeUpdate ([Index As Integer,]Cancel As Integer)

Applies To   DBGrid Control

The parameters to the BeforeUpdate event have the meanings given in the following table.

PARAMETER	VALUE	MEANING
Index	Integer	Uniquely identifies the control in a control array. This parameter is omitted if the DBGrid control is not part of a control array.
Cancel	Integer	Set to nonzero, cancels the action, leaving focus in the DBGrid control. Default is 0.

When the user changes data in the current record and moves to another row (record) or the recordset's Update method is invoked, the BeforeUpdate event is triggered before the data is moved to the bound Data control's copy buffer. If BeforeUpdate does not cancel the action, the data is moved to the Data control's copy buffer and then committed to the underlying database. The AfterUpdate event is triggered after the update completes. You can access the updated record using the Bookmark property of the DBGrid control.

Note: Changing the data via code does not trigger this event!

ButtonClick Event

The ButtonClick event is triggered when a Button object in a Toolbar control is clicked.

Usage   Private Sub *object*_ButtonClick([Index As Integer,]ByVal Button As Button)

Applies To   Toolbar Control

The parameters to the ButtonClick event have the meanings given in the following table.

PARAMETER	VALUE	MEANING
Index	Integer	Uniquely identifies the control in a control array. This parameter is omitted if the Toolbar control is not part of a control array.
Button	Button object	References the Button object that was clicked.

Use the Key property of the Button parameter to determine which button was clicked and then implement the appropriate action. Using the Key property makes the code immune to the rearrangement of the Toolbar buttons.

Change Event

The Change event is triggered when the contents of the control changes. Use the Change event to detect changes so that you can synchronize other controls to the controls that changed.

Usage   Private Sub *object*_Change([Index As Integer])

Applies To   ComboBox Control
                 DBCombo Control
                 DBGrid Control
                 DirListBox Control
                 DriveListBox Control
                 HScrollBar, VScrollBar Controls
                 Label Control
                 PictureBox Control
                 TextBox Control

The Index argument appears only if the control is part of a control array. The index will be set to the number that identifies the member of the control array for which the event is generated. The following table describes how the Change event is triggered for different controls.

CONTROL	EVENT TRIGGER
ComboBox	Occurs when the text in the edit area of the control is changed either by the user or by the setting of the Text property via code. This applies only to ComboBoxes whose Style has been set to vbComboDropdown (0) or vbComboSimple (1). If the code sets the Text property but the old and new values are the same, then no Change events occur.
DirListBox	Occurs when the user changes the selected directory by double-clicking or when code changes the Path property. If the code sets the Path property to its current value, then no Change event will occur.
DriveListBox	Occurs when the user changes the selected drive or when code changes the Drive property. If the code sets the Drive property to its current value, then no Change event will occur.
HScrollBar, VScrollBar	Occurs when the user moves the scroll bars or when code changes the Value properties. If the code sets the Value property to its current value, then no Change event will occur.
Label	Occurs when the label's DDE link updates the label or when code changes the Caption property. If the code sets the Caption property but doing so did not result in a change to the displayed text, the Change event will not be called. In contrast, an update of the DDE link will *always* invoke the Change event.
PictureBox	Occurs when the content of the picture box is updated by a DDE link or when code changes the Picture property.
TextBox	Occurs when the content of the text box is updated by a DDE link or when code changes the Text property. If the code sets the Text property but doing so did not result in a change in the displayed text, the Change event will not be called. In contrast, an update of the DDE link will *always* invoke the Change event.

The following example demonstrates synchronization between controls when values change. It uses three HScrollBar controls as a control array to represent the color values of red, green, and blue. Changing the values of the scroll bars will update the background color of a picture box and display the numeric values in a Label control array.

Example

```
Private Const IDXRED = 0
Private Const IDXGREEN = 1
Private Const IDXBLUE = 2

Private Sub hscColor_Change(Index As Integer)
    Picture1.BackColor = RGB(hscColor(IDXRED), _
        hscColor(IDXGREEN), hscColor(IDXBLUE))
    lblColor(Index) = hscColor(Index)
End Sub
```

You also use the Change event to synchronize DirListBox, DriveListBox, and FileListBox controls, although we recommend that you use the CommonDialog control instead whenever possible.

Example

```
Private Sub DriveDropDown_Change()
    On Error Resume Next      ' Delay error handling
    ' If new drive was chosen, this causes the Dirs box
    ' to update itself.
    DirsBox.Path = DriveDropDown.Drive
    If Err Then               ' If an error occurred, tell user what
        MsgBox (Error$)       ' it was, then reset Drive1.Drive.
        ' DirsBox.Path was not changed, therefore it
        ' still has old drive spec.
        DriveDropDown.Drive = DirsBox.Path
    End If
End Sub

Private Sub DirsBox_Change()
    FileListBox.Path = DirsBox.Path
End Sub

Private Sub FileListBox_PathChange()
    ' Change DirsBox.Path and DriveDropDown.Drive to reflect
    ' the new path.
    DirsBox.Path = FileListBox.Path
    DriveDropDown.Drive = FileListBox.Path
End Sub
```

Be careful when using Change events that you not get into an infinite loop, where the code in your event procedure ends up changing the control so that the Change event is called again and so on and so on. You'll probably end up with an "Out of stack space" error. VB seems to be pretty good at preventing many of these problems because if you change a control via code and the new and old values are the same, the Change event will not be called. As a result, the following code to synchronize two TextBox controls does not result in an infinite loop:

Example
```
Private Sub Text1_Change()
      Text2 = Text1
End Sub

Private Sub Text2_Change()
      Text1 = Text2
End Sub
```

Avoid changing a control's contents in its own Change event. If you must do so, try using a flag to prevent an infinite loop. Save your changes and test well!

 The VB Help file makes these further warnings:

- Avoid creating two or more controls whose Change event procedures affect each other; for example, two TextBox controls that update each other during their Change events.

- Avoid using a MsgBox function or statement in this event for HScrollBar and VScrollBar controls.

But as shown in our example, this first point is not really a problem if you want two TextBox controls to contain the same text. However, you do have to worry if the Change events are making different changes to each other.

As for the second point, we tried it and encountered no problems. Go figure.

Change Event (Toolbar Control)

This Change event is generated after the user customizes a Toolbar control using the Customize Toolbar dialog box.

Usage   *Private Sub object_*Change()

Applies To   Toolbar Control

Click Event

A "click" is the action of a user's pressing and then releasing a mouse button. A Click event is triggered when the user clicks a mouse button over an object. You won't be able to tell which mouse button triggered the event (see the MouseDown and MouseUp events). The Click event can also occur for some types of controls when the Value property of that control changes.

Use the Click event to execute commands or to detect changes to the values of OptionButton and CheckBox controls so that you can change the appearance of other controls on your forms.

Usage   Private Sub Form_Click()
                  Private Sub *object*_Click([Index As Integer])
                  Private Sub *object*_Click([Index As Integer,] Area As Integer)

Applies To   CheckBox Control
                  ComboBox Control
                  CommandButton Control
                  DBCombo Control
                  DBGrid Control
                  DBList Control
                  DirListBox Control
                  FileListBox Control
                  Form Object
                  Frame Control
                  Grid Control
                  Image Control
                  Label Control
                  ListBox Control
                  MDIForm Object
                  Menu Object
                  OLE Container Control
                  OptionButton Control
                  PictureBox Control
                  TextBox Control

The parameters for the Click event have the meanings given in the following table.

PARAMETER	VALUE	MEANING
Index	Positive integer	Appears only if the control is part of a control array. The index will be set to the number that identifies the member of the control array for which the event is generated.
Area	dbcAreaButton or 0	Indicates that the drop-down button of the DBCombo control received the Click event.
	dbcAreaEdit or 1	Indicates that the Edit area of the DBCombo control received the Click event.
	dbcAreaList or 2	Indicates that the List area of the DBCombo control received the Click event.

Note: The Area parameter applies *only* to the DBCombo control.

If the DragMode property of the control is True, then no Click or Mouse events will be generated.

The following list describes the situations in which a Click event is generated for each type of object:

- Form object: When the user clicks the Form or a disabled control of the Form.

- Any control listed under Applies To: When the user clicks the left mouse button over the control.

- The Click event is generated for the right mouse button *only* when the mouse pointer is over the following objects:
  CommandButton
  DBCombo
  DBGrid
  DBList
  Form
  Frame
  Grid
  Image
  Label
  PictureBox

- ComboBox and ListBox controls: When the user selects an item in the control either by using the arrow keys or by clicking the mouse button. If the list is empty, no Click events will be generated.

- CommandButton, OptionButton, and CheckBox controls: When the user presses the spacebar while the control has focus.

- CommandButton, OptionButton, and CheckBox controls: When the user presses the access key for the control.

- CommandButton and OptionButton controls: When the Value property is set to True.

- CheckBox controls: When the Value property is changed.

- CommandButton control: When the user presses the Enter key and a CommandButton's Default property is set to True *and* the focus is not in a OLE Container control.

- CommandButton control: When the user presses the Esc key and the CommandButton's Cancel property is set to True.

When a user clicks a control, the MouseDown event, the MouseUp event, and possibly the DblClick event are also generated. The interaction of all these events can be confusing. The following table summarizes the different behaviors when a user double-clicks a control.

CONTROL	EVENT ORDERING
CommandButton	MouseDown, Click, MouseUp, MouseDown, Click, MouseUp
DBCombo (Style = vbComboSimple), DBGrid, Frame, Form, Image, Label, PictureBox, Textbox	MouseDown, MouseUp, Click, DblClick, MouseUp
DBList, FileListBox, ListBox	MouseDown, Click, MouseUp, DblClick, MouseUp
DirListBox	MouseDown, Click, MouseUp, MouseDown, MouseUp
OptionButton if Value is False before the clicks	MouseDown, Click, MouseUp, MouseDown, DblClick, MouseUp
OptionButton if Value is True before the clicks	MouseDown, MouseUp, MouseDown, DblClick, MouseUp
ComboBox (Style = vbComboDropdown or vbComboDropdownList)	Click
ComboBox (Style = vbComboSimple)	Click, DblClick
DBCombo (Style = vbComboDropdown or vbComboDropodownList)	MouseDown, MouseUp, Click
DBCombo, clicking in text box part of the control	Click, DblClick, MouseUp

For other Custom Controls and Add-In controls, you should test this interaction between the events before using them.

Here's an interesting example that produces somewhat unexpected results in the execution ordering—if you're used to traditional non-event-driven programming:

Example

```
Private Sub Command1_Click()
     Dir1.SetFocus
     Debu.Print "Command1_Click"
End Sub

Private Sub Command1_LostFocus()
    Debug.Print "Command1_LostFocus"
End Sub

Private Sub Command1_MouseDown(Button As Integer, _
  Shift As Integer, x As Single, y As Single)
     Debug.Print "Command1_MouseDown"
End Sub

Private Sub Command1_MouseUp(Button As Integer, _
  Shift As Integer, x As Single, y As Single)
     Debug.Print "Command1_MouseUp"
End Sub

Private Sub Dir1_GotFocus()
     Debug.Print "Dir1_GotFocus"
End Sub
```

What ordering of events would you expect to occur when a user clicks the Command1 button? Here's the result printed in the Debug window:

Returns   Command1_MouseDown
                       Command1_Click
                       Command1_MouseUp
                       Command1_LostFocus
                       Dir1_GotFocus

Note that the MouseUp event of Command1 executes before the focus actually changes, even though the SetFocus method was invoked in Command1's Click event. This is because SetFocus only queues up an event. The event processor will process it after it has processed the events lined up before the SetFocus call.

ColResize Event

The ColResize event is triggered when the user resizes a column in a DBGrid control. It occurs before the Paint event. Use this event to verify the new size.

Usage   Private Sub *object*_ColResize ([Index As Integer,] ByVal ColIndex As Integer,
                       Cancel As Integer)

Applies To   DBGrid Control

The parameters to the ColResize event have the meanings given in the following table.

PARAMETER	VALUE	MEANING
Index	Integer	Uniquely identifies the control in a control array. This parameter is omitted if the DBGrid control is not part of a control array.
ColIndex	Integer	Identifies the column in the DBGrid control being resized.
Cancel	Integer	Set to nonzero, cancels the action, restoring the column size to its original width and also canceling the pending Paint event. Default is 0.

You can accept the change, but adjust the column width by directly modifying the Column-Width property:

Example
```
NewWidth = DBGrid1.Columns(ColIndex).ColumnWidth
NewWidth = NewWidth * 1.05 'Increase by 5%
DBGrid1.Columns(ColIndex).ColumnWidth = NewWidth
```

To cancel the action but force a repaint, set Cancel to 1 and invoke the Refresh method.

ColumnClick Event

The ColumnClick event is triggered when a ColumnHeader object in a ListView control is clicked. Use it to sort the ListItem objects using the selected column (Sorted, SortKey, SortOrder properties). This event occurs only in Report view.

Usage	Private Sub *object*_ColumnClick([Index As Integer,]ByVal ColumnHeader As ColumnHeader)
Applies To	ListView Control

The parameters for the ColumnClick event have the meanings given in the following table.

PARAMETER	VALUE	MEANING
Index	Integer	Uniquely identifies the control in a control array. Omitted if the ListView control is not part of a control array.
ColumnHeader	ColumnHeader object	A reference to the ColumnHeader object that was clicked.

DblClick Event

A "click" is the action of a user's pressing and then releasing a mouse button. A DblClick event occurs when a mouse button is clicked twice in rapid succession over an object. The two clicks must be within the system's double-click time limit; otherwise, two separate Click events will be generated. You won't be able to tell which mouse button triggered the event (see the MouseDown and MouseUp events).

A double-click is commonly used to execute a command when the mouse pointer is over an object that is not a CommandButton object.

Usage	Private Sub Form_DblClick()
	Private Sub *object*_DblClick([Index As Integer])
	Private Sub object_DblClick([Index As Integer,] Area As Integer)
Applies To	ComboBox Control
	DBCombo Control
	DBGrid Control
	DBList Control
	FileListBox Control
	Form Object
	Frame Control
	Grid Control

Image Control
Label Control
ListBox Control
OLE Container Control
OptionButton Control
PictureBox Control
TextBox Control

The parameters for the DblClick event have the meanings given in the following table.

PARAMETER	VALUE	MEANING
Index	Positive integer	Appears only if the control is part of a control array. The index will be set to the number that identifies the member of the control array for which the event is generated.
Area	dbcAreaButton or 0	Indicates that the drop-down button of the DBCombo control received the Click event.
	dbcAreaEdit or 1	Indicates that the Edit area of the DBCombo control received the Click event.
	dbcAreaList or 2	Indicates that the List area of the DBCombo control received the Click event.

Note: The Area parameter applies *only* to the DBCombo control.

If the DragMode property of the control is True, then no Click, DblClick, or Mouse events will be generated.

The following list describes the situations in which DblClick event is generated for each type of object:

- Form object: When the user double-clicks the Form or a disabled control of the Form

- Any control listed under Applies To: When the user double-clicks the left mouse button over the control. For a ComboBox, its style must be vbComboSimple *and* the mouse pointer must be in the list area.

- The DblClick event is generated for the right mouse button *only* when the mouse pointer is over the following objects:

    List area of DBCombo for Style = vbComboSimple
    Drop-down button of DBCombo for Style = vbComboDropdown
    Drop-down button of DBCombo for Style = vbComboDropdownList
    DBGrid
    DBList
    Form
    Frame
    Grid

Image
Label
PictureBox

When a user clicks a control, the MouseDown, MouseUp, and Click events are also generated. The interaction of all these events can be confusing. The table in the Click Event section summarizes the different behaviors when a user double-clicks a control.

The following example uses the DblClick event of a ListBox to activate the default CommandButton object by setting its value to 1. This in turn will invoke the CommandButton's Click event.

Example
```
Private Sub List1_DblClick()
    cmdOK = 1    'Activate the default "OK" CommandButton
End Sub
```

Deactivate Event

The Deactivate event is triggered when a Form or MDIForm becomes inactive because another window in the application is activated. A Form object cannot receive the LostFocus event unless no control on the Form can receive focus, so you can use the Deactivate event as a substitute for the LostFocus event that will always work as expected.

Usage   Private Sub *object*_Deactivate( )

Applies To   Form Object
                 MDIForm Object

An active Form can become inactive by a user's clicking another Form or by code using the Show or SetFocus methods for another Form. The Deactivate event, however, is triggered only if another window in the same application is activated; it will not occur if another application is activated.

The Deactivate event for MDI child forms occurs only when focus is changed *between* child forms. Switching focus from an MDI child form to a non-MDIForm triggers the Deactivate event for the parent MDIForm, *not* the MDI child form.

For a Form object, the LostFocus event occurs before the Deactivate event. But the LostFocus event will not occur if *any* control on the Form can receive focus. The Deactivate event is not triggered when unloading a Form.

DragDrop Event

The DragDrop event occurs for a target control when the user completes a drag-and-drop operation by releasing the mouse button over the target control. It also occurs if the Drag method of the
target object is called with an argument of vbEndDrag (2).

Use the DragDrop event to implement the behavior of a drag-and-drop operation.

Usage   Private Sub Form_DragDrop(Source As Control, X As Single, Y As Single)
                   Private Sub MDIForm_DragDrop(Source As Control, X As Single, Y As Single)
                   Private Sub *object*_DragDrop([Index As Integer,]Source As Control, X As Single, Y
                   As Single)

Applies To   CheckBox Control
                   ComboBox Control
                   CommandButton Control
                   Data Control
                   DBCombo Control
                   DBGrid Control
                   DBList Control
                   DirListBox Control
                   DriveListBox Control
                   FileListBox Control
                   Form Object
                   Frame Control
                   Grid Control
                   HScrollBar, VScrollBar Controls
                   Image Control
                   Label Control
                   ListBox Control
                   MDIForm Object
                   OLE Container Control
                   OptionButton Control
                   PictureBox Control
                   TextBox Control

The DragDrop event has the arguments given in the following table.

PARAMETER	VALUE	MEANING
Index	Positive integer	Appears only if the control is part of a control array. At runtime, this Index argument identifies the member of the control array for which the event occurred.
Source	Object	The control being dragged.
X	Single value	The current horizontal position of the mouse pointer relative to the top-left corner of the target control or form. The unit of measure of the target control or form is used.

PARAMETER	VALUE	MEANING
Y	Single value	The current vertical position of the mouse pointer relative to the top-left corner of the target control or form. The unit of measure of the target control or form is used.

Note: The units of measure may be specified by a control's ScaleHeight, ScaleWidth, ScaleLeft, ScaleTop, and ScaleMode properties.

Use the TypeOf keyword of the If statement in conjunction with the Tag and Name properties to identify the source control. Once a Drag operation has started, no other events are handled except for the DragOver and DragDrop events.

Example

```
Private Sub Text1_DragDrop(Source As Control, X As Single, _
    Y As Single)
    Dim f$, txt$
    If TypeOf Source Is FileListBox Then
        If LCase(Right(Source.filename, 4)) = ".txt" Then
            f$ = Source.path & "\" & Source.filename
            Open f$ For Input Shared As #1
            Do While Not EOF(1)
                Input #1, txt$
                Text1.Text = Text1.Text + txt$
            Loop
            Close #1
        Else
            Beep
        End If
    End If
End Sub
```

In this example, when the user drags a file from a FileListBox control onto the Text1 TextBox control, the DragDrop event first checks that the file has the .txt extension and then reads the contents into the text box. (Actually, the contents of the text box will be poor representation of the file, since the Input function discards most delimiters.)

DragOver Event

The DragOver event occurs for a target control during drag-and-drop operation when the mouse moves the source control over the target control.

Use it to alter the appearance of the drag icon, mouse pointer, or the target control as the mouse passes over the target during a drag-and-drop operation.

Usage   Private Sub *object*_DragOver([Index As Integer,]Source As Control, X As Single, Y As Single, State As Integer)

Applies To   CheckBox Control

ComboBox Control
CommandButton Control
DBCombo Control
DBGrid Control
DBList Control
DirListBox Control
DriveListBox Control
FileListBox Control
Form Object
Frame Control
Grid Control
HScrollBar, VScrollBar Controls
Image Control
Label Control
ListBox Control
MDIForm Object
OLE Container Control
OptionButton Control
PictureBox Control
TextBox Control

Here *object* is either the name of the target control or the literal string, "Form" or "MDI-Form" (for targets that are the Form or MDIForm, respectively). All arguments are inputs to the event procedure.

PARAMETER	VALUE	MEANING
Index	Positive integer	Identifies the control in a control array. If the control is not part of a control array, there is no Index argument.
Source	Object	The source control being dragged.
X	Single	The current horizontal position of the mouse pointer within the target form or control, expressed in terms of the target's coordinate system as set by the ScaleHeight, ScaleWidth, ScaleLeft, and ScaleTop properties.
Y	Single	The current vertical position of the mouse pointer within the target form or control, expressed in terms of the target's coordinate system as set by the ScaleHeight, ScaleWidth, ScaleLeft, and ScaleTop properties.
State	vbEnter or 0	Indicates source control has just been dragged within the range of the target.
	vbLeave or 1	Indicates source control has just been dragged out of the range of the target.
	vbOver or 2	Indicates source control has moved from one position in the target to another.

The following example shows how you can change the DragIcon of the source to the "Do Not Enter" sign when it is dragged over another PictureBox control. It uses the PictureBox's DragIcon property to save the original Source's DragIcon picture.

Example

```
Private Sub Picture3_DragOver(Source As Control, X As Single, _
    Y As Single, State As Integer)
Dim IconDir$

IconDir$ = "C:\APP\vb4\icons\misc\"
Select Case State
  Case vbEnter
    Picture3.DragIcon = Source.DragIcon
    Source.DragIcon = LoadPicture(IconDir$ & _
        "Misc06.ico")
  Case vbLeave
    Source.DragIcon = Picture3.DragIcon
  Case Else
End Select
End Sub
```

DropDown Event

If a ComboBox control's Style property is set to either vbComboDropdown (0) or vbCombo-DropdownList (2), then the DropDown event occurs when the drop-down button is pressed and before the list portion of a ComboBox control is displayed. Use the DropDown event to update the list portion of the ComboBox before displaying it to the user. This allows you to change the contents of the list, based on the settings of other controls on the Form. Don't get carried away, though. If your DropDown event takes too long to run, the user will be confused because the list won't appear until after the event finishes running. If it does have to take a long time, change the mouse cursor or display a status message that asks the user to wait.

Usage   Private Sub *object*_DropDown([Index As Integer])

Applies To   ComboBox Control

The Index argument identifies the control in a control array. If the control is not part of a control array, there is no Index argument.

The following example fills the list with different items, depending on whether the user selects "Beginner," "Intermediate," or "Advanced."

Example

```
Private Sub Combo1_DropDown()
    Combo1.Clear
    If optGrpLevel(0).Value Then        ' Beginner
        For i = LBound(arrBeginner$) To UBound(arrBeginner$)
            Combo1.AddItem arrBeginner$(i)
        Next i
    ElseIf optGrpLevel(1).Value Then    ' Intermediate
        For i = LBound(arrIntermediate$) To _
        UBound(arrIntermediate$)
            Combo1.AddItem arrIntermediate$(i)
        Next i
```

```
        Else                                 ' Advanced
            For i = LBound(arrAdvanced$) To UBound(arrAdvanced$)
                Combo1.AddItem arrAdvanced$(i)
            Next i
        End If
    End Sub
```

Error Event

The Error event occurs only as the result of a data-access error that takes place when no VB code is being executed. This can occur under the following circumstances:

- The user clicks a Data Control button.

- The Data control automatically opens the database to load a Recordset object after the Form_Load event.

- A custom control performs an operation such as the MoveNext method, the AddNew method, or the Delete method.

Usage   Private Sub *object*_Error([Index As Integer,] DataErr As Integer, Response As Integer)

Applies To   Data Control

The Index and DataErr arguments are inputs to the event procedure, and the Response argument is an output from the event procedure to let VB know how it should handle the error.

PARAMETER	VALUE	MEANING
Index	Integer input value	Identifies the control if it's in a control array.
DataErr	Integer input value	The error number.
Response	vbDataErrorContinue or 0	When the *object*_Error() event routine returns with Response set to vbDataErrorContinue, VB continues execution with no interruptions.
	vbDataErrDisplay or 1	The default behavior when no user-defined *object*_Error() event routine is defined. When the *object*_Error() event routine returns with Response set to vbDataErrorDisplay, VB displays the error message.

Expand Event (TreeView Control)

The Expand event is triggered when a Node object in a TreeView control is expanded such that its children become visible. It occurs after the Click and DblClick events. You can cancel the Expand event by explicitly setting the Expanded property of the node to False.

Usage   Sub *object*_Expand([Index As Integer,]ByVal Node As Node)

Applies To   TreeView Control

The parameters for the Expand event have the meanings given in the following table.

PARAMETER	VALUE	MEANING
Index	Integer	Uniquely identifies the control in a control array. This parameter is omitted if the TreeView control is not part of a control array.
Node	Node object	A reference to the Node object that was expanded.

The Expand event occurs when

- the user double-clicks the Node object,

- the Expanded property of the Node object is set to True, or

- a plus/minus image associated with the Node object is clicked.

GotFocus Event

The GotFocus event occurs when an object receives the input focus, as a result of either user action or a call to the SetFocus method. A Form object cannot receive focus unless all of its controls that can receive focus have been hidden or disabled.

You can implement your own context-sensitive help by using the GotFocus event of your controls to display help or status messages. To make your application easier to use, you can also use GotFocus to enable controls that depend on this control and disable those that do not, thereby visually prompting your user to enter the relevant information.

Usage   Private Sub Form_GotFocus( )
                   Private Sub *object*_GotFocus([Index As Integer])

Applies To   CheckBox Control
                   ComboBox Control
                   CommandButton Control
                   DBCombo Control
                   DBGrid Control
                   DBList Control
                   DirListBox Control
                   DriveListBox Control
                   FileListBox Control
                   Form Object
                   Grid Control

HScrollBar, VScrollBar Controls
ListBox Control
OLE Container Control
OptionButton Control
PictureBox Control
TextBox Control

The Index parameter appears only if the control is part of a control array. The index will be set to the number that identifies the member of the control array for which the event is generated.

HeadClick Event

The HeadClick event is triggered when the user clicks a column header of a DBGrid control. You might use this event to re-sort the records based on the entries of the selected column.

Usage   Private Sub *object*_HeadClick([Index As Integer,] ByVal ColIndex As Integer)

Applies To   DBGrid Control

The parameters to the HeadClick event have the meanings given in the following table.

PARAMETER	VALUE	MEANING
Index	Integer	Uniquely identifies the control in a control array. This parameter is omitted if the DBGrid control is not part of a control array.
ColIndex	Integer	Identifies the column in the DBGrid control whose header receives the HeadClick event.

Initialize Event

The Initialize event occurs when an instance of a Form, MDIForm, or Class Module is created. Use this event to initialize any data used by the Form or Class Module.

Usage   Private Sub Form_Initialize( )
                 Private Sub MDIForm_Initialize( )
                 Private Sub Class_Initialize( )

Applies To   Class Module Object
                 Form Object, Forms Collection
                 MDIForm Object

The Initialize event is triggered by the events given in the following table.

OBJECT	TRIGGER FOR INITIALIZE EVENT
Class	The use of the CreateObject function to create an instance of a class, such as `Set cls = CreateObject("Project1.MyClass")`
Form or MDIForm	A reference to a property or event of a form created at design time, such as `Form1.Caption = "Hacker"` The Load event is also triggered.
	The creation of an instance of a Form at runtime, such as `Set frm = New Form1` The Load event is not triggered.

For a Form or MDIForm object, the Initialized event is triggered before the Load event.

The following code tries to establish a connection to the "Word.Basic" OLE Automation object when the Form is created. If there is an error, it makes sure the oWord variable is set to Nothing.

Example

```
Public oWord As Object

Private Sub Form_Initialize()
    On Error GoTo NoConnect
    Set oWord = CreateObject("Word.Basic")
NoConnect:
    On Error GoTo 0
End Sub
```

ItemClick Event

The ItemClick event is triggered when a ListItem object in a ListView control is clicked. This event occurs before the Click event.

Usage   Private Sub *object*_ItemClick([Index As Integer,] ByVal Item As ListItem)

Applies To   ListView Control

The parameters for the ItemClick event have the meanings given in the following table.

PARAMETER	VALUE	MEANING
Index	Integer	Uniquely identifies the control in a control array. This parameter is omitted if the ListView control is not part of a control array.
Item	ListItem object	A reference to the ListItem object that was clicked.

KeyDown, KeyUp Events

The KeyDown and KeyUp events are generated when a user hits a key and an object that supports them has focus. The pressing of a key triggers the KeyDown event, and the release of that key triggers a KeyUp event. Also, for keys that can produce printable output (not modifier, navigation, editing, or function keys), a KeyPress event is triggered between the KeyDown and KeyUp events. The auto-repeat nature of your keyboard will cause KeyDown and KeyPress event pairs to be generated repeatedly after the initial delay. Only when you release the key will the KeyUp event be triggered. For nonprinting keys, only the KeyDown event will be auto-repeated.

Use the KeyDown and KeyUp events to detect special function keys F1 through F12, navigation keys, or the keys on the numeric keypad in order to provide special functionality for your controls. You can also use these events to verify user input, if you want to restrict the input to a specific set of characters.

The TAB key will not generate a keyboard event. Nor will the Enter key if *any* Command-Button object on the form has its Default property set to True. Nor will the Esc key if any CommandButton object on the form has its Cancel property set to True.

Usage   Private Sub Form_KeyDown(KeyCode As Integer, Shift As Integer)
Private Sub *object*_KeyDown([Index As Integer,]KeyCode As Integer, Shift As Integer)
Private Sub Form_KeyUp(KeyCode As Integer, Shift As Integer)
Private Sub *object*_KeyUp([Index As Integer,]KeyCode As Integer, Shift As Integer)

Applies To   CheckBox Control
ComboBox Control
CommandButton Control
DBCombo Control
DBGrid Control
DBList Control
DirListBox Control
DriveListBox Control
FileListBox Control
Form Object
Grid Control
HScrollBar, VScrollBar Controls
ListBox Control
OLE Container Control
OptionButton Control
PictureBox Control
TextBox Control

The parameters of the KeyDown and KeyUp events have the meanings given in the following table.

PARAMETER	VALUE	MEANING
Index	Positive integer	Identifies the control in a control array. If the control is not part of a control array, there is no Index argument.
KeyCode	0 through 255	The key code of the key that triggered the event. See the KeyCode Constants for a list of valid codes.
Shift	0 through 7	A bit-mask that specifies the state of the modifier keys: Shift, Ctrl, and Alt. You can determine the state of any of these keys by performing a bit-wise And operation on the Shift parameter with vbShiftMask, vbCtrlMask, or vbAltMask. This will return nonzero if the associated key is down. If Shift is 0, then no modifier keys are down.

To reject further processing for a key, set the KeyCode parameter of the KeyDown event to 0 and set the KeyAscii parameter of the KeyPress event to 0.

If you do not need your app to respond to both the pressing and the releasing of a key, you may want to use the KeyPress event instead. Use KeyDown and KeyUp event procedures if you need to respond to both the pressing and the releasing of a key.

You cannot reliably determine whether a letter being typed is uppercase or lowercase even if you check the state of the Shift key. This is because you cannot determine the state of the Caps-Lock key. If it's important to determine the case, you might want to use the KeyPress event, whose parameter is the resolved ANSI code of the letter being typed.

Normally, the Form will not receive focus unless there are currently no controls on the Form that can receive focus—i.e., they are either hidden or disabled. This means that, normally, the KeyDown and KeyUp events for the Form will not be triggered. If you set the KeyPreview property of the Form to True, however, the Form's keyboard events will be called before those of the control that has focus.

The KeyDown and KeyPress event routines for the "Text1" text box in this example reject any keys that are not digits or one of the editing keys.

Example

```
Private Sub Text1_KeyDown(KeyCode As Integer, Shift As Integer)
    If Not Shift Then
        Select Case KeyCode
            Case vbKey0 To vbKey9, vbKeyBack, vbKeyEnd, _
                vbKeyHome, vbKeyDelete
                Exit Sub     'Accept key by exiting Sub
            Case Else
        End Select
    End If
    KeyCode = 0     'Reject key
    Beep
End Sub

Private Sub Text1_KeyPress(KeyAscii As Integer)
    If KeyAscii >= Asc(" ") _
        And (KeyAscii < Asc("0") Or KeyAscii > Asc("9")) Then
            KeyAscii = 0     'Reject key
    End If
End Sub
```

Note: You can determine only that a Shift, Ctrl, or Alt key has been pressed. You cannot tell whether the key pressed is the left one or the right one on the keyboard.

 If you press and release the Alt key twice, you will get only three events: KeyDown, KeyUp, and KeyUp.

KeyPress Event

The KeyPress event occurs when the user presses and then releases a key. This key must be one that can generate printable output—not a modifier, navigation, editing, or function key. The parameter passed to the event procedure is the ANSI code of the key.

Use the KeyPress event if you do not need to detect the non-ANSI keys and you do not need to determine explicitly the state of the modifier keys (Shift, Ctrl, and Alt). Also use the KeyPress event—instead of the KeyDown and KeyUp events—if you need to determine reliably the case of the typed letters.

The Tab key will not generate a keyboard event. Nor will the Enter key if *any* Command-Button object on the Form has its Default property set to True. Nor will the Esc key if *any* CommandButton object on the Form has its Cancel property set to True.

Usage   Private Sub Form_KeyPress(KeyAscii As Integer)
                    Private Sub *object*_KeyPress([Index As Integer,]KeyAscii As Integer)

Applies To   CheckBox Control
                    ComboBox Control
                    CommandButton Control
                    DBCombo Control
                    DBGrid Control
                    DBList Control
                    DirListBox Control
                    DriveListBox Control
                    FileListBox Control
                    Form Object
                    Grid Control
                    HScrollBar, VScrollBar Controls
                    ListBox Control
                    OLE Container Control
                    OptionButton Control
                    PictureBox Control
                    TextBox Control

The parameters passed to the KeyPress event have the meanings given in the following table.

PARAMETER	VALUE	MEANING
Index	Positive integer	Identifies the control in a control array. If the control is not part of a control array, there is no Index argument.
KeyAscii	0 to 255	The ANSI keycode of the character that will be sent to the object. Since KeyAscii is passed by reference, you can change the character passed. Set KeyAscii to 0 to cancel the KeyPress altogether.

Use the KeyPress event to intercept keystrokes in a TextBox or ComboBox object so that you can filter the user input or test for valid entry. The event can be caused by any key or key combination that can generate an ANSI key, including Ctrl key combinations. The following example, for instance, may be used to request a password. (Of course, this can be done much easier by using the PasswordChar property of the TextBox control.)

Example

```
Private password$

Private Sub Text2_GotFocus()
    password$ = ""
    Text2.Text = ""
End Sub

Private Sub Text2_KeyPress(KeyAscii As Integer)
    If KeyAscii = vbKeyBack Then        'Backspace
        'Synchronize password$ with entry to erase last character
        If password$ <> "" Then
            password$ = Left$(password$, Len(password$) - 1)
        End If
    Else
        'Build password before changing output character to '*'
        password$ = password$ + Chr$(KeyAscii)
        KeyAscii = Asc("*")
    End If
End Sub
```

Note that you can use the Chr() and Asc() functions to convert between a character and its ANSI number.

Unlike the input parameters for the KeyDown and KeyUp events, the input parameter for the KeyPress event is an ANSI character that is the result of applying the modifier keys Shift and Ctrl to the physical key pressed. For instance, Shift+a with CapsLock *off* will result in KeyAscii's being 65 (uppercase A) and with CapsLock *on* will result in 97 (lowercase a). Because setting KeyAscii to 0 causes the keyboard event to end without passing any keys to the object, you cannot enter Ctrl+@—whose ANSI number is 0—into a control.

Normally, a Form will not receive focus unless there are currently no controls on the Form that can receive focus—(i.e., they are either hidden or disabled). This means that, normally, the KeyPress event for the Form will not be triggered. If you set the KeyPreview property of the form to True, however, the form's KeyPress event will be called before that of the control that has focus.

KeyUp Event

See the KeyDown event.

LinkClose Event

The LinkClose event is triggered by the termination of a DDE conversation. Either the DDE client or server may terminate the conversation at any time. Use the LinkClose event to inform the user that the DDE conversation has been terminated and to clean up.

Usage	Private Sub Form_LinkClose( )
	Private Sub MDIForm_LinkClose( )
	Private Sub *object*_LinkClose([Index As Integer])

Applies To	Form Object
	Label Control
	MDIForm Object
	PictureBox Control
	TextBox Control

The Index argument appears only if the control is part of a control array; it identifies the specific member of the array.

 The information you provide the user should not only indicate that the DDE conversation has been terminated, but also include troubleshooting information, including hints on how to reestablish the conversation.

In the following example the application explicitly terminates the link by setting LinkMode to vbLinkNone or by changing the LinkTopic property.

Example

```
Private Text1Link As Boolean

Private Sub Text1_LinkOpen()
    Text1Link = True
End Sub

Private Sub Text1_LinkClose()
    If Not Text1Link Then Exit Sub
    msg$ = "DDE conversation for " & Text1.LinkTopic & "!" _
        & Text1.LinkItem & " terminated unexpectedly. "
    msg$ = msg$ & "Make sure the server application is " _
        & "still running."
    MsgBox msg$
End Sub
```

LinkError Event

The LinkError Event occurs in response to an error during a DDE conversation (Link). This event is recognized only as the result of a DDE-related error that occurs when no VB code is being executed.

Usage   Private Sub *object*_LinkError([Index As Integer,]Linkerr As Integer)

Applies To   Form Object
                 Label Control
                 MDIForm Object
                 PictureBox Control
                 TextBox Control

The *object* in the Syntax line is the name of the control or the literal strings "Form" or "MDI-Form" (for DDE conversations with the Form or MDI Form, respectively). The LinkError argument is the DDE-related error number passed to the event procedure.

PARAMETER	VALUE	MEANING
Index	Integer	Identifies the control in a control array. If the control is not part of a control array, there is no Index argument.
LinkErr	vbWrongFormat or 1	Indicates the other application requested data in the wrong format. VB may generate several of these errors as it tries different data formats, so you may not want to generate messages based on this error.
	vbDDESourceClosed or 6	Indicates the other application attempted to continue the DDE conversation after the LinkMode property of the source form or control had been set to 0 or vbLinkNone.
	vbTooManyLinks or 7	Indicates all source links are in use. There is a maximum of 128 links per source.
	vbDataTransferFailed or 8	Indicates either that a LinkRequest for a destination control failed to update the control or a Poke failed to update a control.
	11	Indicates not enough memory for DDE.

Use the LinkError event procedure to catch these errors to provide code to run when errors occur.

Example
```
Private Sub MyLinkError(ctl As Control, LinkErr As Integer)
    Dim msg$, item$, r As Integer

    item$ = ctl.LinkTopic & "!" & ctl.LinkItem

    Select Case LinkErr
       Case 11
```

```
        msg$ = "Not enough memory for DDE for: "
      Case vbTooManyLinks
        msg$ = "DDE source has no more available links for: "
      Case vbDataTransferFailed
        msg$ = "DDE request of poke failed for: "
      Case Else
    End Select
    If LinkErr <> vbWrongFormat
        r = MsgBox(msg$ & item$, vbExclamation)
    End If
End Sub

Private Sub Text1_LinkError(LinkErr As Integer)
    MyLinkError Text1, LinkErr
End Sub
```

LinkExecute Event

The LinkExecute event occurs when a DDE client sends a command string to be executed by the server (source) Form or MDIForm. The syntax of the command string is completely arbitrary, and your LinkExecute code must perform all parsing of the string. The syntax should be documented for the client applications.

Usage   Private Sub *object*_LinkExecute(CmdStr As String, Cancel As Integer)

Applies To   Form Object
                 MDIForm Object

The arguments to the LinkExecute event have the meanings given in the following table.

PARAMETER	VALUE	MEANING
CmsStr	String expression	The command string sent by the DDE client (destination) application.
Cancel	0	An output argument. Setting it to 0 accepts the command string.
	−1	The default. Leaving it −1 rejects the command string. The destination application will get a DDE error.
	Nonzero	See comments for −1.

If LinkExecute is not defined, then all DDE Execute requests will be rejected. In the following example, the command strings are expected to be in the form

`[command arguments] ...`

That is, each command and its arguments are enclosed in square brackets and multiple commands may be sent in the same string. Form_LinkExecute performs the parsing into individual command-arguments pairs and then uses the module-level DDEExecute() function to perform the command. If any command fails, further processing is aborted and Cancel is set to True.

Example

```
Private Sub Form_LinkExecute(CmdStr As String, Cancel As Integer)
Dim ind%, ind1%, ind2%
Dim cmd$, arg$, tmpStr$
    If UCase$(CmdStr) = "[QUIT]" Then
        Cancel = False
        End
    End If
    Cancel = True
    tmpStr$ = CmdStr

    Do    'Find each command-argument pairs in brackets
        ind1% = InStr(tmpStr$, "[")
        If ind1% = 0 Then Exit Do
        tmpStr$ = LTrim$(Mid$(tmpStr$, ind1% + 1))

        ind2% = InStr(tmpStr$, "]")
        If ind2% = 0 Then
            Cancel = True
             Exit Sub
        End If

        ind% = InStr(Left$(tmpStr$, ind2% - 1), " ")
        If ind% = 0 Then
            cmd$ = Left$(tmpStr$, ind2% - 1)
            arg$ = ""
        Else
            cmd$ = Left(tmpStr$, ind% - 1)
            arg$ = LTrim$(Mid$(tmpStr$, ind% + 1, _
                ind2% - ind% - 1))
        End If
        Cancel = DDEExecute(cmd$, arg$)
        If Cancel = True Then Exit Do
        tmpStr$ = Mid$(tmpStr$, ind2% + 1)
    Loop While True
End Sub

Private Function DDEExecute(cmd$, arg$)
Dim Cancel As Integer
    Cancel = False
    Select Case UCase$(cmd$)
        Case "TITLE"
            frmPercent.Caption = arg$
            ShowForm
        Case "LABEL"
            lblCaption.Caption = arg$
        Case "Value"
            gagPercent.Value = Val(arg$)
            lblPercent.Caption = gagPercent.Value & "%"
        Case Else
            Cancel = True
```

```
              End Select
              DDEExecute = Cancel
           End Function
```

LinkNotify Event

The LinkNotify event occurs if the LinkMode property of the destination control is set to vbLink-Notify (3) and when the source data has changed in a DDE conversation. The LinkTopic and LinkItem properties identify the data in the source application.

Usage   Private Sub *object*_LinkNotify([Index As Integer])

Applies To   Label Control
                 PictureBox Control
                 TextBox Control

   The Index argument identifies the control in a control array. If the control is not part of a control array, there is no Index argument.
   You can test for conditions in the LinkNotify event procedure to determine if you want to retrieve the data immediately, later, or not at all. To retrieve the data, use the LinkRequest method.

Example
```
           Private Sub Picture1_LinkNotify()
              If AllowingUpdates Then     'Global variable
                 Picture1.LinkRequest
              End If
           End Sub
```

LinkOpen Event

The LinkOpen event is triggered when a DDE conversation is about to be established. Use the LinkOpen event to reject the connection if any conditions for the DDE conversation are not met.

Usage   Private Sub Form_LinkOpen(Cancel As Integer)
                 Private Sub MDIForm_LinkOpen(Cancel As Integer)
                 Private Sub *object*_LinkOpen([Index As Integer,]Cancel As Integer)

Applies To   Form Object
                 Label Control
                 MDIForm Object
                 TextBox Control

   The arguments to the LinkOpen event have the meanings given in the following table.

PARAMETER	VALUE	MEANING
Index	Positive integer	Identifies the control in a control array. If the control is not part of a control array, there is no Index argument.
Cancel	0	The default. This is an output argument. Setting it to 0 allows the conversation to be established.
	Nonzero	Setting Cancel to a nonzero value rejects the connection. The client application will get a DDE error.

If you want to limit the number of DDE conversations accepted by your Form, you can use the LinkOpen and LinkClose events to manage them.

Example
```
Private nDDE As Integer    'Module-level variable
Public Const MaxDDEs = 10

Private Sub Form_LinkOpen(Cancel As Integer)
    If nDDE < MaxDDEs Then
        nDDE = nDDE + 1
    Else
        Cancel = -1
    End If
End Sub

Private Sub Form_LinkClose()
    nDDE = nDDE - 1
End Sub
```

Load Event

The Load event occurs when a form is loaded into memory either by the execution of the Load statement or by a reference to a form's properties or controls. Use the Load event to initialize settings for controls. You can, for example, retrieve settings from the Registry or file—saved in the Unload event—to initialize the controls. This provides the user with a friendly interface that remembers the settings last used for your application.

Usage
Private Sub Form_Load( )
Private Sub MDIForm_Load( )

Applies To
Form Object
MDIForm Object

You can also initialize form-level variables in the Load event. However, you may want to do that in the Initialize event that occurs before the Load event.

When the code references a property or control of an unloaded form, the form is automatically loaded. This triggers the Load event. However, the form is shown (made visible) only if it is an MDIchild form *and* the AutoShowChildren property of the parent MDIForm object is True. The following table summarizes the events that occur when referencing unloaded forms.

FORM TYPE	INITIAL CONDITION	TRIGGERED EVENTS AND VISIBLE STATUS
Form (MDIChild = False)	Form unloaded	Form_Initialize Form_Load Form1.Visible = False
MDIForm	MDIForm unloaded	MDIForm_Initialize MDIForm_Load MDIForm1.Visible = False

Form (MDIChild = True)	Form unloaded
	MDIForm loaded
	MDIForm.Visible = False
		Form_Initialize
		Form_Load
		   If MDIForm's AutoShowChildren is True, then
		      MDIForm1.Visible = True
		      MDIForm_Resize
		      Form1.Visible = True
		      Form_Resize

	Unloaded
	MDIForm Unloaded
		Form_Initialize
		MDIForm_Initialize
		MDIForm_Load
		Form_Load
		   If MDIForm's AutoShowChildren is True, then
		      MDIForm1.Visible = True
		      MDIForm_Resize
		      Form1.Visible = True
		      Form_Resize

Be sure to test the interaction between related events to prevent causing recursion. These include Activate, GotFocus, Paint, and Resize.

The following example uses the Load event of the startup form to load the main forms. Then it hides itself.

Example
```
Private Sub Form_Load()
    Show
    Load frmMain
    Load frmDoc
    frmMain.Show
    frmDoc.Show
    Hide
End Sub
```

LostFocus Event

The LostFocus event occurs when an object loses the input focus either as a result of user action or via code when the SetFocus method of another object has been invoked. This typically means that the GotFocus event of another control or object will follow immediately. Use the LostFocus event to validate the user input or to undo things that the object's GotFocus method set up, such as changing the appearance of a form.

Usage	Private Sub Form_LostFocus( )
	Private Sub *object*_LostFocus([Index As Integer])
Applies To	CheckBox Control
	ComboBox Control
	CommandButton Control
	DBCombo Control
	DBGrid Control
	DBList Control
	DirListBox Control
	DriveListBox Control
	FileListBox Control
	Form Object
	Grid Control
	HScrollBar, VScrollBar Controls
	ListBox Control
	OLE Container Control
	OptionButton Control
	PictureBox Control
	TextBox Control

The Index parameter appears only if the control is part of a control array. The index will be set to the number that identifies the member of the control array for which the event is generated.

The following example expands on the one presented for the KeyPress event. It adds a Lost-Focus event to check that the password has a nonalphabetic character.

Example

```
Private password$

Private Sub Text2_GotFocus()
    password$ = ""
    Text2.Text = ""
End Sub

Private Sub Text2_KeyPress(KeyAscii As Integer)
    If KeyAscii = vbKeyBack Then      'Backspace
        'Synchronize password$ with entry to erase last character
        If password$ <> "" Then
            password$ = Left$(password$, Len(password$) - 1)
        End If
    Else
        'Build password before changing output character to '*'
        password$ = password$ + Chr$(KeyAscii)
        KeyAscii = Asc("*")
    End If
End Sub
```

```
Private Sub Text2_LostFocus()
    Dim a$
    For i = 1 To Len(password$)
        a$ = UCase$(Mid(password$, i, 1))
        If Asc(a$) < Asc("A") Or Asc(a$) > Asc("Z") Then
            Exit Sub
        End If
    Next i
    MsgBox "Your password must have a non-alpha character"
    Text2.SetFocus
End Sub
```

MouseDown, MouseUp Events

The MouseDown event is triggered when a mouse button is pressed, and the MouseUp event is triggered when a mouse button is released. Unlike the Click and DblClick events, the Mouse-Down and MouseUp events tell you which button has been pressed, the state of the modifier keys (Shift, Ctrl, and Alt), and the location of the mouse when the event occurred. See the Click event for a table that describes the interaction between the Click, DblClick, MouseDown, and MouseUp events.

You can use the MouseDown event, for instance, to present a popup menu when the right mouse button is pressed.

Usage	Private Sub Form_MouseDown(Button As Integer, Shift As Integer, X As Single, Y As Single)
	Private Sub MDIForm_MouseDown(Button As Integer, Shift As Integer, X As Single, Y As Single)
	Private Sub *object*_MouseDown([Index As Integer,]Button As Integer, Shift As Integer, X As Single, Y As Single)
	Private Sub Form_MouseUp(Button As Integer, Shift As Integer, X As Single, Y As Single)
	Private Sub MDIForm_MouseUp(Button As Integer, Shift As Integer, X As Single, Y As Single)
	Private Sub *object*_MouseUp([Index As Integer,]Button As Integer, Shift As Integer, X As Single, Y As Single)
Applies To	CheckBox Control
	CommandButton Control
	Data Control
	DBCombo Control
	DBGrid Control
	DBList Control
	DirListBox Control
	FileListBox Control
	Form Object

Frame Control
Grid Control
Image Control
Label Control
ListBox Control
MDIForm Object
OLE Container Control
OptionButton Control
PictureBox Control
TextBox Control

The parameters for the MouseDown and MouseUp events have the meanings given in the following table.

PARAMETER	VALUE	MEANING
Index	Positive integer	Identifies the control in a control array. If the control is not part of a control array, there is no Index argument.
Button	vbLeftButton (1), vbRightButton (2), or vbMiddleButton (4)	Indicates which mouse button triggered the event.
Shift	0 through 7	A bit-mask that specifies the state of the modifier keys: Shift, Ctrl, and Alt. You can determine the state of any of these keys by performing a bit-wise And operation on the Shift argument with vbShiftMask (1), vbCtrlMask (2), or vbAltMask (4). This will return nonzero if the associated key is down. If Shift is 0, then no modifier keys are down.
X, Y	Single values	Give the coordinates of the mouse pointer when the event was triggered. The unit of measure is in terms of the ScaleHeight, ScaleWidth, ScaleLeft, ScaleTop, and ScaleMode of the object *if* the object has these scaling properties; otherwise, the unit is the twip.

It is important to note that the object that receives the MouseDown event grabs *all* mouse events up to and including the MouseUp event, regardless of the location of the mouse pointer and of how many other mouse buttons are pressed after the initial event. This means that when the MouseUp event finally occurs, the pointer may be outside the object.

In the MouseDown and MouseUp events, you cannot tell the current state of the other mouse buttons. You know only that a mouse button has been pressed or released. In contrast, the Mouse-Move event will tell you the current state of all mouse buttons.

Example
```
Private Sub Form_MouseDown(Button As Integer, Shift As Integer, _
    X As Single, Y As Single)
    If Button = vbRightButton Then 'Right button
        PopupMenu mnuPopup, vbPopupMenuRightButton
    End If
End Sub
```

This example displays a popup menu when the right mouse button is clicked on a form.

MouseMove Event

The MouseMove event occurs when the user moves the mouse over the object, regardless of whether any mouse buttons have been pressed.

You can use the MouseMove event to detect the mouse pointer moving over your objects. In response, you can, for instance, change the appearance of the mouse pointer, depending on where it is on your form.

Usage

Private Sub Form_MouseMove(Button As Integer, Shift As Integer, X As Single, Y As Single)

Private Sub MDIForm_MouseMove(Button As Integer, Shift As Integer, X As Single, Y As Single)

Private Sub *object*_MouseMove([Index As Integer,] Button As Integer, Shift As Integer, X As Single, Y As Single)

Applies To

CheckBox Control
CommandButton Control
Data Control
DBCombo Control
DBGrid Control
DBList Control
DirListBox Control
FileListBox Control
Form Object
Frame Control
Grid Control
Image Control
Label Control
ListBox Control
MDIForm Object
OLE Container Control
OptionButton Control
PictureBox Control
TextBox Control

The parameters for the MouseMove event have the meanings given in the following table.

Parameter	Value	Meaning
Index	Positive integer	Identifies the control in a control array. If the control is not part of a control array, there is no Index argument.
Button	0 through 7	A bit-mask that specifies the state of the mouse buttons. You can determine the state of any of these buttons by performing a bit-wise And operation on the Button parameter with vbLeftButton (1), vbRightButton (2), or vbMiddleButton (4). This will return nonzero if the associated mouse button is down. If Button is 0, then no mouse buttons are down.
Shift	0 through 7	A bit-mask that specifies the state of the modifier keys: Shift, Ctrl, and Alt. You can determine the state of any of these keys by performing a bit-wise And operation on the Shift parameter with vbShiftMask (1), vbCtrlMask (2), or vbAltMask (4). This will return nonzero if the associated key is down. If Shift is 0, then no modifier keys are down.
X, Y	Single values	Give the coordinates of the mouse pointer when the event was triggered. The unit of measure is in terms of the ScaleHeight, ScaleWidth, ScaleLeft, ScaleTop, and ScaleMode of the object *if* the object has these scaling properties; otherwise, the unit is the twip.

When no mouse button is down, an object receives a MouseMove event whenever the mouse moves and the mouse pointer is within its borders. If a mouse button is down, the object that received the MouseDown event will continue receiving MouseMove events, regardless of the location of the mouse pointer, *even* if the mouse pointer is outside the boundaries of the Form window.

Be careful when moving a window inside a MouseMove event. MouseMove events are generated when the window moves underneath the mouse pointer, but the pointer remains still. This behavior can cause a cascading event.

The following example implements a simple drawing routine that allows the user to draw straight lines in a PictureBox control.

Example

```
Private OrigX As Single, OrigY As Single
Private SaveX As Single, SaveY As Single

Private Sub Picture1_MouseDown(Button As Integer, _
   Shift As Integer, X As Single, Y As Single)
   If Button = vbLeftButton Then
       OrigX = X: SaveX = X
       OrigY = Y: SaveY = Y
       Picture1.DrawMode = vbXorPen
       Picture1.DrawStyle = vbDot
   End If
End Sub

Private Sub Picture1_MouseMove(Button As Integer, _
   Shift As Integer, X As Single, Y As Single)
   If Button = vbLeftButton Then
```

```
                    Picture1.Line (OrigX, OrigY)-(SaveX, SaveY), vbRed
                    Picture1.Line (OrigX, OrigY)-(X, Y), vbRed
                    SaveX = X: SaveY = Y
                End If
        End Sub

        Private Sub Picture1_MouseUp(Button As Integer, _
            Shift As Integer, X As Single, Y As Single)
            If Button = vbLeftButton Then
                    Picture1.Line (OrigX, OrigY)-(SaveX, SaveY), vbRed
                    Picture1.DrawMode = vbCopyPen
                    Picture1.DrawStyle = vbSolid
                    Picture1.Line (OrigX, OrigY)-(X, Y), vbRed
            End If
        End Sub
```

MouseUp Event

See the MouseDown event.

NodeClick Event

The NodeClick event is triggered when a Node object in a TreeView control is clicked. This event occurs before the Click event.

Usage   Sub *object*_NodeClick([Index As Integer,]ByVal Node As Node)

Applies To   TreeView Control

The parameters for the NodeClick event have the meanings given in the following table.

PARAMETER	VALUE	MEANING
Index	Integer	Uniquely identifies the control in a control array. This parameter is omitted if the TreeView control is not part of a control array.
Node	Node object	A reference to the Node object that was expanded.

ObjectMove Event

The ObjectMove event is triggered immediately after an object in an OLE container control is moved or resized while the object is active for in-place editing. Use this event to determine if you need to resize or move the OLE container control to accommodate changes to the object.

Usage   Private Sub *object*_ObjectMove(Left As Single, Top As Single, Width As Single, Height As Single)

Applies To   OLE Container Control

The parameters of the ObjectMove event have the meanings given in the following table.

PARAMETER	VALUE	MEANING
Left	Single-precision value	The horizontal coordinate of the new left edge of the OLE Container control.
Top	Single-precision value	The vertical coordinate of the new top edge of the OLE Container control.
Width	Single-precision value	The new width of the OLE Container control.
Height	Single-precision value	The new height of the OLE Container control.

Both the ObjectMove and Resize event are triggered when an OLE Container control receives size and location information from its object. The Resize event, however, does not get any information about the new size or position of the object.

Paint Event

If the AutoRedraw property is False, the Paint event is triggered under any of the following conditions:

*   When all or part of a Form or PictureBox is exposed after it has been uncovered by another window

*   After it has been moved or resized

*   When its Refresh method has been invoked from code

Use the Repaint method to redraw any temporary graphics or text that was drawn when the AutoRedraw property was False. If AutoRedraw is True, no Paint events will be generated.

Usage   Private Sub Form_Paint( )
                        Private Sub *object*_Paint([Index As Integer])

Applies To   Form Object
                        PictureBox Control

The Index argument appears only if the control is part of a control array. The index will be set to the number that identifies the member of the control array for which the event is generated.

If the ClipControls property is False, graphics methods used in the Paint event procedure affect only the newly exposed areas; that is, graphics drawn outside the newly exposed area are ignored. If ClipControls is True, then all graphics methods used in the Paint event procedure are applied.

Resizing a Form object always triggers the Resize event, followed by the Paint event—*if* the AutoRedraw property is False; otherwise, only the Resize event is generated. Resizing a Picture-Box control causes a Resize event, but not a Paint event.

To avoid cascading events, avoid performing the following actions inside a Paint event procedure:

- Moving or resizing the object
- Calling the Refresh method

To have your object repainted automatically, set the AutoRedraw property to True. Then you need only implement the Resize event procedure in order to place your graphics and controls properly. When setting AutoRedraw to True is not appropriate, use the Paint event to redraw graphics and the Resize event to move controls around. Since resizing a form will also cause the Paint event, the code in the Paint event does not have to be duplicated in the Resize event. You can avoid duplicating code for a PictureBox control by having the control's Resize event call its Refresh method to invoke its Paint event.

Example

```
Private Sub Form_Paint()
     Cls
     logo$ = "Hacker's Guide"
     Font.name = "Times New Roman"
     Font.Italic = True
     Font.size = 128
     sw = ScaleWidth
     sh = ScaleHeight
     Do
          Font.size = 0.8 * Font.size
          w = TextWidth(logo$)
     Loop While w > sw
     h = TextHeight(logo$)
     CurrentX = (sw - w) / 2
     CurrentY = (sh - h) / 2
     Print logo$
End Sub
```

PanelClick Event

The PanelClick event occurs when you press and release a mouse button over any of the Panel objects of the StatusBar control.

Usage   *Private Sub object*_PanelClick(ByVal *Panel* As Panel)

Applies To   StatusBar Control

Note that when a PanelClick occurs, you still get a regular Click event.

PanelDblClick Event

The PanelDblClick event occurs when you press and release a mouse button twice over any of the Panel objects of the StatusBar control.

Usage   *Private Sub object_PanelDblClick(ByVal Panel As Panel)*

Applies To   StatusBar Control

Note that when a PanelDblClick occurs, you still get a regular DblClick event.

PathChange Event

The PathChange event occurs when the Path property of a FileListBox control is changed via code by the setting of the FileName or Path property.

You can use the PathChange event to respond to Path changes, such as displaying the name of the path in a label.

Usage   Private Sub *object*_PathChange([Index As Integer])

Applies To   FileListBox Control

The Index parameter appears only if the control is part of a control array. The index will be set to the number that identifies the member of the control array for which the event is generated.

Example
```
Private Sub File1_PathChange ()
    lblPath.Caption = File1.Path & ": "
End Sub
```

PatternChange Event

A PatternChange event is triggered when the code either changes the Pattern property or sets the FileName property to a string containing a pattern.

Use the PatternChange event to detect and respond to changes in the pattern.

Usage   Private Sub *object*_PatternChange([Index As Integer])

Applies To   FileListBox Control

The Index parameter appears only if the control is part of a control array. The index will be set to the number that identifies the member of the control array for which the event is.

Example
```
Private Sub File1_PatternChange()
    'Make sure Pattern includes "*.exe"
    If InStr(LCase$(File1.Pattern), "*.exe") = 0 Then
        File1.Pattern = File1.Pattern & ";*.exe"
    End If
End Sub
```

QueryUnload Event

The QueryUnload event occurs before a form or application closes. It gives the form or application a chance to perform some cleanup before closing or even to cancel the unload. The QueryUnload events of *all* affected forms are called before *any* are unloaded. In contrast, the Unload event of each form is called as the form is being closed. When an MDIForm object closes, its QueryUnload event occurs before those for any of its child forms. In contrast, the Unload event of all child forms occur before that for the MDIForm.

Usage   Private Sub Form_QueryUnload(Cancel As Integer, UnloadMode As Integer)
                 Private Sub MDIForm_QueryUnload(Cancel As Integer, UnloadMode As Integer)

Applies To   Form Object
                 MDIForm Object

The Cancel argument is used as *output* from the event routine to cancel the unload process. The UnloadMode argument indicates the reason for the unload. More details are provided in the following table.

PARAMETER	VALUE	MEANING
Cancel	0	An *output* argument. If it is 0 when the subroutine ends, the unload process continues.
	Nonzero	Setting Cancel to nonzero cancels the unload process.
UnloadMode	vbFormControlMenu or 0	Indicates the user chose the Close command from the Control menu on the form.
	vbFormCode or 1	Invokes the Unload statement from code.
	vbAppWindows or 2	Indicates the current Microsoft Windows operating environment session is ending.
	vbAppTaskManager or 3	Indicates the Microsoft Windows Task Manager is closing the application.
	vbFormMDIForm or 4	Indicates an MDI child form is closing because the MDI form is closing.

If you cancel the Unload event in response to the vbAppTaskManager reason, the Task Manager will eventually pop up a message stating, "This program is not responding. . . ." If you then click the End Task button, your application will ignore the cancel and close immediately.

Reposition Event

The Reposition event is triggered after a record becomes the current record. Use this event to initialize any other controls with the data in the record that just became current.

Usage   Private Sub *object*.Reposition ([Index As Integer])

Applies To   Data Control

The Index parameter appears only if the Data control is a member of a control array. It identifies which member of the array received the event.
Note: Unlike the Reposition event, the Validate event is triggered just before moving to another record.

Resize Event

The Resize event is triggered when an object is resized by the user or by code. Also, a Form or MDIForm object's Resize event is called when the object is displayed for the first time. Use the Resize event to reposition the controls on your form to try to maintain a consistent look regardless of the object's size. Use the Paint event to resize and reposition drawn graphics and text. For a PictureBox control, use the Refresh method in the Resize event to trigger explicitly the Paint event. For a Form object—if the AutoRedraw property is False—its Paint event will be triggered automatically after its Resize event.

Usage   Private Sub Form_Resize( )
Private Sub MDIForm_Resize()
Private Sub *object*_Resize([Index As Integer] [[,] HeightNew As Single, WidthNew As Single])

Applies To   Form Object
MDIForm Object
OLE Container Control
PictureBox Control

The parameters of the Resize event have the meanings given in the following table.

Parameter	Value	Meaning
Index	Positive integer	Appears only if the control is part of a control array. The index will be set to the number that identifies the member of the control array for which the event is generated.
HeightNew	Single value	Appears only for an OLE Container control whose SizeMode property is set to vbOLESizeAutoSize (2). It specifies the new height of the control. Your code can change the value to set a different height for the control.
WidthNew	Single value	Appears only for an OLE Container control whose SizeMode property is set to vbOLESizeAutoSize (2). It specifies the new width of the control. Your code can change the value to set a different width for the control.

If an OLE Container control's SizeMode property is set to vbOLESizeAutoSize (2), it will be sized automatically to fit its contents. When the container's object changes size, it triggers the Resize event for the Container control. The HeightNew and WidthNew arguments give the new size of the container's object, but the Resize event procedure can change these values to size the Container control differently.

If all the graphics used by your Form object or PictureBox control are background graphics, you can avoid implementing the Form's Paint event by using the AutoRedraw property to make the graphics "permanent." See the following example:

Example

```
Private Sub Form_Resize()
    AutoRedraw = True
    Cls
    logo$ = "Hacker's Guide"
    Font.name = "Times New Roman"
    Font.Italic = True
    Font.size = 128
    sw = ScaleWidth
    sh = ScaleHeight
    Do
        Font.size = 0.8 * Font.size
        w = TextWidth(logo$)
    Loop While w > sw
    h = TextHeight(logo$)
    CurrentX = (sw - w) / 2
    CurrentY = (sh - h) / 2
    Print logo$
    AutoRedraw = False
End Sub
```

RowColChange Event

The RowColChange event is triggered when the active cell is changed by the user or by code using the Col and Row properties.

Usage   Private Sub *object*_RowColChange ([Index As Integer,][LastRow As String, ByVal
                        LastCol As Integer])

Applies To   DBGrid Control
                        Grid Control

The parameters of the RowColChange event have the meanings given in the following table.

PARAMETER	VALUE	MEANING
Index	Integer	Uniquely identifies the control in a control array. This parameter is omitted if the DBGrid control is not part of a control array.
LastRow	Variant value	(DBGrid only). Specifies the previous row position. It can be a bookmark.
LastCol	Integer	(DBGrid only). Specifies the previous column.

For a Grid control, the SelChange event also occurs (after the RowColChange event) when a user clicks a new cell. But it doesn't occur when you change the selected range via code (using the SelEndCol, SelStartCol, SelEndRow, and SelStartRow properties) without changing the current cell.

For a DBGrid control, the update events for the previous cell will complete before Row-ColChange is triggered. If the user clicks to activate different cells, the RowColChange event is generated without a corresponding SelChange event. If the user clicks a column header to select a column, only the SelChange event is generated. If the user clicks a row header, then the SelChange event is triggered *before* the RowColChange event. Are these bugs? If not, then they *should* be. Use the Col and Row properties to determine the new cell.

RowLoaded Event

The RowLoaded event is *supposed* to be triggered after a DBGrid control loads a row from the underlying database. Use this event to fill in default values for unbound fields and other initialization after a record is loaded.

 This event was obviously something left in the documentation after the feature was removed from VB. You won't see it listed in the code module list for a DBGrid control. We tried to use it anyway and got an immediate GPF.

RowResize Event

The RowResize event is triggered when the user resizes a row in a DBGrid control. It occurs before the Paint event. Use this event to verify the new size.

Usage   Private Sub *Object*_RowResize ([Index As Integer,] Cancel As Integer)

Applies To   DBGrid Control

The parameters to the RowResize event have the meanings given in the following table.

PARAMETER	VALUE	MEANING
Index	Integer	Uniquely identifies the control in a control array. This parameter is omitted if the DBGrid control is not part of a control array.
Cancel	Integer	Set to nonzero, cancels the action, restoring row size to its original height. It also cancels the pending Paint event. Default is 0.

You can accept the change, but adjust the row height by directly modifying the RowHeight property:

Example   `DBGrid1.RowHeight = DBGrid1.RowHeight * 1.05 'Increase by 5%`

To cancel the action, but force a repaint, set Cancel to 1 and invoke the Refresh method.

Scroll Event

The Scroll event is triggered when the scroll box of a scroll bar is being dragged by the user or when the user scrolls a DBGrid control horizontally or vertically. Use the Scroll event to implement "live scroll." This is where you can update dynamically other controls that depend on the value of the scroll bar, rather than just waiting for the Change event, which is triggered by the release of the mouse button once scrolling is complete.

Usage   Private Sub DBGrid_Scroll(Cancel As Integer)
Private Sub *object*_Scroll([Index As Integer])

Applies To   DBGrid Control
HScrollBar Control
VScrollBar Control

The parameters to the Scroll event have the meanings given in the following table.

PARAMETER	VALUE	MEANING
Cancel	Integer value	If the event procedure sets Cancel to nonzero, the scrolling for the DBGrid control is canceled. If you use the Refresh method in the event procedure and set Cancel to a nonzero value, the DBGrid will be displayed momentarily in the new scrolled state and then snap back to the original position.
Index	Positive integer	Identifies the control in a control array. If the control is not part of a control array, there is no Index argument.

Note: Avoid popping up modal forms, including MsgBox dialogs, in this event.

In the following example, three scroll bars are arranged as a control array to get the red, green, and blue (RGB) components of a color request. The scroll event updates the color and labels that are represented by the scroll bars.

Example

```
Private Sub hscColor_Scroll(Index As Integer)
    Picture1.BackColor = RGB(hscColor(0), hscColor(1), _
        hscColor(2))
    lblColor(Index) = hscColor(Index)
End Sub
```

SelChange Event (DBGrid, Grid Control)

The SelChange event is triggered when the selection of cells changes in a grid control.

Usage   Private Sub *object*_SelChange ([Index As Integer,][Cancel As Integer])

Applies To   DBGrid Control
                   Grid Control

The parameters to the SelChange event have the meanings given in the following table.

PARAMETER	VALUE	MEANING
Index	Integer	Uniquely identifies the control in a control array. This parameter is omitted if the DBGrid control is not part of a control array.
Cancel	Integer	(DBGrid only). Set to nonzero, cancels the action, thus restoring the selected cells. Default is 0.

For a Grid control, this event is *not* triggered via code when the SelEndCol, SelStartCol, SelEndRow, and SelStartRow properties are used to change the selected region. Otherwise, the SelChange event occurs after the RowColChange event.

For a DBGrid control, things get weird. If the user clicks to activate different cells, the RowColChange event is generated without a corresponding SelChange event. If the user clicks a column header to select a column, only the SelChange event is generated. If the user clicks a row header, then the SelChange event is triggered *before* the RowColChange event. Also, we cannot find the SelectedRows() property mentioned in the Help file to determine which row is selected. Finally, if the SelChange sets Cancel to True in order to cancel the action, it *still* lets the RowColChange event through. Are these bugs? If not, then they *should* be.

SelChange Event (RichTextBox)

The SelChange event is triggered for a RichTextBox control when the insertion point moves or the current selection changes.

Usage   Private Sub *object*_SelChange([Index As Integer])

Applies To   RichTextBox Control

The Index parameter appears only if the DBGrid control is a member of a control array. It identifies which member of the array received the event.

Use the SelXX properties to examine the current selection in order to update toolbar buttons that set bold, italic, underline, and other characteristics for text.

Terminate Event

The Terminate event is triggered when an instance of a Form, MDIForm, or Class object is about to be removed from memory. This occurs when all variables that refer to the object are set to Nothing (Form and MDIForm objects must be unloaded first) or have fallen out of scope. Use this event to perform final cleanup for a Form or Class Module.

Usage   Private Sub Form_Terminate( )
                 Private Sub MDIForm_Terminate( )
                 Private Sub Class_Terminate( )

Applies To   Class Module Object
                 Form Object, Forms Collection
                 MDIForm Object

If your application calls the End statement, the Terminate event for existing Forms and Classes are *not* triggered. Nor are they triggered if your application ends abnormally.

The following example establishes a connection to the "Word.Basic" OLE Automation object when the Form object is created and then disconnects when the Form is removed from memory.

Example

```
Public oWord As Object

Private Sub Form_Initialize()
    On Error GoTo NoConnect
    Set oWord = CreateObject("Word.Basic")
NoConnect:
    On Error GoTo 0
End Sub

Private Sub Form_Terminate()
```

```
        Set oWord = Nothing
End Sub
```

 Setting a variable that refers to a Form or MDIForm object to Nothing without first unloading it does *not* unload it automatically; nor is the Terminate event triggered. You must first use the Unload command to unload the Form or MDIForm object before setting the variable to Nothing.

Timer Event

The Timer event is triggered when the time interval set for a Timer control has elapsed. The time interval, in milliseconds, is set using the Interval property. The Enabled property must be True and Interval must be nonzero in order for the Timer Event to be triggered.

Use the Timer event to run code at regular intervals, such as when performing animation or background tasks. You can also use the Timer event to implement an alarm, where you specify that code should run at some later time. Because the maximum value for Interval gives you only a time interval of just over a minute, you may need to implement a count of your own in the Timer event in order to use longer time intervals.

Usage   Private Sub *object*_Timer([Index As Integer])

Applies To   Timer Control

The Index argument identifies the control in a control array. If the Timer control is not part of a control array, there is no Index argument.

Note: When you set the Timer control's Enabled property to True, the countdown is reset to the Interval value.

The following example displays a new image from the included resources at every time interval.

Example
```
Private Sub Timer1_Timer()
        Static index
        index = (index Mod 10) + 1
        Image1 = LoadResPicture(index, vbResBitmap)
End Sub
```

UnboundAddData Event

The UnboundAddData event is triggered when a new row is added to an unbound DBGrid control. This allows your application to also add the new row to a database.

Usage   Private Sub *object*.UnboundAddData([Index As Integer,]ByVal RowBuf As
                      RowBuffer, NewRowBookmark As Variant)

Applies To   DBGrid Control

The parameters of the UnboundAddData event have the meanings given in the following
table.

PARAMETER	VALUE	MEANING
Index	Integer	Uniquely identifies the control in a control array. This parameter is omitted if the DBGrid control is not part of a control array.
RowBuf	RowBuffer object	The RowBuffer object contains the (single) row of data added to the DBGrid control.
NewRowBookmark	Variant value	You must assign this parameter to a unique bookmark for the new row of data.

UnboundDeleteRow Event

The UnboundDeleteRow event is triggered when a row is deleted from an unbound DBGrid control. This deletetion allows your application to delete the corresponding row from a database.

Usage   Private Sub *object*.UnboundDeleteRow([Index As Integer,]Bookmark As Variant)

Applies To   DBGrid Control

The parameters of the UnboundDeleteRow event have the meanings given in the following
table.

PARAMETER	VALUE	MEANING
Index	Integer	Uniquely identifies the control in a control array. This parameter is omitted if the DBGrid control is not part of a control array.
Bookmark	Variant value	A bookmark that identifies the row to be deleted.

UnboundReadData Event

The UnboundReadData event is triggered when the DBGrid control needs more data to display,
such as when the control is scrolled.

Usage   Private Sub *object*.UnboundReadData([Index As Integer,]ByVal RowBuf As
                     RowBuffer, StartLocation As Variant, ByVal ReadPriorRows As Boolean)

Applies To   DBGrid Control

The parameters of the UnboundReadData event have the meanings given in the following table.

PARAMETER	VALUE	MEANING
Index	Integer	Uniquely identifies the control in a control array. This parameter is omitted if the DBGrid control is not part of a control array.
RowBuf	RowBuffer object	The data retrieved from the database must be placed in this RowBuffer object (using the Value property) to transfer them to the DBGrid control. The RowBuffer's RowCount property specifies the number of rows to retrieve. A unique bookmark should be set for each row of data by using the Bookmark property of the RowBuffer.
StartLocation	Variant value	Specifies the row immediately before (if retrieving forward) or after (if retrieving backward) the rows to be retrieved. If StartLocation is Null, then the retrieved rows are placed at the beginning (if retrieving forward) or the end (if retrieving backward) of the data set.
ReadPriorRows	True	Retrieves data in the forward direction.
	False	Retrieves data in the backward direction.

If there are *no* RowCount rows to retrieve, you can set the RowCount to the number of rows actually retrieved to inform the DBGrid control.

UnboundWriteData Event

The UnboundWriteData event is triggered when a row of modified data in an unbound DBGrid control must be written to a database. This allows your application to update the corresponding row in a database.

Usage   Private Sub *object*.UnboundReadData([Index As Integer,]ByVal RowBuf As
                     RowBuffer, WriteLocation As Variant)

Applies To   DBGrid Control

The parameters of the UnboundWriteData event have the meanings given in the following table.

PARAMETER	VALUE	MEANING
Index	Integer	Uniquely identifies the control in a control array. This parameter is omitted if the DBGrid control is not part of a control array.
RowBuf	RowBuffer object	Contains the modified data. RowCount is always 1. To cancel the operation, set RowCount to 0.
WriteLocation	Variant value	A bookmark that identifies the row of data.

Unload Event

The Unload event is triggered when a Form or MDIForm window is about to be removed from the screen and all its controls removed from memory. This occurs when the user selects the Close command from the form's Control menu or when the Unload statement is executed from code. Note that this is not the same as making a form invisible by hiding it where no controls are destroyed. Use the Unload event to save settings for controls or even to ask the user to validate data and confirm the unload. You can save control settings in the Registry or a file such that when the form is reloaded, you can recover the settings for your user.

Usage   Private Sub Form_Unload(Cancel As Integer)
                   Private Sub MDIForm_Unload(Cancel As Integer)

Applies To   Form Object
                   MDIForm Object

The Cancel parameter is used as *output* from the event procedure. Its values have the meanings given in the following table.

PARAMETER	VALUE	MEANING
Cancel	0	The default. Leaving this unchanged will allow the form to unload.
	Nonzero	Changing Cancel to a nonzero value in the Unload event will prevent the form from being unloaded. If the Unload event was triggered by the Windows' session ending, then this change will not stop that process. You may want to use the QueryUnload instead to catch these events.

The QueryUnload event for all forms occurs before *any* form's Unload event. To remove a Form or MDIForm completely from memory, you must unload it with the Unload statement before you can set the variables that reference it to Nothing. Otherwise, it is not unloaded from memory and the Terminate event never executes.

The Unload event is triggered by the following:

• Executing the Unload statement from code

- Choosing the Close command from the Form's Control menu
- Using the End Task button of the Windows Task List to end the application
- Closing the parent MDIForm window when the Form is an MDIchild
- Quitting the Windows session

The following example asks the user to confirm save. This gives the user a chance to cancel the unload altogether.

Example

```
Private IsDirty As Boolean      'Form-level variable

Private Sub Form_Unload(Cancel As Integer)
    If IsDirty Then
        msg$ = "Please save the file before exiting"
        r = MsgBox(msg$, vbYesNoCancel  + vbQuestion)
        If r = vbCancel Then
            Cancel = -1
        ElseIf r = vbYes Then
            SaveForm(Me)
        End If
    End If
End Sub
```

Updated Event

The Updated event occurs after an OLE Container control's object has been modified.

Usage   Private Sub *object*_Updated(Code As Integer)

Applies To   OLE Container Control

The input Code argument indicates how the object was updated.

PARAMETER	VALUE	MEANING
Code	vbOLEChanged or 0	The object's data has changed.
	vbOLESaved or 1	The object's data has been saved by the OLE server application that created the object.
	vbOLEClosed or 2	The OLE server application has closed the file containing the linked object's data.
	vbOLERenamed or 3	The OLE server application has renamed the file containing the linked object's data. It's not clear what "renaming" means. We could not get this event to occur by choosing File/SaveAs from OLE server applications.

Example
```
Private Sub OLE1.Updated(Code As Integer)
    FormDirty = True
End Sub
```

Assume FormDirty is a global variable. This example then shows that the Updated event can be used to detect when the OLE1 control has changed.

Validate Event

The Validate event occurs in the following situations:

• Before a different record becomes the current record

• Before the Update method, except when the UpdateRecord method is used

• Before a Delete operation

• Before an Unload operation

• Before a Close operation

Usage   Private Sub *object*_Validate ([Index As Integer,]Action As Integer, Save As Integer)

Applies To   Data Control

The Index argument is an input to the event procedure. On input, the Action argument indicates the action that triggered the event. However, you can change the Action value inside the *object*_Validate() event to convert the action; you can convert only amongst the various Move and AddNew actions. On input, the Save argument indicates whether bound data has changed. On output, the Save argument determines whether the Edit and UpdateRecord methods are executed for data that have changed.

PARAMETER	VALUE	MEANING
Index	Integer input value	Identifies the control if it's in a control array.
Action	vbDataActionCancel or 0	Cancels the operation when the Sub exits.
	vbDataActionMoveFirst or 1	MoveFirst method.
	vbDataActionMovePrevious or 2	MovePrevious method.
	vbDataActionMoveNext or 3	MoveNext method.
	vbDataActionMoveLast or 4	MoveLast method.
	vbDataActionAddNew or 5	AddNew method.

PARAMETER	VALUE	MEANING
Action	vbDataActionUpdate or 6	Update operation (not UpdateRecord).
	vbDataActionDelete or 7	Delete method.
	vbDataActionFind or 8	Find method.
	vbDataActionBookmark or 9	The Bookmark property is set.
	vbDataActionClose or 10	Close method.
	vbDataActionUnload or 11	The form is being unloaded.
Save	True	On input, indicates that bound data has changed. On output, causes data to be saved (and Edit and UpdateRecord methods to run, if data has changed).
	False	On input, indicates that bound data has not changed. On output, causes changed data to be ignored. You can also set the DataChanged property to False to prevent saves.

You cannot invoke any of the Move methods on the same Recordset from the *object_*Validate() event procedure.

APPENDIX: WHAT'S ON THE FLOPPY

So, there's a floppy with this book. Yeah. So, what the heck's on it? Three things:

1. A skeleton for a VB Add-In

2. A demonstration of how to make an OLE client and server with VB

3. A sample application (called Styles) that uses OLE automation

Add-In Skeleton

Use the Add-In skeleton as a starting point for making an Add-In to VB. Section 1 fully describes what this sample does.

VB4 introduced the concept of Add-Ins—programs that extend VB's power. Two Add-Ins come with VB: the Data Manager and the Report Designer. The neat thing is that Add-Ins are really just a special kind of OLE automation server—one that you can create right in VB.

That's the good news. The bad news is that sometimes it's very hard to get VB to do what you want, *how* you want it done. For example, VB hides the features of some of its internal components, notably the editor. So if you want to create an Add-In that somehow supplements the editor (a typical example would be a tool that automatically commented selected code), you may have trouble doing it using standard methods. (We found one example of an application that did comment and uncomment code, but it seemed to rely on SendKeys rather than OLE to work the actual insertion and removal of the ' character.)

VB4 comes with two main examples of Add-Ins: Align and Spy. Play around with them to see how they work. We found them to be fairly clear once you understand them, but they aren't as well documented as they could be. So, here's a skeleton Add-In that shows you the basic pieces you'll probably need to create an Add-In. We call it AddIn. It has four parts:

1. AddIn.vbp (the project file)

2. AddInSetup.cls

3. AddInAction.cls

4. Main.bas

To see what it does (which is basically nothing), run AddIn in one instance of VB. In a second instance, select Add-Ins/Add-In Manager and click the Skeleton Add-In checkbox. Click OK. Then select Add-Ins. At the bottom of this menu, you should see Skeleton Add-In as an option.

OLE Client and Server

Section 1 also has a full description of what the OLE client and server sample does. Put simply, it displays a progress bar. It's useful if you're programming in an environment (such as Word/Excel) that doesn't have fancy progress bars, but you'd like to show one. Unfortunately, Word cannot be a OLEAuto client, so it can't use it, but that's another matter.

The application consists of two parts, the client and the server. The client is made up of these files:

• PrgTest.vbp (the project name)

• frmTest.frm

The server is made up of these files:

- Progress.vbp (the project name)

- frmProgress.frm

- ProgressBar.cls

- modProgress.bas

- Progress.exe

To get this app to work, open Progress.vbp (the server), select File/Make EXE File, and create Progress.exe. Run it. This action will register Progress in your Windows Registry. Now open PrgTest.vbp and run it. Click the Command button. The progress bar shows up and runs.

The Progress.exe contains a class called ProgressBar (so you access it as CreateObject ("Progress.ProgressBar"). Its Instancing property is set to 2 (multiple instances allowed).

The modProgress.bas has the MAIN sub and the global variable, nInstances, that keeps track of how many progress bars are being displayed. This is so that if one is already running, you don't have to run another copy of Progress.exe to get another progress bar. Progress.exe exits when all progress bars have been dismissed.

The ProgressBar class has only properties, no methods. You set its

- caption,

- msg, and

- percent value.

That's it.

Styles

The Styles program is incredibly useful if you're writing Hacker's Guides. See, we (the authors) get a WinWord document template from Addison-Wesley. Said template has about a gazillion styles. And we have to style tag everything. Consequently, we are always going to the little Style pull-down menu in WinWord and scrolling for about twenty minutes.

Vince had a great idea: Write an always-on-top app that pulls the styles out of the current document and enables you to double-click the style you want. It's like having a floating palette of styles.

Styles, as he calls it, uses an OLE connection to a running copy of WinWord to find out all the styles in the current document. It then displays them in a window that will stay on top. When you want to change the style of some part of your document, you select the text and then double-click the style in Styles. No more pulling down the Style menu or typing finger-twisting keyboard shortcuts. Styles sends an OLE command to WinWord to change the style of the selection and then uses AppActivate to make WinWord the active window again. Very clever.

Section 1 contains a more complete explanation.

INDEX

Numbers followed by the letter f indicate figures; numbers followed by the letter t indicate tables.

Addison-Wesley Developers Press publishes high-quality, practical books and software for programmers, developers, and system administrators.

Here are some additional titles from A-W Developers Press that might interest you. If you'd like to order any of these books, please visit your local bookstore or:

FAX us at: 800-367-7198

Call us at: 800-822-6339
(8:30 A.M. to 6:00 P.M. eastern time, Monday through Friday)

Write to us at:
Addison-Wesley Developers Press
One Jacob Way
Reading, MA 01867

Reach us online at:
http://www.aw.com/devpress/

International orders, contact one of the following Addison-Wesley subsidiaries:

Australia/New Zealand
Addison-Wesley Publishing Co.
6 Byfield Street
North Ryde, N.S.W. 2113
Australia
Tel: 61 2 878 5411
Fax: 61 2 878 5830

Southeast Asia
Addison-Wesley
Singapore Pte. Ltd.
15 Beach Road
#05-09/10 Beach Centre
Singapore 189677
Tel: 65 339 7503
Fax: 65 338 6290

Latin America
Addison-Wesley Iberoamericana S.A.
Blvd. de las Cataratas #3
Col. Jardines del Pedregal
01900 Mexico D.F., Mexico
Tel: (52 5) 568-36-18
Fax: (52 5) 568-53-32
e-mail: ordenes@ibero.aw.com
 or: informaciona@ibero.aw.com

Europe and the Middle East
Addison-Wesley Publishers B.V.
Concertgebouwplein 25
1071 LM Amsterdam
The Netherlands
Tel: 31 20 671 7296
Fax: 31 20 675 2141

United Kingdom and Africa
Addison-Wesley Longman Group Limited
P.O. Box 77
Harlow, Essex CM 19 5BQ
United Kingdom
Tel: 44 1279 623 923
Fax: 44 1279 453 450

All other countries:
Addison-Wesley Publishing Co.
Attn: International Order Dept.
One Jacob Way
Reading, MA 01867 U.S.A.
Tel: (617) 944-3700 x5190
Fax: (617) 942-2829

If you'd like a free copy of our Developers Press catalog, contact us at: devpressinfo@aw.com

Visual Basic Database Programming
Second Edition

Karen Watterson and Ibrahim Malluf
ISBN 0-201-48919-8, $39.95 w/CD-ROM

This book shows you how to write database applications quickly
and efficiently with Microsoft's Visual Basic 4.0. Learn how to
work with relational databases, develop client/server applications, use SQL effectively, and work with the Access engine,
other PC databases, OLE 2.0, and more.

Hacker's Guide™ to Word for Windows™
Second Edition

Woody Leonhard, Vincent Chen, and Scott Krueger
ISBN 0-201-40763-9, $39.95 w/disk

This book is the comprehensive, tell-it-like-it-*really*-is reference
for WordBasic, the programming language behind Word for
Windows. Practically every page contains previously undocu-
mented information about Word for Windows, including bugs,
gaffes, gotchas, and workarounds that can save you hours of
frustration. This second edition, which covers both versions 2.x
and 6.0 of WinWord, includes a glossary of the most commonly
asked questions and an all-new section on dynamic dialogs.

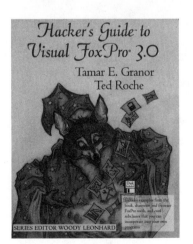

Hacker's Guide™ to Visual FoxPro® 3.0

Tamar E. Granor and Ted Roche
ISBN 0-201-48379-3, $44.95 w/disk

This book is the definitive reference to how all the commands,
functions, properties, events, and methods in Visual FoxPro *really* work. FoxPro experts Tamar Granor and Ted Roche show
you which commands to use, which to avoid, and which ones
don't work quite the way the manual says they do. You'll learn
about common and not-so-common bugs and how to work
around them, plus you get an introduction to OOP, SQL, and
client/server, as well as productivity hints, and advanced cover-
age of OLE and OLE automation.